T0236833

Communications in Computer and Information Science 745

Commenced Publication in 2007
Founding and Former Series Editors:
Alfredo Cuzzocrea, Xiaoyong Du, Orhun Kara, Ting Liu, Dominik Ślęzak,
and Xiaokang Yang

Editorial Board

Simone Diniz Junqueira Barbosa
Pontifical Catholic University of Rio de Janeiro (PUC-Rio),
Rio de Janeiro, Brazil

Phoebe Chen
La Trobe University, Melbourne, Australia

Joaquim Filipe
Polytechnic Institute of Setúbal, Setúbal, Portugal

Igor Kotenko
St. Petersburg Institute for Informatics and Automation of the Russian
Academy of Sciences, St. Petersburg, Russia

Krishna M. Sivalingam
Indian Institute of Technology Madras, Chennai, India

Takashi Washio
Osaka University, Osaka, Japan

Junsong Yuan
Nanyang Technological University, Singapore, Singapore

Lizhu Zhou
Tsinghua University, Beijing, China

More information about this series at http://www.springer.com/series/7899

Daniel A. Alexandrov · Alexander V. Boukhanovsky
Andrei V. Chugunov · Yury Kabanov
Olessia Koltsova (Eds.)

Digital Transformation and Global Society

Second International Conference, DTGS 2017
St. Petersburg, Russia, June 21–23, 2017
Revised Selected Papers

 Springer

Editors
Daniel A. Alexandrov ⓘ
National Research University Higher School
  of Economics
St. Petersburg
Russia

Alexander V. Boukhanovsky
ITMO University
St. Petersburg
Russia

Andrei V. Chugunov
ITMO University
St. Petersburg
Russia

Yury Kabanov ⓘ
National Research University Higher School
  of Economics
St. Petersburg
Russia

Olessia Koltsova ⓘ
National Research University Higher School
  of Economics
St. Petersburg
Russia

ISSN 1865-0929   ISSN 1865-0937   (electronic)
Communications in Computer and Information Science
ISBN 978-3-319-69783-3   ISBN 978-3-319-69784-0   (eBook)
https://doi.org/10.1007/978-3-319-69784-0

Library of Congress Control Number: 2017957555

© Springer International Publishing AG 2017, corrected publication 2018
This work is subject to copyright. All rights are reserved by the Publisher, whether the whole or part of the material is concerned, specifically the rights of translation, reprinting, reuse of illustrations, recitation, broadcasting, reproduction on microfilms or in any other physical way, and transmission or information storage and retrieval, electronic adaptation, computer software, or by similar or dissimilar methodology now known or hereafter developed.
The use of general descriptive names, registered names, trademarks, service marks, etc. in this publication does not imply, even in the absence of a specific statement, that such names are exempt from the relevant protective laws and regulations and therefore free for general use.
The publisher, the authors and the editors are safe to assume that the advice and information in this book are believed to be true and accurate at the date of publication. Neither the publisher nor the authors or the editors give a warranty, express or implied, with respect to the material contained herein or for any errors or omissions that may have been made. The publisher remains neutral with regard to jurisdictional claims in published maps and institutional affiliations.

Printed on acid-free paper

This Springer imprint is published by Springer Nature
The registered company is Springer International Publishing AG
The registered company address is: Gewerbestrasse 11, 6330 Cham, Switzerland

Preface

The international conference Digital Transformation and Global Society (DTGS) is an emerging academic forum in the interdisciplinary field of Internet studies. Held for the second time during June 21–23, 2017, in St. Petersburg, Russia, it brought together more than 80 scholars and experts to discuss the transformative impact of digital technologies on the way we communicate, work, and live. The event was hosted by the ITMO University and co-organized by the National Research University Higher School of Economics, both leading research institutions in Russia.

For DTGS 2017 we received 134 submissions, each of them was reviewed by at least three international Program Committee members. Overall, 38 papers were accepted, with the acceptance rate of 28%. We are happy to mention the increasing quality of papers and poster presentations, and the growing recognition of the conference in Russia and abroad.

The conference started with a plenary session and three insightful keynote reports. Daniel Alexandrov, Professor at the Higher School of Economics and DTGS 2017 co-chair, gave a talk on the interrelationship between the Internet and the modern social sciences. Dr. Ginaluca Demartini from the University of Sheffield and ACM distinguished scholar gave a presentation on the "Power of Big Data" and how data-driven applications transform our everyday life. The keynote lecture by Dr. Sergey Kovalchuk from ITMO University was devoted to the innovations that help to enhance public health decision-making with computational predictive models.

Two more keynote speeches were presented during the conference. Dr. King-wa Fu from the University of Hong Kong shared the results of his research on the Internet censorship in China and the ways to reveal its trends with automatic methods of data collection and analysis. Prof. Carlos Gershenson (National Autonomous University of Mexico) elaborated on the "Future of Urban Mobility" and digital transformations of urban life in the near future.

The conference proceeded with a poster session and panel session. The latter comprised the following DTGS 2017 tracks:

- eSociety: social informatics and cyber activism issues
- ePolity: politics, governance, and civic participation in cyberspace
- eCity: urban environment and Smart City
- eFinance and eEconomy: ICT-enabled finance, economy, and markets
- eHealth: eHealth technologies and their social effects

Based on the results of the Program Committee reviews, the conference chairs selected the following outstanding and best papers of DTGS 2017, one for each track:

- "Measuring Progress in E-Participation in Russia: The Results of a Multi-Method Case Study" by Lyudmila Vidiasova and Yaroslava Tensina (ITMO University, Russia)

- "Developing Social Competence of Preschoolers in Digital Era: Gender Dimensions" by Yuliya Proekt, Alexandra Kosheleva, Voiletta Lugovaya and Valeriya Khoroshikh (Herzen State Pedagogical University, Russia)
- "GAND: Multi-Criteria Decision Analysis Method for Choice the Most Preferable Public Transport Network Designed Using Geospatial Data" by Danila Parygin, Alexey Golubev, Natalia Sadovnikova and Maxim Shcherbakov (Volgograd State Technical University, Russia)
- "Financial Markets Data Collection Using the Information Model of Interagency Cooperation and the International System of Codification of Financial Instruments" by Yuri Lipuntsov (Moscow State University), Richard Beatch and Inessa Collier (Bloomberg AP)
- "Content Sharing in Conflictual Ad-Hoc Twitter Discussions: National Patterns or Universal Trends?" by Svetlana S. Bodrunova, Anna S. Smoliarova, Ivan S. Blekanov (St. Petersburg State University, Russia) and Anna A. Litvinenko (Freie Universität Berlin, Germany)
- "Dynamically Integrating Electronic with Personal Health Records for Ad-hoc Health-Care Quality Improvements" by Aleksandr Kormiltsyn and Alex Norta (Tallinn University of Technology, Estonia)
- "Fashion Bloggers as Cultural Intermediaries: The Meaning of Brand Choices in Style Production" (the best poster) by Margarita Kuleva and Daria Maglevanaya (National Research University Higher School of Economics, Russia)

We express our gratitude to all those who contributed to the success of the event. We thank all the Program Committee members and reviewers, session chairs and authors, as well as the conference staff for their efforts to make DTGS 2017 possible and successful. We believe that DTGS will continue to grow and develop as an international scientific forum.

June 2017

Daniel A. Alexandrov
Alexander V. Boukhanovsky
Andrei V. Chugunov
Yury Kabanov
Olessia Koltsova

Organization

Conference Co-chairs

Alexander V. Boukhanovsky — ITMO University, Russia

Daniel A. Alexandrov — National Research University Higher School of Economics, St. Petersburg, Russia

Organizing Committee

Andrei V. Chugunov (Chair) — ITMO University, Russia

Yury Kabanov — National Research University Higher School of Economics, Russia

Olessia Koltsova — National Research University Higher School of Economics, Russia

Sergei Koltcov — National Research University Higher School of Economics, Russia

Ilya Musabirov — National Research University Higher School of Economics, Russia

Mariia Gruzdeva — ITMO University, Russia

Alyona Suvorova — National Research University Higher School of Economics, Russia

Volume Editors

Daniel A. Alexandrov — National Research University Higher School of Economics, St. Petersburg, Russia

Alexander V. Boukhanovsky — ITMO University, St. Petersburg, Russia

Andrei V. Chugunov — ITMO University, St. Petersburg, Russia

Yury Kabanov — National Research University Higher School of Economics, St. Petersburg, Russia

Olessia Koltsova — National Research University Higher School of Economics, St. Petersburg, Russia

Program Committee

Artur Afonso Sousa — Polytechnic Institute of Viseu, Portugal

Daniel A. Alexandrov — National Research University Higher School of Economics, Russia

Luis Amaral — Universidade do Minho, Portugal

Francisco Andrade	Universidade do Minho, Portugal
Arry Akhmad Arman	STEI - Bandung Institute of Technology, Indonesia
Malay Bhattacharyya	Indian Institute of Engineering Science and Technology, Shibpur, India
Michaël Boireau	Université Libre de Bruxelles, Belgium
Radomir Bolgov	St. Petersburg State University, Russia
Nikolay Borisov	St. Petersburg State University, Russia
Mikhail Bundin	Lobachevsky State University of Nizhni Novgorod, Russia
Ilia Bykov	St. Petersburg State University, Russia
Sunil Choenni	Research and Documentation Centre (WODC), Ministry of Justice, The Netherlands
Andrei Chugunov	ITMO University, Russia
Hernani Costa	LEXYTRAD, University of Malaga, Spain
Esther Del Moral	Universidad de Oviedo, Spain
Florent Domenach	Akita International University, Japan
Isabel Ferreira	Escola Superior de Gestão, Instituto Politécnico do Cávado e do Ave, Portugal
Olga Filatova	St. Petersburg State University, Russia
Enrico Francesconi	Institute of Legal Information Theory and Techniques Italian National Research Council (ITTIG-CNR) and Publications Office of the European Union, Italy
Fernando Galindo	University of Zaragoza, Spain
J. Paul Gibson	Mines Telecom, France
J. Ramon Gil-Garcia	University at Albany, SUNY, USA
Christoph Glauser	Institut für Angewandte Argumentenforschung IFAA, Switzerland
Dimitris Gouscos	National and Kapodistrian University of Athens, Greece
Natalia Grabar	STL CNRS Université Lille 3, France
Ronald Greenberg	Brown & Weinraub, PLLC, USA
Stefanos Gritzalis	University of the Aegean, Greece
Mena Habib	Maastricht University, The Netherlands
Diana Ishmatova	APEC e-Government Center, Japan
Yury Kabanov	National Research University Higher School of Economics, Russia
Christos Kalloniatis	University of the Aegean, Greece
George Kampis	Eotvos University, Hungary
Sanjeev Katara	National Informatics Centre, Government of India, India
Ekaterina Kochmar	University of Cambridge, UK
Sergei Koltcov	National Research University Higher School of Economics, Russia
Olessia Koltsova	National Research University Higher School of Economics, Russia
Alexandra Konradi	ITMO University, Russia
Akmaral Kuatbayeva	Shokan Ualikhanov Kokshetau State University, Kazakhstan

Mariana Lameiras	United Nations University Operating Unit on Policy-Driven Electronic Governance, Portugal
Christine Leitner	Danube University Krems, Austria
Sandro Leuchter	Hochschule Mannheim University of Applied Sciences, Germany
Ignacio Marcovecchio	United Nations University Institute on Computing and Society, Macau SAR
Ilya Markov	University of Amsterdam, The Netherlands
Aleksei Martynov	Lobachevsky State University of Nizhny Novgorod, Russia
Yuri Misnikov	ITMO University, Russia
Harekrishna Misra	Institute of Rural Management Anand, India
Zoran Mitrovic	Mitrovic Development and Research Institute, South Africa
Dmitry Muromtsev	ITMO University, Russia
Ilya Musabirov	National Research University Higher School of Economics, Russia
Robert Müller-Török	University of Public Administration and Finance Ludwigsburg, Germany
Adegboyega Ojo	National University of Ireland Galway, Ireland
Alexander Panchenko	University of Hamburg, Germany
Prabir Panda	Independent Researcher
Zeeshan Pervez	University of the West of Scotland, UK
Dessislava Petrova-Antonova	SU St. Kliment Ohridski, Bulgaria
Lidia Pivovarova	University of Helsinki, Finland
Edy Portmann	Institute of Information Systems (IWI), University of Bern, Switzerland
Surya Prasath	University of Missouri-Columbia, USA
Eugen Ruppert	TU Darmstadt, Germany
Alexander Ryjov	Lomonosov Moscow State University, Russian Presidential Academy of National Economy and Public Administration, Russia
Michael Sachs	Danube University of Krems, Austria
Abdel-Badeeh Salem	Ain Shams University, Egypt
Demetrios Sarantis	National Technical University Athens, Greece
Maria Sigova	International Banking Institute, Russia
Alexander Sirotkin	National Research University Higher School of Economics, Russia
Leonid Smorgunov	St. Petersburg State University, Russia
Alexander Sungurov	National Research University Higher School of Economics, Russia
Alena Suvorova	National Research University Higher School of Economics, Russia
Dmitrii Trutnev	ITMO University, Russia
Christos Tryfonopoulos	University of the Peloponnese, Greece

Mario Vacca	Italian Ministry of Education, Italy
Costas Vassilakis	University of the Peloponnese, Greece
Lyudmila Vidiasova	ITMO University, Russia
Alexander Voiskounsky	Lomonosov Moscow State University, Russia
Nikolina Zajdela Hrustek	Faculty of Organization and Informatics, Croatia
Sherali Zeadally	University of Kentucky, USA
Hans-Dieter Zimmermann	FHS St. Gallen University of Applied Sciences, Switzerland
Vytautas Čyras	Vilnius University, Lithuania

Additional Reviewers

Agbabiaka, Olusegun	Saparkhojayev, Nurbek
Bourlakos, Ioannis	Sideri, Maria
Riabushko, Aleksandr	Yurkov, Alexander
Royzenson, Grigoriy	Zvartau, Nadezhda

Contents

ePolity: Politics of Cyberspace

eCity: Urban Planning and Smart Cities

eSociety: Social Media Analysis

Content Sharing in Conflictual *Ad-Hoc* Twitter Discussions: National Patterns or Universal Trends?

Svetlana S. Bodrunova[1(✉)], Anna S. Smoliarova[1], Ivan S. Blekanov[1], and Anna A. Litvinenko[2]

[1] St. Petersburg State University, 7-9 Universitetskaya nab., 199004 St. Petersburg, Russia
{s.bodrunova,a.smolyarova,i.blekanov}@spbu.ru
[2] Freie Universität Berlin, Garystrasse 55, 14195 Berlin, Germany
anna.litvinenko@fu-berlin.de

Abstract. Recently, the growing role of social network users in content dissemination has brought to life the concept of secondary gatekeeping – selection and republication of content already selected and published by traditional gatekeepers. Secondary gatekeeping is believed to be raising the media in-platform visibility, but it may also have negative effects such as adding to creation of echo chambers and deepening the gaps between conflicting views. Such studies are particularly relevant for emergencies or social conflicts where sharing relevant content may be crucial for lowering social unease. But till today the nature of secondary gatekeeping remains highly understudied. We have conducted a comparative study of three *ad-hoc* Twitter discussions on heated ethnic/racial conflicts in the USA (Ferguson riots), Germany (Köln mass abuse), and Russia (Biryulyovo anti-migrant bashings) to assess the patterns of content sharing by active discussants. We used vocabulary-based web crawling and human coding of over 1,000 tweets in randomized samples. Our results show that, in all cases, there's weak but significant correlation between the type of user and his/her attitude to minority with the attitudes expressed in content, while it is not always true that users prefer the same gatekeeper type, e.g. online or social media. As difference between individual users remains statistically significant, this may mean that the nature of heated *ad-hoc* discussions facilitates formation of 'individual-level filter bubbles' in addition to bigger echo chambers.

Keywords: Content sharing · Secondary gatekeeping · Twitter · Inter-ethnic conflict · Online discussions

1 Introduction

In the last decade, online content selection and news spreading proved to be 'a phenomenon of growing social, economic and political importance' [27: 331] capable, arguably, of subversion of traditional media gatekeeping [12]. In 2010s, research on factors influencing content sharing has dealt with user motivations and content

© Springer International Publishing AG 2017
D.A. Alexandrov et al. (Eds.): DTGS 2017, CCIS 745, pp. 3–15, 2017.
https://doi.org/10.1007/978-3-319-69784-0_1

exposure concepts, among which selective exposure theory shows significant explanatory power; but, till today, these studies provide mixed evidence on which particular factors influence more the selection of shared content, and they remain case-oriented and lack comparative perspectives.

In neighboring research zones, content selection has been studied for decades; thus, of media effects studies, gatekeeping theory is the closest to the studies of content sharing, as it has for long been based on similar sets of research questions. Today, this theory expands to a much greater variety of gatekeeper types, and multi-layer (primary vs. secondary, as well as other divisions) gatekeeping is discussed. But these studies suffer from the same shortcomings; also, the studies do not involve the context of media systems as a variable, while it inevitably casts impact upon the spectra of available content.

This paper aims to partially cover these gaps by analyzing secondary gatekeeping patterns within three Twitter discussions on recent ethnic/racial conflicts in the USA, Russia, and Germany. Here, comparability comes from their *ad hoc* nature [11] as well as from similarity of the cases in terms of political polarization and policy implications.

Using a specially developed web crawler, we collected the bulk of the discussions, ranged the users by the number of tweets, and assessed the links to outer content in 1,000+ tweets by active users for each case by six variables. In Sect. 1, we present the overview of the research approaches, including primary vs. secondary gatekeeping. In Sect. 2, the cases and the hypotheses are presented. In Sect. 3, we describe data collection, sampling, and coding. In Sect. 4, we provide the results and test the hypotheses. In Sect. 5, we discuss our contribution to the existing research and the limitations of the study.

2   Explaining Patterns of Content Sharing: Research Approaches

Today, content sharing encompasses sharing the same content within a platform (e.g. retweeting) and selection and re-publication of media content from outside the platform – or both, with no distinction in many of published works. Since early 2000s, the researchers have tried to conceptualize and empirically assess the motivations and patterns of content sharing on social media platforms. One of the approaches was uses and gratifications theory which focused on user motives for sharing, finding out that these were, primarily, information seeking, socializing, entertainment, and status seeking [27], especially on online networks as content sharing communities [28]. Later, network-based approaches added to this evidence that weakly tied users were more likely to share content if they are tied uni-directedly, rather than bi-directedly, thus forming an evidence of content sharing hierarchies in social media [41].

Another research stream tries to identify the factors that influence content selection beyond user motivation. Recently, a range of works tried to check whether the selective exposure theory [40] works for social media – that is, whether information shared by the users is in line with their values, beliefs, and biases. So far, there is mixed evidence whether this theory works well for content sharing, e.g. on Twitter. For example, authors [46] have shown that, during London riots of 2011, users shared tweets that were in line with their beliefs; in experiment-based research, users do tend to demonstrate bias in news selection [33] – to the extent of formation of echo chambers [20] with the same views reproduced. A group of Italian and American researchers have demonstrated that the selective exposure theory, especially when it comes to personal traits and beliefs, can explain the polarizing effects in echo chambering [38], consumption of (fake) news [4], and in formation of scientific networks [37]. Most echo chambers research is, though, focused on studying in-platform content exchange and its effects (for a review, see [3]), including spreading of online behavior [15] and raising issues via collective intelligence [29, 30]. On the other hand, authors [32] have proved that in sharing news from outside Twitter, users tend to include into their shared links media of various political stands; similar findings were reported for Youtube [22].

But in both cases, the role of content attracted from outside the platform in formation of user echo chambers remains understudied; we still do not know how this or that piece of content is selected and what makes it attractive enough to break the cross-platform boundaries. Also, being well-grounded in theory, this research remains case-oriented and often lacks comparative component; we try to partly cover this gap.

Content Selection and Gatekeeping. Mechanisms of content selection for (re)publication were traditionally studied in media effects research, and in particular – in studies of gatekeeping [48]. In general, gatekeeping helps reduce the complexity of the world turning the incoming unstructured information flow into limited and structured sets of comprehensible messages [44]. Also, as early as in 1975 [24], gatekeeping was associated with objectivity model of journalism based on impartiality and balance, as opposed to advocacy model. But from the very early days of gatekeeping research, it was also considered an oppressive mechanism allowing non-professional intentions in news selection [31].

Media have for decades been studied as major societal information gatekeepers. In 1980s to 1990s, the gatekeeping theory focused on structural constraints of information selection [16], of which time and space pressures, professional values, and organizational routines seemed to be more important than the type of platform, thus forming cross-media understanding of news selection priorities. Also, for international gatekeeping, news values theory was used to explain the choice of local/national vs. international news [39].

The growth of Internet has drastically changed the gatekeeping landscape. Media institutions felt they were losing monopoly in gatekeeping – that is, the control over the relationship with the users they had previously prospered with. Industry predictions ranged from alarmist claims of the 'collapse of gatekeeping' [49] to transformationalism. Among the latter, several ideas deserve mentioning. Thus, the 'gatewatching' concept was suggested [10] assigning the users a capacity to transmit information from media without actual participation in content production. Other concepts were 'network gatekeeping' [9] and 'audience gatekeeping' [43] that described the growing role of information consumers in dissemination of news; soon, these ideas expanded beyond the industry-based structural understanding of 'gatekeeping layers', and *secondary gatekeeping* started to be discussed in media studies [43: 6; 39, 48]. Also, today, the gatekeeping theory meets social network analysis where key nodes (users) who either disseminate information themselves or link discussion zones are considered new gatekeepers [25] or, rather, gatekeepers with smaller gateways [2].

Today, three gatekeeping models are most elaborated (for an overview, see [19]). For the first one, authors define five levels of analysis: individual, that of communication routines, organizational, social-institutional, and social-systemic [43]. For the second [35], primary gatekeepers are those 'who by filtering information and publishing decide what is specifically what we commonly understand as news'; secondary gatekeepers 'are those that filter already available news content'. Thus, it directly links primary gatekeeping to editorial work, and secondary gatekeeping to content sharing (link-, affinity-, or community-based). The third one [46, 47] shifts from selection to 'curation' of content and suggest five types of curators: journalists, strategic communicators, 'social others', computer algorithms, and a reader's self [47: 35].

We, though, need to state that we see the distribution of primary/secondary gatekeeping role to be much more complicated than it comes from the current academic debate, and a 'two-step gatekeeping process' [44] reflecting the idea of two-step communication flow [26], is just one of options. To reduce the complexity, we define them as content producer ('primary gatekeeper'), content re-publisher ('secondary gatekeeper'), and intermediary ('tertiary gatekeeper'). Primary gatekeepers are those who produce pieces of content originally; the content may as well be user-generated. In contrast to this, secondary gatekeepers, when re-publishing, are considering what might be interesting for their core information cocoon. This division seems to be a key one, as their final goals may be similar, as well as factors that shape the individual level of decision-making (from ideology to personality [42]), 'resulting in choices that are organizationally efficient and culturally acceptable inside and outside the newsroom' [44: 56]. Tertiary, or 'algorithmic' [34] gatekeepers, in their turn, use storage, aggregation, and affinity-based algorithms to shape the overall picture.

What differentiates 'new' and 'old' gatekeepers is selection principles as part of the 'content curation' process. For all of them, the issue of subjectivity in selection has never been resolved: in the 50s and 60s, while it was argued that editors were stuck into the machinery of editorial choice based on vigorous criteria [21], other authors [45, 48] argued that subjectivity was the basic principle for content selection. With mediatization of society [17, 23], this gap in understanding has only deepened, as media logic itself has become more subjected to various social pressures, some seen as external for editorial offices and some explicating in subjective editorial decisions. But in online user-level content sharing, user decisions become even more individualized and hectic, also due to combining random/purposeful decisions based on personal traits [3] with the impact of tertiary gatekeepers.

3   Twitter Discussions as Research Object: The Three Cases

Of all social media, Twitter has been under researchers' particular scrutiny due to its bigger feasibility, availability of research software, and platform features. Several works [1, 41] have stated that Twitter is for content dissemination more than other social networks are. Here, we need to discuss how peculiarities of Twitter discussions [13] and relations between Twitter and the outer media system affect content sharing.

First, we need to acknowledge that replicability of our findings to other discussions may be low due to the *ad hoc* nature of the event-based discussions [11]. This may lower the comparative potential and be viewed as a natural limitation of this research, even if we have no empirical proof of non-replicability.

Second, the network structure of the discussion, including echo chambers and influencers [7], may also play a role in content selection – or, rather, content selection helps shape echo chambers, as it is natural to suggest that the logic of consonant reality [36] is shows up in all user decisions, including content sharing. In our previous [6, 8] and ongoing research on Germany and Russia, we have noticed that echo chambers are not only based on attitudes towards immigrants but also on user type. Thus, in Germany in 2014 and 2016, pro-migrant camp is formed around left-liberal media and NGOs, while the pro-nationalist one – around nationalist leaders in Germany and Switzerland who look like 'ordinary users'. In the Russian case, under the cover of intense tweeting by media, we discovered a chain of similar pro-nationalist 'ordinary users' who also acted as gateways for each other's content. We may, thus, hypothesize that cross-platform content sharing is linked to the user type, as well as to his/her attitude towards the minority under question.

Third, what may also matter is the difference of media systems and the role of Twitter in them. Russia differs from both Germany and the US in terms of low trust to print media, competitive social media market, and low hybridization of TV. The US and Russian media markets have a distinct online-only segment, while in Germany dominant positions on offline market survive online. All the media systems have relatively high media-political parallelism, and one can trace political alienations in media content and endorsement: progressive/conservative in the US, left/right in Germany, and pro-/anti-systemic in Russia [5, 6]. As to the Twitter's position on the media markets, its market niche is a bit bigger in the US than in Germany and Russia; there is lack of substantial research on the comparable user profiling in the three countries.

Thus, we formulate the following RQs: (1) is the pattern of content sharing national-bound or universal? Do established media remain the leading primary gatekeeper for Twitter users in *ad hoc* discussions? Do we see any differentiating impact of the outer media systems upon content sharing? (2) Does the type of secondary gatekeeper correlate with the type of primary gatekeeper? (3) Do personal biases of the secondary gatekeeping correlate with the type of the primary gatekeeper and the views in the attracted content?

The Cases Under Scrutiny. To better formulate our hypotheses, we will also shortly describe the cases we look at.

In Russia, in October 2013, a Muscovite Egor Scherbakov was, allegedly, killed by an Uzbek immigrant Orkhan Zeynalov; later, Zeynalov was arrested and found guilty. Before the trial, local residents committed repeated bashings of a major warehouse in the Moscow district of Biryulyovo where the migrant community dwelled and worked; they raised against police and formed 'people's brigades' to monitor the local area. The case became the most resonant conflict between Russians and Southern re-settlers in the recent Russian history.

In the USA, in August 2014, a white police officer Darren Wilson shot dead an unarmed African American youngster Michael Brown. Peaceful protest and violent riots rose repeatedly in Ferguson, Missouri, as well as all over the US. The case has polarized American society not only along white/non-white lines but also across political affiliations.

In Germany, in the New Year night of 2016, mass sexual harassment of women by alleged migrants from Middle East and North Africa took place in Cologne. This made people in many cities protest, mostly under the PEGIDA movement slogans. National media were practically silent on the case, as editorial guidelines prevent journalists from covering ethnics origin of the criminals, while local media reported the case.

Research Hypotheses. Having stated all the mentioned above, we have formulated the following hypotheses:

H1. Across the cases, an 'onion' pattern of content sharing will emerge: social media will be shared most; online-only media will follow, traditional media will come third. In general, structures of media systems will have no visible impact upon content sharing patterns.

H2. The type of secondary gatekeeper will correspond with that of primary gatekeeper in all the three cases.

H3. Personal preferences (pro-/anti-minority) of users will correlate with the type of primary gatekeeper, as well as with pro-/anti-minority bias in shared content.

4 Methodology

To test the hypotheses, we have collected the discussion content, formed tweets datasets for manual coding, coded them, and made calculations for H1 and descriptive statistics (Cramer's V) for H2 and H3.

Data Collection. We have used vocabulary-based web crawling for data collection. To form the vocabularies, we have collected and manually assessed relevant keywords and hashtags at trendinalia.com; all the cases were in Twitter trending topics for at least two days. We have also added keywords found via manual snowballing in 1,000+ popular tweets per case. We used the crawler developed earlier with modules modified for our purposes. The uploading periods included October 1 to 31, 2013 for Russia, August 22 to 31, 2014 for the USA (as the peaking dates of the conflict, August 14 to 21, contained an unfeasible number of tweets for our software), and January 1 to 30, 2016 for Germany. The uploads returned 10715 tweets by 3574 users for Russia, 193812 tweets by 70018 users for the US, and 64874 tweets by 12382 users for Germany.

Sampling of Datasets for Data Annotation. As we were interested in the active users' content sharing patterns, we have formed feasible datasets of tweets for assessment based on user lists ranged by quantity of the published tweets. The collections had to be feasible for manual coding, and thus we were seeking the datasets containing around 1000 tweets; for further research, the datasets are to be enlarged. We had to cut the long tail of the discussion, which may have affected the results in terms of the variety of content shared; but the reason for looking at most active users was that they tend to have more stable patterns of posting and content sharing. Thus, our sample is not representative, but randomized sampling would have even distorted the results in a way, as active users are also those who are retweeted more than others [7], and, thus, the content they share creates impact that goes beyond average.

Cutting the user 'long tail' implied establishing a threshold of user activity – that is, the minimum number of tweets posted in the discussion [14, 33]. Due to very differing user activity, these thresholds (K = Ntweets per user) differed much: for Russia, K = 20, for the USA, K = 66; for Germany, K = 10; K was defined as the point where the graph that ranged users stopped to drop significantly from user to user. After that, randomized samples (certain percentage of tweets) from each user were taken depending on the overall user activity in the discussion, to preserve the comparable volume of the datasets: for Russia, 40%, for the USA, 5%, for Germany, 30%. After cutting out irrelevant tweets, replicas, and foreign-language tweets, the final datasets included: for Russia, 1120 tweets; for the USA, 1095 tweets; for Germany, 911 tweets (since many tweets were in English and had to be cut out). The relatively small sample is explained by the fact that reading of media texts could not be automatized, as so far no sentiment analysis or machine-learning techniques could provide for clear understanding of user attitudes.

Coding. Coding of the datasets was performed by experienced experts and native speakers. Four variables were coded: user type = secondary gatekeeper type ('ordinary user'/political activist/political actor/hybrid media/online-only media/'media' on Twitter/'culture'/other or non-defined); user's attitude to minority (neutral/pro/anti/non-defined); type of primary gatekeeper ('social', online-only, hybrid media, politics, 'culture', other/non-defined); attitude to minority in media content (neutral/pro/anti/non-defined). Links to own content were excluded from the analysis. Also, we excluded the links to Twitter-based photo content (pic.twitter.com). In future, bigger samples may be coded.

5   Results and Discussion

On completing the aforementioned procedures, we have received the following results.

H1. We have calculated the number of links to content outside Twitter in the three datasets in absolute figures and in % (see Table 1).

Table 1. Number of links in the datasets, absolute N

Country	All links, of all tweets		Social media		Online-only media		Hybrid media		Other	
Russia	159	14.2%	62	39%	29	18.2%	62	39%	6	3.8%
USA	280	25.5%	70	25%	96	34.3%	67	23.9%	46	16.4%
Germany	317	34.8%	41	12.9%	41	12.9%	197	62.1%	38	12%

In Table 1, we show political, economic, and cultural links all together, as they are few; everywhere, media are, indeed, the dominant primary gatekeeper, but with very different roles of various types of media. This is why we describe the cases in more detail here.

In the Russian case, we see a picture of rivalry between social and hybrid media – despite low structural online/offline parallelism and low trust to legacy media in Russia. Thus, the idea of the 'onion' pattern of content sharing is not supported; hybrid media are shared more than expected. Social media are represented by blog platforms (Livejournal, Blogspot), the local social network Vkontakte and global Facebook and Instagram, and video hostings (Youtube, Ustream). More interestingly, if we look at online-only and hybrid media in terms of their political bias (and to several political links), we will see that, on Russian Twitter, pro-elite and liberal-oppositional content is shared almost equally, making Twitter much closer an 'opinion crossroads' than, e.g., the Russian Facebook, a distinct platform-wide echo chamber, as stated earlier [6].

For the American case, we see a picture opposite to the Russian one. Here, only 25% of the links is to social media and other 24% – to hybrid media, while online-only comprise over one third. For America, the 'onion' pattern, again, is irrelevant. Also, there are several other features characteristic for the US case. First, all the variety of the mainstream media is shared. The leading print media included *Los Angeles Times, The Nation, The Atlantic, Chicago Tribune, USA Today, Time, The Washington Post*, and *The New Yorker*; of TV, MSNBC, CBS, CNN, and Fox got 2 to 3 links each. Regional media market is well-represented, especially by media of the St.Louis county. Second, there is a striking diversity in formats and political positions of online-only media, many of them being personal or group providers of opinionated writing, grassroots political reporting, and alternative news (like *RawStory.com, Madiaite.com, Vox,* or *Breitbart*). Some outlets balance between politics and journalism (*TheConservativeFreeHouse, ThinkProgress, TalkingPointsMemo, AmericanThinker*). This diversity is supported by that in political links (8% of all links) belonging to activist, human-rights, and petition websites. Third, we have found virtually no African American media. Unlike in the tweets, the 'attracted' discourse, be it pro- or anti-Black, seems to be shaped by 'white' media – except for Youtube that features eyewitnesses' views, African American commentators, and rap music in support of Mike Brown.

The German case is the only that proves H1 right, but, again, the 'onion' logic does not fully work, as social and online media get equal quantity of links – both almost five times less than the hybrid media. 26 links, or 8,2%, belong to political organizations or activists. Surprisingly, 84 of 186 (45%) of German hybrid media links are to advocacy outlets, but this may be explained by the fact that 70% of them lead to a right-wing magazine *Zuerst* and are posted by the same user. Of the rest, 46 are supra-regional general-interest and 50 are regional and local general-interest media. The regional distribution is representative enough; the links are not Cologne-centered. Nearly all the big players are also present: newspapers (*FAZ, Süddeutsche Zeitung,* and *Die Welt* to *Handelsblatt* and the tabloid *Bild*), news magazines (*Spiegel, Focus*), public and commercial TV, and public radio. Due to this, left-right media market polarization reconstructs in the discussion, with right-wing media clearly winning. Online-only media referenced to are also highly politicized. More than half of them (24 out of 41) are the links to advocacy media fostering agendas and news frames alternative to the mainstream media, like *Alternative Dresden News, DortmundEcho,* or *Pi-news.*

Thus, our H1 is fully rejected: the 'onion' pattern of content sharing is absent. Also, national media systems and the state of civil society seem to have a bigger impact than expected upon the sharing strategies of the users. While in the US and Germany 9%

and 8% of the links, respectively, belong to political websites, Russian content sharing is depoliticized. What unites all the cases, though, is an 'opinion crossroads' in terms of political bias present via media links platform-wide, but it is yet unclear whether it is present within 'echo chambers'.

H2 and H3. To assess correlations between secondary gatekeepers' types and attitudes to minorities vs. primary gatekeepers' types and attitudes in their content, we have conducted Cramer's V for the 4 variables described above. The results are shown in Tables 2 and 3.

Table 2. Secondary gatekeeper type vs. ...

	...primary gatekeeper type	...attitude to minority in primary gatekeeper's text
Russia	0.220	0.248*
USA	0.183**	0.208**
Germany	0.219***	0.372***

*Sig.: *p ≤ 0.05; **0.05 < p ≤ 0.001; ***p < 0.001.*

Table 3. Secondary gatekeeper's attitude to minority vs. ...

	...primary gatekeeper type	...attitude to minority in primary gatekeeper's text
Russia	0.288***	0.290***
USA	0.150	0.305***
Germany	0.183**	0.401***

*Sig.: *p ≤ 0.05; **0.05 < p ≤ 0.001; ***p < 0.001.*

As we see from Tables 2 and 3, in all the cases, type and attitude of the secondary gatekeeper (that is, Twitter user) weakly but significantly correlates with bias in the shared text – that is, the hypothesis of selective choice of content is supported in cross-country perspective, and in Germany these ties are the strongest. But at the same time the type of primary gatekeeper (that is, in most cases, media platform) has varying relevance. Thus, in Russia, users of various nature all rely on a variety of media, from hybrid to social, but still choose the content that supports their views; this means they look more at content than stick to their preferred media outlets. In the US, the position of a user towards the minority does not correlate with where a user goes for his/her information supply; it is the particular attitude that will be sought after, and this also may be a sign of occasion-based content consumption and sharing, as there is no stability in linking to the same source. That is, echo chambers in content sharing seem to exist in all the cases, but they are formed via different mechanisms. The type of links seems to be all in all less important for the users than the content, and this supports the idea of active seeking of information rather than 'information cocooning' and passivity in content consumption. But, as already stated, this may also support the idea of occasional sharing as soon as the users run into the content that supports their views. This needs further research.

What is also seen is that our idea of collision of the individual and organizational levels of gatekeeping may be supported in future. What we have definitely seen in case of Germany and for several users in the US and Russian datasets is what one may call 'individual-level filter bubbles' formed not only via posting but also via content sharing. This may amplify the echo chamber concept, as not only network-level inter-user information exchange but also individual-level filtering leads to the rise of closed-up communicative zones. In our future work, we will try to see in detail which gatekeepers were on which side of the conflict, with bigger samples allowing for better conduct of regression analysis.

Discussion and Limitations. Several methodological issues rose in the process of dataset formation and coding. Thus, representativeness of the datasets was considered against feasibility, and the decision was to have more users, rather than more tweets from each user, in the datasets, especially because many most active users were posting or retweeting the same tweets multiple times and had to be almost fully eliminated from the datasets. Also, comparability of the cases and the codebooks was discussed; as stated above, the cases were considered comparable due to their political nature, time structure, and main actors involved. But still one needs to realize that the understanding of political cleavages differs much in the three countries, and in some cases bipolarism of the political spectra does not bring a proper solution in judging the content.

We could not always code the ethnic belonging of the users, and this variable was not used in the research. Manual assessment of the datasets shows much bigger presence of African American population on Twitter than migrant population in Germany or Russia (which is nearly 0), but, as we see from the results, this did not affect the results too much – perhaps due to the structure of the media systems, since they all lack significant representation of the minorities among registered media, and this means that the users share what is available.

And, of course, it was hard not to allow a certain level of subjectivity in coding, but we hope that similarity of the codebooks, cross-checks, and advice from native speakers helped to overcome these limitations.

6 Conclusion

In this paper, we have shown that the complexity of gatekeeping in today's communication flows may be reduced to primary (content producers), secondary (content disseminators), and tertiary ('algorithmic') gatekeepers; thus, content sharing patterns shed light onto the relations between primary and secondary gatekeeping.

We have found that national media markets and the state of civil society still help break the cross-national patterns of content sharing on Twitter, and all the variety of views is presented. But at the same time, across cultures, users share the content they solidarize with in their views; but if in Russia and Germany, user bias is linked to the media they consume, in the USA users are more spontaneous in their choice. Thus, the idea of selective content sharing due to bias and user status is supported cross-culturally, but what is shared depends highly on what national arenas offer.

Acknowledgements. This research has been supported in full by Russian Science Foundation (research grant 16-18-10125).

The authors are grateful to Karl Binger for his help in content coding.

References

1. Bakshy, E., Rosenn, I., Marlow, C., Adamic, L.: The role of social networks in information diffusion (2012). doi:10.1145/2187836.2187907
2. Bastos, M.T., Raimundo, R.L.G., Travitzki, R.: Gatekeeping Twitter: message diffusion in political hashtags. Med. Cult. Soc. **35**(2), 260–270 (2013)
3. Bessi, A.: Personality traits and echo chambers on facebook. Comput. Hum. Beh. **65**, 319–324 (2016)
4. Bessi, A., Caldarelli, G., Del Vicario, M., Scala, A., Quattrociocchi, W.: Social determinants of content selection in the age of (mis)information. In: Aiello, L.M., McFarland, D. (eds.) SocInfo 2014. LNCS, vol. 8851, pp. 259–268. Springer, Cham (2014). doi:10.1007/978-3-319-13734-6_18
5. Bodrunova, S.S., Litvinenko, A.A.: New media and the political protest: the formation of a public counter-sphere in Russia of 2008–12. In: Russia's Changing Economic and Political Regimes: The Putin Years and Afterwards, pp. 29–66. Routledge (2013)
6. Bodrunova, S.S., Litvinenko, A.A., Gavra, D.P., Yakunin, A.V.: Twitter-based discourse on migrants in Russia: the case of 2013 bashings in Biryuliovo. Int. Rev. Manag. Mark. **5**(1S), 97–104 (2015)
7. Bodrunova, S.S., Blekanov, I.S., Maksimov, A.: Measuring influencers in Twitter ad-hoc discussions: active users vs. internal networks in the discourse on Biryuliovo bashings in 2013. In: IEEE Artificial Intelligence and Natural Language Conference (AINL), pp. 1–10. IEEE (2016)
8. Bodrunova, S.S., Litvinenko, A.A., Blekanov, I.S.: Influencers on the Russian Twitter: institutions vs. people in the discussion on migrants (2016). doi:10.1145/3014087.3014106
9. Barzilai-Nahon, K.: Gatekeeping: a critical review. Ann. Rev. Inf. Sci. Technol. **43**(1), 1–79 (2009)
10. Bruns, A.: Gatewatching: Collaborative Online News Production. Peter Lang, Bern (2005)
11. Bruns, A., Burgess, J.E.: The use of Twitter hashtags in the formation of ad hoc publics. In: 2011 Proceedings of the 6th European Consortium for Political Research (ECPR) General Conference (2011)
12. Carr, J.: No laughing matter: the power of cyberspace to subvert conventional media gatekeepers. Int. J. Commun. **6**, 2825–2845 (2012)
13. Cha, M., Benevenuto, F., Haddadi, H., Gummadi, K.: The world of connections and information flow in Twitter (2012). doi:10.1109/tsmca.2012.2183359
14. Chadwick, A.: The Hybrid Media System: Politics and Power. Oxford University Press, Oxford (2013)
15. Centola, D.: The spread of behavior in an online social network experiment. Science **329** (5996), 1194–1197 (2010)
16. Donahue, G.A., Olien, C.N., Tichenor, P.J.: Structure and constraints on community newspaper gatekeepers. Journal. Q. **66**(4), 807–845 (1989)
17. Esser, F., Strömbäck, J.: Mediatization of Politics: Understanding the Transformation of Western Democracies. Springer, Heidelberg (2014). doi:10.1057/9781137275844
18. Flaxman, S., Goel, S., Rao, J.: Filter bubbles, echo chambers, and online news consumption. Public Opin. Q. **80**(S1), 298–320 (2016). doi:10.1093/poq/nfw006

19. Friedrich, K., Keyling, T., Brosius, H.-B.: Gatekeeping revisited. In: Political Communication in the Online World: Theoretical Approaches and Research Designs, pp. 59–72. Routledge (2017)
20. Garrett, R.K.: Echo chambers online? Politically motivated selective exposure among internet news users. J. Comput.-Mediated Commun. **14**, 265–285 (2009)
21. Gieber, W.: Across the desk: a study of 16 telegraph editors. J. Mass Commun. Q. **33**(4), 423–432 (1956)
22. Halvey, M.J., Keane, M.T.: Exploring social dynamics in online media sharing. In: Proceedings of the 16th International Conference on World Wide Web, pp. 1273–1274. ACM (2007)
23. Hjarvard, S.: The mediatization of culture and society. Routledge, New York (2013)
24. Janowitz, M.: Professional models in journalism: the gatekeeper and the advocate. Journal. Q. **52**(4), 618–626 (1975)
25. Jürgens, P., Jungherr, A., Schoen, H.: Small worlds with a difference: new gatekeepers and the filtering of political information on Twitter (2011). doi:10.1145/2527031.2527034
26. Katz, E., Lazarsfeld, P.: The two-step flow of communication: an up-to-date report on a hypothesis. Public Opin. Q. **21**(1), 61–78 (1957)
27. Lee, C.S., Ma, L.: News sharing in social media: the effect of gratifications and prior experience. Comput. Hum. Behav. **28**(2), 331–339 (2012)
28. Lee, J.G., Antoniadis, P., Salamatian, K.: Faving reciprocity in content sharing communities: a comparative analysis of Flickr and Twitter (2010). doi:10.1109/asonam.2010.51
29. Levy, P.: Collective Intelligence: Mankind's Emerging World in Cyberspace. Helix Books (2000)
30. Malone, T.W., Klein, M.: Harnessing collective intelligence to address global climate change. Innov.: Technol. Gov. Glob. **2**(3), 15–26 (2007)
31. Mills, C.: The Power Elite. Oxford University Press, New York (1956)
32. Morgan, J.S., Lampe, C., Shafiq, M.Z.: Is news sharing on Twitter ideologically biased? (2013). doi:10.1145/2441776.2441877
33. Munson, S.A., Resnick, P.: Presenting diverse political opinions: how and how much (2010). doi:10.1145/1753326.1753543
34. Napoli, P.M.: Social Media and the Public Interest: Governance of News Platforms in the Realm of Individual and Algorithmic Gatekeepers. A research paper (2014). https://papers.ssrn.com/sol3/papers.cfm?abstract_id=2481886
35. Nielsen, R.K.: News media, search engines and social networking sites as varieties of online gatekeepers. In: Rethinking Journalism Again: Societal Role and Public Relevance in a Digital Age, pp. 81–97. Routledge (2016)
36. Noelle-Neumann, E.: Die Schweigespirale: öffentliche Meinung-unsere soziale Haut. Riper (1980)
37. Quattrociocchi, W., Amblard, F., Galeota, E.: Selection in scientific networks. Soc. Netw. Anal. Mining **2**(3), 229–237 (2012)
38. Quattrociocchi, W., Caldarelli, G., Scala, A.: Opinion dynamics on interacting networks: media competition and social influence. Sci. Rep. 4, Art. no. 4938 (2014)
39. Roberts, M.S., Bantimaroudis, P.: Gatekeepers in international news: the Greek media. Harvard Int. J. Press/Polit. **2**(2), 62–76 (1997)
40. Sears, D.O., Preedman, J.L.: Selective exposure to information: a critical review. Public Opin. Q. **31**(2), 194–213 (1967)
41. Shi, Z., Rui, H., Whinston, A.B.: Content sharing in a social broadcasting environment: evidence from twitter (2013). Available at SSRN 2341243
42. Shoemaker, P.J., Reese, S.D.: Mediating the Message: Theories of Influences on Mass Media Content. Longman Trade, Harlow (1996)

43. Shoemaker, P.J., Vos, T.P.: Gatekeeping Theory. Routledge, Abingdon (2009)
44. Singer, J.B.: User-generated visibility: secondary gatekeeping in a shared media space. New Med. Soc. **16**(1), 55–73 (2014)
45. Snider, P.B.: 1967. 'Mr. Gates' revisited: a version of the 1949 case study. J. Mass Commun. Q. **44**(3), 419 (1966)
46. Thorson, K., Wells, C.: From two-step to one-step to curated flows: technology, social change and contingent information exposure. In: Annual Meeting of the International Communication Association, Sheraton Phoenix Downtown, Phoenix, AZ, 24 May 2012
47. Wells, C., Thorson, K.: Combining big data and survey techniques to model effects of political content flows in Facebook. Soc. Sci. Comput. Rev. **35**, 33–52 (2015). doi:10.1177/0894439315609528
48. White, D.M.: The gate keeper: a case study in the selection of news. J. Mass Commun. Q. **27**(4), 383–390 (1950)
49. Williams, B.A., Delli Carpini, M.X.: Unchained reaction: the collapse of media gatekeeping and the Clinton-Lewinsky scandal. Journalism **1**(1), 61–85 (2000)

Detecting Interethnic Relations with the Data from Social Media

Olessia Koltsova[1(✉)], Sergey Nikolenko[1,2], Svetlana Alexeeva[1,3],
Oleg Nagornyy[1], and Sergei Koltcov[1]

[1] National Research University Higher School of Economics, Moscow, Russia
{ekoltsova, snikolenko, salexeeva,
onagorny, skoltsov}@hse.ru
[2] Steklov Mathematical Institute, St. Petersburg, Russia
[3] St. Petersburg State University, St. Petersburg, Russia

Abstract. The ability of social media to rapidly disseminate judgements on ethnicity and to influence offline ethnic relations creates demand for the methods of automatic monitoring of ethnicity related online content. In this study we seek to measure the overall volume of ethnicity related discussion in the Russian language social media and to develop an approach that would automatically detect various aspects of attitudes to those ethnic groups. We develop a comprehensive list of ethnonyms and related bigrams that embrace 97 Post-Soviet ethnic groups and obtain all messages containing one of those words from a two-year period from all Russian language social media (N = 2,660,222 texts). We hand-code 7,181 messages where rare ethnicities are overrepresented and train a number of classifiers to recognize different aspects of authors' attitudes and other text features. After calculating a number of standard quality metrics, we find that we reach good quality in detecting intergroup conflict, positive intergroup contact, and overall negative and positive sentiment. Relevance to the topic of ethnicity and general attitude to an ethnic group are least well predicted, while some aspects such as calls for violence against an ethnic group are not sufficiently present in the data to be predicted.

Keywords: Interethnic relations · Ethnic attitudes · Mapping · Social media · Classification · Lexicon

1 Introduction

Social media have become a space where individuals and groups can both cooperate and engage in conflict being highly visible. In particular, judgments about ethnic groups or ethnicity issues in general may be of different valence (as it happens offline), but their dissemination can potentially proceed faster and reach wider audiences than before the internet era. The consequences and thus the importance of this large-scale public visibility of ethnicity related attitudes are still to be fully understood. While the effect of positive online interethnic communication on offline conflict reduction finds a limited proof, there is a large evidence of the impact of negative online content on offline interethnic conflict [15] and hate crime [9]. This creates demand for the methods

© Springer International Publishing AG 2017
D.A. Alexandrov et al. (Eds.): DTGS 2017, CCIS 745, pp. 16–30, 2017.
https://doi.org/10.1007/978-3-319-69784-0_2

of monitoring of ethnicity related online content, in particular for instruments of its automatic mining from large data collections [8].

In this context, Russia, a country with a large number of both "home born" and migrant ethnic groups, has received relatively little attention from researchers [5, 6, 17, 18]. In this paper we seek to measure the overall volume of ethnicity related discussion in the Russian language social media, to compare public attention to different ethnic groups, and to develop an approach that would automatically detect various aspects of attitudes to those ethnic groups.

2 Related Work

Literature on ethnicity and the Internet comes from a large number of disciplines and seems vast, however, there are surprisingly few works that directly address the issue studied here. Most works are devoted to the formation of ethnic identity and boundaries [17, 19, 27, 29], its relation to online intergroup contact or communication [36], as well as ethnic online communities [18, 24] and influence of ethnicity on online connectedness [21] or online access. That said, such studies are most often centered on minority-generated discourse about respective ingroups rather than on their perceptions by the outgroups. There is very little literature on representation of non-dominant ethnic groups on the Internet, notably in the user-generated content [31], although it is a well developed topic in traditional media studies which examine both representations per se [41], and perceptions of those representations by the minorities themselves [33], as well as the relation between representations and public attitudes [34]. Another feature of this stream of studies is that ethnic minorities are usually migrant/diasporic groups [29], or, if they are "indigenous", they are often conceptualized rather as racial than ethnic groups [19]. Most of such research is done either from European or American perspectives [10]. In Europe, for some reason, most research is centered around migrants although usually only migrants of "other" ethnicity are meant. Surprisingly, indigenous ethnic minorities like Catalan in Spain or Irish within the UK and their relation to the Internet have been largely ignored. In the US, on the contrary, all groups except Native Americans can be seen as migrant, but the most problematic division seems to be between races [19] or groups perceived as races rather than as ethnicities [31].

Neither of these approaches fully applies to Russia that comprises a mixture of both migrant and indigenous ethnic groups who clash dependently of their race. Both Russian majority and some other groups may be confused about who is a migrant and who is a local on each given territory, and these notions are constantly being challenged in the public space. Thus, multidirectional interethnic interactions take place in the Russian language internet, and not all of them bare the signs of conflict.

Ethnic communication and conflict online has received its separate attention from researchers. Some studies have sought to compare offline and online interethnic communication [25, 36] and to understand motivations for online interethnic interaction [11]. As mentioned above, quite a number of works attempts to find relation between online interethnic communication and offline conflict prevention [15] or dissemination [9], as well as offline minority mobilization [29]. This research usually does not map, monitor or systematize online attitudes towards various ethnic groups.

When it comes to methods of such mapping, an absolutely separate body of literature exists. This research mostly comes not from social science, but from computer science and computational linguistics, and it overwhelmingly English language oriented, with few exceptions [35]. It is mostly aimed at automatic detecting of hate speech in user-generated content [3], not always specific to the ethnicity issue, while the "positive" side of ethnic representations online misses researchers' attention at all. Hate speech is broadly understood as hostility based on features attributed to a group as a whole, e.g. based on race, ethnicity, religion, gender and similar features.

This research is very different in breadth and scope: some studies seek to perform race- or ethnicity-specific tasks, for instance aim to detect hate speech against Blacks only [23]. Others attempt to capture broader types of hate speech, e.g. related to race, ethnicity/nationality and religion simultaneously [8, 16], or even generalized hate speech [38] and abusive language [28]. Most studies acknowledge that hate speech is domain specific although some features may be shared by all types of hate speech, therefore some try to catalogue common targets of hate speech online [30].

In such works, a large variety of techniques is being offered and developed, including lexicon-based approaches [16], classical classification algorithms [35] and a large number of extensions for quality improvement, such as learning distributed low-dimensional representations of texts [12], using extralinguistic features of texts [40] and others. Some draw attention to the role of human annotators and the procedure of annotations for classification results [2, 39].

This latter topic leads to the problem of definition of hate speech needed to help annotators understand their job. Computer science papers seldom or never address this problem relying on human judgement as the ultimate truth, and when they do address it they mostly focus on making annotators capture the existing definitions of hate speech, not on critically assessing them or developing new ones. Meanwhile, most existing definitions we know are ethically non-neutral which makes them a difficult object for automatic detection. From the overviews we learn that hate speech, or harmful speech is usually defined via such attributes as "bias-motivated", "hostile" "malicious", dangerous" [14], "unwanted", "intimidating", "frightening" [13], which can be summarized as... actually, bad. All the mentioned attributes, as well as the titles of the concepts themselves mark the concepts they seek to define as ethically unacceptable. If so, to correctly detect them, human annotators have to share common values with the researchers, otherwise they would not be able to recognize hate speech in texts. Since not every derogation, disapproval or condemnation is ethically unacceptable (e.g. condemnation of genocide is considered absolutely desirable), language features of disapproval or derogation per se do not necessarily point at what the Western liberal discourse usually means by hate speech, and this makes it especially elusive when applied beyond the Western world. Further below, we elaborate on this problem by offering a number of relatively objective questions that can be answered by annotators of any ethical or political views. We also show how not only negative aspects of ethnicity related speech can be captured.

3   A Note on Ethnicity in Post-Soviet Space

Not only interpretation of results, but even mere cataloguing of Post-Soviet ethnic groups turns to be impossible without prior sociological knowledge. Here we give a brief introduction into the field to make further understanding of our work easier.

Ethnic landscape of Russia is a patchwork inherited from the Soviet Union and earlier Russian Empire that tried to grant each "nationality" a certain degree of autonomy depending on its bargaining capacity. As a result of dissolution of the USSR, Russia has found itself surrounded by 14 countries that under the Soviet rule had been granted the status of "first-order" republics with the right of secession. They include such diverse cultures as the Baltic that are now a part of the EU (Protestant, German or Uralic language group), predominantly Orthodox Slavic Ukraine and Belorussia and Romanian Moldova, as well as Southern Caucasus that includes Christian Georgia and Armenia and Muslim Azerbaijan. The latter together with five Central Asian countries, also Muslim, speaks a language of Turkic group. However, Central Asian countries range from highly secularized predominantly Russian speaking and economically developed Kazakhstan to the underdeveloped Tajikistan whose economy has been subverted by a number of armed conflicts. Former Soviet Union (FSU) countries serve as the major immigration sources for Russia.

Inside Russia the diversity is even higher. Of its 85 administrative units, 22 contain a titular ethnicity in their titles and are termed republics; a few more ethnic-titled units are included inside republics. All the rest, including the "core" Russian provinces, are termed regions and are named after their capital cities or other geographical names. Some ethnic groups have no definite territory, while others that a virtually extinct, do, and one tiny ethnicity has even got two titular regions. Siberia and the European North are populated by small ethnicities of Uralic and some other language families most of whom are close to extinction. Prior to the conquest by the Russian Empire most of them practiced shamanism and hunting-gathering lifestyles. However, many Turkic groups mainly from European Russia, but also from Siberia are much more alive, with Tatars, Bashkirs and Chuvashs being three largest ethnic groups in the country after Russians (and along with Ukrainians). Most of such groups had passed to Islam and sedentary economy prior to the Russian conquest. Tatarstan had even had its own strong statehood, and now it presents a unique combination of strong ethnic identity, industrial development and the ability to integrate. Northern Caucasus, on the contrary, is often described as the powder keg of Russia. Heavy battles have been fought here both between Russian/Soviet forces and the locals and among the locals themselves who had never had any strong tradition of their own statehood. In the 19th century the region became predominantly Muslim which only complicated the situation. Up to date, Northern Caucasian groups have most strongly resisted assimilation, with Chechnya being the leader and the symbol of this strategy (and with Chechens being the next largest group after those aforementioned). Some North Caucasus republics stay beyond the Russian legal and cultural order and at the same time are heavily subsidized. Inhabitants of "core" Russian regions often do not differentiate between Northern and Southern Caucasian ethnicities.

4 Data, Sampling and Lexicon Development

In this study we seek to monitor public representations of ethnic groups available to all or most consumers of user-generated content (UGC) in Russia, and therefore we limit our research to the Russian language texts. This introduces some asymmetry: while Russians in this situation would be mostly speaking to themselves, ethnic minorities would be mostly speaking to the outgroups. However, as political, cultural and "numeric" positions of the dominant nation and of the minorities are fundamentally asymmetric, this only reflects the real communicative situation. In our previous research [1, 5, 26] we adopted a few strategies that we have to abandon here. First, earlier we had sampled either the most popular or random producers of UGC, and then searched for ethnicity related content with topic modeling – an approach close to fuzzy clustering [4]. We found out that it is not optimal for detecting relevant texts as the topic of ethnicity is too rare for the algorithm to work properly. Second, for semi-supervised topic modeling and frequency counts, we had used the most complete list of world ethnic groups and nations. We did not exclude any or differentiate between ethnicities and nations since the boundary between them is thin. What we found out was much more related not to the in-Russia or FSU ethnicities, but to the nations that had major global or regional political influence, first of all – Americans, Germans, Ukrainians and Jews, but also to many European nations. The texts found with our approach in fact were devoted much more to international relations than to ethnicity. We then came to define the texts devoted to the topic of ethnicity as:

1. texts where the major actors were private persons of a given ethnicity or ethnic groups, and not states or their official representatives (e.g. "Russians blocked a UN resolution" is not about ethnicity, while "Russians made a fight at a football match" is);
2. ethnicity is important for the outcomes or is used as an explanation (e.g. "The cook was Tadjik, he knew everything about pilav" is about ethnicity; "We've just returned from an exhibition of a Tadjik painter, let's have lunch" is not).

Based on described above experience, we have come to the conclusion that we, first, should limit our research to FSU ethnicities in order to avoid global politics. Although this does not guarantee avoiding international relations within FSU, but it strongly mitigates this risk because FSU ethnicities are very often present in Russia as private persons or groups, unlike "far-abroad" nations. Second, we have concluded that we should preselect ethnicity related texts using keyword lists. The major goal at this stage able to influence the quality of the subsequent research was developing a comprehensive list of relevant keywords. Keyword search, compared to fuzzy clustering with subsequent labeling, has an obvious limitation: it cannot yield texts that discuss ethnicity without mentioning key words. That is, keyword search can give high precision, but low recall. However, when fuzzy clustering or topic modeling do not work, we consider keyword search as a first step towards elaborating a more sophisticated supervised classification approach that we address further below.

Luckily, in the Russian language all ethnic groups (except Russians) have different words for nouns and for adjectives (e.g. "Turk" vs "Turkish"). By taking nouns only (and generating their female and plural forms), we have been able to increase the relevance of the texts being found. We have also automatically generated bigrams consisting of an ethnic adjective and a noun referring to a person or the nation (e.g. Tatar woman, Chechen people). The most difficult task was to limit our lexicon of ethnonyms – nouns referring to representatives of ethnic groups. Our list includes the following categories:

- Names of all ethnic groups indigenous to the Post-Soviet countries. Some groups are hierarchical: e.g. Mordva includes Moksha and Erzya; some are synonymous, e.g. Alans and Ossetians. Here we mostly used the data from the Russian Census 2010 and the lists of world nations from UN and other international organizations.
- Names of some other significant minorities. Here we had to exclude those groups that were too visible internationally and most often led to the texts on international relations or politics within respective countries (e.g. Germans). We succeeded in including Jews as we had found that while talking about respective international politic another word (Israeli) would be most often used. We included Gypsies as the word "Roma" is virtually unknown in Russian. Here we relied on the data about quantities of different ethnic groups in Russia from its Census 2010.
- Ethnophaulisms: abusive words denoting representatives of ethnic groups. Here we used literature [20, 22, 32, 37] and the lists of top words in ethnicity related topics found in prior topic modeling. A dozen FSU ethnic groups has precise pejorative equivalents (e.g. Jid for Jew); other ethnophaulisms have more blurred meanings: Khach for any Caucasian, or Churka for any Central Asian, but sometimes for any "Eastern" non-Russian. This ambiguity was the major reason why we chose to treat ethnophaulisms and their derivatives as "separate ethnic groups".
- Meta-Ethnonyms. Certain words referring to language groups (Slav, Ugr) or to the regional identity often function as ethnonyms in the Russian language. Some of them are emotionally neutral (Baltic, European, Siberian), but others can sometimes obtain negative connotations, depending on the context (Asian, Central Asian, Caucasian, Highlander). Note that Caucasian in our context means merely a representative of ethnic groups from the Caucasus, not White race in general. Dagestani also belongs to meta-ethnonyms although most Russians do not know that this a regional, not an ethnic name. Lists of top words in ethnicity related topics found in prior topic modeling were used here.
- Cossacks. These were actually a social group in the Imperial Russia with its distinct culture, but no specific language or religion (like Samurai in Japan). Cossacks were free armed peasants who once leaved at Russia's Southern and Eastern borders and were to resist the first blows of steppe nomads. They spoke either Russian or Ukrainian, depending on the region they lived in. As the Russian Empire grew, they lost their "jobs" and benefits and were finally exterminated under the Soviet rule. However, the recent recontructionist movement of Cossacks has demanded to proclaim them an ethnic group. Their half-militarized semilegal groups have been playing an important role in conflicts with ethnic minorities in the Southern Russia and have been often supported by the local authorities.
- Russians. As noted above, "Russian" in the Russian language has no noun. Adjective "Russian" leads to anything but ethnicity topic (e.g. Russian language

school tests and textbooks). Therefore, we included bigrams only, as well as various synonymous nouns (Ross, Rossiyanin etc.).

After forming this list, we checked if the listed items occurred in our Random Sample of user-generated posts. This sample included 74,303 users of VKontakte, the most popular Russian social networking site akin to Facebook. The users had been selected randomly from each of 85 Russian regions, after which we downloaded all messages from each account for all time and obtained 9,168,353 posts and 933,516 comments to them. This sample is large enough to judge which ethnic words are uncommon for the Russian language UGC, and these happen to be only very exotic ethnicities. We thus obtained a list of 4,063 words and bigrams covering 115 ethnic groups.

We then submitted this list to a commercial aggregator of the Russian language social media content and downloaded all messages containing at least on keyword for the period from January 2014 to December 2015. We made small samples from each ethnic group for hand-checking and found out that some ethnonyms had much more frequently occurring homonyms. We had to exclude these words; however, their synonyms stayed in the sample – e.g. "Mariy" that usually led to texts with the female name "Maria" was excluded, but a russified word "Mariets" stayed. After all cleaning we obtained 2,660,222 texts about 97 ethnic groups; we further refer to this collection as Keyword Sample.

5 Ethnic Groups Descriptive Statistics: Frequencies and Co-occurrence

Given that Russian language social media produce several million messages daily, three million messages in a two-year period is a tiny fraction of the entire volume which clearly shows a low interest of the general public in the topic of ethnicity. Mean length of messages with ethnonyms is much higher than that of the VKontakte random sample (332 words compared to 16.7) and 54.6% of texts contain more than 100 words. This suggests that while the vast majority of messages in social media are everyday small talk, texts related to ethnicity are often elaborated discussion pieces. It makes them much more suitable for various machine learning techniques that would fail on random texts due to their shortness. Ten most frequent ethnic groups include Russians, Ukrainians, Jews, Slavs, Asians, Europeans, as well as two largest Muslim minorities in Russia – Tatars and Chechens. The distribution of frequencies is power law, which is not very good for classification tasks if the original proportion is kept. However, we find substantial regional differences. As mentioned above, some regions in Russia are national republics named after their "titular" ethnic groups; when ranked by the number of mentions in respective regions, such ethnic groups on average gain 45 positions compared to their positions in the general frequency list. Almost a half of them finds themselves in top three most frequent groups in the respective region. Smaller groups gain more positions ($r = -0.5$), although in the entire collections larger groups are mentioned more often. This means that discussions about some ethnic groups being hardly noticeable at the national level are in fact quite important at the regional level.

In total, 45% of messages contain more than one ethnic group, with maximum being 60. This may mean that ethnic groups get opposed in the same text which should lead it to have different sentiment patterns. Such mixture would inevitably complicate automatic sentiment analysis, however, interethnic communication, both "positive" and "negative" can be detected only in texts with several ethnic groups. Also, attitudes to ethnic groups in multiethnic texts might differ from those in mono-ethnic messages in an unpredictable way. We thus can not exclude multiethnic texts from the research. We then examined the cooccurrence patterns to decide whether we should sample multi- and mono-ethnic texts separately, or sample clusters of most commonly cooccuring ethnic groups.

We obtain cooccurrence matrix for all 97 ethnicities and calculate a number of distance metrics (cosine similarity, chi square and distributional). We find a large variation in the ethnicities' overall proximity to others – that is, some of them are predominantly mentioned with others while others aren't. We use several algorithms of community detection, that give similar results; Fig. 1 reports the most sound solution based on chi square distance and Infomap algorithm [7]. Nodes depicted as circles with different motives represent ethnic groups, and their sizes reflect the absolute frequencies of those groups in the collection. Distances and edge thicknesses approximate the level of dissimilarity between ethnic groups, while motives of circles denote clusters that were found by the algorithm.

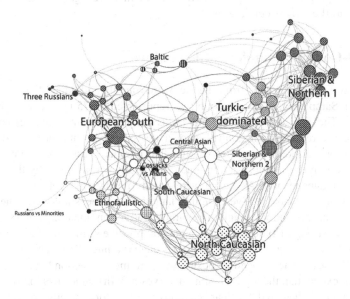

Fig. 1. Cooccurrence of ethnic groups in user posts.

We see that many clusters are formed based on regional and cultural similarity: the Baltic, North and Southern Caucasian, Central Asian (white cluster in the center spread horizontally). Two similar clusters of Northern and Siberian ethnicities and a cluster where in-Russia Turkic peoples prevail are in fact linked by quite a number of non-Turkic ethnicities that were assigned to the "Turkic" cluster. We thus see that in-Russia indigenous ethnicities form a metacluster that is distinct from Central Asia and is very far from the Ethnophaulistic cluster. The latter includes pejoratives for Asian and Caucasian ethnic groups and is closely related to the respective clusters.

Along with Ethnophaulistic cluster, the largest grouping termed "European South" is also not unproblematic. It includes Russians and Ukrainians with their synonyms, including pejoratives, as well as Jews and Gipsies. The latter two groups historically have been connected to the European South, especially Ukraine contributing to its diversity and social cleavages. Russians and Ukrainians have been currently reconnected via a sharp conflict. There are also small clusters of Russians vs non-Russians. To summarize, ethnicities most probably form both problematic and non-problematic clusters, and we can not guarantee capturing conflict by sampling clusters.

We also see that clusters are quite interconnected, and some ethnic groups (e.g. Tatar, Buryat, Turkmen, Alan) demonstrate high betweenness. It is thus hard to sample from clusters both because of their interconnectedness and because they are of very different size; however, from both network and frequency analysis we see that we need small ethnicities to be overrepresented as their infrequency does not mean their unimportance. In fact, two clusters of small Northern and Siberian peoples together are comparable in size with the Central Asian cluster that consists of few large ethnicities. Also, since the distribution of mention frequencies is close to power law training classifiers on proportional sample would teach them to recognize texts related predominantly to the largest ethnic groups.

6   Hand-Coding: Sample and Procedure

We sampled 97 ethnic groups from the Keyword Sample and added the rest 18 from the Random Sample. Each ethnic group was represented by 75 texts except those that were fewer. The final collection for human assessment (Coding Sample) comprised 7,181 texts. We recruited and trained student assessors who first performed training coding that was checked a supervisor. After that unreliable assessors were excluded, and the rest we given more instruction. Each text finally was assessed by three persons who worked independently. Assessors were asked to answer the following questions: (a) is the text understandable? (yes/no/other language); (b) does it contain one, several or no ethnonyms?; (c) how strongly a general negative sentiment is expressed in it, if any? (no/weak/strong); (d) how strongly a general positive sentiment is expressed in it, if any? (no/weak/strong); (e) does the text mention interethnic conflict? (yes/no/unclear); (f) does the text mention positive interethnic interaction? (yes/no/unclear); (g) does the text contain the topic of ethnicity? (yes/no); (h) same question for ten more topics, including "other" and "unclear" (yes/no). Further, for each ethnonym mentioned the following questions were asked: (i) does the author refer to a concrete representative of an ethnic group or to the group as a whole? (former/latter/unclear); (j) what is the overall author's attitude to this group/person? (negative/neutral/positive); (k) does the author belong to the ethnic group s/he is writing about? (yes/no/not mentioned); (l) does the author call for violence against the mentioned ethnic group/person? (no/openly/latently); (m) is the ethnic group or person portrayed as superior or inferior compared to others? (former/latter/unclear/irrelevant); (n) is the ethnic group or person portrayed as a victim or an aggressor in interethnic relations? (yes/no/unclear/ irrelevant); (o) is the ethnic group or person portrayed as dangerous? (yes/no/unclear).

This list reflects our approach to capturing attitudes to ethnicity in UGC. Hate speech as ethnically non-neutral concept was never applied. Neither in written instructions nor during training sessions assessors were told whether it is ethically acceptable to portray ethnic groups as superior or inferior, call for violence against them or engage in conflict with them. The assessors could hold any positions on this matter and be of any ethnic group themselves; their task was to determine if a given feeling or position was present in the text. Moreover, they were explicitly told that making their own ethical judgement about text authors or text characters was not their job.

For this codesheet, a web interface was developed that works both from stationary computers and mobile devices. It has several questions per screen and the checkboxes with the most frequent answer checked by default. This makes the work of assessors much faster and minimizes errors. The interface also allows deleting the answers would an assessor find a mistake after submitting the work.

The results of coding present a "vortex". If an assessor found the text uninter-pretable, no other questions were shown. We obtained 4,947 texts that were unani-mously considered understandable, and 6,719 texts understood by at least one assessor (of them the vast majority was understood by two persons). Further, there were 6,383 texts in which at least one assessors found an ethnonyms. It means that the rest contained homonyms (e.g. reference to actor Alan Rickman instead of Alans). In particular, among mentions of eleven Siberian/Northern ethnic groups as much as 48-97% in fact were found to contain no ethnonym. For 86% of ethnicities, however, this rate of false-positives was below one-third. As a result, we obtained 4,121 texts that were found both understandable and ethnonym-containing unanimously. Only these texts got answers to questions c-f. Finally, of them only 2291 were unanimously considered to contain the topic of ethnicity. It means that the rest only mentioned an ethnonym – (e.g. "Ukrainian Ivan Petrenko won the gold medal in sprinting"). Therefore, only 2,291 texts got three answers on questions i-o.

It thus has been virtually impossible to work only with the most reliable data – that is, the texts that got three independent grades for each question. Although their reli-ability might have improved the quality of classification, their small quantity would have played against it. We therefore chose to work with texts that had received at least one grade. Even then, for some questions the "yes" answers were too rare (e.g. call for violence). Finally, we trained classifiers only for questions c, d, j (negative and positive sentiment and author's attitude); e, f (conflict and positive interaction), and g (presence of ethnicity as a topic). The latter was made to improve selection of relevant texts compared to simple keyword search that, as mentioned in the beginning, gave a rel-atively good precision but supposedly poor recall.

7 Classification and Results

The experiment procedure was the following. At first, for feature selection, a lexicon of bigrams was trained on the Keyword Sample with non-lemmatized texts with Gensim phrases function. The final lexicon included only words and bigrams that occurred not less than 5 times in the collection (7,307 unigrams and 6,514 bigrams). After that we experimented with extracting words and bigrams from texts lemmatized with pymorpthy2. The final lexicon included 6,364 words and 7,039 bigrams.

The hand-coded texts were also lemmatized and transformed into the vector form using both absolute word frequencies and their tf-idf weights. As the target variables were the mean assessors' scores, they were often non-integer; therefore, they were either binarized or trinarized depending on the number of initial values that the corresponding variable could take. The thresholds for this procedure are given in Table 1.

Table 1. Quality of automatic classification of users' texts on ethnicity

Does the text contain:	Texts	Binarization/ trinarization	Avg precision	Avg recall	Avg F1	Avg accuracy & variance	Gain over base., target class, %
General negative sentiment	6,674	<0.3 = 0; ≥0.3 = 1	0.75	0.75	0.75	74.67 ± 1.50	20
General positive sentiment	6,688	<0.3 = 0; ≥0.3 = 1	0.71	0.66	0.68	75.1 ± 1.69	21
General attitude to an ethnic group	5,970	<1.3 = 0; [1.3; 2.35] = 1; >2.35 = 2	0.55	0.47	0.49	66.54 ± 1.74	21; 7
Interethnic conflict	6,701	<0.3 = 0; ≥0.3 = 1	0.72	0.71	0.71	75.22 ± 1.60	26
Positive interethnic interaction	6,711	<0.3 = 0; ≥0 = 10.80	0.71	0.61	0.63	82.80 ± 1.58	18
Topic of ethnicity	5,970	<0.8 = 0; ≥0.8 = 1	0.67	0.66	0.66	66.81 ± 1.82	16

The sample was 100 times randomly divided into a training set (90%) and a test set (10%). The classifier (logistic regression with scikit-learn library) was trained on the training sets and tested on the test sets. The results were averaged over all 100 runs.

The following quality metrics were calculated: (a) precision: the share of texts correctly assigned to a given class among all texts assigned to this class; (b) avg precision: mean of all values of precision over all classes; (c) recall: the share of texts assigned to a given class among all texts assigned to this class by assessors; (d) avg recall: mean of all values of recall over all classes; (e) F1-score (a variant of F-measure): F1 = 2 * (precision * recall)/(precision + recall); (f) avg F1: mean of all values of F1 over all classes; (g) accuracy: the share of correctly predicted cases, %, that is the share of texts that were assigned to the same class as decided by the assessors; (h) avg accuracy & variance – mean of all values of accuracy over all classes and its variance; (i) gain over baseline for the target class, the baseline being the probability of assigning an item from a class of interest to its true class by a random classifier that keeps the true class proportion. That is, for each target class this probability equals its share in the collection. The target class was each time the one that possessed the feature (e.g. texts that contain negative sentiment as opposed to those that do not). For the three-class task r there were two target classes: text with positive attitude and with negative attitude to ethnic groups as opposed to the neutral.

These metrics were calculated for classifiers trained on: lemmatized and non-lemmatized texts; texts vectorized with absolute word frequencies and tf-idf weights; with a word-only lexicon and with a lexicon that includes both words and bigrams. The best results were obtained on lemmatized texts with tf-idf weights and bigrams, and only they are reported below (see Table 1).

We find that general positive and negative sentiments, as well as interethnic conflict are reasonably well predicted. Positive sentiment detection, however, gains much more in terms of precision than recall compared to the baseline, while the prediction of the other two variables is more balanced. This is a common problem with the positive "end" of the sentiment spectrum: lexical features for it are much scanter than for the negative "end", and positive sentiment is much more often expressed indirectly. We can see the same tendency with detecting positive interethnic contact as compared to conflict. It, too, gains mostly in precision rather than in recall.

Prediction of the ethnicity topic yields modest results for a similar reason: the predicted feature is quite vague and hard to define. In fact, this was the question that aroused the largest share of doubts and disagreement among assessors. Finally, predicting attitude to an ethnic group faces the largest problems. We can see that while negative attitude get predicted fairly well with 20% gain over the baseline, detection of positive attitude gains 16% in precision and zero in recall. This most probably happens because nearly half of the texts contain more than one ethnic group. There are, however, several important arguments against excluding those texts for attitude prediction. First, we do not know how attitude formation in multiethnic texts substantially differs from that in mono-ethnic one: it may happen that different speech features are used in those two types of texts. Second, even if it is not the case, a classifier trained on "pure" mono-ethnic cases would inevitably "average" attitude scores for different ethnicities if they get different attitudes in the same text.

8 Conclusion and Future Work

In this work we find that although ethnicity related hate speech online is an important concern both for the public and the policy makers, ethnicity relevant discourse constitutes a tiny fraction of user-generated content. This makes a task of retrieving relevant content similar to finding a needle in a haystack. Furthermore, attitudes expressed in such short informal texts are, unsurprisingly, not easy to predict, as humans, too, diverge in their understanding of various aspects of those attitudes. We conclude that at present researchers of ethnicity representations in the Russian language social media can rely on our general negative sentiment and conflict detection classifiers to look for problematic texts, and (with more caution) on positive sentiment and positive interaction detection classifiers to find texts that can potentially contribute to interethnic understanding and peace. While these instruments can still be improved, their quality is already reasonably high. However, prediction of the other two variables should be improved.

Apart from obtaining more marked-up data (which is currently being done), several directions for improvement may be outlined. First, it is necessary to set stricter criteria for classifying a text as truly devoted to ethnicity. With more data is will become possible to select only texts on which the opinion of at least two persons coincided. Further, adding a more contrastive collection of non-relevant texts might improve the quality of topic classification. Next, predicting other variables based only on relevant texts might influence quality – in particular, excluding texts where ethnonyms were only mentioned, but the topic of ethnicity was absent, might bring forward lexical features used to express attitudes to ethnic groups.

In general, however, improvement of attitude detection should follow a different path. This task similar to opinion mining from consumer reviews with multiple entities, e.g. that compare several products. For such cases the existing approaches usually recommend to perform sentence-level analysis. A problem with social media texts is that often sentence division is not clear. Furthermore, ethnic groups, unlike most consumer goods, can interact, and this is usually expressed in the same sentence. It is thus necessary to do manual linguistic work to adjust the size of the window for left and right contexts of ethnonyms. It may be also useful to exclude ethnic groups that get rarely covered in highly opinionated pieces. However, as different groups may be described in different terms, to avoid a bias after such exclusion, it may make sense to further develop the approach of sampling from clusters – e.g. a cluster of small Siberian ethnicities might get represented by those that arouse more sentiment. Finally, it may worth trying to predict attitudes to each ethnic cluster separately (with conflict-driven clusters being divided).

We also find that attention to ethnic groups varies greatly by region and by group; we therefore expect that sentiment, attitudes and conflict levels also vary. It thus makes sense to detect not the absolute values aggregated by region, group or ethnicity cluster, but their change compared to the average level or to the previous period.

Acknowledgements. This work was done at the Laboratory for Internet Studies, National Research University Higher School of Economics (NRU HSE), Russia. It was supported by the Russian Research Foundation grant no. 15-18-00091.

References

1. Apishev, M., Koltsov, S., Koltsova, E.Y., Nikolenko, S., Vorontsov, K.: Mining ethnic content online with additively regularized topic models. Computacion y Sistemas **20**, 387–403 (2016). doi:10.13053/CyS-20-3-2473
2. Attenberg, J., Ipeirotis, P.G., Provost, F.J.: Beat the machine: challenging workers to find the unknown unknowns. In: Proceedings of 11th AAAI Conference on Human Computation, pp. 2–7 (2011)
3. Bartlett, J., et al.: Anti-Social Media. Demos, London (2014)
4. Blei, D.M., Ng, A.Y., Jordan, M.I.: Latent Dirichlet allocation. J. Mach. Learn. Res. **3**, 993–1022 (2003)
5. Bodrunova, S., Koltsova, O., Nikolenko, S.: Are migranty all the same? Attitudes to re-settlers from post-soviet South in the Russian blogosphere (2016). Unpublished manuscript

6. Bodrunova, S.S., Litvinenko, A.A., Gavra, D.P., Yakunin, A.V.: Twitter-based discourse on migrants in Russia: the case of 2013 bashings in Biryulyovo. Int. Rev. Manag. Mark. **5**, 97–104 (2015)
7. Bohlin, L., Edler, D., Lancichinetti, A., Rosvall, M.: Community detection and visualization of networks with the map equation framework. In: Ding, Y., Rousseau, R., Wolfram, D. (eds.) Measuring Scholarly Impact, pp. 3–34. Springer, Cham (2014). doi:10.1007/978-3-319-10377-8_1
8. Burnap, P., Williams, M.L.: Cyber hate speech on Twitter: an application of machine classification and statistical modeling for policy and decision making. Policy Internet **7**, 223–242 (2015). doi:10.1002/poi3.85
9. Chan, J., et al.: The internet and racial hate crime: offline spillovers from online access. MIS Q.: Manag. Inf. Syst. **40**(2), 381–403 (2016)
10. Daniels, J.: Race and racism in Internet studies: a review and critique. New Media Soc. **15**, 695–719 (2013). doi:10.1177/1461444812462849
11. Dekker, R., Belabas, W., Scholten, P.: Interethnic contact online: contextualising the implications of social media use by second-generation migrant youth. J. Intercult. Stud. **36**, 450–467 (2015). doi:10.1080/07256868.2015.1049981
12. Djuric, N., Zhou, J., Morris, R., Grbovic, M., Radosavljevic, V., Bhamidipati, N.: Hate speech detection with comment embeddings. In: Proceedings of the 24th International Conference on World Wide Web, pp. 29–30. ACM (2015). doi:10.1145/2740908.2742760
13. Faris, R., Ashar, A., Gasser, U., Joo, D.: Understanding harmful speech online. Berkman Klein Center Research Publication No. 2016-21 (2016). doi:10.2139/ssrn.2882824
14. Gagliardone, I.: Mapping and Analysing Hate Speech Online. Social Science Research Network, Rochester (2014)
15. Gibson, S., Lando, A.L.: Impact of Communication and the Media on Ethnic Conflict. IGI Global, Hershey (2015)
16. Gitari, N.D., Zuping, Z., Damien, H., Long, J.: A lexicon-based approach for hate speech detection. Int. J. Multimed. Ubiquit. Eng. **10**, 215–230 (2015). doi:10.14257/ijmue.2015.10.4.21
17. Gladkova, A.: Linguistic and cultural diversity in Russian cyberspace: examining four ethnic groups online. J. Multicult. Discourses **10**, 49–66 (2015). doi:10.1080/17447143.2015.1011657
18. Glukhov, A.P.: Construction of national identity through a social network: a case study of ethnic networks of immigrants to Russia from Central Asia. AI Soc. **32**, 101–108 (2017). doi:10.1007/s00146-016-0644-9
19. Grasmuck, S., Martin, J., Zhao, S.: Ethno-racial identity displays on Facebook. J. Comput.-Mediat. Commun. **15**, 158–188 (2009). doi:10.1111/j.1083-6101.2009.01498.x
20. Grishhenko, A.I., Nikolina, N.A.: Expressive ethnonyms as markers of hate speech [Jekspressivnye jetnonimy kak primety jazyka vrazhdy]. In: Hate Speech and Speech of Consent in the Socio-Cultural Context of Modern Society [Jazyk vrazhdy i jazyk soglasija v sociokul'turnom kontekste sovremennosti], pp. 175–187 (2006). (in Russian)
21. Kim, Y.-C., Jung, J.-Y., Ball-Rokeach, S.J.: Ethnicity, place, and communication technology: effects of ethnicity on multi-dimensional internet connectedness. Inf. Technol. People **20**, 282–303 (2007). doi:10.1108/09593840710822877
22. Korobkova, O.S.: Hate speech indicators in ethnic membership nominations: sociolinguistic aspect [Markery jazyka vrazhdy v nominacijah jetnicheskoj prinadlezhnosti: so-ciolingvisticheskij aspekt]. Izvestia: Herzen Univ. J. Humanit. Sci. [Izvestija Rossijskogo gosudarstvennogo pedagogicheskogo universiteta im. AI Gercena] 200–205 (2009). (in Russian)

23. Kwok, I., Wang, Y.: Locate the hate: detecting tweets against blacks. In: Proceedings of the 27th AAAI Conference on Artificial Intelligence, AAAI 2013, pp. 1621–1622 (2013)

24. McLaine, S.: Ethnic online communities. In: Cyberactivism: Online Activism in Theory and Practice, pp. 233–254 (2003)

25. Mustafa, H., Hamid, H.A., Ahmad, J., Siarap, K.: Intercultural relationship, prejudice and ethnocentrism in a computer-mediated communication (CMC): a time-series experiment. Asian Soc. Sci. **8**, 34–48 (2012). doi:10.5539/ass.v8n3p34

26. Nikolenko, S.I., et al.: Topic modelling for qualitative studies. J. Inf. Sci. **43**(1), 88–102 (2017)

27. Nakamura, L.: Cybertypes: Race, Ethnicity, and Identity on the Internet. Routledge, Abingdon (2013)

28. Nobata, C., Tetreault, J., Thomas, A., Mehdad, Y., Chang, Y.: Abusive language detection in online user content. In: Proceedings of the 25th International Conference on World Wide Web, pp. 145–153. International World Wide Web Conferences Steering Committee (2016). doi:10.1145/2872427.2883062

29. Parker, D., Song, M.: New ethnicities online: reflexive racialisation and the internet. Soc. Rev. **54**, 575–594 (2006). doi:10.1111/j.1467-954X.2006.00630.x

30. Silva, L., Mondal, M., Correa, D., Benevenuto, F., Weber, I.: Analyzing the targets of hate in online social media. In: Proceedings of the 10th International Conference on Web and Social Media, ICWSM 2016, pp. 687–690 (2016)

31. Steinfeldt, J.A., Foltz, B.D., Kaladow, J.K., Carlson, T.N., Pagano Jr., L.A., Benton, E., Steinfeldt, M.C.: Racism in the electronic age: role of online forums in expressing racial attitudes about American Indians. Cult. Divers. Ethnic Minor. Psychol. **16**, 362–371 (2010). doi:10.1037/a0018692

32. Sternin, I.A.: Politically incorrect national names in language consciousness of language's possessor [Nepolitkorrektnye naimenovanija lic v jazykovom soznanii nositelja jazyka]. Polit. linguist. [Politicheskaja lingvistika] **1**, 191–193 (2013)

33. Trebbe, J., Schoenhagen, P.: Ethnic minorities in the mass media: how migrants perceive their representation in Swiss public television. J. Int. Migr. Integr. **12**, 411–428 (2011). doi:10.1007/s12134-011-0175-7

34. Tukachinsky, R., Mastro, D., Yarchi, M.: Documenting portrayals of race/ethnicity on primetime television over a 20-year span and their association with national-level racial/ethnic attitudes. J. Soc. Issues **71**, 17–38 (2015). doi:10.1111/josi.12094

35. Tulkens, S., Hilte, L., Lodewyckx, E., Verhoeven, B., Daelemans, W.: A dictionary-based approach to racism detection in Dutch social media. arXiv preprint arXiv:1608.08738 (2016)

36. Tynes, B.M., Giang, M.T., Thompson, G.N.: Ethnic identity, intergroup contact, and outgroup orientation among diverse groups of adolescents on the Internet. CyberPsychol. Behav. **11**, 459–465 (2008). doi:10.1089/cpb.2007.0085

37. Vepreva, I.T., Kupina, N.A.: The words of unrest in the world today: unofficial ethnonyms in real usage [Trevozhnaja leksika tekushhego vremeni: neoficial'nye jetnonimy v funkcii aktu-al'nyh slov]. Polit. linguist. [Politicheskaja lingvistika] 43–50 (2014). (in Russian)

38. Warner, W., Hirschberg, J.: Detecting hate speech on the world wide web. In: Proceedings of the Second Workshop on Language in Social Media, pp. 19–26. Association for Computational Linguistics (2012)

39. Waseem, Z.: Are you a racist or am I seeing things? Annotator influence on hate speech detection on Twitter. In: Proceedings of the 1st Workshop on Natural Language Processing and Computational Social Science, pp. 138–142 (2016)

40. Waseem, Z., Hovy, D.: Hateful symbols or hateful people? Predictive features for hate speech detection on Twitter. In: Proceedings of NAACL-HLT 2016, pp. 88–93 (2016)

41. Zhu, Z.: Making the "invisible" a "visible problem"—the representation of Chinese illegal immigrants in US newspapers. J. Chin. Overseas **10**, 61–90 (2014). doi:10.1163/17932548-12341268

Analysis and Classification of Multi-opinionated Content in the Era of Cyber Activism

Priya Dhawan[✉], Gopika Bhardwaj, and Rishabh Kaushal

Indira Gandhi Delhi Technical University, Delhi, India
priya.dhawan767@gmail.com

Abstract. Today, the use of Online Social Media (OSM) is not restricted to merely networking and socializing. Recent events all around the globe attest to the prevalence of use of OSM sites for bringing about dramatic and drastic reforms in real world, phenomenon being referred as *Cyber Activism*. The real world is marred with various turmoils and people hold myriad variety of views and judgments regarding various issues. Their opinions are often poorly backed by facts. We refer to such inconclusive judgements that users generate and propagate on OSM platforms as *Multi-Opinionated Content*. One of the greatest challenge in such an environment is to analyze and classify such content into multiple opinion classes. In this work, we propose a generic semi-supervised classification based methodology for analyzing and classifying multi-opinionated content. We have used widely known off-the-shelf classifiers namely KNN, decision tree and random forest in our approach. To implement and validate our methodology, we have mined opinions on content in various forms, namely videos, tweets and posts on three popular social media platforms namely Youtube, Twitter and Facebook, respectively. In our validation, we have taken the Kashmir conflict between India and Pakistan as our case study. We have used plethora of features in building the classification model. Our experiments show that Random Forest classifier gives maximum accuracy of 90.02% and user level features give the best results. Our work can be used to process large amount of multi-opinionated content for effective and accurate decision making in the era of cyber activism generating multi-opinionated content.

Keywords: Online social media · Opinion mining · Semi-supervised learning

1 Introduction

Twitter, Facebook and YouTube are widely used online social media platforms for discussing and sharing views. As per recent statistics, there are numerous indicators demonstrating huge growth of these social networking sites with Twitter allowing 100 million users to post around 500 million tweets per day, YouTube having over 6 billion hours of videos watched every month and Facebook with its 1.86 billion monthly users. These statistics clearly suggests that these online

© Springer International Publishing AG 2017
D.A. Alexandrov et al. (Eds.): DTGS 2017, CCIS 745, pp. 31–44, 2017.
https://doi.org/10.1007/978-3-319-69784-0_3

social media (OSM) platforms enable millions of users to upload large amount of content. Users are often inclined to upload content which is sensational, at times with an objective of sensitizing and sometimes inciting others in support of their views, opinons and agenda.

1.1   Era of Cyber Activism and Multi-opinionated Content

Since the advent of social media platforms, the inter-connectedness between the people has undoubtedly reached unprecedented levels. With barely any restrictions, Internet in general and OSM platforms in particular have become powerful medium for free speech and activism. The accessibility of such OSM platforms and their ability to provide anonymity for their users have encouraged increased participation, as is evident during the political protests against the World Trade Organisation in Seattle in 1999 and the mobilisation of citizens during the Arab Spring [1]. We refer to such an environment as an era of *Cyber Activism*, defined as *the process of using Online Social Media tools to create, operate and manage activism for any cause.* In such an era of cyber activism, people have varying views about varying subjects and contradictory opinions regarding contentious situations. This has led to the rise of what we refer as *Multi-Opinionated Content.* Such multiplicity of opinions are expressed on all forms of content namely posts, photos, videos, audio, etc. on OSM platforms. But in a world that is rapidly changing, people do not hold on to steadfast and rigid opinions. Often this multi-opinionated content is inconclusive, lacks authority and is devoid of facts. However, it has a capacity to form popular opinions and maneuver narratives. It is therefore important and a challenge to develop and build systems that could automatically analyze and classify user generated content into multiple opinion categories.

1.2   Our Contributions, Validation and Results

In this work, we have made an attempt to build a *generic* semi-supervised classification model that analyses and classifies multi-opinionated content on OSM platforms into multiple opinion classes. We have extracted all representative opinions revolving around a particular topic using a number of keywords. Further, we have identified and extracted all possible features for the opinionated content, categorized these features into content-level, user-level and so on. We feed these features into standard off-the-shelf learning algorithms (classifiers) namely K-Nearest Neighbour (KNN), Random Forest and Decision Tree. Our usage of semi-supervision meant that we require only a small set of manually annotated content. In our work, we had addressed a lot of challenges, for instance, clearly identifying the multiple opinion classes in the multi-opinionated content present in the era of cyber activism.

We have tested our model on the Kashmir conflict between India and Pakistan. Such conflicts often leads to people making contrary opinions and expressing strong sentiments. These remarkably varying opinions and sentiments makes the Kashmir conflict an apt case study for experimental setup to test, validate and evaluate our generic model for classification. We have extracted a large number of Facebook posts, Twitter tweets and Youtube videos based on popular keywords on these OSM platforms. In terms of sentiment classes, we identied five classes namely Pro-India, Anti-India, Pro-Pakistan, Anti-Pakistan and Pro-Kashmir. Our results include the accuracies of various classication algorithms used to classify content on the three popular OSM platforms namely Youtube, Twitter and Facebook. Additionally, we have analyzed the distribution of content in all the classes based on popularity and engagement metrics. Through our work, we have come to the conclusion that this generic model can be applied to the myriad of similar conflicts situation which precipitate multi-opinionated content on OSM platforms in this era of cyber activism.

2   Related Work

Our problem is at the cross section of various overlapping domains of opinion mining and classification, often performed using classification models based on semi-supervised learning. In this subsection, we briefly describe some of the most important prior works.

2.1   Opinion Mining

Wu et al. [2] applied text mining to analyze unstructured text content on Facebook and Twitter sites. The result reveals that the text mining is an effective technique to extract business value from vast amount of available social media data. Maynard et al. [3] described the challenges faced in opinion mining and developed a rule-based approach that performs linguistic analysis that builds on linguistic sub-components to calculate opinion polarity and score. Cambria et al. [4] developed an opinion mining source called SenticNet that performs mining of natural language text at semantic level. Deriving from these works, we used python libraries to mine opinions from various Online Social Media Platforms.

2.2   Classification

Papadopoulos et al. [5] performed the community detection and classification of existing algorithms and also assessed the performance of existing methods in terms of computational complexity and memory. Khan et al. [6] have presented an algorithm for twitter feeds classification based on a hybrid approach. The proposed method includes various pre-processing steps before feeding the text to the classifier - filtering english tweets, removal of duplicates, special characters, URL, hashtags, punctuation and usernames. Spell checker is applied to correct the spellings. Slang words are replaced with correct words and abbreviation with complete word. After performing pre-processing, data is fed to classifier which performs classification. Noferesti and Shamsfard [7] evaluated indirect opinion for drug reviews to improve classification process. We have used scikit-learn to perform classification on our data.

2.3 Semi-supervised Learning

Bodo and Minier [8] have compared kNN and semi-supervised kNN algorithms empirically on 2 data sets for multi-label classification. Zhu and Grahramani [9] investigated the use of unlabeled data to help identify labeled data in classification. They have proposed a simple iterative algorithm, label propagation, to propagate labels through the data set along high density areas defined by unlabeled data. We have also used the same to label our unlabelled data.

3 Methodology

In this section, we will elucidate our proposed generic methodology that we have designed to analyze and classify multi-opinionated content in the era of cyber activism. Figure 1 gives a pictorial description of data processing pipeline.

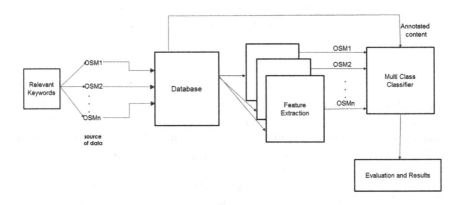

Fig. 1. Pipeline of data processing for proposed generic methodology for analyzing and classifying multi-opinionated content over popular OSM platforms

3.1 Phase I: Information Gathering

First phase involves understanding the background of the topic (conflict situation), identifying relevant keywords for data collection over various OSM platforms. Data collected is pre-processed before feature extraction phase can begin.

– **Understanding the background.** In this step, we thoroughly understand our topic (conflict situation) which had lead to generation of multi-opinionated content on various OSM platforms. So, we read up the background history pertaining to the topic and major events related to it. It is very important to have a general understanding of topic so as to make sense of the multi-opinionated content generated by users.

- **Identifying opinion classes and associated keywords.** Once we have completely understood the topic, we identify multiple classes of opinions being expressed by users and the commonly used words or phrases by them, referred as keywords. These keywords must be concise in number and must fully reflect the various opinions of the topic.
- **Data Collection.** Using these keywords, we collect data from various OSM platforms using their application programmer interfaces (APIs). For multi-opinionated content, we limit ourselves to textual data (and meta-data) associated with *posts* on Facebook, *tweets* on Twitter and *video title, description and comments* on Youtube. The data is stored in a database which supports unstructured data (for instance, mongoDB).

3.2 Phase II: Features Engineering and Annotation

In second phase, we perform **feature engineering** which involves identification of numeric features in various OSM platforms and formulate the process of **annotation** which is to be done manually. Given that we are using semi-supervised learning approach, the manual annotation work is significantly reduced. Detailed list of features for each OSM platform are explain in sections later.

3.3 Phase III: Semi-supervised Learning

Annotation of opinionated content manually would require lot of time and patience. Therefore, in our proposed generic methodology, we employ a standard learning technique called **semi-supervised learning**. Semi-supervised learning makes use of unlabeled data for training, typically a small amount of labeled data with a large amount of unlabeled data. Using this technique, we can ensure that our entire data gets annotated. We make use of off-the-shelf learning algorithms namely K-Nearest Neighbor, Decision Tree and Random Forest for classification. This is followed by the process of **feature selection** where important features in our data that contribute most to the accuracy are identified. Finally, we evaluate the accuracy of learning algorithms using k-fold cross validation process.

4 Experimental Study

In this section, we have implemented the generic methodology proposed in the above section on Jammu-Kashmir Conflict.

4.1 Phase I: Information Gathering

Our case study is based on the plethora of opinions and facts revolving around the resolution of the conflict through various activist movements started by various stakeholders on Facebook, Twitter and Youtube.

– **Understanding the background.** We have tested our model on the age-old conflict of Kashmir occupation by India and Pakistan. Parts of Kashmir are occupied by India, Pakistan and China. While the countries involved refuse to release their stronghold on the beautiful alley, the people of the region suffer untold pain. The resolution of the conflict is intensely difficult due to the multiple opinions garnered by the people.
– **Identifying opinion classes and associated keywords.** As we scoured the online social media platforms for relevant activist movements pertaining to the Kashmir conflict, we were able to narrow down to the following keywords in Table 1 which aptly represent the situation on multiple online social media platforms.

Based on our review of the opinionated content revolving around our chosen keywords, we are able to narrow down the opinions to 5 class labels for Youtube and Facebook and 6 class labels for Twitter.

(i) Anti-India: Content generated by people having an Anti-India outlook. They believe that India should relinquish its hold over Kashmir.

(ii) Pro-India: Opinionated content that supports Indian presence in the valley and rallies for the full occupation of Kashmir by India.

Table 1. Keywords pertaining to Jammu-Kashmir conflict

Platform	Related keywords
Youtube	Kashmir terrorism
	Kashmir hate speech
	Kashmir violence
	Kashmir clashes
	PakistanoccupiedKashmir
	Kashmir people about India
	Kashmir people about Pakistan
Twitter	@JammuKashmir5
	kashmirSOS
	freekashmir
	kashmirlovesIndia
	burahwani
	Kashmirissue
	KashmirUnrest
	KashmirKillings
Facebook	Proud to be a Kashmiri
	Kashmir.Page
	KashmirCrisis
	Freedom of Kashmir

(iii) Anti-Pakistan: Sentiments that hold Pakistan in a negative view, includes posts by people who protest against Pakistan's Occupation of Kashmir.

(iv) Pro-Pakistan: Opinions that supports Pakistan's control and sensitize others to cause of Pakistan being in control of Kashmir.

(v) Pro-Kashmir: Public opinion that emphasizes direct vigorous action in support of Kashmir secession from both India and Pakistan.

(vi) Undecidable: For Twitter, we needed to form another class label because we were only able to annotate tweets, while in Facebook and Youtube, our annotation was quite comprehensive, since we annotated posts, comments and video title, description, comments, channel title and description for the platforms respectively. Hence, for Twitter, we introduce class 'Undecidable' for tweets containing vague and ambiguous data that does not fall into any of our label buckets.

Following pie-charts show the distribution of various videos, posts and tweets across different classes (Fig. 2).

– **Data Collection.** We have collected our opinionated content derived from the above mentioned keywords and public pages from the repective platforms and have stored it in mongoDB. As written in Table 1, using YouTube Data API, 5396 videos were collected along with their metadata which were reduced to the count 4396 after removing duplicate videos. Additionally, we have collected near to 50 comments per video and we have 111121 comments in our database.

We collected 4732 tweets using Twitter library Tweepy.

Using Facebook Graph API, we collected facebook posts and like our collection in Youtube, we also collected around 50 comments per post, making total collected Facebook data sum up to 120457. Along with the opinionated content, we also collected various attributes for each platform which are in later sections, defined as features. Our aim is to form an exhaustive data set. Data cleaning is done by removing punctuation marks, hashtags () and @ from the data set. Stop words are not removed because they play an importance role in defining the opinionated content given by the users.

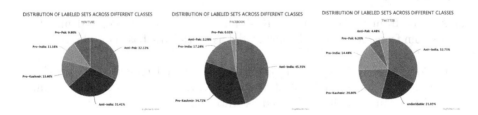

Fig. 2. Distribution across classes

4.2   Phase II: Features Engineering and Annotation

The most optimum results are achieved when we construct a set of features. This process is called Feature Engineering. A feature is a piece of information that might be useful for prediction. All the collected attributes which we deemed useful for our generic model have been used as features.

After having identified our various classes - we move on to the task of putting our opinionated content - each video, post and tweet into its respective class. This task of Manual annotation has been performed by a team of 2 (Fig. 3).

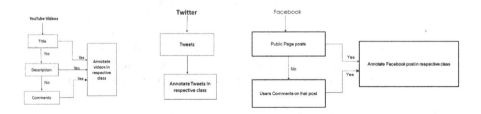

Fig. 3. Manual annotation techniques - Youtube, Twitter and Facebook

Facebook - For Facebook, we read the entire post as well as its commnents, and with a completely rational point of view, classify the post in any of the above mentioned classes its opinionated content majorly belongs to. We annotated 360 posts manually.

Twitter - For Twitter, we read the entire tweet. Since Twitter is a microblogging site with a mandate of just 140 characters per tweet, we came across some content that was distinctly unopinionated which we classified as Undecidable. We annotated 370 tweets.

Youtube - For Youtube, we first review the video title and description. If the opinions reflected in the above features are vague, we move on to comments garnered by the video. If ambiguity persists in the comments, we review the title and description of the channel that posted the video and only after accomplishing these comprehensive steps, we classify the video under the afore mentioned classes. We annotated 350 videos.

For example -

(1) A video from Indian occupied Kashmir - Thousands of people demanding freedom from India - Can be annotated as Anti-India based on phrase "freedom from India".
(2) In PoK, locals raise anti-Pakistan slogans, demand removal of Army. Peoples in Baluchistan and Pakistan occupied Kashmir are protesting against Pakistan can be easily annotated as Anti-Pak.

This data forms our ground truth data for implementation of Semi-supervised Learning.

Feature Extraction. We analysed our collected attributes and reduce the vast attribute set by applying feature extraction. Now, we have a smaller yet richer set of attributes. Our model which is built on extracted features is of a higher quality, because the data is described by fewer and meaningful attributes. Feature Extraction enhances the speed and effectiveness of supervised learning.

We started from our initial data - all the attributes we have collected - and built informative and non-redundant features to facilitate the subsequent semi- supervised and supervised learning steps. We have identified and extracted various relevant numerical features pertaining to our content. The Tables 2, 3 and 4 contain the rich set of numerical features that will form our training set for applying classification algorithms.

Table 2. Exhaustive feature set for Facebook

Type	Features
Post-level	Post age, post length, comment count, like count, number of top-k bigrams in post $k = 5$, share count

Table 3. Exhaustive feature set for Twitter

Type	Features
Tweet-level	Tweet age, favourites count, tweet length, retweet count, hashtag count, mention count, number of top-k bigrams in tweet $k = 5$
User level	No of followers No of following

4.3   Phase III: Semi-supervised Learning

Taking into consideration that labeled data must be significantly less than unlabeled data, we performed semi-supervised learning in iterations. Taking 350, 360 and 370 labeled data for Youtube, Facebook and Twitter respectively, we applied Label Spreading technique for an unlabeled data set of 500. In the next iteration, we used the labeled data of 850, 860 and 870 for the three platforms and increment our data set by 500, checking the accuracy of the process at every iteration. We implemented the procedure using Label Spreading mode of Semi-Supervised module of Python Library - scikit-learn. We checked the accuracy of this semi-supervised learning technique by applying supervised learning algorithms - KNN, Decision Tree and Random Forest.

Sometimes, too much information can reduce the effectiveness of a model. Irrelevant features add noise to the data and affect the accuracy of the model. To improve the accuracy of our classifiers, we performed feature importance and identified 10 most important features pertaining to the classifiers employed. We implemented the same using feature importance method of scikit-learn Python library which ranks features according to their contribution to accuracy of the classifier.

Table 4. Exhaustive feature set for Youtube

Type	Features
Video-level	View count, like count, dislike count, comment count, video age, title length, description length, number of top-k bigrams in title, number of top-k bigrams in description
Channel-level	Channel age, views, comment count, channel subscriber count, total number of videos
Comment level	Number of top-k bi-grams in top-N comments, reply count of top-N comments, like count received of top-N comments

5   Results

5.1   Analysis

In context of Youtube, the popularity of the Activism movement can be gauged by various factors whose characterization study is depicted in Fig. 4 comprising Comment Count, View Count and Like Count received on all videos. Similarly for Facebook and Twitter, we can understand the relevance of key distinguishing features that numerically characterize our opinionated content.

In Figs. 5 and 6, the engagements have been captured as Comment Count, Like Count, Share Count for Facebook and as Favourite count and Retweet Count for Twiiter and these are represented in cumulative distribution function curves.

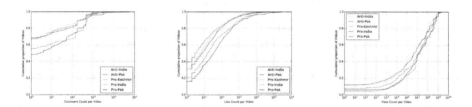

Fig. 4. Characterization of videos based on their popularity and engagement metrics

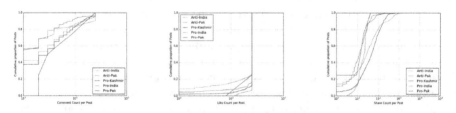

Fig. 5. Characterization of posts based on their popularity and engagement metrics

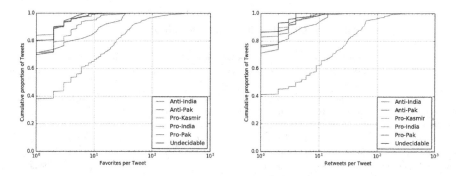

Fig. 6. Characterization of tweets based on their popularity and engagement metrics

5.2 Classification

We have applied Decision Tree, Random Forest and KNN classifiers on all 3 platforms on different combination of features unique to each platform.

To avoid over-fitting, we performed cross-validation. Applying k-fold cross validation, $k = 10$, we trained our model using $k-1$ of folds as training data and the resulting model was validated on the remaining part of the data. The performance measure reported by k-fold cross validation is computed as the average of values in the loop.

We have implemented Decision Tree and Random Forest using both the metrics for splitting the tree - Gini Impurity and Entropy. Table 5 contains the measures of the maximum accuracies we were able to get using these classifying algorithms.

Figs. 7, 8, 9, 10, 11 and 12 represent results for Youtube, Facebook and Twitter. We have the results for Decision Tree Classification for different feature sets among the data on which we have implemented both Gini Impurity and Entropy parameters. Similar results have been obtained for Random forest. We have evaluated Nearest Neighbour values for different values of k. Along with Classifier accuracies, we hae included Feature Importance results for a variety of feature set combinations for Decision Tree and Random forest. Feature Importance is not implemented in KNN.

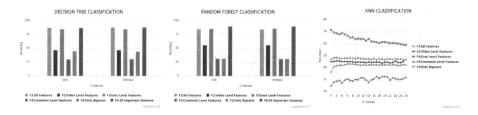

Fig. 7. Youtube - decision tree, random forest and KNN results

Table 5. Classification results for all platforms

Dataset	Decision tree			K-nearest neighbour			Random forest		
	Criterion	Accuracy	Precision	k-value	Accuracy	Precision	Criterion	Accuracy	Precision
Youtube									
F1: All features	Entropy	88.17	87.07	3	48.56	47.12	Gini	85.10	85.34
F2: Video-level	Gini	46.83	46.89	3	45.90	44.40	Entropy	56.01	55.82
F3: User-level	Gini	84.71	85.23	1	71.38	72.93	Entropy	86.05	86.74
F4: Comment-level	Entropy	30.70	26.54	20	33.00	25.91	Gini	31.48	26.61
F5: Only bigrams	Gini	45.06	43.13	7	43.15	43.19	Gini	31.66	26.77
F6: Ten important	Entropy	88.19	88.31	-	-	-	Gini	90.02	89.93
Facebook									
F1: All features	Entropy	83.51	83.60	4	71.92	72.33	Gini	85.54	85.78
F2: Without bigrams	Entropy	83.21	83.91	7	72.28	72.53	Entropy	86.64	86.66
F3: Only bigrams	Entropy	45.64	43.13	21	48.42	36.73	Entropy	47.28	46.92
F4: Ten important	Entropy	83.78	84.42	-	-	-	Entropy	86.07	86.04
Twitter									
F1: All features	Entropy	61.33	462.33	5	41.09	42.80	Entropy	62.37	62.549
F2: Tweet and user	Entropy	60.76	61.99	9	39.58	58.17	Entropy	65.23	65.88
F3: User-level	Gini	62.13	63.21	1	60.83	62.27	Entropy	64.44	64.18
F4: Only bigrams	Gini	37.51	46.5	17	34.63	33.26	Gini	38.32	43.80
F5: Ten important	Entropy	59.48	62.02	-	-	-	Gini	65.93	66.47

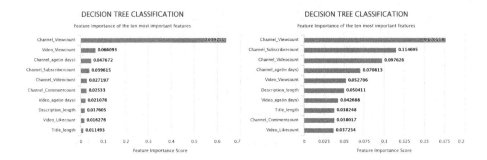

Fig. 8. Youtube feature importance

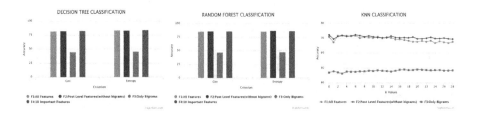

Fig. 9. Facebook - decision tree, random forest and KNN results

Fig. 10. Facebook feature importance

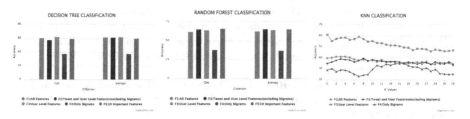

Fig. 11. Twitter - decision tree, random forest and KNN results

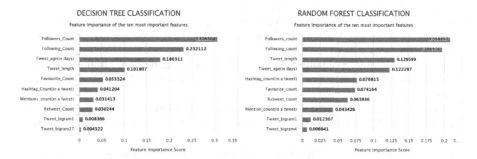

Fig. 12. Twitter feature importance

6   Conclusion

Through our research, we can ascertain that OSM has indeed become quite a popular platform for creating and managing activism of any kind. Our proposed generic methodology can be applied to any such OSM which is contributing to Cyber Activism to analyze the content and classify the varying opinions of the involved parties. The results obtained can prove crucial to resolution of conflicts and maintenance of peace. Our world is rife with all sorts of turmoil and people today easily turn to social media to air their anguish and sorrow. As social media connects millions of people, many rise to join the cause of a better world and start all kinds of long-distance movement, organised on the internet - leading to the proliferation of Cyber-Activism. Governments and Peace-keeping organisations like the United Nations need to keep a check on such Cyber Activism activities lest they turn into violence and causes for terrorism. Our generic model is simple to implement and very effective in gauging the multiple sentiments fuelling the cyber activists. The results of analysis and classification can be used to take preemptive action to prevent any kind of mishap as well as for clear solid decision making especially while resolving conflict situations. In the future, we are working on detecting influencers who initiate activism on the Internet.

References

1. Eltantawy, N., Wiest, J.B.: The Arab spring—social media in the Egyptian revolution: reconsidering resource mobilization theory. Int. J. Commun. **5**, 18 (2011)
2. He, W., Zha, S., Li, L.: Social media competitive analysis and text mining: a case study in the pizza industry. Int. J. Inf. Manage. **33**(3), 464–472 (2013). doi:10.1016/j.ijinfomgt.2013.01.001
3. Maynard, D., Bontcheva, K., Rout, D.: Challenges in developing opinion mining tools for social media. In: Proceedings of the@ NLP can u tag# usergeneratedcontent, pp. 15–22 (2012)
4. Cambria, E., Speer, R., Havasi, C., Hussain, A.: SenticNet: a publicly available semantic resource for opinion mining. In: AAAI Fall Symposium: Common-Sense Knowledge, vol. 10, no. 0, November 2010
5. Papadopoulos, S., Kompatsiaris, Y., Vakali, A., Spyridonos, P.: Community detection in social media. Data Min. Knowl. Disc. **24**(3), 515–554 (2012). doi:10.1007/s10618-011-0224-z
6. Khan, F.H., Bashir, S., Qamar, U.: TOM: Twitter opinion mining framework using hybrid classification scheme. Decis. Support Syst. **57**, 245–257 (2014). doi:10.1016/j.dss.2013.09.004
7. Noferesti, S., Shamsfard, M.: Resource construction and evaluation for indirect opinion mining of drug reviews. PLoS ONE **10**(5), e0124993 (2015). doi:10.1371/journal.pone.0124993
8. Bod, Z., Minier, Z.: On supervised and semi-supervised k-nearest neighbor algorithms. In: Proceedings of the 6th Joint Conference on Mathematics and Computer Science, p. 1 (2008)
9. Zhu, X., Ghahramani, Z.: Learning from labeled and unlabeled data with label propagation (2002)

Fashion Bloggers as Cultural Intermediaries: The Meaning of Brand Choices in Style Production

Margarita Kuleva[1,2(✉)] and Daria Maglevanaya[1]

[1] National Research University Higher School of Economics, Saint Petersburg, Russia
mkuleva@hse.ru, dvmaglevanaya@edu.hse.ru
[2] Centre for German and European Studies,
SPBSU - Bielefeld University, Saint Petersburg, Russia

Abstract. The paper focuses on fashion bloggers as cultural interme- diaries, which taste origins connect different audiences and groups in the fashion industry. Our sample consists of 15 blogs, which were nom- inated for two major awards for fashion bloggers Bloglovin.com and Stylight.com in 2015. We analyzed 1223 looks they produced for 1 year (brand choices for every look). We created a two-mode network (blogger - brand) and converted it to the one-mode network (brand- brand). The main research question is whether fashion bloggers as cul- tural intermediates tend to follow professional community and replicate its hierarchies or rebel against it by creating their owns. The analysis con- sists of 2 steps. First, we look at three dimensions of brand combination (a) mass-market and haute-couture brands (b) brands oriented to male or female audiences (c) global and local brands. Second, we apply the association rules algorithm to extract combinations of brands matching with not only by the quantity of coupling but probabilistically explore brand unions.

Keywords: Fashion bloggers · Cultural intermediaries · Digital fash- ion · Brand choice

1 Introduction

The paper investigates the meaning of fashion bloggers and their brand choices in the process of fashion system democratization. In particular, we analyze how award-winning bloggers combine different type of garments (varied by country of production, the price, and uniqueness) in their looks. By identifying the prin- ciples of clothing combination, we see whether fashion bloggers replicate the existing hierarchies of the professionalized field of fashion or create alternative ones.

The fashion industry is known as a hierarchized one, both on levels of produc- tion [6,8] and consumption. This perspective follows classical theories of fashion diffusion, i.e. trickle-down theory [9,15]. However, in the second part of 20th cen- tury scholars emphasize various evidences on democratization of fashion system: trickle-up consumption [4], street-fashion [8] and subcultural styles [17]. "New

© Springer International Publishing AG 2017
D.A. Alexandrov et al. (Eds.): DTGS 2017, CCIS 745, pp. 45–54, 2017.
https://doi.org/10.1007/978-3-319-69784-0_4

cultural intermediaries" - makers of taste, redefining the value of a (cultural) product through their judgments - become a key figure in the process of democratization of fashion. Bourdieu mentioned the group in "Distinction" within following passage "the new cultural intermediaries (the most typical of whom arc the producers of cultural programmes on TV and or the critics of 'quality' newspapers and magazines and all the writer-journalists and journalist-writers) have invented a whole series of genres half-way between legitimate culture and mass production ('letters', 'essays', 'eye-witness accounts')" [2]. Later on, other authors stressed on the increasing importance of new cultural intermediaries in the postindustrial world: the formation of the principles of postmodernist consumption culture [5], the redefinition of the market, the reduction of the distance between consumers and producers [12].

A contemporary fashion industry is characterized by multiple forms of cultural mediation. Some of these activities can hardly be called "new" and are well-known in the history of fashion: for example, models, sales consultants. Others ones have been institutionalized only recently, for example, [10] mentions 'buyers' and 'cool hunters'. Defining features of fashion blogging in this series are, on the one hand, its mass character (thanks to web 2.0 platforms, huge numbers of young people have got technical opportunities for broadcasting their own ideas about fashion and style), on the other - a small connection with the professional fashion industry (the most high-valued bloggers before their recognition did not have a special education or sufficient professional experience in the industry).

The "golden age" of fashion blogs began in 2006 when fashion professionals of haute couture segment began to invite bloggers to their shows and force various forms of cooperation with them. Some of the bloggers were hired by major fashion magazines as Vogue or Dazed & Confused as columnists [11]. To date, one can speak about the formation of a research direction around the fashion blogging. In particular, some researchers focus on the careers of bloggers, atypical for the fashion industry [13], others - on the influence of bloggers on brand consumption (see [7,14,16,18]). Significantly less is analyzed not only the economic but also the symbolic meaning of fashion bloggers, which is the focus of this paper. In particular, the main research question for this paper is whether fashion bloggers as cultural intermediates tend to follow professional community and replicate its hierarchies or rebel against it by creating their own.

In particular, in this ongoing research, we interested how fashion bloggers (re)connect the hierarchical world of fashion producers and the broader audience of fashion consumers. We know that they use that trends which are translated on runways, but actually, it remains unknown to what outcome it leads to style production. And how the bloggers select and combine clothes from different brands that have various position in the field of fashion for their outfits.

2   Methodology

This research is based on secondary network data collected in 2016. In our case we couldn't detect clear borders of bloggers' professional community [3], our choice was to use "experts lists". We made a sample of 15 nominee and winners from 2 international fashion-bloggers awards of the 2015 year (www.blog.bloglovin. com and www.influencerawards.stylight.com). Then we took a massive of brands which were used in their outfits from January 2015 to September 2015 and after that, we filtered all their posts from the beginning of their blogs to the last post in September. In our analysis, we use materials from 1223 blog posts, to which we applied filtration on 300 brands of clothes, shoes, and accessories. This amount was due to the fact that of the 600 brands that were collected in January-September were taken only recurring in previous years. In our sample, award-winning bloggers are represented by different continents and also 4 of 15 have their own business connected with jewelry or clothing production (Table 1).

Table 1. Bloggers nominees and their locations

Nickname	Gender	Country	Own business
harperandharley	F	Australia	
thechroniclesofher	F	Australia	
lookdepernille	F	Denmark	+
leblogdebetty	F	France	
dandydiary	M	Germany	
katelovesme	M	Spain	
dulceida	F	Spain	
andreaswijk	M	Sweden	
angelicablick	F	Sweden	
blankitinerary	F	USA	+
oraclefox	F	USA	+
liketheyogurt	F	USA	
thriftsandthreads	F	USA	
iamgalla	M	USA	
mdvstyle	M	USA	+

There no information about their educational or professional trajectories, so it is not possible to detect their background in fashion, media or art industries and control this parameter. As we mentioned above, we have 300 brands and to move in our analysis we need to separate them into groups of different brands classes by previously fixed categorization in Aspers and Godart research of fashion production field [1]: lux brands—haute couture, which belongs to high-fashion and collections of this brands shown on catwalks. Premium brands—clothing producers, which shown collections which call ready-to-wear, and production volumes are calculated on mass consumption. Mass-market brands—companies that produce clothes in large volumes, and sales are going through chain stores.

After the initial acquaintance with the field the last category "designers brands" was added by us: that are mostly independent designers who produce limited and unique clothes collections and still almost not recognized by the major fashion media. They do not work on fashion houses, but the prices on their clothes are between premium and lux.

The following analysis was separated on 3 steps. Firstly we did networks of brands where the connection was defined as use couple of brands in the one outfit and made comparisons with ERGMs. Then we use a method of association rules on this connection to extract different levels of mixed-types clothing couples not only by the frequency of brand couples but using probabilistic methods.

3   Result

Firstly we had a two-mode network with bloggers and clothes they used in their posts. Then we created a bipartite projection and in the further analysis, we used a network with brand-brand connections. As a result of Newman algorithm clusterization, we had 7 base communities (Fig. 1). Modularity of this graph is equal to 0.371 and after that, we compared this network with the Erdos-Renyi random graph model (modularity = 0.0626) with the same parameters, so in our network formed clusters are weakly connected with one another, but the nodes within them are closely linked. We suppose, that brands separated on clusters by

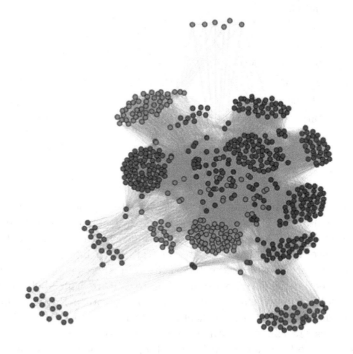

Fig. 1. Communities of brands

the frequency of joint usage in the same outfits, so at this stage, we interpret this division as based on stylistic repertoires. In particular, We can observe designer Spanish brands in the dark-green community, or blue community, where brands collaboration with each other are located.

Let's pay attention to the strength of the connections between certain nodes (Fig. 2), which is mapped in the thickness of the links that connects them. It can be seen on the network that there is a share of "strong unions" formed between brands that are not used in a generalized picture for the entire sample, or whether such links are formed between a "popular" brand that is at the core of the network and a brand from the periphery. We can interpret this as legitimation strategy of bloggers, who try to the extent a high symbolic prestige of a core brand to its 'unpopular' associate.

It is also worth looking at the location of brands in the network (Fig. 3), depending on their belonging to the previously created classification of brand types. There are the colors of the vertices are indicated in accordance with the

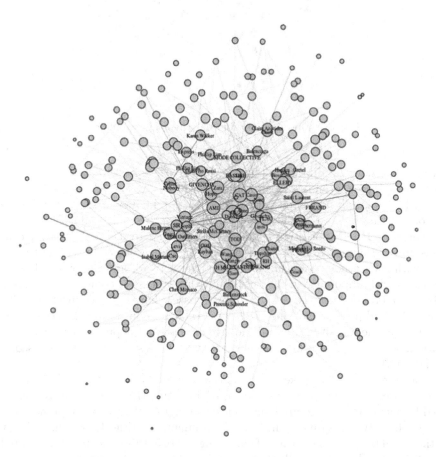

Fig. 2. The strength of the links between brands

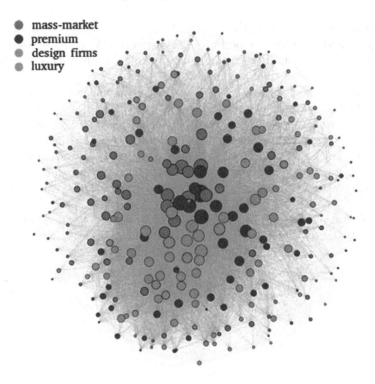

mass-market
premium
design firms
luxury

Fig. 3. Brand type attribution (Color figure online)

specified parameters of brand affiliation: luxury class—red, premium brands—blue, mass-market brands - green and design firms—yellow [1]. The size of the vertex in the graph is defined with respect to the number of shortest paths to the others. In the core of the graph there are represented brands of different categories and the assortativity index there is equal to 0.057. The latter confirms previous observation, that brands with the higher degree linked mostly not only with each other "powerful" brands in the network and unpopular brands matching with unpopular in the outfits but this process of combining clothes is mixed. So, brands from the core are approximately have equal connections with unpopular and popular clothing producers. Talking about brand choices in style production, there is situation that mostly common and popular for trendsetters clothing joining in the outfits with elements which are specific (regional designer brands etc.).

On the next step let's take a closer look at the core of the network (we reduced it to vertices with more than 180 links). Highlighting this segment of frequently used bloggers brands, and applying to it clustering by the Newman method, the core of the network is divided into 2 main communities (Fig. 4). The modularity of the graph based on the results of clustering is 0.025, this indicator is considered insufficient to allow us to talk about meaningful relationships between agents in groups. But based on the results of the algorithm and the classification table of

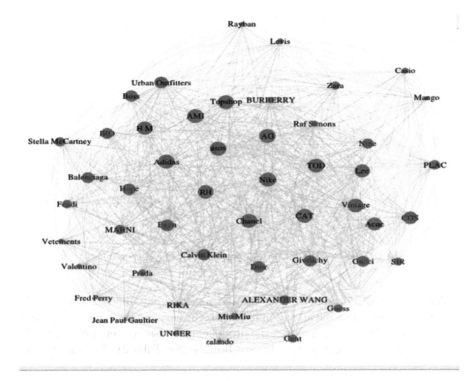

Fig. 4. The core of the network (Color figure online)

brands, the groups in a result can be divided into those in which luxury brands (orange cluster) or mass market (blue cluster). However, there are deviations, for example, the brand "Chanel", belonging to the category of luxury, is associated with a blue cluster.

To test the assumption that the matching of clothing and luxury accessories with other types, as opposed to combinations of clothing only from the luxury class, a binomial test was used. The results showed that the acquisition of looks combining luxury and mass-market, premium or designer clothes is not accidental, and the probability of such an event is 59% ($Y > 64078$, n = 108353, p-value $< 2.2e - 16$, 95% CI = [0.588, 0.594]). Proceeding from this, one can assume about the processes of transformation of the "canonical" mode propagation and a strict hierarchy of consumption of its products.

The next step was to apply association rules method to extract "non-trivial" transactions with different types of brands. We regulated it by "lift" parameter to detect cases with brand mixing and there are such observations. Looking at how the combinations between brands are formed, translating their use in bloggers looks into the category of transactions, we also see a picture of mixing different categories of brand types. It can be noted that, in addition to canonical rules, combining luxury brands with each other, like Chanel and MARNI, or Chanel, Givenchy and Dior, there are associations of luxury and mass-market brands like Topshop and Givenchy (Fig. 5).

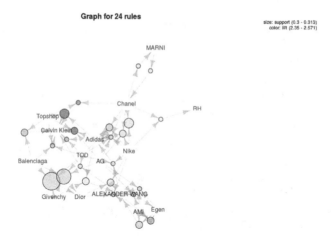

Fig. 5. Association rules with brand to brand transactions

The last step of this analysis was devoted to geography dimension on brands presented in blogs. Drawing attention to North America and the USA at all, there are concentrated to a greater extent the producers of mass-market clothing, while in Europe there are concentrated luxury brands (see Table 2). The interaction

Table 2. Distribution of countries with clothing production

LUX	Country	N	PREM	Country	N	M-M	Country	N	DES	Country	N
	France	18		USA	29		USA	37		Australia	10
	USA	16		UK	12		UK	13		USA	10
	Italy	12		Australia	7		Australia	10		Sweden	6
	UK	9		France	6		Sweden	10		Spain	5
	Australia	7		Sweden	6		Spain	9		Denmark	3
	Denmark	5		Denmark	5		Germany	4		UK	2
	Germany	1		Germany	5		China	3		Finland	1
	Korea	1		Italy	5		Denmark	3		France	1
	CHE	1		Japan	2		Canada	2		Ireland	1
				New Zeland	2		France	2		Italy	1
				Greece	1		Japan	2		NLD	1
				Netherlands	1		NLD	2		Singapore	1
				Spain	1		New Zeland	2		CHE	1
				Switzerland	1		Bangladesh	1			
							Italy	1			
							Norway	1			
							CHE	1			
							Turkey	1			
		70			83			104			43

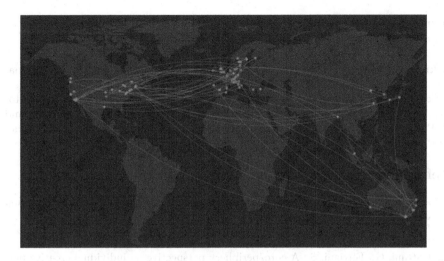

Fig. 6. Brand types worldwide distribution.

of producers and professional consumers (bloggers) in the clothing market also includes Australia, which is characterized by designer brands, whose production is not mass or belonging to the institute of fashion houses. In addition, it is worth noting the west and east coast of North America, which are not connected with each other but interact with European producers. Next map displays the brands from previous analysis and their headquarters (Fig. 6).

4   Discussion

In conclusion, it's should be said that fashion bloggers can definitely be recognized as democratizers of fashion: at all levels of analysis, we have obtained a combination of luxury brands with cheaper and less symbolically prestigious ones. We can not meet such combinations in more habitual places of production, dissemination, and consumption of clothing (fashion catwalks, magazines, clothing stores). Nevertheless, we come to the conclusion about the complexity and non-randomness of combinations of types of brands, beyond which we can trace the moves of bloggers as agents of the field of fashion. In particular, the presence of the luxury segment, which was combined with all other types of brands, provided both legitimization of these brands, and the blogger himself/herself. The global nature of the use of brands by bloggers is also of a note, despite this global picture is limited by North America, Europe, few Asian countries, and Australia and excludes most countries of Global South and Russia as well. As further prospects for the development of this study lie the expansion of the sample, based on expert lists and replenishment of the base of nominees and winners of the awards for 2016. In addition, it is a priority to upgrade methodology with defining economic interactions of bloggers with different brands (sponsorships or promotions). This will allow examining in detail the components of the style as a product of bloggers through consumption of brands.

Acknowledgements. The paper benefited from the support of The Russian Foundation for Humanities (15-03-00722 Coevolution of knowledge and communication networks: structural dynamics of creative collectives in European cultural capitals, 2015-ongoing), and the Centre for German and European Studies (Bielefeld University and St. Petersburg State University) supported by the DAAD with funds from the German Foreign Office.

References

1. Aspers, P., Godart, F.: Sociology of fashion: order and change. Ann. Rev. Sociol. **39**, 171–192 (2013)
2. Bourdieu, P.: Distinction: A Social Critique of the Judgement of Taste. Harvard University Press, Cambridge (1984)
3. Cattani, G., Ferriani, S.: A core/periphery perspective on individual creative performance: Social networks and cinematic achievements in the Hollywood film industry. Organ. Sci. **19**(6), 824–844 (2008)
4. Crane, D.: Fashion and its Social Agendas: Class, Gender, and Identity in Clothing. University of Chicago Press, Chicago (2012)
5. Featherstone, M.: Consumer Culture and Postmodernism. Sage, Thousand Oaks (2007)
6. Entwistle, J., Wissinger, E.: Keeping up appearances: aesthetic labour in the fashion modelling industries of London and New York. Sociol. Rev. **54**, 774–794 (2006)
7. Halvorsen, K., Hoffmann, J., Coste-Manière, I., Stankeviciute, R.: Can fashion blogs function as a marketing tool to influence consumer behavior? Evidence from Norway. J. Glob. Fashion Mark. **4**(3), 211–224 (2013)
8. Kawamura, Y.: Japanese teens as producers of street fashion. Curr. Sociol. **54**(5), 784–801 (2006)
9. King, C.W.: Fashion adoption: a rebuttal to the 'trickle down' theory. In: Greyer, S.A. (ed.) Towards Scientific Marketing, pp. 108–125. American Marketing Association, Chicago (1963)
10. Mora, E., Rocamora, A.: Letter from the editors: analyzing fashion blogs-further avenues for research. Fashion Theory **19**(2), 149–156 (2015)
11. Mora, E.: Collective production of creativity in the Italian fashion system. Poetics **34**(6), 334–353 (2006)
12. Negus, K.: The work of cultural intermediaries and the enduring distance between production and consumption. Cultural Stud. **16**(4), 501–515 (2002)
13. Pedroni, M.: "Stumbling on the heels of my blog": career, forms of capital, and strategies in the (sub) field of fashion blogging. Fashion Theory **19**(2), 179–199 (2015)
14. Reddy, S.L.: Fashion blogging and personal style bloggers. Int. J. Costume Fashion **13**(1), 1–10 (2013)
15. Simmel, G.: Fashion. Int. Q. **10**(1), 130–155 (1904)
16. Stankeviciute, R.: Occupation fashion blogging: relation between blogs and luxury fashion brands. In: Hoffmann, J., Coste-Manière, I. (eds.) Global Luxury Trends. Palgrave Macmillan, UK (2013)
17. Steele, V.: Anti-fashion: the 1970s. Fashion Theory **1**(3), 279–295 (1997)
18. Zhang, C.: Fashion blogs: the new member in fashion industry. J. Digit. Res. Publ. **3**(1), 153–161 (2010)

Online Socioeconomic Activity in Russia: Patterns of Dynamics and Regional Diversity

Dmitry Verzilin[1]([⊠]), Tatiana Maximova[2], and Irina Sokolova[3]

[1] St. Petersburg Institute for Informatics and Automation
of the Russian Academy of Sciences (SPIIRAS),
14th Lin. V.O., 39, St. Petersburg 199178, Russia
modusponens@mail.ru
[2] Saint Petersburg National Research University of Information Technologies,
Mechanics and Optics (ITMO University),
Kronverksky pr., 49, St. Petersburg 197101, Russia
maximovatg@gmail.com
[3] St. Petersburg State University,
Universitetskaya emb., 7-9, St. Petersburg 199034, Russia
i_sokolova@bk.ru

Abstract. The paper focused on analysis of heterogeneous panel data characterizing recourses, conditions, levels, habits, and effects of online communication between people, enterprises and public organizations. The data were obtained from open access sources of federal and regional government bodies, social media, and service providers, and included statistics on key word searches, communities in social networks, demography of organizations, online purchasing, public online services, indicators of socioeconomics development, and ICT recourses. Multidimensional classification of regions and statistical analysis of dependencies between time-series data items let determine main factors of online socioeconomics activities and provided a technique of their forecasting.

Keywords: Cluster analysis · Internet-communication · Key word searchers · Performance factors · Public online services · Regression analysis · Russian regions · Service providers · Social media

1 Introduction

The development of information and communication technologies and their integration into industrial production, the financial sector, the economy, trade, public administration, everyday life and human interaction leads to a blurring of the boundaries between the physical, digital and social spheres, generates new organizational structures - cyberphysical, cybereconomic, socio-cybernetic and, finally, socio-cyberphysical and socio-cyber-economic systems.

Known to date examples of such systems suggest that these systems have a high potential for enforcing economic growth, their functioning can be considered as an intensive factor of economic growth.

© Springer International Publishing AG 2017
D.A. Alexandrov et al. (Eds.): DTGS 2017, CCIS 745, pp. 55–69, 2017.
https://doi.org/10.1007/978-3-319-69784-0_5

Realizing the high importance of information and communication technologies for economic development, the European Union developed the Digital Single Market Strategy[1]. The goal of the strategy is to make Europe the world leader in the digital economy, ensuring global growth for European companies. The main objectives of the strategy are to improve access for businesses and consumers to online goods and services, to remove barriers to cross-border online activity, to create the conditions for the further development of digital networks and services.

Thereby, the idea of increasing the competitiveness of industry through the integration of information and communication technologies into production processes initiated the emergence of the management concept of "cyberphysical systems." The concept of "cybereconomic systems" and "socio-cybereconomic systems" can become an actual methodological basis for studying social and economic relations and interactions arising in the markets using digital technologies and Internet communications. Taking into account the global world trends in the development of digital technologies and their diffusion into the economic and social space, the study of the online social and economic activity of the population of the Russian regions, the quantitative assessment of the state of the regional infrastructure for the development of digital networks and services are relevant scientific tasks.

2   Research Problem

To date, the Russian regions are significantly different in terms of the development of information and communication infrastructure, eGovernment services and eCommerce. Distribution among the population of digital devices differs significantly in the regions. Terms of conducting business in the regions are also different. These and other reasons determine the differences in spreading of online activity of the population and business. In addition, there is a regional specificity in the choice of topics and areas of online activity. To assess these differences and determine the direction of development of online socio-economic activity we can use data from open access sources of federal and regional government bodies, social media, and service providers, and statistics on key word searches, communities in social networks, demography of organizations, online purchasing, public online services, indicators of socioeconomics development, and ICT recourses. Multidimensional classification of regions and statistical analysis of dependencies between time-series data items let determine main factors of online socioeconomics activities and provided a technique of their forecasting.

Our goal was to find out qualitative and quantitative differences between Russian regions in online socioeconomic activity, to explain these differences, and to determine desirable regional patterns of transformations in cyber space.

---

[1] https://ec.europa.eu/digital-single-market/en.

3 Literature Review

The transition from an industrial society to an information society, the development of a digital economy lead to the necessity of developing a new paradigm and management principles, initiate scientific research in the fields of the theory of systems and neo-cybernetics. Articles [1, 13] consider the possibility of using the theory of complex systems and the theory of dynamical systems for a formalized description and analysis of social processes. Mancilla [10–12] discusses the basics of describing social systems in cybernetics of the third and fourth order.

In our papers with co-authors [15, 17–19] we discussed general schemes of management of socio-cybereconomic systems. Particularly, we introduced techniques for combining graph models representing casual relations between socioeconomic characteristics, dynamic modals, and statistical models. Here we attract attention to the statistical component.

Social systems can be the object of cybernetic research. For this purpose, it is expedient to distinguish three groups of characteristics in them: the elements of the system, the control actions and the use of cyberspace. Elements of the system can change their behavior spontaneously, regardless of the state of the external environment. Interaction of elements among themselves usually leads to self-organization, the result of which is the dynamic equilibrium of the system.

Self-organization of economic entities takes place under the influence of such objects and systems as competitors, business partners, suppliers, customers; state and municipal authorities; criminal structures [16].

Specific manifestations of self-organization depend on the degree of external and internal factors of economic entities. The basis of self-organization are economic and other interests of the self-organizing subsystems and objects (business entities, legal entities and individuals, their communities and associations), as well as the relationships between them.

Under the conditions of rapid changes, of increasing uncertainty and unpredictability in the environment, the future of open systems can not be precisely predetermined, and they usually have several potential lines of development. The systems are in a situation of constant selection, the search for solutions to meet changing conditions. There is a constant diffusion of resources and services, most often from the outside. It blurs spontaneously the boundaries of emerging systems, removes them from the original state of balance and stability, and creates the state of a dissipative order and initial self-organization.

The peculiarity of the socio-cyberphysical system is that it does not have centralized control [15]. The response of the system to the control actions is difficult to predict. At the same time, various responses to the control action can lead to different dynamic equilibrium. The system can have an impact on the external environment.

Market mechanisms have key potential to self-organization and evolution of social systems. The idea of market self-organization as a mechanism of evolution and technological progress was thoroughly developed in the works of the Russian economist Nikolai Kondratiev [9]. The concepts of economic dynamics and market sharing are fundamental to determine the economic environment. In certain periods market relations contribute to the expansion of production, intensification of trade, growth of economic sectors. There are periods unfavorable for the development of economic activity.

Before the start of the upward stage, that is, during the depression, "there is a revival in the field of technical inventions." At the beginning of the growth and just before it widespread applications of these innovations in the industry inevitably cause a change of production relations. In a period of growth the social activity, leading to a disruption in social life, is much higher than in the downward phase. According Kondratiev social upheavals, on the one hand is one of the manifestations of a major cycle; from another hand is a factor that determines to a large extent the direction of economic dynamics [9].

Social factors have decisive importance in the transition from downward to up-stage of the wavelength. The period of depression and crisis is accompanied by high unemployment and low incomes. At the same time in this period the basic innovations should be established, which will determine the economic growth in the upward phase of a long cycle. Therefore, it is obvious that to overcome the crisis, along with incentives for technological innovations, the social innovation must necessarily be supported.

Using cyberspace for communication by the elements of the system (for example, social networks, communication Internet sites, information platforms for the exchange of opinions, purchase of goods, ordering services, etc.) accelerates the process of self-organization of the system [15] and enhances its "intelligence". The self-learning of the system occurs as a result of processing of large data collected by the system from its elements. The result of self-learning may be the impact on the external environment through the elements of the system.

For example, the authors of the article [4] consider the development of the Internet as a means of empowering citizens, meeting their consumer goals. The substantiation of this thesis is carried out using data from mass observations of the online social activity of the population of Russia, Mexico, Chile and Uruguay.

An example of the directive management impact, which resulted in an online communication platform, is given in the Kabanov and Sungurov study [7]. The authors show that the emergence of eGovernment in the regions of Russia is largely a result of the vertical influence of the federal government, but regional disparities in the work of eGovernment are explained by the dependence on regional factors, for example, investments in information and communication technologies. The work of eGovernment is a good example of the impact on the external environment through the elements of the system. Dobrolyubova and Alexandrov [6], using sociological surveys, argue that citizens who use electronic means to apply for public services demonstrate a higher satisfaction with the quality of public services than those who use traditional personal communication procedures.

The influence of socio-cybernetic systems on the external environment is considered in articles [2, 5]. It is shown that the data collected automatically from the portals of the electronic petition can be used for research in several areas: the influence of the media and PR on political participation, the identification of factors influencing online political activity and voting, and the analysis of the influence of the portals of electronic petitions on making of political decisions.

The problems and directions of development and use of the infrastructure of cyberspace (information and communication infrastructure) in Russia were discussed in detail [3, 4, 6]. A significant gap between Russia and OECD countries exists in the provision of public services in electronic form [6]. A comparative analysis of the development of the information society in Russia and in other countries of the world was carried out in the article [3]. Four main indexes were analyzed: eGovernment Development Index, Network Readiness Index, Knowledge Economy Index, ICT Development Index. As a result of gap-analysis, Russia's strong and weak positions in the world information society development rankings have been identified. Thematic areas specific of online activity have been found for Russia [4]: social, communication and entertainment activities.

4 Methodology

The methodological basis of the study of online socio-economic activity in Russian regions is a systematic approach to the study of the economy. In a concentrated form, this approach is described in articles of G.B. Kleiner and co-authors, combined in a monograph [8]. Kleiner develops a new theory of economic systems. The economy is represented as a set of interdependent processes of the emergence, functioning, inter-action, transformation and liquidation of economic systems of different levels, size, location and purpose. This direction is the development of the system paradigm pro-posed in the late 1990 s by János Kornai as an addition to the neoclassical, institutional and evolutionary paradigms. Each system is dual: the "internal" definition of the system by Ludwig von Bertalanffy is inseparable from the "external" definition of the system as relatively stable in time and in space of the supersystem. In system analysis, this duality is reflected in the concepts of "structure" (internal description) and "function" (external description).

The concept of "life economy" is described in the article [14]. This concept can be used as an addition to the above system methodology for describing the functioning and interaction of socio-cybereconomic systems. The authors of the concept of "life economy" propose to consider the economy as a "living organism", in the center of which there is a certain self-organized society, taking into account historical, ethnic, cultural peculiarities.

In the statistical analysis of the manifestations of online socio-economic activity and the construction of statistical models describing the patterns of online socio-economic activity and the factors affecting it, we were guided by the following methodological positions.

Socio-economic activity is due to both the economic needs of the elements of society and the economy, and the technical conditions for its manifestation in online form. Demonstrations of needs can be assessed by indicators of keyword searches and access to online services.

The conditions for manifesting online social and economic activity are determined, first of all, by the level of development of the infrastructure of cyberspace. To assess this level, can be used official statistical indicators such as prevalence of personal computers, expenses for information and communication technologies, proportion of population using Internet for obtaining state and municipal services in electronic form, etc. When constructing statistical models, regions, virtual communities in social networks, thematic search requests can be used as objects of statistical observation.

5 Data Description and Analysis

5.1 Data Description and Methods

The data were obtained from open access sources of federal and regional government bodies[2], social media, and services providers[3], and included statistics on keyword searches, communities in the most popular social network[4] in Russia, demography of organizations, online purchasing, public online services, indicators of socioeconomics development, and ICT recourses. Multidimensional classification of regions and statistical analysis of dependencies between time-series data items let determine main factors of online socioeconomics activities and provided a technique of their forecasting.

5.2 Infrastructure of Cyberspace

We observe a reliable growth of indicators, characterizing the infrastructure of Russian cyberspace (Table 1). To characterize the infrastructure of cyberspace in Russian regions we analyzed nine indicators. We performed factor analysis with varimax normalized rotation method and obtained three latent factors explaining 72% of the data variation. Factor loading (correlations between the factors and the initial indicators) let interpret the factors as the resources of ePopulation, eOganization, and eGovernment correspondingly (Table 2). We used factor scores to perform a three-dimensional classification of Russian regions. Four clusters were obtained with different average values of factors (Fig. 1). The clusters contained respectively 24, 9, 29, 23 regions with the most typical representatives: The Republic of Buryatia, Magadan Region, Tula Region, Sakhalin Region. The classification provides clues for region patterns of socioeconomic transformations in the cyber space.

Regions of cluster 2 with high purchasing capacity produce dissatisfied needs of online services. Development of eGoverment is urgent here. Regions of cluster 1 and cluster 4 with low purchasing capacity can be stimulated with advanced development of ITC in educational organizations.

The data on the demography of Russian organizations, carrying out activities related to the use of computers and information technologies and to software development and consulting in this field, demonstrate a considerable growth of number of the organization and the rate of newly established ones (Table 3).

A rough bottom estimate of the lifetime duration of these organizations is about 8.6 years.

---

[2] https://fedstat.ru/.

[3] https://wordstat.yandex.ru/, https://adwords.google.com/.

[4] https://vk.com/.

Table 1. Dynamics of statistical indicators characterizing the infrastructure of cyberspace (data from https://fedstat.ru/indicator/33631)

Statistical indicator	2009	2010	2011	2012	2013	2014	2015	2016
Number of personal computers per 100 people of labor resources (an able-bodied working-age population and a working population of other age groups, value of the indicator for the year)	10	10	11	12	12	13	13	–
Expenses for information and communication technologies (rubles per unit of labor recourses, value of the indicator for the year)	4 584	5 607	6 552	9 076	13080	12768	12774	–
The proportion of organizations that had a website in the total number of organizations (percentage, value of the indicator for the year)	–	28.5	33	37.8	41.3	40.3	42.6	–
The proportion of organizations using the Internet for placing orders for goods and services in the total number of organizations (percentage, value of the indicator for the year)	–	35	39.2	41.1	43.4	41.7	41.3	–
The proportion of organizations using broadband Internet access in the total number of organizations (percentage, value of the indicator for the year)	–	–	–	–	79.4	81.2	79.5	–
The proportion of electronic document circulation between public authorities and local governments in the total volume of interdepartmental workflow (percentage, value of the indicator for the year)	–	–	–	51.5	49.3	61.7	44.9	–
The proportion of population using Internet for obtaining state and municipal services in electronic form (percentage, value of the indicator for the year)	–	–	–	–	30.8	35.2	39.6	51.3
The proportion of population who used the Internet to order goods and/or services (percentage, value of the indicator for the year)	–	–	–	–	15.3	17.8	19.6	23.1
The proportion of the population that are active users of the Internet (percentage, value of the indicator for the year)					61.4	64.9	68.3	71.5

Table 2. Factor loadings (varimax normalized). extraction: principal components

Statistical indicator	ePopulation	eOrganization	eGovernment
Number of personal computers per 100 people of labor resources (an able-bodied working-age population and a working population of other age groups, value of the indicator for the year)	0.81	0.00	−0.05
Expenses for information and communication technologies (rubles per unit of labor recourses, value of the indicator for the year)	0.77	0.03	−0.10
The proportion of organizations that had a website in the total number of organizations (percentage, value of the indicator for the year)	0.11	0.90	0.10
The proportion of organizations using the Internet for placing orders for goods and services in the total number of organizations (percentage, value of the indicator for the year)	0.52	0.72	−0.07
The proportion of organizations using broadband Internet access in the total number of organizations (percentage, value of the indicator for the year)	0.00	0.93	0.03
The proportion of electronic document circulation between public authorities and local governments in the total volume of interdepartmental workflow (percentage, value of the indicator for the year)	0.03	−0.17	0.83
The proportion of population using Internet for obtaining state and municipal services in electronic form (percentage, value of the indicator for the year)	−0.08	0.29	0.77
The proportion of population who used the Internet to order goods and/or services (percentage, value of the indicator for the year)	0.83	0.13	0.06
The proportion of the population that are active users of the Internet (percentage, value of the indicator for the year)	0.82	0.23	0.06
Expl.Var	2.90	2.38	1.30
Prp.Totl	0.32	0.26	0.14

We can see a dramatic increment in officially liquidated organizations in 2016. However, it was compensated with greater numbers of newly created organizations. That was distinct from the highly negative overall date on organizations' demography, as the "death" level of Russian organizations exceeded the "birth" level by 55.5% in

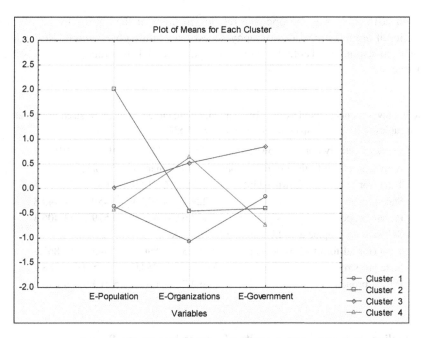

Fig. 1. Means for each cluster, unit

Table 3. Dynamics of the number of organizations (data from https://fedstat.ru/indicator/42969)

Statistical indicator	2012	2013	2014	2015	2016
Number of organizations according to state registration data (units)					
Total	4 866 620	4 886 432	4 843 393	4 886 007	5 043 553
Activities related to the use of computers and information technology	71 445	75 571	78 567	82 463	87 822
Number of newly created organizations (units)					
Total	434 661	440 734	449 333	492 627	455 820
Activities related to the use of computers and information technology	8 422	8 597	8 742	9 474	10 691
Software development and consulting in this field	3 252	3 125	3 382	3 762	6 150
Number of officially liquidated organizations (units)					
Total	420 952	412 255	399 273	325 698	711 424
Activities related to the use of computers and information technology	4 794	4 805	5 059	4 277	9 849
Software development and consulting in this field	1 661	1 643	1 785	1 536	3 638
Number of individual entrepreneurs according to state registration (person)					
Total	4 059 706	3 533 511	3 608 844	3 689 805	3 770 550
Activities related to the use of computers and information technology	51 975	48 953	54 303	61 947	72 440
Software development and consulting in this field	13 824	14 131	16 670	20 598	28 455

2016. In 2015 there was the opposite relation in favor of the "birth" by 52.4%. The instability of organizations' demography necessitates future observations. Now we can see that investments (Table 4) show a good potential for future growth of the infrastructure.

Table 4. Investments in fixed assets (Russian federation, large and medium-sized organizations) million rubles (data from https://fedstat.ru/indicator/40534)

Types of activity/Forms of ownership	2013	2014	2015	2016
Activities related to the use of computers and information technology				
Total (for all forms of ownership)	10 378	16 812.8	28 642.5	30 739.5
State property	5 224.9	4 835.3	7 450.9	7 449.8
Private property	2 124.6	3 428.9	10 579.7	13 406.3
Software development and consulting in this field				
Total (for all forms of ownership)	2 136.3	2 890.2	7 443.7	11 865.5
State property	33	258.6	55.9	88.7
Private property	894.7	1 069.7	5 503.9	9 810.2

5.3   Online Socioeconomic Activity of People in Russian Regions

We used the Google correlate tool[5] to describe essential growth of the interest among Russian users to internet purchases (Fig. 2). We can see a synchronized dynamics of search activity with the keywords "Yandex Market" (the online tool aggregating internet markets of goods), "City Link" (All-Russia discounter of internet purchases) and "Joint purchases" (a tool for self-organizing crowd purchases with wholesale discounts).

We chose the keywords "Yandex Market" because they denote the main aggregator of links to Russian Internet stores. Additional keywords were determined through searchers synchronize across time.

We analyzed online socioeconomic activity in Russian regions in tree main fields: internet purchases, remote/internet jobs, distant/online education/courses. We used Yandex wordstat tool[6] to collect search activity data. Then we calculated relative indicators of search activities per 100 people of labor resources (an able-bodied working-age population and a working population of other age groups). Three relative indicators corresponding to three fields provided only one factor (Table 5) characterizing more than 82% of the data variation. According to the values of the factor we could select the regions with the highest level of activities: Moscow and Moscow region, St. Petersburg and the Leningrad Region, Nizhny Novgorod Region, Novosibirsk Region, Sverdlovsk Region.

---

[5] https://www.google.com/trends/correlate.

[6] https://wordstat.yandex.ru/.

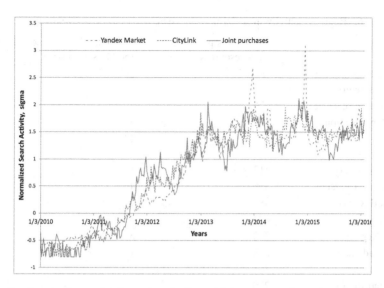

Fig. 2. Synchronized growth of searches dealing with internet purchases in Russia (data from https://www.google.com/trends/correlate)

Table 5. Factor loadings (unrotated). extraction: principal components

Initial indicators	Factor loadings
Market	−0.940356
Job	−0.924520
Education	−0.853170
Expl.Var	2.466906
Prp.Totl	0.822302

To characterize the relative popularity of actions in the three fields described above we used the affinity index (the ratio of search activity in the field to overall search activity in the region). The results obtained characterized needs and habits of population rather than links to the regional infrastructure of cyberspace.

The diversity of needs and habits can be confirmed with a statistically significant regression between the online education and online job popularity:

$$education\_activity = -0.898\,job\_activity + 2.038, R = 0.41 \qquad (1)$$

We analyzed popularity of regional communities in the social network vk.com (Table 6) and ranked regions from St. Petersburg to Republic of Bashkortostan. The regions not included in the ranking do not have mass communities.

Table 6. Regional activity in social network (date from https://wordstat.yandex.ru)

Region	Subscribers per 1000 labor resources	Communities with more than 150000 subscribers
St. Petersburg and the Leningrad Region	1870	28
The Republic of Dagestan	676	2
Novosibirsk Region	534	3
Moscow and Moscow region	521	22
Murmansk Region	512	1
Republic of Tatarstan	500	4
Novgorod Region	487	1
Perm Region	424	3
Samara Region	332	3
Kaliningrad Region	318	1
Omsk Region	307	2
Volgograd Region	270	2
Bryansk Region	265	1
Saratov Region	256	2
Vologda Region	242	2
Arhangelsk Region	237	1
Ryazan Oblast	233	1
Udmurt Republic	220	1
Orenburg Region	216	1
Ulyanovsk Region	208	1
Voronezh Region	202	1
Sverdlovsk Region	200	2
Chelyabinsk Region	187	1
Tyumen Region	135	2
Krasnodar Region	104	1
Krasnoyarsk Region	102	1
Rostov Region	97	1
Stavropol Territory	95	1
Republic of Bashkortostan	64	1

6 Discussion of Results and Conclusion

Internet sites providing new technologies for social communications and self organization have good opportunities for eCommerce. These opportunities are reflected in the rapid growth of search activity with new notions such as joint purchases for wholesale discounts.

The infrastructure of cyberspace in Russian regions has three distinct components revealed through factor analysis of a broad set of indicators. These components are:

digital resources of population, stimulating new investment in ICT, resources of eCommerce organizations, and resources of eGovernment.

The level of online socioeconomic activities in Russian regions, particularly in the field of remote work and distant education depends upon the infrastructure of the cyberspace. That can be confirmed with the results of ANOVA for the clusters obtained in the multidimensional classification of regions according to three factors of infrastructure.

In contrast to the level of online activities, the relative popularity of themes in cyberspace depend mostly on the needs and habits of population. For example, we observed statistically significant negative dependencies between the popularity of remote work and distant education.

The data on search queries and virtual communities refute stereotypes of regional online activities. For example, Moscow is far from the first place in adherence to big communities in a social network, while Dagestan outruns it.

Socio-economic relations are increasingly manifested in a digital form. Information and communication technologies integrated into the economy and social relations, become the basis of competitive advantages in global markets, transforming production systems into cyber-physical systems, economic and social relations and interactions into interactions in socio-cybereconomic systems. These trends provide opportunities for innovation and economic growth through the development of cyberspace.

The digital single market is a technological platform for realization of digital opportunities of innovative development and economic growth. Such a market should provide citizens and businesses with access to online activities, fair competition conditions and protection of personal data. A free virtual flow of labor, goods, services and capital should be ensured in the market.

The basic principles of building the market are the following:

- ensuring good access for the population and enterprises of all regions to online goods and services;
- creation of favorable conditions for the development of information and communication infrastructure in the regions;
- a constant increase in the return on investment in the development of the information and communication infrastructure by increasing the competitiveness of domestic goods and services, the availability of online public services and educational services for the public.

The data on investments in activities related to ITC infrastructure show very high rate of growth amidst stagnation of Russian economy. The opportunities of online activity can be a driver of perspective economic transformations. The abovementioned classifications of regions can be used for regional patterns of such transformations.

Acknowledgments. The research described in this paper is partially supported by the Russian Foundation for Basic Research (grants 15-08-08459, 16-07-00779, 17-08-00797, 17-06-00108), Russian Humanitarian Found (grants 15-04-00400).

References

1. Becerra, G., Amozurrutia, J.A.: Rolando García's "Complex Systems Theory" and its relevance to sociocybernetics. J. Sociocybern. **13**(15), 18–30 (2015)
2. Bershadskaya, L., Chugunov, A., Golubtsova, E.: Measurement techniques for e-participation assessment: case of ussian e-petitions portal. In: International Conference Proceeding Series, vol. 2014, pp. 395–398. ACM (2014)
3. Bershadskaya, L., Chugunov, A., Trutnev, D.: Information society development in Russia: measuring progress and gaps. In: Proceedings of the 2014 Conference on Electronic Governance and Open Society: Challenges in Eurasia, EGOSE 2014, pp. 7–13. ACM, New York (2014)
4. Brodovskaya, E., Dombrovskaya, A., Synyakov, A., Batanina, I.: Online social activity in latin america (Mexico, Chile and Uruguay) and Russia: cross-national research. In: Chugunov, Andrei V., Bolgov, R., Kabanov, Y., Kampis, G., Wimmer, M. (eds.) DTGS 2016. CCIS, vol. 674, pp. 26–34. Springer, Cham (2016). doi:10.1007/978-3-319-49700-6_4
5. Chugunov, A.V., Kabanov, Y., Zenchenkova, K.: E-participation portals automated monitoring system for political and social research. In: Chugunov, Andrei V., Bolgov, R., Kabanov, Y., Kampis, G., Wimmer, M. (eds.) DTGS 2016. CCIS, vol. 674, pp. 290–298. Springer, Cham (2016). doi:10.1007/978-3-319-49700-6_27
6. Dobrolyubova, E., Alexandrov, O.: E-government in Russia: meeting growing demand in the era of budget constraints. In: Chugunov, A.V., Bolgov, R., Kabanov, Y., Kampis, G., Wimmer, M. (eds.) DTGS 2016. CCIS, vol. 674, pp. 247–257. Springer, Cham (2016). doi:10.1007/978-3-319-49700-6_23
7. Kabanov, Y., Sungurov, A.: E-government development factors: evidence from the Russian regions. In: Chugunov, A.V., Bolgov, R., Kabanov, Y., Kampis, G., Wimmer, M. (eds.) DTGS 2016. CCIS, vol. 674, pp. 85–95. Springer, Cham (2016). doi:10.1007/978-3-319-49700-6_10
8. Kleiner, G.B.: Economy. Modeling. Mathematics. Selected works. Russian Academy of Sciences, Central Economic-Mathematics In-t.-M.: CEMI RAS, 856 p. (2016). (in Russian)
9. Kondratiev, N.D.: The major economic cycles. Moscow. Translated and published as The Long Wave Cycle. Richardson & Snyder, New York, 1984, 138 p. (1925). (in Russian)
10. Mancilla, R.G.: Introduction to sociocybernetics (part 1): third order cybernetics and a basic framework for society. J. Sociocybern. **9**(1/2), 35–56 (2011)
11. Mancilla, R.G.: Introduction to sociocybernetics (part 2): power, culture and institutions. J. Sociocybern. **10**(1/2), 45–71 (2012)
12. Mancilla, R.G.: Introduction to sociocybernetics (part 3): fourth order cybernetics. J. Sociocybern. **11**(1/2), 47–73 (2013)
13. Nebbitt, V.E., Tyuse, S.W., Vaughn, M.G., Perron, B.E.: Conceptual tools for research on race and social problems: an overview of dynamic theory and model development. J. Hum. Behav. Soc. Environ. **20**(7), 909–923 (2010)
14. Safonov, A.L., Popkov, S.Y., Slobodchikov, I.M., Smirnov, V.M., Yastrebova, E.V.: Life Economy (in Russian) Business in Law. Econ. Leg. J. **1**, 7–25 (2016)
15. Sokolov, B., Yusupov, R., Verzilin, D., Sokolova, I., Ignatjev, M.: Methodological basis of socio-cyber-physical systems structure-dynamics control and management. In: Chugunov, A.V., Bolgov, R., Kabanov, Y., Kampis, G., Wimmer, M. (eds.) DTGS 2016. CCIS, vol. 674, pp. 610–617. Springer, Cham (2016). doi:10.1007/978-3-319-49700-6_61

16. Verzilin, D.N., Mamonov, S.A., Corbunova, I.R.: Modelling coherent and self-organization behaviour of social and economic system. In: XVI International Conference "Dynamical System Modeling and Stability Investigations" (DSMSI-2013), p. 422, 29–31 May 2013. Taras Shevchenko National University of Kiev, Ukraine (2013)
17. Verzilin, D.N., Maximova, T.G.: Models of social actors' reaction on external impacts. St. Petersburg State Polytechnical University. J. Comput. Sci. Telecommun. Control Syst. **2** (120), 140–145 (2011). (in Russian)
18. Verzilin, D.N., Potapychev, S.N., Ryzhkov, N.A.: The use of simulation to evaluate the response of social and economic systems to external influences. In: V Conference "Simulation. Theory and Practice", IMMOD 2011, St. Petersburg, 19–21 October 2011, pp. 115–119 (2011). (in Russian)
19. Verzilin, D.N., Shanygin, S.I., Chereshneva, A.V.: Conceptual bases of modelling of social systems and estimation of stability of social processes. St. Petersburg State Polytechnical University. J. Comput. Sci. Telecommun. Control Syst. **5**(133), 123–128 (2011)

Digital Inequality in Russia Through the Use of a Social Network Site: A Cross-Regional Comparison

Yuri Rykov[✉], Oleg Nagornyy, and Olessia Koltsova

Laboratory for Internet Studies,
National Research University Higher School of Economics,
Saint Petersburg, Russia
rykyur@gmail.com, nagornyy.o@gmail.com,
ekoltsova@hse.ru

Abstract. An important role of digital inequality for hindering the development of civil society is being increasingly acknowledged. Simultaneously, differences in availability and the practices of use of social network sites (SNS) may be considered as major manifestations of such digital divide. While SNS are in principle highly convenient spaces for public discussion, lack of access or domination by socially insignificant small talk may indicate underdevelopment of the public sphere. At the same time, agenda differences between regions may signal about local problems. In this study we seek to find out whether regional digital divide exists in such a large country as Russia. We start from a theory of uneven modernization of Russia and use the data from its most popular SNS "VK.com" as a proxy for measuring digital inequality. By analyzing user activity data from a sample of 77,000 users and texts from a carefully selected sub-sample of 36,000 users we conclude that regional level explains an extremely small share of variance in the overall variation of behavioral user data. A notable exception is attention to the topics of Islam and Ukraine. However, our data reveal that historically geographical penetration of "VK.com" proceeded from the regions considered the most modernized to those considered the most traditional. This finding supports the theory of uneven modernization, but it also shows that digital inequality is subject to change with time.

Keywords: Digital inequality · Social network site use · Online user behavior · Topic modeling · Russian regions · VK.com

1 Introduction

An important role of digital inequality for hindering the development of civil society is being increasingly acknowledged. Simultaneously, differences in availability and the practices of use of the Internet and social network sites (SNS) may be considered as major manifestations of such digital divide. While SNS are in principle highly convenient spaces for public discussion, lack of access or domination by socially insignificant small talk may indicate underdevelopment of the public sphere. At the same time, agenda differences between regions may signal about local problems. In this

© Springer International Publishing AG 2017

D.A. Alexandrov et al. (Eds.): DTGS 2017, CCIS 745, pp. 70–83, 2017.
https://doi.org/10.1007/978-3-319-69784-0_6

study we seek to find out whether regional digital divide exists in such a large country as Russia. We start from a theory of uneven modernization of Russia and use the data from its most popular SNS "VK.com" as a proxy for measuring digital inequality.

2 Literature Review

Related literature covers at least two research fields: (1) digital divide and (2) socioeconomic development of Russian regions. The literature on digital divide discusses benefits and social implications of Internet use among different groups of population. Works about differences in development of the Russian regions can form a basis to explain contemporary digital inequality.

2.1 The Digital Divide

The main focus of the studies on digital divide concerns penetration and accessibility of the Internet among different groups of population. The initial assumption of these studies is that the access to the Internet and information is a valuable resource and an undoubted good expanding social opportunities and life chances of users compared to non-users. The digital divide is a factor of social inequality additional to traditional sources of inequality. The unequal Internet access depends on demographic and socioeconomic differences such as gender and age, income and education, race and ethnicity, location and type of settlement. According to the study of Pew Internet and American Life Project, the most accurate predictors of intensity and diversity of Internet use are levels of income and education [20].

There are three hypothetical scenarios of social inequality implications under the influence of Internet use [10]: (a) if Internet access is provided mainly for upper classes of society, social inequality grows ("the rich get richer" model); (b) if equal Internet access is provided, inequality remains the same; (c) if deprived and marginal groups of population benefit from the Internet use in the first place, inequality is reduced. Finally, the relation between socioeconomic status and access to the Internet is reciprocal, the traditional forms of inequality and digital inequality could strengthen each other [17].

Early research used quite basic indicators of digital divide and limited them to the material dimension of Internet use: availability and quality if computer equipment, Internet access, signal speed and quality, number of places with Internet access, time spent on the Internet. When the Internet penetration in developed countries reached saturation, more refined indicators related to user qualities and behavior came to the forefront: user skills and abilities, use goals, topics of information search and so on. Furthermore, rate of social media content activity was used as an indicator of digital inequality and applied in the study of unevenness of urban space [12]. Thus, nowadays digital divide has evolved into a complex concept that includes at least two levels. The digital divide of the first level is connected with the material characteristics of access to ICT, the second level accounts for the characteristics of use (goals, skills, activity). Furthermore, the uneven access to users' attention is an additional aspect of second level digital divide [8].

Approached from the digital divide perspective, two main dimensions of SNS use —contents and online user engagement—could be considered as indicators of digital inequality. Topic variation on the SNS could point at digital inequality because greater attention to socially significant topics in a particular region (such as human rights, economy, social policy, housing and utilities, urban planning and so on) indicates a stronger online public sphere and could lead to potential benefits for population, while greater presence of everyday topics (such as sports, celebrities, cars, cooking recipes and so on) might mean lack of SNS-mediated public sphere. Likewise, differences in online user engagement on the SNS could be an indicator of digital inequality because greater online activity and social involvement may lead to a larger amount of social capital [9] and stronger communication power of the population [6].

2.2 Socioeconomic Development of Russian Regions

According to [1] Russia is a fundamentally segmented society, and one of the most well-known theories explaining unequal development of Russian regions is a so-called "Theory of four Russias" [21]. Zubarevich distinguished four types of Russian settlements, that differ from each other in terms of population and socioeconomic modernization. The "First Russia" is represented by large cities with population over 500,000 and is characterized with high speed of the post-industrial transformation. The majority of Internet users are concentrated in these cities. The "Second Russia" can be found in industrial cities with population between 20,000 and 500,000. Inhabitants of these cities are employed at industrial, often state-owned companies; they keep struggling for economic well-being and are indifferent to the problems of the middle class. The "Third Russia" is conservative and passive population from rural periphery and small towns of most of the regions. They have the lowest level of education and mobility, are employed in the state-owned organizations and agriculture, and are completely focused on their own problems [22]. Finally, Zubarevich singles out North Caucasus and southern Siberia republics and places them into the "Fourth Russia". The population of these regions is said to exercise traditional, pre-industrial lifestyles and often retreat to subsistence farming. The "Four Russias" theory is close to the more general theory of post-materialism [13], which argues that the growth of economic well-being causes transition to the so-called post-materialist values including self-expression and greater participation of the individual in public life.

Bodrunova and Litvinenko [3] used Zubarevich's classification to analyze the fragmentation of communication in the Russian public sphere. The authors examined the contribution of online media to the split of Russian public sphere in the electoral cycle 2011–2012 and found that the split in the online media reproduces social divisions from the "Four Russias" theory. Thus, territorial differences have been related to the differences in media consumption. Authors assigned the main role in this split to the confrontation between the "First" and "Second Russia", which differ in their values, attitudes and behaviors. The "Third" and "Fourth Russia" are much less represented in the online media and the public sphere. However, as this elation has not been tested quantitatively neither in Bodrunova and Litvinenko [3] nor in any other research on Russia, it needs further investigation.

3 Research Questions

This study seeks to find a meaningful regional variation in SNS use. As the latter is a complex phenomenon we split it into two dimensions regarding contents and formal online user behavior. Online content is characterized and measured through its topical structure. Topic variation as an important feature of the second level digital divide because it reflects uneven distribution of public attention towards different social issues, and uneven practice of use of an SNS as a media outlet in different Russian regions.

RQ1: What are the differences in representation of online content topics across Russian regions?

Formal online user behavior is represented as the aggregate of elementary user actions such as posting messages and comments, giving "likes", making "friends", reposting and so on. All these elementary actions form digital user biography and patterns of socially oriented using of an SNS. Differences in patterns of SNS use are also an important feature of the second level digital divide because they reflect different purposes of SNS use, and uneven user activity and social engagement.

RQ2: What are the differences in online social engagement of the SNS users across Russian regions?

4 Data and Methods

In this research we use the data from the most popular Russian SNS "VK.com", a Russian replication of Facebook. At the time of the study "VK.com" had over 350 million registered users. Since the "VK.com" user ID is generated incrementally (the first registered is assigned ID 1, the second is 2 and so on.), we were able to generate a random sample by selecting the required number of random numbers from a range of 1 to 350 million and download user information filtering out removed profiles. However, due to the extremely uneven distribution of users across regions, we refused from random sampling, because users from Moscow, accounted for almost a quarter of all registered accounts, and Saint Petersburg accounted for 11%, while some regions were represented by a tiny fraction. Since one of the main objectives of the research was to disclose the topic structure of "VK.com" users' posts and to identify interregional differences, we needed that the number of texts in each region was approximately the same. Otherwise, we would examine the agenda of users from several large cities. To avoid such bias the upper limit of 1000 users per region was set.

The data was collected by using the "VkMiner" software developed in The Laboratory for Internet Studies. Only publicly available data on "VK.com" users were collected, such as information from the profile and records from the "walls". Some regions were excluded from the analysis because user data from these regions were incorrectly downloaded during the data collection[1]. Thus, the final sample included

---

[1] Amur Oblast, Astrakhan Oblast, Ingushetia, Kaliningrad Oblast, Mari El, Nenets Autonomous Okrug, Perm Krai, Ryazan Oblast, Sakha Republic, Sverdlovsk Oblast, Tver Oblast, Udmurtia, Khanty-Mansi Autonomous Okrug, Chuvashia, Chukotka Autonomous Okrug, Yamalo-Nenets Autonomous Okrug.

7,827,384 entries from the "walls" of 42,459 users from 69 out of 85 regions of the Russian Federation. They represent all "four Russias".

Our task of topic detection was solved with an approach known as topic modeling. We used the most popular topic modeling algorithm—latent Dirichlet allocation (LDA) with Gibbs sampling, implemented in the TopicMiner[2] software. The output of the LDA consists of the matrix of probabilities of words in topics and the matrix of probabilities of topics in texts [16]. In other words, it is assumed that each document belongs to all topics and each word has the potential to generate any topic, but with highly different probabilities. Top words form interpretable sets that can be easily labeled by human analysts.

One of the research questions was the detection of topical profiles of users, but the data was collected from the "walls" of users. A "wall" is the main message board of the user's profile and the place for public communication with user's "friends", followers and other visitors. "Wall" works as a personal media outlet, because posts from the "wall" appear in the news feed of the user's "friends" and followers. Users can also make posts on each other's walls. So we decided to group the texts not by the "wall" but by the author. The preliminary selection of the texts thus included 5,392,586 entries from the "walls" of 74,303 users including those who posted only on the walls of others.

To reduce the dimensionality of the data and to improve the results of topic modeling we set a time limit for the texts. It reflects the need to take into account the fact that the topical profile of the author changes over time. It can occur as a result of changes in the author's preferences or as a result of changes in the policy of the SNS. In particular, since October 20, 2010 "VK.com" has changed its communication concept: the walls of users have ceased to be a place for communication, the focus of the service has been transferred from users' pages to the news feeds with updates of records, statuses and friends' photos[3]. At the time a new functionality was introduced that has made it more convenient to receive news from public pages. Since then "VK.com" has become less focused on communication between private users. As the change in the technical features has definitely influenced patterns of social interaction, from the analysis the entries older on October 21, 2010 were excluded.

All texts were preprocessed with the TopicMiner software and passed through the following stages: (1) removing of HTML-tags, (2) tokenization, (3) lemmatization, and (4) stopwords removing. Thereby the dictionary of our text corpus comprises about 220,000 unique words.

The next modification of the original sample was performed due to difficulties of topic modeling of short texts from SNS. Since the topics are formed by words that often occur together within one document and in short texts too few words co-occur, modeling on these texts led to the emergence of uninterpretable topics.

There are several ways to deal with topic modeling of short texts that can be divided into two groups: (1) modification of the source data; (2) modification of the topic modeling algorithms. In the absence of ready-to-use implementations of topic

---

[2] https://linis.hse.ru/soft-linis.

[3] https://vk.com/blog/blog154.

modeling algorithms for short texts, the first approach was chosen. This group of methods is easier to implement, and therefore it is more popular [11, 19]. We, first, merged all texts of the same user, and, second, filtered out all users whose merged texts contained fewer than fifty words. As a result, the final sample consisted of texts from 36,396 authors. For a model with 150 topics it allowed us to achieve more than a hundred interpretable topics, which was much better than the result obtained with the initial texts.

Finally, we got rid of unstable topics in our model. The algorithms of topic modeling have a well-known limitation: each time they are run on the same texts and with the same parameters, slightly different topics are obtained. To fight this, we used normalized Kullback-Leibler similarity measure [14]. Thus we ran our algorithm three times and selected only the topics that appeared in all three runs. The two topics from different runs were considered identical if the similarity between them exceeded the 95% threshold. As a result, we obtained 33 stable topics almost all of which were easily interpreted.

5 Results

5.1 Topic Modeling

After determining the stable topics, they were manually labeled. The following topics were identified: (1) Tips for cleaning and washing; (2) Recipes of baking; (3) Strength exercises; (4) Music; (5) Babies; (6) Automatically generated messages from "VK.com" applications; (7) Recipes of desserts; (8) Competitions and prizes; (9) War, the Great Patriotic War; (10) Obscene vocabulary; (11) Movies; (12) Football; (13) Musical events; (14) Patterns of behavior of men and women; (15) Beauty, make-up, manicure; (16) Automatically generated messages from "VK.com" applications; (17) City events; (18) Cars; (19) Russian-Ukrainian relations; (20) Tourism; (21) Christianity; (22) Physical exercises; (23) Recipes of main dishes; (24) Uninterpretable; (25) Automatically generated messages from games; (26) Recipes of main dishes; (27) Salad recipes; (28) Malady fundraising for children; (29) Search for hosts for stray animals; (30) Recipes of desserts; (31) Islam; (32) Gardening; (33) Knitting.

It can be clearly seen that the VK user-generated agenda is dominated by consumption, everyday small talk and private approach to problem-solving. Most of these topics are related to such everyday activities as games, listening to music, cooking, solving everyday problems. People use "VK.com" SNS mainly as a place where they can save interesting information about an unusual culinary recipe, recommendations for body care and garden management, select new films and music. This huge part of user' records is created with the instrumental aim to ensure quick access to potentially useful information. Another significant part of the texts is automatically generated by numerous applications, most often for advertising purposes.

Together with uninterpretable and non-subject topics, these topics centered on private life comprise the bulk of the content of "VK.com" SNS. At the same time, we have identified a small number of public affairs topics that are especially interesting for sociological analysis. Such topics are "Christianity", "Islam", "Ukraine-Russia relations", "City events" and "Malady fundraising for children". These topics touch socially significant and potentially problematic phenomena of the public life.

To account for regional differences, we have aggregated the Russian regions into seven Federal Districts (traditional semi-formal administrative division in Russia, Table 1) and calculated the average probability of topics in each of them. As the revealed topic composition has seemed gender-sensitive, we have done the same for male and female users. As seen from it, the topic preferences of men and women are very different. In their posts users of "VK.com" reproduce the common gender stereotypes. The most typical topics for women are those about cooking recipes, children, needlework and beauty, while men engage in the talk about football, games, cars and politics. This finding can significantly supplement previous studies in this area [2, 15]. In particular, Bischoping claims that "consistent patterns can be seen in the gender differences for most topic areas, with women holding the majority of conversations about people and relationships and appearances, and men typically holding the majority of conversations about work and money and issues". We confirm some of these findings—women indeed give more attention to talks about their appearance and men are more interested in topics about "issues" (war, politics). But we also identify other patterns of gender behaviour. According to our data, women talk a lot more about cooking and men take the lead in games, including football and computer games.

Table 1. Distribution of users in sample dataset among Federal districts of Russia

Federal districts	Users	
	N	%
Center FD	17117	22
North West FD	10096	13
South FD	7196	9
Caucasus FD	5795	8
Volga FD	13980	18
Ural FD	6200	8
Siberia FD	11055	14
FarEast FD	5597	7
Total	77036	100

Regarding regional differences, we have found that the most unevenly distributed topic is "Islam" (Fig. 1). It is much more pronounced in North Caucasian Federal District of Russia, which consists of republics whose population has traditionally practiced Islam—Dagestan, Ingushetia, Chechnya and others.

Another interesting finding concerns topic called "Ukraine-Russia relations". It is more vivid in the Southern Federal District, that has a common border with Ukraine (Fig. 2). This may indicate the concern of residents of this border district with recent events in Ukraine. In particular, the regime change in Ukraine and subsequent military actions led to the influx of refugees into Russia.

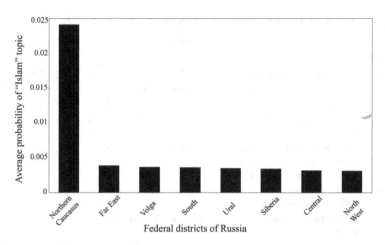

Fig. 1. Topic modeling results: distribution of "Islam" topics by Federal districts of Russia

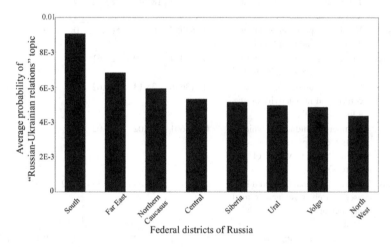

Fig. 2. Topic modeling results: distribution of "Ukraine-Russia relations" topic by Federal districts of Russia

5.2   Formal Online User Engagement

Distribution of user meta-data and indicators of online user activity are extremely uneven and right-skewed (Table 2).

Boxplots on Fig. 3 indicate that pioneer users of "VK.com" were inhabitants from North West Federal district. Users from the other regions registered later, and the latest were those from the republics of North Caucasus and Far East. These data reflect the process of "VK.com" penetration through the geographical space of Russia after being originated in Saint Petersburg. The boxplots of SNS usage duration (Fig. 4) also illustrate this process. Boxplots from Fig. 5 show the distribution of birth years of users among Russian regions and indicate the age of inhabitants from the North West region

Table 2. Descriptive statistics of online user behavior indicators

		Min	Max	Mean	Std.dev	1st Q	Median	3rd Q
User meta-data								
Birth year	Birth year from a user profile	1902	2002	1986	13.18	1982	1989	1995
Friends	Number of user's "friends"	0	8895	45.8	178.44	0	1	35
Followers	Number of user's followers	0	18235	23.5	146.28	0	0	9
Groups	Number of groups joined by a user	0	4681	24.7	89.63	0	0	13
Duration	The duration of VK.com use computed as difference between dates of the first and the last user posts on the "wall"	0	3254	663.2	685.51	32	460	1072
Indicators of public user engagement								
Posts	Total number of posts on a user's "wall"	0	53285	113.04	585.45	0	3	33
Comments	Total number of comments on a user's "wall"	0	15513	11.20	115.05	0	0	0
Likes	Total number of "likes" on a user's "wall"	0	71304	181.49	985.12	0	1	28
In reposts	Number of posts reposted by the user on the own "wall"	0	52957	68.18	502.26	0	0	3
Out reposts	Number of posts reposted by other from the a user's "wall"	0	4374	8.60	57.61	0	0	0
Contributors	Number of unique users who contributed into activity on the a user's "wall"	0	13656	35.13	151.62	0	2	17
Sources	Number of unique IDs which posts were reposted by a user on his "wall" (diversity of sources)	0	3601	14.02	60.02	0	0	2
Originality	Share of original (authored by a user himself) posts among total number of posts on a user's "wall"	0	1	0.684	0.374	0,32	0.93	1
Other' posts share	Share of posts authored by other users among total number of posts	0	1	0.347	0.394	0	0.133	0.75
Other' comments share	Share of comments authored by other users among total number of comments	0	1	0.601	0.319	0,42	0.6	1
Other' likes share	Share of "likes" leaved by other users among total number of "likes"	0	1	0.831	0.242	0,76	0.94	1

is slightly shifted to the older side. Such distribution could be explained with geographical paths and dynamics of SNS penetration and by the innovation diffusion theory [18]. According to the latter technologies first spread among younger population and further are adopted by the older. Older population of the North West region had received an advantage comparing to their peers from other regions because of the earlier start of "VK.com".

Table 3. ANOVA test results

		Sum of squares	df	Mean square	F	Sig. (p-value)
ID	Between groups	1.303e19	7	1.862e18	291.425	0.000
	Within groups	4.922e20	77028	6.390e15		
	Total	5.052e20	77035			
Duration	Between groups	3.601e8	7	5.145e7	111.187	0.000
	Within groups	2.283e10	49338	462698.284		
	Total	2.319e10	49345			
Birth year	Between groups	58896.728	7	8413.818	49.217	0.000
	Within groups	3359569.600	19652	170.953		
	Total	3418466.327	19659			
SNS "Friends"	Between groups	6741415.327	7	963059.332	30.326	0.000
	Within groups	2.446e9	77028	31757.260		
	Total	2.453e9	77035			
Others' posts share	Between groups	105.128	7	15.018	97.709	0.000
	Within groups	7988.100	51971	0.154		
	Total	8093.227	51978			

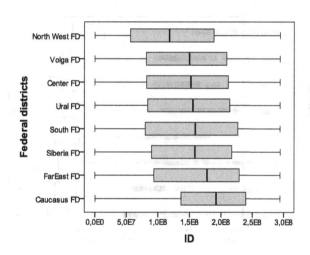

Fig. 3. Boxplots of user ID distribution among Federal districts of Russia

A one-way between subjects ANOVA was conducted to estimate the effect of geographical location (Federal districts of Russia) on users' IDs, SNS usage duration, users' age, number of users' SNS "friends" and share of others' posts on a user's "wall". There were significant effects in all tests (Table 3). Boxplots from Fig. 6 indicate differences, albeit not very pronounced, in the number of users' SNS "friends" among Russian Federal districts. The rank of each district roughly corresponds to the order of VK's geographical dissemination: users from North West regions tend to have more "friends" compared to all other regions, while users from republics of North Caucasus and Far East tend to have fewer SNS "friends". The most "friendly" regions are Nenets Autonomus Okrug and Vologda Oblast. This result is similar to the findings

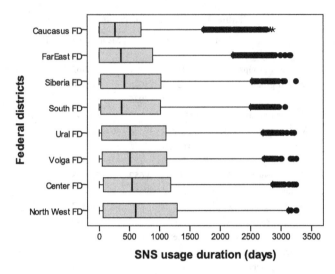

Fig. 4. Boxplots of SNS user duration distribution among Federal districts of Russia

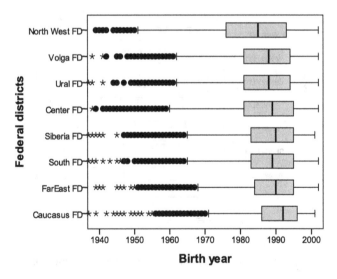

Fig. 5. Boxplots of users birth years distribution among Federal districts of Russia

obtained in the other study of Russain VK.com users [23]. Since the number of SNS "friends" could be a component of social network capital these differences may be interpreted as display of digital inequality.

The measure from Fig. 7—share of others' posts on a user's "wall"—indicates the extent of users' online involvement and public engagement with others. Boxplots show significant differences in the distribution of shares among Russian regions: Central and North West regions have the highest scores for online social engagement, while Caucasus Federal district has the lowest. Previous research found that directed public

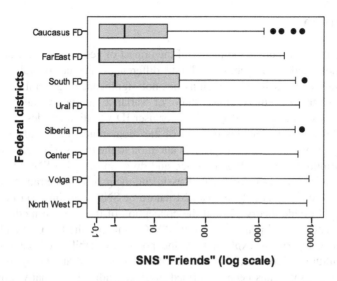

Fig. 6. Boxplots of user SNS "friends" distribution among Federal districts of Russia (logarithmic scale)

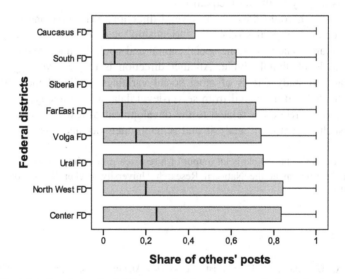

Fig. 7. Boxplots for share of others' posts distribution among Federal districts of Russia

communication is positively linked to higher levels of bridging social capital [9]. Therefore, uneven distribution of this measure among Federal districts actually indicate the divide in online social capital.

Other indicators of online social engagement such as number of unique contributors, other' comments and likes shares did not indicate any significant or interpretable differences.

6   Conclusion

Obtained results contribute to the theory of the impact of geographic location on online communication and user behavior. First, differences in the overall activity of "VK.com" users across Russian regions are not significant in general. The regional level explains the extremely small share of variance in the overall variation of behavioral user data (the max ICC = 0.04 for user ID variation and less than 0.01 for other variables). This evidence is in favor of the geographical independence of online users' engagement. A notable exception is attention to the topics of Islam and Ukraine. Second, distributions of user IDs, user age and duration of active SNS use reflect the natural process of SNS diffusion across Russia and the gradual penetration into various regions of the country. The dynamics and nature of SNS spreading can be explained with the digital divide theory [7] and the conception of the unequal modernization of Russia [21]. The delayed penetration of the "VK.com" into the Far East and republics of the North Caucasus is explained by the poorer availability of the Internet and significant cultural differences. The delayed and weak representation of these regions in the online media space has been confirmed in other studies [3]. Finally, this research shows the uneven distribution of users' online involvement measure among Federal districts of Russia, which indicates the divide in online social capital and could be interpreted as display of digital inequality.

Further research could develop in several directions. The first one is an investigation of structural properties of users' "friendship" networks [4, 5] among Russian regions which are related to online social capital and could be interpreted as indicator of the second level digital divide. Another direction is to go beyond geographical dimension and to study effects of other social variables of digital inequality which could be collected and measured from server-level data: age, ethnicity, education and so on. One more direction is related to the development of text mining methods and techniques such as sentiment analysis and semantic network analysis.

Acknowledgements. This article is an output of a research project implemented as part of the Basic Research Program at the National Research University Higher School of Economics (HSE) in 2017.

References

1. Auzan, A., Belyakov, E.: Economist Aleksander Auzan: "Rossia prevraschaetsa v stranu menedzherov, ohrannikov, migrantov i pensionerov" [Economist Alexander Auzan: 'Russia is turning into a country of managers, security men, migrants and pensioners']. Komsomolskaya pravda (2011). http://www.kp.ru/daily/25782.5/2766102/. Accessed 21 Apr 2017. (in Russian)
2. Bischoping, K.: Gender differences in conversation topics, 1922–1990. Sex Roles **28**(1–2), 1–18 (1993)
3. Bodrunova, S.S., Litvinenko, A.A.: Four Russias in communication: fragmentation of the Russian public sphere in the 2010s. In: Dobek-Ostrowska, B., Glowacki, M. (eds.) Democracy and Media in Central and Eastern Europe 25 Years On, pp. 63–80. Peter Lang, London (2015)

4. Bohn, A., Buchta, C., Hornik, K., Mair, P.: Making friends and communicating on Facebook: implications for the access to social capital. Soc. Netw. **37**, 29–41 (2014)
5. Brooks, B., Hogan, B., Ellison, N., Lampe, C., Vitak, J.: Assessing structural correlates to social capital in Facebook ego networks. Soc. Netw. **38**, 1–15 (2014)
6. Castells, M.: Communication Power. Oxford University Press, Oxford (2013)
7. Deviatko, I.F.: Digitizing Russia: the uneven pace of progress toward ICT equality. In: Ragnedda, M., Muschert, G.W. (eds.) The Digital Divide: The Internet and Social Inequality in International Perspective, pp. 118–133. Routledge, New York (2013)
8. DiMaggio, P., Hargittai, E., Neuman, W.R., Robinson, J.P.: Social implications of the Internet. Annu. Rev. Sociol. **27**, 307–336 (2001)
9. Ellison, N.B., Vitak, J., Gray, R., Lampe, C.: Cultivating social resources on social network sites: Facebook relationship maintenance behaviors and their role in social capital processes. J. Comput-Mediat Comm. **19**, 855–870 (2014)
10. Hargittai, E., Hsieh, Y.P.: Digital inequality. In: Dutton, W.H. (ed.) The Oxford Handbook of Internet Studies. Oxford University Press, Oxford (2013)
11. Hong, L., Davison, B.D.: Empirical study of topic modeling in Twitter. In: Proceedings of the First Workshop on Social Media Analytics, pp. 80–88. ACM, New York (2010)
12. Indaco, A., Manovich, L.: Social media inequality: definition, measurements, and application. Urban Stud. Pract. **1**, 11–22 (2016)
13. Inglehart, R.: Modernization and democracy. In: Inozemtsev, V., Dutkiewicz, P. (eds.) Democracy versus Modernization: A Dilemma for Russia and for the World, pp. 123–144. Routledge, New York (2012)
14. Koltcov, S., Koltsova, O., Nikolenko, S.: Latent dirichlet allocation: stability and applications to studies of user-generated content. In: Proceedings of the 2014 ACM conference on Web science (WebSci 2014), pp. 161–165. ACM, New York (2014)
15. Moore, H.T.: Further data concerning sex differences. J. Abnorm. Psychol. **17**(2), 210–214 (1922)
16. Steyvers, M., Griffiths, T.: Probabilistic topic models. In: Landauer, T., McNamara, D., Dennis, S., Kintsch, W. (eds.) Latent Semantic Analysis: A Road to Meaning. Lawrence Erlbaum, New Jersey (2006)
17. Van Dijk, J.A.M.G.: The Deepening Divide: Inequality in the Information Society. Sage, London (2005)
18. Wejnert, B.: Integrating models of diffusion of innovations: a conceptual framework. Annu. Rev. Sociol. **28**, 297–326 (2003)
19. Weng, J., et al.: TwitterRank: finding topic-sensitive influential twitterers. In: Proceedings of the Third ACM International Conference on Web Search and Data Mining, pp. 261–270. ACM, New York (2010)
20. Witte, J.C., Mannon, A.P.: The Internet and Social Inequalities. Routledge, New York (2010)
21. Zubarevich, N.: Perspectiva: Chetire Rossii [Four Russias]. Vedomosti, 3014 (2011). https://www.vedomosti.ru/opinion/articles/2011/12/30/chetyre_rossii. Accessed 21 Apr 2017. (in Russian)
22. Zubarevich, N.: Chetire Rossii i novaya politicheskaya realnost' [Four Russias and a New Political Reality]. Polit.ru (2016). http://polit.ru/article/2016/01/17/four_russians/. Accessed 21 Apr 2017. (in Russian)
23. The most friendly regions — Virtual Population of Russia, http://webcensus.ru/vmap/внутренняя-дружба/. Accessed 21 Apr 2017. (in Russian)

eSociety: ICTs in Education and Science

Developing Social Competence of Preschoolers in Digital Era: Gender Dimensions

Yuliya Proekt[(✉)], Alexandra Kosheleva, Violetta Lugovaya, and Valeriya Khoroshikh

Herzen State Pedagogical University of Russia,
Saint-Petersburg, Russian Federation
proekt.jl@gmail.com, alkosh@inbox.ru,
violetta_lugovay@mail.ru, vkhoroshikh@gmail.com

Abstract. In this study authors examined the relationships between preschoolers' usage of digital technologies and their social competence. Previous research has shown that there aren't many connections between children's ICT using and their social competence. Social competence was measured through three types of a source of information (children, parents, kindergarten teachers). The impact of two independent variables (gender and engagement if ICT usage) on social competence of preschoolers was considered. The findings revealed impact of gender on children's social competence's development regarding their engagement in ICT usage.

Keywords: Development · Social competence · Preschool age · Gender · Digital technologies · Electronic devices · Cognition · Emotion · Motivation · Social behavior

1 Introduction

Modern psychologists pay strong attention to essential transformations of life environment that have basically changed sociocultural landscape of Childhood [1, 24, 34, 39, 45, 51, 65]. Nowadays a child develops and lives in hybrid space contained a physical and a virtual reality inseparably [20]. Interactions of the child with the virtual space begin at any moment of time when he or she uses technical tools for communication, searching information, viewing photos and video and so on. Such interaction adds distant contexts to everyday life of the child even then he or she moves through the physical space. Emphasizing Vygotskian ideas [63] we can say that new types of cultural tools strongly affect developing child's cognition, emotion and social behavior. Digital technologies have become the strongest input variable that influences a social situation of child's development. The first generation of digital natives is becoming parents themselves and easily let their children use mobile devices and other ICT. If imitation of adult behavior is the important part of children's social learning [5], parents who constantly use ICT set an example for modeling of behavior by their children. In spite of this, there are not enough empirical studies focused on connection between children's using of digital devices and their social behavior.

© Springer International Publishing AG 2017
D.A. Alexandrov et al. (Eds.): DTGS 2017, CCIS 745, pp. 87–101, 2017.
https://doi.org/10.1007/978-3-319-69784-0_7

2 New Technologies and Children's Development

In the recent years anxieties about wide digital technologies pervasiveness in human life were occurred in psychological and pedagogical literature more and more often. Moreover experts tend to alarm that digital technologies influence negatively on cognitive development and self-control of modern children. Scholars have pointed out at the formation of an inadequate image of the world, decrease of cognitive activity and decline of mnemonic abilities, attention skills and imagination [10, 17, 24, 34, 58, 60]. Mental transformations of modern children also reveal itself in an expressed polarization of developmental levels, reduction of children with average intellect [24, 58]. The distinct phenomenon of modern children's cognition is so-called "clip thinking" as a transition from linear model of cause-effect relationships to net model of thinking [27, 59]. Extreme point of view has been reflected in an elaboration of the «digital dementia» concept that combines cognition states of young ICT users and similar states of brain with cognitive disabilities [29, 61].

Nonetheless empirical findings don't confirm so negative perspective but they are rather contradictory. The numerous studies have been revealed extremely weak connections between time of watching TV and school achievements of children [25, 35, 49, 57, 69]. The content of the watched programs is more significant than watching time. For example watching of learning programs (such as the "Sesame Street") tends to influence positively on language and cognition development [16, 32, 33, 36] and school achievement [7, 66]. The studies suggest that computer learning games may positively affect visual spatial and spatial reasoning skills, reaction time and multi-tasking [13, 37, 42, 43, 70].

Thus assessment of ICT impact on cognition development and school achievement has been often speculative and reflected rather beliefs of scholars than empirical facts. As shown in the O'Neil et al. [44] thorough review of studies of the educational potential of games, only nineteen articles among thousands of published between 1990 and 2005 contained qualitative or quantitative data.

Scholars admit that digital environment fundamentally changes conditions of child cognitive development but they still discuss a meaning of those changes. Put in terms of Wertsch [67] modern children's cognition conducts a lot of mediated actions as thinking with help of cultural tools including digital technologies. Dennett [19] discusses digital technologies as a part of situated cognition that includes external tools in internal cognitive processes. So "technologisation" of childhood [47, 48] has led to appearance of new cognitive phenomenon in children development. But what happens with social development when technical tools have been becoming one of the main cognitive tools and communicative mediators for children?

Increasing communicative distance between children and adults, digital divide between generations are the distinctive features of modern cultural situation of growing up. These circumstances have inevitably changed conditions of modern socialization processes. Thus an issue of young ICT user's social competence's development might be considered as an urgent psychological question.

3 Social Competence

Scholars often define child capabilities to succeed in meeting societal standards and in social relationships, as well to feel him- or herself positively in society as "social competence" [4, 41, 50, 71]. The key function of social competence is to organize social behavior for achieving desired effects of social interactions [3]. There are many aspects of this theoretical construct. Social competence reflects cognition about social life, emotion regulation in communication, social skills in sustaining contacts, achieving goals, dealing with communicative problems, coping with peer pressure and so on [11, 28, 52]. Zigler and Trickett [71] suggest that social competence reveals in two interrelated dimensions: intrapersonal or "self-actualizing" and interpersonal or "social expectancy". Another viewpoint associated with division between social performance which could be viewed by other people and social skills that could be used or not by the child in different social situations [12, 30].

At the same time, most scholars in this domain tend to define social competence like complex multifaceted concept that includes cognitive, emotional, motivational and behavioral components. Summarizing of theoretical and empirical findings let us suppose a structural model of social competence in preschool age (see Table 1).

Table 1. Description of social competence components

Social competence components	Traits and abilities of preschooler that strengthen social competence
Motivation [2, 28, 50, 54]	- *Desire to enter new contacts* - *Interest in company* - *Aspiration to cooperation* - *Communicate orientation*
Cognition [2, 28, 38, 50, 54]	- *Social knowledge* - *Social perception* - *Awareness of own social self* - *Adequate self-esteem*
Emotion and emotion regulation [2, 4, 31, 50, 54]	- *Respect for other people's values* - *Ability to recognize emotional states of peers, adults and him/herself* - *Anger management skills* - *Developed self-control* - *Ability to listen other people* - *Ability to accept the results of social interactions*
Behavior [2, 4, 38, 50, 54]	- *Helping behavior, co-operation, altruism* - *Formation of communicative ethic* - *Assimilation of norms of social relations* - *Ability to change communicative style depends on situation of interaction with adults and peers* - *Communicative skills*

Many external and internal factors influence development of social competence. Some of them connected with cultural conditions [15, 18], other reveal basic gender differences. There are enough empirical evidences that female preschoolers tend to be more empathic and cooperative and have better developed social skills than their male peers [6, 22, 23, 26, 56, 64]. Boys often demonstrate more aggressive behavior and seem to prefer physical than social activity [6, 8, 40, 68] that could slow down their social competence's development.

Social competence is the important indicator of socialization processes' success. Quality of social environment plays a key role in that processes. Family, kindergartens communities, peer systems are the main sources for children to learn about social roles and their identities, to form expectations to social interaction and cooperation [9, 14]. Nowadays mobile devices and mass media have become mediators for children to learn patterns of social behavior [53]. Concerning this issue we conducted a study that main purpose was to explore correlation between social competence of preschoolers and their engagement in using of digital technologies. Another aim was to study gender differences in that correlation. In this study we consider the engagement in using of digital technologies by children through screen time (such as time spent for television viewing, computer, tablet, smartphone and other electronic devices usage).

4 Method

4.1 Participants

The study involves 69 families with children aged between 5 and 6 (36 girls (52.2%), mean age 5.19 SD = 0.4). None of the children has any disabilities or developmental delays. The parents' mean age was 33.35 (SD = 4.55). All parents who took part in the study were women. 43 women have higher education (65.2%), 10 women are divorced (15.2%). 46 children have siblings (69.7%). 5 children have families with single parent. All of the children have been receiving education at kindergartens in Saint-Petersburg (Russia). The kindergartens were located in three different districts of the city (downtown area, outskirts, and suburb). 7 kindergarten teachers also were involved to the sample for assessment of children's social competence. Data from 3 families was removed as a result of problem with completing their forms.

4.2 Measures

4.2.1 Social Competence

In this study social competence was measured through three types of a source of information. Social Competence Evaluation Scale was used to receive information from kindergarten teachers, Parent Questionnaire Form was filled by mothers, and Child Test Anxiety was used with children for determining their experience and comprehension of social situations.

4.2.1.1 Social Competence Evaluation Scale (SCES)

The Scale involves 20 items that were created based on Table 1. The scale was developed by the authors within the scope of the study. A five-pointed Likert scale (1-almost never; 2-rarely; 3-sometimes; 4-often; 5-constantly) was used for evaluation frequency of social competence demonstration by a child during his or her staying in kindergarten (see all items in Table 2). Below we propose factor structure of scale and discuss its reliability.

Table 2. Factor loading and factor structure of social competence's evaluation by kindergarten teachers (Note. SI = social interaction, CO = communicative orientation, SC = social cognition)

Items	SI	CO	SC
The child is able to listen to another person and to be careful about another's opinions and values	**0.87**	0.04	0.04
The child can gently react to conflict situations, knows how not to quarrel	**0.86**	−0.13	0.01
The child effectively interacts with the social environment and is able to act how it could be accepted in a cultural community	**0.84**	−0.03	0.38
The child is able to correlate his/her own desires with other people's interests	**0.82**	0.28	0.18
The child can be aware of and understand other people's emotion and feelings	**0.79**	0.16	0.07
The child has necessary skills for collective behavior and an activity, he/she is able to move towards the common goals	**0.69**	0.26	0.37
The child yearn for showing higher, positive human traits and social feeling (joy, love, sympathy, empathy and so on)	**0.59**	**0.54**	−0.01
The child can keep a simple conversation with adults and peers (reach an agreement, exchange of stuff, propose actions and so on)	**0.57**	0.24	**0.59**
The child acquaints with basic rules of social relationships	**0.55**	0.38	0.43
The child is able to help and is ready to accept help from other people	**0.53**	0.23	0.43
The child has an adequate self-esteem	**0.52**	0.46	0.27
The child can present and defend his/her point of view without insulting other communicants	0.17	**0.79**	0.11
The child is focused on social interaction with peers and adults	0.17	**0.75**	0.25
The child has an expressed desire to take up a place among those who are significant for him/her (peers and adults)	−0.04	**0.70**	0.44
The child can be aware of and express ethically his/her own emotion and feelings	0.15	**0.70**	0.22
The child has a need for communication and approval	−0.21	**0.58**	0.22
The child has necessary capacities for cognitive activity in the social scope	0.25	0.09	**0.82**
The child can get needed information in conversation	0.10	0.25	**0.78**
The child has elementary knowledge about social world, other people and him or herself	0.20	0.39	**0.70**
The child is aware of his/her own personality	0.11	**0.57**	**0.57**
Explored variance	5.76	4.00	3.58
Unique variance accounted for by factors	28.8%	20.0%	17.9%

4.2.1.2 Parent Questionnaire Form (PQF)

The Questionnaire involves questions about social skills and traits of the children. Parents were suggested to evaluate such traits and skills as social confidence, spacious mind, the richness of inner world, spirituality, jocundity, self-confidence, sense of purpose, savvy, emotional openness, responsiveness, leadership skills, and the richness of imagination. A five-pointed Likert scale (1-not at all; 2-slightly; 3-moderately; 4-very; 5-extremely) was used for their assessment of trait presence in the child personality. Also parents could add any traits of their children that how they mean contributed social success of the child and evaluate them by the same way.

4.2.1.3 Child Test Anxiety (Temml, Dorca, Amen) [21]

Experimental material contains 14 pictures in size 8.5 * 11 cm. Each picture presents some typical situation from preschooler's life. There are two set of pictures. Pictures for girls demonstrate a girl in situation; pictures for boys demonstrate a boy. Face of the child doesn't draw clearly. Picture has only a contour of the child's head. Each picture contains two additional images of child's head corresponding with sizes of the contour of the child's head in basic image. One of them is a smiling face, another is a sad face. Pictures depict different situations (interaction with adults, with peers and being alone). Each of situations has one of the three emotional meanings (positive, negative, and neutral). A child is shown a picture and then asked what kind of face could a picture' child have (smiling or sad). The index of anxiety is defined as an amount of sad face's choices. We also used 5 additional indicators. Three indicators revealed the negative experience of the child in different social situations (with adults, with peers, being alone). Other two indicators evaluated an adequacy of choice sad or smiling faces in accordance with emotional meaning of situations.

4.2.2 Engagement in Digital Technologies Usage

4.2.2.1 Using of Time Scale (Rubinshtejn) [55]

The scale was used to determine how usually children spend their time. The Scale include a set of typical children activity (eating, sleeping, strolls, games with peers, games with adults, joint reading, being in a kindergarten, sport, visiting entertainment places, visiting museum, theaters, circus, watching TV, using computers, tablets, smartphones and other electronic devices). Parents were asked to assess timing for each type of the child's activity in percentages of usual week time. The screen time was used as a key indicator.

4.2.2.2 Parent's Attitudes Forward ICT Using of a Child Form

The Form includes questions about factual and desired children's age for beginning to use ICT, to have smartphones and tablets, to watch TV, children's interest in digital tools, how often and what for children use ICT and what are other activities their children prefer. Five-pointed Likert scales (1-not important at all; 2-of little importance; 3-of average importance; 4-very important; 5-absolutely essential) also were suggested to evaluate the meaning of digital technologies (TV, computer, smartphone, tablet) for social competence development. Last part of the form includes questions about socio-demographic profiles of family (children's age, gender, parent's age, gender, educational level).

4.3 Procedures

The data was gained from kindergarten teachers, parents and children. Parents were explained goals and objectives of study, presented information about participation in the study their children and given written form for decision-making. Then parents who agreed to participate themselves and give permission to participate their children were given forms for filling at home. The data gaining from children were conducted in kindergartens during children's free activity time. Each child was examined individually, apart from others in a separate room. Children's spontaneous sayings were also recorded by experimenters. Teachers filled the Social Competence Evaluation Scale for each child in their kindergarten group separately.

4.4 Data Analysis

In this study gender and engagement in ICT were determined as independent variables. We first conducted the median split to divide children into high and low engagement in ICT usage groups using the screen time indicator (mdn = 4, range = 0–13). Next step was performed for analyzing the data by the One Sample Kolmogorov–Smirnov Test. The results of the analysis of the Kolmogorov–Smirnov Test have showed a normal distribution (p > 0.05) for independent variable screen time (K–Ñ d = 0.16), and dependent variables indicating social competence - social interaction (K–Ñ d = 0.14), communicative orientation (K–Ñ d = 0.10), social cognition (k–ñ d = 0.17), total SCES (k–ñ d = 0.09), total evaluation of the child's social competence by parents (K–Ñ d = 0.11). Then we used descriptive analyses and correlations of all the study variables. Also factor analysis and analysis of variance were conducted. All analyses were computed in Statistica v. 6.1 (StatSoft Inc.).

5 Results

At the first step we conducted exploratory factor analysis for developing SCES, Principal components analysis with varimax raw rotation was computed for initial 20 items. Follow recommendation for extraction of factor number [62] we used an analysis of the Scree plot and an analysis of Eigenvalues greater than one. Their results let us extract three factors.

There was a theoretical distinction between cognitive, emotional, motivational and behavioral components of social competence. But the empirical results supported a three-factor solution, with common factor of Social Interaction and two partial factors Communicative Orientation and Social Cognition. Emotion and motivation did not independently contribute to social competence of preschoolers. There were only three cases with cross loading of items across factors with items loaded above .50 on two factors. See Fig. 1 for Principle Components Scree Plot. See Table 2 for factor loadings and factor structure. See Table 3 for reliability, means, and standard deviations of the scale items.

Factor 1: Social Interaction (Expl. Var = 5.76). The Social Interaction factor was one of three empirical factors and it captured different aspects of preschooler's behavior in social situations. This factor consisted of 11 items and accounted for 28.81% of the

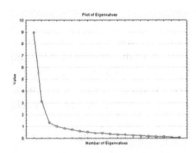

Fig. 1. Principle components scree plot

variance in the sample. These items involve social skills of the child that let him or her build strong relationships with people. Some items reflect social cognition (e.g. "The child acquaints with basic rules of social relationships") and motivation to communicate (e.g. "The child yearn for showing higher, positive human traits and social feeling (joy, love, sympathy, empathy and so on)"). See Table 3 for alphas, means, and standard deviations of the scale items.

Table 3. Cronbach's alpha, split-half reliability, means and SDs of. Questionnaire items for overall SCES and its subscales

Factor	Number of items in each scale	Cronbach's Alpha (standardized)	Split-half reliability	Mean	SD
Social interaction	11	0.93	0.95	41.19	6.57
Communicative orientation	7	0.85	0.89	27.54	4.06
Social cognition	5	0.86	0.87	20.39	2.85
Total SCES	20	0.88	0.94	77.59	10.09

Factor 2: Communicative orientation (Expl.Var = 4.00). The second factor captured the child's interests in communication, his or her self-control skills. This factor consisted of 7 items and accounted for 20.02% of the variance. These items involve child's desires to emphasize his or her individuality and needs for communication and approval. In the other hand, this factor includes respect to feeling of other people and self-control capacities.

Factor 3: Social Cognition (Expl.Var = 3.58). The third factor comprised items that reflect cognitive abilities of the child needed for communication. This factor consisted of 5 items and accounted for 17.88% of the variance. These items involve examples of knowledge or skills that suggest the child would be successful in conversations. For instance "The child can keep a simple conversation with adults and peers (reach an agreement, exchange of stuff, propose actions and so on)" and "The child can get needed information in conversation".

These three factors are consistent with theoretical framework and they correspond with cognitive, emotional, motivational and behavioral components of preschooler's social competence.

Apparently the results disclose three main domains of revealing social competence of a child in different social situations. All factors and the whole Scale had a high internal reliability. All subscales have strong correlation between each other (SI&CO – r = 0.51; SI&SC – r = 0.64; CO&SC – r = 0.70).

Girls were evaluated significantly more social competent then boys (F (4, 58) = 5.52, p < 0.001). But significant gender difference in subscales was revealed only for the social interaction scale (F (1, 63) = 12.27, p < 0.0001). Significant differences in engagement in ICT usage weren't appeared for any subscale or the whole Scale (F (4, 58) = 2.16, p = 0.085). The biggest variance was revealed for the communicative orientation scale, especially for children who highly involved in ICT usage (Table 4).

Table 4. Means and SD of subscales SCES for gender and engagement in ICT usage

Factor	Gender				Engagement in ICT usage			
	Girls		Boys		Low		High	
	Mean	SD	Mean	SD	Mean	SD	Mean	SD
Social interaction	43.66	5.16	38.27	7.19	41.05	3.97	41.36	4.42
Communicative orientation	27.77	4.08	27.33	4.32	28.06	5.95	26.76	7.89
Social cognition	20.77	2.69	19.97	3.17	20.23	3.08	20.68	2.70
Total scale	80.20	9.22	74.63	10.89	77.88	10.15	77.24	10.80

Another effect in evaluations of children's social competence was appealed in case of parents' scores comparison (see Table 5).

Table 5. Means and SD of traits evaluation by parents for gender and engagement in ICT usage

Traits and abilities of the child	Gender				Engagement in ICT usage			
	Girls		Boys		Low		High	
	Mean	SD	Mean	SD	Mean	SD	Mean	SD
Spacious mind	3.83	0.75	3.80	0.71	3.88	0.76	3.72	0.68
Social confidence	3.77	0.91	3.77	1.04	3.75	1.01	3.80	0.91
The richness of inner world	3.80	0.80	3.67	0.92	3.73	0.82	3.76	0.93
Spirituality	3.31	0.83	3.37	0.96	3.40	0.87	3.24	0.93
Jocundity	4.20	0.72	4.17	0.75	4.25	0.63	4.08	0.86
Self-confidence	3.74	0.98	3.37	1.22	3.70	1.11	3.36	1.08
Sense of purpose	3.49	0.89	3.23	1.25	3.55	1.04	3.08	1.08
Savvy	4.00	0.80	3.93	0.87	4.15	0.77	3.68	0.85
Emotional openness	4.06	0.87	4.03	1.10	4.00	1.04	4.12	0.88
Responsiveness	4.23	0.73	4.07	0.87	4.00	0.85	4.40	0.65
Leadership skills	3.49	1.01	3.17	1.21	3.38	1.15	3.28	1.06
The richness of imagination	4.29	0.99	4.23	0.94	4.08	1.10	4.56	0.58
Total scale	46.20	6.27	44.80	6.41	45.85	6.44	45.08	6.23

Children with high engagement in ICT usage were evaluated by parents as more responsive (F (1, 61) = 4.08, p < 0.05) and having the richer imagination (F (1, 61) = 4.15, p < 0.05), but less savvy (F (1, 61) = 5.28, p < 0.05). There were no gender differences in parents' evaluation of social competence of their children. Total scale of social competence's evaluation by parents had a high internal reliability (Cronbach's Alpha (standardized) α = 0.82, split half r = 0.83).

The findings of this study didn't reveal any statistically significant correlation between children's engagement in ICT usage and indicators of social competence (see Table 6). This is important to note that the results didn't show significant correlation between evaluations of the child's social competence by parents and kindergarten teachers but there are connections between the evaluations of the child's social competence by parents and kindergarten teachers and children understanding of negative social situations. More competent children were less likely to select smiling faces for negative social situations.

Table 6. Correlation coefficients between indicators of social competence and engagement if ICT usage (Note: *p < 0.05; **p < 0.01)

Variables	1	2	3	4	5	6	7
1. Evaluation of the child's social competence by kindergarten teachers	–						
2. Evaluation of the child's social competence by parents	0.09	–					
3. Adequacy of choices in negative social situations	0.27*	0.28*	–				
4. Adequacy of choices in positive social situations	0.02	0.15	0.13	–			
5. Time of watching TV	0.005	0.07	−0.01	−0.09	–		
6. Time of using computers	0.12	0.16	−0.05	−0.17	0.30*	–	
7. Time of using smartphones, tablets	−0.08	−0.14	−0.15	−0.16	0.22	0.42**	–
8. Screen time	0.01	0.04	−0.09	−0.18	0.74**	0.74**	0.71**

Notwithstanding lack of significant correlations for all children interest connections between children engagement in ICT usage and social competence were appeared in gender groups. So for boys' evaluation of the social competence by kindergarten teachers was positively associated with factual age of beginning to watch TV (r = 0.40, p < 0.05) and frequency of using tablet for learning (r = 0.47, p < 0.01). For girls an adequacy of choices in negative social situations was inversely correlated with time of using smartphones and tablets (r = −0.43, p < 0.05), and screen time overall (r = −0.51, p < 0.01). Similar results were conducted by using analysis of variance (ANOVA) with gender and engagement in ICT usage as independent factors (see Fig. 2). A main effect for both factors was found (F(1, 62) = 13.666, p < 0.001). There weren't any effects for gender (F(1, 62) = 0.56, p = 0.46) or engagement in ICT usage (F(1, 62) = 0.49, p = 0.48) separately.

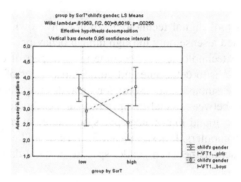

Fig. 2. Effects of gender and engagement in ICT usage on adequacy of choices in negative social situations

6 Discussion

There are two typical approaches to explore associations between ICT usage and behavior of young children. First of them is linked with a qualitative study (case-study, interviews, close observation and so on). The second approach contains quantitative study and often contains methods that received information about children from adults (parents, kindergarten teachers, other experts). We have realized the second approach and not so many connections were revealed between engagement in ICT usage and social competence of preschoolers. Our results provide support for the reports of other researchers. For example Ogelman et al. [46] conducted a study that aim was to reveal predicted effects of technology devices' use durations of children the same aged on their social skill levels, social impact and social preference. Their finding also didn't reveal significant correlations between digital technologies usage and children's social behavior. We agree with one of the results' explanations given by the authors that kindergarten teachers and parents' evaluations might be incorrect. In other hand family practices and a content of digital technologies might play a crucial role in their impact on social competence's development. There are many evidences for such an assumption in qualitative studies. So Plowman et al. [48] found that parents' cultural practices and values affected a family communicates, plays together, or supports their child's learning more than the technologies usage. In this study significant correlations between content of ICT usage and children's social competence were appeared only in male sample. Depressed social competence of girls with high engagement in ICT usage is a very interest result that might reflect specific of social situation of girls' upbringing and gender preference's formation. Girls' games often focus on social situation modeling, they are more sociable. If ICT usage becomes predominant occupation for girls it could decline their social activity and delay their social competence's development. ICT usage by boys might provide more opportunities for communication with peers and adults in opposite of cases of traditional boys games or other activities.

7 Conclusion

As any other cultural tool digital technologies don't have own positive or negative meaning, they are gained a sense only through human behavior. And want we it or not interaction with digital technologies has become integral part of children life. In this case a key task of adults is to determine and utilize those types of children interaction with ICT that could be suitable and useful for their development. In this study we examined connections between social competence of preschoolers and their engagement in ICT usage. We found that gender plays an important role in the association with ICT usage by preschoolers. It is significant for further studies to explore this issue in the context of interactions between gender specific of child day-to-day activity and ICT usage.

References

1. Abramenkova, V.V., Bogatyreva, A.: Deti i televizionnyj ehkran. J. Vospitanie shkol'nikov **6**, 28–31 (2006)
2. Antonova, T.N.: Social'naya kompetentnost' rebenka-doshkol'nika: pokazateli i metody vyyavleniya. J. Detskij sad ot A do YA **5**, 54–69 (2004)
3. Argyle, M.: Development of social coping skills. In: Frydenderg6, L. (ed.) Learning to Cope, pp. 81–106. Oxford University Press, New York (1999)
4. Asmolov, A.G.: Lichnost' kak predmet psihologicheskogo issledovaniya. Izd-vo MGU, Moskva (1984)
5. Bandura, A.: Social Foundations of Thought and Action: A Social Cognitive Theory. Prentice-Hall, Englewood Cliffs (1986)
6. Bendas, T.V.: Gendernaya psihologiya: Uchebnoe posobie. Piter, Saint-Petersburg (2006)
7. Borgh, K., Dickson, W.P.: Two preschoolers sharing one microcomputer: creating prosocial behavior with hardware and software. In: Campbell, P.F., Fein, G.G. (eds.) Young Children and Microcomputers, pp. 37–44. Prentice Hall, Englewood Cliffs (1986)
8. Braza, F., Braza, P., Carreras, M.R., Muñoz, J.M.: Development of sex differences in preschool children: social behavior during an academic year. J. Psychol. Rep. **80**(1), 179–188 (1997)
9. Bronfenbrenner, U.: The Ecology of Human Development: Experiments by Nature and Design. Harvard University Press, Cambridge (1979)
10. Buckingham, D.: After the Death of Childhood: Growing Up in the Age of Electronic Media. Polity Press, Oxford (2000)
11. Burt, K.B., Obradović, J., Long, J.D., Masten, A.S.: The interplay of social competence and psychopathology over 20 years: testing transactional and cascade models. J Child Dev. **79**, 359–374 (2008)

12. Cavell, T.A.: Social adjustment, social performance, and social skills: a tri-component model of social competence. J. Clin. Child Psychol. **19**, 111–122 (1990)
13. Chatters, L.B.: An assessment of the effects of video game practice on the visual motor perceptual skills of sixth grade children. Unpublished doctoral dissertation, University of Toledo, Toledo, OH (1984)
14. Cicchetti, D., Toth, S.L.: The role of developmental theory in prevention and intervention. J. Dev. Psychopathol. **4**, 489–493 (1992)
15. Cole, P.M., Tan, P.Z.: Emotion socialization from a cultural perspective. In: Grusec, J.E., Hastings, P.D. (eds.) Handbook of Socialization, pp. 516–542. The Guilford Press, New York (2007)
16. Comstock, G.A.: Television and the American Child. Academic Press, San Diego (1991)
17. Cordes, C., Miller, E. (eds.): Fool's Gold: A Critical Look at Computers in Childhood. Alliance for Childhood, College Park (2000)
18. Damon, W.: Social and Personality Development. SAGE Publication Inc., London (1983)
19. Dennett, D.C.: Kinds of Minds: Towards an Understanding of Consciousness. Weidenfeld and Nicholson, London (1996)
20. de Souza e Silva, A.: From cyber to hybrid: mobile technologies as interfaces of hybrid spaces. J. Space Cult. **9**(3), 261–278 (2006)
21. Denisova, N.D.: Diagnostika emotsionalno-lichnostnogo razvitiya doshkolnikov 3-7 let. Uchitel, Volgograd (2014)
22. DiPrete, T.A., Jennings, J.L.: Social and behavioral skills and the gender gap in early educational achievement. J. Soc. Sci. Res. **41**(1), 1–15 (2012)
23. Duckworth, A.L., Seligman, M.E.P.: Self-discipline outdoes IQ in predicting academic performance of adolescents. J. Psychol. Sci. **16**, 939–944 (2005). doi:10.1111/j.1467-9280. 2005.01641.x
24. Fel'dshtejn, D.I.: Glubinnye izmenenija sovremennogo Detstva i obuslovlennaja imi aktual-izacija psihologo-pedagogicheskih problem razvitija obrazovanija. J. Vestnik prakticheskoj psihologii obrazovanija **1**(26), 45–54 (2011)
25. Fetler, M.: Television viewing and school achievement. J. Commun. **35**, 104–118 (1984)
26. Fortin, N.M., Oreopoulos, P., Phipps, S.: Leaving boys behind: gender disparities in high academic achievement. Technical report, National Bureau of Economic Research (2013). http://www.nber.org/papers/w19331.pdf
27. Girenok, F.I.: Metafizika pata. Kosnoyazychie ustalogo cheloveka. Labirint, Moskva (1995)
28. Gogoberidze, A.G.: Predshkol'noe obrazovanie: nekotorye itogi razmyshlenij (Koncepciya obrazovaniya detej starshego doshkol'nogo vozrasta). J. Upravlenie v DOU **1**, 10–19 (2006)
29. Greenfield, S.: Mind Change. Random House, New York (2014)
30. Gresham, F.M.: Conceptual and definitional issues in the assessment of children's social skills: implications for classification and training. J. Clin. Child Psychol. **15**, 3–15 (1986)
31. Halberstadt, A.G., Denham, S.A., Dunsmore, J.C.: Affective social competence. J. Soc. Dev. **10**(1), 79–119 (2001). doi:10.1111/1467-9507.00150
32. Huston, A.C., Wright, J.C.: Mass media and children's development. In: Sigel, I.E., Renninger, K.A. (eds.) Handbook of Child Psychology, pp. 999–1058. Wiley, New York (1997)
33. Huston, A.C., Wright, J.C.: Children's processing of television: the informative functions of formal features. In: Bryant, J., Anderson, D.R. (eds.) Children's Understanding of Television: Research on Attention and Comprehension, pp. 35–68. Academic Press, New York (1983)
34. Karabanova, O.A.: Social'noe konstruirovanie detstva. J. Obrazovatel'naja politika **5–6**(43–44), 52–61 (2010)

35. Keith, T.Z., Reimers, T.M., Fehrmann, P.G., Pottebaum, S.M., Aubey, L.W.: Parental involvement, homework, and TV time: direct and indirect effects on high school achievement. J. Educ. Psychol. **78**, 373–380 (1986)
36. Kirkorian, H.L., Wartella, E., Anderson, D.R.: Media and young children's learning. J. Future Child. **8**, 63–86 (2008)
37. Kuhlman, J.S., Beitel, P.A.: Videogame experience: a possible explanation for differences in anticipation of coincidence. J. Percept. Motor Skills **72**(2), 483–488 (1991)
38. Kunicyna, V.N., Kazarinova, N.V., Pogol'sha, V.M.: Mezhlichnostnoe obshchenie: Uchebnik dlya vuzov. Piter, Saint-Petersburg (2002)
39. Livingstone, S., Haddon, L., Görzig, A., Olafsson, K.: Risks and safety on the internet: the perspective of European children. Full findings. LSE, EU Kids Online, London (2011)
40. Maccoby, E.: Gender as a social category. J. Dev. Psychol. **24**, 755–765 (1988)
41. Masten, A.S., Coatsworth, J.D., Neemann, J., Gest, S.D., Tellegen, A., Garmezy, N.: The structure and coherence of competence from childhood through adolescence. J. Child Dev. **66**, 1635–1659 (1995)
42. McClurg, P.A., Chaille, C.: Computer games: environments for developing spatial cognition. J. Educ. Comput. Res. **3**, 95–111 (1987)
43. Miller, G.G., Kapel, D.E.: Can NonVerbal, puzzle type microcomputer software affect spatial discrimination and sequential thinking of skills of 7th and 8th graders? J. Educ. **106**, 160–167 (1985)
44. O'Neil, H.F., Wainess, R., Baker, E.: Classification of learning outcomes: evidence from the computer games literature. J. Curric. **16**, 455–474 (2005)
45. Obuhova, L.F., Korepanova, I.A.: Sovremennyj rebenok: shagi k ponimaniju. J. Psihologicheskaja nauka i obrazovanie **2**, 5–19 (2010)
46. Ogelman, H.G., Güngör, H., Körükçü, Ö., Sarkaya, H.E.: Examination of the relationship between technology use of 5–6 year-old children and their social skills and social status. J. Early Child Dev. Care (2016). doi:10.1080/03004430.2016.1208190
47. Plowman, L., McPake, J., Stephen, C.: Just picking it up? Young children learning with technology at home. J. Cambridge J. Educ. **38**, 303–319 (2008)
48. Plowman, L., McPake, J., Stephen, C.: The technologisation of childhood? Young children and technology in the home. J. Child. Soc. **24**(1), 63–74 (2010). doi:10.1111/j.1099-0860.2008.00180.x
49. Potter, J.W.: Does television viewing hinder academic achievement among adolescents? J. Hum. Commun. Res. **14**, 27–46 (1987)
50. Proekt, Y.L.: Model' social'noj kompetentnosti v mladshem podrostkovom vozraste. In: Sbornik nauchno-metodicheskih statej Obrazovanie XXI veka: model' novoj shkoly. Vypusk 4. Sbornik nauchno-metodicheskih statej, pp. 85–97. SAGA, SPb. (2010)
51. Proekt, Y.L., Bogdanovskaya, I.M., Koroleva, N.N.: Razvitie setevyh tekhnologij kak faktor transformacij zhiznennogo prostranstva sovremennogo cheloveka. J. Universum: Vestnik Gercenovskogo universiteta **1**, 89–96 (2014)
52. Raver, C.C., Zigler, E.F.: Social competence: an untapped dimension in evaluating Head Start's success. J. Early Child. Res. Q. **12**, 363–385 (1997)
53. Richert, R.A., Robb, M.B., Smith, E.I.: Media as a social partner: the social nature of young children's learning from screen media. J. Child Dev. **82**, 82–95 (2011). doi:10.1111/j.1467-8624.2010.01542.x
54. Rose-Krasnor, L.: The nature of social competence: a theoretical review. J. Soc. Dev. **6**, 111–135 (1997)
55. Rubinshtejn, S.Y.: Ispol'zovanie vremeni (fakticheskoe i zhelatel'noe) kak pokazatel' napravlennosti lichnosti. In: Portnov, A.A. (ed.) Eksperimental'nye issledovaniya v patopsihologii, pp. 245–253. Akademiya, Moskva (1976)

56. Ruble, D.N., Martin, C.L., Berenbaum, S.A.: Gender development. In: Eisenberg, N. (ed.) Social, Emotional, and Personality Development, pp. 858–932. Wiley, Hoboken (2006)
57. Schmidt, M.E., Vandewater, E.A.: Media and attention, cognition, and school achievement. J. Child. Electron. Media **18**(1), 63–85 (2008)
58. Smirnova, E.O.: Doshkol'nik v sovremennom mire. Drofa, Moskva (2006)
59. Soldatova, G., Nestik, T., Rasskazova, E., Zotova, E.: Cifrovaya kompetentnost' rossijskih podrostkov i roditelej: rezul'taty vserossijskogo issledovaniya. Fond Razvitiya Internet, Moskva (2013)
60. Soldatova, G., Zotova, E., Chekalina, A., Gostimskaya, O.: Pojmannye odnoj set'yu: social'no-psihologicheskoe issledovanie predstavlenij detej i vzroslyh ob Internete. Fond Razvitiya Internet, Moskva (2011)
61. Spitzer, M.: Antimozg. Cifrovye tekhnologii i mozg. AST, Moskva (2014)
62. Tabachnick, B.G., Fidell, L.S.: Using Multivariate Statistics, 5th edn. Allyn & Bacon: Pearson Education Inc., Boston (2007)
63. Vygotskij, L.S.: Problemy razvitiya psihiki. In: Vygotskij, L.S. (eds.) Sobranie sochinenij: v 6-t., T.3. Pedagogika, Moskva (1983)
64. Walker, S.: Gender differences in the relationship between young children's peer-related social competence and individual differences in theory of mind. J. Genet. Psychol. **166**(3), 297–312 (2005)
65. Walrave, M., Heirman, W.: Cyberbullying: predicting victimisation and perpetration. J. Child. Soc. **25**(1), 59–72 (2009)
66. Wenglinsky, H.: Does it compute? The relationship between educational technology and student achievement in mathematics. Educational Testing Service, Princeton. https://www.ets.org/Media/Research/pdf/PICTECHNOLOG.pdf
67. Wertsch, J.V.: Voices of the Mind: A Sociocultural Approach to Mediated Action. Harvard University Press, Cambridge (1991)
68. Whiting, B., Edwards, C.P.: A cross-cultural analysis of sex differences in the behavior of children aged three through eleven. J. Soc. Psych. **12**, 171–188 (1973)
69. Williams, P.A., Haertel, E.H., Haertel, G.D., Walberg, H.J.: The impact of leisure time television on school learning: a research synthesis. Am. Educ. Res. J. **19**(1), 19–50 (1982)
70. Yuji, H.: Computer games and information-processing skills. J. Percept. Motor Skills **83**, 643–647 (1996)
71. Zigler, E.F., Trickett, P.K.: IQ, social competence, and evaluation of early childhood intervention programs. J. Am. Psychol. **33**, 789–798 (1978)

The Effectiveness of Leading Russian Universities in Achieving Graduate-Level Employability from Social Network Data

Oksana Pavlova, Philip Kazin[(✉)], Nikolay Butakov,
and Steven Hagen

ITMO University, St. Petersburg, Russia
pavlova.ifmo@gmail.com, kazin@corp.ifmo.ru,
alipoov.nb@gmail.com, hagen@mail.ifmo.ru

Abstract. The 'VKontakte' social network is increasingly becoming a useful source of data for studying many aspects of Russian social life. This research paper uses this source to investigate one of the most crucial issues for many young Russians – how successful are Russia's leading universities in the employability rates of their graduates on completion of their studies. Official data from the Ministry of Education and Science of the Russian Federation show fairly high rates of employment, but the methodology used gives us little indication of the extent to which their employment corresponds to the professional or occupational specialism they acquired at their university. The analysis with the use of the 'VKontakte' network provides significant insight into this question. This paper presents results about the employability of graduates from the leading Russian universities participating in the 5–100 Competitiveness and Growth Program specifically in the subjects of "Mathematics and Information Technology" and "Engineering" where a high degree of correlation between subject specialism and employment is expected (The Russian Academic Excellence Project aiming at bringing 5 Russian Universities into their list of the Top 100 world universities (For more details see: http://5top100.com/)).

Keywords: Higher education institutions · Graduate employment and employability · Professional and occupational competencies · ICT for employment evaluation · Social networks · Quality of education

1 Introduction

We purport that one of the key quality indicators of university education is graduate employability. In our definition, 'effective graduate employability' means that institutions have supported the student knowledge, skills, attributes, reflective disposition and identity that graduates need to succeed in the workforce. This can be tested by the correlation between subject specialism and relevant professional employment. Different approaches to the concept of 'effective graduate-level employability' are described in the academic literature [1–12]. Androsova is correct in her assertion that employment by itself does not signify effective graduate-level employability [1]. Most graduates seek work which allows them to make use of the specialist knowledge and skills they

© Springer International Publishing AG 2017
D.A. Alexandrov et al. (Eds.): DTGS 2017, CCIS 745, pp. 102–112, 2017.
https://doi.org/10.1007/978-3-319-69784-0_8

have acquired on their university course. The graduates' task is generally not only to find a job, but also to establish themselves professionally in society and contribute to the economy as a whole. In other words, if 100% of graduates from a specific Masters' courses find employment, it is not necessarily follow that the employability is 'effective' neither for (a) the graduates themselves nor for (b) the economy.

Social networks are a unique and rich source of data for analyzing effective graduate-level employability as they reveal not only the fact of employment, but also the graduate's attitude to this fact. Therefore, in this paper we present the information, obtained from the analysis of data derived from the popular Russian social network "VKontakte", on the employment data of graduates of those leading Russian universities which participate in the "Project 5-100", since these universities aspire to achieve global competitiveness, are classified as the top-performing universities in Russia and have in some cases achieved high rankings in the world top hundred ratings[1]. Graduates of Russian universities provide data on their employment in open access on their personal pages and these data (usually published to inform friends and contacts about status and activities) provide a unique source of live, relevant information about the quality of the employment and the graduate's reaction to their job.

In this paper, we analyze effective graduate-level employability from individual graduates' point of view; namely, by (a) evaluating the extent to which the graduate's course of studies, and skills acquired, are directly relevant to his or her employment (the 'rational constituent of effective employability') and (b) the individual graduate's willingness to reveal his/her workplace in the social network ('the emotional constituent'). Section 2 contains a summary of latest research on employability and in the third Section, we review the recent data available on graduate employment from Russian universities giving a critical appraisal of the strengths and weaknesses of their data collection methods. In Sect. 4, we present our own methodology and tools used to analyze the data derived from the 'VKontakte' social network and provide our conclusions.

2 International Studies on the Employment of University Graduates

Graduate-level employability has become a key indicator of university quality round the world and is included in the profiles of many universities. It is often a key criterion for selecting universities by students, their parents and employers. It is a component of state planning in various countries: for example, governments round the world require certain numbers of professions to join the economy annually, such as: engineers, IT-specialists, physicians, surgeons, accountants and so on.

The fact that graduates frequently do not practice their specialism leads to mismatches within the economy leading to a shortage of manpower in certain sectors and a

---

[1] Ratings of Universities Reputation (RA Expert). Rating "100 best Russian universities", 2016 http://raexpert.ru/rankings/vuz/vuz_2016/#3. Russian Education. Federal Portal. http://www.edu.ru/ratings/reyting-vuzov-rossii-2016/.

rise in immigration, which has become politically unacceptable in some countries. Governments are therefore reluctant to invest in training individuals if they do not practice their specialism. Shortages of professionals in certain fields compromises the effectiveness of the education system. This has also led some governments, such as the UK government, to intervene by offering financial support to encourage individuals to study for certain professions such as Math and Science teaching.

The most important latest studies on this topic include works of Boden and Nedeva [4], Pegg et al. [13], Jackson [9], Unay-Gailhard [18] dedicated to reconceptualization of the role of higher education, which analyze the notion of "capabilities and possibilities of employment", the essence and constituents of employment, its interconnection with its constituents and impact of social factors on employment. Comparative research of this topic in different countries include the work of Blackmore et al. [3], Baldry [2], Imdorf et al. [8].

Another direction of graduate employment investigation is the study of technologies and training methods that improve capabilities, career opportunities and one's chances of employment. Studies focused on the role of career guidance and career self-management for successful employment of university graduates include Bourner and Millican [5], Jackson and Wilton [10], Bridgstock [6]. Our article presents the Russian case of effective graduate-level employability in a comparative perspective within the context of these studies.

3 Analysis of Russian Public Sources of Information on Effective Graduate Employability

Russian sources of public information on graduate employment all possess gaps and flaws in their data and in their methodology. These are explained below.

3.1 SuperJob Ranking (See Table 1. Level of University Graduate Employment in Respect to Their Specialism, Column 1), Data of 2000–2005

In Table 1 the rating [17] is based on the data from the site Superjob.ru. The rating is formed on the basis of an analysis of all resumes of universities graduates available in the Superjob.ru database over 5 years (2000–2005). The graduates' degree specialisms are compared with their positions and responsibilities in their latest workplace. The positive feature of this approach is the acknowledgement and measurement of a correlation between a graduate's career-path and his or her specialism.

On the other hand, these data are incomplete as they include only those graduates who were seeking employment through a recruitment agency whose data appear in their database. Not all graduates use recruitment agencies, and do not include Superjob. Many graduates are looking for employment independently or with the help of their acquaintances, and they also tend to seek work locally in line with the industrial development in their region.

Table 1. Graduate employment (using data from various sources)

	SuperJob, 2000–2005, %	Ministry of education and science, 2014, %	Social navigator, 2015, %	Expert RA, 2016, ranking (out of 100)	Expert RA, 2016, ranking (out of 100)
	Employment in line with subjects studied	Total graduate employment	Obtained the official job offer from the industry	Criteria for high quality education	Employers demand for graduates
HEI	1	2	3	4	5
ITMO	–	85	71.30	13	40
LETI	–	90	94.8	32	76
SSAU	–	90	24.10	41	15
UNN	–	85	9.60	31	63
KFU	–	85	39.00	16	31
MIPT	15–30	85	0	3	3
SPbPU	30–45	85	7.0	14	10
NSU	–	85	24.50	4	20
MEPhI	30–45	85	88.80	7	6
TPU	–	85	67.20	4	20
UrFU	45–60	85	68.20	22	4
MISIS	30–45	80	70.20	11	14
HSE	More 60	80	0.40	6	7
TomskSU[1]	–	80	42.60	19	21
TyumenSU[2]	–	80	37.60	83	86
SUSU	–	80	97.20	50	88
IKBFU	–	75	0	75	122
FEFU	–	75	37.40	34	67
SFU	–	75	16.90	24	8
MSMU	–	70	0	28	17
RUDN	45–60	70	44.80	15	33

Where ITMO - ITMO University; LETI – St. Petersburg Electrotechnical University; SSAU - Samara University; UNN - Lobachevsky State University; KFU - Kazan Federal University; MIPT - Moscow Institute of Physics and Technology; SPbPU - Peter the Great St. Petersburg Polytechnic University; NSU - Novosibirsk State University; MEPhI - The National Research Nuclear University; TPU - Tomsk Polytechnic University; UrFU - Ural Federal University; MISIS - The National University of Science and Technology; HSE - NRU Higher School of Economics; TSU[1] - Tomsk State University; TSU[2] - Tyumen State University; SUSU - South Ural State University; IKBFU - The Immanuel Kant Baltic Federal University; FEFU - Far Eastern Federal University; SFU - Siberian Federal University; MSMU - Sechenov First Moscow State Medical University; RUDN - RUDN University.

3.2   Rating Compiled by the Ministry of Education and Science of the Russian Federation Presented on the Site "Graduate Employment Monitoring" (See Table 1, Column 2), 2014 [11]

This official data source is derived from the Pension Fund of Russia (PFR), but data for 2015–2016 are absent there, and it includes no data on the correlation between an individual's employment and their specialism, which is a major gap.

The methodology used by the Ministry of Education and Science of the Russian Federation is as follows: The Ministry sends a depersonalized request to PFR. PFR responds positively provided at least one tax payment has occurred. Graduates, however, can change their workplace, but the Ministry makes only a single request in a given year. For example, after completing his or her studies a graduate may take employment in line with their specialism but only on a temporary basis. Then he/she quits the job and starts to work in a different profession unrelated to his/her degree subject (e.g. as a sales assistant or a sales manager in a supermarket) with a labor contract without making any payments to the tax office or to the pension fund.

This kind of example shows that the following flaws in the dataset: in the first case: the graduate is considered to be employed according to his specialism (if the request for information came during the relevant time or on the basis of his first payment). In the second case, she or he is considered to be employed no longer in accordance with his or her specialism (but came after he or she quit his/her job). In the third case, she/he is considered to be unemployed (as his work generates no tax payments). The latter case does not contradict the data of the Russian Federal State Statistics Service that shows increasing unemployment among people with higher education.

Therefore, this set of ratings is misleading: while it takes into account all employed graduates and gives information about their degree specialism, it gives no information on extent to which these job profiles correlate to specialisms acquired in universities. In this way, we have the general employment data, but no data on employment utilizing degree specialisms.

3.3   The Rating of Demand for University Graduates by Employers Based on the Social Navigator "Russia Today" (See Table 1, Column 3), 2016 [16]

The object of this data-gathering exercise is to identify demand for specialists (i.e. graduates with specialist qualifications) on the labor market, as this demonstrates the demand of employers. Accordingly, it measures the number of specialist graduate jobs offered by particular employers including graduate assignments and contracts for training specialists in given organizations.

However, there is one major shortcoming: they do not reflect the full picture of the profile of the employment of university graduates with a particular specialism, but rather reflects how effective a particular university is in networking with companies and finding posts for its graduates in particular industries.

If 75% of a graduate cohort have offers of employment from particular companies, this does not mean that the remaining 25% are not employed in an organization relevant to their specialism. This means that the university has an agreement and has concluded contracts on cooperation with particular organizations.

3.4   Data Provided by the Rating Agency Expert RA

Rating devoted to the conditions for acquiring education of high quality (see Table 1, column 4), 2016
This ranking [14] is based on universities' own results and attestations of a quality education, which are evaluated by groups of indicators: i.e. "level of teaching", "international integration", "resource provision", "demand among applicants". However, high ratings according to the quality of education or student experience do not necessarily correlate to a higher percentage of employment in line with the relevance of the graduate's degree subject to a particular job.

Rating of employers' demand for graduates (see Table 1, column 5), 2016
In 2016, 144 higher education institutions participated in a survey. Sources of statistical information [15] were data from university questionnaires, scientometric indicators and data from open sources.

The basis for the ranking is the response of universities to two groups of indicators: "cooperation with employers" and "quality of graduate careers." In particular, the following target groups are analyzed: students and graduates, representatives of academic and scientific communities, representatives of employers' companies. In 2016, more than 28,000 respondents took part in the surveys.

The data were partially defective because neither employment in line with graduate subject specialisms nor demand for particular graduates by employers were included.

Nonetheless, we do not know the sociological sample, the veracity of respondents' answers during questioning, methods of data collecting (indicators presented on the websites of higher educational institutions can be overestimated).

As it can be seen from Table 1, the data on the employment of Russian university graduates differ significantly depending on the source as the data collection methods vary widely. According to unofficial & unconfirmed data (publications in the media referring to select polls among the population), the number of graduates employed in jobs relevant to their specialist degree studies is much lower than it is stated in official statistics. So, according to the MK.RU (2013), 55% of the Russian graduates polled do not have employment in line with their subject specialism.

Moreover, statistics provided by official sources, for example the Ministry of Education and Science, are not comprehensive. At best, the Ministry of Education and Science present only the average percentage of graduates in employment, without taking into account graduates in non-professional employment (that is, employment in non-standard occupations), which gives only a vague perspective on the actual extent of graduate-level employment. In addition, universities carry out training in various subject-areas (Natural Sciences, ICT, Engineering, etc.), and the proportion/share of people employed within jobs which reflect their field of study also varies according to the specific field or branch of science.

Accordingly, the official data presented on the non-professional employment of graduates or graduate employment in general, do not give a complete picture of the level of graduate employment from subject-specific courses (educational programs) within the same university.

4 Case Study of the Effectiveness of Graduate-Level Employability in Russian Universities in the Areas of "Mathematics (Including Applied Math) and Information Technology" and "Engineering" According to the Social Network "Vkontakte"

4.1 The Description of the Case Study

The objectives of the Case Study were (1) to study data on employment, jobs and positions held by users of the social network "VKontakte", who are graduates of Russian universities (participating in the "5-100" program) in the subject-areas of "Mathematics and Information Technology" and "Engineering" between 2011 and 2016; (2) to carry out a comparative analysis of data on professional employment/ non-professional employment from official sources and unofficial ones obtained from the social network "VKontakte".

Our hypothesis is that, judging from the information in social media, the percentage of Russian graduates finding employment in a job where they apply their specialist degree skills and knowledge is only 45% of the total number of graduates.

4.2 Results of the Case Study and Their Interpretation

Table 2 presents statistics on employment in the specialisms of graduates of leading Russian universities (participants of Project 5-100) in the subject-areas of "Mathematics and Information Technology" and "Engineering" in the period of 2011–2016 according to data mined from the social network "Vkontakte".

According to the data from Table 2, only 51.2% of graduates of "Mathematics and Information Technology" and 48% of "Engineering" graduates are employed in jobs where they can apply their subject specialist knowledge. Also in the table there are data on each of the 21 leading universities in Russia, so that they can be compared with each other.

Thus, after analyzing the statistics derived from the social network "Vkontakte" we came to the following conclusions:

Not all graduates are willing and/or have the desire to inform the public about the place of their employment. This phenomenon may have different causes:

1. Users do not trust social networks (e.g. due to data leakage [7]); or do not have a serious attitude towards social networks (see Table 2).
2. Some users post jokes instead of information. Jokes can be different for different reasons.

Table 2. The effectiveness of graduate-level employability in Russian universities (participating in the program "5-100") in the areas of "Mathematics and Information Technology" and "Engineering" according to the data from social network "Vkontakte".

I.	Educational programs on mathematics and information technologies					
	Employment in accordance with acquired profession	Among them with leading positions in industry	Unclear	Non-professional employment	Among them having leading posts	Irony or joke instead of information
ITMO	62.0	1.0	13.9	14.6	1.1	6.6
UNN	46.0	0.9	8.0	29.0	3.0	4.0
LETI	54.5	0.0	13.8	20.0	2.1	9.7
IKBFU	40.0	2.2	13.3	33.3	2.2	8.9
FEFU	28.3	2.2	23.9	39.1	4.3	2.2
KFU	28.2	0.0	21.7	40.9	2.0	7.3
MISIS	48.2	0.0	16.5	24.6	1.0	9.7
MIPT	68.2	0.0	9.8	14.1	3.1	4.7
SPbPU	47.8	2.5	6.3	37.1	0.0	6.4
NSU	44.6	0.0	13.4	23.2	0.3	18.5
HSE	68.4	0.0	15.8	15.8	0.0	0.0
MEPhI	55.2	0.0	10.4	23.4	1.3	9.7
MSMU	–	–	–	–	–	–
RUDN	28.0	0.0	12.0	44.0	0.0	16.0
SSAU	68.0	3.0	1,0	18.0	2.0	8.0
TSU[1]	70.5	0.0	3.2	14.2	0.0	12.2
TPU	55.0	1.0	7.0	28.0	4.0	4.0
SFU	38.0	2.5	19.5	29.5	0.0	9.5
TSU[2]	60.0	0.0	6.0	34.0	0.0	0.0
UrFU	65.0	0.0	18.0	12.0	0.0	6.0
SUSU	49.1	1.7	18.4	16.1	5.5	9.1
Average	**51.2**					
II.	Educational programs on engineering					
ITMO	39.4	0.0	13.2	31.0	3.0	12.9
UNN	–	–	–	–	–	–
LETI	53.2	0.0	9.5	23.0	2.0	12.5
IKBFU	27.6	0.0	13.8	37.9	3.4	17.2
FEFU	28.3	2.2	23.9	39.1	4.3	2.2
KFU	–	–	–	–	–	–
MISIS	54.8	0.1	6.1	32.5	0.7	4.9
MIPT	58.0	0.0	9.6	23.7	0.7	8.0
SPbPU	56.6	1.7	12.9	23.8	0.0	5.1
NSU	–	–	–	–	–	–
HSE	–	–	–	–	–	–

(*continued*)

Table 2. (*continued*)

I.	Educational programs on mathematics and information technologies					
	Employment in accordance with acquired profession	Among them with leading positions in industry	Unclear	Non-professional employment	Among them having leading posts	Irony or joke instead of information
MEPhI	55.8	0.0	3.9	23.4	3.9	13.0
MSMU	–	–	–	–	–	–
RUDN	37.4	0.0	11.0	36.0	3.0	12.7
SSAU	47.7	0.5	9.0	33.0	7.0	7.5
TSU[1]	53.3	0.0	13.3	23.3	0.0	10.0
TPU	59.9	0.0	7.6	23.0	1.5	8.1
SFU	56.3	0.3	8.4	27.6	0.9	6.5
TSU[2]	–	–	–	–	–	–
UrFU	41.2	0.4	12.0	36.1	3.9	6.4
SUSU	45.2	0.0	17.2	26.4	0.9	10.3
Average	**48**					

Where ITMO - ITMO University; UNN -Lobachevsky State University; LETI - Saint Petersburg Electrotechnical University; IKBFU - The Immanuel Kant Baltic Federal University; FEFU - Far Eastern Federal University; KFU - Kazan Federal University; MISIS - The National University of Science and Technology; MIPT - Moscow Institute of Physics and Technology; SPbPU - Peter the Great St. Petersburg Polytechnic University; NSU - Novosibirsk State University; HSE - NRU Higher School of Economics; MEPhI - The National Research Nuclear University; MSMU - Sechenov First Moscow State Medical University; RUDN - RUDN University; SSAU - Samara University; TSU[1] - Tomsk State University; TPU - Tomsk Polytechnic University; SFU - Siberian Federal University; TSU[2] - Tyumen State University; UrFU - Ural Federal University; SUSU - South Ural State University.

- Kind jokes - users have a sense of humor, treat the world around them with humour. It indicates a good mood, a desire to praise, add a playful note on a typical day.
- Also, a joke can mean a defensive reaction, a desire to cope with the negative. It is an attempt to relieve tension under difficult living conditions. Graduates are not proud of the place of employment or the job they have.
- Another meaning is compensation for a personal defect such as social disinterest, isolation. This type of behavior is characteristic of closed, silent, shy people who, therefore, try to attract the attention of others.
- Aggressive, evil jokes indicate a desire to humiliate or insult. When a person shows ill-will, this is due to low self-esteem. It turns into hardness/severe attitude towards the world around them, and means dissatisfaction with life. Graduates are not proud of the place of their work, there is no self-realization in professional activity.

*In general, **less than half of graduates** in the subject-areas of "Mathematics and Information Technology" and "Engineering" work in their specific field after graduating from university (49.6%).*

This suggests that the leading universities of the country may not be providing the necessary level of interaction with employers, despite the high demand for graduates in these subject-specialisms on the labor market.

Judging by the data on the rate of economic growth in the country, the development of industrial production, the growth of Russia's position in the main indices of innovation activity, the cause of the problem may not simply be connected with adverse economic conditions but an underlying cause may be a mismatch between the subject specialisms taught at university and the demands of the labor market.

Based on the results of the analysis, we can extrapolate that the issue of the poor correlation between graduate-level employability and the labor market may concern most Russian higher educational institutions and regard different subject specialisms in all regions of the country to a greater or lesser extent to the point of being systemic.

5 Conclusions

The study undertaken suggests that the Russian Higher Education system, with reference to graduate-level employability in key science-based subjects, is underperforming and is less effective than commonly believed with regard to the supply of graduates with specialist subject knowledge into the economy. In our case study, half the graduates of two science-based subjects did not find relevant employment where used the specialist skills and knowledge acquired from their degree-courses.

This suggests that further research is needed to investigate the extent to which these findings apply to graduates in other specialist subject-areas. At the level of labor supply, an integrated approach to the organization of labor force planning is required, in particular, mapping the content of the specialist curriculum to employer and broader economic needs. Some early steps in forecasting this direction are already being made by institutes of development (e.g. the Agency for Strategic Initiatives or the Skolkovo Foundation). However, it may be some time before this work will have a noticeable impact on planning the training and education of the future labor force in Russian universities.

Acknowledgements. We would like to thank Professor Alexander V. Boukhanovsky without whom this research would not be possible.

References

1. Androsova, E.V.: Evaluation of the effectiveness of employment universities graduates (gender aspect) In: Economic Science and Practice: Materials II International. Scientific Conference, pp. 60–62. Publishing House: Young Scientist, Chita (2013)
2. Baldry, K.: Graduate unemployment in South Africa: social inequality reproduced. J. Educ. Work **29**(7), 788–812 (2016). doi:10.1080/13639080.2015.1066928
3. Blackmore, J., Gribble, C., Rahimi, M.: International education, the formation of capital and graduate employment: Chinese accounting graduates' experiences of the Australian labour market. J. Crit. Stud. Educ. **58**(1), 69–88 (2017). doi:10.1080/17508487.2015.1117505

4. Boden, R., Nedeva, M.: Employing discourse: universities and graduate 'employability'. J. Educ. Policy **25**(1), 37–54 (2010). doi:10.1080/02680930903349489

5. Bourner, T., Millican, J.: Student-community engagement and graduate employability. J. Widening Participation Lifelong Learn. **13**(2), 68–85 (2011)

6. Bridgstock, R.: The graduate attributes we've overlooked: enhancing graduate employability through career management skills. J. High. Educ. Res. Dev. **28**(1), 31–44 (2009)

7. Hi-Tech Mail.ru: Panic in social networks: Russians massively close their accounts. https://hi-tech.mail.ru/news/social_network_danger/

8. Imdorf, C., Helbling, L.A., Inui, A.: Transition systems and non-standard employment in early career: comparing Japan and Switzerland. J. Educ. Work (2016). doi:10.1080/13639080.2016.1243234

9. Jackson, D.: Re-conceptualising graduate employability: the importance of pre-professional identity. High. Educ. Res. Dev. **35**(5), 925–939 (2016). doi:10.1080/07294360.2016.1139551

10. Jackson, D., Wilton, N.: Perceived employability among undergraduates and the importance of career self-management, work experience and individual characteristics. J. High. Educ. Res. Dev. (2016). doi:10.1080/07294360.2016.1229270

11. The ministry of science and education. http://vo.graduate.edu.ru/#/?year=2014

12. On the employment status of graduates of vocational education institutions, in demanded specialties, required competencies and expected forecast of staffing requirements (based on monitoring results conducted in 83 constituent entities of the Russian Federation): analytical report. Voronin, A.V., Gurtov, V.A., Serova, L.M. (eds.) Publishing House: PetrSU, Petrozavodsk (2012)

13. Pegg, A., Waldock, J., Hendy-Isaac, S., Lawton, R.: Pedagogy for Employability. Higher Education Academy, York (2012)

14. Rating agency "Expert RA": HEI rating of conditions for acquiring education of high quality. http://raexpert.ru/rankingtable/university/2016/tab02/

15. Rating agency "Expert RA": rating of demanded graduates in employers' opinion. http://raexpert.ru/rankingtable/university/

16. Social navigator "Russia Today". https://ria.ru/sn/

17. Super job. The rating of higher educational institutions on the graduates employment in accordance with trained profession. https://www.superjob.ru/research/articles/496/rejting-vuzov/?order_by=2&order_dir=0&order_by_prev=0&order_dir_prev=0#t

18. Unay-Gailhard, İ.: Job access after leaving education: a comparative analysis of young women and men in rural Germany. J. Youth Stud. **19**(10), 1355–1381 (2016). doi:10.1080/13676261.2016.1166189

Analyzing Web Presence of Russian Universities in a Scientometric Context

Anastasiya Kuznetsova$^{(\boxtimes)}$, Stanislav Pozdniakov, and Ilya Musabirov

National Research University Higher School of Economics, Saint-Petersburg, Russia
adkuznetsova13@gmail.com, pozdniakov.stanislav@gmail.com,
ilya@musabirov.info

Abstract. In this paper, we analyse the strategies and stratification of Russian universities in the Northwestern region. By enriching traditional social network analysis scientometric tools, we developed web presence indicators focused on the contexts in which universities are linked with businesses and are mentioned in media. We treat resulting groups in terms of Gouldner's cosmopolitans versus locals theory, based on differences in their publication strategies, and embeddedness in business connections and media contexts.

Keywords: Russian universities · Northwestern region · Webometrics · Altmetrics · LDA · Topic modelling

1 Introduction and Related Work

One of the most important factors for university performance assessment is their publication activity. Universities in Russia are not exceptions from this trend. Because of this "publish or perish" mentality, a highly competitive environment appeared [1], and Russian universities are stratified in their publication activity. Researchers can target their publications either to an international audience of Web of Science (WoS) and Scopus-indexed journals; high-profile Russian journals, which are included in newly developed Russian Science Citation Index (RSCI), or less internationally oriented Russian journals. The majority of Russian journals are excluded from international science communication [3]. However, more and more Russian papers are indexed in the Web of Science Core Collection [8].

The aim of our research is to define strategies, that universities use to increase performance indicators. The focus is on the web data extracted from companies and news websites, which show the business and media context. In addition, we consider data about publications and universities domain-related data. We suggest that additional data from various sources is valuable for analysing and understanding universities agencies.

The difference in strategies allows universities to be considered within the locals and cosmopolitans theory. Gouldner applied this theory to academics, where locals are the group of individuals who interact within this group and use

© Springer International Publishing AG 2017
D.A. Alexandrov et al. (Eds.): DTGS 2017, CCIS 745, pp. 113–119, 2017.
https://doi.org/10.1007/978-3-319-69784-0_9

interpersonal channels to spread the information. Oppositely, cosmopolitans are connected with several communities; consequently, they have weaker connections within these groups and use organizational and head channels for spreading information [5]. In Puttens study [10], universities faculties are considered to follow one of the roles of the introduced theory (cosmopolitan or local). Moreover, in [11] the importance of different orientations for scientists as locals and cosmopolitans is revealed. The concept of productivity is divided into scientific productivity, such as the sum of journal publications and presentations and organizational productivity: laboratory technical reports and memoranda. Cosmopolitan orientation is related primarily to the scientific productivity dimension, while locals orientation is positively associated with organizational productivity.

2   Data and Method

One of the common ways of university research assessment is scientometrics, which applies quantitative analysis to the following aspects of publications: citation indexes, authors, subjects and sources. More recent advances in the field have built on social network analysis methods, including analysing co-authorship and bibliographical coupling data from the network perspective, which is targeted to find structurally important authors, works, organizations and publication venues in their interconnections.

An alternative approach to assess scientific activity and impact is webometrics or cybermetrics [7].

Webometrics uses a toolkit of methods and approaches to judge a publications' web presence, including web impact factor (WIF) - the normalized number of unique in-links to the domain [6]. Researchers have demonstrated that the total number of links on a page of the website and the average number of links on a page could be indicators of the value and importance of the information on these pages. According to Thelwall [12], WIF correlates positively with the offline research activity of the university. The Webometrics Ranking of World Universities Project is the largest academic rating of higher education institutions and it is based on webometrics - the amount of web content (the number of pages and files) and the apparent impact of publications on the number of citations in social media.

However, the choice of ranking approach, while important for applications, limits the understanding of the structure and the strategies employed by the agents. Moreover, it influences the agents' desire to manipulate the system in various ways [4].

While web ranking methodologies pay considerable attention to universities' domains, we suggest that important information about universities can be gathered from their structural connections with other types of agents, including industrial companies and media.

We used the case of 51 universities from the Northwestern region of Russia, focusing on their research in Economics and Management. We focus on distinguishing agents' strategies based on the following metrics:

- The number of unique incoming links to the university's domain.
- Representation in major regional media – the frequency of mentioning a single university on media sites.
- Representation on the sites of business companies: the frequency of mentioning a university on the websites of Top-50 companies of the Northwestern Federal District according to the Expert magazine ranking.

To understand whether Northwestern universities prefer to be published in international or Russian journals, we extracted the number of RSCI and WoS publications in the fields of economic, business, management, and finance. We use hierarchical clustering with complete linkage method to reveal stable groups of universities characterized based on a number of WoS/RSCI indexed publications and on the number of unique external links to the university web domain.

To analyse the context, in which universities activity was mentioned on media and companies websites, we used the latent Dirichlet allocation algorithm (LDA) [2] with a 50-topic model.

During the data gathering process, it became clear, that some institutions are frequently mentioned on media purely in the negative context, so thematic context was considered in our analysis. Using Pearsons residuals we chose several prominent topics strongly associated with the universities in our sample.

3   Analysis and Results

Figure 1 shows that Northwestern region universities are differentiated in publication activity strategies, since they have different proportions of publications in Web of Science Core and RSCI journals.

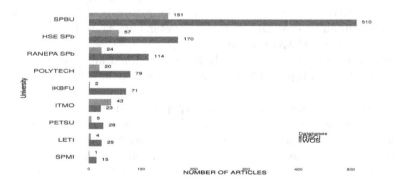

Fig. 1. The number of economics and management publications in WoS and RSCI, Russian Northwestern Universities

Hierarchical clustering of webometrics indicators reveals three groups of universities (Fig. 2). For RANEPA and HSE campuses in Saint-Petersburg, indicators were multiplied by the percentage of researchers in these campuses (0.294

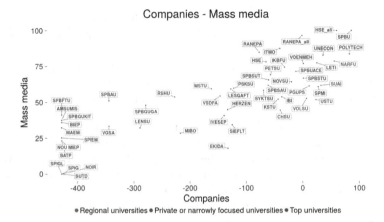

Fig. 2. Map of Russian Northwestern universities based on normalized frequency of mentioning on media and companies websites (Color figure online)

and 0.133 respectively). In addition, non-corrected indicators for these institutions as a whole are marked "HSE_all", and "RANEPA_all" on Fig. 2.

Some universities appear in news more often than others, simultaneously, being out of the of top regional companies attention at all (green cluster). This could be a sign of a low level of business connections and a lack of collaboration with these universities, for example, they could have a lack of collaborative educational programmes and internships.

The red cluster consists of both technical and economic universities occupying top positions in the region. The most popular and presented in media universities are well-known, highly reputed ones e.g. HSE University, St. Petersburg State University, The Russian Presidential Academy of National Economy and Public Administration (RANEPA), St. Petersburg State University of Economics (UNECON), ITMO University.

The blue cluster includes narrowly focused regional universities, which are connected with local topics. They are also more visible in RSCI than in Scopus and WoS.

The green cluster is occupied by narrowly specialized small universities, which are not highly represented in scientometric databases and they strongly differentiate on Media-Company coordinates. Generally, they are less frequently discussed in media than universities in red and blue clusters; however, some of them (Saint-Petersburg State University of Architecture and Civil Engineering, Immanuel Kant Baltic Federal University, and Novgorod State University - Fig. 2, right side) indicate a high level of embeddedness within the industrial sector. Meanwhile, another group of institutions (the Baltic University of Ecology, Politics, and Law; Murmansk Academy of Economics and Management; and St. Petersburg Institute of Economics and management - Fig. 2, left side) demonstrates no visible web traces of collaborations with top companies.

Prominent topics associated with universities from red and blue clusters are shown in Table 1.

Universities from the red cluster with specialization in social science and economics are related to the topics about industry, innovations, science, research, business executives, and education. They are treated as makers and producers of scientific and innovative knowledge [9]. They are also mentioned in the context of business, finance, investments and entrepreneurship. This indicates that they have close ties with the business sector through consulting, business incubators and other collaborative initiatives.

Table 1. Results of LDA applied to media texts

Group of universities	Topics	Context
Top universities with specialization in social sciences and economics red cluster	monitoring_education, directors_researchers, research (social sciences), economics, prices, finances	"this data was presented in the report of the Director of the Institute of Social Analysis and Forecasting (RANEPA) and professor of HSE Tatiana Maleva "Man in the solidarity pension system" "issues under monitoring openness of Russian universities for applicants" "The second lecture in the framework of the HSE and Jaguar Land Rover was devoted to the future of the banking sector"
St. Petersburg universities with specialization in STEM disciplines red and blue clusters	industry, innovations, research2 (science)	"Chemists from ITMO University have developed a colorless ink for color printing" "boosting the competitiveness of innovative industries by establishing strong out-sectoral and in-sectoral linkages and the general infrastructure"
Regional universities or narrowly focused universities blue cluster	local, arctics, transport	"The core of this long-standing debates is whether the butter "Vologda" is the unique product of Vologda region..." "Research Expedition "Floating University" started from Arkhangelsk and is going to the Arctic on the board of the research vessel"

The universities with STEM specialization are unsurprisingly related to research in science, industry and innovations. These universities are related to the topics about technological research and developments in this area.

Regional or narrowly specialized universities from the blue cluster are connected with local topics. For example, Arctic University (NARFU) was mentioned in the context of the Arctic Research Programme.

We found no prominent topics for universities from the green cluster.

4   Conclusion

In this paper, we enriched the scientometric analysis of university research activity with the set of webometric indicators. In addition, we investigated at the context in which universities are mentioned in media. Northwestern universities are stratified across different dimensions. Based on the connections with companies and publication strategies we revealed several groups of universities.

The cluster of top universities invests in high-profile publication ties development. They are linked in business and media as expert centers, business education providers and innovation leaders, with a saliency in LDA topics on research, innovations, business and industry development.

The second group is characterized by more narrowly focused universities with an advanced level of publication activity and performance in the region. They demonstrate the same exposure in the media and collaborations with top companies.

The third cluster consists of universities with low publication activity in economic and management. These universities may be oriented to satisfy the needs of regions and smaller regional companies, and they tend to be out of the attention of the media. Instead, they focus on building strong connections with particular industrial partners.

Acknowledgements. The article was prepared within the framework of the Academic Fund Program at the National Research University Higher School of Economics (HSE) in 2017 2018 (grant No. 17-05-0024) and by the Russian Academic Excellence Project "5-100".

We are grateful to Viktor Karepin for his help with this research.

References

1. Altbach, P.: Anarchy and exploitation in scientific communication - university world news, March 2017. http://www.universityworldnews.com/article.php?story=20170328140116938
2. Blei, D.M., Ng, A.Y., Jordan, M.I.: Latent dirichlet allocation. J. Mach. Learn. Res. **3**(Jan), 993–1022 (2003)
3. Dyachenko, E., Fursov, K.: Russian scholarly journals in science communication. High. Educ. Russia Beyond **11**, 7–9 (2017)
4. Espeland, W.N., Sauder, M.: Rankings and reactivity: how public measures recreate social worlds 1. Am. J. Sociol. **113**(1), 1–40 (2007)
5. Gouldner, A.W.: Cosmopolitans and locals: toward an analysis of latent social roles. I. Adm. Sci. Q. **2**, 281–306 (1957)
6. Ingwersen, P.: The calculation of web impact factors. J. Doc. **54**(2), 236–243 (1998)
7. Ingwersen, P., Björneborn, L.: Methodological issues of webometric studies. In: Moed, H.F., Glänzel, W., Schmoch, U. (eds.) Handbook of Quantitative Science and Technology Research, pp. 339–369. Springer, Dordrecht (2004). doi:10.1007/1-4020-2755-9_16
8. Kasyanov, P.: Russian academic publishing landscape. High. Educ. Russia Beyond **11**, 9–11 (2017)

9. Kim, E.H., Zhu, M.: Universities as firms: the case of us overseas programs. In: American Universities in a Global Market, pp. 163–201. University of Chicago Press (2010)
10. Putten, J.V.: Cosmopolitan and local faculty orientations: a reanalysis of historical data. Paper presented in the Open Track at the EAIR 36th Annual Forum in Essen, Germany (2014)
11. Stahl, M.J., McNichols, C.W., Manley, T.R.: Cosmopolitan-local orientations as predictors of scientific productivity, organizational productivity, and job satisfaction for scientists and engineers. IEEE Trans. Eng. Manag. 2, 39–43 (1979)
12. Thelwall, M., Harries, G.: The connection between the research of a university and counts of links to its web pages: an investigation based upon a classification of the relationships of pages to the research of the host university. J. Assoc. Inf. Sci. Technol. **54**(7), 594–602 (2003)

Challenges of the Digital Economy in the Context of Globalization: Training of PhDs in Software Engineering in Russia

Vladimir G. Khalin[1](✉), Alexander V. Yurkov[1](✉), and Yury V. Kosov[2](✉)

[1] St. Petersburg State University, St. Petersburg, Russia
{v.halin,a.v.yurkov}@spbu.ru
[2] North-West Institute of Management - Branch of the Russian Presidential Academy of National Economy and Public Administration,
St. Petersburg, Russia
kosov-yuv@sziu.ranepa.ru

Abstract. Creation of an information and communication infrastructure of the digital economy requires specialists capable of initiating, developing, and implementing projects in the field of information technologies and communications. In Russia there is still no scientific specialty exactly named Software Engineering for the training of post-graduate students and doctoral candidates. Moreover, such a specialty is missing in the list of scientific specialties on which the degrees of the candidate and the doctor of sciences are defended. The article provides an analysis of the current status of Russian higher education in the field of bachelor's and master's training in Software Engineering and related specialties and formulates a proposal to include Software Engineering in the Nomenclature of Specialties of Scientists of the Russian Federation. To solve this problem, it is necessary to organize training for specialists in this area at the third level of higher professional education, namely the training of PhDs - candidates and doctors of sciences - in the field of Software Engineering.

Keywords: Digital economy · Software Engineering · PhD training · Higher education · Scientific specialties

1 Introduction

The key resources for the modern development of society are knowledge, information, and education. These resources are called upon to be created by the modern research universities which rightly rank among the main institutions of the knowledge economy of the 21st century [1]. In the context of globalization [17], information and communication technologies (ICT) have become the subject of special attention of universities seeking to meet the challenges of the future digital economy [19]. However, within recent years the Russian education skewed towards ICT only as a means of educational activity, but not as a subject of special study [21] and the industrial sector, has led to the fact that, as it turns out, there is no Software Engineering in the list of areas for training specialists of higher scientific qualification [13]. At the same time, the creation of an

© Springer International Publishing AG 2017
D.A. Alexandrov et al. (Eds.): DTGS 2017, CCIS 745, pp. 120–129, 2017.
https://doi.org/10.1007/978-3-319-69784-0_10

information and communication infrastructure of the digital economy definitely requires specialists - including those with the highest scientific qualifications: candidates and doctors of sciences - for whom software engineering would be the subject of their professional activity, because they are called to initiate, develop and implement ICT projects of the digital future [23].

2 Globalization and Higher Education

The problem of the influence of globalization on the development of education in the world community is very important. Globalization is understood in the modern science as one of the most important trends in the development of the present-day world [20]. In a broader sense, globalization is understood as the homogenization and universalization of the world, which is associated with the creation of large unified economic spaces and with the increasing political interdependence of states and regions of the contemporary world, with the development of integration processes in the sphere of education [12].

Integration processes in the field of higher education became especially noticeable at the end of the last century, when there was a reduction in governmental financial support in the industrially developed countries. The strategy for the adaptation of higher education institutions of foreign countries to the reduction of governmental financial support was to increase the income from tuition fees, including those paid by foreign students [4].

The university's ability to attract foreign students has become an important indicator of educational activity [14]. The ability of the university to attract foreign students depends not only on its financial situation. The attractiveness of the university for foreign students is seen as an indicator of the effectiveness of the university, its prestige. According to many experts, in the contemporary world, competition for attracting foreign students between universities is increasing, as well as their share in this segment of the educational market [10].

Under such conditions, the impact of globalization on education has become especially noticeable. This process increases the mobility of students and teachers, imposes new demands on the quality of training specialists, and the importance of international (and even "global") component in the training of specialists with higher education is growing [15].

The wide dissemination of information and communication technologies has established a material and technological base for the globalization of education, created scientific and technical prerequisites for the generation of an international level in education [11]. This level is manifested in the real mobility of students and mobility in the virtual educational space as a promising direction of expanding the internationalization of education. Under these conditions, compliance with the world level of education, primarily in the range of training areas that provide technical progress and challenges for the future digital economy, is an objective necessity for Russian higher education.

3 Software Engineering Education in Russia: Federal Background

Analyzing what has been done in recent years, it should be noted that in the Russian higher school, the Federal state educational standards for the training of bachelors and masters in Software Engineering (SWE) were developed and approved in 2011 by the Ministry of Education and Science. This allowed starting the training of bachelors and masters in the direction of Software Engineering in our country. At the moment, 91 universities of Russia are training bachelors and masters in Software Engineering, including training in higher education institutions from the top ten of the acceptance quality rating:

- St. Petersburg State University - SPbSU[1]
- National Research University "Higher School of Economics" - HSE[2]
- Moscow State Technical University named after N.E. Bauman - MSTU named after N.E. Bauman[3]
- National Research Nuclear University - MEPhI[4]
- National Research Tomsk Polytechnic University - TPU[5]
- National Research Tomsk State University -TSU[6]
- St. Petersburg State Polytechnic University - SPbSPU[7]
- Ural Federal University - UrFU[8]
- St. Petersburg National Research University of Information Technologies, Mechanics and Optics - ITMO University[9]
- St. Petersburg Electrotechnical University - LETI[10]
- South Ural State University (National Research University) - SUSU[11]

By the Order of the Government of Russia from 06.01.2015 No. 7 «*On the approval of the list of specialties and areas of higher education corresponding to the priority areas of modernization and technological development of the Russian economy*» [18], training of specialists in the field of Software Engineering was named the priority area of modernization and technological development of the Russian economy.

---

[1] www.spbu.ru.

[2] www.hse.ru.

[3] www.bmstu.ru.

[4] www.mephi.ru.

[5] www.tpu.ru.

[6] www.tsu.ru.

[7] www.spbstu.ru.

[8] www.urfu.ru.

[9] www.ifmo.ru.

[10] www.eltech.ru.

[11] www.susu.ru.

4 Training in Software Engineering in Saint Petersburg State University

St. Petersburg State University has a license for training of bachelors and masters in Software Engineering, starting from 2011. Training of bachelors and masters in this direction in St. Petersburg State University is conducted at the Department of Software Engineering of the Mathematics and Mechanics Faculty [9] under the programs No. 09.03.04 (for bachelors) and No. 09.04.04 (for masters). The following key departments of the faculty take part in the implementation of these educational programs: Software Engineering[12]; Analytical Information Systems[13]; Computer Science[14]; Parallel Algorithms[15]; Operations Research[16]. Programs include profile disciplines [22]:

- Structures and algorithms for computer data processing
- Practice of Programming
- Software Engineering
- Computer Graphics
- Software Project Management
- Formal Languages and Automata Theory
- Databases
- Architecture of Computational Systems
- Algorithms and Complexity

The List of key professions of graduates:

- Programmer
- Software architect
- Database administrator
- Information Systems specialist
- Project manager in Information Technology
- Testing expert in the field of Information Technology
- Head of Software Development projects
- Technical writer
- Systems analyst
- Technical support specialist in Information and Communication Systems
- Systems programmer.

More than 30 professors - doctors of sciences - take part in the implementation of the programs, including: Andrey N. Terekhov[17] - Head of the Software Engineering

---

[12] http://math.spbu.ru/en/chairs/dep11.html.

[13] http://math.spbu.ru/SD_AIS/index.shtml.

[14] http://math.spbu.ru/en/chairs/dep10.html.

[15] http://www.math.spbu.ru/en/chairs/dep22.html.

[16] http://math.spbu.ru/en/chairs/dep09.html.

[17] http://www.math.spbu.ru/user/ant/.

department, Boris A. Novikov[18], Nikolay K. Kosovsky[19], Demyanovich Yu.K.[20], Vladimir O. Safonov[21], and others.

In addition to training in the area of Software Engineering for bachelors and masters, SPbSU provides postgraduate, masters and bachelor's training in a number of specialties close to the professional field of SWE [2], among them:

- Educational programs for graduate students:
  - 02.06.01 - Computer and Information Sciences
  - 09.06.01 - Informatics and Computer Engineering
  - 27.06.01 - Control in Engineering Systems.
- Educational programs for the training of masters:
  - 01.04.02 - Applied Mathematics and Informatics
  - 02.04.02 - Fundamental Informatics and Information Technologies
  - 02.04.03 - Information Systems Administration and Mathematical Support
  - 03.04.01 - Applied Mathematics and Physics
  - 09.04.03 - Applied Informatics
  - 27.04.03 - Systems Analysis and Control
  - 38.04.05 - Business Informatics.
- Educational programs for bachelor's training:
  - 01.03.02 - Applied Mathematics and Informatics
  - 01.03.04 - Applied Mathematics
  - 02.03.01 - Mathematics and Computer Science
  - 02.03.02 - Fundamental Informatics and Information Technologies
  - 02.04.03 - Information Systems Administration and Mathematical Support
  - 03.04.01 - Applied Mathematics and Physics
  - 09.04.03 - Applied Informatics
  - 27.04.03 - Systems Analysis and Control
  - 38.04.05 - Business Informatics.

The implementation of educational programs for training of masters and bachelors in the areas of Fundamental Informatics and Information Technology and Systems Analysis and Control is carried out by the following departments of the Faculty of Applied Mathematics–Control Processes:

- Computer Applications and Systems [5]
- Computer Modelling and Multiprocessor Systems [6]
- Electromechanical and Computer Systems Modelling [7].

Educational programs for the training of masters and bachelors in the direction of Business Informatics are implemented at the Faculty of Economics of St. Petersburg State University by the Department of Information Systems in Economics [8]. Basic

---

[18] http://www.math.spbu.ru/user/boris_novikov/index.shtml.

[19] http://www.math.spbu.ru/user/kos/kos.html.

[20] http://www.math.spbu.ru/parallel/demjanovich_priv_en.php.

[21] https://sites.google.com/site/vosafonov/.

courses of this educational program, correlating with those listed in the Software Engineering Body of Knowledge SWEBOK [3], are as follows:

– Databases
– Object-Oriented Analysis and Programming
– Business Information Analysis
– Information Systems
– Analysis and Modeling of Business Processes
– IT-infrastructure Management
– Information Law
– Simulation Modeling
– Decision support systems
– Decision theory.

According to the statistics of the period of 2011–2016, the graduates worked in the following positions:

– Database administrator
– Computer Network administrator
– Business analyst
– Systems analyst
– Specialist in the Implementation of Information Systems
– Systems programmer
– Information Systems designer
– Information Systems consultant
– Service engineer for Information Systems
– Economist in Planning
– Director for Economics,

that is, in the professions which create the digital economy of the future.

5   Problem and Contradiction

No matter how reassuring the above-mentioned background seems, it is necessary to state that at the moment there is no scientific specialty in Russia exactly called Software Engineering, which should be used to train postgraduate and doctoral students - see Nomenclature of Specialties of Scientists of the Russian Federation [13] approved by the Order of the Ministry of Education and Science of Russia on 10.01.2012, No. 5, in which the defense of candidate and doctoral theses takes place in Russia, as well as the awarding of scientific degrees of candidate and doctor of science. At the same time, in Russia education system there is a considerable experience in the training of highly qualified personnel (postgraduate and doctoral students) with the award of scientific degrees of a candidate and a doctor of science in scientific specialties close to the professional field of Software Engineering. It is possible, for example, to name the following scientific specialties, for which postgraduate students, candidates and doctoral students are trained in Saint Petersburg State University, as well as dissertational councils for awarding scientific degrees of candidate and doctor of sciences work:

- Computer Science, Computer Engineering and Management
  - 05.13.01 - Systems Analysis, Control and Information Processing
  - 05.13.11 - Mathematical Support and Software of Computers, Complexes and Computer Networks
  - 05.13.17 - Theoretical Bases of Computer Science
  - 05.13.18 - Mathematical Modeling, Numerical Methods and Program Complexes
- Physics and Mathematics
  - 01.01.07 - Computational Mathematics
  - 01.01.09 - Discrete Mathematics and Mathematical Cybernetics
- Economics
  - 08.00.13 - Mathematical and Instrumental Methods of Economics.

Professor Terekhov[22] believes that in Russia the actual training of highly qualified specialists (candidates and doctors of sciences) in the field of SWE is carried out exactly in the scientific specialty 05.13.11 - Mathematical Support and Software of Computers, Complexes and Computer Networks [24]. At the same time, the passport of such scientific specialty states that: (1) scientific, theoretical and economic importance of solving the problems related to this specialty is the improvement of efficiency of data and knowledge processing using computers, complexes and computer networks and in shortening of the time of their creation; (2) scientific degrees of candidate and doctor of sciences are awarded: in technical sciences - for studies containing results the use and implementation whereof provide significant technical effect; and in physics and mathematics - for achievement of results in the form of new mathematical methods and proven properties of algorithmic languages or programming systems qualified as a contribution to the development of mathematical programming theory and data or knowledge processing systems. Analysis of foreign and domestic practices of training of scientific personnel of the highest level in SWE shows that the closest scientific specialty in Russia, corresponding to the European specialty PhD SWE is the specialty 05.13.11 - Mathematical Support and Software of Computers, Complexes and Computer Networks (Technical sciences).

6 European Support

The challenges of globalization promote European cooperation in the field of SWE education. As a good example of international cooperation in the field of higher qualification scientific personnel training in SWE one should mention the *Joint Programs and Framework for Doctoral Education in Software Engineering* project conducted within the EU Erasmus + Program *Capacity building in higher education*[23]. The overall aim of the project is to support the development, modernization, and internalization of SWE higher education in the target countries, including Russia,

---

[22] Also the President of the Nation wide Association of the most technically competent Russian software developing companies RUSSOFT http://russoft.org/, and ACM and IEEE CS member.

[23] http://fase.it.lut.fi/.

according to the SWEBOK international standard, and, at the same time, to help all partner countries strengthen their PhD programs and make them more attractive for international students. Starting in 2015, eleven European universities, including the Saint Petersburg State University, have been sharing their experience in creating educational environment according to the international standards. The project offers training for qualified teaching staff of all partner universities and for PhD students in the target countries in the framework of 7 two-week intense schools organized in partner universities every 6 months. Thus the project facilitates are building and offering sustainable multidisciplinary and multi-regional perspective programs to educate the next generation of software engineering professors. PhD students and their supervisors are offered courses on advanced techniques of SWE and reviews of the best practices of research projects. Assistance is provided in preparation of high-quality scientific publications on the subject, which includes the following areas:

- Research Methods in the age of Software as a Service
- Advanced methods and tools of SWE
- Problem-based learning in the field of SWE
- Human-computer interaction in SWE
- Models of SWE and modeling
- Mathematical and computational foundations of SWE
- SWE: A View from the point of view of economics and business.

The last area of research is widely represented in the Faculty of Economics of Saint Petersburg State University, where it is taught for several years by highly qualified personnel in the field of business informatics. Training is conducted in the following areas:

- Investment analysis of SWE projects
- Risk analysis and Risk management of SWE projects
- Business Intelligence for SWE costing
- Techniques and methodology of simulation modeling in SWE
- Competences of a perfect software engineer
- Economics and Competitiveness of SWE education.

7   Proposal and Prospects

It seems advisable to prepare a reasonable petition to the Ministry of Education and Science of Russia on the engagement of a new specialty "Software Engineering" in the Nomenclature of Specialties of Scientists on behalf of Saint Petersburg State University and other leading Russian universities. This will provide an opportunity to carry out the defense of candidate and doctoral dissertations in Russia and award scientific degrees of candidate and doctor of science in the Software Engineering scientific specialty. The addition of the two existing levels of higher professional education - bachelor and master's - to the currently absent third level - postgraduate course in Software Engineering will comply with the logic of the Bologna process, in which the Russian education is gradually blending in. This will be an important system-building solution would create the conditions for the training of personnel, designed to implement a variety of ICT projects for the digital future.

To substantiate the formulated proposal, the following specific studies should be performed:

1. Detailed substantiation of the petition to the Ministry of Education and Science of Russia for the inclusion of the new specialty "Software Engineering" in the Nomenclature of the specialties of scientific workers of the Russian Federation in the sections: relevance, draft passport of the new specialty, its uniqueness and difference compared with the already existing ones.
2. Economic estimates of the costs of training of specialists in Software Engineering in Russia and foreign universities.
3. Identification and recognition of management risks in the Russian higher school in the context of opening of a new scientific specialty "Software Engineering" in order to answer the question: how to create a favorable management system [16] in the leading Russian universities for effective training of specialists of higher scientific qualification - PhD and doctors of sciences - in the field of Software Engineering.

Acknowledgements. The research is partially supported by the Russian Foundation for Basic Research (RFBR), grant 16-06-00221. Authors are sincerely grateful to Ms. Ekaterina Morozova for her invaluable help in translating this article.

References

1. Altbach, P.G., Salmi, J. (eds.): The road to academic excellence: the making of world-class research universities. World Bank Publications (2011). http://documents.worldbank.org/curated/en/584591468324279676/pdf/646680PUB0Russ0371975B00PUBLIC00PDF.pdf. (in Russian)
2. Appendix No. 1.1 to the License of Saint Petersburg State University for the right to provide educational services for the implementation of educational programs. http://spbu.ru/files/upload/Structure/documents/licenzia/pril-1-1-2016.pdf. (in Russian)
3. Bourque, P., Fairley, R.E. (eds.): Guide to the Software Engineering Body of Knowledge, Version 3.0. IEEE Computer Society (2014). www.swebok.org
4. Edwards, C., McCluskey, N.: Higher Education Subsidies. https://www.downsizinggovernment.org/education/higher-education-subsidies. Accessed 24 Apr 2017
5. Department of Computer Applications and Systems of the Saint Petersburg State University. http://www.apmath.spbu.ru/ru/structure/depts/kts/
6. Department of Computer Modelling and Multiprocessor Systems of the Saint Petersburg State University. http://www.apmath.spbu.ru/ru/structure/depts/kmms/
7. Department of Electromechanical and Computer Systems Modelling of the Saint Petersburg State University. http://www.apmath.spbu.ru/ru/structure/depts/mems/
8. Department of Information Systems in Economics of the Saint Petersburg State University. http://www.spbu-bi.ru/ru/
9. Department of Software Engineering of the Saint Petersburg State University. http://se.math.spbu.ru/SE

10. Stuen, E.T., Mobarak, A.M., Maskus, K.E.: Foreign Graduate Students and Knowledge Creation at U.S. Universities: Evidence from Enrollment Fluctuations. http://www.vanderbilt.edu/econ/conference/gped-conference-06/papers/stuen.pdf. Accessed 24 Apr 2017
11. Cornalia, F., Tirocchib, S.: Globalization, education, information and communication technologies: what relationships and reciprocal influences. Procedia Soc. Behav. Sci. **47**, 2060–2069 (2012). http://pages.erau.edu/~andrewsa/Project_2/Micheletti_Sam/Micheletti%20Project%202/GEIM_micheletti.pdf. Accessed 24 Apr 2017
12. Held, D., McGrew, A., Goldblatt, D., Perraton, J.: Global Transformation: Politics, Economics and Culture. Polity Press, Cambridge (2000). 515 p.
13. Higher Attestation Commission of the Russian Ministry of Education and Science (VAK)/ Reference. http://vak.ed.gov.ru/help_desk. (in Russian)
14. Akareem, H.S., Hossain, S.S.: Determinants of education quality: what makes students' perception different. Open Rev. Educ. Res. **3**(1), 52–67 (2016). http://www.tandfonline.com/doi/full/10.1080/23265507.2016.1155167. Accessed 24 Apr 2017
15. Knight, J.: Higher education crossing borders: a guide to the implications of the general agreement on trade in services (GATS) for cross-border education. A Report Prepared for the Commonwealth of Learning and UNESCO (2006)
16. Khalin, V.G.: Modernization of National System of Higher Education in the Context of Making Administrative Decisions. St. Petersburg University Press, St. Petersburg (2008)
17. Kosov, Y.: The concept of a "gateway to the global world" in relation to Saint Petersburg – Moscow Axis of Development. In: Symposium Between Shanghai Administration Institute and the North-West Institute of Management of Russia, Shanghai, pp. 38–46 (2014)
18. Order of the Government of the Russian Federation of 6 January 2015. No 7-p O Perechne spetsial'nostei i napravlenii podgotovki vysshego obrazovaniya, sootvetstvuyushchikh prioritetnym napravleniyam modernizatsii i tekhnologicheskogo razvitiya rossiiskoi ekonomiki [About the List of specialties and directions of training of the higher education corresponding to priority directions of modernization and technological development of the Russian economy] (2015). http://www.garant.ru/products/ipo/prime/doc/70742752/. (in Russian)
19. ROADMAP for Implementing the Global Competitiveness Programme of the National Research University "Higher School of Economics" in 2013–2020 (SUMMARY). https://strategy.hse.ru/en/summary. Accessed 16 Mar 2017
20. Scholte, J.A.: Globalization: A Critical Introduction, p. 492. Palgrave Macmillan, New York (2005)
21. Shilova, O.N., Yurkov, A.V.: Ob informatsionnykh tekhnologiyakh v obrazovanii v kontekste obespecheniya global'noi konkurentosposobnosti universiteta [On information technologies in education in the context of ensuring the global competitiveness of the university]. In: X International Forum FROM SCIENCE TO BUSINESS «Academia–Industry–Government: The Results of a Decade Cooperation». 11–13 May 2016 Saint Petersburg, Russia, Proceedings, pp. 140–142 (2016). http://elibrary.ru/download/elibrary_26157161_19167764.pdf. (in Russian)
22. Software Engineering: Competent-oriented curriculum of the basic educational program of higher education of the baccalaureate in the direction 09.03.04 Software Engineering. http://math.spbu.ru/ru/mmeh/PLANS/1/15_5080_090304bPrIng_16_12_15.pdf. (in Russian)
23. Soroka, E.G.: To the question about the education of future IT professionals in software engineering as a tool for developing high-quality software products. Herald Siberian Inst. Bus. Inf. Technol. **2**(14), 85–92 (2015). http://www.sibit.sano.ru/assets/files/docs4/01-09-2015/2015_2(14).pdf. (in Russian)
24. Terekhov, A.N.: What is the program engineering? [Programmnaya Ingeneria]. J. Softw. Eng. **1**(1), 40–45 (2010). (in Russian)

Estimation of Relationship Between Domains of ICT Semantic Network

Ravil I. Mukhamediev[1(✉)], Ramiz M. Aliguliyev[2], and Jelena Muhamedijeva[3]

[1] KazNRTU, KBTU, Almaty, Kazakhstan
ravil.muhamedyev@gmail.com
[2] Institute of Information Technology of Azerbaijan
National Academy of Sciences, Baku, Azerbaijan
muhamedijeva@gmail.com
[3] IICT, Almaty, Kazakhstan
muhamedijeva@mail.ru

Abstract. This article discusses the domains of information and communication technologies such as Big Data, Computational Biology, Cloud Computing, Cyber-Physical Systems, Embedded Systems, Information Security, Internet of Things, Human-Machine Systems, Mobile Computing, Machine Learning, Machine-to-Machine, Multi-Agent Systems, Neural Networks, Robotics, Visualization, Augmented Reality, SDN, 5G, e-Governance, Smart City, Smart Grid. The assessment of link strength in ICT research domains is made; refined and formalized semantic networks of ICT domains are constructed based on the metrics of the normalized (information) distance and the semantic similarity proposed in the literature. These semantic networks show the relative values of the research domain and their relation to each other.

Keywords: ICT · Bibliometric analysis · Semantic network · Science direct

1 Introduction

The research domain being determined with a general term 'information and communication technologies (ICT)', features remarkable dynamism, rapid emergence of new entities and change of conventional research domains. Over the last years ICT domain has been joined by new directions in research, which include Big Data, Bioinformatics (Computational Biology), Cloud Computing, Cyber-Physical Systems, Embedded Systems, Information Security, Internet of Things, Human-Machine Systems, Mobile Computing, Machine Learning, Machine-to-Machine, Multi-Agent Systems, Neural Networks, Robotics, Visualization, Augmented Reality, SDN, 5G, e-Governance, Smart City, Smart Grid, etc.

When designing the scientific research it is interesting to estimate the prospective of subdomain development. Bibliometric analysis of ICT research entities by the way of

---

The original version of this chapter was revised: The author correction was updated. The erratum to this chapter is available at https://doi.org/10.1007/978-3-319-69784-0_39

© Springer International Publishing AG 2017
D.A. Alexandrov et al. (Eds.): DTGS 2017, CCIS 745, pp. 130–135, 2017.
https://doi.org/10.1007/978-3-319-69784-0_11

determination of publication count in the mentioned subdomains allows to reveal the most significant research domains count-wise and assess the dynamics of their growth. Although, discovering patterns by publication count provides only the overall assessment of one or another of research domains. Furthermore, significant number of new results is achieved at the domain interface. To that end it is important to estimate the correlation between domains and dynamics of change in their scientometric parameters. As a convenient way of entity and link visualization between them semantic networks are applied. With this regard the source [1] builds the semantic network of ICT domains according to EBSCO data. The sources [2, 3] present later data and make certain formalization for building the ICT entity semantic network including individual sub domains. Still the mentioned sources do not formalize strictly the strength of links between domains, which hinders comparison of semantic networks built from different datasets. At the same time, the sources [4–6] introduce the entities of similarity and strength of links between semantic entities, which could be used for further formalization of the semantic network.

This paper provides findings on assessment for strength of links of ICT research domains and builds the updated and formalized semantic network of ICT domains based on the metrics of normalized distance and similarities between the entities from the literature. The assessment of change dynamics in scientometric parameters of the listed above domains has been provided earlier in the paper [7].

The paper consists of three parts.

The second part describes formal parameters of the assessment of strength of links between ICT domains.

The third part presents application results of the suggested metrics, achieved from bibliometric base Science Direct and features the semantic networks developed based on this data.

The achieved results are briefly discussed in the conclusion.

2 Assessment of Links Between ICT Research Domains

To visualize the relative value of ICT components and their links the source [2] suggests the semantic network of new ICT domains. The semantic network is set by nodes (presenting entities in our case) and semicircular arcs, defining links between entities. The binary connection network is used, where the network nodes have different size, but semicircular arc have normalized thickness, which allows to visualize more properly as publication count as links between entities.

The paper [3] uses the following formal definitions to build the semantic network. Firstly, to illustrate the scope of publication a logarithmic measure was applied, as publication count for various domains differs by hundreds of time – $r_i = \log k$, where r_i – radius of i-network node, k- publication count for a selected domain. Secondly, the strength of links between entities is described by thickness of a semicircular arc $w(i,j) = r(i,j),$ where w(i, j) – "strength" of links between entities. In the simplest case r(i,j) = n(i,j), where n(i, j) – publication count for cases of two search terms at once relevant to the domains i and j.

To calculate the strength of links between entities this paper uses similarity between entities, suggested in the paper [4]:

$$sim_{NGD}^{local}(t_i, t_j) = \exp\left(-diss_{NGD}^{local}(t_i, t_j)\right) \tag{1}$$

Which, in its turn, is based upon the value of normalized distance Google [5], determined with the following Eq. [6]:

$$diss_{NGD}^{local}(t_i, t_j) = \frac{\max\{\log n_i, \log n_j\} - \log n_{ij}}{\log n_{BB} - \min\{\log n_i, \log n_j\}} \tag{2}$$

where n_i - article count in some bibliometric base, containing a search term t_i;

n_j - article count in some bibliometric base, containing a search term t_j

n_{ij} - article count in some bibliometric base, containing search terms t_i and t_j

n_{BB} - article count, indexed in some bibliometric base throughout all search terms being under research

Note that the entity 'search term' is considered as a nonempty set of words, defining some research domain.

The tables given below illustrate the results of parameter data application in the assessment of correlation between ICT domains.

To evaluate links between ICT research domains the matrix of binary links between domains was built. For this purpose, scientific articles were searched for both one and two key words in Science Direct (the bibliometric database of scientific publications).

The results are given in Table 1, where main diagonal shows the number of publications in the selected research domain. Numbers below the main diagonal show the amount of publications with two keywords. In turn, the numbers above the main diagonal reflect the similarity between entities, calculated by formula (1) and multiplied by a certain weighting factor (w = 10/0.65) for convenience of subsequent rounding and visualization. To eliminate the division error by zero, the zero values are replaced by values less than 1. The data given in table corresponds to 10-year period (from 2006 to 2015).

For the convenience of graphical representation for ICT semantic network, the domain values are presented on logarithmic scale (logarithm for base 10) and rounded according to the expression Round $\left((\text{Log}(n_j, 10) - 2), 1\right)$.

As a result, the following relative domain values were obtained (Fig. 1).

To build a semantic network, the strength of the links between domains was normalized. As a result, a semantic network is constructed (Fig. 2), based on the data obtained. Arcs with the strength less than 4 are not shown.

Table 1. Links between ICT research domains (ScienceDirect).

Keywords	augmented reality	big data	bioinformatics	cloud computing	cyber-physical systems	embedded systems	information security	internet of things	human-machine systems	mobile computing	machine learning	machine to machine	communication	multi-agent systems	neural networks	robotics	visualization	Intelligent transport	e-government	software defined networking	IMT advanced	smart city	smart grid
smart grid	6.334	5.546	5.335	7.825	9.225	5.731	6.202	7.222	3.564	6.633	6.524	8.446	5.41	6.171	6.104	5.443	5.224	4.037	3.653	0.813	8.388		20623
Smart city	4.707	3.571	3.533	5.01	6.144	3.176	4.055	5.424	2.078	4.585	3.973	5.761	3.93	3.506	3.509	3.154	3.319	2.494	1.499	1.335		21356	264
5G	1.7786	0.8658	2.5896	2.0245	2.6832	1.1078	0.8164	1.901	0.4485	1.6229	1.3577	3.9633	0.8926	1.6738	1.5403	1.3227	0.245	0.0881	0.4456	177708		2	6
SDN	3.728	1.8711	3.9675	4.9585	5.3119	2.2635	3.1067	3.6388	0.6078	2.4029	4.2238	6.8767		4.5182	3.1832	0.8285	1.4342	0.798	200187	9	2		6
E-Governance	2.722	2.709	2.431	4.229	4.2	2.703	3.908	3.1	0.904	2.378	2.517	4.026	2.296	2.139	1.991	2.262	1.889	48469	1	1E-04	8		3
ITS	4.155	3.356	3.443	5.073	6.487	3.793	4.237	5.274	2.314	4.479	4.43	6.846	4.625	4.477	4.908	3.307	17492	1	148	1E-04	6		7
Visualization	3.9012	0.3653	3.2317	2.9934	3.7543	0.755	1.3691	2.2099	0.8144	3.1095	2.776	4.9393	1.2203	3.0605	402684	148	148	148	392	159	71		217
Robotics	4.2331	1.4303	2.4994	3.2061	5.0714	2.3197	1.751	2.8096	0.9545	3.0194	3.4987	6.518	2.951	5.3368	105997	1822	297	23	1033	81	71		131
Neural Networks	2.6271	1.1242	3.2464	2.9649	3.7384	1.3617	1.4812	2.1733	1.5	2.1625	4.8131	7.0886	1.7344	250330	1837	2127	437	73	9078	474	167		335
Multi-agent systems	2.9951	1.2952	3.1416	3.7331	4.7651	1.771	2.1793	4.3854	1.0682	2.786	2.9618	5.3041	184222	567	738	342	380	72	1126	59	216		95
Machine to machine	5.4395	4.1272	5.7127	6.9968	6.6936	4.6629	5.0523	5.172	5.5721	5.0188	8.5355	50179	2363	10516	3159	3859	779	199	7428	692	390		652
Machine Learning	4.288	2.7416	4.0955	4.8743	5.3182	2.6647	3.32	3.7191	3.028	3.4727	103389	9286	717	4999	723	1260	171	59	2575	50	128		207
Mobile computing	5.0342	2.8283	2.6024	5.7625	5.8126	3.1538	3.9945	4.7222	1.0947	70867	392	725	306	161	238	236	124	32	765	39	178		160
Human-machine systems	4.3763	2.3447	4.0193	5.5462	5.4723	2.5696	3.1231	3.8627	119483	6	501	1875	34	138	11	31	7	1	6	2	6		3
Internet of things	4.398	3.259	2.829	5.473	6.214	2.948	4.668	47633	392	290	551	1022	76	93	131	373	220	194	513	31	276		200
Information Security	3.3954	2.0804	2.5704	5.1172	5.4333	2.1597	167224	1201	980	956	1758	653	291	117	373	586	220		1975	37	229		232
Embedded systems	3.4155	0.8058	2.887	3.448	4.7461	408599	1411	438	1261	1080	1114	3094	981	991	732	960	304	313	2281	241	167		320
Cyber-Physical systems	4.94	4.22	3.68	6.65	6543	303	284	185	212	182	154	306	140	43	118	71	88	17	296	4	77		161
Cloud computing	4.513	3.703	3.679	43382	253	724	1578	600	683	1106	794	1782	457	234	138	392	144	204	1653	33	169		324
Bioinformatics	3.389	2.369	70783	165	11	774	205	64	782	91	726	1230	479	736	117	1164	32	35	1248	224	49		33
Big Data	1.333	4E+05	335	889	134	859	1150	602	863	652	1113	1705	372	559	132	162	147	287	1237	109	271		229
Augmented reality	21037	2	39	99	20	234	93	96	234	278	183	289	55	39	176	446	25	9	177	4	60		34

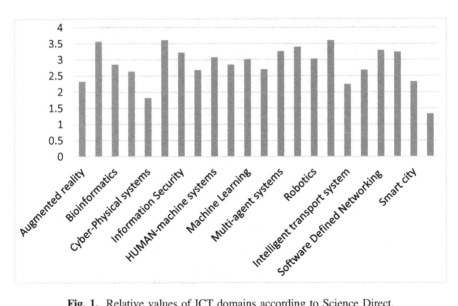

Fig. 1. Relative values of ICT domains according to Science Direct.

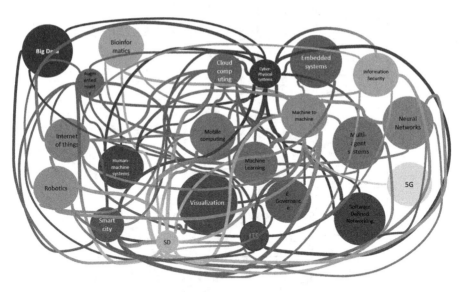

Fig. 2. Semantic network of ICT domains according to Science Direct data.

3   Conclusion

This paper considered the assessment for strength of semantic links of some ICT research domains. We used a measure of similarity between entities, based on Google's normalized distance value. The result of Science direct database analysis is presented and visualization in the form of semantic networks is performed. Considering the obtained semantic network, we can note a significant difference in the number of links between research domains. The network allows us to visualize and formalize the presentation of semantically close scientific entities. The researches at the intersections of technologies are displayed.

The connection between Smart City and M2M is a vivid example, which shows the scope of M2M applications. In turn, M2M, Neural Networks and Machine Learning are strongly connected. We can conclude that these technologies play a significant role in the development of Smart City.

We can offer a number of ways for the development of this visualization method. Firstly, we can compare networks obtained using other databases. The second is the mapping dynamics of domain changes.

It is clear that semantic networks cannot fully characterize research domains. An expert opinion is needed. However the proposed approach can be used to support expert decision-making in a view of their visibility.

Acknowledgments. The work was partially funded by grant No. 0168 GF4 of the Ministry of Education and Science of the Republic of Kazakhstan. Work by Ramiz M. Aliguliyev was supported by the Science Development Foundation under President of the Republic of Azerbaijan – Grant № EIF-2014-9(24)-KETPL-14/02/1.

References

1. Muhamedyev, R.I., Kalimoldaev, M.N., Uskenbayeva, R.K.: Semantic network of ICT domains and applications. In: Proceedings of the 2014 Conference on Electronic Governance and Open Society: Challenges in Eurasia, New York, pp. 178–186 (2014)
2. Muhamedyev, R.I., et al.: Revelation of new ICT domains for upcoming Kazakhstan's participation. In: Proceedings of the 2014 Conference on Electronic Governance and Open Society: Challenges in Eurasia, New York, pp. 178–186 (2014)
3. Muhamedyev, R.I., Amirgaliyev, Y.N., Kalimoldayev, M.N., Khamitov, A.N., Abdilmanova, A.: Selection of the most prominent lines of research in ICT domain. In: Proceedings of the 2015 Twelve International Conference on Electronics Computer and Computation (ICECCO), pp. 36–42. IEEE (2015)
4. Alguliev, R.M., Aliguliyev, R.M.: Evolutionary algorithm for extractive text summarization. Intell. Inf. Manag. **1**(1), 128–138 (2009)
5. Cilibrasi, R.L., Vitányi, P.M.B.: The Google similarity distance. IEEE Trans. Knowl. Data Eng. **19**(3), 370–383 (2007)
6. Aliguliyev, R.M.: A new sentence similarity measure and sentence based extractive technique for automatic text summarization. Expert Syst. Appl. **36**(4), 7764–7772 (2009)
7. Abdilmanova, A., Alyguliev, R., Muhamedyev, R.: Differential metrics for assessment of bibliometric indicators of ICT domains. Cloud Sci. **3**(3), 366–379 (2016)

eSociety: Legal, Security and Usability Issues

Blocking Social Media. Reasoning and Legal Grounds

Ekaterina Shireeva[1]([✉]), Aleksei Martynov[1], Andrei Kaplunov[2], and Vladimir Ukhov[2]

[1] Lobachevsky State University of Nizhny Novgorod (UNN),
Nizhny Novgorod, Russia
shireevaekaterina@yandex.ru, avm@unn.ru
[2] Saint-Petersburg University of MIA, Saint Petersburg, Russia
{editor62,spb-u-mvd.kaf-ap}@yandex.ru

Abstract. Use of social media represents now a global trend that also contaminates the sphere of public administration and other governmental activities. Despite so wide use and popularity of social media among individuals, business and social institutes, they become more and more subject for censorship and blocking with different reasoning and outreach. Recent incidents all over the world show an emerging tendency to restrict social media use by companies, employers and the governments. It is worth noting, that not only China or North Korea which are traditionally famous for their restrictive policies towards Internet activities are spotted for blocking social media but a large part of African countries and even countries rather close to Europe, e.g. Turkey, Ukraine, Russia. The authors are seeking to provide a brief review of reasoning and legal grounds for social media blocking used by the governments.

Keywords: Social media · Internet blocking · Censorship · e-Democracy

1 Introduction

Social media become an inherent part of our life and are used now for many purposes from private intercourse to providing public services. The auditory of social networks platforms exceeds 1/3 of world population with a total number of active users amounting to 2.3 billion. Average Internet user has now approximately 5.54 social media accounts [33].

The government and public officials are also becoming active users of social media for different purposes and reasons but mostly for policies' promotion and intercommunication with the society. Those tendencies and a possible influence of social media on forming public opinion make think not only about positive but also about negative factors of social networks' use. Employers are trying to assert that using of social networks may impair working activities of the employees and to decrease their productivity. The government and the society are aware of a possibility to manipulate public opinion, when social media are used for separatist, extremist, terrorist or, sometimes, merely illicit activities, which endanger national security and legal order. It is clear that the pretexts for blocking social media are mostly common and are widely

© Springer International Publishing AG 2017
D.A. Alexandrov et al. (Eds.): DTGS 2017, CCIS 745, pp. 139–147, 2017.
https://doi.org/10.1007/978-3-319-69784-0_12

used by the governments. This situation logically draws to a very appropriate question whether those reasons really take place and whether they affect human rights and may probably shift the existing balance of interests. If truth to be told, most of those cases could allegedly make think of some kind of hidden motives to control public opinion or oppress democratic values. The authors suggest making a brief review of existing governmental practice of blocking social media in the world in order to reveal urgent issues to address in the nearest future.

2   Literature Review

The use of social media is now widely studied by scholars from different countries and could be regarded as a new challenge for many areas of modern science.

Large part of the researches acknowledge the fast penetrating of social media across government organizations [20, 23, 34, 35] that represents new opportunities for building government-citizens relationship [11, 15], providing public services [19], public engagement, government transparency [2–4, 18].

Nevertheless, the usage of social media by governmental organizations may confront different negative factors - security risks [12], reputation damage [1], deviant behavior [25], privacy risks [11] etc.

The influence of social media on developing and promoting of e-democracy is largely discussed and confirmed by many researches [6, 8, 22, 26, 30]. Thus, a considerable growth of social networking activities and widespread use of technologies and methods of bypassing national Internet filtering and censorship represent a serious challenge for authoritarian and non-democratic regimes [13, 14, 18, 23]. On the other hand, democratic countries in return with strong traditions to respect freedom of expression face an unprecedented activity of terrorist and extremist groups using social media for recruiting new members, planning their attacks or promoting terrorism and extremism [32].

The widespread practice of blocking or restricting access to the Internet and social networks sites by certain national authorities is examined by many scholars and researchers, e.g. China [10], North Korea [29], ex-USSR countries [16, 24], etc.

Despite a majority of researches dedicated to the national practices of blocking social media, they do not treat attentively the problematics of legal reasoning and grounds for the cease of access to social network sites. The latter explains the actuality of such a research.

3   Current Tendencies in Social Media Use and e-Democracy

It is reasonably presumed that social media are becoming a powerful tool for shaping public opinion. This tendency does not go unseen by state authorities as well as by the society and political groups.

From one side, the intention to increase public participation and government transparency makes public authorities and top leaders be present on social media platforms. Even in 2012, in the USA, about 700 Federal departments had about 3000 pages in Facebook and 1000 microblogging on Twitter, 700 YouTube channels and 500 pages on Flickr. All those accounts were official and belonged to Federal departments, agencies, programs and certain high rank officials. The same tendency is for the UK, where about 90% of local officials use Twitter, 80% - Facebook and only 3% of them do not have any account in social networks. In Sweden quite a popular channel of communication are blogs: about half of the local municipalities have their blogs, and only 43% use Twitter and about 80% - Facebook [21]. In Russia, the President of the State and the Prime Minister as well as Deputy Prime Ministers, Federal Ministers have social media accounts and actively use them. The President Vladimir Putin constantly uses Twitter and YouTube and has a personal website. His account in Twitter is followed by about 3.4 millions of subscribers and more than 29 thousands of users are subscribed to his YouTube blog. The Prime Minister is an absolute leader in Russia for using social media and have profiles in Facebook, Twitter, Instagram, Vkontakte. His Twitter account has an enormous number of subscribers - 5.1 millions. For comparison, the ex-US President Barack Obama obtained Facebook account only in 2015. Previously, he had used only Twitter and the White House official microblogging.

On the other hand, citizens have also intended to use social media for political reasons. Recent statistics on popularity of e-petitions shows a considerable growth of number of individuals involved in filing and signing their claims [27]. This tendency also is becoming a global trend [8] and even makes governments to consider them and to adopt special legal frameworks allowing to do it officially with obligatory response from an appropriate authority [9].

Another tendency is the influence of social media on inner national democratic climate. The interconnection between Facebook & Twitter and fomenting civil protests during Arab Spring do not leave the minds of scholars and politicians [14, 26, 28]. Moreover, social networking sites are used now both for promoting democratic values as well as for terrorism propaganda. This phenomenon makes authoritarian and non-democratic regimes be aware of what is happening on social media, especially in the cases where their citizens are involved, and, at the same time, democratic regimes be aware of terrorism and extremism propaganda, planning attacks and recruitment. The latter explains a large number of gossips about social media users being under lens of state security agencies even in countries with strong democratic traditions [5].

4   Recent National Practice of Blocking Social Media

Recent studies and researches on the current national practices of social media blocking show a substantial growth of countries using it for different purposes and with different reasoning.

According to the Freedom on the Net 2016 Report the Internet freedom declined for six recent years. Two-thirds of all internet users are living in the countries where expressed criticism of the government, military or ruling family are subject to censorship and sometimes may cause a severe punishment [31].

Regardless the fact that the practice of social media blocking could vary from state to state, there are some tendencies and common traits making possible to suggest a certain classification.

The quick review of the phenomena of blocking social media shows that according to territorial area of blocking it could be national, local and inner.

The national blocking could be suggested as a lack of technical access in all areas of the country to specific or all social media. This is the case of DPRK (North Korea), Iran, China, and some countries that block constantly particular social networks. For example, since 2010 Bangladesh, Pakistan, Saudi Arabia have been blocking access to Facebook and Wikipedia. Russia since August 2016 constantly blocked LinkedIn.

The local blocking of social networks can be of several types. Thus, social networking can be blocked locally on a certain territory (part of territory) of the country, as well as some providers do not provide access to social networks. It should be named here the same case of China. In 2015 Chinese Government blocked the social network Vkontakte from several parts of its territory - Beijing, Shenzhen, Inner Mongolia and the provinces of Heilongjiang and Yunnan. In May 2015, five Tajik Internet providers blocked access to various social networks (it seems to be that the number of ISPs in Tajikistan, more than five, and therefore, access was not quite full).

The inner blocking of social networking usually takes place in separate organs, institutions and organizations. In many countries, employers are trying to block access for employees to social networking during working hours or from working devices. In Russia in 2011, according to national statistics about 63% of employers blocked access to social networks like Facebook, Vkontakte, Odnoklassniki, to compare – in 2008 their number had not exceeded 54%. Companies at the time of 2011–2013 usually named "saving Internet traffic" as a main reason for denying access to social networks for the employees, however nowadays this reasoning could not be as obvious as most of organizations use flat rate tariffs. Thus blocking social media for the employees becomes mostly a part of inner corporate policy with its proper reasoning and justification, e.g. information security (protection of classified or limited access information), health protection, need to concentrate on working duties, corporate or service ethics. The practice of adopting specific regulation or corporate rules – Guidelines, Codes of Conduct, etc. is becoming a certain trend for business as well as for governmental agencies. According to those documents in some cases or for some categories of employees, using of social media could be prohibited and even blocked from working devices. On the over hand, there is a lot of current and recent researches underlining the lack of an explicit connection between employees' productivity and usage of social networking during working hours [7].

Taking into consideration, the period of blocking social media, it could be permanent, prolonged or temporary.

The permanent blocking of social networking may be suggested as a lack of technical access throughout the country for an extended period of time (over 1 year). Here could be named a large part of countries denying constantly access to specific or all social networks such as DPRK (all social media), China (Facebook, Twitter, etc.), Saudi Arabia (Facebook), Iran (Facebook & Twitter) and Pakistan (Youtube).

The prolonged blocking social networking may be the lack of access from several weeks to 1 year. The term prolonged could be equally used when the same social network has been blocked repeatedly during the year. Thus, Tajikistan repeatedly blocked social networks Youtube, Facebook, Odnoklassniki, Vkontakte for the period from 28 May 2015 to 9 Jun 2015, 24 August 2015 to 22 September 2015. In 2016,

Tajikistan blocked Facebook three times - in June, July, and October. In 2014, China for 4 months blocked Instagram.

The temporary blocking of social networking sites is short-term (from several hours to several days) the lack of access to social networking sites. For example, Kazakhstan for one day (27.11.2014) blocked social network Vkontakte, Facebook, Twitter, Instagram. For more than 12 h on May 29 2013, there was no access to a social network Vkontakte from the whole territory of the Russia.

5 Legal Grounds and Reasoning for Blocking Social Media

The decision to cease access to social networks may be made by executive bodies (the head of the state, a ministry responsible for media or information technologies, law enforcement agencies etc.). Mostly this is typical for authoritarian regimes as it is in North Korea where those decisions are taken by the Ministry of Post and Telecommunications of the DPRK, requiring national mobile and Internet providers to block access to certain sites.

In vast majority of states, the blocking of Internet sites and social media is possible under court order. For example, in 2014 Turkish court ruled to cease access to several Internet resources (Twitter & Youtube) disseminating an audio record, where allegedly the President Recep Tayyip Erdogan discusses with his son Bilal a corruption scheme. In March 13 2016, the court issued another order to block social media but this time in connection with the terrorist attack in Ankara.

The reasoning and legal grounds for blocking access to social media platforms is a very wary ground and could not be easily detected in some cases and depend on many factors. The analysis of the existing practice of blocking social networks in different countries allows us to differentiate these causes.

Firstly, legally justified and clearly declared reasons for the blocking of social networks. Thus, the blocking of social networking may be due to a direct and continuous violation of national legislation, protection of rights and freedoms of citizens, lawful interests of individuals and legal entities. This could be the case of:

– massive violation of copyright (piracy), when the social network is illegal proliferation of books, films, music, audio and video records without an authorization from right holders. For example, at the end of 2013 Russian court blocked social network Vkontakte on receiving the legal order issued by Italian court;
– uncontrolled dissemination of pornography, including illegal child pornography. In 2012, precisely for this reason Vkontakte was completely blocked on the territory of Turkey;
– fraud or other criminal activity. In 2016 Algeria and Ethiopia blocked social networks to exclude national exam fraud;
– preventing terrorism or extremism actions (planning or terrorist actions, recruitment of terrorists, militants, members of illegal armed formations, terrorist accomplices). Those reasons are more and more often proclaimed for blocking social media. Thus, Tajikistan in June 2015 ceased the access to Facebook and Turkey in April 2015 blocked Twitter and Youtube due to "massive and uncontrolled propaganda of terrorism and extremism".

Secondly, non-obvious and controversial reasons for blocking social networks. In these cases, there is strong presumption that the officially expressed opinion and legal ground are used essentially to veil the true one. Among those reasoning with a very vague formula could be mentioned: "unstable political situation" (Tajikistan - from 28 May to 9 June 2015; 5 October to 11 October 2014); "impossibility of censorship" (Thailand, 2014); "violation of the inviolability of private life" (Iran, 2014); "content of the social network do not correspond to moral values, accepted in society" (Saudi Arabia, 2010). Recent events in Turkey related to the coup attempt (16 June 2016), were also accompanied by blocking social networks. This time Turkish authorities blocked access to Facebook, YouTube, Twitter but remained unblocked Instagram and Vimeo.

Among non-obvious reasons and legal grounds could be considered blocking social networks in the aim of hiding information about the terrorist act. In Turkey, it becomes an ordinary practice for the judicial bodies after major terrorist acts to issue court orders to block social networking to prevent distribution of photos and videos depicting victims of the attack and the moment of the explosion. It should be noted that the Turkish authorities also impose restrictions on the coverage of terrorist attacks in all mass media. The restriction applies to all demonstrations of the right scene of the act as well as broadcasting the explosion and what happened after it.

Thirdly, there could be arbitrary or ill-grounded reasoning for blocking social networks. This is initially the case of countries with authoritarian or non-democratic regimes. Social networks blocking usually regarded by them as part of their national policy aimed to suppress essential human rights such as freedom of speech, freedom of expression, privacy and is aimed to exclude any "foreign influence" on the population of the state [29]. North Korea on 22 June 2015 blocked Instagram in order to conceal the major emergency incident. In April 2016, the DPRK government indefinitely blocked access to social networks Facebook, YouTube, Twitter under the pretext to ban "propaganda against the DPRK and blocking of websites containing information of a sexual nature". In both cases, the blocking occurred without any formal declaration of it. In September 2014, China blocked the same social networks to hide political protests in Hong Kong [17]. In May 2014, Thailand also ceased access to Facebook to hide political protests. Turkey in 2015 repeatedly blocked Twitter, Facebook, Youtube pursuing purely political reasons.

6 Conclusion

The analysis of the practice of blocking social media urge to suggest several issues to address from the point of law.

1. Still existing inner ambiguity of legal nature of social network initially created as a space for private communication obviously has evolved to some new phenomena and social network platforms has become more a public area. Its actors have received an unseen before possibility to communicate with a whole world. On the other hand, all the actions undertaken in social media are considered to be made in public and draw to the appropriate responsibility from the point of law and sometimes to a rather severe punishment [31].

2. Global character of social media and diversity of information circulating inside them make modern governments and national societies be aware of it. Usually states are rather keen in regulating, controlling information flows inside their territory, and all traditional mass media are bound by inner national regulation, ethical and moral rules. On the other hand social media content represents a mixture of all possible data even those that could be unacceptable in some countries for religious, cultural, political and other reasons. This awareness and sometime an openly expressed antagonism explain the increasing practice of blocking social media on national level.

3. The owners of social media are becoming more and more considerable actors influencing and shaping public opinion globally. The implemented inner policies and practices of filtering and censuring communication content could possibly affect individuals rights and free information flow. In this situation, the governments sometimes are feeling useless being aware of losing control over information flows that draws to inappropriate and inadequate reaction of blocking social networking entirely. The only suitable solution here is to make inner policies of filtering and censuring of content of social networks more transparent for governments and the society. While drafting those policies social media owners should take into consideration the diversity of regulation, ethical and moral standards in different countries and cooperate closely with their governments. Moreover, to some extend those Internet companies should understand their responsibility and accountability for disseminating of illegal and harmful content in social media accepting more the role of intermediaries between governments, societies and individuals.

4. The government allegedly could use alternative methods to prevent dissemination of undesirable information without blocking completely the access to social networks. The very example of it could be the situation in Germany in May 2016 when the government called their nationals to avoid from publishing any photo or video from the place of terroristic act especially about police actions in order not to provide any information about security and antiterrorism actions undertaken in response to the attack. This time, citizens started to post photos of their cats and dogs supporting at the same time the police actions and their unity with the attack's victims. Unfortunately, those examples are very few, most governments, like Turkey, prefer to block social media not relying on good will of their citizens, depriving them from the possibility to express themselves.

References

1. Bekkers, V., Edwards, A., De Kool, D.: Social media monitoring: responsive governance in the shadow of surveillance? Gov. Inf. Q. 30(4), 335–342 (2013). doi:10.1016/j.giq.2013.05.024

2. Bertot, J.C., Jaeger, P.T., Hansen, D.: The impact of polices on government social media usage: Issues, challenges, and recommendations. Gov. Inf. Q. 29(1), 30–40 (2012). doi:10.1016/j.giq.2011.04.004

3. Bonson, E., Torres, L., Royo, S., Flores, F.: Local e-government 2.0: social media and corporate transparency in municipalities. Gov. Inf. Q. **29**(2), 123–132 (2012). doi:10.1016/j.giq.2011.10.001

4. Castells, M.: The new public sphere: global civil society, communication networks, and global governance. Ann. Acad. Polit. Soc. Sci. **616**(1), 78–93 (2008)

5. Danish Ministry Releases Plan to Block Online Propaganda of Terrorism (2017). https://sputniknews.com/europe/201701121049539296-denmark-government-online-propaganda/

6. DeNardis, L., Hackl, A.M.: Internet governance by social media platforms. Telecommun. Policy **39**(9), 761–770 (2015). doi:10.1016/j.telpol.2015.04.003

7. Dimov, D.: Restricting social media at work (2013). http://resources.infosecinstitute.com/restricting-social-media-at-work/

8. Dumas, C.D., Atrey, A., Lee, J., Harrison, T.M., Fake, T., Zhao, X., Ravi, S.S.: E-petition information diffusion in online social networks. In: Proceedings of 17th International Digital Government Research Conference on Digital Government Research (dg.o 2016), pp. 515–517. ACM, New York (2016). doi:10.1145/2912160.2912227

9. E-Petitions of UK Government and Parliament. https://petition.parliament.uk/

10. Feng, G.C., Guo, S.Z.: Tracing the route of China's internet censorship: an empirical study. Telemat. Inform. **30**(4), 335–345 (2013). doi:10.1016/j.tele.2012.09.002

11. Hong, H.: Government websites and social media's influence on government-public relationships. Publ. Relat. Rev. **39**(4), 346–356 (2013)

12. Hrdinová, J., Helbig, N., Peters, C.S.: Designing social media policy for government: eight essential elements (2010). https://www.ctg.albany.edu/publications/guides/social_media_policy/social_media_policy.pdf

13. Imani Giglou, R., d'Haenens, L., Ogan, C.: Turkish diasporic responses to the Taksim square protests: legacy media and social media uses in Belgium, the Netherlands and Germany. Telemat. Inform. **34**(2), 548–559 (2017). doi:10.1016/j.tele.2016.09.012

14. Kharroub, T., Bas, O.: Social media and protests: an examination of Twitter images of the 2011 Egyptian revolution. N. Media Soc. **18**(9), 1973–1992 (2015). doi:10.1177/1461444815571914

15. Kim, S.K., Park, M.J., Rho, J.J.: Effect of the government's use of social media on the reliability of the government: focus on Twitter. Publ. Manag. Rev. **17**(3), 328–355 (2015)

16. Kozhamberdiyeva, Z.: Freedom of expression on the internet: a case study of Uzbekistan. Rev. Central East Eur. Law **33**(1), 95–134 (2008). doi:10.1163/092598808X262542

17. Lee, F.L.F., Chen, H., Chan, M.: Social media use and university students' participation in a large-scale protest campaign: the case of Hong Kong's Umbrella Movement. Telemat. Inform. **34**(2), 457–469 (2017). doi:10.1016/j.tele.2016.08.005

18. Lee, G., Kwak, Y.H.: An open government maturity model for social media-based public engagement. Gov. Inf. Q. **29**(4), 492–503 (2012). doi:10.1016/j.giq.2012.06.001

19. Linders, D.: From e-government to we-government: defining a typology for citizen coproduction in the age of social media. Gov. Inf. Q. **29**(4), 446–454 (2012). doi:10.1016/j.giq.2012.06.003

20. Mergel, I., Bretschneider, S.I.: A three-stage adoption process for social media use in government. Publ. Adm. Rev. **73**(3), 390–400 (2013)

21. Mickoleit, A.: Social media use by governments: a policy primer to discuss trends, identify policy opportunities and guide decision makers. In: OECD Working Papers on Public Governance, vol. 26. OECD Publishing, Paris (2014). doi:10.1787/5jxrcmghmk0s-en

22. Mossberger, K., Wu, Y., Crawford, J.: Connecting citizens and local governments? Social media and interactivity in major U.S. cities. Gov. Inf. Q. **30**(4), 351–358 (2013). doi:10.1016/j.giq.2013.05.016

23. Nam, T.: A tool for liberty or oppression? A cross-national study of the internet's influence on democracy. Telemat. Inform. **34**(5), 538–549 (2016). doi:10.1016/j.tele.2016.11.004

24. Nurullaev, R.: Website blocking in Russia: recent trends. Comput. Law Secur. Rev. **33**(20), 211–222 (2016). doi:10.1016/j.clsr.2016.11.010

25. Picazo-Vela, S., Guitiérrez-Martínez, I., Luna-Reyes, L.F.: Understanding risks, benefits, and strategic alternatives of social media applications in the public sector. Gov. Inf. Q. **29**(4), 504–511 (2012). doi:10.1016/j.giq.2012.07.002

26. Poell, T., Abdulla, R., Rieder, B., Woltering, R., Zack, L.: Protest leadership in the age of social media. Inf. Commun. Soc. **19**(7), 994–1014 (2016). doi:10.1080/1369118X.2015.1088049

27. Rath, K.: E-petitions get 6.4 million signatures in a year (2012). http://www.bbc.com/news/uk-politics-19266497

28. Said, G.R.E.: The internet social media and the Arab spring: a study of Egyptian users' usability. In: Vision 2020: Innovation, Development Sustainability, and Economic Growth - Proceedings of 21st International Business Information Management Association Conference, IBIMA, p. 615 (2013)

29. Seliger, B., Schmidt, S.: The hermit kingdom goes online ⋯ information technology, internet use and communication policy in North Korea. North Korean Rev. **10**(1), 71–88 (2014). doi:10.3172/NKR.10.1.71

30. Servaes, J.: The many faces of (soft) power, democracy and the internet. Telemat. Inform. **30**(4), 322–330 (2013). doi:10.1016/j.tele.2013.04.001

31. Silencing the Messenger: Communication Apps Under Pressure. Freedom on the Net 2016 Report (2016). https://freedomhouse.org/sites/default/files/FOTN_2016_Full_Report.pdf

32. Staniforth, A., Nitsch, H.: Preventing terrorism together. A framework to provide social media anti-radicalization training for credible community voices. In: Emerging Trends in ICT Security, pp. 549–556 (2013). doi:10.1016/B978-0-12-411474-6.00034-7

33. We Are Social's. Digital in 2016, Special Report (2016). http://wearesocial.com/uk/special-reports/digital-in-2016

34. Zheng, L., Zheng, T.: Innovation through social media in the public sector: information and interactions. Gov. Inf. Q. **31**(Suppl. 1), S106–S117 (2014). doi:10.1016/j.giq.2014.01.011

35. Zheng, L.: Social media in Chinese government: drivers, challenges and capabilities. Gov. Inf. Q. **30**(4), 369–376 (2013). doi:10.1016/j.giq.2013.05.017

Computer Games in Focus of Modern Russian and American Legislation

Olga Kononova[1(✉)] and Aleksa Grant[2]

[1] St. Petersburg National Research University of Information Technologies, Mechanics and Optics (ITMO University), the Sociological Institute of the Russian Academy of Sciences, Birzhevaya St. 14, 199034 St. Petersburg, Russia
kononolg@yandex.ru
[2] Versany, 235 E 95th St, New York, NY 10128, USA
aleksagrant@yahoo.com

Abstract. The article examines the legal issues of dissemination and use of children computer games. Computer games industry affects the interests of many stakeholders. There are various factors that determine the need for introduction of state regulation of legislative measures in this area. The article compares the laws of Russia and America in the field of children computer games provided the protection and rights of children. The research showed the existence of common characters, tendencies and issues in this field, in spite of differences between two countries legislation. The study established legal uncertainty of the 'computer game' concept; revealed the scientific community opinion contradiction about the nature of computer games and their valid influence on behavior, health and mentality of children and teenagers; identified the instability of society interest in the legislative initiatives connected with computer games.

Keywords: Computer games · Scientific review · Content analysis · Scientific journals · Query · Law · Legislation · Legislation initiatives

1 Introduction

Nowadays computer games are in fact the global industry with a rising trend. The industry affects the interests of many stakeholders. All the countries admit it. The industry importance is confirmed by statistics of computer games market; as the Russian Federation statistics as the United States of America statistics.

Global games market showed the great growth from $66.3 Bn in 2012 to $101.1 Bn in 2016 (Newzoo reports, 2015, 2016, 2017). In accordance with J'son & Partners Consulting data, in the period 2014–2016 global games market rose 17% and reached $95.2 Bn. At the same period Russian share in global games market rose 16% and reached $1.89 Bn; the online gaming users' quantity doubled.

The US has a very robust computer gaming industry, with earnings over 23.5 billion dollars last year – slightly less than China, and account for about 25% of the world market. Statistics from Entertainment Software Association (ESA) stipulated that the last years the video games industry in the country experienced exponential growth

© Springer International Publishing AG 2017
D.A. Alexandrov et al. (Eds.): DTGS 2017, CCIS 745, pp. 148–158, 2017.
https://doi.org/10.1007/978-3-319-69784-0_13

four times faster than that of the entire American economy. On average, this industry achieves 9% annual growth. There are many factors contributing towards this accelerated growth. According to Deloitte, trends that contribute to growth in the games industry over the next five years include increased Mergers and Acquisitions activity, international growth, online and mobile usage, technological enhancements, and regulating changes. Many investors are venturing to this industry because it is highly lucrative [1]. Ibis world research shows games industry has a low market share concentration, with the top four operators contributing 33.8% of total industry revenue in 2016. Higher concentration exists within each type of business, though, as GameStop dominates the retail market; Microsoft, Nintendo and Sony dominate the hardware market and Activision Blizzard and Electronic Arts (EA) dominate the software market.

Tax incentives from local, state and federal governments play a critical role in helping computer game developers launch more games into the market. In addition to this, there is a general preference for computer game development as projects in American college and universities [2]. These enhance the popularity of computer games in the country further. The modern generation, especially the young adults and children have had a high appreciation of the computer games [3]. The computer games industry has also become a great employer and absorbs specialists in programming, designing, modeling, production and testing of the computer games. Besides being pursued as a career, gaming has also become a source of livelihood for the hobbyist who produce own games and sell them to the public [4].

There are two groups of factors associating with computer games. The first group of factors includes: market size, usage areas, kinds of products and services, consumers categories, types of devices and technologies, list of professions, number of people employed in game sector, and others. The corresponding stakeholders are: creators, producers and distributors of computer games and other actors of computer game market. The second group of factors includes: content, themes, forms of visualization, target audience or categories of gamers. The corresponding stakeholders are: gamers (classified by age, gender, professions and others), parents of young gamers who have not reached the age of majority, informal groups including online networks, civil society institutions, and the state.

Stakeholders groups influence the legislative base creation and speed of the adoption of legislative initiatives. The legislative acts have usually restrictive character, if it is aimed at the first stakeholder's group, and protective character, if it is related to the second stakeholder's group. The legislative acts and initiatives maintain positive games playing effects and protect from negative ones.

Positive aspects of playing computer games, according to Paul R. Kearney, are improving learning abilities, imagination and critical thinking.

Negative aspects of Playing Computer Games:

– Computers harm children's health (overweight, little activity aggressiveness and nervousness).
– No time control, little popular books reading and undone homework.
– Children addiction to the games.

It should be acknowledged that the legislation aimed at regulating the relations concerning exclusively computer games and computer games use does not exist as in Russia as in America. The reasons are undetermined.

The second group of factors and corresponding stakeholders are allocated in research. The child-gamers and parents, state, society institutes supported their interests are separate category of actors. The research demonstrated that the interest to the computer games theme in context of the legislation is changeable. It depends on the variety of reasons. The research purposes are to show the fact of interest changeability, to describe regularities of appearance legislation initiatives.

2 Computer Games and the Russian Legislation: Scientific Publications Content-Analysis

To evaluate the dynamics of research interest to legislative aspects of computer games expansion the study consists of the review of the Russian scientific journals. Discourse analysis can be seen as the theoretical basis of study. The idea was that the language of scientific publications as well as the mass media language is included in the formation of the 'agenda-setting'. Scientific agenda manifested the fact that the importance of certain issues, ideas, approaches determined by the frequency of their reference in journal publications. It creates set of scientific topics that are understood as the most important by research community.

The fact of interest changeability has been fixed by studying and analysis of scientific publications placed in the Russian public domain - Scientific Electronic Library (http://elibrary.ru/). Totally 604 files in years 2005–2015 have been selected for analysis and then transferred to multifunctional library «Humanitariana» by designed ITMO University (St. Petersburg). E-library «Humanitariana» has contextual search services, different types of queries, automated knowledge ex-traction from the scientific texts. «Humanitariana» provides reproducibility and interpretability of results, allows proving the relevance and practical significance of the proposed study subject matter.

The relative-frequency query is for the construction of frequency-ranked words list, 'terminogramma', relatively user-selected 'reference term'. A query is done in four stages:

(1) The user generates a query by filling two fields - "reference term" and "depth of sampling frequency ranking". The query depth can be arbitrary. By default, the query depth is 30.
(2) The user selects the array of resources (publications) for analysis and distributes them into baskets (from 1 to 3).
(3) As a result of the query the system forms only the set of those documents paragraphs that contain user-specified reference term.
(4) Final frequency-ranked list of nouns reduced to the normal form (nominative case, singular number) is based on the selected paragraphs set.

Query allows setting the terms that are mostly often found in the paragraphs contained user-selected 'reference term'. Thereby macro-context of 'reference term' use in a separate document or documents set, for example, in the articles of a particular author or in a full-text database as a whole is revealed.

Two relative-frequency queries on a scientific publication range of the category "Computer games" were performed [5]. The first one was done with respect to the law 'reference term' (Table 1). The second has focused on the legislation 'reference term'. The depth of the sampling frequency ranking was established as 30.

Table 1. Terminogramma: fragment (top 15).

Resources baskets					
2005–2007		2008–2012		2013–2015	
Word	Quantity	Word	Quantity	Word	Quantity
Law	32	Game	87	Game	267
Process	20	*Law*	72	World	87
Party	15	World	28	*Law*	84
Activity	11	Gamer	21	Gamer	57
Education	8	Person	16	Man	51
System	7	Teenager	16	Reality	48
Knowledge	6	Computer	12	Children	34
Time	6	Activity	11	Object	33
Result	6	Group	11	Offence	31
Image	6	Opportunity	11	Product	28
News	5	Development	11	Development	28
World	5	Internet	10	Time	27
Person	5	User	10	Schoolchild	26
University	5	Individual	10	Action	25
Russia	5	Children	10	Restriction	25

Terminogramma was built on an array of scientific publications relative to the law 'reference term'. It consisted three documents baskets: '2005–2007', '2008–2012', '2013–2015'.

The final list was generated in the table form; each term is indicated next to the number of its use in the selected 'resources basket' in absolute terms (Table 1). The table head 'Quantity' means "how many times this word is met in context of user-selected 'reference term'." The user-selected 'reference term' is highlighted in the color. In Table 1 the user-selected 'reference term' law is highlighted in color and the *Italic*.

Query has allowed defining macro-context of the law 'reference term' use in the documents array. The Table 1 demonstrates the query results - words that are most often found in the paragraphs that contain the term 'law'.

The first basket of document, 2005–2007, connects the 'law' term (within a paragraph) with the concepts of process, activity, system or with the concepts of education, knowledge. The concepts connected with games participants (gamer, person, man, child, boy and so forth) have beyond the frequency-ranked list; Top 30, Top

100 and even Top 200. Macro-context of the 'reference term' law is unassociated with the subjects of gaming relations including children 'reference term'. Moreover, the macro-context of the law 'reference term' is unassociated with the game 'reference term' during the considered time period. The result indirectly received says lack of sharpness of problems connected with a gamification in social society and scientific communities of separately taken Russia country.

Analysis of documents baskets ('2008–2012' and '2013–2015') gave similar results. However, common picture of baskets content is different from the previous one. In these case, the link of the 'law' term with the concepts game, gamer, person, man, teenager, schoolchild, children was clearly established.

The 'legislation' term has been met in text even less often. Documents basket '2005–2007' showed the absence of the association between the 'legislation' and 'computer games' concepts. Documents baskets "2008–2012" and "2013–2015" indicated a poor association among 'legislation', 'computer games' and 'computer gamers' concepts.

It should be noted, that the absolute-frequency query (depth in 100 and 200 words) made the entire documents array ('2005–2015') has revealed an absence of the 'law' and 'legislation' words. Therefore, the authors of publications rarely have addressed the topic of legislation for ten years.

In addition, the research included a short analysis of English-language scientific publications. There is the list of the scientific editions on the Digital Games Research Association (DiGRA) website [6]. This list includes 65 periodicals in which games are either only the main subject, or one of the main subjects for articles. Magazines, which were the first to form the social and humanitarian theory of computer games were reviewed; English-language scientific journals: «Game Studies» (since 2001), «Games and Culture» (since 2006). «Humanitariana» allows putting only an absolute-frequency query for English-language texts, the result of which is a frequency-ranked list of nouns included in the search area resources. The result of query has shown the lack of the 'law' and 'legislation' terms in the list (Top 100). The authors of English-language professional publications have rarely addressed the topic of legislation as well.

3 Russian and American Computer Games Legislation Issues

There are two ways in the Russian legislation for presentation of computer games as the subject of law. In certain cases, the games are attributed to software. In other cases, in the field of copyright in particular, the computer games are complicated, integral object where the computer program presents only one of several elements.

The computer games are often recognized as the complex subject of intellectual activity, namely multimedia products. It should be acknowledged that there is no legislation aimed at regulating the relations concerning exclusively computer games and their use in the Russian Federation. At the same time, certain articles of codes and other documents of the Russian legislation can be applied to computer games or situations associated with them [7]. For example, Russian Federation laws:

- "On Basic Guarantees of The Rights of the Child in The Russian Federation"; N 124–FZ, 1998.
- "On Information, Information Technologies and Information Protection"; N 149-FZ, 2006.
- "On Protection of Children from Information Harmful to Their Health and Development"; N 436-FZ, 2010.

The lawmakers from different countries, especially American, pay much attention to legal regulation of computer game influence children. There are two general ways of the regulation. The first is an adoption (enactment) of a law connected with children interests' protection [8]. American laws are applied to computer games or situations associated with them:

- "Child Abuse Prevention and Treatment Act (CAPTA)"; 1974.
- "Children's Online Privacy and Protection Act (COPPA)"; 1998, 2013 (amended to account for changes in technology since its original passage.) It requires all web-sites, mobile applications, networked video game services, and interactive online services that are directed towards children under the age of 13 to comply with very specific rules and regulations.
- "The 21 Century Media Market Responsibility Act"; 2000.
- "Child Online Protection Act (COPA)"; 47 U.S.C. § 231, 2004, 2007, 2008. COPA has never taken effect because a federal district court found COPA unconstitutional and issued a permanent injunction against its enforcement.
- "The Family Entertainment Protection Act (FEPA)"; 2005.
- "The Children's Internet Protection Act (CIPA)"; 2006. Law applies only to public libraries and schools and mandates that they employ software filters to restrict access by minors to inappropriate material.
- "Video Game Decency Act"; 2007.
- "Video Games Ratings Enforcement Act"; H.R.287, 2013.

The governments have also paid attention the regulation of the industry through legislation. While video games are classed as functional software with a graphical interface in Russia, United States take a more pragmatic approach, recognizing the complexity of video games and favoring a "distributive classification", whereby each creative element of a game is protected separately according to its specific nature. The law is clear that the minors would not be exposed to violent or sexually explicit computer games. Through developed rating practices, the government classifies the games appropriate for minors or other. The restricted sales strategy has been in use in many states to control the exposure of the violent and sexually explicit computer games on minors as well [3].

Out of the top 10 selling computer games of 2014, five of them are rated for mature audiences with many children still having access to these hardcore games that ulti-mately compromise their morality. The American Federal government has not per-formed exemplarily in developing legislations purposely structured to fight against the exposure of children to mature content and violence in computer games. The Family Entertainment Protection Act (FEPA) was introduced into the Senate to help curb this problem in 2005. Although it was unapproved, it plays a critical role in shedding light on the laxity that exists in the American government when it comes to enforcing computer gaming legislations. There is a similar legislation in Congress now titled H.R.287 – Video Games Ratings Enforcement Act. It was introduced in 2013.

The responsibility of restricting the access of minors to mature computer game content lies entirely with the Entertainment Software Rating Board (ESRB). This non-profit entity is tasked with the responsibility of setting both content and age ratings on all computer games being sold on the US market. It relies on legislations passed by state governments to enforce its recommendations. This often undermines its effectiveness in ensuring that children only gain access to their designated games. As a result, more American teenagers continually purchase mature rated games and play them, resulting in a growing culture of violence and immorality. States such as California have made positive progress in developing appropriate laws that support ESRB's mission. The state has banned all sales of computer games that are perceived to be violent to minors within its jurisdiction. Such actions will play a very important role in protecting children from mature rated games. Federal courts have repeatedly struck down proposed legislations aimed to regulate sales of games to minors due to its violation of the First Amendment, and argued. It creates a whole new regulation of speech. Another thing that the industry leaders point out is a lack of research and subsequently evidence, linking computer games and dangerous responses in players.

In addition to the aforementioned protections, federal and state legislators of U.S. have enacted several criminal provisions designed to punish Internet users who hurt minors physically. Some laws that traditionally protect children have been expanded to apply to situations where an individual uses the Internet and computer to facilitate the crimes [9–11].

Russian Federal law on protection of children from harmful information is connected with the three-level rating system of films functioned in the USSR. All Russian or foreign films should get the certificate with age category: for any audience (0+); for any audience except special child sessions (6+); for persons over 16 years of age. In 2001 extra age categories "12+" and "18+" appeared. In 2005 the category "14+" was added. Rating system protects children and teenagers from audio and video products which can harm children' health, emotion and intellectual development. Federal law "On Protection of Children from Information Harmful to Their Health and Development" presented a new rating system which spreads on films and computer games.

There are Russian and American video games content rating systems (Table 2).

Table 2. Computer games and age classification

Country	The age classification name	Adoption year	Age classification
The United State of America	Entertainment Software Review Board (ESBR)	1994	0+, 6+, 10+, 13+, 17+, 18+
The Russian Federation	Russian Age Rating System (RARS)	2012	0+, 6+, 12+, 16+, 18+

There are other video production rating systems in the world, which have the same aim and the tools to achieve it. The rating systems assign ratings for video games and apps to empower consumers, especially parents, with guidance that allows them to make informed decisions about the age-appropriateness and suitability of video games and apps. It reports about violence, sexual scenes or using drugs in video product. Systems of games classification are useful only in that measure in what use it. In the USA polls have shown that 66% of parents don't know about a games classification system.

The major stakeholders in the computer games industry include the creators of computer games, like Electronic Arts (EA) Corporation, the regulators, such as the government, the investors and finally the consumers. A 2015 report from ESA presents the consequential facts about the culture of gaming in the American society. Millions of Americans enjoy computer games as a way of passing time. On average, 4 out of 5 American households have a gaming device that can be utilized to play computer games. An incredible 42% of Americans attest to regularly play video games, usually for more than 3 h every week. Another interesting statistic revealed by the EA was the age profile of American gamers. The identified average age of gamers is 35. However, there is still an exceptionally high number of children who indulge in video games. In fact, the report reveals that 26% of American game players are under the age of 18 years. The report goes to state that parents play a very important role in controlling the content that their children are exposed to when playing game. 91% of them use the parental control features available to protect their children from violence, obscenities and nudity in games. Shooter and action games are the most prominent type of games enjoyed by the American population with 21.7% and 28.2% of market share respectively.

Entertainment Software Review Board (ESBR) was created by Entertainment Software Association - ESA. Every year ESA makes investigates facts about computer games players. Among other factors they examine gamer's age, favorite games and average time spent for them. In 2016, they discovered that the average age of American computer game player is 35 years old. Meanwhile, 27% of American players is under the 18 years old. ESA also found out that 62% of parents who have kids-gamers also play computer games [12].

Company «Mail.Ru Group» observed Russian gamers. Online games are popular among people of all ages, but the biggest group from 25 to 34 years old (30%) plays computer games more often than others and prefer to use smartphones or tablets. This is due to the young adults' high interest in the new technologies and mobility pref-erences. Only 15% of Russian gamers are elder 12 are students and pupils [13].

Russian and American computer gamers' age distribution is presented at Table 3.

Significant percent of gamers are minors, who are also under the influence of developing technologies and adult gamers. Nevertheless, the most important question is connected with the consequences of passion for computer games.

The diversity of statistic information, society information and science initiatives speaks about an attention of different actors to the computer games playing issue [14–16]. Actors struggle for the attention to problems which they are interested in and to the exact interpretation of the computer games playing (if it is good or not) at different public arenas (legislature, mass media). The statements won in this «fight» at legis-lature arena become legal acts. Nowadays the statement saying that computer games can be dangerous wins.

Table 3. Computer games and age of computer gamers distribution

Age groups	The United State of America (%)	Age groups	The Russian Federation (%)
Under 18 y.o.	27%	**12–24 y.o.**	25%
18–35 y.o.	29%	**25–34 y.o.**	30%
39–49 y.o.	18%	**34–44 y.o.**	21%
50+ y.o.	26%	**45–54 y.o.**	12%
		55+ y.o.	12%
The average game players' age	35 y.o.	**The average game players' age**	33 y.o.

In 2015 American Psychological Association (APA) presented the results of the study "could violence in computer games be the reason of crime behavior". The scientists discovered the link between playing in computer games and decrease the empathy level and prosocial behavior. ASA concluded that computer games is one of the risk factors like depression, family problems etc., which can be the reason of the high level of aggression [17].

Four national organizations of health care of the USA among which there is American Medical Association have established that virtual violence is directly connected with real. Games turn violence into attractive and ordinary thing [18].

At the same time the public notes the possibilities of computer games. In 2010 Russian deputies suggested that computer games could help to maintain the level of patriotism in country. For example, BBC informed about cases when computer games helped people. In 2016 the game «Pokemon Go» had helped a few autistics to adapt to the society [19].

Talmedzh Wright and Paul Bridenbakh, Loyola's university, Chicago: "Games help to build up the relationship in usual life, teach effective team work, and discharge the mental energy which is saved up during aggressive self-affirmation of teenagers. Games can compensate shortages in emotional life, give a support for overcoming fear" [18].

Researches data of Institute of psychology of RAS of the Russian Federation also taped no symptoms of alienations or computer dependence. Moreover, researches established that players adapt among the peers easier. Large scale Russian researches about dependence of aggression of children and teenagers on "bloody" computer games still were unconducted.

4   Conclusion

The following conclusions were made during the study.

The interest to the computer games theme in reference to legislation is ever-changing.

Legislative initiatives in both countries appear only during critical situations or crises; usually, crime cases committed by minors, which society attributes to computer game addiction. Similar incidents cause a temporary increase of society interest in the problem of computer games for children. Such incidents temporarily attract attention to issues within the game industry. Mass media and online communities become involved, with the issue rising and public beginning to discuss the problem. Further the problem rises to the legislative level. Unfortunately, legislative initiatives, as a rule, receive weak support. Legislators postpone the decision until the next incident, or take partial steps.

Minor-gamers group makes insignificant percent from total number of computer gamers as in America as Russia.

The connection of behavioral cruelty among minors and their interest in computer games is little investigated, demands confirmations and additional research.

Underage gamers make up a small percentage of overall gamers in America, and in Russia alike. The correlation of behavior cruelty among minors and computer games is vague, and therefore, requires further research.

Acknowledgements. The reported study was funded by RFBR according to the research project "Scientific methods in research of computer game experience" № 16-06-00368 a, 2016–2017.

References

1. Wesley, D., Barczak, G.: Innovation and Marketing in the Video Game Industry: Avoiding the Performance Trap. Routledge, London (2016)
2. Gaudiosi, J.: The top 10 U.S. states for video game development jobs. http://fortune.com/2015/02/24/10-successful-states-video-game-development/
3. Toffler, A., Toffler, H.: Revolutionary wealth. N. Perspect. Q. **30**(4), 122–130 (2013)
4. Bellotti, F., Kapralos, B., Lee, K., Moreno-Ger, P., Berta, R.: Assessment in and of serious games: an overview. Adv. Hum.-Comput. Interact. **2013**, 11 (2013). Article ID: 136864. http://dx.doi.org/10.1155/2013/136864
5. Kononova, O.V., Sergeeva, O.V., Krut'ko, E.A., Oreh, E.A.: Play computer experience as a subject of the scientific periodical press in focus of the automated context search. In: IV International scientific and practical conference «Communications in Social and Humanitarian Knowledge, Economy, Education», Minsk, pp. 251–253 (2016)
6. Digital Games Research Association. http://digrastudents.org/games-research-journals/
7. Kotenko, E.S.: The legal regime of computer games. Actual Probl. Russ. Law **2**, 422–430 (2010)
8. Protection of Children Online: Federal and State Laws Addressing Cyberstalking, Cyberharassment and Cyberbullying. https://epic.org/crs/RL34651.pdf
9. Rose-Steinberg, J.: Gaming the system: an examination of the constitutionality of violent video game legislation. Seton Hall Legislative J. **35**(1), 7 (2010). Article ID: 7. http://scholarship.shu.edu/shlj/vol35/iss1/7
10. Ford, W.K.: The law and science of video game violence: what was lost in translation? Cardozo Arts Ent. Law J. **31**, 297 (2013)
11. Calvert, C., Richards, R.D.: Precedent be damned – it's all about good politics & sensational sound bites: the video game censorship saga of 2005. Tex. Rev. Ent. Sports Law **6**, 80–155 (2006)
12. Essential facts about the computer and video game industry. http://www.theesa.com/wp-content/uploads/2016/04/Essential-Facts-2016.pdf

13. Mail.Ru group research: the profile of the Russian gamer. https://corp.mail.ru/ru/press/infograph/9576/
14. Clements, C.: Protecting protected speech: violent video game legislation Post-Brown v. Entertainment Merchants Ass'n. BCL Rev. **53**, 661 (2012)
15. Channov, S.E.: On the issue of the criteria for the prohibition and restrictions of computer network games in the territory of the Russian Federation. Inf. Law (4), 20–24 (2016). Publishing: "Lawyer", Moscow (2016)
16. Ivanov, A.V.: Negative influence of modern television and computer games on the crime of minors. Vestnik TISBI **2**(50), 165–172 (2012). Publishing house: University of Management "TISBI", Kazan
17. Do violent video games lead to criminal behavior? http://www.cbsnews.com/news/do-violent-video-games-lead-to-criminal-behavior/
18. About the problem of cruel games. http://sd-company.su/article/games/violence-game
19. Can Pokémon Go help people with autism open up to the world? http://www.bbc.com/russian/features-36855029

Problems of Legal Regulation of Games with Augmented Reality (Example of the Russian Federation)

Roman Amelin[1]([✉]), Sergey Channov[2], and Galina Komkova[1]

[1] National Research Saratov State University named after N. G. Chernyshevsky, 83 Astrakhanskaya Street, Saratov 410012, Russia
ame-roman@yandex.ru
[2] The Russian Presidential Academy of National Economy and Public Administration, 23/25 Sobornaya Street, Saratov 410031, Russia

Abstract. The article analyzes the issues related to the legal regulation of games with augmented reality. The authors summarized the numerous incidents, the statements of politicians and legislative initiatives caused by the global fascination with such games. They identified two groups of problems, not typical for the previous generation of computer games. First, the threat to life and health of the player. Second, the threat to the rights and interests of other people and the public interest. The authors proposed the criterion of the prohibition (restriction) of distribution of such games – stimulation of illegal behavior of players. Bodies authorized to apply the appropriate restrictions, as well as means to ensure the ban – legal acts, state information systems – are considered by the example of the Russian Federation law.

Keywords: Augmented reality · Video games · State information systems · Administrative Code · Legal liability · Federal Service · A threat to life and health · Ban on the dissemination · Real world · App store · Game Pokemon

1 Introduction

Computer games exist for a long time, but the legal issues related to their regulation, still exist and continue to accumulate. New games appear and old questions arise. In what cases do these games represent a social danger? Whether to limit their spread? How to implement it?

From the perspective of the issues and problems of legal regulation of computer games, there is reason to talk about the two conditional "eras" of their evolution.

The first "era" associated with classic single player games. Two key issues were raised. Firstly, the potential harm from the game to the consumer (effects on the psyche, computer addiction, etc.) So, Manhant (the purpose and the meaning of the game is murder) was banned in many countries. Carmageddon gameplay consisted killing

This work was supported by grant 17-03-00082 from the Russian Foundation for Basic Research.

© Springer International Publishing AG 2017
D.A. Alexandrov et al. (Eds.): DTGS 2017, CCIS 745, pp. 159–169, 2017.
https://doi.org/10.1007/978-3-319-69784-0_14

pedestrians, and the game was allowed in the UK under the condition that the blood will be green, and people will be replaced by zombies or robots with oil instead of blood. Secondly, the game can be considered as an information product that carries certain messages to users - and fall under the prohibition in connection with the spread of forbidden information. For example, Fallout 3 banned in Australia for the promotion of drugs (the protagonist can take drugs to achieve a variety of positive effects). Football Manager 2005 is banned in China over the threat to the sovereignty and territorial integrity, as Taiwan and Tibet were included in the list of football teams as a separate country i.e. "declared as independent states".

Restriction of games which represent a public danger from the point of view of a particular state is achieved by prohibition or restriction of their sales within the state. With the development of the Internet, eliminating the territorial restrictions, law adopts an approach of "accessibility of the Internet resource test". According to this approach, the national court may resolve litigation related to relationships in the Internet if you have access from territory of the state to the appropriate site. It is understood that the substantive law of the State, from which you can access the specified resource is applied to the site content [1]. We cannot say that the approach is common, but it is used widely enough since 1990s. Thus, the German authorities prosecuted subsidiary CompuServe manager. CompuServe provided technical access to US web resources, among which were the games Doom and Heretic (contributing, according to the German authorities, the socio-ethical disorientation) and Wolfenstein 3D (containing Nazi symbols forbidden to spread) [2].

The popularity of multiplayer online games (mainly MMORPGs) marked the beginning of the second "era". Legal problems associated with the single-user games, supplemented with problems of user interaction in the virtual world as well as the relationship of users and game administration.

From a legal point of view, the most interesting aspect is the problem of user interaction. In what cases do the relationship in the virtual space produce legal effects in the real world? For example, whether the theft in the virtual world be regarded as causing harm, if it is not provided by the rules of the game? [3, 4] Can the rules of real right and property rights specifically apply to virtual property? [5] Can a virtual game currency be considered as "electronic money" or only as "cash equivalents" (forbidden under Russian law)? [6] It should be stated that the global legal science is currently not developed a universal approach to the solution of these problems. There is a disconcerting number of women complaining of being sexually harassed by male players in virtual chat rooms and multiplayer online games.

As for the relationship between the players and the administration of multiplayer online games, there is no common approach as well, although practice of law application is gradually accumulated. Thus, in the Russian Federation courts apply to relations arising from participation in multiplayer RPGs provisions for games and betting established by Chapter 58 of the Civil Code. In particular, the courts take the position that, in accordance with para. 1, Art. 1062 of the Civil Code, the demands of citizens and legal entities related to the organization of games and betting or participating in them, are not subject to judicial protection, except for the requirements of persons who took part in the games or betting under the influence of fraud, violence, threats, etc.

Restricts access to inappropriate online games can be carried out by blocking the Internet resources, on which game servers are located. Thus, in the Russian Federation, addresses of sites, which are conducted by Gambling ("online casino"), blocked by inclusion in the "Register of banned sites" in accordance with Art. 15.1 Information Act. We do not know on the prohibition of any multiplayer role-playing games at the state level, but such restrictions are imposed by the developers for users residing in the territory of a certain state repeatedly. For example, due to the US sanctions inhabitants of the Crimea and Sevastopol could not play the game Word of Warcraft; the players of Iraq previously faced with the same problem. It should be noted that in both cases, users have the technical ability to bypass a blocking using proxy-servers, replacing the information on your location and posing as citizens of another state.

Currently, due to the worldwide popularity of the game Pokemon Go, published in July 2016, we can speak about the occurrence of the third "age" of computer games – games with augmented reality, that give rise to new and unique legal problems.

2   Games with Augmented Reality: Legal Problems

Games with augmented reality have been considered in the literature in many aspects: design [7, 8], education [9] (about university education see also [10]), art [11] etc. Also, ethical and legal problems associated with such games were discussed [12]. However, in reality, these problems manifested itself only in 2016 due to the mass popularity of games tied to the user's geolocation.

To achieve the results of such game (Pokémon capture, portal activation, etc.), the player has to move to a specific point of the real world. Only in this case respective capabilities are activated in the game. In addition, the phone or tablet camera widely used in the game. Player observes the virtual objects on the background of the real situation. Although in Pokemon Go camera can be turned off (and this greatly simplifies the process), there is no doubt that in the near future, these games will use recognition technology to their full capacity, and the virtual game objects will not just show up on a background of real objects, but will interact with them.

Thus, now games with augmented reality stimulate the players to go out, travel on certain routes, use the camera. We can only assume what other features will appear in the new games. However, analysis of numerous incidents of mass Pokemon Go enthusiasm (as well as politicians' propositions and legislative initiatives) reveals quite a significant range of emerging threats.

Conventionally, they can be classified into two groups:

1. Danger to life and health of the player. In addition to the traditional debate about the harmful effects of computer games ("computer addiction", "social disorientation", etc.) in the case of games with augmented reality, there is a real risk associated with the need to reach a certain place (in some cases - for a limited time).

   Inspired by the game, some players enter into forbidden territory. That's what happened the first death of a player in Pokemon Go in Guatemala - teenagers included in the protected object and had been shot by police. In pursuit of Pokémon players inadvertently fall under cars, break away from the cliffs, become victims of criminals (who specifically ambushes in deserted places with game objects).

2. Causing harm the legitimate rights and interests of other persons as a result of actions of the players.

The most common problem associated with inattentive drivers, massive violation of traffic rules by pedestrians hurrying to the desired location and other traffic accidents. In addition, there are the following threats associated with passion the game:

- infringement of privacy in connection with the massive use of cameras and distribution of images of the gameplay;
- infringement of privacy in connection with the penetration of the private area (for example, a resident of Canada has sued the company Niantic Inc. for the "involvement" of players to her house);
- threat of confidentiality, industrial espionage (for this reason, the Volkswagen management has banned its employees to play Pokemon Go inside the plant);
- threat to national security (for example, the US Department of Defense banned the game Pokemon Go at its facilities due to the fear of industrial espionage); game banned in Iran at the state level "for security reasons";
- violation of ethical behavior by players in cultural places and religious institutions. Thus, the Cathedral of St. Nicholas in Vienna sued the company Niantic Inc. and demanded to remove Pokémons from the temple. The Russian blogger deliberately hunt for Pokemon in the church and distribute video was arrested.

The fundamental question of this study is whether the reason of a special legal regulation of relations about games with augmented reality exist. Is it reasonable to ban or restrict the distribution and use of the games in the state? If so, what should be the legal mechanism of this prohibition (limitation)? And what organizational and technical means may be used for this purpose?

3 Protection of the Game: A Threat to the Interests of the Player

The first step is to analyze the threats to the interests of the players coming from the game. As noted above, these problems are not new to computer games. Moreover, there are cases (and repeated) the death of the players, who, in their enthusiasm, forget about sleep and food. However, games with augmented reality, obviously, opens up a new level of danger.

In principle, it should be noted that modern society is based on the fact that people need some protection from the goods and services that could be harmful to his health. However, it should also distinguish between different options.

It's one thing if the product or service creates an implicit threat to the consumer. If we talk about computer games (including network), it is considered that it is technically possible to create games that have a hidden impact on the players' subconscious [13]. Such games, of course, should be prohibited (even if it does not cause obvious harm to life and health).

Another situation occurs if the user is aware of the danger of harm to life and health when using a particular product or service, but he ignores it. In general, the legislation of the various states in relation to the ban, and (or) restrictions of such products is ambiguous. For example, cigarettes and alcohol are such products. Despite repeatedly proven harm from consumption of these products, and efforts to reduce their consumption taken by the government and various non-governmental organizations, the majority of people consciously reconciled with the possibility of causing harm to their health. Most states of the world set different restrictions on the production and sale of tobacco and alcohol products, but a complete ban is set only in a few of them.

On the other hand, the position of the majority of states in respect of psychotropic and narcotic drugs is tougher: they are banned completely or partially. However, it should be noted that the main reason for the ban on the manufacture, sale and use of drugs is not the harm that may be caused to health of the consumer, but the potential danger posed by consumers to other persons.

Returning to the computer online games, we note that some of them undoubtedly threaten harm to life and health of the player. Pokemon Go gameplay entails injury, and even death for players (however it does not stop them).

Is this sufficient reason to ban such games? It is rather difficult to give an unambiguous answer to this question, we think, it must be individually in each case. In any case, this criterion should be interpreted too broadly, because any computer game has the potential harm to the health of the player (e.g. visual impairment).

At the same time, it appears that the potential risk of harm to the life and health of players can act as a basis for limiting the distribution and use of such games.

4   The Harm to the Rights and Legitimate Interests of Other Persons, Caused by the Actions of the Player

The essential feature of games with augmented reality is the fact that their ubiquity affects the interests of people who are not involved in the gameplay, as well as the public interest. As shown above, the players may infringe on the right to privacy, confidentiality, public security, the feelings of believers, etc.

Wondering how the law should respond to these circumstances, it is necessary to make an important point. Following gaming purposes, the players perform actions in the real world (movement, videography, etc.) - and at the same time they are quite able to realize the meaning and social danger of their actions, even if they are passionate about the gameplay. Regardless of whether a person is playing a game or talking on the phone while driving, whether he catches a Pokemon or makes selfie on the background of documents containing confidential information - such acts must obviously be qualified identically. And at first glance the game with augmented reality does not entail anything new from the legal point of view.

At the same time, in our opinion, there is a very important point - as a game promotes unlawful behavior of users.

For example, consider the games that are obviously extremist. One of them is the so-called "Great Game "Break the system", the materials of which have been placed on a number of Internet sites. The essence of this game project is to obtain a certain status (for example, "Street Fighter" or "Internet-fighter"). To do this, players receive the task of varying difficulty through the Internet and perform them in real life. The higher the level of fighter in the online game, the more difficult and dangerous jobs available for its off-line prototype. For example, the first level of "street fighters" print out leaflets with the symbols of the pagan god Svarog and the words "Big Game", and then paste over a variety of subjects and objects in the city of residence. And on the sixth level fighters must upload the video clip to prove the implementation of actions in the real world - for example, the destruction of barracks and trade tents, where the "aliens" are deployed. Creators of the project called visitors from the regions of the Caucasus and the former Soviet republics "aliens" [14]. As can be seen from this description, the game "Break the system" is not a computer network game in the literal sense, but, nevertheless, appears obvious example of "game" being implemented in the real world, but with the use of Internet resources (and the corresponding technical devices), while it is clearly an extremist game.

Let us imagine that rare Pokemon (or other objects with which cooperation is important for success in the game) appear only on highways, areas protected by military units and religious institutions. There will be a situation similar to the current state in the field of copyright, when the violation is committed by a large number of people, but to attract each offender to justice is physically impossible.

For the game Pokemon Go for the first time was available map created by third-party developers. Map showed the location of Pokemon in real time on the map, not just near the player (as it is supposed to play). As a result, the players learned about the appearance of a rare Pokémon in a certain place. After that, a crowd of people (hundreds or even thousands of players gathered in the capitals parks in summer) raced to a specified point on the map, causing inconvenience to passers-by and interfering traffic. This effect is classified as definitely undesired, although not provided by the game developers (we note that currently developers have substantially increased the security protocols used, and the new map is not created yet).

Returning to the question of the stimulus for the players to be in a certain place in order to achieve success in the game, we note that developers of Pokemon Go seek to avoid the possible threats. So, without knowing the exact location of a rare Pokémon, players do not need to choose a path that leads to the territory of the protected object. Objects are very rare along the highways and in the wilderness. Developers blocked the appearance of Pokémon in a certain territory at the request of organizations and individuals. Of course, every state has the right to believe that such measures are not sufficient to ensure safety.

According to the authors, the creation of games with the potential to cause damage to national security is theoretically possible. Of course, they should also be subject to a total ban on the territory of the state. At the same time, this criterion must be used with great caution and not broadly in any case. In particular, citing the threat to the game Pokemon Go, officials pointed out that the citizens in the framework of the gameplay can perform recording secret objects. Foreign governments, allegedly controlling the game, will have access to secret snapshots [15]. According to the authors, this argument is unfounded. If the government and the relevant intelligence agencies cannot ensure the security of sensitive sites from the citizens themselves, who work there, it says more about the systemic problems in the organization of these special services, and not about the potential dangers of any games. In any case, in our opinion, if, for example, a soldier consciously carries out filming a secret military base in defiance of a ban (including during gameplay) - it is an occasion of his discipline, or possibly criminal liability, but not a reason to ban the game.

On the other hand, it seems quite reasonable possible restrictions on the implementation of the gameplay on the objects of this type because, for example, the appearance of Pokémon may lead to a dramatic increase in the number of persons wishing to enter into the territory. This will complicate the work of security services and systems.

In general, it seems to us that the establishment of various restrictions on the distribution and use of computer network games is quite possible, and in some cases, necessary. Such restrictions may affect the location and time of game play (for games with augmented reality); the circle of participants (for example, age limits), etc.

5 The Bodies Authorized in the Field of Prohibition and Restrictions of Network Games

It follows that, in certain cases, where the game encourages players to commit illegal acts, there is an objective need to limit distribution and use of this game. This raises the question: which authorities may be authorized to adopt such decisions.

The Russian Federation is currently the executive authorities have the greatest powers in limiting the spread of various kinds of information. Among them, a special role is played by the Federal Service for Supervision of Communications, Information Technology, and Mass Media. The powers of the Federal Service, in particular, include: state control and supervision over compliance with requirements of Russian legislation in the sphere of protection of children from information harmful to their health and (or) development; creation, formation and maintenance of the "Registry of banned sites"; etc. [16].

On the other hand, if you apply directly to the procedures prohibit the dissemination of certain information in the Russian Federation can be seen that the Federal Service makes independent decisions on the prohibition access only to certain types of information, directly specified in Art. 15.1 Information Act. In all other cases the court decision prohibits the dissemination of information (in particular, on access to relevant sites).

It seems that as a general rule judicial authority decision should be established bans on the dissemination and use of network computer games on the territory of the Russian Federation. The Federal Service for Supervision of Communications, Information Technology, and Mass Media can be endowed with the power to ban the distribution and use of games only in the obvious and exceptional cases, for example, if the game is able to push the player to commit suicide (by analogy with the ban on access to relevant sites).

In general, it appears that the ban on the distribution and use of computer games in a democratic state should always be individual. Well-defined (in the law) criteria should be the basis for the ban. The ban should be set by enforcement act, as a general rule - by the court decision.

As for the introduction of restrictions on the distribution and use of games on the territory of the Russian Federation, the case and the reasons of such restrictions, of course, must be established by a federal law (otherwise would be contrary to Art. 55 of the Constitution). Executive authority should apply specific restrictions on a particular game. If distributors or the players violate the restrictions, this should entail the legal responsibility under the law.

6 Legal Means to Restrict the Spread and Use of Games, Creating Danger for the Player and Other People

The next important question is about method for implementing of decisions taken by a judicial authority or executive authority. This question has both legal and organizational, and technical nature.

First of all, it should be noted that the ban on the distribution and use of network computer games on the territory of the Russian Federation can be implemented by issuing appropriate orders to the following subjects (and establish sanctions for non-compliance): (1) organizers/creators/distributors; (2) consumers/members/players; (3) both categories.

The first way seems more promising. Currently most computer network games distributed through specialized app stores, the number of which is relatively small (App Store, Windows Store, Google Play, and other). A certain difficulty of execution of decisions on prohibition is that currently, the complete technical blocking of access to these app stores from the territory of the Russian Federation is impossible, therefore there is a question to compel the owners of these shops to perform the judgment. It seems, however, that this problem is not of a very serious nature, as app stores that distribute online games for mobile applications, are owned by large corporations with offices in Russia, which are aimed at compliance with Russian laws.

But here arises another problem: the jurisdiction of the Russian court extends, quite naturally, only on the territory of the Russian Federation. That is, the prohibition on the distribution of a particular game on the territory of the Russian Federation will not act globally. Accordingly, the competent authority cannot demand from app store owners to remove the game from the store complete. They can demand only to make it inaccessible for the residents of a particular country (option - persons on its territory).

Binding to the place of residence, in practice does not work, because at the moment users can specify as the location of their primary residence, any state without any problems.

Another option is to establish a ban on the installation of certain games on the device, located on the territory of the state. However, different locking methods that are linked to IP-address, geolocation data etc. can also be bypassed. In addition, there is a question about the possibility and permissibility lock games installed on the user's device outside of the state, which was then moved to its territory.

In recent years, in the Russian legislation, state information systems (SIS) have become a kind of legal instrument. The government regulates the responsibilities and capabilities of the actors through the creation and implementation of such information systems [17]. In particular, one of the main ways to block unwanted information is to enter the address of the Internet resource into a special SIS (Registry of banned sites). Telecommunications operators providing Internet access services in the territory of the

Russian Federation are obliged to block access of their users to the addresses contained in the registry. Extension of this measure to the addresses of prohibited online game servers is quite logical. But, as practice shows, this option does not guarantee results, because there are many technical ways to get around this lock.

Thus, the implementation of measures to prohibit the spread of networked computer games on the territory of the state require the search for new technical solutions.

There is another embodiment of the ban on the dissemination and use of unwanted games in the state. It is to establish the legal liability for players. The advantage of this option is its relative simplicity: its implementation does not require any new technical solutions; it can be legally done through a simple supplement of the Administrative Code.

Disadvantages of this approach are also evident. Number of players of the popular game can be hundreds of thousands or millions. Attract them all to administrative responsibility is problematic.

Yet the introduction of such measures of responsibility, in our view, could give a certain result - the very existence of appropriate formulations of administrative offenses would give the effect of general prevention. Our objection to the use of this option is based on other considerations.

Firstly, in our view, the establishment of administrative responsibility for users of network computer games would be too cumbersome and, consequently, excessive restriction of their rights. With the introduction of such provisions in the domestic laws, each user before install a new game on his (her) phone, tablet, computer, or other device would have forced yourself to find out whether or not this game banned in the territory of the state. Although this can be realized through the establishment of the register of forbidden games and placing it on a public site, it seems, such a requirement goes beyond the permissible limits.

Secondly, the social danger of the installation and use of banned games is much lower than the danger of the development and spread of such games. For example, the user's behavior, playing in extremist game (e.g., exciting intolerance to certain social groups) is not desirable, but not sufficient to bring him to legal liability (assuming, of course, that he does not carry his actions on the real representatives of these social groups). At the same time, the developer and (or) disseminator of such a game, obviously, is intended to have an impact on the minds of players. This behavior deserves punishment.

Instead of ban, specific restrictions with regard to certain games can be installed. For violation of these restrictions, players are also liable to legal responsibility. In some cases, new regulations are not required, existing ones are enough. For example, the penetration of the protected object during the game may result in administrative liability (Article 20.17 of the Administrative Code of the Russian Federation: "Violation of access control protected object", Article 20.19 of the Administrative Code "Violation of special regime in the Closed City", etc.).

Administrative responsibility may serve as a means of ensuring compliance with the restrictions by the game developers. For example, the game organizers can be held responsible for the placement of game objects in inappropriate places. In some instances, the existing rules on administrative offenses can also be used. For example,

Art. 20.2.2 of the Administrative Code: "organization of mass simultaneous holding and (or) the movement of citizens in public places, which caused a public nuisance".

7 Conclusion and Prospects

Games with augmented reality will be widely disseminated in the next few years. New technologies that allow virtual objects on the screen of the smartphone to interact with the environment will appear. Millions of players will make gaming activities in the real world. The law should promptly respond to this reality by setting the boundaries of proper behavior for players and developers to minimize the danger - for the players themselves and those around them, the public interests and even the state interests. Some studies on this subject already posted. For example, Donald J. Kochan has researched conflicts between augmented reality and real property [18].

Currently, some common approaches can already be generated, including the liability base for the players and the developers of these games, the base and methods of restrictions (ban) of their distribution and use. *The principle of evaluation of the behavior "required" by the players to succeed in the game can be the basis.* We offer developers of computer games to take this principle into consideration as part of the ethical code. As the distribution and development of games with augmented reality, this code can form the basis of international law.

Games that stimulate illegal behavior must be unequivocally prohibited, the responsibility for dissemination must be established. If players commit wrongful acts (deliberately or inadvertently) in the game that does not require such behavior, only those persons should be brought to justice - for the relevant offense and regardless of the game (although we do not exclude the possibility that the game could be an aggravating factor, by analogy with alcohol intoxication).

Of course, quite a serious work on the formalization of the principle and check it by practice is required.

Also authorities responsible for conducting the examination (assessment) of games in terms of behavior stimulated need to be determined. Specific ways to limit the spread of unwanted games need to be settled. Bases and measure of responsibility need to be fleshed out. This research is only a first step in this important and responsible process.

References

1. Azizov, R., Arkhipov, V.: Relations in the internet format WEB 2.0: the problem of the correspondence between the network architecture and the legal regulation. In: Law, no. 1, pp. 90–104 (2014)
2. Rosenblatt, B.: Principles of Jurisdiction. Berkman Center for Internet & Society at Harvard University (2016). http://cyber.law.harvard.edu/property99/domain/Betsy.html
3. Izbachkov, Y.: Theft in the style of "fantasy". In: Culture: Management, Economics, Law, no. 1, pp. 8–12 (2012)
4. Lin, H., Sun, C.-T.: Cash trade within the magic circle: free-to-play game challenges and massively multiplayer online game player responses. In: Proceedings of DiGRA 2007 Conference, pp. 335–343 (2007)

5. Bartle, R.A.: Pitfalls of Virtual Property, p. 1. The Themis Group (2004). http://themis-group.com/uploads/Pitfalls%20of%20Virtual%20Property.pdf
6. Arkhipov, V.: Virtual property: systemic legal issues in the context of the development of computer games industry. In: Law, no. 9, pp. 69–90 (2014)
7. Lanham, M.: Augmented Reality Game Development. Packt Publishing Ltd., Birmingham (2017)
8. Cawood, S., Fiala, M.: Augmented Reality: A Practical Guide. Pragmatic Bookshelf, Raleigh (2008)
9. Diegmann, P., Schmidt-Kraepelin, M., van den Eynden, S., Basten D.: Benefits of augmented reality in educational environments – a systematic literature review. In: Wirtschaftsinformatik Proceedings, vol. 103 (2015)
10. Rassolov, I.M., Sidyacheva, N.V., Zotova, L.E., Salitova, F.S., Konyushenko, S.M., Gzhemskaya, N.K.: Socio-pedagogical priorities of the educational process at the university: the didactic aspect of information technology. Int. J. Environ. Sci. Educ. 11(18), 10987–10997 (2016)
11. Geroimenko, V.: Augmented Reality Art. Springer, Cham (2014)
12. Wassom, B.: Augmented Reality Law, Privacy, and Ethics. Elsevier Science, Amsterdam (2014)
13. Prokofiev, V.: The secret weapon of information warfare: attack on the subconscious. SINTEG, Moscow (2003)
14. The nationalists blew up the internet by "big game" (2016). http://vkrizis.ru/obschestvo/nacionalisty-vzorvali-internet-bolshoy-igroy/
15. Hasan, T.: Is Pokemon Go Really Posing a Global Threat to National Securities? (2016). http://www.opednews.com/articles/Is-Pokemon-Go-Really-Posin-by-Tazeen-Hasan-Global-Capitalism_Global-Hegemony_Global-Outreach_Globalization-CAFTA-160812-442.html
16. The Federal Service for Supervision of Communications, Information Technology, and Mass Media. Official site (2017). http://eng.rkn.gov.ru/
17. Amelin, R., Channov, S.: State information systems in e-government in the Russian Federation: problems of legal regulation. In: Proceedings of 2nd International Conference on Electronic Governance and Open Society: Challenges in Eurasia (EGOSE 2015), pp. 129–132. ACM, New York (2015)
18. Kochan, D.: Playing with real property inside augmented reality: Pokemon Go, trespass, and law's limitations. Whittier Law Rev. (2017)

Protection Against Information in eSociety: Using Data Mining Methods to Counteract Unwanted and Malicious Data

Igor Kotenko[1,2(✉)], Igor Saenko[1,2], and Andrey Chechulin[1,2]

[1] St. Petersburg Institute for Informatics and Automation of the Russian Academy of Sciences, 39, 14 Liniya, Saint Petersburg, Russia
{ivkote,ibsaen,chechulin}@comsec.spb.ru
[2] St. Petersburg National Research University of Information Technologies, Mechanics and Optics, 49, Kronverkskiy prospekt, Saint-Petersburg, Russia

Abstract. Despite the positive aspects of usage of the Internet and social networks within the concept of eSociety, huge data collections available for viewing and analysis to the user of the Internet can contain information which can be unwanted or malicious. The paper considers the problem of protection of users in the "electronic society" infrastructure against such information. The paper discusses the nature of the problem and possible approaches to its solution. To solve the problem it is proposed to use modular approach to construction of automated systems of protection against information, based on application of Data Mining methods. We consider the implementation of the system of protection against unwanted and harmful content, based on the classifier with three-level hierarchical architecture. Its experimental evaluation, which confirmed high efficiency of functioning of the system for most of the analyzed categories of web sites, are also discussed.

Keywords: eSociety · Information security · Protection against information · Data Mining · Web classification · Classifier · Information retrieval

1 Introduction

Currently, the ubiquity of information technologies in social sphere and formation of the new level of information interaction between citizens on the basis of the concept of eSociety is a rather strong trend that determines the accelerated development of all aspects of the public sphere and is a powerful factor of economic growth. The Internet and social networks, as the technical basis for eSociety, play the role of a powerful source of information that is necessary to solve many problems in social life, as they contain great amount of information available to users around the world. The access to this information is available to any person. This is an advantage for the development and implementation of the concept of eSociety in our daily life.

At the same time, despite the positive aspects of the Internet and social networks' usage within the frames of the eSociety concept, it should be noted that the huge flows and collections of data, available to be viewed and analyzed by every user of the Internet, may contain information that is undesirable or harmful for certain groups of

© Springer International Publishing AG 2017
D.A. Alexandrov et al. (Eds.): DTGS 2017, CCIS 745, pp. 170–184, 2017.
https://doi.org/10.1007/978-3-319-69784-0_15

individuals. Such information may include, for example, the information contained on the web sites of organizations that are prohibited on the territory of the Russian Federation or other countries, as well as on the web pages that distribute unlicensed content or promote violence and the use of narcotic substances.

Not less important is separating of juvenile users from information which may harm their health and development. Therefore, at present, in global information networks, along with the problem of information security, the other challenge arises: protection of users against unwanted or malicious information. The urgency of this problem causes no doubts, and the need for its fast solution increases significantly [1–4].

The aim of the research, which results are presented in this paper, was consideration of the nature of the declared problem, possible approaches to its solution, discussion of the proposed approach and the results of its experimental evaluation.

The main *theoretical contribution* of the paper is the following: (1) the justification for the existence of the problem of protection against information in eSociety and necessity to create automated systems protecting against information, intended for the solution of the problem; (2) formation of a system of efficiency indicators for systems of protection against information; (3) design, implementation and experimental evaluation of the new approach to construction of systems of protection against information.

The *novelty* of the obtained results is determined by hierarchical and integrated application of various Data Mining methods to estimate and classify heterogeneous information in the course of analyzing of web sites and social networks. The distinctive feature of the approach is the use of the classifier with three-level hierarchical architecture, based on accounting of complexity of various sources of information – text content, structural features, website's URL and others. The solution proposed in this paper allows you to create reliable systems for protection against information due to high accuracy of classification and availability of the category "unknown", the decision on access to which can be taken separately.

This paper differs from the other related papers of the authors [4–7] in several aspects: the problem of protection against information in eSociety was discussed; the architecture of the system was extended; new experiments were fulfilled and the results of experiments were improved.

Further structure of the paper is as follows. In Sect. 2 the results of analysis of the problem of protection against unwanted and harmful content are given, and the system of effectiveness indicators for the proposed protection system is substantiated. Section 3 considers various approaches to construct individual elements of the system for protection against information, and the proposed approach to its implementation is substantiated. Section 4 discusses implementation issues and experimental evaluation of the developed system. Conclusions and future research directions are given in Sect. 5.

2 Analysis of the Problem of Protection Against Information in eSociety

First of all, it should be noted that in Russia the problem of unwanted and malicious information is now being mentioned at the legislative level. In particular, this problem is reflected in the "Doctrine of information security", in the Federal law "On information, information technologies and protection of information" and in the Federal law "On protection of children from information that is harmful to their health and development". This signifies that at the state level this issue is in the focus.

At that the concept of information object in general case is rather indefinite and may include any class of entities access to which could harm the information security of the user.

Considering the current situation, these classes can include web sites or their individual pages, e-mail messages, social networks, sources of information containers for various data exchange systems (logical nodes of peer-to-peer networks, mail networks, physical hosts) and so on. The main danger to the user at the moment is presented by objects that are shared, the download of which can lead to receiving unwanted information.

Thus, in accordance with the requirements of the aforementioned laws, in formation of eSociety the organization of protection against unwanted and harmful content can be divided into two main areas: (1) protection of juveniles against inappropriate content; (2) blocking content that violates the law.

However, implementation of these activities is complicated, first of all, by large amounts of information in the Internet and, in particular, in the social networks, and by high variability of the content of the sites and complexity of the structure of these sites.

The main direction of solving the given problem, allowing to obtain high recognition quality of unwanted and harmful information, is manual assessment of web pages by experts. However, it is worth noting that often even expert conclusion on belonging of the web page to one category or another may be misleading. In addition, the performance of any expert is much lower than the growth of the number of websites and modification of information, presented on them.

However, the specificity of software systems for protection against information, aimed at ensuring certain (rather high) level of information security is that the typical user is not able to give an adequate assessment of the degree of danger himself. Thus, the role of users in such systems is significantly reduced, and the first place is taken by automated rating systems, managed by a small number of experts in the field of information security and based on the relevant sources of primary information about the information objects.

In this case, the quality of web page analysis as compared to their expert assessment could be lower, but it is obvious that automated systems can significantly increase efficiency and reduce the complexity of web site analysis [1].

The need to use automated systems to protect against unwanted and harmful content is now clearly understood by software developers, resulting in the appearance of software tools for this purpose. So, in many social networks (e.g., in the network "Vkontakte"), and global information search systems (Yandex, Google), the means of secure information retrieval are implemented. Similar functionality has domestic browser "Sputnik", which provides detection of unwanted and dangerous information as well as content filtering. In addition, there are modules for parental controls that are included into antivirus software, and fully independent decisions, ensuring fencing of juveniles from unsuitable content. More private task, which nevertheless is also connected with unwanted information, is the definition of advertising content sent to users by e-mail (anti-spam).

However, often all of these approaches demonstrate their inefficiency: compiled "black" and "white" lists do not cover all the variety of options that distinguish unwanted information. This situation is further complicated by high variability of information in the Internet, frequent appearance of new sites and rapid updates of content even within the same web page.

The difficulty of revealing of unwanted information from huge amounts of diverse, often contradictory and volatile data is due, in particular, to the constructive particularities of web resources. Usually they have complex hierarchical structure and are composed of many elements: formatted text and graphical content, software code, links to other documents, etc. That is why unwanted content is not always determined on the basis of only textual signs: often in determination of the direction of the site the information about its URL or structural features helps.

The disadvantage of systems based on predefined rules or lists is that they cannot learn on their own. However, in this situation you can use methods of machine learning (Data Mining). Then the basic idea will be in transition to the classification problem, existing in this domain, which is formulated as follows: it is required to attribute the object under study to one class out of the set of pre-known classes.

Thus, considering the aspects of functioning of automated content assessment systems, it is possible to outline functional requirements for them.

First of all, it should be noted that the calculation of the indicators, characterizing information stored on web sites, should be conducted not only in the context of the data received from the user (from the user workstation), but accounting all the rest of available information (the experience of other users; white/black/grey lists; text and graphic content; structural features; links between objects; external data provided by communities of users, experts and other companies specializing in information security) [2, 3].

Further, analysis of the information contained on the web site must be performed by centralized means of technological infrastructure that is hosted "in the cloud". The process of analyzing of a web site should begin at the fact of registration of events, initiated by the user, the consequences of which may result in risks of his information security. Finally, the speed of decision making about the information provided on the web site should be comparable at least with the speed of a standard antivirus application working on the user's workstation. The indicators, characterizing the information, stored on the web sites, are considered as a set of values (estimates) that define numerically the degree of affiliation of the web site to the set of controlled categories (Fig. 1). A grade of affiliation is ranging from 0 to 1.

To assess the effectiveness of the content assessment system we introduce into consideration relevant quantitative indicators.

To the greatest extent for this purpose the indicators that are used to assess the effectiveness of information retrieval systems, are suitable. We divide the set of all elements of the sample (the set of the analyzed web sites) into four possible groups based on relevancy of the web site and the correctness of its choice. Then we give the notation for the number of elements in each group.

We denote the number of correctly detected elements in the sample using the *TP* (true positive), and the number of correctly rejected items of the sample through *TN* (true negative). Then the number of elements not belonging to the category, but incorrectly

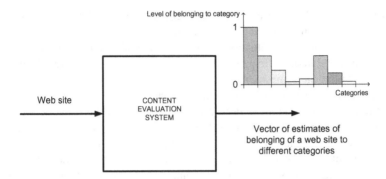

Fig. 1. The input and output of the content assessment system

assigned to it (a "false alarm" or error of the first kind) will receive the designation of *FP* (false positive), and the number of elements belonging to the category, but wrongly rejected ("skip events" or type II error) is denoted as *FN* (false negative).

Let us consider the effectiveness indicators for content assessment systems:

- *Precision, p*. This parameter is defined as the ratio of correctly classified sites of a certain category to the total number of sites that the classifier affiliated to this category. It is calculated for each category separately.
- *Recall, r*. This parameter is defined as the ratio of correctly classified sites of a certain category to the total number of sites actually belong to this category. Ii is calculated for each category separately.
- *F-measure, F*. This parameter represents the harmonic mean between precision and completeness. It is calculated for each category separately.
- *Accuracy, a*. This parameter is defined as the ratio of correctly classified sites in all categories to the total number of sites. Ii is calculated for entire test sample.

It should be noted that depending on the specific task been solved the imposed indicators have different importance for different tasks. For example, for the web pages analysis module, included in the antivirus software, the primary value belongs to high accuracy, since the large number of false positives is not allowed.

In the case of parental control the indicator of "fullness" is more important because of the need to protect children from inappropriate content, to which will be affiliated as well the sites that have doubtful information, but that are not assigned to any specific category.

3 Approach to Building of the Automated System for Protection Against Information Based on Data Mining Methods

To develop the approach for construction of automated system for protection against information, let us first examine the existing solutions that are applied to the analysis of web sites and that are implemented in known automated systems. There are solutions, which are based on verification of occurrence of pre-defined keywords and their combinations, as well as other rules that are specified, for example, using regular expressions. On their basis the decision to allow or block a website is taken. The disadvantage of this method is its low accuracy, because words can be replaced with synonyms that will lead to skipping of unwanted information, and the presence of the prohibited words that are used in "legal" context may lead to ban of access to websites not containing inappropriate content.

Another approach involves the use of the safe search mode on search sites Yandex or Google. Their main disadvantage is limited applicability. The user can go to a less popular search engine, in which this mode is not provided, or go to the unwanted web page from an external link.

Many systems use the maintenance and analysis of the "white" or "black" lists. In the first case, connecting to all sites is disallowed, except for a pre-specified white list. In the second case the blocking is carried out only when it is present in the "black list". However, both of these approaches have a significant drawback, due to the high variability of web sites. After the formation of the lists the subject of websites can change, which will lead to receiving unwanted or blocking necessary information.

The difficulty of revealing of unwanted information from huge volumes of varied, often contradictory and volatile data is caused, among other things, by particularities of web sites building. Usually they have complex hierarchical structure and are composed of many elements: formatted text and graphical content, software code, links to other documents, etc. Therefore, the unwanted information is not always determined on the basis of only textual signs. Often to determine the site orientation the information about the link (address) of the web site (URL) or its structural features helps.

The general disadvantage of the systems using predefined words, rules, or lists, is the absence of self-learning possibility. Therefore, in some systems it is proposed to use approaches based on methods of machine learning. The main objective of these methods is formulated as follows: it is required to affiliate the object under study to one of the plurality of pre-known classes. With regard to the protection against unwanted information the example of such application of machine learning methods can be functioning of a parental control system that categorizes web pages by categories and blocking those that were unwanted ("adult websites", "weapons", "drugs", etc.).

When considering the proposed approach to the construction of the automated system for protection against information we will focus on two aspects: (1) the overall architecture of the proposed classifier and (2) the mechanism of data extraction for the analysis of web pages.

As it was mentioned above, web pages are different from usual text documents by higher complexity and, above all, by the fact that they are partially structured (semi-structured) using HTML tags of markup, are linked between each other by links, contain snippets of code executable both on the server side and the client. Therefore, it is proposed to consider these aspects of web pages in the classification process.

The classifier is an essential component of the automated system of protection against information, implementing methods of Data Mining. On its basis the analytical module of the system is functioning. The peculiarity of the proposed *architecture of the classifier* is that it is, in fact, has a three-level hierarchical structure.

Figure 2 shows that within each of the web page aspects (text content, structural features, website URL and others) there are classifiers of the first level. Their number coincides with the number of categories of the classification. Each of them makes decision about affiliation of the incoming input data to its category.

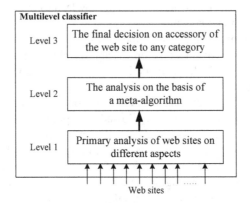

Fig. 2. The hierarchical architecture of the classifier

The results of the classifiers of the first level serve as input to the classifier of the second level – meta-algorithm (e.g., Stacking), which makes decision based on the information from the classifiers of the first level.

The results of the classifiers of the second level for each of the aspects are analyzed by the classifier of the third level, issuing the final decision on affiliation of the web page to a particular class.

This approach is modular and, consequently, allows you to easily add new aspects and categories. Moreover, each of the classification algorithms is a "black box" with inputs and outputs, allowing you to easily replace some of the algorithms by others on each of the levels.

Another advantage of this architecture is the localization of changes, as re-training may occur only for the separate classifiers. In addition, the advantage of this approach is ability to additionally train classifiers. Over time, information becomes outdated, for example, with the appearance of new types of substances in the category "drugs" the classifier trained on the old data will work worse. However, using the proposed architecture, it is possible to update individual classifiers, training them with the updated information. At that the remaining system components would not be affected.

The proposed *mechanism of extraction of data* to analyze web pages is based on analysis of the following features: textual content [4, 5]; address of location of the site in the Internet (URL); structural attributes (HTML tags) [6–8]; history of site (age of the site, country in which the site was registered, the organization providing website hosting, history of servers on which the site was placed); external sources of information ("black" or "white" lists, the responses from the search engines).

All of the above characteristics in one way or another have been used in several well-known classification methods.

Classification by text is the most widely used method, consisting of two stages. At the first stage the preparation of data with their translation into the form perceived by the classifier is performed. At this stage, removal of the markup tags, extraction of text content of web pages, stemming (i.e. the preservation of the foundations of words with dropping their endings), the exclusion of punctuation and stop words in the form of prepositions, conjunctions, pronouns, etc. are done. The second stage consists of sending the preprocessed data to one or another standard text classifier based on known Data Mining methods (Naïve Bayes, SVM, etc.).

Most of the known methods of text classification are based on dividing the sample into two parts: test and training (supervised method). The example is the SVM method [9]. More promising is the method without pre-training (unsupervised method) [10], intended to classify text with little resources requirements, and for generating training samples. In this method the document is splitted into sentences, and then each sentence is mapped to a category based on pre-prepared keywords' lists and metrics of similarity of sentences.

To define spam the method of categorization that is based on the analysis of the total number of words on the page, average word length, affiliation of the web page to the set of most frequent words and statistics of n-grams (combinations of n symbols) is successfully used [11].

Alternative in text classification is the method in which they move from the consideration of documents as sets of words to the analysis of their values, which are taken from lexical databases. However, experiments have shown that although consideration of the meaning of words slightly increases the value of accuracy, it does not lead to significant improvement in the accuracy and completeness of the classification [12].

Text classification may not be considered sufficient. It does not take into account the structural features of web pages. HTML document is usually linked by links to other documents and can contain pictures and other non-text elements. In addition, the difficulty may appear from categories that have similar text content, but differ in their structure (for example, "blogs", "forums", "chats").

So the method based on the analysis of URL got its development. It is based on the assumption that a web page will rarely be visited if its address does not reflect in some way its topic [13]. One way to do this is to break the URL into its component parts to be analyzed later. This approach has been successfully used to protect against phishing sites [14]. Each URL fragment is represented as a two dimensional vector containing the fragment and its position, which are then fed to the input of a trained classifier.

Another way is to use the length of the host name and that of the entire URL, calculate the number of different symbols in it (e.g., dots) and analyze the fragments of the URL between these symbols. At that the characteristics based on information about the host (geographical features, date of registration, the value of the maximum period of time for which a packet can exist before his disappearance (TTL), etc.) are used. All these attributes are the input to the standard classifier using Data Mining techniques (Naïve Bayess, SVM, Logistic Regression, Decision Trees) [15].

One option to further split the URL into fragments is usage of entropy. This approach allows you to split into component parts the domain names in which some words are merged together. The test partitioning, which has the smallest entropy among the rest, will be the most likely new fragment [16]. Additionally, you can use the analysis of sequences of n-grams for which the frequency of occurrences is calculated [17]. This method is able to show good results of categorization in solving specific problems ("spam"/"mail", "phishing"/"benign"), but in the general case, with arbitrary number and composition of categories, the quality of the classification decreases. The main reason is that not always the page address in the Internet coincides with its contents.

Thus, to identify categories based on structural characteristics, it is necessary to look for other methods, one of which may be usage of information about the HTML tags of the website. Here also there are different approaches to analysis. An important source can be the information contained in such tags as <title> or <meta>, which, along with the textual content of web pages, have been extracted by the special parser [18, 19]. On the other hand, there are methods based on counting the number of tags on the page [20].

Thus, the construction of automated system for protection against information should be done on the basis of the following principles: (1) extraction of information that is most relevant to the analysis of the information content of the web site out of all available data; (2) search for most important external sources of information for performing analysis; (3) integrating heterogeneous information from multiple sources into general representation of the web site; (4) minimizing the load on the hosts of end users at information collecting; (5) counteraction to intentional and accidental distortions (noises) in information, received from external sources; (6) search for effective methods of identifying the web pages' categories with desired values of performance, computational complexity and accuracy of decision making.

A possible implementation of the automated system of protection against information on the back-end server (servers) can be based on combination of the following two approaches: (1) use of robots-spiders, evaluating the sites to the possible extent; (2) usage of the module that evaluates each requested page at the user's requests.

On the client side (front-end) of the system it is expected to use additional analysis module. This module is required in the case of a disconnection with the server, normally it is disabled. In addition, for greater system reliability and flexibility it is possible to conduct a simple keyword search.

The advantages of this approach are its high performance (additional costs other than possible equipment costs are not required), protection against sites that do not hide their affiliation to any category, as well as the ability to assess all of the requested sites. The disadvantages include: the possibility of cheating the system (creating a website in such a way that the automatic system gives incorrect assessment); false positives; the need to use powerful computing equipment at large number of requests to the sites; aging of assessment (in the case of automated searching and compiling black and white lists).

It is expected that this system will improve the overall quality of information on the Internet (by eliminating sites containing information prohibited by law) and will protect end users against inappropriate content (due to blocking of web sites that are unacceptable to certain groups of users).

4 Implementation and Experimental Evaluation of the System for Protection Against Information for eSociety

Based on the analysis of possible ways of constructing the automated system of protection against information for eSociety, it was decided to present its software infrastructure as a set of software modules with clearly defined inputs and outputs, consistent work of which will provide the whole process of classification of web sites.

The particularities of this infrastructure are as follows [7]: (1) built-in analytical module, combining different algorithms and methods of machine learning that will not only follow preset rules, but will train itself; (2) use of various aspects of web pages (text content, structural features, URL); (3) modularity of structure.

In the implemented software prototype of this infrastructure at the initial stage the download from the Internet of categorized lists of websites is performed. We used the following data sources: URLBlacklist[1], Shalla's Blacklist[2] and DMOZ[3]. Each of them has its own data format. For example, URLBlacklist consists of a set of folders whose names correspond to the classification categories, and within each of them there is a file called domains, containing the URL of the specific web sites that belong to this category. Shalla's Blacklist has a similar structure, however, allows presence of nested subfolders. DMOZ has a hierarchical structure and is provided as two XML files, one of which contains the list of all available categories and subcategories, and the second is the URL of websites, corresponding to these categories.

After the end of download the content of the list is extracted and placed into the database. Then according to the available URLs of websites the downloads of their HTML representation is done.

After loading from the saved HTML representation, different characteristics, used in the analysis process, are extracted. Sources for these characteristics are the following aspects of web pages: textual (the full text of web pages and the text extracted from the HTML tags, for example, the contents of the <meta> tag); structural (statistics of HTML tags); the URL of the page (for subsequent analysis of n-grams).

Other aspects that may be analyzed (their analysis is one of directions for future work) are: images; information from WHOIS servers that allow you to retrieve registration information about the owners of domain names and IP addresses as well as other information; dynamic content generated on the page using JavaScript.

Once all data is collected, their cleaning is performed. In particular, we delete from the received text of web pages all characters except spaces and letters of the alphabet, which are then converted to lower case. After cleaning, the stage of building the dictionary and the transformation of characteristics into formats that are perceived by specialized software for data analysis. RapidMiner[4] is the specialized tool used in this research. In the process of its work it performs building of the models and training of

---

[1] http://urlblacklist.com.

[2] http://www.shallalist.de.

[3] https://www.dmoz.org.

[4] https://rapidminer.com.

the classifiers from the first to the third levels. The reports, got on the results of the classification of web pages, are then displayed in Microsoft Excel format.

The following limitations were set on source data used for training the system and its operation testing:

1. Length of the main text of the web pages after the cleaning procedure needs to be in the range of from 500 to 5000 bytes. This value, established experimentally, allows to exclude the sites with too short content from sampling (which is usually not classified, for example, it may be a message prompting you to enable JavaScript or update Flash Player) and too large volume sites (which will contain words of all categories, which will reduce the quality of training).
2. The sample included only those web pages whose primary language is English. This restriction is due to the peculiarities of the Porter's lexical analyzer (stemmer) [21], which works best with English words.

In accordance with the restrictions imposed there were allocated two sets of data. The first of them included the following categories: "Sites for adults" (adult), "Alcohol" (alcohol), "Sites about medicine" (medical) and "Sites about religion" (religion), while into the second set there were added "Online game" (gamesonline), "Hunting" (hunting) and "Music" (music). They all can be used in the process of protecting juveniles against inappropriate content and counteract the spread of unlicensed content.

In addition to these sites, in each of the sets there was also additionally introduced category, indicating an unknown result, received the name "Unknown". The number of web pages in each dataset was taken the same and equal to 1200.

The results of experimental evaluation of the proposed approach to classification of web sites with respect to these two selected datasets are shown in Figs. 3 and 4.

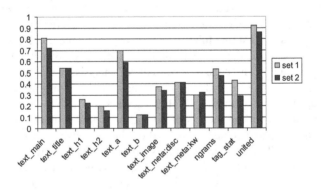

Fig. 3. Evaluation of "accuracy" on the web sites' datasets

Figure 3 presents the experimental evaluation of "accuracy" for each dataset in the context of various analyzed classification criteria. The figure shows that the "accuracy" of the classifiers reaches the greatest values at the analysis of the main text (81.7% and 73.0% for the first and second set, respectively). The classifier that focuses on content analysis of references is on the second place (70.7% and 58.6%).

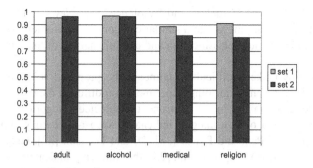

Fig. 4. Evaluation of F-measure on datasets from web sites

These results show that the analysis of the specifics of web documents has fairly high efficiency. Internet resources are usually linked with other sites of similar subjects, therefore, the accounting for such specificity is the factor that distinguishes the classification of web pages classification from plain text documents.

Other features with high values of accuracy are: the text from the tag <title> and n-grams. For the first dataset the results are 53.6% and 53.6%, respectively, and for the second dataset – 53.6% and 47.2%, respectively.

Figure 3 also shows the generalized assessment of "accuracy". We can see that for both datasets the proposed approach demonstrates quite high "accuracy". During the experiments on the first dataset it is equal to 92.7%, and for the second – 86.1%. For the second dataset this value was less because it has more categories (7 vs. 4) that makes classification more difficult.

Figure 4 presents the results of experimental evaluation in terms of F-measure, that is a combined measure of accuracy and completeness.

The figure shows that the proposed approach is generally characterized by high value of F-measure. The exceptions are the sites in the "Medicine" category for the first dataset and the category "Religion" for the second. For these categories in the future we plan to add classifiers based on the new dimensions that will improve the effectiveness of the system of protection information.

Thus, the experiments show that the joint analysis of various characteristics allows to achieve high values in accuracy and completeness of the classification, due to the unification and combination of classifiers that analyze their criteria. As a result, the system for protection against information sufficiently rarely affiliates websites to unknown (high completeness), and the number of false positives is low enough (high precision).

Despite all the advantages, the proposed approach has its drawbacks. Thus, the quality of classification depends very much on the quality of the training sample. At the same time, since training samples are usually formed by experts, these samples very much depend on the experts' point of view on the belonging of the sites to categories. For example, the same site can be classified as "Drugs", "Medicine", "Forum", etc. This disadvantage can be eliminated by increasing the volume of training samples, but then there is a problem with the creation of such samples. In addition, the quality of the classification depends on the initial choice of the category list. For example, if you select certain categories of "Cruelty" and "Violence", or "News" and "Weapons," a frequent mistake is placing the site in a similar category. This problem can be partially eliminated by applying multi-classification and careful analysis of the semantic content of categories.

These problems make it difficult to compare the proposed solution with similar approaches, because when performing experiments on different data, the quality of the classification depends on the initial data and the selected categories. Therefore, the comparison was carried out by integral indicators, such as accuracy and F-measure. Thus, in the papers of Patil and Pawar [18], Qi and Davison [22], Chakrabarti et al. [23], Calado et al. [24], and Liparas et al. [25], the following indicators of the accuracy of the classification of sites were given: 89.0, 91.4, 75.0, 81.6% and 86.2%, respectively. The values obtained with the proposed approach approximately correspond to or exceed these results (92.7% for 5 and 86.1% for 7 categories). At the same time, the quality of classification by certain categories reached 95%. In addition, it is important to note that those sites that were not properly classified were often labeled as "Unknown". The percentage of direct errors (i.e., false positives and false negatives attributing the site to the wrong category) did not exceed 4% and 7%, respectively. Mangai et al. [26] shows the values of F-measures for different parameters of the classification algorithms. The presented results range from 91 to 96%, which corresponds to the results obtained in our paper.

5   Conclusion

In this paper it is shown that protection against unwanted and harmful content in eSociety is a rather big problem, the main focus of solving of which can be to create and use automated systems capable of performing classification of websites according to different characteristics using Data Mining methods. The proposed approach to creation of the classifier of web sites implements the three-level hierarchical architecture. The classifier allows to add easily new categories and to replace algorithms on each of levels. Experimental evaluation of the developed prototype of the system for protection against information showed sufficiently high values of indicators of efficiency of classification for different categories of websites. These results show that the proposed in this paper approach can be used in the systems for protection against information within the concept of eSociety. At the same time, such systems can be used by Internet providers to protect end users (by blocking or allowing viewing of information in the browser) and public organizations (to search for unwanted information on the Internet and build lists of forbidden sites on the territory of the Russian Federation). We should highlight the development of decision making mechanisms based on other types of features that characterize web sites (information about domain, links between sites, etc.) as our future research directions.

Acknowledgements. This research is being supported by the grant of RSF#15-11-30029 in SPIIRAS.

References

1. Qi, X., Davison, B.D.: Web page classification: features and algorithms. ACM Comput. Surv. **41**(2), 12 (2009). Article 12. doi:10.1145/1459352.1459357
2. Dumais, S., Platt, J., Heckermann, D., Sahami M.: Inductive learning algorithms and representations for text categorization. In: Proceedings of 7th International Conference on Information and Knowledge Management, pp. 148–155. ACM, New York (1998). doi:10.1145/288627.288651
3. Resnick, P., Zeckhauser, R., Friedman, E., Kuwabara, K.: Reputation systems. Commun. ACM **43**(12), 45–48 (2000). doi:10.1145/355112.355122
4. Kotenko, I., Chechulin, A., Shorov, A., Komashinsky, D.: Analysis and evaluation of web pages classification techniques for inappropriate content blocking. In: Advances in Data Mining: Applications and Theoretical Aspects. In: Proceedings of 14th Industrial Conference, ICDM 2014, St. Petersburg, Russia, 16–20 July 2014, pp. 39–54 (2014). doi:10.1007/978-3-319-08976-8
5. Kotenko, I., Chechulin, A., Komashinsky, D.: Evaluation of text classification techniques for inappropriate web content blocking. In: 2015 IEEE 8th International Conference on Intelligent Data Acquisition and Advanced Computing Systems: Technology and Applications (IDAACS), pp. 412–417. IEEE Press, New York (2015). doi:10.1109/IDAACS.2015.7340769
6. Novozhilov, D., Kotenko, I., Chechulin, A.: Improving the categorization of web sites by analysis of HTML-tags statistics to block inappropriate content. In: Novais, P., Camacho, D., Analide, C., El Fallah Seghrouchni, A., Badica, C. (eds.) Intelligent Distributed Computing IX. SCI, vol. 616, pp. 257–263. Springer, Cham (2016). doi:10.1007/978-3-319-25017-5_24
7. Kotenko, I., Chechulin, A., Komashinsky, D.: Categorization of web pages for protection against inappropriate content in the internet. Int. J. Internet Protocol Technol. (JIPT) **10**(1), 61–71 (2017). doi:10.1504/IJIPT.2017.10003851
8. Elsas, J., Efron, M.: HTML tag based metrics for use in web page type classification. In: American Society for Information Science and Technology Annual Meeting. Providence, Rhode Island, USA (2004)
9. Joachims, T.: Text categorization with support vector machines: learning with many relevant features. In: 10th European Conference on Machine Learning, pp. 137–142 (1998). doi:10.1007/BFb0026683
10. Ko, Y., Seo, J.: Automatic text categorization by unsupervised learning. In: 18th Conference on Computational Linguistics, pp. 453–459 (2000). doi:10.3115/990820.990886
11. Ntoulas, A., Najork, M., Manasse, M., Fetterly, D.: Detecting spam web pages through content analysis. In: 15th International World Wide Web Conference (WWW), pp. 83–92 (2006)
12. Kehagias, A., Petridis, V., Kaburlasos, V.G., Fragkou, P.: A comparison of word- and sense-based text categorization using several classification algorithms. J. Intell. Inf. Syst. **21**(3), 227–247 (2003). doi:10.1023/A:1025554732352
13. Attardi, G., Gulli, A., Sebastiani, F.: Automatic web page categorization by link and context analysis. In: 1st European Symposium on Telematics, Hypermedia and Artificial Intelligence, pp. 105–119 (1999)
14. Khonji, M., Iraqi, Y., Jones, A.: Enhancing phishing e-mail classifiers: a lexical URL analysis approach. Int. J. Inf. Secur. Res. **6**, 236–245 (2012)

15. Ma, J., Saul, L.K., Savage, S., Voelker, G.M.: Beyond blacklists: learning to detect malicious web sites from suspicious URLs. In: Proceedings of 15th ACM SIGKDD international conference on Knowledge discovery and data mining (KDD 2009), pp. 1245–1254. ACM, New York (2009). doi:10.1145/1557019.1557153

16. Kan, M.-Y., Thi, H.O.N.: Fast webpage classification using URL features. In: Proceedings of 14th ACM International Conference on Information and Knowledge Management (CIKM 2005), pp. 325–326. ACM, New York (2005). doi:10.1145/1099554.1099649

17. Geide, M.: N-gram character sequence analysis of benign vs. malicious domains/URLs. http://analysis-manifold.com/ngram_whitepaper.pdf

18. Patil, A.S., Pawar, B.V.: Automated classification of web sites using naive Bayesian algorithm. In: Proceedings of International MultiConference of Engineers and Computer Scientists, pp. 466–470 (2012)

19. Riboni, D.: Feature selection for web page classification. In: Proceedings of Workshop on Web Content Mapping: A Challenge to ICT, pp. 121–128 (2002)

20. Meshkizadeh, S., Masoud-Rahmani, A.: Webpage classification based on compound of using HTML features & URL features and features of sibling pages. Int. J. Adv. Comput. Technol. 2(4), 36–46 (2010)

21. Porter, M.F.: An algorithm for suffix stripping. Program 14(3), 130–137 (1980)

22. Qi, X., Davison, B.D.: Knowing a web page by the company it keeps. Proceedings of CIKM 2006, 228–237 (2006)

23. Chakrabarti, S., Dom, B., Agrawal, R., Raghavan, P.: Scalable feature selection, classification and signature generation for organizing large text databases into hierarchical topic taxonomies. Int. J. Very Large Data Bases 7(3), 163–178 (1998)

24. Calado, P., Cristo, M., Moura, E., Ziviani, N., Ribeiro-Neto, B., Goncalves, M.A.: Combining link-based and content-based methods for web document classification. In: Proceedings of CIKM 2003, New York, USA, pp. 394–401 (2003)

25. Liparas, D., HaCohen-Kerner, Y., Moumtzidou. A., Vrochidis, S., Kompatsiaris, I.: News articles classification using random forests and weighted multimodal features. In: Proceedings of 7th Information Retrieval Facility Conference (IRFC 2014), Copenhagen, Denmark, pp. 63–75 (2014)

26. Mangai, J.A., Wagle, S.M., Kumar, V.S.: A novel web page classification model using an improved k nearest neighbor algorithm. In: Proceedings of 3rd International Conference on Intelligent Computational Systems (ICICS 2013), Singapore, pp. 49–53 (2013)

Assessing Subjective Quality of Web Interaction with Neural Network as Context of Use Model

Maxim Bakaev[(⊠)], Vladimir Khvorostov, and Tatiana Laricheva

Novosibirsk State Technical University, Novosibirsk, Russia
{bakaev,xvorostov}@corp.nstu.ru, tatka_all1994@mail.ru

Abstract. Despite certain advances in automation of software quality assurance, testing and debugging remain the most laborious activities in the software development cycle. Evaluation of web interaction quality is still largely performed with traditional human effort-intensive methods, particularly due to the inevitable association of website usability with particular contexts of use, target users, tasks, etc. We believe that testing automation in this field may ultimately lead to better online experience for all and are important in promoting e-society development. We propose to employ artificial neural networks to predict website users' subjective impressions, whose importance is widely recognized but that are somehow overshadowed by the effectiveness and efficiency dimensions. We justify the structure of the network, with the input layer reflecting context of use, while the output layer consisting of the subjective evaluation scales (*Beautiful, Evident, Fun, Trustworthy,* and *Usable*). The experimental session with 82 users and 21 university websites was undertaken to collect the evaluation data for the network training. Finally, we verify the validity of the model by comparing it to a certain baseline, analyze the importance of the input factors, and provide recommendations for future evaluations-collecting sessions.

Keywords: User satisfaction · Methods for software analysis · Usability engineering · Testing automation

1 Introduction

As e-society develops, the swift advance of web-based software brought a new dimension to the classic software engineering process, with the extreme growth in the number of websites, the pressure for rapid development, the possibility of frequent updates, etc. At the dawn of the online era, most of web services and applications had relatively low complexity and were developed by small and/or inexperienced teams. This has clearly changed, as websites are becoming not only numerous and ubiquitous, but also complex, as basically any software is turning into web software. The special feature of web interfaces that shape the modern e-society is that their users are by and large impatient novices: web users are experienced with neither website in particular, and they leave easily, unless their very first impressions of the website are positive and pleasant ones. Let us then recount which popular web software quality assurance (QA) techniques currently address this issue and if their automation is done.

© Springer International Publishing AG 2017
D.A. Alexandrov et al. (Eds.): DTGS 2017, CCIS 745, pp. 185–195, 2017.
https://doi.org/10.1007/978-3-319-69784-0_16

Testing visual appearance of a page and ensuring its reasonable correspondence to the design prototype is yet another type of testing, specific for the web. In principle, screenshots of the page rendered in various browsers can be auto-compared to design mockups, but in practice this is rarely done, due to complexity and ambiguity of image analysis tasks. In contrast, **load testing** is naturally automatable, since high number of relatively unsophisticated requests can be generated by a dedicated tool straightforwardly and quickly, unlike by manual workforce. As for **usability and interaction quality testing** automation, it does use approaches and tools of the functional-, visual appearance-, and load testing – but to a limited coverage. Indeed, a usable application **necessarily** corresponds to the functional and design specifications and responds promptly, but this isn't **sufficient** for its high usability. Meanwhile, the advance of web-based software is due not just to its universal availability, maintainability, and other similar factors, but is also associated with the technological development and standardization of web interfaces.

In contrast to most other software quality attributes, such as reliability, maintainability, etc. [1], interaction quality is **relative** to a context of use (see e.g. the ISO 9241-11 1998 specification for usability), which obviously thwarts attempts towards its testing automation. It is not by chance that existing techniques are mostly able to assess user- and task-independent quality aspects, such as e.g. validating correctness of HTML code or its correspondence to accessibility guidelines [2], but not attributes like learnability (being easy to grasp and start using a product), attractiveness, satisfaction, etc. Although there remains certain conceptual ambiguity both in literature and in practical QA in respect to usability (see our review in [3]), its three commonly recognized dimensions are identified as **effectiveness, efficiency,** and **satisfaction**. The subjective dimension of satisfaction is still somehow disfavored compared to the other two, even though the role of aesthetic impression, trust, pleasure, etc. is widely recognized for websites' success. Also, for better or for worse, qualitative usability evaluations prevail, understandably hindering automation and leading to unavoidable involvement of costly usability engineers, and the results depend heavily of their expertise level. Meanwhile, employment of real users, experts or specialists is not always the most effective way, especially if evaluations are needed for a great number of website versions. For example, in web engineering based on evolutionary algorithms, repeated assessment of the candidate solutions' quality would be unfeasible through interactive means only (i.e. by humans), and introduction of certain computable fitness function representing the environment (i.e. context of use) is essential [4].

So, in our paper we consider the problem of automated assessment of web interaction subjective quality – i.e. predicting user's subjective evaluation of a website **without an actual user**. Among the advantages of automated evaluation of website usability the following ones are commonly noted [5]: lower costs, reduction of human expertise needed, better consistency and coverage, emerging capabilities to predict losses from usability problems and to promptly evaluate different design versions, etc. Thus we believe that advances in this field may ultimately lead to better online experience for all and are important in promoting e-society development. Section 2 is dedicated to general overview of web usability evaluation and assessment methods, with special focus on artificial neural networks (NN), which is the method we apply in our current work. Particularly, we explain about potential feasibility of the method and justify the structure of the network, with the input layer reflecting context of use, while the output layer consisting of popular subjective evaluation scales. In Sect. 3, we describe how we collected the evaluations and then constructed and trained the network. We also verify the validity of the model by comparing it to a baseline and analyze the importance of the input factors, providing recommendations for scheming future evaluation-collecting sessions.

2   Methods

Before anything else, we'd like to note that since there seems to be little consensus in conceptual application of "quality evaluation" and "quality assessment" terms, we are going to use them as close synonyms, the former rather relating to approximate values and only certain aspects of quality, while the latter being more quantitative and involving more rigorous process. Also, we equal "interaction quality" to "usability" in the assumption that functional requirements are met and the **effectiveness** dimension of the latter is ensured. In the current section, we provide overview of existing methods and tools for web usability assessment and engineering, and then describe the proposed neural network-based approach.

2.1   Traditional and Automated Web Interaction Quality Assessment

Though it is said that "Each method [for assessing usability]... is unique, and relies heavily on the skills and knowledge of evaluators" [6], the set of web usability evaluation methods universally includes the following kit [3]:

- **User observation** – may be explicit, i.e. watching real users performing real tasks in a real context, or implicit, such as analyzing logs or even videos of user behavior on a website. Major web analytics services (Yandex.Metrica, Google Analytics, etc.) increasingly provide the means for tracking and analyzing user interactions with respect to usability.
- **Usability testing** – while both users and tasks are "replicated" to match the real ones, the method is consistently listed among the most effective methods in usability engineering. Lately, as broadband channels became capable of streaming video in real time, numerous web services for performing remote usability testing emerged (Userlytics, OpenHallway, etc.), many of which also aid in recruiting participants and generally allow saving costs and time.
- **Surveys and inspections** – either with real users (e.g. with a feedback form) or with usability experts (heuristic evaluation), but without guaranteed fulfillment of the actual tasks. Nowadays, free or freemium services such as Usabilityhub, Usabilla, or Askusers.ru aid in specifying usability-related questions and obtaining the answers from users. Heuristic evaluation can be semi-automated via specifying checklists of design guidelines/heuristics and even auto-validating those that are user- and task-independent.

The interest towards automating web interaction quality assessment increased in the 2000s [7], together with dramatic growth of the online economy and the number of websites. Currently, the respective approaches may be divided into the following major groups (see more detailed review in [3]), summarized as shown in Table 1:

Table 1. Approaches towards automated web interaction quality assessment

Approach	Users, website, interaction	Limitations
Interaction-based	Real or representative users Real or prototype website (dynamic) Real interaction (reflected in logs)	In scope – mostly "owned" websites In pace – enough users must visit In disservice – potential losses from poor quality
Metric-based	No users Real website (static) No interaction (code or design analysis)	In generalization – metrics and their weights are specific to use context In expertise – may need human assessors/annotators
Model-based	Model or simulated users Model, prototype, or real website Simulated interaction, analysis of other interactions' data	In resources – collected data, up-to-date models, computational powers In knowledge – models must be created and trained

- **Interaction-based** ones use data obtained from real or test interactions with the assessed website. These may involve analysis of mouse actions, keyboard inputs, "optimality" of user paths on website, detection of "usability threats" [8], etc.
- **Metric-based** – rely on operational website characteristics that presumably reflect its usability. These are generally extracted from available website source code or design [9], with subsequent quantitative evaluations or comparisons against "good practices" – established design guidelines (see e.g. [2] or [7]).
- **Model-based** – seek to obtain usability evaluations from models (mainly Domain, User, and Tasks [10]) as well as through general knowledge about human behavior and web technologies [11].

Thus, no single method or tool is the ultimate solution (lack of the universally accepted operationalization of usability surely adds to this as well), so combining them often yields better results, particularly in terms of ROI. The hybrid approaches often rely on AI and machine learning methods, which may include real-time processing of interaction data (including eye-tracking or brainwave analysis), model-based evolutionary approaches [12], usability models trained with data obtained from both interaction and surveys [13], and so on. The possible outcome ranges from merely the assessed quality value to identification of potential usability problems [8], to linking to relevant design guidelines [14], to even on-the-fly augmentation (re-generation) of the interface [15]. So, in our current work we are considering the application of artificial neural networks, which are generally recognized as a promising method in software testing [16], to assess subjective quality of web interaction.

2.2   Neural Network-Based Web Interaction Quality Assessment

Basically, a NN is a sophisticated way of specifying a function, and they are naturally used in increasingly popular evolutionary algorithms to specify fitness function that evaluates the quality of the candidate solutions, at least preliminarily [17]. NNs also have very reasonable computational effectiveness compared to other AI or statistical methods and are self-adapting, which allows accommodating the problem of ever-changing software requirements [18]. NNs are first trained and then tested on real data, attempting to generalize the obtained knowledge in classification, prediction, decision-making, etc. The available dataset is generally partitioned into training, testing, and holdout samples, where the latter is used to assess the constructed network – estimate the predictive ability of the model. The network performance is estimated via percentage of incorrect predictions (for categorical outputs) or relative error that is calculated as sum-of-squares relative to the mean model (the "null" hypothesis).

Neural networks have long history in software testing automation, but they generally focus on functional requirements. A notable "social" exception is the works applying the popular Kansei Engineering method in web design, which establish connections between design factors (input neurons) and users' subjective evaluations per emotional scales (output neurons) [9, 19]. However, this "emotional engineering" has no emphasis on user interaction, so for our purposes, i.e. prediction of web interaction subjective quality, it makes more sense to have quality attributes as output neurons. The input, since usability is an "emergent property of usage" [6], should necessarily include factors of use context – i.e. User, Platform, and Environment attributes. The final consideration is the diversity of input data that is essential for proper NN training [16] and thus its ultimate feasibility for the quality prediction, so the input factors' importance should be studied to better design future data collection sessions.

In our current work, we are going to use websites from a single domain and a relatively uniform target user group. So, the proposed structure of the NN input is the following:

- **User-related** factors: age, gender, and language/cultural group. The selection of the factors is based on general knowledge of important user attributes. We did not include the user experience factor, since (a) it's hard to identify unambiguously, and (b) it would rather define a separate target user group in our settings.
- **Platform-related** factors: website country group, number of website sections (major chapters), Flesch-Kincaid Grade Level (as assessed by https://readability-score.com), and number of errors plus warnings (reported for a website by https://validator.w3.org code validator).
- **Environment-related** factors: page load time, global rank in terms of visitors, and bounce rate (all of these provided by http://alexa.com).

The NN output is the following evaluation scales representing popular dimensions of subjective interaction quality: *Beautiful, Evident, Fun, Trustworthy*, and *Usable*. In the following section we describe the experimental research that we undertook to collect data, create and train the NN, and estimate the accuracy of the model.

3   Experimental Results

3.1   The Experimental Setup

For the assessment, we employed 21 websites, all relating to a single fixed domain –
Career and Education: 11 websites of German universities and 10 of Russian ones (for
both groups, English versions were used), with sufficiently diverse designs with respect
to layout, colors, images, etc. The website country factor was assigned two possible
levels: German and Russian. The evaluators were 82 students from a German and a
Russian university, virtually all of them majoring in Computer Science/Informatics, but
the level of the program, i.e. Bachelor or Master, was not included as an input factor.
More detailed data on the participants are presented in Table 2.

Table 2. The data on the two user groups in the experiment

Total number of participants		German users	Russian users
		40	42
Gender	Male	90%	71.4%
	Female	10%	28.6%
Program	Bachelor	35%	54.8%
	Master	65%	45.2%
Age	Range	19–33	20–28
	Mean	24.5	21.7
	SD	3.19	0.89
Native language	Common	German: 75%	Russian: 90.5%
	Others	25%	9.5%

The language group of the participants was assigned 3 levels: German, Russian and
Other (Chinese, Arabic, Turkish, Yakut, Mongolian, or Kazakh). The experiment was
performed at the universities' computer rooms in several sessions, with participants
using diverse equipment to evaluate the websites through specially developed web
software (http://ks.khvorostov.ru). Each user was asked to evaluate 10 websites randomly selected from the 21 and presented in random order, by the five subjective
scales, with values for each ranging from 1 (worst) to 7 (best).

3.2   Descriptive Statistics

In total, data sets for 820 full evaluations of websites were recorded in the experimental
software database. The mean evaluations with standard deviations per the scales are
presented in Table 3 (SPSS software was used for statistical analysis and construction
of the NN). We applied ANOVA to assess statistical significance of differences
between evaluations by the two user groups – the significant ones at $\alpha = .06$ are
marked in bold, while the p-values are provided in the respective column. In Table 4
we present pair-wise Pearson correlations between the user evaluations per the subjective quality scales – all correlations are significant ($p < 0.001$).

Table 3. Mean (SD) evaluations per the scales for the two user groups

Scale	German users	Russian users	Difference
Beautiful	3.83 (0.59)	4.10 (0.98)	
Trustworthy	**4.10** (0.37)	**4.53** (0.76)	p = 0.058
Fun	**3.54** (0.50)	**4.20** (0.97)	p = 0.025
Evident	**3.79** (0.27)	**4.60** (0.66)	p < 0.001
Usable	**3.78** (0.36)	**4.52** (0.79)	p = 0.003

Table 4. Correlations between the subjective quality scales

Scales	Beautiful	Trustworthy	Fun	Evident	Usable
Beautiful	1	0.670	0.767	0.563	0.605
Trustworthy		1	0.673	0.648	0.675
Fun			1	0.638	0.661
Evident				1	0.813
Usable					1

More complete description of the data can be found in the relevant technical report [20].

3.3   The Neural Network

The neural network was constructed in SPSS with the following settings: *Multilayer Perceptron*, 1 hidden layer with 10 neurons (half of the sum neurons of input layer and output layer), optimization algorithm – *gradient descent*, activation functions – *sigmoid* for the hidden layer and *identity* – for output layer. The partition of the data was 80% for training data, 10% – test, 10% – holdout (81 evaluations). We transformed the output scales from Ordinal to Scale, since we were interested in average predicted evaluations rather than their exact values. The average overall relative errors for the resulting NN model are presented in Table 5.

Table 5. Average overall relative errors for the subjective quality scales

Scale	Error
Beautiful	0.656
Fun	0.707
Evident	0.762
Trustworthy	0.786
Usable	0.792
Model	**0.737**

The average overall relative error value of 0.737 does not allow us to conclude that the constructed NN model is by all means good in predicting subjective evaluations of users. The errors are quite diverse for different scales, and seemingly the model better predicts impressions for the scales that users understand clearer: compare 0.656 for *Beautiful* and 0.707 for *Fun*, quite common terms, versus 0.786 for *Trustworthy* and 0.792 for *Usable*, which are much more specialized. This highlights again the necessity to pay close attention to exact names of the subjective scales (the fact known well in Kansei Engineering) and calls for the use of simpler and less ambiguous terms.

As a baseline for the NN-induced assessment accuracy, we'd like to use the data and the algorithm from one of our previous works [21], in which we employed a guideline-based method for website quality evaluation, with 24 users and 6 e-commerce websites. The subjective quality values assessed with the proposed fuzzy relations algorithm based on correspondence to guidelines and the actual user evaluations obtained via usability testing sessions are presented for comparison in Table 6.

Table 6. Assessed and evaluated subjective interaction quality for the websites

Website id	Website description	Assessed quality	User evaluation
#1	A web forum for pensioners	64.97%	62.99%
#2	A non-state pension fund	77.01%	66.07%
#3	A business education center	65.28%	82.32%
#4	An online medical shop	62.35%	72.95%
#5	A web development company	78.26%	74.62%
#6	An educational website for seniors	88.03%	87.50%
Average:		72.65%	74.41%

The correlation between the quality values assessed by the algorithm and evaluated by users is thus relatively low, at 0.448, but we would also like to obtain the relative errors for the comparison. In calculating the error, as the null model we propose to use the average value of assessed quality, since users are known to be often biased in their evaluations and the "real null" of 50%, i.e. the truly average value between the worst and the best value in the scale, is rarely reported in studies. The relative error value calculated this way equals to 1.066, which is considerably worse than the 0.737 we got for the NN model. We'd like to note, however, that this example is only given as an illustrative baseline, but not to actually assess quality of any websites, since the number of employed users, guidelines and websites was too low, and the training set in that research was not different from the assessed set of websites. In Table 7 we present the results of the importance analysis for the independent variables (inputs).

We can see that the factors related to *User*, *Platform*, and *Environment* dimensions of the use context are quite mixed in terms of their importance. Still, some potentially useful recommendations could be made for future evaluation sessions (within the considered domain of *Career and Education*):

- When selecting users, make sure that age diversity is maintained in the sample, but it's hardly necessary to represent both genders, since the latter factor was not important with respect to the evaluations provided.

Table 7. The independent variables' (factors') importance

Factor	Importance	Normalized importance
Flesch-Kincaid grade level	0.177	100.0%
User age	0.161	90.9%
Alexa bounce rate	0.135	75.9%
Page load time	0.130	73.0%
Website group	0.109	61.4%
Errors + Warnings	0.105	59.4%
User language group	0.069	39.0%
Alexa global rank	0.054	30.6%
Number of sections	0.044	24.6%
User gender	0.016	8.8%

- For cross-cultural generalization to be feasible, it is important to employ websites from different countries and users of different cultures.
- The employed websites don't have to be different in scale (reflected as the number of sections and number of visitors in our experiment), but the diversity of content (grade level) and of technical quality (response speed, code validity) should be maintained.

4   Conclusions

Web interfaces continue to gain popularity in software engineering and their development and testing constitute a very significant share in modern web projects – in terms of not just website design, but the whole web interaction quality assurance. Analysis and testing automation, which is widely recognized as very much desirable, in this field implies assessing usability without users or experts, since though websites are abundant, human effort and time are not. In our paper, we explored capabilities of an artificial neural network in predicting subjective evaluations of a website, within a fixed domain (university websites) and target user group (students). For that, we conducted an experimental session with 82 users and 21 websites, collecting 820 full evaluations and using them to train the NN (80%) and estimate the predictive ability of the model.

The relative errors (average 0.737) suggest moderate predictive potential of the model, which however was better that the fuzzy relations algorithm from one of our previous works used as a baseline for comparison [21]. The "common-sense" subjective evaluation scales (*Beautiful* and *Fun*) had considerably lower errors compared to more complex and specialized ones (*Usable* and *Trustworthy*). So, one may be recommended to ensure that the employed adjectives are clear and unambiguous for the users. The analysis we performed with the context of use factors (*User*, *Platform*, and *Environment* dimensions) showed their mixed importance, and we provided recommendations on user and website selection in future evaluation data gathering sessions.

Among the limitations of our research are fixed domain of websites and a single target user group. It also remained unclear whether the obtained number of evaluations was reasonable, or should more data be collected for the network training. The prospects of our future research work should include varying the amount of richer training data with respect to users and websites and analyzing the quality of the resulting NN models.

Acknowledgement. The reported study was funded by RFBR according to the research project No. 16-37-60060 mol_a_dk. The authors also thank M. Gaedke and S. Heil from TU Chemnitz who facilitated the collection of user evaluations.

References

1. Glass, R.L.: Facts and Fallacies of Software Engineering. Addison-Wesley Professional, Boston (2002)
2. Gay, G., Li, C.Q.: AChecker: open, interactive, customizable, web accessibility checking. In: 2010 International Cross Disciplinary Conference on Web Accessibility (W4A 2010), no. 23 (2010)
3. Bakaev, M., Mamysheva, T., Gaedke, M.: Current Trends in automating usability evaluation of websites. In: International Forum on Strategic Technologies (IFOST), NSTU, pp. 510–514 (2016)
4. Bakaev, M., Gaedke, M.: Application of evolutionary algorithms in interaction design: from requirements and ontology to optimized web interface. In: IEEE ElConRusNW, pp. 125–130. LETI, St. Petersburg (2016). doi:10.1109/EIConRusNW.2016.7448138
5. Dingli, A., Mifsud, J.: Useful: a framework to mainstream web site usability through automated evaluation. Int. J. Hum. Comput. Interact. (IJHCI), 2(1), 10–30 (2011)
6. The Encyclopedia of Human-Computer Interaction, 2nd edn. (2016). https://www.interaction-design.org/literature/book/the-encyclopedia-of-human-computer-interaction-2nd-ed. Accessed 07 Apr 2017
7. Vanderdonckt, J., Beirekdar, A., Noirhomme-Fraiture, M.: Automated evaluation of web usability and accessibility by guideline review. In: Koch, N., Fraternali, P., Wirsing, M. (eds.) ICWE 2004. LNCS, vol. 3140, pp. 17–30. Springer, Heidelberg (2004). doi:10.1007/978-3-540-27834-4_4
8. Grigera, J., Garrido, A., Rivero, J.M., Rossi, G.: Automatic detection of usability smells in web applications. Int. J. Hum.-Comput. Stud. 97, 129–148 (2017)
9. Lin, Y.C., Yeh, C.H., Wei, C.C.: How will the use of graphics affect visual aesthetics? A user-centered approach for web page design. Int. J. Hum.-Comput. Stud. 71(3), 217–227 (2013)
10. Feuerstack, S., Blumendorf, M., Kern, M., Kruppa, M., Quade, M., Runge, M., Albayrak, S.: Automated usability evaluation during model-based interactive system development. In: Forbrig, P., Paternò, F. (eds.) HCSE/TAMODIA-2008. LNCS, vol. 5247, pp. 134–141. Springer, Heidelberg (2008). doi:10.1007/978-3-540-85992-5_12
11. Palanque, P., Barboni, E., Martinie, C., Navarre, D., Winckler, M.: A model-based approach for supporting engineering usability evaluation of interaction techniques. In: 3rd ACM SIGCHI symposium on Engineering Interactive Computer Systems, pp. 21–30 (2011)
12. Pleuss, A., Wollny, S., Botterweck, G.: Model-driven development and evolution of customized user interfaces. In: 5th ACM SIGCHI Symposium on Engineering Interactive Computing Systems, pp. 13–22 (2013). doi:10.1145/2494603.2480298

13. Speicher, M., Both, A., Gaedke, M.: Ensuring web interface quality through usability-based split testing. In: Casteleyn, S., Rossi, G., Winckler, M. (eds.) ICWE 2014. LNCS, vol. 8541, pp. 93–110. Springer, Cham (2014). doi:10.1007/978-3-319-08245-5_6
14. Viswanathan, S., Peters, J.C.: Automating UI guidelines verification by leveraging pattern based UI and model based development. In: ACM CHI 2010 EA on Human Factors in Computing Systems, pp. 4733–4742 (2010). doi:10.1145/1753846.1754222
15. Barrera-León, L., et al.: TUKUCHIY: a dynamic user interface generator to improve usability. Int. J. Web Inf. Syst. **12**(2), 150–176 (2016)
16. Vanmali, M., Last, M., Kandel, A.: Using a neural network in the software testing process. Int. J. Intell. Syst. **17**(1), 45–62 (2002). doi:10.1002/int.1002
17. Dias, J., et al.: A genetic algorithm with neural network fitness function evaluation for IMRT beam angle optimization. Central Eur. J. Oper. Res. **22**(3), 431–455 (2014)
18. Yao, X.: Evolving artificial neural networks. Proc. IEEE **87**(9), 1423–1447 (1999)
19. Guo, F., et al.: Optimization design of a webpage based on Kansei engineering. Hum. Factors Ergon. Manuf. Serv. Ind. **26**(1), 110–126 (2016). doi:10.1002/hfm.20617
20. Bakaev, M., Gaedke, M., Heil, S.: Kansei engineering experimental research with university websites. Technical report, TU Chemnitz, CSR-16-01 (2016)
21. Bakaev, M., Avdeenko, T.: User interface design guidelines arrangement in a recommender system with frame ontology. In: Yu, H., Yu, G., Hsu, W., Moon, Y.-S., Unland, R., Yoo, J. (eds.) DASFAA 2012. LNCS, vol. 7240, pp. 311–322. Springer, Heidelberg (2012). doi:10.1007/978-3-642-29023-7_31

ePolity: Electronic Governance and Electronic Participation

eGov Services' Consumers in the Process of Innovations' Diffusion: The Case from St. Petersburg

Lyudmila Vidiasova$^{(\boxtimes)}$ and Andrei Chugunov

ITMO University, Saint Petersburg, Russia
bershadskaya.lyudmila@gmail.com,
chugunov@egov-center.ru

Abstract. In this paper, we contribute to the research of e-government development from a demand-side. The study was carried out in groups of online services' consumers, per E. Rogers adopter categories: innovators, early adopters, early majority, late majority, and laggards. The sociological survey has been conducted with the purpose to reveal differentiation of online services' users. 450 respondents have been interviewed during the research.

The study concentrated on the following indicators connected with citizens or a demand-side: IT skills and Internet usage, online services usage, awareness of new services, level of satisfaction, and reasons of dissatisfaction with the portals.

The survey detected a frequent Internet usage, growth of citizens' awareness of online services portal, interest to the interactive part of the portal, and 4 times increase of satisfaction with online services.

The authors proved recommendations for a smoother online services' adoption by the late majority and laggards groups.

Keywords: E-government · Adoption · Diffusion of innovations · Online services · Demand-side · Users' characteristics

1 Introduction

E-governance adoption is often accompanied by a proclamation of its potential social and economic benefits: convenience of governmental services, cost-efficiency in administration, reduced corruption, increased citizen satisfaction with government [1], and openness to business in different spheres of activity [2].

The level of adoption has been measured in researches addressing to normative indicators [3], political regime [4] or administrative efforts in the field of efficiency [5, 6].

In the studies above, picture from the point of view of offering services is clearly presented. In foreign practice, it is called the "supply-side", but one should not lose sight of the opinions of end-users of electronic services - "demand-side" [7]. Foreign researchers emphasize the serious influence of factors of both types on the development of e-government technologies and their real use [8].

© Springer International Publishing AG 2017
D.A. Alexandrov et al. (Eds.): DTGS 2017, CCIS 745, pp. 199–208, 2017.
https://doi.org/10.1007/978-3-319-69784-0_17

We have selected the Russian Federation as a case of a country attempting to follow international trends in e-governance development while facing considerable barriers, or institutional traps, built into its legal framework and bureaucratic structures and traditions. In this study, we addressed our attention to the demand-side of online services production and looked at the Russian citizens' adaptation to new services. The case of St. Petersburg has been selected for the study as a pilot region for testing the proposed survey questionnaire. The results of the Russian region ranking of citizens' registration in "Unified system of identification and authentication" (USIA) could be an indirect evidence of e-government services usage and adoption. This proportion means that registered citizens have the intention or have already applied for electronic public services. St. Petersburg occupies the 22nd place among 85 Russian regions in this ranking with 25% of population being already registered in USIA.

St. Petersburg citizens have an opportunity to use the St. Petersburg portal of government and municipal services (hereinafter - the Portal) located at https://gu.spb.ru/. In 2014 the Portal's authentication system was linked with the USIA, that could help to integrate 3 levels of services together - federal, regional and municipal. The portal consists of two main part - the informative and interactive ones. In addition, the portal's operators provide different feedback channels to collect citizens' opinions: opinion polls, online forms, online applications etc.

We believe that the research results shed light on the ways in which citizens adopt the new services provided by the government.

2   Literature Review

We started our research from the analysis of e-government demand-side and the process of e-services implementation in the studied area.

The introduction of e-government technologies has been studied by foreign scientists for a long time. According to their opinion, the process of implementing e-government technologies faces many barriers of an organizational, technological and financial nature. Certain difficulties in the use of new technologies lie in the development of human capital of one or another community [9]. In research practice, serious attention is paid to the assessment of technological components [10] as well as the processes of providing public services in electronic form [11]. Organizational barriers are explored in the framework of the analysis of the compliance of the stated objectives and implemented initiatives [12], assessment of the authorities' readiness for reform [13] and innovation [14], balance of resources, needs and political decisions [15, 16].

The topic of e-services adoption focuses on the opposite side of the e-government phenomena. We found examples of the studies conducted at federal [17, 18], regional [19] and municipal [20] levels as well. The human-centered characteristics are also in focus counting IT skills and qualification [21], level of trust [22], expectations connected with the cultural and social significance of technology adaptation [23]; as well as heterogeneity of users who can benefit from new services [24].

In Russian practice, several studies are also being conducted on the proposal of electronic public services. Official web resources are a source of knowledge of the degree of openness of government bodies [25]. The attention of researchers is attracted by factors that affect the state of satisfaction of services consumers [26] as well as determining the expectations of citizens [27] and users' categories [28]. There are separate studies aimed at assessing the quality of public and municipal services [29], conditions in MFC [30], perception of corruption factors in interaction with government agencies [31].

The demand for electronic government services mostly depends on the solution of the problem of information inequality (the availability of the Internet in the regional context and in various types of settlements, as well as the inclusion in electronic interaction, depending on the age group of the population). According to the monitoring data of the HSE [32], 39% of the population in rural areas has never used the Internet, and representatives of the older generation show very low rates. In 2014 31% of citizens aged 45 to 54 have never used the network (in 2013 - 35%), 55% of the people in the group 55–64 (in 2013 - 57%) and 79% of the older age group from 65 to 72 years (in 2013 - 81%). These data and especially insignificant dynamics to decrease are alarming in the context of the need to meet the targets related to the demand for electronic services by all segments of the population.

The provided literature review underlines the lack of unified techniques assessing e-services' adaptation in Russia. We propose a sociological survey approach for measuring citizen's attitude to online government services and tested it on a case of St. Petersburg.

3   Research Design

The methodology of the study is determined by the provisions of the innovation diffusion concept. In this framework, the implementation of electronic services is a new, innovative way of interaction between government and citizens. According to Rogers, the diffusion of innovation includes five stages: knowledge, beliefs, decisions, implementation, confirmation [33]. In this study, attention was paid to the diffusion of this innovation among citizens by the example of St. Petersburg.

According to the concept of innovations' diffusion, the five categories of consumers of innovations are distinguished (so called—adopting categories) [34]:

1. Innovators (2.5%) - those who are the first to adopt innovations, usually a young age group;
2. Early adopters (13.5%) - usually social leaders, popular, highly educated people;
3. Early majority (34%) - more cautious than early followers, but accepting innovation earlier than others;
4. Late majority (34%) - as a rule, skeptics accepting innovations after the majority have already mastered them;
5. Laggards (16%) - conservatives, who take innovations in the last place, usually this is the oldest age category.

We conducted a questionnaire survey among St. Petersburg citizens. The research included 2 waves of opinion polls hold in 2014 and 2015. The same questionnaire was used each year. We used a random, unrepeated, stratified sample for a survey, and the total number of respondents reached 450 people each year (95.4% confidence level, error no more than 5%). The developed questionnaire was presented in two forms (all the same): offline and online. The offline poll was organized as personal interviews with the visitors of seven Multifunctional centers of public services (hereinafter MFC) located at different city districts. The online poll collected opinions of Internet users and was placed on an open resource. The information about the online survey was distributed by active online communities and official web-pages of local authorities.

The demography of respondents is the following: 58% - women, 42% - men. The age presentation was divided into 3 main groups (33% for each): 18–30 year, 31–45 year, and 46 years and more. More than a half of respondents (66%) got higher education, 18% - incomplete higher education, and 16% - secondary education and less.

Based on the literature review, we selected a list of factors that influence on online services adoption. These factors related to the citizen or demand-side and counted: IT skills, Internet usage, online services usage, awareness of new services' portals, level of satisfaction, reasons of dissatisfaction with the portals. In this paper, we proved a comparative analysis of the results achieved in 2014 and 2015.

4 Findings

The research findings allowed to make some conclusion on the citizens' adoption to new electronic forms of interaction with the government.

4.1   IT Skills and Internet Usage by St. Petersburg Citizens

The research revealed a high-level of Internet technology adoption by St. Petersburg citizens. The percentage of active Internet - users has grown (Table 1). The respondents from online survey demonstrated higher points of activity (48% to 38% of MFC's respondents).

Table 1. Frequency of Internet usage by respondents, %

The intensity	2014	2015
Always online	28	31.7
Every day	46.7	52
Once in a week	2	3.7
Twice in a week	3	1.4
Once in a month	1	2
Rarely	4	2.2
Don't have access to the Internet	10	14.1

The fact that an average user spends more hours online also underlines the growth of IT-skills and reduction of a possible fear of new technologies.

4.2   Users' Preferences in Government Services Receiving

Many respondents (94%) applied for government services at least once a year. The most active group of users consisted of 18–30 y.o. respondents (62%). The popularity of government services (according to citizens' responses) is presented at Table 2.

Table 2. Application for government services by respondents, %

Government services	2014	2015
Social sphere	42.3	49.8
Healthcare	48.9	43.2
Tax services	28.1	37.2
Migration services	40	33
Education	15.1	17.4
Registration	14.7	14.1
Entrepreneurial services	8.1	9.9

The survey revealed an important trend in citizens' adoption: for 2 years of the survey they showed a preference in online services and MFC (Table 3).

Table 3. Citizens'preferences in receiving government services, %

Way to receive a service	2014	2015
MFC	60.6	82.8
Visit to the authorities	65.8	49.3
Federal e-services portal (gosuslugi.ru)	28.5	40.5
St. Petersburg e-services portal	14	24.9
Call centers	7.2	6.6
Info-kiosks	4.1	1.5
E-cards	0.5	0.2

4.3   The Level of Involvement in Online Services Portals' Usage

To identify the level of citizens' awareness of functioning the State online services portal (UPGS) in the questionnaires relevant questions were included. The level of St. Petersburg citizens' awareness reached 78% in 2015.

In comparison, the level of awareness of St. Petersburg portal is a little bit low-60%. Also 23% had a registration at the Portal, and this number is almost 2 times higher in the group of online respondents. Table 4 shows level of awareness between the respondents of different age groups. We want to stress that in 2015 even the respondents of the oldest group showed some knowledge about the Portal.

With the general growth of registered respondents in both government and municipal portals, not all respondents could explain the difference between the portals. This circumstance can be explained by the fact that only 15% of all respondents have

Table 4. Citizens awareness with the State online services portal, age groups, %

Years of respondents	Yes, and already registered	Yes, I know what is it	I've heard smth	No
18–30	26	29	10.1	34.9
31–45	32.6	26.4	16.7	24.3
46–60	14.9	18.2	18.3	48.6
60+	1.6	1.6	5.2	91.6

experience of registration on both portals at once. Thus, this group of respondents was able to independently assess the capabilities and functionality of the two portals. In addition, the level of awareness of their differences is higher among users registered on the Portal, 40% of whom could explain what the difference is. On the contrary, less than 1/3 of the respondents registered at the UPGS were able to explain the difference between the portals.

Among the respondents and aware of the existence of the regional Portal, 47% at least once used it. Over the past year there has been a positive trend: more and more respondents turned to the Portal repeatedly: the proportion of citizens' who used the Portal 2–3 times reached 22%, and 5 times and more – 15%. According to the survey, residents of St. Petersburg at the age of "31–45 years" use the Portal more than 5 times more often. For younger users ("18–30 years"), as well as for respondents from older age groups (from 46 years and older), it is typical, on average, 1–3 visits to the Portal.

In the survey, we compared the interest to informative and interactive parts of the Portal. According to survey results, the information search was used by 32% of respondents, compared to 53% of those who applied for a service electronically. Information services are more demanded by citizens of 30–45 years, and the interactive part received much attention from the younger users.

4.4   Users' Satisfaction with the Portal

We checked the services adoption through the level of citizens' satisfaction with the Portal. For this purpose, we asked the respondents who already had an experience in online services, if they were satisfied with them, and 80% answered in the affirmative.

The highest satisfaction level was detected in the group of 18–45 y.o. participants. Also, those respondents who received registration services were the most satisfied (86%) among the rest. The level of satisfaction with tax, health and migration services was also rather high - 70% of positives responses. The respondents highlighted the following factors that influenced positively on the Portal's adoption: time saving, clear presentation of a service, step by step instructions provided. According to the survey, more than a half of responded would recommend the Portal to their friends, relatives, and colleagues. This number increased 4 times from 2014.

The most critical factor that influenced negatively on online services adoption belonged to the Portal's registration system. The citizens complained about its difficulties including the complexity of procedures (25%) and need to prove the identification by a personal visit to an organization. Also 4% worried about the safety of personal data and hackers' attack, and 3% didn't get enough information on a certain service they needed.

4.5 Conlusions

The study allowed to determine the following categories of consumers of e-government services:

- Innovators - a group of citizens aged 31–45 from among businessmen who actively use services in the sphere of economy, business, taxes, traffic police;
- Early adopters - representatives aged 18–30 years, 1/5 of whom already had a registration at UPGU at the time of the first wave of the survey in 2014;
- Early majority - citizens in the age group of 31–46 years who learned about the portals via the Internet, having specific needs for receiving services in education, health, social; having higher or incomplete higher education, occupying leading positions, or being specialists;
- Late majority - broader group aged 18 to 45 years, including that group of users (18–30), who less often than others, apply for public services;
- Laggards - a group of users from 46 years and older, representatives of various fields, they learn to use new technologies, master them on the recommendation of their friends and relatives.

The study revealed that a larger number of residents of St. Petersburg began to use the Portal repeatedly. The received data testify to a steady passage of three stages of diffusion of innovations (knowledge, conviction, decision). At the same time, the number of respondents confirming its practical implementation and confirmation is growing every year, which is reflected in repeated appeals on portals for receiving services.

The possibility of such a speed of development and the demand for electronic channels of interaction with the authorities is directly related to the rapid growth of the Internet audience in Russia. In 2003 the monthly audience of Internet users in the Russian Federation was 9.9 million people, or 9% of the adult population of Russia, and the daily audience - 3.2 million or 3% of citizens. In 2016, these figures were, respectively, 81, 2 million people or 70% for a monthly audience and 69.2 million for a person or 59% for a daily audience. Also, the users' adoption is strengthened by a massive registration in USIA that reached 33,6 million in 2016, as well as the number of government services provided online - 220 million [35].

For a smoother online services' adoption, we strongly recommend paying more attention to the laggards group and the late majority group addressing its' special needs, for example providing learning workshops on online services usage. It's also reasonable to provide workshops on the selected government services that could be of interest to these groups: for instance, preparation for retirement, receiving benefits, appointment for a doctor, looking for a part-time job etc. Moreover, it's necessary to use those communication channels that are preferable by different groups of adopters.

We understood some limitations of the conducted research due to the regional specific. However, the questionnaire could be applied at different regions and municipalities to detect the groups and users and proved the specified recommendation for better e-services adoption. The study demonstrated a separation between new technologies' adopters. Focusing on different groups could be helpful in addressing the programs for e-participation, e-consultations and e-decision-making development.

We also believe that such segregation influence on social effectiveness from new technologies usage. This could be a prominent topic for further research.

Acknowledgments. This work was conducted with support of RFBR grant №. 16-36-60035 "The research of social efficiency of e-participation portals in Russia".

References

1. Government 3.0: Opening a New Era of Hope and Happiness for All the People Korean Ministry of Security and Public Administration (2013)
2. Janssen, M., Shu, W.S.: Transformational government: basics and key issues. In: Proceedings of the 2nd International Conference on Theory and Practice of Electronic Governance, pp. 117–122. ACM Press, New York (2008). doi:10.1145/1509096.1509120
3. Tolbert, K., Mossberger, K., McNeal, R.: Institutions, policy innovations, and e-government in the American states. Public Adm. Rev. **68**(3), 549–563 (2009). doi:10.1111/j.1540-6210.2008.00890.x
4. Chadwick, A., May, C.: Interaction between states and citizens in the age of the internet: e-government in the United States Britain and the European union. Governance **16**(2), 271–300 (2003). doi:10.1111/1468-0491.00216
5. Luna-Reyes, L.F., Gil-Garcia, J.R.: Using institutional theory and dynamic simulation to understand complex e-government phenomena. Gov. Inf. Q. **28**(11), 329–345 (2011). doi:10.1016/j.giq.2010.08.007
6. Weerakkody, V., El-Haddadeh, R., Sabol, T., Ghoneim, A., Dzupka, P.: E-Government implementation strategies in developed and transition economies: a comparative study. Inf. J. Inf. Manag. **32**(1), 66–74 (2012). doi:10.1016/j.ijinfomgt.2011.10.005
7. Nielsen, M.: Identifying e-government success factors: an analysis of selected national governance models and their experience in digitizing service delivery. In: Proceedings of EGOSE 2014, pp. 19–26 (2014). doi:10.1145/2729104.2729111
8. Delopoulos, H.N.: Barriers and opportunities for the adoption of e-governance services. Int. Scholary Sci. Res. Innov. **4**(6), 883–886 (2010)
9. Heeks, R.: Implementing and Managing Egovernment: An International Text. Sage Publications, London (2006)
10. Thorson, S., Ragland, J.: E-Governance in the Americas and Europe. Final report of the Electronic Governance Research Institute of the University of Seul (2002)
11. UN E-Government Survey. E-Government in Support of Sustainable Development. UN Department of Economic and Social Affairs; UN Division for Public Administration and Development Management. United Nations (2016). http://workspace.unpan.org/sites/Internet/Documents/UNPAN96407.pdf
12. Nour, M.A., AbdelRahman, A.A., Fadlalla, A.: A context-based integrative framework for e-government initiatives. Gov. Inf. Q. **25**(3), 448–461 (2008). doi:10.1016/j.giq.2007.02.004
13. Alreemy, Z., Chang, V., Walters, R., Wills, G.: Critical success factors (CSFs) for information technology governance (ITG). Gov. Inf. Q. **36**(6), 907–916 (2006). doi:10.1016/j.ijinfomgt.2016.05.017
14. Savage, R.L.: Policy innovativeness as a trait of American states. J. Politics **40**(1), 212–219 (1978). doi:10.2307/2129985

15. Mooney, C.Z., Lee, M.: Legislative morality in the American states: the case of pre-roe abortion regulation reform. Am. J. Pol. Sci. **39**(3), 599–627 (1995). doi:10.2307/2111646

16. Nagi, E., Hamdan, M.: Computerization and e-government implementation in Jordan: challenges obstacles and successes. Gov. Inf. Q. **26**(4), 577–583 (2009). doi:10.1016/j.giq. 2009.04.003

17. Okunoye, A., Bada, O.A., Frolick, M.: IT innovations and e-services delivery: an exploratory study. In: Proceedings of the 9th International Conference on Social Implications of Computers in Developing countries, Brazil, May 2007 (2007). https://pdfs. semanticscholar.org/d9c5/b8d926425dddadaa7194ec0a3e7b8f36c6b9.pdf

18. Arduini, D., Nascia, L., Zanfei, A.: Complementary approaches to the diffusion of innovation: empirical evidence on e-services adoption in Italy. Int. J. E-Services Mob. Appl. (2012). doi:10.4018/jesma.2012070103. http://www.igi-global.com/article/complementary-approaches-diffusion-innovation/68829

19. Al Zaabi, H.: Adoption, Diffusion and Use of E-government Services in the Abu Dhabi Police Force. Ph.D. thesis. University of Hertfordshire (2013). http://uhra.herts.ac.uk/bitstream/handle/2299/10757/05115377%20Al-Zaabi%20Hassan%20final%20PhD%20submission.pdf;sequence=1

20. Henriksen, H.Z.: The diffusion of e-services in Danish municipalities. In: Traunmüller, R. (ed.) EGOV 2004. LNCS, vol. 3183, pp. 164–171. Springer, Heidelberg (2004). doi:10. 1007/978-3-540-30078-6_28

21. Carter, L., Belanger, F.: The utilization of e-government services: citizen trust, innovation and acceptance factor. Inf. Syst. J. **15**(1), 5–25 (2005). doi:10.1111/j.1365-2575.2005. 00183.x

22. Carter, L., Weerakkody, V.: E-Governemnt adaption: a cultural comparison. Inf. Syst. Frontiers. **10**(4), 473–482 (2008). doi:10.1007/s10796-008-9103-6

23. Vekantesh, V., Morris, M., Davis, G, Davis, F.: User acceptance of information technology: toward a unified view. MIS Q. **27**(3), 425–478 (2003). http://www.jstor.org/stable/30036540

24. Gil-Garcia, R., Helbig, N., Ferro, E.: Understanding the complexity of electronic government: implications from the digital divide literature. Gov. Inf. Q. **26**(1), 89–97 (2009). doi:10.1016/j.giq.2008.05.004

25. Dmitrieva, N.E.: Communications in social networks: results of the monitoring of openness of federal bodies of the executive power in social networks. Public Adm. Issue. **2**, 123–146 (2015). https://vgmu.hse.ru/2015-2/151702618.html. (In Russian)

26. Reshetnikova, D.S.: Factors of public assessment of civil servants' performance in providing civil services. Public Adm. Issues. **2**, 131–164 (2016). https://vgmu.hse.ru/en/2016-2/185040575.html. (In Russian)

27. Trahtenberg, A.D.: E-government: a technocratic utopia or a demanded structure. Nauchnyy ezhegodnik Instituta filosofii i prava Ural'skogo otdeleniya RAN **11**, 253–269 (2011). (In Russian)

28. Trakhtenberg, A.D.: E-government and e-services: operationalization of administrative ideology and citizens' tactics. Sci. Yearbook Inst. Philos. Law Ural Branch Russian Acad. Sci. **16**(2), 63–79 (2016). (In Russian)

29. Evaluation of the Quality of Public Services Provided by the State (Municipal) Institutions. Obzor Instituta regional'nogo razvitiya. Pskov, 25 p. (2014). (In Russian)

30. Mitrofanova, S.V., Mal'kova, V.A.: The state of affairs of multifunctional centers providing public and municipal services in the City of Stavropol. Vestnik Severo-Kavkazskogo federal'nogo universiteta, **2** (47), 270–277 (2015). (In Russian)

31. Study of the Views of people in the Republic of Tatarstan on Corruption. Report of the Republic of Tatarstan Committee on Social and Economic Monitoring. Kazan (2016). (In Russian)

32. Abdrahmanova, G.A., Gohberg, L.M., Kovaleva, G.G. et al. (eds.): Information Society: Demand of the population in Russia for Information and Communication Technology. Analytic report (2015). http://issek.hse.ru/news/150039251.html. (In Russian)
33. Rogers, E.: Diffusion of Innovations, 5nd edn., 512 p. The Free Press, New York (2003)
34. Nosonov, A.M.: Theory of diffusion of innovations and innovative development of Russian regions. Pskovskiy regionologicheskiy zhurnal **25**, 3–16 (2015). (In Russian)
35. Deputy Minister of Communications and Mass Communications of Russia Alexander Kozyrev's Presentation at the Conference TAdviser IT Government DAY. http://www.tadviser.ru/index.php/Статья:Конференция_IT_Government_Day_2016/. Accessed 22 Oct 2016. (In Russian)

Common Government Services Portal of Russian Federation: How do People Use It? What is the Attitude Towards It?

(A Case Study of Materials for the Region of Russia)

Evgeniya Petrova[(⊠)] 🄳

National Research University Higher School of Economics,
2/8 Khitrovskiy Pereulok, Building 5, 109028 Moscow, Russia
evpetrova@hse.ru

Abstract. The present article explains the prospects of an anthropological approach to study the effects of the technological innovations.

This article is focused on the empirical research of using the Common Government Services Portal in South Russia Region. In the study we used such methods as the in-depth interviews, observation, and experiment. The research guide included four conceptual blocks: Familiarity; Experience in the use of Internet technologies; Interaction with the government authorities; and Experience in the use of Common Government Services Portal.

As a result of research, it became clear that many portal users do not realize its connection with the State, but classify it as a part of Internet environment. If the user realizes that the portal is a technological intermediary between the State and the citizen, the practice of using it varies considerably with respect to general Internet practices.

Keywords: Internet · Common Government Services Portal of Russian Federation (CGSP) · Public Services Portal of the Russian Federation · Media studies · Media anthropology

1 Introduction and Background

The English version of gosuslugi.ru uses two variants for translating its title. The first is Public Services Portal of the Russian Federation (this title was used on https://www.gosuslugi.ru/foreign-citizen?lang=en). The web page indicates that Public Services Portal of the Russian Federation "is a part of the infrastructure which provides data exchange and technological interaction of information systems used for rendering state and municipal services in electronic form".

But there is also another title - Common Government Services Portal of Russian Federation (this title was used on www.gosuslugi.ru/foreign/). The following information is given on the website: "Common Government Services Portal of Russian Federation is part of the infrastructure that provides for the information and technological interaction of information systems used for rendering government and municipal services in electronic format".

© Springer International Publishing AG 2017
D.A. Alexandrov et al. (Eds.): DTGS 2017, CCIS 745, pp. 209–218, 2017.
https://doi.org/10.1007/978-3-319-69784-0_18

At the stage of collecting empirical data in our study, we did not need to use the titles in English. We communicated with the respondents about the "gosuslugi". In preparing this article, the question arose of the need to define the exact terms. We decided to rely on the title "Common Government Services Portal of the Russian Federation", because such a translation, in our opinion, is closer to the Russian official name of the portal.

In January 2017, the Ministry of Communications and Mass Media of the Russian Federation reported that the number of Russians, who are registered on the gosuslugi. ru, had reached 40 million (data from the Official Internet resource of the Ministry of Communications and Mass Media of the Russian Federation) [9]. It means that every second user of the Russian Internet segment (Runet) can receive the government services electronically. In 2016 the Common Government Services Portal had almost 18 million new users.

Increasing number of the Common Government Services Portal users is a process based on a large-scale informatization, which has been conducted in Russia for several decades. According to the Federal Law of February 3, 2014 No. 9-FZ «On Amendments to the Federal Law "On Communications"», signed by the President of the Russian Federation Vladimir Putin, all residents shall be guaranteed the equal access to the communication services, it is planned to create the access points in the settlements with a population of 250 to 500 people and to provide the public Internet access at a speed of at least 10 Mbit/s. According to the report "Runet Today: Analytics, Figures, Facts", Audience of the Russian Internet is 80.5 million users (the in-crease amounted to 9.2% compared with the previous year), and 66.5 million people (57%) go online every day (+9,3% compared with the previous year) [16].

The experts believe that by 2020 three quarters of Russians will become the Internet users. The number of mobile Internet users is increasing, and the time spent by users on the network is growing as well [6]. All these data prove that quantitatively Russia shows a significant dynamics of the new information technologies development, and an infrastructure is designed to significantly increase the number of users with the various electronic systems, including those that are promoted by then Government.

The most important element of e-government system in Russia is Common Government Services Portal. The scientific and expert community has become interested in this resource since its development, and was keeping this interest at all stages of the portal development. In our opinion, at the present stage the Common Government Services Portal (www.gosuslugi.ru) is an important link in the system of electronic interaction between the State and citizens, which determines many of its characteristics, and the core of e-government system in its Russian version.

Common Government Services Portal creates a system of traditional practices mediation for interaction between the State and citizens. According to Knut Lundby's article, the mediated communication turns into a process of mediatization, when the ongoing mediations mould the long-term changes in the social, cultural, or political environment [8]. The long-term and multicomponent process of government services mediatization is not limited to the result only. Mediatization is a change. It is a transformation. The scale and complexity of such a phenomenon as the mediatization of public services require the appropriate approaches to study them.

An analysis of academic literature, paying attention to the Internet-resources of e-government has allowed us to reveal that the main direction for the portal learning is based on obtaining the empirical data from Internet sources. This way you can get a wide range of data about the portal itself, attendance, discussion of the portal in the Internet environment. This approach is the basis for understanding the electronic system of state-to-citizens connectivity. We consider that this direction will develop rapidly of all others in the nearest future.

There are different examples of such kind of the research [15, 3, 1 and et al.]. The demonstrative example is the annual "United Nations E-Government Survey". In 2012, this research was called "E-Government for the People". According to the Russian experience, the researches made it possible to review the basic online services. They remarked that "the public services portal is one of the key elements" of the project, allowing to create the "E-government" in the country. «The portal provides a single point of access to all reference, which are based on the state and municipal services, through the Internet and provides citizens and organizations with the opportunity to receive these services electronically». By way of illustration they used the print-screen of a page from www.gosuslugi.ru [17, p. 39].

As previously mentioned, more and more people are involved in the use of portal, but their experience is insufficiently studied, and therefore the qualitative characteristics of interaction between citizens and the government through the Common Government Services Portal are not extremely clear.

How do the government bodies learn about the citizens' satisfaction with the mediated government services? What do the authorities know about the practices of using the portal? One of the most popular method of gathering information about that is a population survey. However, this traditional method often does not allow us to obtain the truthful answers. "For two decades the Russian industry of mass polls showed a much more stable habit of lying", - noted Dmitry Rogozin, Director of the Federal Research Methodology Center, the Russian Academy of National Economy and Public Administration under the President of Russian Federation, - "Its basis is the substitution of product with packaging, the development of technology for the presentation of cardboard descriptions of research activity. Talking about the half-literary technology of lie is inconvenient to anyone: neither customers, nor sociologists, nor inter-viewers, nor respondents, therefore we live with a figure of silence and reasoning about the "as if" polls" [7].

As previously noted, we think that the most perspective direction or the empirical studies concerning the media are based on Internet sources (both, the resources themselves and social networks, blogs, etc.). But at the same time, we understand that the representation of data in the Internet environment has its own specifics, and we cannot equate the actual behavior (evaluation) in the Internet environment and offline. It seems important to study the relationship between a person and technologies using such methods that make it possible to get as close to a person as possible: communicate, observe, be included in his environment. We consider that such methods can expand the understanding the deep processes and effects.

2 Research Problem and Methodology

Methodologically, the project presented in this article is close to the interdisciplinary study of media practices for the residents of Russian rural settlements (in Kostroma, Rostov, Irkutsk regions and in Tatarstan), which was conducted by the Media Researches Laboratory of National Research University - Higher School of Economics in 2012–2014.

The researchers were interested not only in the media preferences of the villagers, but also how the media fits into the circle of people's everyday activities, what place they have in the house interior, how the TV-view takes place and what functions are used in the new communication media; how media influence the assessment of surrounding reality and perception of its place and society. By using the separate direction, we revealed the features of the Internet consumption in Russian rural settlements [for more details, see 4].

When studying the media consumption of inhabitants in the Russian province, we repeatedly faced with the significant contradictions in the collection of information by various methods. The respondents may give one answer in the questionnaire, and then (in a deeper study) refute what was said. Observing the respondents, we often received the completely different information, sometimes even the opposite of the one that was originally announced.

Understanding these features led us to the decision to study the actual aspects of electronic interaction between the government and citizens through the Common Government Services Portal by using the tools of anthropological approach. In the research methodology, we have combined the in-depth interviews, observations and experiments. During the research the author of this article lived in the Rostov-on-Don and had wide possibilities to observe the different practices of everyday life and formed the guide of the interviews with the understanding of the local specification.

It's not easy to talk about innovation with the ordinary people. For the majority of our respondents the CGSP is an example of new technology, which is still very little came into their lives. With the ability to combine interviews, observation and experiment we can obtain data that cannot be obtained with only one tool.

We proceed from the premise that one of the main goals of the Common Government Services Portal is to improve the quality of citizens' life. So, it is necessary to investigate the resource through the optics, which the citizens use themselves.

What is the attitude towards CGSP? How does it fit into the lives of respondents (their daily practices)? What are the meaningful assesments? Such an approach adjoins to the anthropological paradigm of media researches - a rather new and promising, in our opinion, research direction in Russia [for more details, see 10].

To move to a higher level of electronic interaction with the government the fundamental importance has a citizens' interest. It is important to understand how they use the portal, what the perception of services is, etc. After all, the e-government mechanisms should be turned into the electronic assistants, rather than the unfeeling electronic barriers between the man and the government officials, which are essentially impervious to the human emotion, sympathy, empathy, the desire to support a person in a problem situation. Otherwise, we will just see with you, according to the apt expression of Bogdanov, "the birth of a new IC bureaucracy" [2].

3 Data Description

Based on the media studies outlined above, in 2016 a unit of research was developed to study the practices of using the Common Government Services Portal by the residents of regional center. This project was implemented by the staff of Media Communications and Multimedia Technologies Department of the Don State Technical University, which is a partner of the National Research University "Higher School of Economics".

Only those respondents, who already had experience in using the Common Government Services Portal, were selected for the study. The interviews took place in the respondents' households. It was collected 51 in-depth interviews (62 h of audio recordings) and photographic materials (pictures of the main premises of households, and media consumption devices).

The research guide included four conceptual blocks: Familiarity, Experience in the use of Internet technologies, Interaction with the government authorities, and Experience in the use of Common Government Services Portal.

During the interview and after it, the researcher filled out the observer's questionnaire. If it was possible to obtain the consent of respondents, the researchers took pictures of the household interior, paying a special attention to the placement of media devices.

Each interview ended with the following appeal to the respondent: "Imagine that now you have a need to use the website www.gosuslugi.ru. Please, show, how would you do it? Let's try to simulate this situation." The respondents responded to this proposal quite willingly. This way it was possible to include the elements of experimental approach in the research methodology.

4 Territorial Context of the Study

Rostov-on-Don - the city, where the study took place, is a capital of Rostov region. This is the tenth largest city in Russia, the first in the Southern Federal District and the first in the region. Rostov region borders Ukraine in the west and northwest.

In 2016 the population of Rostov-on-Don was amounted to 1119.9 thousand people (data as of December 1, 2016 the Official website of the Territorial Agency of the Federal State Statistics Service for the Rostov Region) [5].

According to the information of the Official portal of Rostov region Government, the Internet connectivity in Rostov region is 80% [17]. According to the Industry study by the company "Yandex", in particular, 77% of users surf the Internet every day [13].

In 2016 there was a significant increase in the number of residents of the Don capital registered on the Common Government Services Portal. As of 2016/01/01, the number of users registered in the Unified Identification and Authentication System (UIAS) in Rostov-on-Don were 33,977 people. That is 3.5% of the urban population over 14 years old. And already on 2016/11/09 the number of such users registered was 293 309 people, i.e. 30.4% of the urban population over 14 years old (the data from the Official website of Rostov-on-Don Administration) [14]. Such registration is necessary to gain access to the Common Government Services Portal. How were these indicators achieved? The Official website of Rostov-on-Don Administration says that "more than

2,500 conferences and meetings have been held in the teams of various organizations; the outdoor advertising of Common Portal was placed in the streets of Southern capital, the advertising products (booklets, leaflets, posters) is provided to the organizations, and the mass media are actively involved in the process" [14].

According to our information, which we received in Rostov-on-Don during the empirical study, in 2016 the administrative resource was actively involved to increase the number of portal users. For example, the respondents showed us the letters that were distributed in their schools, Universities, enterprises. We were told that the heads of organizations collect data on how many employees are registered on the portal, and "strongly recommend to register on it as soon as possible" (quote from an interview with the respondent).

5   Discussion of the Results

The following two groups are clearly distinguished among the users of Common Government Services Portal: adherents of the network communications (active users of the new media) and traditionalists (the dominant type of communication is hierarchical, in media consumption the priority is given to watching TV).

This division is close to the classification proposed by Marc Prensky. He identified two groups of the digital residents - "Digital Immigrants" - are those of us who were not born into the digital world but use the new technologies, and "Digital Natives" - a generation, which was born during the digital revolution and since the birth is under the influence of digital technology [12].

"Digital Immigrants" use the Internet resources cautiously, but, at the same time, the access to network resources is very important for them. The respondents, who have only used the portal several times, expressed regret for that. They felt themselves clearly uncomfortable. They are ashamed of their small digital experience. Access to the Internet resources for this group of people is endowed with an additional sense of socialization, transition to the more progressive communities through the use of common information resources and communication channels.

For the "Digital Natives" the Internet is a territory, where they feel themselves quite freely. Trust in the Internet environment among the representatives of this group is very high. We made other conclusions by analyzing the answers in the interview block devoted to interaction with the government authorities. In this part the respondents are more restrained in the assessments, they are critical. There are many contradictory statements therein, and the stereotypes are strong. The terms of "authority"- "state" - "government" (and "government officials") have a clear personification. The distinction of these terms is chaotic, and often contradictory.

We should note that the peculiarities of groups were little discernible in that part of interview, where the conversation was about the experience of interaction with the authorities. Here the interviews were permeated with the stereotypes common for the both groups, which were demonstrated by both active TV audience and Internet users.

Below we will show you, for example, what the respondents say:

Authority is something that is above me, above the people
(*a student, always on-line*);
Government is a fat-fat man, who is fed by a waster
(*a young man, 18 years old, is preparing to enter the University, an active Internet user);*
Officials – figures of the "Dead souls"[1], everyone is trying to create the appearance of work
(*a man, a military officer, who uses the Internet several times a week*);
Through the government services, you can do something on trifles. But any important things need to be done personally, to look into the eyes of a person, to understand what he needs
(*a woman, 30 years old, an entrepreneur*)

It should be noted that in none of the interviews any conscious ideas related to the concept of the government-service was heard. Several times the respondents mentioned that this way, through the services, the government interacts with the citizens, and it needs the feedback. But this idea was mentioned not accented, only in passing. The ideas of a government - the ruler of justice and the state - a system that provide the security (internal and external) are much more popular among the respondents.

The young respondents (all of them are the active Internet users) often responded that they are trying to interact as little as possible (the term given by the respondents "en-counter") with the government.

In our opinion, the most important observation is that the majority of respondents (42 of 51) do not consider the Common Government Services Portal as a part of interaction system between the government and the citizens. For them it is more a person's interaction with the Internet environment. For the majority of respondents, the "authority"- "state" - "government" (and "government officials") concept exists in a separate meaning, which has a few intersections with the everyday practices of people in the perception of respondents.

Below there are some examples what the respondents say:

"I'm very glad that this site has appeared. To go to all those officials, ask them... it's really good that now you can do everything without all that stuff"
(a woman, 33 years old, a housewife)

I, generally, try not to get involved in all sorts of things with the government. It's good that now you can do it through the Internet.
(*a man, 28 years old, didn't say his official status)*
The fewer officials you see, the more you sleep. So, this site is just the ticket. I'm thinking about how to delete my data after I got what I needed. The less authorities know about you, the better.
(*a man, 21 years old, a programmer)*

---

[1] It is a novel by the famous Russian writer Nikolai Gogol.

Public authorities are aiming to increase the number of portal users. Above we mentioned the dynamics of growth in the number of portal's users. As a result of our research, we found out that it is not always clear for people that when they use the portal, the same officials - representative of authorities - help to solve their problem. The respondents believe that through the portal they could do everything they need without the authorities involvement.

We believe, there is a significant potential for interaction between the authorities and citizens through such tools as the Common Government Services Portal. To do this, it is necessary to create an agenda in the information field that unites the meanings of "Internet", "authorities", "citizens". As a matter of interest, in a conversation about the Internet the respondents feel more freely than when it comes to interaction with the government, authorities, and government officials.

When listening to the dictaphone records of conversations, we noticed that in different blocks the rate of speech is changing. Thus, in the part, where the respondents talk about the Internet, the speech flows faster, pauses are shorter. Conversation about the state, authorities and government officials passes more slowly, with significant pauses, short answers, the respondents are joking less. The interviewers characterized this block as the heaviest for conversation. After it the conversation about the Common Government Services Portal was held, normally, more at ease and easily.

We are faced with the fact that there are some topics that are especially difficult to be formulated by the respondents: innovation and relations with the authorities. Both of these topics have a unifying feature - the lack of conscious language, the poor vocabulary for such a conversation. If, in the case of innovation, there is not enough words, then, when it comes to the authorities, the respondents gush with the stereotypes and clichés said by the other people.

During the interview, the interviewers noted the following peculiarity: when passing to these topics, the respondents' speech speed slows down, the speech becomes more viscous, the respondents react less reactively to the questions and try to get off the subject. If the respondents treated the Common Government Services Portal exclusively as an "Internet website", the conversation was held effortlessly.

After each interview, we asked the respondents to simulate the situation, where the website www.gosuslugi.ru is used: "Imagine that now you have a need to use gosuslugi.ru. Please, show, how would you do it? Let's try to simulate this situation...". Almost all the respondents supported the proposal. This method gave us the interesting observations and examples. For example, one of the participants of the study said that at first she "needs to change into another robe, before log in the government services" (52 years old woman). Many respondents needed the additional actions to start using the website (to sit to another chair, to put things in order at the workplace, to thrust out chest to and so on).

Repeatedly in the experimental situation, the respondents passed to another computer, to use www.gosuslugi.ru. Here is one of the examples. Throughout the interview, the iPad was laying next to the participant in the study (a student, 20 years old). Several times she checked the messages there, showed the photos from her page in a popular social network, when it came to talk about the Internet resources usage. However, when she was offered to use the website of Government Services, the respondent invited the interviewer to another room to "connect to the government services on the main home computer" (quote from an interview with the respondent). Through the material world, people often more impartially express their attitude, formulate their opinion. There is less internal censorship, which is common for the verbal forms.

When studying the media consumption in the Russian regions, we repeatedly pointed out that the number of media consumption devices is higher than the number of family members, even in the poor homes. The media devices are often the center of home space [for more details, see 11]. They are endowed with an additional meaning and value.

In the living room, there is the newest and most modern TV, even if they more often watch another one (in the kitchen, in the bedroom, etc.). The model of cell phone (or tablet) is important for the respondents. For them this is a subject of special status, belonging to the desired social group. We can see a displacement of meanings for the material, symbolic, virtual and real worlds.

Also, we noted such displacements in the course of our study on the Common Government Services Portal. It is very difficult to catch such combinations by using only the quantitative methods and studying the portal itself. However, perhaps it is namely those features of perception and attitude are the answers to questions about the portal popularity (or its unpopularity), about the use of only its separate services and capabilities, etc.

6 Conclusion

According to the data that we have, the respondents allocate the CGSP among other Internet resources, if they realize its connection with the authorities. They use it differently compared to any other resources. That is, the data obtained as a result of Internet environment researches may not be sufficient, when it comes to the systems, where the several important semantic fields intersect.

The other part of respondents, on the contrary, does not realize that the CGSP is an intermediary for rendering the government services to the citizens. That such mediation is an important government function. They perceive their experience as interaction with the Internet environment, with the technologies. And here a very important topic of interaction between the government and the citizens, which addressing the issues of serious scale, arises: why do citizens need the government? And, please note, this technology is developed by the government, which spends the considerable resources on it. Does it count on this effect?

It seemed to us that the chosen interdisciplinary approach has proved its productivity, let us to expand the perception of how the Common Government Services Portal is perceived and evaluated by those for whom it was created. In the long term we hope to reach a comparative analysis in terms of the territorial perspective and to study the ongoing processes in the dynamics.

References

1. Bershadskaya, L., Chugunov, A., Filatova, O., Trutnev, D.: E-governance and e-participations services: an analysis of the discussions in Russian social media. In: Proceedings of the International Conference for E-Democracy and Open Government, CeDEM14, 21–22 May 2014, Danube University Krems, Austria (2014)
2. Bogdanov, V.S.: Elektronnoye upravleniye v obshchestve: sotsial'nyye i poz-navatel'nyye Problemy [E-government in the society: social and cognitive problems]. Universitetskaya kniga, Moskva (2016)
3. Maria, D.J., Richard, S., Tony, C., James, M.: A study of e-government and e-governance: an empirical examination of municipal websites. Public Adm. Q. **35**(1), 3–25 (2011)
4. Davydov, S.G., Logunova, O.S., Petrova, E.: Features of internet consumption in Russian rural settlements. J. Print Media Technol. Res. **3**(2), 85–93 (2014)
5. Goroda s chislennost'yu naseleniya 100 i boleye tysyach chelovek [Cities with a population of 100 thousand people and more]. http://rostov.gks.ru/wps/wcm/connect/rosstat_ts/rostov/ru/statistics/population/. Accessed 29 Dec 2016
6. Internet v Rossii: dinamika proniknoveniya. Leto-2016 (Otchet ob issledo-vanii Fonda «Obshchestvennoye mneniye») [Internet in Russia: the connectivity dynamics. Summer-2016 (Report on Studing the Fund "Public Opinion)]. http://fom.ru/SMI-i-internet/13021. Accessed 25 Feb 2017
7. Lgut li oprosy obshchestvennogo mneniya v Rossii? [Do the public opinion polls lie in Russia?].   http://www.chaskor.ru/article/lgut_li_oprosy_obshchestvennogo_mneniya_v_rossii. Accessed 18 Nov 2016
8. Knut, L.: Mediatization of communication. In: De Gruyter, M. (ed.) Handbooks of Communication Science, vol. 21, pp. 3–36 (2014)
9. Na Yedinom portale gosuslug zaregistrirovan kazhdyy vtoroy pol'zovatel' Runeta [Every second user of the Runet is registered in the Common Gov-ernment Services Portal]. http://minsvyaz.ru/ru/events/36373/. Accessed 01 Mar 2017
10. Novikova, A.A.: Antropologiya media v Rossii: istoki i perspektivy [Media Anthropology in Russia: Origins and Prospects]. Etnograficheskoye obozre-niye **4**, 3–12 (2015)
11. Petrova, E.V.: Vzaimodeystviye mediakontenta i kul'tury povsednevnosti Poseleniya Yuga Rossii: problema novogo vremeni i prostranstva [Interaction of the media content and the daily life culture of the rural settlement in the South of Russia: the problem of new time and space]. Observatoriya kul'tury **1**(1), 36–42 (2016)
12. Prensky, M.: Digital natives, digital immigrants. Horizon **9**(5) (2001). MCB University Press. http://www.marcprensky.com/writing/Prensky%20%20Digital%20Natives,%20Digital%20Immigrants%20-%20Part1.pdf. Accessed 11 Nov 2016
13. Razvitiye interneta v regionakh Rossii [Internet development in the regions of Russia]. https://yandex.ru/company/researches/2015/ya_internet_regions_2015. Accessed 11 Nov 2016
14. Rostovskaya oblast' - v desyatke liderov po registratsii na portale «Gosuslugi» [Rostov region is in the top ten on the registration in the "Government Services Portal"]. http://rostovgorod.info/press_center/news/139/45065/. Accessed 28 Dec 2016
15. United Nations E-Government Survey 2012: E-Government for the People. United Nations, New York (2012)
16. Runet segodnya: Analitika, Tsifry, Fakty [Runet today: Analytics, Figures, Facts]. http://2016.russianinternetforum.ru/news/1213/. Accessed 03 Jan 2017
17. Vosem'desyat protsentov protsentov territorii Rostovskoy oblasti obespechennykh dostupom v Internet [Eighty percent of the territory of Rostov Region is provided with the Internet access]. https://www.donland.ru/Donland/Pages/View.aspx?pageid=125269&mid=130586&item. Accessed 27 Nov 2016

Measuring Progress in E-Participation in Russia: The Results of a Multi-method Case Study

Lyudmila Vidiasova[(⊠)] and Yaroslava Tensina

ITMO University, Saint Petersburg, Russia
bershadskaya.lyudmila@gmail.com,
tensina.yaroslava@mail.ru

Abstract. The paper describes a scientific research on e-participation development in Russia. The portal "Russian Public Initiative" has become the research object. This e-participation portal considers to be an official e-petition portal in Russia and was launched in 2013. However, the results of its work are not obvious.

In the research, we appealed to the international practice and the national context (revealed after an expert poll) and conducted an analysis of an e-petition portal by using a combination of factors and criteria. The data describing the institutional factors, the results of previously conducted expert poll on e-participation barriers, and applied automated tool to assess the portal operation for the period 2013–2017 was used in the survey.

The results show the efficiency through analysis of quantitative data on petitions' publication, votes for and against the petitions, as well as a qualitative assessment of regulations and decision-making on the petitions that collected the necessary number of votes.

Keywords: E-petition portal · Success factors · Social efficiency · Case-study

1 Introduction

Electronic participation, representing new mechanisms of interaction between government and society, includes various tools, methods and technologies. This variation complicates the issue of evaluating its effectiveness due to the necessity to take into account specific sets of parameters. International research practice counts examples of techniques providing a framework of e-participation assessment. Russia makes efforts to follow these global trends; however there is still a lack of a complex system for e-participation evaluation.

In this paper, we present the results of a multi-method case study aiming at measuring progress in e-participation with a focus on Russian state e-petition portal. We believe that proposed approach could be useful for assessment e-participation tools efficiency in other countries as well.

© Springer International Publishing AG 2017
D.A. Alexandrov et al. (Eds.): DTGS 2017, CCIS 745, pp. 219–230, 2017.
https://doi.org/10.1007/978-3-319-69784-0_19

2 State of the Art

For the research, we provided an analysis of scientific and analytical publications describing e-participation measurement techniques.

At the global scale, we have an example of the UN developed a unified methodology for an e-participation index, including assessment of e-information, e-consultation and e-decision-making [1]. This index is used now for cross-countries assessment in e-participation development by measuring web-presence.

Medaglia analyzed a complex of parameters including activities actors, effects, contextual factors [2]. Different researchers underlined a great role of measuring institutional factors' impact [3] and governmental form [4] influencing e-participation. There is also an approach focusing on web 2.0 parameters count such as: web-presence, media diversity, synchronous and asynchronous communication channels and used modeling [5]. This approach showed the benefits of Web 2.0 network. The framework proposed in this work allowed a quantitative evaluation of different e-participation projects.

Macintosh and Whyte proposed an evaluation framework [6] consisted of democratic (representation, engagement, transparency, conflict and consensus, political equality, community control), project (engaging with wider audience, obtaining better informed opinion, enabling more in-depth consultation, cost effective analysis of contribution, providing feedback to citizens), and socio-technical (social, acceptability, usefulness, usability) criteria.

A qualitative approach has been applied by the German scientists who conducted semi-structured interviews, qualitative research, and document analysis for measuring the value of public participation through the categories of expectancy, transparency, acceptance, fairness, effectiveness, and efficiency, own impact, satisfaction [7]. Another research team tested public values using the standard criteria (content, usability, quality), and public value indicators (accessibility, citizen engagement, transparency, responsiveness, dialog, balancing of interests) [8]. An economic approach counts the costs caused by web 2.0 and direct costs (development of new services, additional staff, data management, indirect human costs, limited participation of users, indirect organizational costs, loss of control over the system, professional education and training of personnel, introduction of a new organizational policy), and the associated risks (political, legal, technical, social, weak social media policy, data ownership, information, freedom, reputation, critical reviews, digital divide) [9].

The other researchers paid special attention to the role of international drivers in the state e-participation policy [10], as well as the government readiness to reforms [11] and the whole level of democracy within the country [12]. Technological development is an important condition for e-participation [13], but it's not enough without the sufficient level of human capital characteristics [14], including computer literacy, mechanisms for breaking the digital divide, level of income and social welfare [15]. Citizens' trust in e-participation tools [16] reinforced by trust in government institutions [17] creates new benefits for all of the stakeholders as well.

At the previous stage of our research we conducted an expert poll aiming at detection the factors that influence e-participation in Russia [18]. The experts underlined a great importance of administrative barriers and lack of proper regulations in e-participation field. The experts put emphasis on the importance of such barriers as low level of trust in e-participation tools, inadequate usability of existing tools, lack of personal/public benefits from the use of tools and high public and political indifference in society.

The experts were asked to formulate the criteria that are applicable for measurement the effectiveness of e-participation tools. The experts unequivocally expressed support for the inclusion of quantitative and qualitative criteria. According to experts' proposals, quantitative criteria included the number of participants involved in the tool, the number of years of a tool's operation, the number of applications/petitions/initiatives being submitted, the number of active users, the proportion of successful cases (solved problems, completed initiatives), the speed of petitions' implementation, the time for a solution, the number of satisfied users, the percentage of regulatory acts adopted by the authorities on citizens' initiatives, and the number of portal visits.

Qualitative criteria counted the detailed analysis of discussion, constant updating of design, freedom of discussion, simplicity and convenience of registration and participation, security of registration and participation, real confirmation of a solution, logic of interface, presence of high quality assessments of the provided services (citizens' surveys, users' evaluation), a high level of integration with social networks.

In our research, we tried to appeal to the international practice and the national context and conducted an analysis of an e-petition portal by using a combination of factors and criteria.

3 Research Design

The conducted research aimed at understanding whether e-petition portal's operation in Russia result into a real policy making. For the case study, we selected the state e-petition portal titled "Russian Public Initiative" (RPI). This portal has been developed in 2013 and is placed at https://www.roi.ru. According to the portal's terminology, the citizens' applications are called "initiatives" and aggregate proposals on federal, regional and municipal levels.

The portal presents all the published initiatives and provides an opportunity for citizens to vote for or against the initiative. The portal requires a registration on the federal online services portal.

During the research, we applied a methodology of a multi-method case study that involved a view to the research task from a qualitative and quantitative sides, as the expert survey suggested. We operated only with data published in open access.

We summarized the parameters being used for the research in Table 1.

For operations with quantitative data, we used an automated system for e-participation portals' monitoring. The system downloaded the required data from the portal's API. For qualitative analysis we manually worked with information form the section "Decisions" on the portal- (https://www.roi.ru/complete/).

The research counted data for the following period: April 2013–March 2017.

Table 1. Data sources in the research

Quantitative data	Qualitative data
Number of petitions being submitted Petitions' dissemination by level, categories and regions Progress of voting for and against each petition Proportion of successful petitions	Data on regulations related to e-participation field in Russia and RPI operation Information about the petitions collected a required number of votes

4 Findings

The research findings reflect an empirically collected data on qualitative and quantitative criteria, and showing the specific functioning of the portal.

4.1 Analysis of the Regulation Framework for RPI Operation

To determine the regulative framework for e-participation functioning in Russia, we studied the documents that reflected the related topics. The study revealed several documents in e-participation filed, but not a single strategy, program or anything like that.

The federal law 59 "On the order debated the requests of citizens of the Russian Federation" from 21.04.2006 (the latest edition from 18.07.2012 №19-P) [19] regulates the implementation of the constitutionally citizen's rights to appeal to the state and municipal authorities. This document guarantees the right to make an individual or a collective request. Article 4 of this document describes the electronic method as one of the equally ways of citizens' treatments. According to this law, all requests must be examined by the authorities within 30 days.

The President of the Russian Federation decree "On the main directions of governance improvement" №601 from 07.05.2012 [20] covers the e-participation issues in more details. It provides the development of the RPI as an e-petition portal, as well as a platform for bills' discussion, open data publishing and citizens' assessment of the authorities. The key efficiency indicators for such activities development include the level of citizens' satisfaction with online services, the percentage of citizens with ability to get online services, the percentage of citizens who receive online services, reducing the time in the queue while contacting the authorities.

The state program "Information Society" (2011–2012) [21] has been developed for the clear establishment of goals and tasks, as well as the financing for all the initiatives connected with them. The progress in information society buildings should be measured by the Russia's place in the international ICT rankings, percentage of citizens who use government e-services, level of the Internet usage, overcoming digital divide between Russian citizens.

The decree of the President of the Russian Federation №183 of 4.03.2013 "On consideration of public initiatives directed by citizens of the Russian Federation using the Internet portal "Russian Public Initiative" [22] regulates the rules of the portal operation. The public initiative posted on the Internet resource should receive the necessary support during the voting using the Internet resource. The initiative considers to be supported, if within 1 year it receives:

(A) for a federal level- at least 100 thousand votes;
(B) for a regional level- at least 5 percent of the votes of citizens permanently residing in the territory of the relevant region;
(C) for a municipal level- at least 5 percent of the votes of citizens permanently residing in the territory of the respective municipality.

The RPI presents a combination of the responsibilities of the legislative and executive branches. The public initiative, which received the necessary support during the voting, is being sent electronically to an expert working group of the appropriate level (federal, regional or municipal) to conduct an examination and provide a decision on whether to draft a relevant normative legal act or other measures to implement this initiative.

4.2 Russian Public Initiative Development Characteristics

During the research we detected more than 9.5 thousand initiatives on the RPI. The majority belonged to the federal level and reached 86%, however regional and municipal levels collected only 7% and 6% respectively. Figure 1 presents the collected initiatives by their field.

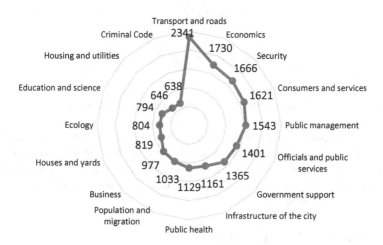

Fig. 1. Number of initiatives published at RPI by category, 2013–2017

The study revealed quite an impressive level of citizen's interest in the beginning of the portal's operation when a record flow of proposals was recorded (Fig. 2). This trend is more for federal and regional initiatives.

At the same time, the trend of municipal initiatives' publication is opposite. Despite a very small amount of proposal at this level, the frequency of such publications has extreme changes, but on the average, it fluctuates from 4 to 25 initiatives per month (Fig. 3).

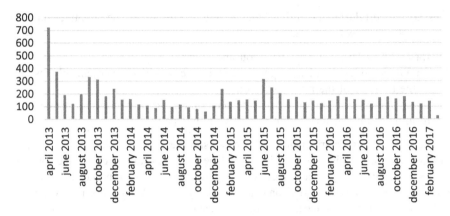

Fig. 2. Dynamics of initiatives number, 2013–2017 (initiatives of all levels)

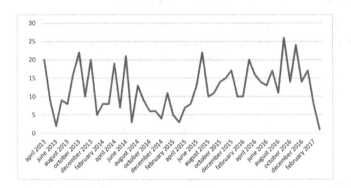

Fig. 3. The dynamics of initiatives number at the municipal level, 2013–2017

As the portal gives an opportunity for a citizen to leave the voice for or against the initiative, we have compared the dynamics of collecting the votes of both types. The research revealed the prevalence of the supporting voices. It means, from one side, a certain level of users' solidarity, and from the other side, some reasonableness of the initiatives to be discussed (Fig. 4).

4.3 Analysis of the Voting Progress

The process of an initiative's "life cycle" begins with its' publication on the RPI portal (www.roi.ru) and an assignment of a unique number. Then the initiative becomes open for voting. If the initiative receives the required number of votes, it goes to an expert working group at the federal, regional or municipal level. Further, the expert group adopts a motivated decision on the implementation or rejection the initiative.

First of all, we analyzed the votes' collection by those initiatives that were on voting at the period of research. Table 2 accumulates the analysis results by categories and shows a low number of initiatives overcoming the barrier of 50% of the required level.

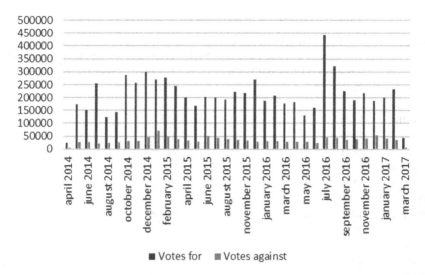

Fig. 4. Votes "For" and "Against" the initiatives published at Russian Public Initiative, 2014–2017

At the municipal level, among 576 placed initiatives, only 4 initiatives (0.69%) were able to get more than 10% of the required number of votes. The categories of these initiatives are "Ecology", "Public management", "Houses and yards", "Security", "Infrastructure of the city", "Officials and public services ", "Population and migration" and "Economy". At the regional level, among the 745 initiatives, only 5 initiatives (0.67%) were able to get more than 10% in the categories "Transport and roads", "Infrastructure of the city" and "Housing and utilities".

4.4 Qualitative Analysis of Successful Petitions' Fate

After that, we analyzed the history of portal's operation and paid attention to the initiatives that collected more than 100, 000 votes. We provide below the description of each case.

(1) Prohibition to officials and employees of companies with state (municipal) property to purchase cars worth more than 1.5 million rubles. The voting ended on July 15, 2013 (100 807 votes for, and 279 against). On September 10, the working group reviewed the initiative and recommended that the Russian government to prepare the regulations that determine the marginal prices of purchased cars. The requirement of 1,5 million rubles was declined. In November 2013 the State Duma adopted in the first reading a law prohibiting officials to buy cars more than three million rubles. On July 2014, the Russian Prime Minister signed a decree prohibiting officials from buying foreign cars and equipment (not counting international brands manufactured in Russia). On October 2014, the Russian government issued a decree limiting the purchase of cars for federal officials with a sum of 2,5 million rubles.

Table 2. Distribution of initiatives by % of votes, categories

Category	Number of initiatives	Number of initiative, collecting more than 50% of required votes	Percentage of initiatives that received more than 50% of the vote to the total number of initiatives on category
Transport and roads	2341	7	0.30%
Economics	1730	3	0.17%
Security	1666	2	0.12%
Consumers and services	1621	4	0.25%
Public management	1543	3	0.19%
Officials and public services	1401	4	0.29%
Government support	1365	0	0.00%
Infrastructure of the city	1161	0	0.00%
Public health	1129	2	0.18%
Population and migration	1033	2	0.19%
Business	977	3	0.31%
Houses and yards	819	0	0.00%
Ecology	804	1	0.12%
Education and science	794	1	0.13%
Housing and utilities	646	0	0.00%
Criminal code	638	2	0.31%

(2) Cancelation of the law on random blocking of Internet resources. The voting ended on August 9, 2013 (100 057 votes for, 346 against). The working group considered the initiative to abolish the federal law inexpedient, and recommended the State Duma to take into account the remarks of the authors while improving the legislation. Also, there was a recommendation to the Public Chamber of the Russian Federation to consider in the format of public hearings the issue of improving the regulatory and legal mechanisms for protecting the rights of rights holders in the Internet.

(3) My home is my castle. The initiative assumes to recognize any defensive actions by a citizen in his own house as a necessary self-defense. The voting ended on February 20, 2014 (100 458 votes for, and 552 against). The expert group recognized the importance of the problem and recommended the government to

implement this initiative. The authorities ignored the recommendations of the working group. The activists were forced to publish a petition on the non-government e-petition portal "Change.org" demanding to consider the already approved initiative in the State Duma.

(4) Cancellation of the right of priority passage of all vehicles, except for vehicles of operational services. The voting ended on March 17, 2014 (100 108 votes for, and 327 against). The working group concluded that the initiative be implemented with the help of normative acts, but not at the legislative level.

(5) The initiative against the introduction of additional taxes on purchases in foreign online stores, and against the reduction of the customs limit to 1000 euros for the purchase of goods for personal needs. The voting ended on July 15, 2014 (100 251 votes for, 978 - against). On July 2014, the Ministry of Finance suspended the preparation of a resolution. In the Ministry of Economic Development the draft was criticized and then returned to the Ministry of Finance for a revision. On October 2014, the federal working group supported the initiative and recommended the Government to consider this issue once again. On October 2014, the Ministry of Economic Development promised that the threshold of duty-free trade would be above 150 euros. By the decision of the Eurasian Economic Commission, the duty-free threshold remained unchanged until 2016.

(6) On the criminal liability for the illegal enrichment of officials and other persons obliged to report on their incomes and expenditures. The voting ended on December 9, 2014 (100,092 votes for, and 123 against). On February 2015, the working group recognized the development of an appropriate normative legal act as inexpedient. The working group only recommended the activists to provide an analysis of the current anti-corruption legislation. In spring 2015, the initiative's supporters made attempts to submit proposals to the State Duma through regional parliaments.

(7) Making the Russian Football Union and the Ministry of Sport to conduct a rating Internet voting on candidacies for the post of head coach of the Russian national football team, as well as the candidates for the Russian national football team before the world competition. The voting ended on March 31, 2015 (100,002 votes for, 2,060 against). Despite the negative evaluation of the initiative by representatives of the Russian Football Union and the Ministry of Sport, the expert group supported the idea and recommended conducting a rating vote. However, the expert groups' decision was more of a recommendation than a mandatory nature.

(8) Making changes in the Labor Code, providing a mandatory indexation of the wages of employees at least once a year, not lower than the level of actual inflation. The voting ended on April 7, 2015 (100 049 votes, 1975 against). On June 2015, the expert group found it inappropriate to include in the Labor Code of the Russian Federation. A similar petition was published on the portal "People's Initiative" (operated by the Communist Party), and by the research time it collected 1,492 votes out of 20,000 required.

In addition, we revealed 12 initiatives being detected as successful but not collected the required number of votes. These cases relate to the parallel adoption of the sufficient law in the state Parliament or municipal administration, and the decision was actually made not due to the merits of the portal.

5 Conclusions

As a research result, the conclusions on the specificity of e-participation portal in Russia functioning were received. The conducted research revealed a working capacity of the proposed approach. The quantitatively observed trends corresponded with the qualitative analysis' results.

The regulations' analysis showed the areas that are regulated right now – the process of working with citizens' initiatives, a trend to strengthen effective ICT communication and clearly description of the RPI operation. However, the rest of the existed e-participation tools just partly relates to the proposed actions. The lack of a complex document describing e-participation aims and features also does not contribute to the development of these mechanisms. RPI has a clearly understandable mechanism of operation and the description of a petition "life-cycle". At the same time, the founded documents did not have the criteria for evaluation the effectiveness of a portal's work.

The revealed quantitative parameters of the portal showed the operation cycle, the distribution of citizens' attention to different spheres of life, and the progress of voting. The case of RPI visually demonstrated an extremely growth of the interest to the portal at the very beginning of the start. However, this interest also fell by the first anniversary of the portal. These data showed that citizens' trust and efforts met a resistance that significantly cooled the enthusiasm of activists.

The comparison of votes for and against the initiatives showed quite a high level of solidarity among the portal users: the published petitions face more with a support than an opposition. That's why increasing the motivation to use the portal could lead to the collection of the required number of supportive votes.

A detailed analysis of the "successful petitions" underlined the indirect evidence of a possible citizens' dissatisfaction: less than 1% of the published petitions were satisfied. The citizens could also be annoyed by the decisions of the expert group regarding those petitions that received an appropriate number of votes. These factors could reduce citizens' motivation to use e-participation tools and loosen their belief in the effectiveness.

The practice of non-government portals (for instance, Change.org) demonstrates an active promotion of the successful cases – when the adopted petition is sent by e-mail to a wide list of subscribers. Such actions attract attention and expand the circle of participants. The positive cases of raiding citizens' motivation should be applied at the RPI.

The major limitation of the research belonged to the case focus on e-petition portal, which is just a one type of e-participation tools. While studying e-voting, or online applications, discussions and crowdsourcing for the state issues, it's necessary to accumulate more wide range of parameters.

Moreover, a satisfaction level could be measured by conducting polls or interviews with the portals' users. By now, we do not have such data in Russia, and due to the

RPI's anonymity, we couldn't make a social portrait of the Russian e-petitioners. The research team is going to test the proposed methodology and the automated monitoring system to compare the results on e-participation tools at different levels.

Acknowledgments. This work was conducted with support of the Grant of the President of the Russian Federation to young scientists №MK-5953.2016.6 "The research of e-participation tools development factors in Russian Federation".

References

1. E-Government Survey. UN Report (2016). http://workspace.unpan.org/sites/Internet/Documents/UNPAN96407.pdf
2. Medaglia, R.: eParticipation research: moving characterization forward (2006–2011). Gov. Inf. Quart. **29**, 346–360 (2012). doi:10.1016/j.giq.2012.02.010
3. Jho, W., Song, K.: Institutional and technological determinants of civil e-Participation: solo or duet? Gov. Inf. Quart. **32**, 488–495 (2015). doi:10.1016/j.giq.2015.09.003
4. Zheng, Y., Schachter, H.L., Holzer, M.: The impact of government from e-participation: a study of New Jersey municipalities. Gov. Inf. Quart. **31**, 653–659 (2014). doi:10.1016/j.giq.2014.06.004
5. Ter'an, L., Drobnjak, A.: An evaluation framework for eParticipation: the VAAs case study. Int. Sch. Sci. Res. Innov. **7**(1), 77–85 (2013)
6. Macintosh, A., Whyte, A.: Towards an evaluation framework for e-Participation. Transform. Gov.: People Process Policy **2**(1), 16–30 (2008). doi:10.1108/17506160810862928
7. Schroetera, R., Scheel, O., Renn, O., Schweizer, P.: Testing the value of public participation in Germany: theory, operationalization and a case study on the evaluation of participation. Energy Res. Soc. Sci. **13**, 116–125 (2016). doi:10.1016/j.erss.2015.12.013
8. Karkin, N., Janssen, M.: Evaluating websites from a public value perspective: a review of Turkish local government websites. Int. J. Inf. Manag. **34**, 351–363 (2014). doi:10.1016/j.ijinfomgt.2013.11.004
9. Sivarajah, U., Irani, Z., Weerakkody, V.: Evaluating the use impact of Web 2.0 technologies in local government. Gov. Inf. Quart. **32**, 473–487 (2015). doi:10.1016/j.giq.2015.06.004
10. Akrivopoulou, C.A.: Human Rights and the Impact of ICT in the Public Sphere: Participation, Democracy, and Political Autonomy. Information Science Reference, USA (2014). doi:10.4018/978-1-4666-6248-3
11. Alreemy, Z., Chang, V., Walters, R., Wills, G.: Critical success factors (CSFs) for information technology governance (ITG). Gov. Inf. Quart. **36**(6), 907–916 (2016). doi:10.1016/j.ijinfomgt.2016.05.017
12. Karlsson, F., Holgersson, J., Soderstrom, E., Hedstrom, K.: Exploring web participation approaches in public e-services development. Gov. Inf. Quart. **29**, 158–168 (2012). doi:10.1016/j.giq.2011.07.009
13. Astrom, J., Karlsson, M., Linde, J., Pirannjad, A.: Understanding the rise of e-participation in non-democracies: domestic and international factors. Gov. Inf. Quart. **29**, 142–150 (2012). doi:10.1016/j.giq.2011.09.008
14. Satish, K., Teo, T.S.H., Lim, V.K.G.: Contextual factors, e-participation, and e-government development: testing a multiple-mediation model. In: Proceedings of PACIS 2012, p. 113 (2012). http://aisel.aisnet.org/pacis2012/113

15. Lancee, B., Van der Werthorst, H.G.: Income inequality and participation: a comparison of 24 European countries. Soc. Sci. Res. **41**(5), 1166–1178 (2012). doi:10.1016/j.ssresearch.2012.04.005

16. Scherer, S., Wimmer, M.: Trust in e-participation: literature review and emerging needs. In: Proceedings of ICEGOV 2014, pp. 61–70 (2014). doi:10.1145/2691195.2691237

17. Charalabidis, Y., Tsitsanis, T., Koussouris, S., Matzakou, I.: Momentum Deliverable 2.7: E-Participation Projects Consolidated Results (2013). http://www.epomentum.eu/LinkClick.aspx?fileticket=3pkZY45Ect8%3d&tabid=57&mid=492

18. Vidiasova, L., Mikhaylova, E.: E-participation tools: barriers for development in Russia. Inf. Resour. Russ. **6**, 31–33 (2016). in Russian

19. Federal law №59: On the order debated the requests of citizens of the Russian Federation. From 21.04.2006 (2006)

20. Presidential decree of the Russian Federation № 601: On the main directions of governance improvement. From 07.05.2012 (2012)

21. State Program "Information Society" (2011-2010). The Russian government regulation №313 from 13.04.2014 (2014)

22. The decree of the President of the Russian Federation №183 of 4.03.2013: On consideration of public initiatives directed by citizens of the Russian Federation using the Internet portal "Russian Public Initiative" (2013)

Public Service Ethics vs. Social Media Use in Russia

Mikhail Bundin[1(✉)], Aleksei Martynov[1], and Yury Avrutin[2]

[1] Lobachevsky State University of Nizhny Novgorod (UNN),
Nizhny Novgorod, Russia
mbundin@mail.ru, avm@unn.ru
[2] Saint-Petersburg University of MIA, Saint Petersburg, Russia
axx2006@mail.ru

Abstract. The wide use of social media by public authorities and officials is now an international trend now. Modern political and government leaders find here great opportunities to promote their policies and boost citizens' participation. On the other hand, recently adopted legal and official documents e.g. Guidelines, Codes of Conduct demonstrate that the use of social media by public servants and employees is not so encouraged or sometimes explicitly prohibited even when it is for purely 'personal' purposes. Thus, it becomes evident that national governments seek now to control online activities of their employees explaining it mainly by ethical reasons in order to guarantee fairness, impartiality and neutrality of public service and to avoid any adverse interference. For this purpose, Russia adopted in 2016 a federal law creating an obligation of public servants to declare any use of social media before their authority. This new initiative could shift the existing balance between the right to privacy and public service ethics especially in absence of any coherent and explicit regulation on social media use by public employees in Russia.

Keywords: Public administration · Open Government · Social media · Public service ethics · Russia

1 Introduction

Extreme popularity of social networking sites (hereinafter – SNS) contaminates also the public sector. The intention to enlarge the auditory makes public authorities and officials become active users of social media. It is not a secret that many high rank officials, including President of United States or Russian President have accounts on SNS and use them to deal with a large audience. Many official governmental platforms are interconnected with social media accounts with a considerable number of followers, users or subscribers. Moreover, social media are now considered to be a rather powerful e-democracy tool for discussing vital political and social issues. The government and public authorities use SNS platforms for promoting their policies and decisions. This tendency is an international trend common for all modern societies.

Regardless so wide use of SNS by public authorities and high-ranking officials, social media on-line activities of public servants evoke various ethical and legal

© Springer International Publishing AG 2017
D.A. Alexandrov et al. (Eds.): DTGS 2017, CCIS 745, pp. 231–242, 2017.
https://doi.org/10.1007/978-3-319-69784-0_20

problems. Most of them are caused by an ambiguous nature of SNS. From one point, they were originally designed and destined for personal or private communication and from the beginning were the spaces where everyone could freely express himself. From the other point, the recent practice shows great interest of the state and public authorities in regulating and participating in on-line activities. The latter draws to acknowledgment of SNS as a public space. Every comment or a 'post' in your account is treated now as something said in public with appropriated consequences and responsibility. In Russia, some online activities including allegedly those on social networking sites sometimes need registration at Federal Service on Communication and Mass Media Control (Roskomnadzor). Thus, all Internet page holders that have more than 3 000 visits per day should declare themselves and be included in a special register as 'bloggers'. Failure to meet those requirements is subject to the administrative responsibility (a considerable fine). The bloggers are also responsible for any illegal activity on their pages even for materials placed by third parties.

In this case, several issues are to be suggested to analyze the problematics of on-line activities of public servants on SNS:

1. Is there could be private or public use of SNS by public employees?
2. Should the government monitor public servants accounts on SNS? How should the government respond to their on-line activities there?
3. Should on-line activities on SNS of a person be considered in case of his/her joining the public service or obtaining a new public post?
4. What measures of responsibility could be applied to public servants using SNS and in what cases?

2   Literature Review

The problematics of governmental use of social media is now widely studied by scholars from different countries and represents a new challenge for many areas of modern science.

Most of researchers acknowledge the fast penetrating of social media across government organizations [22, 27, 32, 43, 45, 53, 54] that represents new opportunities for building government-citizens relationship [20, 23], providing public services [25], public engagement, government transparency [3–5, 24].

On the other hand, the usage of social media by governmental organizations could also confront different negative factors: security risks [21], reputation damage [2, 52], deviant behavior [35], privacy risks [21] etc.

Those positive and negative factors make some scholars speak for the necessity of social media governance [26, 29, 34, 36, 48] and the best possible tool here could be the adoption and implementing of social media policies [27, 48]. Thus, social media policies and guidelines are suggested to be an effective mechanism to clarify objectives and accountability of social media [14], helping to align their use with the mission, procedure, and values of governmental organizations [48] and include them into organizational processes [28].

Despite the large number of the researches concerning governmental use of social media they are usually confined to enumerating possible legal issues, e.g. privacy, freedom of speech, freedom of information, public records management, public disclosure, accessibility, copyright etc. [21]. In some documents, legal aspects are limited to requiring the usage of disclaimers aimed to separate public employee's opinion from the official one [44].

The existing studies on public service ethical problems are focused mainly on general problems of corruption, bribery, conflict of interests, abuse of function, and disclosure of information [38, 50]. Nevertheless, it does not mean that Ethical Codes could not be used for SNS and especially when regulating public servants social media activities.

Thus, the legal problematics of public employees' use of social media seems to be not studied enough especially in connection with ethical and legal problematics.

3 Current State of Use of Social Media in Public Sector

It is a global trend for public authorities and state top leaders to be present on SNS. In 2012 in the USA, about 700 Federal departments had about 3000 pages in Facebook, 1000 microblogging on Twitter, 700 YouTube channels and 500 pages on Flickr. All those accounts were official pages of federal departments, agencies, programs and certain high rank officials. Even in 2011, about 2/3 of us government employees had accounts in social networks, 90% of them gave preference to Facebook. Their blogs had only 20% of officials. Similar statistics is for the UK: about 90% local officials use Twitter, 80% of Facebook and only 3% do not have any account in social networks. In Sweden quite a popular channel of communication are blogs: about half of the local municipalities have their blogs, and only 43% are using Twitter and about 80% Facebook [30].

In Russia, the President of the State and the Prime Minister as well as Deputy Prime Ministers, Federal Ministers have social media accounts. The President Vladimir Putin is registered in Twitter and YouTube and has a personal website. His Twitter account is followed by 3,36 millions of subscribers and more than 29 thousands of users follow his YouTube blog. The Prime Minister is evidently even more active user of SNS and has profiles in Facebook, Twitter, Instagram, Vkontakte. His Twitter account's number of subscribers has outrun the President's one and achieved 5.1 millions of users. For comparison, the US President Barack Obama has got Facebook account only in 2015 [51]. Previously, he used only Twitter and official the White House microblogging.

Among most recent announces of social media use was made by the Federal Attorney's office that officially enlarged considerably its presence in social media and created in 2016 accounts in Vkontakte, Facebook, Instagram and Classmates that were added to existing Twitter profile functioning since 2010.

The latest research on the usage of social media by the Federal Executive in Russia showed from one side a considerable growth of number of SNS accounts created by federal agencies and on the other side a huge gap in preferences of citizens and those of federal authorities while choosing social media sites [6].

The existing practice in Russia shows that most of governmental agencies prefer not to welcome the presence of their employees in social media. State agencies and officials use social media for providing official information about their activities or, generally speaking, news. Only 10% of politicians and state bodies interact effectively with the society, most of them – about 61% presented on various SNS remain alien to all that is happening within those sites keeping a semblance of any activity. The quality of the content of official accounts also leaves much to be desired remaining purely professional, absolutely impersonal, dry and official, while citizens prefer a human side or a user's oriented approach, that could significantly increase the loyalty towards the state official or agency policy [49]. A "human face" of official accounts seems to be a general problem and is common for many countries [54].

General observation shows now apparent that state and municipal bodies and employees in Russia are reducing activities on SNS or even withdrawing from them. This process started to happen from late 2014 – early 2015. Currently, a large number of state and municipal employees have removed their accounts from social networks or depersonalized them. The situation has not had any official comment but the authors are presuming it to be an inner policy inside state body and agencies based on some codes of behavior with no public access to.

Most recent decisions of the Federal Government show a considerable interest in regulating social media use by public employees. In 2015, the State Duma announced a bill prohibiting the usage of social networking services and applications by public servants from their working devices. In 2016, the scope of the bill was enlarged for the whole public sector. The employer would have the right to ban using SNS during the working hours. The latest legal initiative goes even further and seeks to make public employees to reveal their usage of social media for the last 3 years when obtaining a new post [16, 17]. This situation makes think about the possible consequences of such legal novelties for the Russian society and the government in order to suggest a coherent policy on using social media for public sector from the point of law and ethic.

4   Code of Ethics for Public Sector and Social Media Use

Public service ethics is an intrinsic part of legal status of every public official. The global character of the fight against corruption drove to the elaboration of Model Codes of Conduct for public sector on international and regional levels. Most of them have general provisions concerning the information sharing activities of public servants evidently including those in mass media and social media.

The Model Code of Conduct for Public Officials of Council of Europe adopted in 2000 [15] contains series of obligations that are common for a large part of similar documents adopted in Europe. According to this document public officials:

- should act in neutral political manner and should not attempt to impair the existing policies, decisions or actions (art. 4);
- serve loyally and lawfully a state or municipal body (art. 5);
- be courteous in his or her relations with citizens he or she serves, as well as to his superior, colleagues or subordinate staff (art. 5);

- should avoid conflict of his private interests with his or her duties (art. 13);
- conduct in a manner that public's confidence and trust in integrity, impartiality and effectiveness of the public service are preserved and enhanced (art. 9);
- should disclose information only according to rules and requirements applying to the authority he or she is employed for, avoiding disclosure of confidential or classified information (art. 11, 22);
- should not conduct in his or her official capacity or in private life that makes him or her susceptible to improper influence of others (art. 20).

Similar documents have been adopted in Russia for many spheres of the public sector: Model Code of Ethic and Conduct for Civil State and Municipal Servants of Russian Federation [31]; Code of Ethic and Conduct of Servants of Central Bank of Russia [10]; Codes of Professional Ethic of Notaries in the Russian Federation [13]; Code of Judicial Ethic [12]; Code of Ethic of Procuratura [11]; Code of Ethic and Conduct for Civil Servants of the Investigative Committee of the Russian Federation [9].

Brief analysis of them reveals more detailed regulation of public officials' activities when dealing with mass media and public appearance. The Model Code of Ethics and Conduct for Civil State and Municipal Servants of Russian Federation as a more general document and a sample of many others existing regulations states that a public servant should:

- refrain from any behavior that could cause doubt in the faithful execution of state (municipal) servants official duties and avoid conflict situations capable of inflicting damage to reputation of a state or local authority;
- refrain from public statements, judgements and estimations concerning activity of the state or local authority, its head if it's not part of his or her official duties;
- comply with the government body or body of local self-government rules of public speaking and dissemination of service information;
- abstain in public statements, including in mass media, evaluating in a foreign currency goods, works, services and other objects of civil rights, the sums of transactions between residents of the Russian Federation, budget indicators of all levels, state and municipal bonds, government and municipal debt, except cases when it is required for accurate information dissemination according to the law, international treaty or customary business practices.

For some public sectors could exist additional and specific regulation of professional conduct, e.g. judicial and law enforcement agencies employees have normally obligations to refrain from any actions including public statements that could affect the independence and impartiality of the Justice. Normally judges are required not to comment the course of any affaires before the final decision is taken.

Thus, professional code of ethics and conduct for public sector usually are based on the following principles, that public employee should not commit actions:

- contrary to the interests of service duties;
- that could affect reputation of the public authority;
- that could affect reputation and dignity of the profession;
- undermining the trust in a government employee's impartiality and independence;
- that could draw to conflict of interests.

Those principles could be easily applicable for public employees actions on SNS but do not provide sometimes detailed and coherent answer to practical issues. To deal with them governmental agencies elaborate special policy documents: guidelines, guidance, policy documents, recommendations, strategies, standards, protocols etc.

5 Social Media Policies as a Main Tool

5.1 Elements of Governmental Social Media Policies

Social media policies are named often as a common tool for detailed regulation of social media use and not only for public sector [54]. Government agencies create them for different goals, e.g. social inclusion, good governance [3]. One of the most cited research of Hrdinová et al. [21], where 26 publicly available social media policies were analyzed, underlines that most of them include eight common elements: employee access, account management, content management, acceptable use, employee conduct, citizen conduct, security concerns and legal issues. This approach was criticized because of ambiguity of its boundaries [39]. Other scholars suggested some new components – organizational responsibility and rules of "online netiquette" [28]. Special report released by Bureau of Justice Assistance states that social media policies should deal with the following issues: compatibility with over laws and policies, authorized use, information evaluation, information archiving, procedure of dissemination and purpose of use [7]. A special survey conducted by National Association of State Chief Information Officers (NASCIO) [33] examined thirty-one state policies identified that confidentiality (84%), ethical conduct (74%), security and privacy (65%), personal use (55%), public commenting (45%) and transparency (39%) were the most mentioned elements. The document also suggested that social media policies should address: demand evaluation, acceptable use, organizational concerns, policy scope, principles of interactions, record management, relationship with current policies and employee training.

Although policy elements vary in different studies, at least six elements are common and generally used by a considerable part of them: account management, content management, resource arrangement, employee conduct, citizen conduct, security concerns [39].

5.2 Official vs. Private Use

The general analysis of implemented Social Media Policies shows also that they treat the above mentioned elements in two main dimensions or ways how social media are used by public employees:

"Official use" – an employee acts on behalf of the state agency through its or his/her official profile;

"Personal use" – for private or personal goals not in connection with his working activities or official duties [21].

In most cases, Social Media policies are more concentrated on the first part prescribing how a public servant should act when using an official account (account or profile created and operated on behalf of a state authority). Normally this type of use is possible under direct authorization from the public body and this should be included in servant's duties. All interactions are to be formal. The account should be well labeled and interconnected with other official resources (sites, other social media, e-mails etc.). Sometimes regulation here is very detailed concerning cases of responses to public comments or providing services [44].

Personal use is a more sensible category. This part contains mostly restrictions on using social media in order to avoid any connection of employee's personal or private activities with the authority. Thus, a public servant should avoid any: reference to his current post, comment or reply on behalf of the agency. If any of this happens he is obliged to post a disclaimer with a special formula that all his actions taken and views expressed are his own and do not reflect the official views or policies of the agency. Furthermore, an employee is usually asked to behave in an honorable and responsible manner avoiding illegal or indecent actions (disseminating classified information, copyright infringements, insult, defamation etc.) [44]. More specific element could be found in this part of Social Media Policies for military, defense or police agencies where regulation is more concentrated on disclosure of confidential information on special operations and security risks during personal use of SNS [18].

Thus, personal use of social media by public employees represents an interesting issue where the existing practice varies and is differently regarded from the point of law and ethics. The UK Social Media Guidance for Civil Servants emphasizes that a civil servant should follow general ethical conduct rules that demand from any employee to act in accordance with principles of integrity, honesty, objectivity and impartiality. On the other hand, the Guidance clearly states the right of a civil servant for personal use of SNS during his own time or sometimes during working hours and from any device including a working one. Instead, he should be mindful of his duties not to disclose official information without authorization, and not to take part in any political or other public activity, which compromises, or might be seen compromising, his impartial service to the government of the day or any future government [41].

Employer's control and monitoring of social media activities of public employees represents another considerable challenge for the freedom of information and privacy rights applicable here [42]. Surely, this case is more relevant to 'Personal use' that have two different aspects: the usage of social media during working hours and use of them outside job activities. For the first case, even in private sector we are observing a common tendency for toughening regulation. Employers not only in public sector want to restrict, control or monitor their employees' activities in social media during working hours and this position found support from the state authorities. The other case, when an employee uses SNS for initially private purposes outside his working place and hours is differently treated in private and public sector. It becomes a general tendency that public employees right for personal using SNS are more limited. Government while drafting Social Media Policies, Guidelines and Code of Conduct is seeking to enlarge their scope to personal or private activities of public servants on SNS that could also engage responsibility for actions in discrepancy of their official post or duties.

5.3   Public Servants' Responsibility

Despite the absence of any legal basis for official surveillance of on-line activities of public employees on SNS in Russia it exists in practice and numerous cases shows it.

Autumn 2010 the ex-governor of Tver Region of Russia posted on his Twitter account a photo of a worm that he had allegedly found on his plate during the official meeting of the Germany President at Kremlin residence. The post gave place to a serious investigation that proved its incorrectness and despite a rather humorous comment made in response by the Prime-Minister, Dmitriy Medvedev, the governor was dismissed in a half of a year [16].

Another curious case happened to Vice-Governor of Orel Region Alexander Ryavkin who posted in Facebook a photo of restaurant in Karlovy Vary with a comment that 'the divine fois-gras is served there'. The post and the photo caused very sharp reaction from the public and made him resign [16].

The considerable support from the public also could not save from reassignment the other high-rank Russian official Deputy Minister on Economic development Sergei Belyakov. In 2014, on his page in Facebook he admitted that he was deeply ashamed of the recent government's decision on social security policy and received in return a vast majority of positive comments from citizens [47].

Similar cases but with different connotation continue to happen and not only in Russia [1, 37]. The international tendency was perfectly described in memos disseminated during election campaign in Canada in 2015 that "you are public servants 24/7" and have "a duty of loyalty" [46]. Those examples clearly demonstrate that "personal use" of social media by public officials is now under question.

5.4   Drafting Russian Social Media Policy

Unfortunately, the creation of Social Media Policies for public sector in Russia continues to face various difficulties. Existing regulation and policy documents are focused on more general aspects, e.g. Open Government, Open Data, e-Democracy etc. One of the key legal instruments regulating the use of social networks by public servants and bodies is the Guidelines on the Implementation of the Principles of Openness by the Federal Executive Authorities [19]. Though it has only an advisory power, the Guidelines suggest clearly that social networks are an important information platform for non-formal communication between the Federal Executive and citizens. Existing Codes of Ethic for public sector do not regulate specifically the usage of social media by public employees regarding it as a particular case of media activities.

Russian companies are also rather shy in revealing their policies towards using social media by their employees. According to some surveys, one third of Russian companies is banning the usage of social media by their staff during working hours [16, 43]. Half of companies uses SNS to control and monitor their staff activities and considers this information for career promotion [8].

Public bodies mostly keep silence on their social media policies' documents and strategies despite the number of rather vague and loose provisions and general intention to communicate with the public through SNS. Most recent decisions show on the other hand strong emphasis of the public authorities on different levels to control and monitor 'personal use'. The recently adopted and above mentioned Federal Law obliges public employees to declare their online activities is one of the most obvious examples. Some local authorities go in the same directions and adopt similar provisions on municipal levels.

The absence of coherent rules of play for using social media by public authorities and officials represents a potential risk for both citizens and public employees. The undertaken steps towards regulation of governmental use of social media look very awkward and contribute mostly interests of state and local authorities instead of finding a true balance of interests for government, citizens and employees.

The head of the National Strategy Council Valery Khomyakov believes that the initiative on "declaring" of the Internet accounts of civil servants fits into the general trend on the "crackdown" in the country. However, the expert doubts that the rule will be workable, as it would need a special agency or a department for tracking social media activities of public servants [16].

6 Conclusion

It becomes clear that social media have changed considerably our social landscape. They are now an indispensable part of our life and a place where people share and express opinion on different political and social issues and a powerful e-democracy tool. This explains why SNS platforms are becoming more and more a public space with a large potential auditory. Despite, the existing positive and negative factors of using social media for public duties governmental agencies and employees are inclined to use them in order to develop communication and e-participation of the citizens. Taking into account that all interactions of the government with citizens are formal and need a coherent set of rules, many countries introduced special ethic and policy documents to help and organize governmental use of SNS. Thus, Social Media Policies and Guidelines become an inherent part of Open and E-Government system. It should be admitted that an 'official use' of social media by public employees has a coherent regulation that seems to be reasonable and well based as they act on behalf of a state or local authority in the line of their duty. In this case, state officials should stick to existing legal and ethical regulation. On the other hand, 'personal use' of social media by public officials seems to be a wary ground. It becomes a general tendency that the government wants to monitor and control public servants' actions on SNS and to make them responsible for unethical behavior, especially during working hours or at working place. Moreover, recent governmental initiatives not only in Russia point out that a public servant should be so 24/7 and is responsible even for actions on SNS outside his duties or job hours. Application of so general rule could affect considerably public servant's rights to privacy and freedom of information. Besides, Social Media Policies and other documents do not make any distinction for public officials' ranks and duties. It is commonly recognized that high-rank officials should be more used to interference in their private life or to be in the limelight. Ordinary public employees in return should be treated more sensibly leaving them more discretion for using social media exclusively for their personal needs.

All those issues should be also addressed while drafting Social Media Policies for the government. The present situation in Russia and considerable growth of social media use in national public sector are forming now an urgent need of a policy document that would solve many existing problems and provide a coherent regulation in this sphere.

References

1. Ariel, B.: Belgian Muslim official resigns after comparing Israel to ISIS (2016). http://www.israelnationalnews.com/News/News.aspx/217438
2. Bekkers, V., Edwards, A., De Kool, D.: Social media monitoring: responsive governance in the shadow of surveillance? Gov. Inf. Quart. 30(4), 335–342 (2013)
3. Bertot, J.C., Jaeger, P.T., Hansen, D.: The impact of polices on government social media usage: issues, challenges, and recommendations. Gov. Inf. Quart. 29(1), 30–40 (2012)
4. Bertot, J.C., Jaeger, P.T., Grimes, J.M.: Using ICTs to create a culture of transparency: E-government and social media as openness and anti-corruption tools for societies. Gov. Inf. Quart. 27(3), 264–271 (2010)
5. Bonson, E., Torres, L., Royo, S., Flores, S.F.: Local e-government 2.0: social media and corporate transparency in municipalities. Gov. Inf. Quart. 29(2), 123–132 (2012)
6. Bundin, M., Martynov, A.: Use of social media by the federal government in Russia. In: ACM International Conference Proceeding Series, pp. 394–395 (2016)
7. Bureau of Justice Assistance. Developing a Policy on the Use of Social Media in Intelligence and Investigative Activities: Guidance and Recommendations (2013). http://www.iacpsocialmedia.org/Portals/1/documents/SMInvestigativeGuidance.pdf
8. Chernokojeva, I.: Every Second Employer monitors his staff activities in social media (2014). https://versia.ru/supejob-kazhdyj-vtoroj-rabotodatel-sledit-za-svoimi-sotrudnikami-v-socsetyax
9. Code of Ethic and Conduct for Civil Servants of the Investigative Committee of the Russian Federation. http://sledcom.ru/document/1060
10. Code of Ethic and Conduct of Servants of Central Bank of Russia. http://www.cbr.ru/anticor/zip/kodex.pdf
11. Code of Ethic of Procuratura. http://genproc.gov.ru/documents/orders/document-14294/
12. Code of Judicial Ethic. http://www.garant.ru/products/ipo/prime/doc/70201432/
13. Codes of Professional Ethic of Notaries in the Russian Federation. http://www.consultant.ru/document/cons_doc_LAW_189129/
14. Criado, J.I., Sandoval-Almazan, R., Gil-Garcia, J.R.: Government innovation through social media. Gov. Inf. Quart. 30(4), 319–326 (2013)
15. Draft Recommendation No. R of the committee of ministers to member states on codes of conduct for public officials (2000). https://search.coe.int/cm/Pages/result_details.aspx?ObjectID=09000016804d065a
16. Ezhov, S.: Officials, Open your Nicks! (2016). http://www.newizv.ru/lenta/2016-06-23/241490-chinovniki-raskrojte-niki.html
17. Gorbunova, A.: Candidates for a municipal post would be obliged to declare their social media activities (2016). https://opennov.ru/news/27837-kandidaty-na-municipalnuyu-sluzhbu-budut-otchityvatsya-o-deystviyah-v-socsetyah
18. Guide de Bon Usage des Mediaux Sociaux du Ministère de l'Intérieur. http://fichiers.acteurspublics.com/redac/pdf/Aout/2014-guide-medias-sociaux-agents-mi.pdf

19. Guidelines on the Implementation of the Principles of Openness by the Federal Executive Authorities. http://open.gov.ru/upload/iblock/830/830154385b151a308d6d820ff8fa03bd.doc

20. Hong, H.: Government websites and social media's influence on government-public relationships. Public Relat. Rev. **39**(4), 346–356 (2013)

21. Hrdinová, J., Helbig, N., Peters, C.S.: Designing social media policy for government: eight essential elements (2010). https://www.ctg.albany.edu/publications/guides/social_media_policy/social_media_policy.pdf

22. Kavanaugh, A.L., Fox, E.A., Sheetz, S.D., Yang, S., Li, L.T., Shoemaker, D.J., Natsev, A., Xie, L.: Social media use by government: from the routine to the critical. Gov. Inf. Quart. **29** (4), 480–491 (2012)

23. Kim, S.K., Park, M.J., Rho, J.J.: Effect of the government's use of social media on the reliability of the government: focus on Twitter. Public Manag. Rev. **17**(3), 328–355 (2015)

24. Lee, G., Kwak, Y.H.: An open government maturity model for social media-based public engagement. Gov. Inf. Quart. **29**(4), 492–503 (2012)

25. Linders, D.: From e-government to we-government: defining a typology for citizen coproduction in the age of social media. Gov. Inf. Quart. **29**(4), 446–454 (2012)

26. Macnamara, J., Zerfass, A.: Social media communication in organizations: the challenges of balancing openness, strategy, and management. Int. J. Strateg. Commun. **6**(4), 287–308 (2012)

27. Mergel, I., Bretschneider, S.I.: A three-stage adoption process for social media use in government. Public Adm. Rev. **73**(3), 390–400 (2013)

28. Mergel, I., Greeves, B.: Social Media in the Public Sector Field Guide: Designing and Implementing Strategies and Policies. Jossey-Bass/Wiley, San Francisco (2012)

29. Mergel, I.: Social media adoption and resulting tactics in the U.S. federal government. Gov. Inf. Quart. **30**(2), 123–130 (2013)

30. Mickoleit, A.: Social Media Use by Governments: A Policy Primer to Discuss Trends, Identify Policy Opportunities and Guide Decision Makers, OECD Working Papers on Public Governance, No. 26, OECD Publishing, Paris (2014). doi:http://dx.doi.org/10.1787/5jxrcmghmk0s-en

31. Model code of ethics and conduct for civil state and municipal servants of Russian Federation. http://base.garant.ru/55171108/

32. Mossberger, K., Wu, Y., Crawford, J.: Connecting citizens and local governments? Social media and interactivity in major U.S. cities. Gov. Inf. Quart. **30**(4), 351–358 (2013)

33. National Association of State Chief Information Officers (NASCIO). Examining State Social Media Policies: Closing the Gaps (2013). http://www.nascio.org/Portals/0/Publications/Documents/NASCIO_2013SocialMediaIssueBrief.pdf

34. Noesselt, N.: Microblogs and the adaptation of the Chinese party-state's governance strategy. Governance **27**(3), 449–468 (2014)

35. Picazo-Vela, S., Guitiérrez-Martínez, I., Luna-Reyes, L.F.: Understanding risks, benefits, and strategic alternatives of social media applications in the public sector. Gov. Inf. Quart. **29**(4), 504–511 (2012)

36. Piotrowsky, S.J., Zhang, Y., Lin, W., Yu, W.: Key issues for implementation of Chinese open government information regulations. Public Adm. Rev. **69**(SUPPL. 1), S129–S135 (2009)

37. Portnoy, J.: Va. GOP official resigns after controversial Facebook post. Washington post (2014). https://www.washingtonpost.com/local/virginia-politics/va-gop-official-resigns-after-controversial-facebook-post/2014/08/07/d41fcec0-1ddd-11e4-82f9-2cd6fa8da5c4_story.html

38. Puiu, S.: Ethics management in public sector – background and tools. Procedia Econ. Finance **23**, 604–607 (2015). doi:10.1016/S2212-5671(15)00566-3

39. Qiang, C., Xiaolin, X., Bolin, C., Wei, Z.: Social media policies as responses for social media affordances: the case of China. Gov. Inf. Quart. **33**(2), 313–324 (2016). doi:10.1016/j.giq.2016.04.008
40. Schlaeger, J., Jiang, M.: Official microblogging and social management by local governments in China. China Inf. **28**(2), 189–213 (2014)
41. Social media guidance for civil servants. https://www.gov.uk/government/publications/social-media-guidance-for-civil-servants/social-media-guidance-for-civil-servants
42. Social Media in the Work Place. Around the World 3.0. http://www.proskauer.com/files/uploads/social-media-in-the-workplace-2014.pdf
43. Social Media: only for official use. http://hr-portal.ru/article/dlya-sluzhebnogo-polzovaniya-socialnye-seti
44. Social Security Administration. Social Security Administration's Social Media Policy. https://www.ssa.gov/socialmedia/SSA_Social_Media_Policy_Final.pdf
45. Tedeev, A.A., Usanova, V.E.: Elektronnoe gosudarstvo: Monografiya. "Elit", Moscow (2008)
46. Tejas, A.: Canada Government Attempts to Stifle Public Servants' Social Media use Ahead of Election: Union Leaders. International Business Times (2015). http://www.ibtimes.com/canada-government-attempts-stifle-public-servants-social-media-use-ahead-election-2057846
47. The Deputy Minister was fired for shame. https://www.gazeta.ru/politics/2014/08/06_a_6163433.shtml
48. Vaast, E., Kaganer, E.: Social media affordances and governance in the workplace: an examination of organizational policies. J. Comput.-Mediat. Commun. **19**(1), 78–101 (2013)
49. Vasilenko, L.A., Tarasova, E.V., et al.: Modeli dialoga vlasti i obschestva v internet-kommunikatsiyah: metodicheskoe posobie. Prospekt, Moscow (2015)
50. Wright, B.E., Hassan, S., Park, J.: Does a public service ethic encourage ethical behavior? Public service motivation, ethical leadership and the willingness to report ethical problems. Public Adm. **94**(3), 647–663 (2016)
51. Zaru, D.: President Obama joins Facebook, addresses climate change in first post (2009). http://edition.cnn.com/2015/11/09/politics/barack-obama-joins-facebook/index.html
52. Zavatarro, S.M., Sementelli, A.J.: A critical examination of social media adoption in government: introducing omnipresence. Gov. Inf. Quart. **31**(2), 257–264 (2014)
53. Zheng, L., Zheng, T.: Innovation through social media in the public sector: information and interactions. Gov. Inf. Quart. **31**(SUPPL.1), S106–S117 (2014)
54. Zheng, L.: Social media in Chinese government: drivers, challenges and capabilities. Gov. Inf. Quart. **30**(4), 369–376 (2013)

Requisites for Open Budgeting: A Comparison of the 'Budget for Citizens' in Russian Regions Using QCA

Leonid Smorgunov[⊠]

St. Petersburg State University, Universitetskaya Nab.,
7/9, St. Petersburg 199034, Russia
l.smorgunov@spbu.ru

Abstract. The practice of citizens' involvement in the process of the formation, monitoring and evaluation of performance of the public budget has become one of the most important forms of cooperation of citizens and government. Of particular importance is acquiring a digital form of government where the public use of data creates a solid platform for the modern type of "co-production" of public budgets. Modern budgeting based on cooperation transforms designs of budgetary policy, accountability systems, processes of identifying public values, and others. Ensuring citizen-oriented data relating to the budget here gets particular importance, and sharing the learning of citizens and the government for inclusive budget process becomes the main requisite for successful collaboration. This paper analyzes the Russian practice of open budget and "budget for the citizens" in the context of different requisites: social-economic and informational, which construct an inclusive capacity of the regions. This practice was introduced in 2013 at the federal and regional levels. Though institutions of "budget for the citizens" inure for legitimating regimes, they are also good factors for mutual learning for cooperation. Transparency of budgetary data, its transformation for the citizens, and budgeting, initiated by citizens, affect the character of Russian designs for inclusive budgeting in the regions. On the basis of different ratings of open budgeting and requisites, this paper explains the complex configuration of requisites for the open budget and the 'budget for citizens' and three models of introducing forms of e-participation. The main hypothesis of the study is the higher the level of inclusive capacity of the region, the higher the openness of budget data and the "budget for citizens". For a comparison of 22 Russian regions, the QCA method has been used.

Keywords: Open budget · Participatory budgeting · Requisites for open budget · Inclusive capacity · Russian regions · QCA method

1 Introduction

Today the process of political and administrative activity has become saturated with new forms and mechanisms, which include such unusual components for older models as public examination and evaluation, public forums, public-private commissions, etc. There are different names for these new forms of public engagement into policy and

© Springer International Publishing AG 2017
D.A. Alexandrov et al. (Eds.): DTGS 2017, CCIS 745, pp. 243–256, 2017.
https://doi.org/10.1007/978-3-319-69784-0_21

decision-making processes. Warren for example, categorizes many of these developments as "governance-driven democratization" [25]. Some scholars use the term "collaborative governance". Paying attention to citizen engagement and participation in public governance, Walker and Shannon give this development the name "participatory governance" [24]. This partly independent trend in modern theory of public governance take characteristics of the new development from process of community engagement into policy, decision-making, and public service delivery. This direction elaborates the concepts of "governance through community engagement", "community engaging government" or "integrated public governance" [2, 9]. In general we can say that the traditional problem of the relationship between politics and governance in these new concepts has been turned in the direction of finding the relationship of citizens and state institutions. Although questions of cost-effectiveness remain, some new ones come to the fore: the problem of sensitivity and responsibility of government, political stability and absence of violence, skillful organization (quality control), the rule of law and fighting corruption.

One of the forms of involving citizens in public policy is participatory budgeting. We find the first experience of such budgeting in the 1980s in Brazil [23]. In the future, participatory budgeting was adopted by many countries and regions. The study of budgeting for citizens, as a rule, refers to the internal mechanism of citizens' participation in the development of the budget at various levels of public policy [3], the process of discussing budget data, and the development of deliberative democracy [7], and the effectiveness of spending the budget in terms of civic participation [5]. A number of researchers agree that participatory budgeting is a form of inclusive institutions [21] that contribute to raising the overall justification for budget spending and forming a new cohort of citizens interested in participating in the affairs of the municipalities, regional authorities and government of the country.

In the study of participatory budgeting, one can find work that describes the conditions for its emergence, and the contextual factors that influence its inclusion in the overall design of public policy, which determine its integrity and effectiveness [20]. Part of the work describes the specifics of the diffusion of the experience of participatory budgeting in the country, highlighting here such forms as learning, competition, pressure, and imitation [10]. In our work, we follow this line of study of the budget for citizens, drawing attention to the basic requisites that contribute to the formation of the opportunity and willingness of citizens to participate in budgeting. These opportunities and readiness are associated with the use of conditions and the construction of institutions that determine the participatory capacity of citizens.

For these purposes, the article uses a special method of qualitative comparative analysis – QCA/fs [14], which allows not only to study the complex diversity of the conditions of an event, process or object, but also to formulate certain ideas about the causal mechanism involved in order to achieve some result. As an object of research, 22 regions of Russia were taken, which received the highest ratings in the process of monitoring the openness of budget data and the formation of a "budget for citizens."

2 Conceptualization of the Russian 'Budget for Citizens'

In Russia, the policy of involving citizens in the budget process began in 2013. In July, the Minister of Finance of the Russian Federation approved the Working Group on "Budget for Citizens". The joint order of the Ministry of Finance, the Ministry of Regional Development and the Ministry of Economic Development on August 22, 2013 approved the Methodological Recommendations on the submission of budgets of the constituent entities of the Russian Federation, local budgets, and reports on their implementation in an accessible form for citizens. The Budget Message of the President of the Russian Federation on Budget Policy in 2014–2016 stated that "from 2013 onwards, at all levels of the administration, a brochure" Budget for Citizens "should be published (posted on the Internet). This will make it possible to inform the population in an accessible form about the relevant budgets, planned and achieved results of using budget funds" [4]. In October, a model of the first federal "Budget for Citizens" in the Russian Federation was published. And in December the updated version of the "Budget for Citizens" to the Federal Law of December 2, 2013 No. 349-FZ "On the Federal Budget for 2014 and for the Planning Period of 2015 and 2016" was presented. This addition to the law was recommended by the State Duma and the Federation Council of the Federal Assembly of the Russian Federation. On the portal of the open government, a specialized website "Budget for Citizens" (http://budget.open.gov.ru/) was created, which became the organizing start for the dissemination of the practice of the open budget in the regions and municipalities of Russia. Currently, all 85 regions have open budgets for citizens (see Fig. 1) and hundreds of municipalities use the practice of civil budgeting. At the same time, pilot projects on the introduction of a "budget for citizens" at the municipal level in cities such as Sosnovy Bor, Cherepovets, Mirny and others were begun. In subsequent years, the concept of a "budget for citizens" developed in the direction of not only improving the presentation of budget data to citizens, but also to expand the practice of involving citizens in the budget process itself.

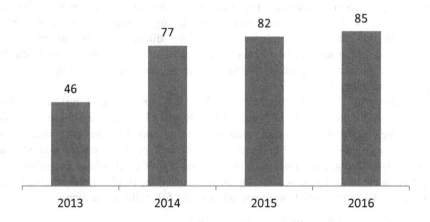

Fig. 1. 'Budget for citizens' in the regions of Russia

The budget for citizens in Russia is a simplified version of the budget document that uses informal language and accessible formats to make it easier for citizens to understand the budget, explain to them the plans and actions of the government during the budget year, and show their forms of possible interaction with the government on issues of public expenditure finance.

The general requirements for reporting data for the civil budget are defined in the "Methodological Recommendations". The following sections are usually included in the budget for citizens: a glossary explaining the basic concepts used in the budget process; a general description of the region; the main indicators of the socio-economic development of the region in accordance with the forecast of its socio-economic development; the main tasks and priority directions of the budgetary policy of the region for the next financial year and planning period; the main characteristics of the budget (in absolute and relative terms), including information on incomes and expenditures, intergovernmental transfers planned to be received from the federal budget (budget of the constituent entity of the Russian Federation, local budget), as well as budget deficit/surplus; basic information on the intergovernmental fiscal relations of the region, including information on transfers to be received from the federal budget (the budget of the constituent entity of the Russian Federation) sent to local budgets planned to be received from local budgets; level of debt burden on the regional budget, including the structure of its debt; information on the position of the region in the ratings of the openness of budget data, the quality of management of regional finance; information on the holding and participation of the region in the competitions of projects on the presentation of budgets for citizens, on the implementation of projects of proactive budgeting, as well as projects aimed at increasing the budget literacy of the population.

At the same time, information must correspond to a number of criteria: (1) sufficiency, (2) clarity, (3) relevance, (4) reliability, (5) accessibility, (6) timeliness. The budget for citizens is targeted at a certain target groups of citizens. The target group and its composition may be determined by the criteria for assigning citizens and/or organizations receiving support (or other forms of payment) from the budget to a particular target group. Such criteria can include qualitative characteristics of representatives of target groups, the number of representatives of the target group and its social significance, and the amount of budgetary allocations directed to support the target group. The target group can be a group of citizens and/or organizations to which the activities of the state program of the subject of the Russian Federation (municipal program) are directed.

Beginning in 2015, the Research and Development Financial Institute (NIFI), commissioned by the Ministry of Finance of the Russian Federation has been rating the Russian regions according to their criteria for open budgets. The methodology for assessing the regions establishes benchmarks for best practices on the content and accessibility of budget documents, as well as the use of mechanisms for public participation in the budget process. For our study, we used the results of the ranking of the regions for 2015 [19], which were compiled in the following main areas:

- characteristics of the originally approved budget,
- annual performance report,

- amendments to the law on the budget,
- interim reporting on budget execution and analytical data,
- draft budget and materials for it,
- financial control,
- public information on the activities of state institutions of the subject of the Russian Federation (planned and actual performance indicators),
- budget for citizens (the law on the budget, the annual report on the budget execution, the draft budget),
- public participation (quarterly).

In practice, the level of openness of budget data in the regions and the implementation of the "Budget for Citizens" program were to a certain extent determined by the activity of regional authorities in fulfilling the tasks assigned to them by the federal government. At the same time, it should be noted that the differentiation of regional development in its various dimensions - economic, social, and digital - did not at first sight affect the pace and intensity of introducing new approaches to budgeting. In the rating table, regions with different degrees of social and economic development (in Table 1) fell into Sect. 1 (regions with very high level of open budget data) and Sect. 2 (regions with a high level of openness of budget data). Statistical analysis of the correlation between the openness of budget data and the level of socio-economic development (expressed in regional GDP per capita) shows low results (r is 0.25). What is the unifying factor of influence on the openness of budget data in the regional context? In our opinion, this complex factor will be such an indicator of regional development as the capacity for "inclusiveness". Under the inclusiveness of regional development, we will understand a level of regional development when citizens are aimed at participating (and have the opportunity for such participation), public authorities are open to participation, and citizens themselves use the results of development. Under the capacity for inclusiveness, we mean institutions and positions that provide the opportunity for participation. *The main hypothesis of the study, therefore, is that the higher the level of inclusive ability of the region, the higher the openness of budget data and the "budget for citizens".* Of course, to a certain extent, the open budget itself is a factor of inclusiveness, that is, can act as an independent variable. However, in this case, we take into account the time period when the open budget was a goal, rather than a means of achieving any result. At least in respect to the policy of open budgeting, we can say that it is still a task that needs to be addressed effectively.

Four characteristics of the inclusive capacity of the region in the aspect of the topic under study are, in our opinion, significant. *First*, inclusivity implies a high level of opportunities for citizens to use information. This level is determined, on the one hand, by the development of new means of communication and information, and on the other, by the openness of state and municipal authorities. To this end, we formulated two variables: *inf* - the level of development of the information society in the region, and *serv* – the share of citizens who are ready to use e-services. Both variables include the content of openness of authorities and the development of information infrastructure. *Secondly*, inclusive ability is provided by the state of the middle class in the region (*income*) and the quality of life (*life*). The operationalization of these variables, and therefore their metric values, are taken from various sources. The development of the

Table 1. 22 highest positions in the rating of the Russian regions on open budgeting for 2015

Region	Place	Total marks	GRP per capita, thousand rub.	The share of households with a personal computer
Max of possible marks		*210.0*		
Krasnodar Kray	1	185.00	355.0	67.5
Orenburg Oblast	2	184.00	387.8	70.1
Omsk Oblast	3	182.50	312.0	71.7
Krasnoyarsk Kray	4	178.00	565.3	72.0
Murmansk Oblast	5	164.00	510.8	88.6
Adyghe Republic (Adygea)	6	162.00	183.4	59.8
Hanty-Mansiysky Autonomous Okrug - Yugra	7	157.50	1937.0	84.6
Moscow Oblast	8	154.00	441.8	78.6
Stavropol Kray	9	153.00	217.6	65.9
Vladimir Oblast	10	147.00	255.4	71.5
Udmurt Republic	11	132.00	328.0	68.8
Irkutsk Oblast	12	130.00	419.9	76.0
Bashkortostan Republic	13	119.50	323.6	70.6
Astrakhan Oblast	14	114.00	314.5	77.4
Penza Oblast	15	111.00	248.9	67.8
Kirov Oblast	16	109.00	212.5	66.5
Vologda Oblast	17	108.00	394.1	64.0
Ulyanovsk Oblast	18	104.50	239.2	63.0
Arkhangelsk Oblast	19	104.00	352.0	78.5
Altai Kray	20	102.50	206.7	67.8
Voronezh Oblast	21–22	102.00	352.9	73.7
Tambov Oblast	21–22	102.00	326.5	68.1

information society (*inf*) is determined by the data of the Ministry of Communications of the Russian Federation [17]. The share of citizens registered in the Unified Register of Public Services (URPS) (*serv*) is also determined according to the data of the Ministry of Communications [12]. The state of the middle class in the region (*income*) is calculated by the median income per capita according to Rosstat. And, finally, the quality of life (*life*) is according to the quality of life rating in the Russian regions on the Riarating portal [18].

As dependent variables in our study, we took (*open*) general rating data on the state of openness of budget data in the regions of Russia and (*cit*) general characteristics of the rating relative to the development of the "budget for citizens". The variable "open" allowed to talk about the general state of the region regarding the implementation of the principle of openness of budget data for citizens, which was wider than the budget for citizens, but covered the basic level of the region's readiness for initiative budgeting. The variable "cit" characterized the level of development of the special program "Budget for Citizens" at the regional level.

There is a problem of choosing boundary criteria. The objectives of the study affect the choice and argumentation, although, of course, a well-founded theory will be here at the right time. In our case, we use the principle of relativity, subordinating the choice of criteria to situational conditions. The study assumes that the entire volume of studied cases breaks up into two relatively equal sets of developed and insufficiently or undeveloped cases, taking into account the hypothesis of a normal distribution. For analysis purposes, the metric data for the independent and dependent variables were recoded according to the QCA analysis, where one means quality, zero - no quality. The boundary criteria for the availability of quality were determined by the average values, i.e. among the values above ones characterized the presence of quality (1), below the average values indicated by the lack of quality (0). It was hypothetically assumed that there is a normal distribution of metric data. In this case, the designation of variables with a capital letter indicates the presence of quality, i.e. 1; lowercase letters indicate a lack of quality (0).

The general hypothesis of the research is expressed by the following model, if we use QCA operators - qualitative comparative analysis [14].

$$Open\,(Cit) \ = \ Inf + Serv + Income + Life$$

The openness of budgetary data in the region is determined by a combination of four conditions: the information development of the region *or* the share of citizens registered in the URPS *or* the availability of the middle class *or* the quality of life of the population.

The object of the study is the regions that received the highest scores on the openness of budget data in 2015. In 2015 there were 22 regions.

3 Method of Research

To analyze the relationship between "open budgeting" and the conditions for its formation in the regions of Russia (capacities for inclusiveness), we will use a configurable qualitative analysis proposed and developed by Ragin [13–16]. This approach is based on Boolean algebra. Boolean algebra began to be used as a qualitative methodology for analyzing empirical material presented in categorical form with the help of a non-metric categorical scale. At the same time, it turned out that this methodology makes it possible to perform a number of tasks that earlier in the political study, based on statistical analysis, caused difficulties.

Boolean algebra originated as historically the first section of mathematical logic in the middle of the 19th century and was named after George Boole (1815–1864) – an Irish mathematician and logician, who first introduced logic as an algebra of classes connected by the operators "and", "or" and " not". From his works the algebra of logic begins and its component part is the algebra of statements, in which algebra methods are used to study operations on statements, in respect of each of which one can assert only that its content is true or false. In political science, Boolean algebra (as a synonym for the whole algebra of logic) began to be used in the 1980 s, and the first was Charles Ragin, whose work immediately attracted the attention of researchers [8]. There are other publications that reveal the essence of the use of algebra of logic in political studies [1, 11]. Algebra of logic has begun to be used in studies of various phenomena of political life, including public policy [6].

As Charles Ragin pointed out, there is no need to consider Boolean algebra in its entirety in order to understand its possibilities in social science; Boolean principles used in c very simple [14: 85]. The sense of using logic algebra in qualitative research is that the researcher analyzes empirical data, formalizing their qualities in statements that are judged as false (lack of quality) or true (the presence of quality). Thus, the causes and consequences of phenomena are formalized, which then are reduced to truth tables, analyzed by a special procedure for minimizing logical expressions. George Romme wrote that Boole's logic allows us to limit the subjectivity of the interpretation of the data obtained, although it does not solve this problem completely: "Qualitative analysis of, for example, interviews or documentary data intends to capture the underlying meaning and patterns embodied in the data. This kind of inductive analysis appears to address concerns for (external) validity, because by arguing from the parts to the whole, the real meaning behind the data may emerge. However, it also relies to a great extent on subjective interpretation and judgment, and thus introduces a tradeoff in terms of validity. This problem can be somewhat reduced by using double coding procedures and other measures to cross-check potentially subjective interpretations. Nevertheless, the reliability of measures and conclusions obtained in the qualitative analysis of social processes tends to remain subject to severe challenge" [22: 317–18].

This crisp-analysis is important for us in two aspects. First, in essence, this approach starts with the premise of maximizing causal complexity, whereas the statistical method begins with the premise of the simplicity of the relationship. Of course, the Boolean analysis, compared to the "case-study" approach, is not characterized by maximum attention to historical details, but it allows including in the consideration the maximum number of possible combinations of conditions, and it is more reliable from the point of view of obtaining theoretical generalizations. "Note, writes Ragin, that the Boolean approach accomplishes what case-oriented investigators attempt, but on much larger scale. In case-oriented studies, investigators analyze similarities and differences in order to identify common underlying patterns and types.... However, the web of similarities and differences frequently gets out of hand. The Boolean truthtable approach and its rules for simplifying complexity provide a basis for managing this complicated web. It allows case-oriented investigators to see and comprehend complex patterns and conjunctures" [14: 122]. At the same time, this technique allows (if it is necessary) to economically explain causal interdependencies. An economical explanation is achieved by determining the largest classes of conditions for which a certain result is characteristic. Secondly, the Boolean analysis technique contributes simultaneously to research in the integrity of the causes and effects of the phenomenon being studied, as well as to study the individual components of this integrity. In this respect, it includes an orientation toward holism and inductive analysis. Ragin writes: "In Boolean analysis cases are seen as combination of parts. These combinations can be interpreted as different situations. The fundamental principle of holism provides a metatheoretical basis for this way of seeing cases: to alter any single part of a whole, any element, is - potentially at least – to alter the character of the whole. This approach contrasts directly with most statistical approaches, where the goal is to estimate the average effect of each variable (the causal significance of each part) across all values of other variables" [14: 122].

For the sake of investigation, an advanced program called QCA/fs (Qualitative Comparative Analysis/fuzzy set) has been developed. The latter program is specially adapted to social data and is actively used today in comparative studies. The QCA/fs • program has more possibilities and itself generates a truth table from the data matrix coming in at the input.

4   Crisp-Analysis Results of the Relation Between the Russian Open Budget and 'Budget for Citizens' and Its Requisites

To conduct the Crisp-analysis, we have generated an initial truth table, which included codified indicators of the dependent and independent variables for each individual case, which are the regions of Russia. Using a special computer program QCA/fs, a basic truth table was created for 22 cases (see Table 2). It shows all the independent variables (*Life, Income, Inf, Serv*), as well as the number of cases that correspond to a particular configuration of the requisites. A separate column shows the values of the dependent variable (*Open*). In this case, all configurations of the requisites are represented by the presence of the result. This is evidenced by 1 in this column and the raw consistency parameters, which for all rows are the same 1.000000. Consistency indicates that all the cases examined fall under the corresponding configuration; there are no contradictory results. According to the table, there are ten conditional configurations that satisfy the result. This complex configuration can be simplified using qualitative comparative analysis techniques. This simplification does not deprive the conclusion of the justi-fication, but only allows creating a picture of the regular configurations of causes.

Table 2. Truth table for relations between open budget and its requisites, 22 Russian regions in 2015

Life	Income	Inf	Serv	Number of cases	Open (QCA characteristics of outcomes)	Raw consistency
1	0	1	1	7	1	1.000000
1	1	1	1	3	1	1.000000
1	0	1	0	2	1	1.000000
1	0	0	0	2	1	1.000000
0	0	1	0	2	1	1.000000
0	0	0	1	2	1	1.000000
1	1	1	0	1	1	1.000000
1	1	0	0	1	1	1.000000
0	1	1	1	1	1	1.000000
0	0	1	1	1	1	1.000000

Analysis of the truth table using the Quinn-McCluskey algorithm yields the following result of the configuration of the conditions (1) that determine the presence of high openness of budget data in the regions of Russia.

$$Open = Inf \bullet income + serv \bullet Life + Serv \bullet Inf + Serv \bullet income \bullet life \qquad (1)$$

As can be seen from the ten possible configurations of reasons for the openness of budget data, four configurations are natural for 22 regions. Note that the configuration of causes should be considered in the integrity of the presence and absence of quality, although the presence of a condition indicates its generating power. Thus, from the logical proposition (1), it can be concluded that the openness of budget data (*Open*) is the result of the information society, and the absence of a middle class (*Inf* • *income*) or a minor inclusion of the population in the use of electronic services, but with a high level of quality of life (*serv* • *Life*), or significant inclusion of the population in the use of electronic services and Developed information society in the regional context (*Serv* • *Inf*), or a significant inclusion of the population in the use of electronic services with insignificant quality of life indicators and development of the middle class (*Serv* • *income* • *life*). Using the factorization of Boolean expressions, we can obtain an even more economical formula (2).

$$Open = Inf \bullet income + serv \bullet Life + Serv \bullet (Inf + incom \bullet life) \qquad (2)$$

It (2) shows that an open budget requires three basic requisites. First, the high development of the information society is conditionally necessary; second, the high quality of life in the region; thirdly, the availability of experience in the use of electronic services by citizens. True, all these requisites are necessary conditionally, but insufficient reasons, because we see their combination with other factors (their presence or absence).

The same procedure for working with the truth table for 22 regions will be conducted, using as a result the development of the "budget for citizens" program. From the truth table (Table 3), you can see that the configuration of the conditions is the same as for the budget openness. However, there are contradictory results encoded by the letter C in the sixth column, when this configuration generates the result and does not generate it. It is also obvious when we look at the raw consistency. Contradictory results require specific work with them. Charles Ragin says that their use is determined by theoretical considerations, which should be justified. It is clear that if we take into account that all the contradictory configurations give a positive result and include them in the analysis, then we will get the same final conclusion as in the case with the study of the openness of budget data. In this respect, formulas (1) and (3) will be similar.

$$Cit = Inf \bullet income + serv \bullet Life + Serv \bullet Inf + Serv \bullet income \bullet life \qquad (3)$$

The relevance of the corresponding contradictory configurations to obtain the result ("budget for citizens") is not obvious. Using the logic of experimental analysis, we can say that these configurations are not necessary and sufficient for a "budget for citizens",

Table 3. Truth table for relations between 'budget for citizens' and its requisites, 22 Russian regions in 2015

Life	Income	Inf	Serv	Number of cases	Cit (QCA characteristics of outcomes)	Raw consistency
1	0	1	1	7	1	1.000000
1	1	1	1	3	1	1.000000
1	0	1	0	2	C	0.500000
1	0	0	0	2	1	1.000000
0	0	1	0	2	C	0.500000
0	0	0	1	2	C	0.500000
1	1	1	0	1	1	1.000000
1	1	0	0	1	1	1.000000
0	1	1	1	1	1	1.000000
0	0	1	1	1	1	1.000000

so we can neglect them. Then the result of the investigation will be a formula (4) which gives a definite new result: in the configuration of conditions, a significant '*Income*' variable appears.

$$Cit = Serv \bullet Inf + serv \bullet inf \bullet Life + serv \bullet Income \bullet Life + Inf \bullet Income \bullet Life \quad (4)$$

$$Cit = Serv \bullet Inf + Life \bullet (serv \bullet inf + serv \bullet Income + Inf \bullet Income) \quad (5)$$

$$Cit = Serv \bullet Inf + servinfLife + Income(servLife + InfLife) \quad (6)$$

In formula (4), using factorization, the conditions of the information society, the inclusion of the population in the use of electronic services, and the quality of life are significant for the "budget for citizens", but are neither necessary nor sufficient. Where then we see the unification of the existence of conditions, somewhere presence is adjacent to the absence. In formula (5), which is equivalent to formulas (3) and (4), the 'Income' variable is singled out, which along with other conditions also becomes neither necessary nor sufficient.

Using qualitative comparative analysis, we showed one or another significance of the influence of independent variables, such as information and socio-economic requisites, on the openness of budget data and the introduction of a "budget for citizens." However, the hypothesis of the direct influence of the co-existence of these conditions has failed. None of them is either necessary or a sufficient reason for the result. However, the study revealed that each independent variable performs its task of stimulating the movement to open budget data or to a "budget for citizens." The question of what none of them poses separately indicates the complex structure of the configuration of variables.

How can we use the obtained empirical result in a positive sense else? In our opinion, the results of a qualitative comparative analysis speak of *different types or models of introducing open budget data and a "budget for citizens" in the Russian regions*.

5 Three Models of Implementation of an Open Budget and 'Budget for Citizens'

It was mentioned above that the implementation of open budget data and the 'budget for citizens' are determined by two basic conditions: the socio-economic state of citizens, which create opportunities for participation, and the information level of the regional development, which, of course, also functions as a capacity building, but is still a significant factor in the readiness for electronic participation. The latter is determined, in our opinion, by the learning process to use electronic resources to solve personal and public problems. In this regard, the first and second programs of "Electronic Russia", together with initiatives to create e-government, platforms for e-services, open government, open data platforms, etc., have for nearly 20 years served as a process of gradual learning for officials and citizens to use electronic means effectively. It should be noted that the introduction of electronic platforms and their use is becoming an important indicator of citizens' quality of life.

Analysis of the configuration of conditions leads to the allocation of three basic models for the formation of an open budget and a "budget for citizens" (Table 4). *The first model* can be conditionally called *technocratic*. In this model, great importance is attached to the formation of information infrastructure and electronic services. At the same time, for various reasons, the socio-economic factors that provide free opportunities for participation are pushed back to the back-end plan. This refers to the low quality of life and fair distribution of income. These regions include the Astrakhan Oblast, the Kirov Oblast, and the Altai Kray.

Table 4. The models of introducing open budget and 'budget for citizens'

Model	Complex configuration	Cases
Technocratic model	*Inf • income* *Serv • Inf* *Serv • income • life*	Astrakhan Oblast, Kirov Oblast, Altai Kray
Evolutionary model	*serv • Life* *serv • inf • Life* *serv • Income • Life*	Krasnodar Kray, Orenburg Oblast, Republic of Adygea
Inclusive model	*Inf • Income • Life*	Omsk Oblast, Krasnoyarsk Kray, Murmansk Oblast, Moscow Oblast, Bashkortostan, Voronezh Oblast

In *the second model*, a passive approach to the formation of conditions for an open budget and a "budget for citizens" is observed. High quality of life and more or less favorable conditions for income distribution are considered more important than the development of e-democracy for citizens. The last questions are solved *evolutionarily* together with the general policy of the development of the region. There is no active learning and the desire to mobilize for participation. These regions include the Krasnodar Kray, Orenburg Oblast, Republic of Adygea and, to a lesser extent, Khanty-Mansiysk Autonomous Okrug, Stavropol Kray, and Udmurt Republic.

Most of the regions surveyed follow the *third strategy* of combining conditions. This model can be conditionally designated *inclusive*. For inclusive development, not only the opportunities for participation that are being formed are important, but also the combination of these opportunities with the capabilities that are provided in this case by e-democracy. In these regions, information development, provision of electronic services, quality of life and fair distribution are combined in a complex configuration of conditions. These regions include the Omsk Oblast, Krasnoyarsk Kray, Murmansk Oblast, Moscow Oblast, Bashkortostan, and the Voronezh Oblast.

Of course, in this study, only one in 2015 was taken, and only the most developed regions in terms of the degree of openness of budget data and the development of a "budget for citizens" were studied. However, the selected object of research was designed to search for more or less stable relationships between the requisites of electronic citizens' participation based on open budget data. More developed regions show more pure conditions for a complex combination of factors and models of transition.

6 Conclusion

This study examined complex configurations of factors that are associated with the development of open budget data and a "budget for citizens" in the Russian regions. The main hypothesis that these factors have a direct impact on the process of formation of participatory budgeting was corrected in the sense that each factor generated a certain configurational link with other requisites of the studied processes. In its pure form, none of the factors has shown its effectiveness. Based on the complex configuration of dependencies, it was concluded that we can talk about three models for creating conditions for an open budget and a budget for citizens: technocratic, evolutionary and inclusive. These conclusions are based on the study of the 22 most developed regions in terms of the level of openness of budgets. To analyze the dependency configuration, a qualitative comparative analysis method (QCA) was used. Of course, further studies of a greater variety of conditions and cases may lead to a refinement of these findings and the formation of new conceptual approaches.

References

1. Abell, P.: Foundations for a qualitative comparative method. Int. Rev. Soc. Hist. **34**(1), 105–115 (1989)
2. Ansell, C., Gash, A.: Collaborative governance in theory and practice. J. Public Adm. Res. Theory **18**(4), 543–571 (2008)
3. Boukhis, I., Ayachi, R., Eloedi, Z., Mellouli, S., Amor, N.B.: Decision model for policy makers in the context of citizens engagement: application on participatory budgeting. Soc. Sci. Comput. Rev. **34**(6), 740–756 (2015)
4. Budzhetnoe Poslanie Presidenta Rossiyskoy Federatsii o Budzhetnoy Politike v 2014–2016 godah 13 Iyunia 2013. http://kremlin.ru/acts/news/18332. Accessed 20 Apr 2017
5. Cabannes, Y.: Participatory budgeting: a significant contribution to participatory democracy. Environ. Urban. **16**(1), 27–31 (2004)

6. Rihoux, B., Ragin, C. (eds.): Configurational Comparative Methods: Qualitative Comparative Analysis (QCA) and Related Techniques. Sage, Thousand Oaks (2009)
7. Ganuza, E., Frances, F.: The deliberative turn in participation: the problem of inclusion and deliberative opportunities in participatory budgeting. Eur. Polit. Sci. Rev. 4(2), 283–302 (2012)
8. Rihoux, B., Grimm, H. (eds.): Innovative Comparative Methods for Policy Analysis: Beyond Quantitative-Qualitative Divide. Springer, New York (2006)
9. Kernaghan, K.: Moving towards integrated public governance: improving service delivery through community engagement. Int. Rev. Adm. Sci. 75(2), 239–254 (2009)
10. Krenjova, J., Raudla, R.: Policy diffusion at the local level: participatory budgeting in Estonia. Urban Aff. Rev. 3(4), 1–29 (2017)
11. Markoff, J.: A comparative method: reflections on Charles Ragin's innovations in comparative analysis. Hist. Methods: J. Quant. Interdiscip. Hist. 23(4), 177–181 (1990)
12. Po raschetam Rosstata. http://d-russia.ru/rosstat-zafiksiroval-perevypolnenie-plana-dostich-v-2016-g-50-dlya-pokazatelya-dolya-grazhdanispolzuyushhih-elektronnye-gosuslugi.html. Accessed 19 Apr 2017
13. Ragin, C. (ed.): Issues and Alternatives in Comparative Social Research. E. J. Brill, Leiden (1991)
14. Ragin, C.: The Comparative Method: Moving Beyond Qualitative and Quantitative Strategies. University of California Press, Berkeley (1987)
15. Ragin, C.: The logic of the comparative method and the algebra of logic. J. Quant. Anthropol. 1(4), 373–398 (1989)
16. Ragin, C., Meyer, S., Drass, K.: Assessing discrimination: a Boolean approach. Am. Sociol. Rev. 49(2), 221–234 (1984)
17. Rating po urovniu razvitia informatsionnogo obschestvaza 2015 god. http://minsvyaz.ru/ru/events/35027/. Accessed 21 Apr 2017
18. Rating rossiyskyh regionov po kachestvu szizni-2015. http://riarating.ru/regions_rankings/20160225/630011011.html. Accessed 10 Apr 2017
19. Rating sub'ektovRossiyskoyFederatsiipourovniuotkrytostybudgetnyhdannyhza (2015). https://www.nifi.ru/ru/rating/2015/rezultaty-rejtinga-2015.html. Accessed 21 Apr 2017
20. Rios, A.-M., Bastida, F., Benito, B.: Budget transparency and legislative budgetary oversight: an international approach. Am. Rev. Pub. Adm. 46(5), 546–568 (2014)
21. Rocker, A.: Framing Citizen Participation: Participatory Budgeting in France, Germany and the United Kingdom. Palgrave Macmillan, Basingstoke (2014)
22. Romme, A.: Boolean comparative analysis of qualitative data: a methodological note. Qual. Quant. 29(3), 317–329 (1995)
23. Souza, C.: Participatory budgeting in Brazilian cities: limits and possibilities in building democratic institutions. Environ. Urban. 13(1), 159–184 (2001)
24. Walker, P., Shannon, P.: Participatory governance: towards a strategic model. Commun. Dev. J. 46(2), ii63–ii82 (2011)
25. Warren, M.E.: Governance-driven democratization. Crit. Policy Stud. 3(1), 3–13 (2009)

ePolity: Politics of Cyberspace

Ideological Segregation in the Russian Cyberspace: Evidences from St. Petersburg

Denis Martyanov and Il'ia Bykov[✉]

St. Petersburg State University, St. Petersburg, Russia
dsmartyanov@mail.ru, i.bykov@spbu.ru

Abstract. This paper is devoted to the study of political attitudes of Internet-users in Russia. The study is based on empirical data obtained by a survey conducted in 2015 in St. Petersburg. The authors have identified groups of political ideologies' supporters in St. Petersburg which compose a political spectrum of communists, social-democrats, conservatives, liberals, and nationalists. These ideologically motivated groups tend to be unlike in terms of online news consumption, political online activities, and political approaches to regulate cyberspace. The authors were able to identify ideological groups that can be described as *cyber-leftists* and *cyber-rightists* in the Russian Internet.

Keywords: Political ideology · Online media · Russia · Cyberpolicy · Digital divide · Ideological segregation

1 Introduction

Despite the periodical critique of political ideology in modern society, the ideological views remain to be an important element of political process throughout the world [1,2]. The modern information society facilitates transformation of political ideas and changes in political values, that turns to the emergence of new social movements. We believe that the development of Internet technologies involves several challenges for political ideologies at once. They include such important questions as a role of online media, problems of digital inequality, Internet governance, copyright issues, and the points of interaction between traditional political ideologies and the values of cyberculture.

Of course, classification of political ideologies is traditionally important issue for political researches. This issue has gained new aspects since the emergency of new ideological approaches such as feminism and environmentalism. In result, traditional ideologies are being modernized and transformed to the new forms of cyberanarchism, cyberlibertarianism, and cyberconservatism. From the ordinary Internet-users' point of view it is really hard to find ideological ground. There are at least two reasons for this. First of all, Internet agenda tends to differ from offline mainstream communication. 'Virtual reality' has its own values, reference groups, and political hierarchy. Second, there is a huge difference between

© Springer International Publishing AG 2017
D.A. Alexandrov et al. (Eds.): DTGS 2017, CCIS 745, pp. 259–269, 2017.
https://doi.org/10.1007/978-3-319-69784-0_22

political position in real society and imaginary position in cyberspace. Therefore, contemporary studies in political ideologies have been challenged with new topics and new research methods.

This paper aims to analyze ideological views of Internet users in Russia by means of public opinion survey. The study focuses on three research questions about ideologically motivated Internet usage, ideologically motivated online media consumption, and ideological views on the problem of Internet governance.

2   Research Background

There are many studies in the field of ideological views of Internet users. One part of them tends to focus on one nation data [13]. The others try to apply comparative approach, having in common hard criticism of modern liberal politics and the idea of cybersecurity as a factor of political decisions. For example, Sarikakis and Thussu considers cyberethics and feminism to play important role in the development of political ideologies [17]. McLachlan analyzes early cybercommunitarian ideas based on the earlier thoughts of Reingold [14]. Wong and Altman focuses on the problem of copyrights which provides ideological background for cyberpiracy movement [19]. Gurumurthy and Chami argue that Internet governance is a three-party process which includes influences from governmental structures, private businesses, and non-governmental organizations [11]. It is worth to notice that attempts to reduce ideology to technological standards are still in discussion [12].

As we mentioned previously, researchers sometimes critically assess the role of the Internet for ideological thinking. In such cases, the Internet is claimed to be either a factor for liberalism to reconstruct concept of privacy or a tool of neo-colonialism, which uses Internet technologies for globalization and ideologically protect right of IT-companies to licensing and copyrights [3,8,16]. These authors tend to criticize modern version of liberalism for supporting economic development which, de facto, forms a new version of colonialism.

Also, we were able to identify a special thematic cluster about ideological segregation on the Internet [11]. Sunstein founded out that online behavior is associated with an ideological views, which implies ideological predisposition to communicate with like-minded people [18]. Sunstein's study prompted a number of scientists to analyze the phenomena associated with ideological segregation and echo chambers in the Internet, which based on the desire to communicate with people with a similar point of view [5]. Probably, it is ideological segregation that is an essential factor for the formation of virtual communities. In a study of ideological online groups, researches founded out that the Internet encourages violent groups to propagate radical ideologies banned by traditional media channels [6]. At the same time, Gentzkow and Shapiro think that digital news have enormous potential for 'democratic politics' [9, p. 2].

However, Byrne and many others underline a fact that online news is not dominant at the moment [6]. For this reason, traditional media forms political consciousness, determining consumption of digital news and dictating users' way to digital platforms. This problem corresponds mainly with the phenomenon of echo chambers. Echo chambers serve as ideological spaces in which like-minded people have the opportunity to receive news and discuss them only when these discussions do not create inconvenience to them. Thus, digital media can perform the function of maintaining latent patterns and radical ideologies.

Investigating the relationship of American news media and ideology, Gentzkow and Shapiro demonstrated the effect of a horizontal model of news consumption, according to which the ideological views of users form a left-right spectrum of news consumption [9,10]. Internet users with opposite views apply various online resources and practically not crosses on web-sites with each others. This is due to the desire to be limited to resources that support their own point of view. In the modern Internet, the role of such sites is played by numerous personal blogs, public pages, and online communities. Thus, the Internet forms an ideological segregation, which to a certain extent is softened by a small number of popular 'centrist sites'.

We believe that similar analysis of this kind of segregation is also relevant for the Russian Internet. There is a small number of studies in the field of online news consumption which reveals significant disproportions in political communication online and offline in Russia [4,7]. However, the measurement of ideological segregation in Russia is associated with some additional difficulties. The fact is that the binary division according to the American model on the left and right in Russia does not work just as well. The ideological spectrum of political system in Russia is far from completing in terms of institutionalization, and the variability and polarization of the ideological space is very different from the American model.

3   Research Design

Empirical data were obtained in result of a sociological survey that was conducted in May 2015 in St. Petersburg. The project was implemented on the basis of the Resource Center for Sociological and Internet Research of St. Petersburg State University. The survey method was a telephone interview. The sample size was 1200 people permanently residing in St. Petersburg. The sample was random, non-repetitive with the quotation on the following signs: sex, age, education, district of residence. Bearing in mind the size, randomness, and quatation of the sample, we estimate the results to be statistically significant (p-value less than 0.05). The data were analyzed with IBM SPSS programm.

It is possible to hypothesise that ideological views are able to influence Internet use, online media consumption, and approaches to regulate cyberspace. The complexity of ideological identification has been discussed in special literature. In result, the list of political ideologies actual for today Russia has been revealed by previous studies [15]. However, we think that there is a big problem with the accuracy of the ideological identification among Russian citizens. 'Liberalism' and 'communism' are sufficiently compromised political labels, while social-democracy and conservatism have no vivid institutional incarnations in Russia that would make it possible to produce ideological identification without problems. Due to this reason, it makes sense to ask two questions about ideological views. One of them seeks for self-identification, the other would identify political views of the respondent according to their answer on key issue of the governmental role in politics and economy.

In other words, the ideological factor in our study was measured by using two indicators. The first one corresponds to the way in which respondents identify himself ('nominal' ideology), and the second - to what statements that characterize the model of the state, typical for the modern political ideologies, the respondents agree with the most ('real' ideology). To identify 'nominal' ideology our questionary included the question 'In terms of your political outlook, do you think of yourself as … communist/social-democrat/liberal/conservative/nationalist/mixes/hard to tell?' To identify 'real' ideological views of the respondent who, for example, is a communist the principle of a state 'where there is no private property, there is no sharp property stratification between people, but there is very rigid ideological control over people' should be chosen. The other 'real' ideological views were checked by similar questions.

The data obtained within survey allow us to apply Chi-square tests and calculate standardized residuals in order to understand how political views impact digital divide, mass media consumption, and views on cyberpolicy. Standardized residuals usually are used to indicate the degree of deviation of the observed frequencies from the expected ones. This statistical procedure has revealed a number of deviations among the positions of certain socio-demographic and political-ideological groups of respondents issues related to the use of the Internet. In the course of the study, a significant discrepancy was found in these two parameters, so they both allows us to identify a specific parameters of the Internet users' political views.

4   Research Results

First of all, we have found that there are four large groups of inhabitants in St. Petersburg with political views: communists, social-democrats, liberals, and conservatives (see Fig. 1). It was a big surprise to find so many 'real' liberals and so few 'real' communiststs in St. Petersburg, though we should take into consideration that voting and ideological views are hardly interconnected in Russia. We did not ask a question about voting in last elections and now have no way to verify if liberals tend to vote less. However, we also expected bigger share of nationalists, predicting that mainstreem TV-propaganda should free nationalistic point of view. It is unclear if true nationalists gave 'fake' answers in survey or conservative political views are actually better describes the situation. We think that we should study these results however surprising they are.

Ideological views	Nominal (self-appointed)	Real (question-driven)
Communists	10,42 %	6,83 %
Social-Democrats	14,75 %	21,58 %
Liberals	13,92 %	32,17 %
Conservatives	13 %	15,92 %
Nationalists	1,67 %	1,92 %
Mixed political views	33,57 %	14,75 %
Hard to tell	12,67 %	6,83 %

Fig. 1. Ideological views in St. Petersburg, N = 1200, 2015.

4.1 Digital Divide and Political Ideologies

To begin with, it is necessary to take into account such traditional factors as age and sex. The main factor of the digital divide is traditionally the age of potential Internet users. Our study supports this (see Figs. 2 and 3).

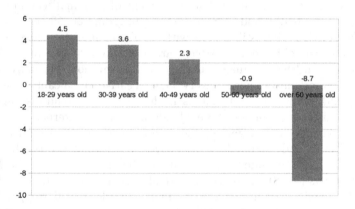

Fig. 2. Age and statement 'I use the Internet every day', St. Petersburg, 2015, standardized residuals, p-value less than 0.05.

We have found a stable correlation the age and the frequency of Internet use. Significant standardized residuals were found in most groups. For example, for a daily Internet users of up to 29 years old the standardized residual is 4.5, and for people over 60 is −8.7. The gap between those who use the Internet and those who do not use it, mainly relates to the oldest residents of St. Petersburg. 77 percent of people who do not use the Internet at all belongs to the age group '60 and older'.

Less significant, although still significant, is the gender factor. Among men, the daily Internet audience is 80.2 percent, while women - 68.5 percent. Here, a significant standardized residual was found: +1.8 for men who go online every day.

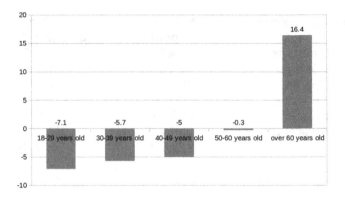

Fig. 3. Age and statement 'I never use the Internet', 2015, St. Petersburg, 2015, standardized residuals, p-value less than 0.05.

Based on the analysis of socio-demographic data, it can be assumed that the age gap will correlate with the ideological characteristics of more active and less active users. For example, more than 40 percent of 'nominal' communists are people over 60 years old, and 58.8 percent are in group '50–59 years old'. This trend is less obvious, but still traced with 'real' communists - 26.8 percent of them over 60 years old and 47.5 percent are in group of '50–59 years old'. The analysis of standardized residuals confirmed this assumption. The daily audience of 'nominal' communists shows a very high negative significant standardized balance (−2.5), while group of 'not users' has +5. This trend also applies to 'real' communists: +1.8 among those who do not use the Internet.

On the contrary, high negative of standardized reseduals were detected for 'nominal' liberals and 'nominal' conservatives who do not use the Internet at all (both −2.5). At the same time 'nominal' liberals tend to use the Internet more than others (+1.8). However, this trend does not extend to 'real' liberals. It looks like 'nominal' group makes a core for 'real' ideological groups. At some point, it has a sense since self-identification is a spontanious process which tells that respondent is used to think about political questions.

4.2   Mass Media and Political Views

The next block of questions deals with idelogically motivated use of mass media. We measured the audiences of several types of media (news agencies, online newspapers, political blogs, and online communities). The potential audience of these sites was measured. The amount of time that the user spends on the site has not been taken into account. The spectrum of mass media included mainstream news-agencies (RIA-Novosti, REGNUM, ITAR-TASS, RBC), online newspapers and radio (Gazeta.Ru, Fontanka.Ru, Echo of Moscow, Lenta.Ru, Lifenews.Ru), public accounts in social networks ('Anti-Maidan', 'Sputnik i Pogrom', 'Svobodnye novosti'), and political blogs (Navalny, ColonelCassad).

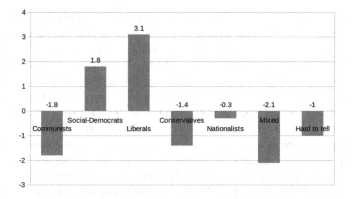

Fig. 4. 'Echo of Moscow' and 'nominal' ideological views of its audience, St. Petersburg, 2015, standardized residuals, p-value less than 0.05.

According to our data there are ideologically motivated differences in using mass media. For example, 'Echo of Moscow', a well-known opposition radio, in fact tends to be media for liberals and social-democrats (see Figs. 4 and 5). 'Nominal' liberals actually like to use various popular online-newspapers and news-sites (RBC +2.2; Gazeta.ru +2.3; Fontanka.ru +3.0; Echo of Moscow +3,1, Lenta.Ru +2,3, Kommersant.Ru +6,6). 'Real' social-democrats also are interested in various popular online-newspapers and news-sites (RBC +2.7, Gazeta.Ru +2.1, Fontanka.ru +3.8, 'Echo of Moscow' +4.8, Lenta.Ru + 3.7, Lifenews.Ru +1.9, Kommersant +4.2). Thus, among the ideologically motivated readers of the sites we were able to identifed two overlapping groups - 'nominal' liberals and 'real' socialists, who are interested in the same mass media.

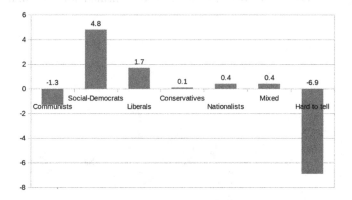

Fig. 5. 'Echo of Moscow' and 'real' ideological views of its audience, St. Petersburg, 2015, standardized residuals, p-value less than 0.05.

We measured three public communities in 'Vkontakte', the most popular social network in Russia. All of them have extremely low interest from potential

visitors (7.7 percent for 'Anti-Maidan', 2.5 percent for 'Sputnik i Pogrom' and
9.3 percent for 'Svobodnye novosti'). However, several interesting dependencies
were revealed. For example, 'Anti-Maidan' has negative views among 'real' liberals (-2.1) and positive among communists ($+3.3$) and conservatives ($+2.2$).
'Sputnik i Pogrom', obviously, injoys support from 'real' nationalists ($+6.3$), but
'real' communists do not express interest in its content (-2.3). A negative standardized residuals (-2.4) were found among 'real' social-democrats and positive
among communists ($+3.9$) and conservatives ($+2.9$) for the 'Svobodnye novosti'.

Political blogs have a lower interest comparing to the information sites. The
most famous of them (the blog of Alexei Navalny) by the degree of interest of
the audience does not exceed 3 percent. Interestingly, among the Internet users,
the blog of Aleksei Navalny is popular among 'nominal' liberals ($+4.6$) and 'real'
nationalists ($+4.8$).

4.3   Ideological Aspects of Cyberpolicy

An important issue of contemporary politics deals with the problem of Internet
governance. We investigated the attitudes of ideologically motivated groups to
the models of Internet governance asking questions 'Who do you think should
regulate the Russian segment of the Internet?' There were several answers
available: 'Russian government', 'Russian non-governmental organizations', and
'International non-governmental organizations'. The following dependencies were
identified (see Figs. 6 and 7). Among the supporters of the idea of Internet regulation by government authorities were identified a standardized residuals of $+1.9$
for 'real' conservatives and $+1.8$ for 'real' communists, $+2.8$ for 'nominal' socialists, and a negative standardized residuals of -2.3 for 'nominal' liberals. The
only significant standardized residuals for supporters of the idea of the Internet
regulation by international organizations were identified for 'nominal' liberals
($+2.5$).

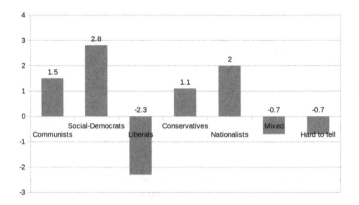

Fig. 6. Agreement with the statement 'Russian government must control the Internet'
and 'nominal' ideological views, St. Petersburg, 2015, standardized residuals, p-value
less than 0.05.

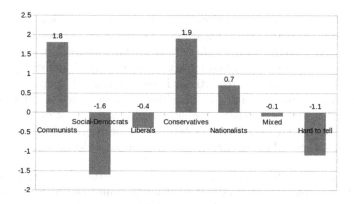

Fig. 7. Agreement with the statement 'Russian government must control the Internet' and 'real' ideological views, St. Petersburg, 2015, standardized residuals, p-value less than 0.05.

Also, we attempted to investigate another issues in the field of cyber policy. Respondents were asked to indicate their attitude to the following statements: 'Everything should be free on the Internet', 'The Internet should provide an opportunity to earn in it', 'For greater security on the Internet, people should register under their own names', 'The Internet should not have a political censorship', etc. The most interesting results involves liberals, on the one hand, and communists and conservatives, on the other hand. For example, 'real' liberals do not like the idea of censorship on the Internet (+1.9), while 'nominal' communists think that everything should be free on the Internet (+1.7).

5   Conclusion

The study confirmed our assumption of a divergence of positions on key issues related to Internet activity and Internet policy in groups that identify themselves with a certain ideology and in groups that share the values of the respective ideologies. First, among the bearers of classical ideological views, there is a group of cyberconservatives with some level of cyberphobia - people who either do not use the Internet or use network resources by the logic and values of the 'real world'. The greatest number of cyberconservatives was found among the communists (primarily in the group of 'nominal' communists). For this group, the Internet enhances the action of traditional media and produces an opportunity to obtain additional information from already familiar hands. But these people do not perceive the Internet as a second reality with alternative sources. For cyberconservative 'nominal' communists the Internet exists only with confirmation in real practice or in traditional media. Online events, flesh mobs and virtual reality are outside the scope of their world view.

Secondly, the group of 'nominal' liberals has a great interest for these users of the Internet demonstrate the greatest number of deviations in terms of cyberactivity. This group consists of the most active Internet users. It has very few people who do not use the Internet and an increased concentration of daily users. An important point here is that this group positions itself as liberals but in reality does not share liberal values. This group is characterized by anomaly high rate of interest in online media and foreign web-sites, which indirectly indicates their ideology as 'westerners' rather than classical liberals. This group is the target audience for the most significant opposition political blog - the blog of Alexei Navalny. It is worth to note that 'nominal' liberals are against of Internet regulation by the state, but they want the Internet to be regulated by international public organizations, which confirms their 'westernist' orientation.

Acknowledgments. This research was supported by St. Petersburg State University (project 106-120 'Political self-identification of online-communities in St. Petersburg'). Also, for this study we utilized facilities provided by the Center for Sociological and Internet Research at Saint-Petersburg State University (Russia).

References

1. Anderson, D.M., Cornfeld, M. (eds.): The Civic Web: Online Politics and Democratic Values. Rowman and Littlefield, Lanham (2003)
2. Baranov, N.A.: The main directions of an ideological discourse in modern Russia. Polit. Expert.: POLITEX **8**(2), 19–34 (2012)
3. Birdsall, W.F.: The ideology of information technology. Queen's Q. **104**, 287–299 (1997)
4. Bodrunova, S.S., Litvinenko, A.A., Gavra, D.P., Yakunin, A.V.: Twitter-based discourse on migrants in Russia: the case of 2013 bashings in Biryulyovo. Int. Rev. Manag. Mark. **5**(Special Issue), 97–104 (2015)
5. Boutyline, A., Willer, R.: The Social Structure of Political Echo Chambers: Variation in Ideological Homophily in Online Networks (2015). https://www.ocf.berkeley.edu/~andrei/downloads/echo.pdf
6. Byrne, C., et al.: Online ideology: a comparison of website communication and media use. J. Comput. Mediated Commun. **18**, 137–153 (2013)
7. Chugunov, A., Filatova, O., Misnikov, Y.: Citizens' deliberation online as will-formation: the impact of media identity on policy discourse outcomes in Russia. In: Tambouris, E., Panagiotopoulos, P., Sæbø, Ø., Wimmer, M.A., Pardo, T.A., Charalabidis, Y., Soares, D.S., Janowski, T. (eds.) ePart 2016. LNCS, vol. 9821, pp. 67–82. Springer, Cham (2016). https://doi.org/10.1007/978-3-319-45074-2_6
8. Cohen, J.E.: Privacy, Ideology, and Technology: A Response to Jerey Rosen Georgetown University Law Center (2001). http://scholarship.law.georgetown.edu/facpub/809/
9. Gentzkow, M., Shapiro, J.M.: Ideology and online news. In: Chicago Booth and NBER (2013). http://web.stanford.edu/~gentzkow/research/echo_structural.pdf
10. Gentzkow, M., Shapiro, J.M.: Ideological segregation online and offline. Q. J. Econ. **126**(4), 1799–1839 (2011). https://doi.org/10.1093/qje/qjr044
11. Gurumurthy, A., Chami, N.: Internet governance as 'ideology in practice' India's 'free basics' controversy. Internet Policy Rev. **5**(3) (2016). https://doi.org/10.14763/2016.3.431, https://policyreview.info/articles/analysis/internet-governance-ideology-practice-indias-free-basics-controversy

12. Kelly, B., Dunning, A., Guy, M., Phipps, L.: Ideology or pragmatism? Open standards and cultural heritage web sites. In: International Cultural Heritage Informatics Meetings (ICHIMs) (2003). http://opus.bath.ac.uk/12622/
13. Lu, Y., Chu, Y., Shen, F.: Mass media, new technology, and ideology: an analysis of political trends in China. Glob. Media China 1(1–2), 70–101 (2016)
14. McLachlan, S.F.: The Utopian Fallacy of Web 2.0: Community, Ideology and Exploitation on the Social Web (2011). https://minerva-access.unimelb.edu.au/handle/11343/37116
15. Popova, O.: Studing the problems of political self-identification in Russia. Polit. Expert.: POLITEX 9(2), 205–219 (2012)
16. Sarikakis, K.: Ideology and Policy: Notes on the Shaping of the Internet. In: First Monday 9(8) (2004). https://minerva-access.unimelb.edu.au/handle/11343/37116
17. Sarikakis, K., Thussu, D.K. (eds.): Ideologies of Internet. Hampton Press, Broadway (2006)
18. Sunstein, C.R.: Republic.com 2.0. Princeton University Press, Princeton (2009)
19. Wong, S., Altman, E.: Restricting internt access: ideology and technology. In: Proceedings of the 2nd International Conference on Communication Systems and Networks, pp. 260–267. India, Bangalore (2010)

Russian Anti-corruption Protests: How Russian Twitter Sees It?

Valerii Nechai[✉] and Dmitry Goncharov

National Research University Higher School of Economics,
Saint-Petersburg, Russian Federation
{vnechai,dgoncharov}@hse.ru

Abstract. This article explores the map of political preferences of Russian Twitter users in the wake of March 2017 anti-corruption protests. So far there is little research on the political aspects of Twitter in Russia and our paper seeks to fill this gap in the scholarship. It is based on content analysis of over 45,000 tweets published during a week after March 26 events. According to the project preliminary results, political attitudes of Russians remain fairly moderate, though evidence points to some polarization among the politically involved. The research also reveals a variety of value patterns shared by politically active users and investigates corresponding clusters of users that are taking shape in the ongoing online discussion and networking. The article concludes with an interpretation of how these clusters might relate to menu of political participation during current electoral cycle in Russia.

Keywords: Politics · Social media · Twitter · Political protest · Connective actions

1 Introduction

In March 2017 Russian opposition leader Alexey Navalny issued a film made by his Anti-corruption Foundation. The film accused prime-minister Dmitry Medvedev and his close circle of amassing property using suspicious and distrustful deals. Navalny claimed that Medvedev uses a network of charity organisations headed by his friends to control palaces, a castle with a vineyard in Europe and luxurious assets. After the film was issued, the biggest Russian street protests in five years took place. According to independent Echo Moskvy radio station, the number of the protesters on March, 26 was close to 80 000 people all over the country.

Some observers considered these protests to be an unofficial start of Alexei Navalny's Presidential Campaign. This is a part of strategy designed to fight against electoral campaigns pattern when incumbent regime actors tend to postpone the official start of the pre-election race, in order to get a head start. Navalny made an attempt to seize the initiative, increasing the tone of political discussion and claiming to be the leading figure in Russian opposition at this time period.

© Springer International Publishing AG 2017
D.A. Alexandrov et al. (Eds.): DTGS 2017, CCIS 745, pp. 270–281, 2017.
https://doi.org/10.1007/978-3-319-69784-0_23

During and especially after these protests, social media played an important role allowing users to spread the information concerning the Medvedev's case investigation and organize the protest activities. One of the key platforms here was Twitter. Whereas Twitter is used by only a minority of Russians, we assume that its influence extends beyond mere numbers of users as it serves as a poweful tool of alternative political communication. During the protests Twitter was used to complement information provided by mainstream (state controlled) media and to channel the communication related to the political outcomes of the March rallies.

We can observe that social media (Twitter including) do play a part in framing Russia's contentious politics, though the exact mechanisms of social influence which are behind that need thorough exploration. The ultimate ambition of the research is to shed some light on the matter, focusing on variety of the engagement discursive patterns of the politicaly active social media users. In order to do so we collected more than 45 000 of tweets published from the mid-day of March, 26 until April, 2 and related to the protests.

The research question we would like to answer in this project is: what kind of discursive polarisation could be identified within Twitter community emerged in the aftermath of the anti-corruption protests? The secondary questions are:

- What are the dominant discoursive patterns that could be identified in the discussions? (Q1)
- To what extent corruption isssue' is important for patterns' framing? (Q2)

In order to reach the goal of the research, we decided to employ the next methods: (a) topic analysis of the tweets and (b) social network analysis of the community under study.

This paper is organized as follows: in the first part we will explore a conceptual framework for study social media in contentious politics, second part will describe the project methodology, data collection and data analysis, then we will proceed with data interpretation and conclude with some findings and suggestions for the further research.

2   Related Work

The nature of public protests is very well studied for both democratic and authoritarian regimes (Levitsky and Way 2002; Almeida 2003; Levitsky and Way 2002). In the first case non-violent protests serve the purpose of social and political communication, complementing electoral procedures and other forms of conventional political and civic engagement. In authoritarian political contexts public protest imply complex institutional meaning. In paradoxical logic of hybrid authoritarianism limited protests may favour regime consolidation increasing trust in government (Frye and Yakovlev 2016). They also can work as an efficient channel of information exchange, mitigating information problems resulted from democracy degradation (Lorentzen 2013). But protests (especially when they occur at critical points of electoral cycles) are not all good for "new authoritarianisms".

They feed the specter of colored revolutions – the worst nightmare of the Post-soviet autocrats. Business of hybrid authoritarian games is pretty tricky one and requires great sophistication in balancing between strong political monopoly and democracy imitation. Even limited opportunities provided within imitative institutional framework may grow potential for regime change. So, it is quite relevant to address the key question of contentious politics theory: what kind of social and cultural mechanisms could be identified behind protest mobilization (McAdam et al. 1996)?

Political activists use social media platforms as forceful mean of coordination. They also share information via such digital media. Moreover, activists employ social media in order to increase their visibility of their actions and accomplishments as well as sharing the ideological message they want to propagate. This platforms are highly exploited in authoritarian regimes where media are controlled by government. The Internet, blogs, microblogging tools and messengers is considered to be a unique opportunity to seize the initiative from authoritarian leaders and to develop free public discussion in the virtual world.

There is already a fairly large bulk of research on the links between online communication and offline protest activities (Gaffney 2010; Kavanaugh et al. 2011). Digitalization has provided political activists with new powerful instruments of networking and mobilization. It lead to emergence of new patterns of activism/public opinion leadership identified as solo organizers or lone wolfs (Earl and Kimport 2011). Social media alow activists to start campaigns of civic or political mobilization having much less money, time and other resources than if it would have been spent in the past. The new logic of connective action "makes it much easier to build networks and do first steps in mass social mobilization" (Bennett 2012). From the Arab Spring to the Occupy Wall Street movements such digital networks were highly exploited by opposition activists. In other words, the Internet has replaced mass media in the function of being a connective tissue of democracy, as Gunther and Mughan (2000) used to call.

Today people use social media platforms like Facebook, Twitter, etc. for not only private but also for public conversation. The Twitter has about 320 million active users per month, 1 million of them are Russians. Takes-up in Twitter's global coverage made it an important platform for public communication. It has become a real-time global news network for current events as well as a site of debate and discussion about political, social and cultural issues. Twitter data is also relatively straightforward to collect and analyze, especially in comparison to ephemeral social media platforms like Snapchat or social networking sites like Facebook, which blend together closed, private modes of communication with public ones.

Being one of the most widespread and influential online social networks, Twitter has many controversies. Originally, it was created as a site for social conversation between friends and like-minded individuals; however, now Twitter became a place for many other forms of discourse and action. "The example of "#BlackLivesMatter" demonstrates the importance of social media to contemporary social movements, civil initiatives and campaigns for social justice and political change" (Duchess and Edwards 2016). Others highlight the role of Twitter during the Arab Spring (Bruns et al. 2013). Still, there are different views on the role of Twitter for the society. Some think that it is a place for online hate, bullying and mob justice (Losh 2014), whereas others call it as a primarily identity-blind, libertarian, free speech-dominated Internet platform (Burgess 2016).

The availability of data on activities of users who use the Application Programming Interfaces (APIs, Twitter's case) makes it possible to employ new research methods which "allow bridging the gap between humanities-oriented Internet studies and the big data research" (Burgess and Bruns 2012). According to Weller 2014, this type of research "is seen by some scholars as representing a computational turn" (Berry 2011). Whereas, others prefer the idea of "the development of more scientistic models in media, cultural, and communication studies" (Hartley 2009).

"The key modes of communication on Twitter are linked to the specific technological affordances of Twitter as a platform, and can be understood as corresponding to micro, meso, and macro layers of information exchange and user interaction" (Weller 2014). Twitter and other social networks are almost freely used having a great deal of autonomy and, consequently, providing some possibilities for conversation within pro- and anti-government groups or between both of them.

One of the key components of a successful protest mobilization is the consolidation of patterns of identity within large protest groups (Crabtree 2005; Bennett 2012). This research is to help us to uncover the possible identity patterns across all political orientations – either anti-governmental or pro-governmental ones.

As Downing (2000) argues media can be pivotal in the struggle for power in all regimes, including non-democratic systems. Media of all types interferes and powerfully impacts on competition between social movements and the authoritarian state. Sure enough, it is important to keep in mind that, though being a key actor in the process of the protest mobilization, media is not a main driving force behind a regime change – to make it happen there should be serious influences rooted in economical and social transformations. Still, the identity and cultural analysis may shed the light on the issues related to the potential of successful mobilization in Russia's contentious politics.

3   Data and Method

The datasets were extracted by the Twitter Archiving Google Sheet (TAGS).

The datasets were created stating the following keywords in the Query field: 'protest', 'Dimon will reply', 'Navalny', 'He isn't just a Dimon'; the date parameters were set from March 26th, 2017 to April 2th, 2017, the minimum of followers a person must have to be included in the list was set at 200. As a result the initial datasheet contains more than 45 000 of tweets.

In order to get a quick characterization of the tweets types the table is provided with the total number of tweets, the number of retweets and the number of unique users. The table also contains numbers of tweets sent, the number of users mentioned, the number of followers and followees. Such information 'allows structural analysis of relationships between entities and are particularly useful for locating actors (users or domains) in relation to issues (hashtags)' (Marres et al. 2013). For example, we can get a list of the most retweeted messages. Such data would allow us 'to reconstruct and narrate the timeline of an event' (Rogers 2014).

For analyzing the data we exploited Tableaue software. Since there is a large number of data, we decided to stick to the top 10 results of each category (hashtags, mentions, retweets and users).

For carrying out preliminary social network analysis we use the Force Atlas 2 algorithm by Gephi. This method was used by Bruns and Burgess (2014) in Queensland University of Technology. This algorithm "simulates gravitational attraction between connected nodes in a network" as Bruns and Burgess (2014) stated. "Force Atlas 2 is able to visualize large and complex networks, and is optimized to highlight densely interconnected clusters in the networks it visualizes" (Bruns and Burgess 2014).

In order to do topic modelling, we employ Latent Dirichlet Allocation (LDA), which is widely used for such goals. "LDA is an unsupervised machine learning technique which identifies latent topic information in large document collections" (Blei et al. 2003). It uses a bag of words approach, which treats each document as a vector of word counts. A detailed explanation of LDA method and its usage for topic modelling in Twitter analysis was given by Hong and Davison (2010). However, this approach has some limitations, which result in the instability of the results. In order to make the results to some extent closer to the reality, at least five repetitions for each topic models were done.

4   Analysis and Discussion

According to social network analysis carried out over the network of users, several communities were found. All of them are highly interconnected (Fig. 1). Moreover, they are connected to each other, which means that there is a high level of communication between different parties. After excluding the distant communities we allocated the two largest and four smaller clusters. Based on the topic modelling of the tweets published by the communities we came to a conclusion that the top groups could be marked as: anti-government and pro-government. What is also exciting is that these groups are fairly equal in terms of the user quantity.

We found out that the Russian twitter audience didn't widely exploited hashtags (Fig. 2). Only 3 911 (8,6%) tweets contained a hashtag with the total number of hashtags 63. We created a subset of the 10 most used hashtags. According to this subset, the most widely exploited tag 'He isn't just a Dimon' was used about 200 times at March, 26 and then this number dramatically decreased. Interestingly, both parties used hashtags; however, pro-governmental groups preferred to use informative tags: news and Navalny's pupils, whereas others put more radical

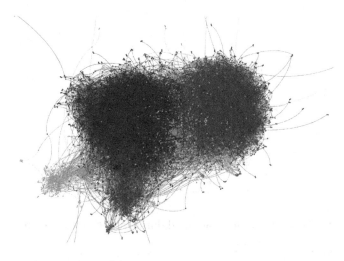

Fig. 1. Community structure of the Twitter users made with GEPHI software. The colors show political polarisation, blue (and bluish) for anti-government; red (and reddish) for pro-government; yellow - neither pro- or anti-government (Color figure online)

and mobilizing labels, such as: Putin's a chief, 'Dimon will give an answer', He isn't just a Dimon, etc. Finally, there was no evidence of mobilizing campaign for the future protests (Table 1).

Table 1. The top popular communities in the data set

Community	Leaders	Number of users	Percentage
Anti-government	Navalny, Lubov Sobol	2458	37.2%
Pro-government	Violetta Volkova, Ilya Remeslo	2110	32.8%
Not-into politics bloggers	Danila Poperechniy, Vlad Rozenthal	645	10.0%
English-speaking, pro-Navalny	DarthPutinKGB	399	6.2%
State-oriented nationalists	Sergey Kurginyan	280	4.4%
Independent	—NONE—	180	2.8%

Looking at Fig. 3 we may conclude that pro-governmental Twitter users are less active in using hashtags than anti-government ones. In other words, the regime loyalists were not ready to react to the protest actions. We argue that Alexey Navalny group was much more active in propagating their ideas than the pro-governmental community.

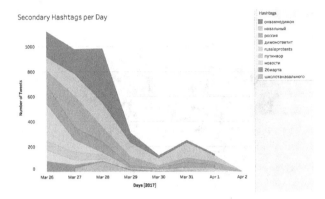

Fig. 2. The secondary hashtags used during a week after the protests

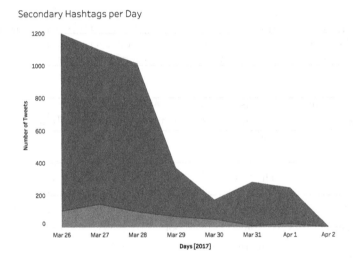

Fig. 3. The dynamics of using hashtags by pro-government users (red zone) and anti-government (blue zone) (Color figure online)

The dynamics of the discussion was decreasing (Fig. 4). The number of the tweets which mentioned the keywords descended sharply despite of the continuing discussion in traditional independent media (Radio Liberty, Echo of Moscow, etc.) and state-controlled media (VESTI channel), which started covering the protests on the next day they had taken place. We believe that the flow of the discussion changed the second-topic and focused on the events which happened after the protests (magistrate trials, punishment for protesters, etc.), which could not be identified with the initial keywords settings. Moreover, the participants returned to their routine: their offices, classes, homes. Although, this phenomenon couldn't be seen a an evidence of decline in protest activity. We believe that the protest became more passive in order to gain much more energy.

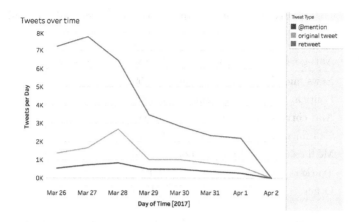

Fig. 4. The dynamics of tweets containing the keywords on Navalny anti-corruption protests

One of the limitations of the LDA method is the question of the 'right' number of topics. We followed the rule described by Nagorny and Koltsova in their work (2017) and applied a metric proposed by Cao et al. 2009. For the corpus of tweets marked as "anti-government" the optima Cao Juan's measure was 45 topics, whereas for "pro-government" corpus the method evaluated k as 50 topics. The example of topic modeling results is given in the Table 2.

Table 2. Examples of topics for anti-government cluster

Protests in regions	The new protests will be held	Children against corruption
0.035*DimonWillAnswer	0.019*Protest	0.042*Protest
0.032*Peterburg	0.018*New	0.035*Children
0.028*Ekaternburg	0.154*Again	0.030*Crusade
0.022*Kazan	0.141*Streets	0.028*Corruption
0.200*Police	0.086*Programme	0.027*Youngsters
0.015*Square	0.083*Project	0.010*Pupils
0.014*Scan	0.042*Repeating	0.010*Toddlers

After careful consideration, every topics in both Anti-governmental and Pro-governmental clusters were grouped into several bigger ones. The allocation of topics groups for both clusters are given in Tables 3 and 4.

As we can see from the main topics in the Anti-government cluster, three approximately equal groups of publications could be distinguished (except a fraction of news covering tweets which could be omitted from the analysis, since this group doesn't relate to the research design). The outcomes show that the

Table 3. The most discussed by anti-government cluster topics ranked by salience (in descending order)

Anti-government cluster	Index of topic's salience
News and the protest coverage	0.2859
Political alogans and opinions	0.1595
Anti-corruption theme	0.1544
Call for new protests	0.1413
Media silence and propaganda	0.0666
Truckers' protest	0.063
Other	0.1294

Table 4. The most discussed by pro-government cluster topics ranked by salience (in descending order)

Pro-government cluster	Index of topic's salience
Negative characteristics of Navalny as a person	0.4234
Negative characteristics of Navalny's deeds	0.1697
Jockes and Irony	0.1239
Child theme	0.1231
Call to punish Navalny	0.0822
Other	0.0777

protesters widely employed a mixture of political slogans, anti-corruption statements and calls for new public actions (the index of topic's salience varies from 0.1413 to 0.1595). This data gives some grounds to describe the main features of the political campaign by Navalny: his supporters sent to the elites three main messages: demand for political change, deep dissatisfaction with corruption, and that the protests will continue.

Meanwhile, pro-Kremlin users spread predominantly negative assesment of Navalny ('He's a criminal', 'Nazi', 'thief', etc.) and his acts ('He bribed people', 'He lied to people', etc.). The rest of tweets could be grouped as: jokes and irony about protesters (including trolling), covering a theme of minors' involvement with a negative connotation ('Youngsters as cannon fodder for Navalny', 'Children should study better instead of protesting', etc.) and request to punish the protesters. Surprisingly, only the last fraction of tweets could be described as 'having a political connotation' and it was the least popular group of tweets. Therefore, we can conclude that the vast magority of the publications in this sector contained tweets which could be considered as 'fake news' (here we use a definition of 'fake news' given by Allcott and Gentzkow (2017): 'rumors that do not originate from a particular news article; conspiracy theories; satire that is unlikely to be misconstrued as factual'); whereas, political statements weren't widespread.

5   Conclusion

The results reported in this chapter shed some light on the affordances of Twitter platform and how users create and share meaning during political protests. The most important finding is a high level of polarization of politically active users. We can clearly see two large groups of users who confront each other: anti-regime participants and regime loyalists.

Both camps employed Twitter. However, it was done in different ways. The difference between topics shared by the fractions is extremely striking. The anti-government community employed Twitter mainly as a channel of communication and spreading information between users predominantly via retweets mechanism. Surprisingly, the number of direct political statements, including anti-corruption claims, was much lower. Nevertheless, some activists continue inviting people to take part in the future protests, which shows an organisational role of Twitter communication. In contrary, the pro-government group prefered spreading messages containing 'fake news' features and exploited trolling methods. The main goal of such communication could be seen as 'putting as much of black paint at his portrait as possible'. Besides this, the users also called to punish Navalny and the protesters. In other words, in their hands Twitter played only a role of a communication tool; they didn't use its organisational capacities.

These observations may lead to a number of preliminary conclusions. First of all, we do see that Twitter communication provides politicaly active users with an instrument for developing their social and political identities across highly polarized spectrum of the Russian political and civic engagement. The big question here is it possible to uncover any potetntial for political mobilization in this kind of identity-building communication?

We suggest that the answer to this question could be found in the musing on group differences related to value orientations and intention to use online communication for the offline networking and mutual action. There are quite solid grounds to believe that regime loyalists use Twitter communication just to confirm and consolidate their identity based partly on anti-liberal cultural consensus and partly on more or less pragmatic support of regime policies. They reveal no intention to translate this shared identity into offline networking or action.

Anti-regime identity-building communication seems to be much more instrumental in consolidating offline community of politically active individuals. Here we may expect an institutional evolution which would fit into the logic of contentious politics development through less resourse consuming framework of *connective action*. At the same time it is important to mention that our research does not allow to come to clear conclusions concerning the value structure of the anti-regime communication. Anti-regime users demonstrate rather strong dissatisfaction with corruption and general social and political frustration. But value content of this identity is rather vague and may be compared to general mood of social disillusionment shared by the most in the very late period of the Soviet history.

Finally, authors have to admit that there is no enough solid evidence to conclude whether this communicative potential for social would have some influence on the way the politics in Russia is made. Alike, we cannot conclude whether Twitter could be a mean of political mobilisation or it is just an extra tool for 'spreading the word'. These questions are points for the further research.

References

Allcott, H., Gentzkow, M.: Social media and fake news in the 2016 election. In: Working Paper, National Bureau of Economic Research, January 2017

Almeida, P.D.: Opportunity organizations and threat-induced contention: protest waves in authoritarian settings. Am. J. Sociol. **109**, 345–400 (2003)

Bennett, W.L.: The personalization of politics political identity, social media, and changing patterns of participation. ANNALS Am. Acad. Polit. Soc. Sci. **644**(1), 20–39 (2012). Sage Publications

Berry, D.: The computational turn: thinking about the digital humanities. Cult. Mach. **12**, 1–22 (2011). Open Humanities Press

Blei, D.M., Ng, A.Y., Jordan, M.I.: Latent dirichlet allocation. J. Mach. Learn. Res. **3**, 993–1022 (2003)

Bruns, A., Highfield, T., Burgess, J.: The Arab Spring and social media audiences: english and Arabic Twitter users and their networks. Am. Behav. Sci. **57**, 871–898 (2013)

Burgess, J., Bruns, A.: (Not) the Twitter election: the dynamics of the #ausvotes conversation in relation to the Australian media ecology. Journal. Pract. **3**, 384–402 (2012)

Cao, J., Xia, T., Li, J., Zhang, Y., Tang, S.: A density-based method for adaptive LDA model selection. Neurocomputing **72**, 1775–1781 (2009)

Crabtree, J.: Patterns of Protest: Politics and Social Movements in Bolivia. Latin American Bureau, London (2005)

Downing, J.D.: Radical Media: Rebellious Communication and Social Movements. Sage Publications, Thousand Oaks (2000)

Earl, J., Kimport, K.: Digitally Enabled Social Change: Activism in the Internet Age. MIT Press, Cambridge (2011)

Frye, T., Yakovlev, A.: Elections and property rights: a natural experiment from Russia. Comp. Polit. Stud. **49**, 499–528 (2016)

Gaffney, D.: # iranElection: quantifying online activism (2010)

Gunther, R., Mughan, A.: Democracy and the Media: A Comparative Perspective. Cambridge University Press, Cambridge (2000)

Duchess, H., Edwards, S.B.: Black Lives Matter. ABDO, Minneapolis (2016)

Hartley, J.: From the consciousness industry to the creative industries: consumer-created content, social network markets, & the growth of knowledge. In: Media Industries: History, Theory & Method, pp. 231–244. Wiley-Blackwell (2009)

Hong, L., Davison, B.D.: Empirical study of topic modeling in Twitter. In: Proceedings of the First Workshop on Social Media Analytics, pp. 80–88. ACM (2010)

Kavanaugh, A.L., Yang, S., Li, L.T., Sheetz, S.D., Fox, E.A.: Microblogging in crisis situations: mass protests in Iran, Tunisia. Egypt. In: CHI. ACM (2011)

Levitsky, S., Way, L.: The rise of competitive authoritarianism. J. Democr. **13**, 51–65 (2002)

Lorentzen, P.L.: Regularizing rioting: permitting public protest in an authoritarian regime. Q. J. Polit. Sci. **8**, 127–158 (2013)

Losh, E.: Hashtag feminism and Twitter activism in India. Soc. Epistemol. Rev. Reply Collect. **3**, 11–22 (2014)

Marres, N., Gerlitz, C., Weltevrede, E., Borra, E., Rieder, B.: Mapping WCIT with Twitter: issue and hashtag profiles (2013)

McAdam, D., Tarrow, S., Tilly, C.: To map contentious politics. Mobil.: Int. Q. **1**, 17–34 (1996)

Nagornyy, O., Koltsova, O.: Mining media topics perceived as social problems by online audiences: use of a data mining approach in sociology (2017)

Rogers, R.: Debanalising Twitter. Twitter and Society (2014)

Weller, K.: Twitter and society: an introduction. In: Weller, K., Bruns, A., Burgess, J., Mahrt, M., Puschmann, C. (eds.) Twitter and Society 2014, vol. 89, pp. xxix–xxxviii. Peter Lang, New York (2014)

Interaction Between the Internet and the Political Regime: An Empirical Study (1995–2015)

Yury Kabanov[(✉)] and Bogdan Romanov

National Research University Higher School of Economics,
St. Petersburg, Russia
ykabanov@hse.ru, baromanov@edu.hse.ru

Abstract. This ongoing paper is devoted to the empirical study of the interaction between the Internet and the political regime. Departing from several theoretical assumptions, we aim to explore the correlation between the development of the Internet and democracy from 1995 to 2015. Our findings suggest that although the Internet is associated with democracy, this link has been losing its significance over time, and more consolidated autocracies are utilizing the potential of the Internet.

Keywords: Internet · Information technology · Democratization · Quantitative methods · Regression analysis

1 Introduction

Despite the extensive body of works, the Internet remains underexplored in terms of its relation to the political regime, mainly due to its ever-changing nature and ambiguous evidence. On the one hand, recent events, such as the Arab Spring have shown some mobilization, and consequently, democratization potential of the social media [1]. On the other hand, some authoritarian countries seem to have successfully utilized the Internet in order to pursue their own goals of regime legitimation and surveillance over citizens [2, 3]. The debate between cyber-optimists and cyber-pessimists on the role of the Internet in political change remains vivid [4], since there are cases and empirical results that can support both parties' positions. In this regard, further research is needed, first to evaluate the theoretical and empirical basis of these positions, and second to trace the dynamics between the Internet development and the political regime variations.

The paper presents preliminary results of the empirical research, aiming to explore the relationship between the Internet development and the political regime during 1995–2015. Based on the literature review of the existing analytical approaches, we distinguish several hypotheses that are tested by statistical methods.

The paper's content is structured as follows. Firstly, we conduct a literature review, providing different viewpoints on the Internet – political regime interaction and its possible causal mechanism. Secondly, we conduct an empirical quantitative analysis, and subsequently provide the results and their interpretation. In conclusion we summarize our findings.

© Springer International Publishing AG 2017
D.A. Alexandrov et al. (Eds.): DTGS 2017, CCIS 745, pp. 282–291, 2017.
https://doi.org/10.1007/978-3-319-69784-0_24

2 The Internet, Democracy and Autocracy: A Review

When the active Internet diffusion began, studies have emerged to consider its possible preconditions and outcomes in the context of political regimes. Several approaches to this problem could be distinguished. Firstly, there is a split between the *cyber-optimistic* and *cyber-pessimistic positions.* The former advocate for a democratizing potential of the Internet, while the latter state that the Internet can also be a tool for sustaining the autocratic rule [4: 4–5]. Secondly, because the casual link between the Internet and the political regime remains unclear, there are different interpretations of its direction. Some scholars argue that the Internet is independent variable affecting the regime, whereas others suppose the regime type affects the Internet diffusion itself. As a result, we have a matrix of different approaches (Table 1).

Table 1. Matrix of approaches towards the Internet and the political regime research

	Optimists	Pessimists
Internet -> Regime	(1) *Liberation technology* [5]	(3) *Authoritarian consolidation* [2], *repression technology* [27]
Regime -> Internet	(2) *Democracy advantage* [21]	(4) *Authoritarian catching-up* [21]

The first position states that the Internet is an instrument of democratization in its own right, or, as coined by Larry Diamond, a *liberation technology*, i.e. a means to facilitate mobilization and civic participation [5]. In this respect, the Internet is viewed basically through its Web 2.0 dimension. Such technology facilitates democratization in several ways, but basically through collective action promotion [6] and new communication opportunities [7], and the *demonstration effect* [8], whose core idea is that the successful democratization is related to the diffusion of power via communication.

But it is not only the communicative power of the Internet that matters. The economic development could be a moderator between the Internet spread and democratization. Such mechanism can be derived from Lipset's theory of democratization, which claims that prosperous countries are more likely to be democratic. In detail, he suggests four factors, which contribute to the democratic transition: urbanization, industrialization, education and revenue. Urbanization and industrialization cause the raise of the educated and relatively wealthy middle class, interested in politics and demanding political changes and civic rights [9]. The Internet seems to become an important supplement to this theory, as the current global economy and the Internet development are now closely interconnected. The middle class now employs the benefits of the Internet, as an education and economic tool and a political instrument not to allow the violation of their rights and freedoms in a long-run perspective [8], and hence to foster political changes.

The third optimistic causal mechanism has much in common with the previous one. Inglehart [10] in his modernization theory assumes that the economic development leads to the value shift from materialist values to post-materialist values of self-expression and life quality. Post-materialism, characterized by mass participation, trust, tolerance and civic freedoms, also includes the right to access information and use technologies for development, possible via ICTs [11]. Despite internal processes, new cultural values are also formed by globalization, when liberalization ideas circulate freely on the Internet, influencing citizens' attitude and involvement in the political life [12]. One example of how post-material values and the Internet are interconnected is the spread of *pirate parties:* as empirically shown by Kabanov [13], the institutionalization and popularity of these organizations are determined by both the Internet spread and the value shift, both having mutually significant correlations. Furthermore, in practice, post-material values positively affect offline and online political engagement [14].

The fourth mechanism that seems to be an important link is the development of various electronic tools of citizens' engagement, i.e. the electronic government and participation. The Internet is becoming not only the source of information or a means of communication, but also a public sphere of dialogue and deliberation. As argued by Polat, these three dimensions of the Internet can enhance public participation in the scope [15]. At the moment, governments around the world are launching online forums that provide technologies to aggregate citizens' contribution to the decision-making process [16], leading to e-democracy [17]. Even non-democratic countries do not constitute an exception from the global trend of e-government and e-participation implementation, although the results of such policies are ambiguous [3].

Overall, some empirical evidence backs the abovementioned assumptions. First of all, there is a plethora of cases on how autocracies can be challenged by the Internet-led protest mobilization [18]. Secondly, several time-series analyses have been conducted to trace the relationship between the Internet and democratization. For instance, Best and Wade consider the Internet as an independent variable, evaluating its explanatory power of democracy from 1992 to 2002. In their opinion, the democratizing potential of the Internet started in 2000. Although such effect varies across regions, the Internet and democracy positively and significantly correlates with each other [19].

At the same time, such positive link was found in the studies that consider the inverse relationship, when the Internet diffusion was considered a result of political variables (i.e. the second position in the matrix). For example, Milner, having analyzed the diffusion patterns from 1991 to 2001 in 190 countries, concluded that democracies are more likely to adopt the new technology, hence the "spread of democracy... may thus help reduce the digital divide" [20]. The results spoke well for a "democracy advantage" [21] approach stating that democracies are more successful in promoting new policies and technologies, like e-government.

Nevertheless, the optimistic viewpoint has been questioned from the very beginning. The third and forth positions in the matrix are quite the same in its instrumentalist view of the Internet. The latter, according to them, may be utilized by autocracies as successful as by democracies without inevitable subversion risks. Groshek, for instance, found little support that the Internet was a democratization driver in 1994–2003 [22], while Corrales and Westhoff [23] argued that strong and economically advanced autocracies were successfully introducing the Internet, subverting its potential democratization effects. In other words, authoritarianism is not a total and unquestionable obstacle to the Internet, neither the Internet automatically fosters democratization in a country. Even more, as argued by some scholars, ICTs can prolong the authoritarian regime instead of democratizing it. As Goebel puts it, "popular access to ICT might or might not help undermine authoritarian rule, but if skillfully used, will definitely make a regime more resilient" [2]. Rød and Weidmann found no evidence of the Internet's democratizing influence on political institutions; on the contrary, preference is given to the view of the Internet as a tool for autocrats, and in fact as a dependent variable [24]. More and more autocracies are introducing various pseudo-democratic instruments, like electronic participation and online deliberation forums, for the sake of legitimacy and state control of the new media [25, 26], transforming a democratizing potential of the Internet into the "Big Brother 2.0" model [27].

In general, the interaction of the Internet and the political regime remains unclear in the academia. Although the approaches mentioned above present their own causal mechanisms, it is still not yet clear whether the Internet determines democratization, democracy is a prerequisite for the Internet spread, or it is just a correlation and both factors are preconditioned by other variables. It seems that the actual link is very case-specific and dependent on the time period of the research. In this respect, in this paper we consider the relationship between the Internet and the political regime as multidirectional, although we technically view the former as an independent variable in the regression analysis. Our main goal is to find out how the interaction between the Internet and democracy is changing over time, and if the Internet can be a factor of democratization.

Based on the theoretical approaches, we propose several hypotheses:

- **H1:** The Internet spread is positively associated with the level of democracy, being a factor of democratization.
- **H2:** The Internet has an important moderating effect on the level of democracy and its predictors, such as economic wealth, post-materialist values and electronic mechanisms of engagement (e-government and e-participation).
- **H3:** As more autocracies are adapting the Internet to serve the ends of authoritarian consolidation, the democratizing potential of the Internet will weaken over time and across countries.

3 Empirical Study

Research Design. To test the hypotheses, we use the statistical methods of correlation analysis and linear regression. While the first one helps to explore the statistical significance of the variables' interaction, the latter helps to see the causal relationship when testing for other factors. The period of study is 20 years, from 1995 to 2015. The dependent variable is the political regime (REGIME). It is calculated by using the Polity IV[1] data on political regimes – the level of democracy (DEMOC) and autocracy (AUTOC) institutionalization. We subtract the measure of AUTOC from the measure of DEMOC, and get the value within [−10; 10], where 10 is for the most democratic country, and −10 for the most authoritarian.

---

[1] Polity IV Project, Political Regime Characteristics and Transitions, 1800-2015, INSCRdata. [Electronicresource]. URL: http://www.systemicpeace.org/inscrdata.html (retrieved: 26.02.2017).

Our main independent variable is the percentage of Internet users, calculated by the World Bank (INTERNET). We also take the logged data from the World Bank for GDP per capita, which is used as a measure of the national economic wealth (GDP_log) in accordance with Lipset's theory. To measure the e-government and e-participation influence we use the data from the UN E-Government Index, particularly such sub-indices as the E-Participation Index (E-PART), Online Services (E-GOV) and Human Capital Index (HUMAN).[2] To measure the interaction effect of the Internet and GDP we first calculate the centered variables to reduce the problem of multicollinearity, and second multiple the centered variables (INTERNET_GDP).[3]

To access the cultural explanation, we take another dataset with cross-section data, as values' measurements are not available for all years and countries cover. As a proxy for post-materialist values, we use the data on the 12-item post-materialist index from Inglehart's World Values Survey (VALUES),[4] and run an analysis with the medium estimations of the abovementioned variables.

Correlation Analysis. We start our quantitative analysis from the correlation analysis between the Internet users, levels of democracy, autocracy and the overall regime estimation. The results are presented in Fig. 1, denoting the correlation coefficients between INTERNET, DEMOC, AUTOC and REGIME. The results show that the Internet development and the level of democracy are in fact significantly correlated phenomena. However, this relationship is changing over time. In the 1990s, the Internet was developing predominantly in democracies, and the peak is traced at the beginning of the millennium, when there was the strongest positive correlation between the level of democracy and the overall regime estimation, and the strongest negative correlation with the institutionalization of autocracy. It means that in time we could expect the Internet to be well developed in established democracies and to be least developed in established autocracies. However, the situation changed, and the Internet began to lose its democratizing potential: the correlation between the Internet and democracy is still statistically significant, but the coefficients are smaller overtime. What is also important, the link between the level of autocracy (AUTOC) and the Internet has also been missing its significance, and since 2011 it has not shown a statistically important interaction. It means that although we can still expect the Internet to be developed in democracies more likely, we cannot deny that consolidated autocracies also use the benefits of the new technologies.

To exemplify the changes of the interaction between the Internet and political regime we draw three scatter-dot charts using the data of three periods 1995, 2005 and 2015 (pic. 2–4). It is clear that in 1995, the Internet was a privilege of democracies, and the relationship between the Internet and democracy was quite linear and positive. But in 2005 we can see several authoritarian countries (such as Singapore, UAE etc.) that are

---

[2] UN E-GovernmentSurvey 2016 [Electronicresource]. URL: https://publicadministration.un.org/egovkb/en-us/reports/un-e-government-survey-2016 (retrieved: 08.04.2017).

[3] WVS Database. [Electronicresource]. URL: http://www.worldvaluessurvey.org/WVSOnline.jsp (retrieved: 26.02.2017).

[4] WVS Database. [Electronicresource]. URL: http://www.worldvaluessurvey.org/WVSOnline.jsp (retrieved: 26.02.2017).

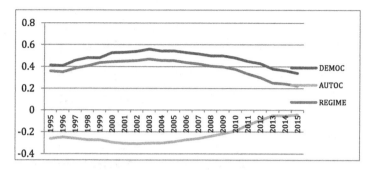

Fig. 1. Correlation coefficients of INTERNET with DEMOC, AUTOC, REGIME. **Source**: Authors' Calculations. **Note**: For DEMOC and REGIME all coefficients are statistically significant at the 0.01 level, for AUTOC all coefficients during the period 1995–2009 are statistically significant at the 0.01 level, in 2010 – significant at the 0.05 level, during the period 2011–2015 – not significant.

quite successful in the Internet promotion. In 2015, we observe a J-curve: the Internet is mostly developing either in strong democracies or in strong autocracies, while the so-called hybrid regimes are lagging behind. It is quite in line with the assumption that capable authoritarian countries are now taking advantage of using the Internet.

Hence, the correlation analysis confirms the plausible hypotheses that although the Internet can be associated with democracy and considered at least its correlate (H1), such democratizing effect is fading and the most consolidated autocracies are not threatened by the *liberation technology* (H3) (Figs. 2, 3 and 4).

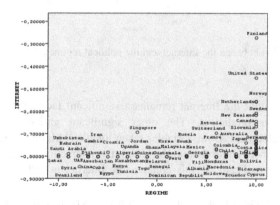

Fig. 2. The correlation between the Internet and the political regime in 1995. **Source**: Authors' calculations.

Regression Analysis. To explore the interaction between the Internet and the political regime in interaction with other variables, we run several regression models, where REGIME is a dependent variable. The summary of models is presented in Table 2.

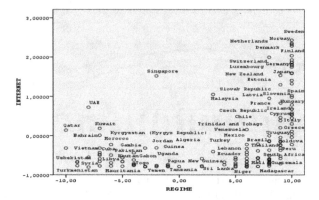

Fig. 3. The correlation between the Internet and the political regime in 2005. **Source**: Authors' calculations.

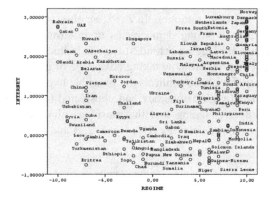

Fig. 4. The correlation between the Internet and the political regime in 2015. **Source**: Authors' calculations.

The analysis shows that the Internet remains a significant factor in all models, when controlled for other predictors. The other significant variable is the level of e-government development. Both variables taken together, Model 4 explains about 14 per cent of the variance. Other factors, including the interaction between the GDP and the Internet, are insignificant. In this context, the Internet is still associated with the democratic regime.

However, when the variance includes non-democracies, the situation changes. Table 3 contains models for those countries having [−10; 0] on the REGIME scale, meaning they are either hybrid or autocratic. The only significant variables are GDP_log and HUMAN, meaning that the Internet is neither associated with the regime, nor boosts an economic-enabled democratization. The GDP and human capital are negatively correlated with democracy in this variance, meaning that wealthier and more developed countries are stronger autocracies. So, while generally the Internet is related

Table 2. The results of the regression analysis (dependent variable – REGIME), all cases. **Source**: Author's calculations

	Model 1	Model 2	Model 3	Model 4
	Standardized Beta-coefficients (p-value in parentheses)			
INTERNET	.303 (.000)	.270 (.000)	.222 (.000)	.238 (.000)
GDP_log	−.038 (.546)	–	–	–
INTERNET_GDP	−.046 (.303)	−.050 (.288)	–	–
E-PART	−.050 (.391)	–	–	–
E-GOV	.177 (.006)	.136 (.002)	.148 (.001)	.175 (.000)
HUMAN	.068 (.092)	.065 (.077)	.066 (.069)	–
Adjusted R-square	.144	.145	.146	.144
Standardized error	5.816	5.813	5.85	5.86

Table 3. The results of the regression analysis (dependent variable – REGIME), non-democracies. **Source**: Author's calculations

	Model 5
	Std. Beta-coefficients (p-value in parentheses)
INTERNET	.026 (.805)
GDP_log	−.443 (.000)
INTERNET_GDP	−.001 (.989)
E-PART	.042 (.679)
E-GOV	.101 (.303)
HUMAN	−.320 (000)
Adjusted R-square	.321
Standardized Error	2.318

to democracy, consolidated authoritarian regimes seem to have learnt how to use it to gain an economic advantage. To test another causal mechanism based on values, we use the cross-section data with VALUES. The results are presented in Table 4. Again, in all cases (Model 6) we see that the Internet is the most significant factor when

Table 4. The results of the regression analysis (dependent variable – REGIME). **Source**: Author's calculations

	Model 6 (all cases)	Model 7 (non-democracies)
	Std. Beta-coefficients (p-value in parentheses)	
INTERNET	.763 (.000)	.161 (.557)
GDP_log	−.369 (.060)	−.466 (.112)
VALUES	.193 (.106)	−.320 (.752)
INTERNET_VALUES	−.091 (.476)	−.066 (.837)
Adjusted R-square	.253	.000
Standardized Error	5.492	3.1

controlled to the GDP, values and Internet-values interactive variable. However, when we explore non-democracies (Model 7), all factors lose their significance.

Although the interaction effect hypothesis has not been confirmed directly in the regression analysis (except for e-government), we need to admit that there is a strong and significant correlation between the Internet and other predictors of democracy (Table 5). It means that a more elaborate technique is still needed to evaluate this interaction.

Table 5. Correlation analysis between the GDP, Internet and post-materialist values. Source: Authors' calculation.

	GDP_log	VALUES
INTERNET	.753** (3239 cases)	.383** (88 cases)
GDP_log	–	.515** (88 cases)
VALUES	.383** (88 cases)	–

Note: ** - correlation is significant at the 0.01 level.

4   Conclusion

Our findings suggest that the relationship of the Internet and political regime is ambivalent and varies over time. In fact, the positive correlation between the variables could have been a proof of the Internet democratization potential. Now the link is weakening though, indicating that the optimistic viewpoint needs to be changed into a more neutral, instrumentalist, version. Modern autocracies, especially consolidated ones, have learnt to use the Internet as a tool for economic modernization. The regression analysis shows that although the spread of ICTs is a statistically significant predictor of democracy, when changing the sample to autocracies only, it is losing its significance, putting the validity of the cyber-optimistic position at question. However the strong and significant correlation between the Internet and other predictors of democracy, like economic growth and values, leaves space for further elaboration on this topic, and more research is needed to trace these multi-level links.

Acknowledgements. The paper was prepared within the framework of the Academic Fund Program at the National Research University Higher School of Economics (HSE) in 2016 (grant No. 16-05-0059) and supported within the framework of a subsidy granted to the HSE by the Government of the Russian Federation for the implementation of the Global Competitiveness Program.

References

1. Howard, P.N., Hussain, M.M.: Democracy's Fourth Wave: Digital Media and the Arab Spring. Oxford University Press, New York (2013)
2. Göbel, C.: The information dilemma: how ICT strengthen or weaken authoritarian rule. Statsvetenskaplig tidskrift **4**, 385–402 (2013)
3. Karlsson, M.: Carrots and sticks: Internet governance in non–democratic regimes. Int. J. Electron. Gov. **6**, 179–186 (2013). doi:10.1504/IJEG.2013.058405

4. Oates, S.: Revolution Stalled: The Political Limits of the Internet in the Post-Soviet Sphere. Oxford University Press, New York (2013)
5. Diamond, L.: Liberation technology. J. Democr. **21**, 69–83 (2010)
6. Farrell, H.: The consequences of the Internet for politics. Annu. Rev. Polit. Sci. **15**, 39–42 (2012). doi:10.1146/annurev-polisci-030810-110815
7. Weare, C.: The Internet and democracy: the causal links between technology and politics. Int. J. Public Adm. **5**(25), 659–691 (2002). doi:10.1081/PAD-120003294
8. Hill, K.A., John, E.H.: Is the Internet an instrument of global democratization? Democratization **6**, 99–127 (1999). doi:10.1080/13510349908403613
9. Lipset, S.M.: Some social requisites of democracy: economic development and political legitimacy. Am. Polit. Sci. Rev. **53**, 69–105 (1959). doi:10.2307/1951731
10. Inglehart, R., Wayne, E.B.: Modernization, cultural change, and the persistence of traditional values. Am. Sociol. Rev. **65**, 19–52 (2000)
11. Lehdonvirta, V.: Online spaces have material culture: goodbye to digital post-materialism and hello to virtual consumption. Media Cult. Soc. **32**, 883–889 (2010). doi:10.1177/0163443710378559
12. Nisbet, E.C., Stoycheff, E., Katy, E.P.: Internet use and democratic demands: a multinational, multilevel model of Internet use and citizen attitudes about democracy. J. Commun. **62**, 249–265 (2012). doi:10.1111/j.1460-2466.2012.01627.x
13. Kabanov, Y.: Piratskie partii: mirovie tendencii razvitiya. Politiya **77**, 128–143 (2015). in Russian
14. Vanderhill, R.: Limits on the democratizing influence of the Internet: lessons from post-soviet states. Demokratizatsiya J. Post-Soviet Democr. **23**, 31–56 (2015)
15. Polat, R.K.: The Internet and political participation: exploring the explanatory links. Eur. J. Commun. **20**, 435–459 (2005). doi:10.1177/0267323105058251
16. Macintosh, A.: Characterizing e-participation in policy-making. In: Proceedings of the 37th Annual Hawaii International Conference on System Sciences, pp. 1–10. IEEE Press (2004)
17. Theocharis, Y.: Young people, political participation and online postmaterialism in Greece. New Media Soc. **13**, 203–223 (2011). doi:10.1177/1461444810370733
18. Ruijgrok, K.: From the web to the streets: Internet and protests under authoritarian regimes. Democratization **3**(24), 498–520 (2017). doi:10.1080/13510347.2016.1223630
19. Best, M.L., Wade, K.W.: The Internet and democracy: global catalyst or democratic dud? Bull. Sci. Technol. Soc. **29**, 255–271 (2009). doi:10.1177/0270467609336304
20. Milner, H.V.: The digital divide: the role of political institutions in technology diffusion. Comp. Polit. Stud. **2**(39), 176–199 (2006). doi:10.1177/0010414005282983
21. Stier, S.: Political determinants of e-government performance revisited: comparing democracies and autocracies. Gov. Inf. Q. **3**(32), 270–278 (2015). doi:10.1016/j.giq.2015.05.004
22. Groshek, J.: A time-series, multinational analysis of democratic forecasts and Internet diffusion. Int. J. Commun. **4**, 142–174 (2010). doi:10.1177/1748048508100909
23. Corrales, J., Westhoff, F.: Information technology adoption and political regimes. Int. Stud. Q. **4**(50), 911–933 (2006). doi:10.1111/j.1468-2478.2006.00431.x
24. Rød, E.G., Nils, B.W.: Empowering activists or autocrats? The Internet in authoritarian regimes. J. Peace Res. **52**, 338–351 (2015). doi:10.1177/0022343314555782
25. Åström, J., et al.: Understanding the rise of e-participation in non-democracies: domestic and international factors. Gov. Inf. Q. **2**(29), 142–150 (2012). doi:10.1016/j.giq.2011.09.008
26. He, B., Warren, M.E.: Authoritarian deliberation: the deliberative turn in Chinese political development. Perspect. polit. **2**(9), 269–289 (2011). doi:10.1017/S1537592711000892
27. Zeng, J.: China's date with big data: will it strengthen or threaten authoritarian rule? Int. Aff. **6**(92), 1443–1462 (2016)

eCity: Urban Planning and Smart Cities

Strategic Planning of Science City Socioeconomic Development

Alexander N. Raikov$^{(\boxtimes)}$ ⓘD

Institute of Control Sciences of Russian Academy of Sciences,
Profsoyuznaya St., 65, 117997 Moscow, Russia
Alexander.N.Raikov@gmail.com

Abstract. A Science City (SC) is an urban development vision of a Smart City that includes a powerful city-forming scientific-industrial complex in an advanced fashion with a view to managing a city's assets and human capital. Therefore, the strategic planning of the SC's socioeconomic development requires as special scientific-industrial and cultural marketing analysis involving citizens in strategic processes (civic participation). Certain factors should be considered, such as the fact that SC strategic planning must be coordinated with the federal government and regional authorities, as citizens are demanding more accountability from the government and it is necessary to create conditions for networked group self-organization. So, SC strategic planning has become a transparent networked multilevel decision-making process where marketing analysis and civic participation are the challenge for Smart City strategic planning methodology. Under such conditions this paper aims to develop the author's convergent approach (CA), which would help to accelerate the networked strategic meetings by applying Situational Center, Cognitive Modeling, Genetic Algorithm, and Big Data analysis technology for the verification of cognitive models. This study is an attempt to address the issue of applying CA for accelerating SC strategic planning with civic participation and marketing analysis. To portray the issue of scientific-industrial complex and cultural marketing analysis in these terms, Quality Function Deployment was used. This ground was tested in the SC strategic planning process in the SCs of Korolev and Fryazino, Moscow Region, Russia. It was shown that the CA helps to speed up the traditional strategic planning significantly.

Keywords: Civil participation · Convergence approach · Decision-making · Networked strategic meeting · Science City · Smart City · Strategic planning

1 Introduction

The strategic planning of the socioeconomic development of an e-City (Smart City) is especially challenging in relation to a Science City (SC). Regular state strategic planning in Russia began in 2014 when the relevant federal law, number 172, was adopted. Special laws (in 1999, number 70; in 2015, number 100) were adopted for the SC. The laws ensure strategic forecast, planning and programming processes through special rules on the federal, regional and municipal levels.

© Springer International Publishing AG 2017
D.A. Alexandrov et al. (Eds.): DTGS 2017, CCIS 745, pp. 295–306, 2017.
https://doi.org/10.1007/978-3-319-69784-0_25

The modern system approaches to city development planning have been considered (see, for example, [1, 2]). But it was shown that the SC has its own distinctive features for strategic planning. So, according to the above-mentioned laws, the SC includes a city-forming science-industrial complex. It develops and approves the strategy of social and economic development that has to be coordinated with the federal government and regional authority and includes a section with the characteristics of the scientific-industrial complex and innovative potentials of SC's organizations, such as the methods and mechanisms of their development. The road map for this strategy must be based on: the development of the science-industrial complex, including small and medium-sized enterprises; the implementation of innovative projects aimed at the creation and development of the production of high-tech industrial products; the preservation and development of Science City infrastructure. The relative number of scientific workers (researchers) from the science and production complex must exceed a certain threshold.

A Scientific and Technical Council of the Science City and a board of directors from leading city companies could be created to support the strategy-making processes. The chameleonic science and technology market dynamic must be taken into consideration in a special way. As the strategy is created to ensure the improvement of the quality of SC life and its citizens, it is very important to organize civil communities and civic participation to discuss different issues. Civic participation is the individual and collective actions designed to address and discuss strategic issues of public concern.

So, the strategic planning in the SC is a networked multilevel decision-making process that could take into account a lot of (up to 100) poorly predictable factors, such as: global science and technology market dynamics, nuances of domestic and foreign policy, financial constraints, civil groups' requirements and experts' opinions, digital technology development, etc. There are about 50 well-known models for strategic thinking [3], the Mintzberg's 10 schools of strategic thought [4] and other different approaches in the field of strategic management [5] and decision analysis for unstructured problems [6]. The scientific and technical council, groups of people and experts, and city citizens are the participants of the strategic processes; and it is required to get high-level agreement between the participants, including civil communities. Such an abundance of strategy-making approaches, inside and outside factors can make this strategic planning process unsustainable and divergent.

To make strategic management more efficient, sustainable and purposeful, managers of various companies around the world implement special management innovations, such as: introducing agile technology into the strategic process; reducing the number of control hierarchy levels; encouraging horizontal links; using project methods and technologies; increasing team confidence; implementing permanent and self-education principles; replacing salary with rewards; covering everybody with strategic planning processes; reducing financial control losses; creating broadcasting networks to improve transparency; placing more emphasis on intellectual property and intangible assets; organizing strategic conferences and conversations; creating and developing special networked expertise (e-expertise) decision support systems, etc.

But the dynamically segmented science and technology market is getting more complicated and faster developing. Its predictability is reducing. Consequently, it requires new strategic planning approaches and additional resources to keep SC development more sustainable and purposeful, and its business more competitive. In previous practice, building the strategy for a city has taken about 5–9 months and its administration had to keep special strategic planning and information technology departments. The new reality does not always allow this to happen; the duration of the strategic planning process may be restricted to 1–2 months and the process may be realized by the city administering themselves with invitations to 2–3 consultants with their special group strategy-making methodology.

To accelerate the SC strategic planning agreement and to make the strategic planning process with compulsory civic participation more purposeful and sustainable, the special author's *convergent approach* was applied and tested.

2   Convergent Approach for SC

Strategic decision-making in socioeconomic subjects is usually supported by different methods. It may be the well-known SWOT analysis (Strengths, Weaknesses, Opportunities, and Threats) method, the Analytic Hierarchy method [7], experts' procedures [8], marketing analysis, or statistical and sociological investigations. The strategic socioeconomic planning for the SC involves many groups of people, participants of social networks, crowds, etc. They develop their claim during the long-term strategic planning.

The success of strategic planning with civil participants depends on solving a set of issues from the fields of politics, economy, sociology, finance, technology, etc. Furthermore, the proposed mechanisms have to support the digital democracy processes of citizens' strategic discussions and decision-making, taking into account the possibilities of modern digital and networked technologies, including artificial intelligence.

One of the main restrictions to advancing the CA is the established traditions and laws that govern the citizens' processes of strategic discussion and decision-making. The development of democratic processes is very conservative. This domain seems impervious to the transformative effects of digital and networked technologies. Models of representative democracy, administration hierarchy, elections and experts' processes have not been changed much for a long time. The way in which authority interacts with the public and experts hasn't changed much either. The processes of public participation rarely involve effective virtual collaboration technology for giving citizens the power to make decisions [9].

Countries' leaders have designed the e-government activity around interconnection, openness, transparency and cybersecurity. Citizens have used e-voting in their national elections. The networked technology gives them a way to develop a pure market, driven by supply and demand, with the possibility of being decentralized and free from government control. In their turn, networked opportunities and thoughts that governments are dysfunctional and corrupt are pushing more to make social decisions outside the current state decision-making system, not by voting. Voter turnout is dropping in a lot of countries.

Blockchain and bitcoin technology has begun to support the development of democratic processes. Blockchain drives different transformations, such as: integrity, when trust and transparency become the most important characteristics of social activity; citizen power, when people take more responsibility for their communities and collaborations. A number of hidden factors influence SC strategic processes. On the whole, the SC socioeconomic decision-making processes can be characterized by the following specific features:

- Poorly predictable and chaotic behavior of the environment and participants;
- Boundary fuzziness of groups and areas of their interest;
- Weakly formalized and ill-defined problems;
- Unsustainable and divergent discussion and decision-making processes;
- Unique problematic situations;
- Stealthiness of participants' intentions;
- Deviations of the global strategic plan realization;
- Importance of small actions, and others.

The convergent approach focuses on two essential aspects, namely: the stability (sustainability) and purposiveness of group strategic planning and control [10]. The convergent approach integrates:

- Strategic SWOT analysis methods for identifying and formulating the factors that influence strategic development;
- Networked strategic conversation technology [8] for speeding up obtaining the strategic agreement between the members of the authority team (administration) and groups of experts;
- Cognitive modeling and genetic algorithms for incorrect problem solving [10, 11];
- Big Data analysis for cognitive model verification [12];
- The logic of breakthrough thinking [13], etc.

The creation strategy for the SC requires taking into account the above-mentioned specific features of the SC such as citizens' opinions, which are to be agreed with the decision-making activity of the SC administration and groups of experts. The main components of the strategic decision-making processes in the SC are illustrated in Fig. 1.

The different features of the participants of strategic decision-making processes in the SC appear to suggest that the strategic planning has to be structured in a special convergent way to get the synergy of strategic decision-making processes on different levels. The convergent approach just provides this synergy. It ensures the control process of the various strategic meetings, discussions or conversations so that they are converging toward strategic goals. The convergent processes become purposeful in spite of the fact that the goals could be fuzzy. The processes become ill-defined because no formalized participants' activities (dreams, intentions, interests, feelings and thoughts, mimicry and gestures) are expressed by means of discontinuous and discrete words and images. At the same time, in the strategic meeting where these activities predominate, the duration of the process of getting an agreement may be excessively long and result in failure.

The convergent approach creates necessary conditions for ensuring the convergence of the discussion processes. This is achieved mainly by applying cognitive modeling and the genetic algorithm that help to solve incorrect problems in the cognitive model [10, 11]. These conditions may look like requirements for the special

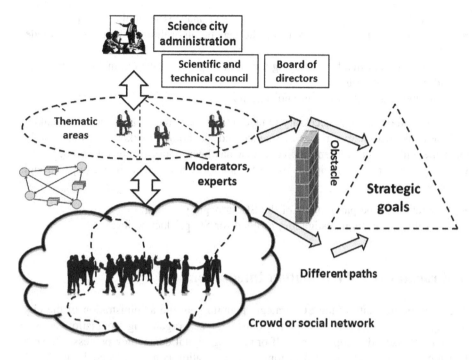

Fig. 1. The components of strategic decision-making processes in the Science City.

structuring of information processes and taking the mandatory steps. The requirements for structuring the special information helps to increase the stability of the consent attainment process in a team or group of people during the formation of the strategy. The moderator who is conducting strategic conversations needs to know certain rules and make sure they are adhered to, such as:

- Information openness and transparency of the discussion process;
- Stringency of the conversation schedule;
- Changing rates of information openness and of stringency in a special way;
- Support for the special level and rate of internal chaos generated during the discussion process, etc.

There are mandatory steps (algorithm) in the strategic conversation between the participants of the SC authority team and groups of experts:

- Separate goals, resources and actions;
- Create of a goals tree by categorizing goals as: main, internal and external;
- The goals are to be ranked by using, for example, the above-mentioned Analytic Hierarchy method [7];
- Decompose the resources into a finite number of parts by using, for example, the well-known SWOT analysis method;
- Define a few strategic directions (priorities) by using the SWOT analysis method;
- Create a strategic cognitive model [10];

- Verify the cognitive model by using Big Data analysis technology [12];
- Define the optimal actions by using the genetic algorithm on the cognitive model [10];
- Identify mechanisms for managing the strategy implementation, including financial and investment tools;
- Write the strategic document and road map.

At the same time, it is necessary to take into account the citizens' decision-making and the consumer characteristics of science and technology market forces to complement the author's convergent approach that has been applied only for strategic conversation between the participants of the SC authority team and expert groups through two new components:

- Integration of the participants of the SC strategic planning;
- Marketing analysis investigation, adapted for SC product policy.

3   Fractal Civic Participation Integration

The main participants of the SC strategic planning are the administration of the city, management of enterprises, expert groups and self-organizing population activity (crowd). The self-developing and self-organizing digital democracy processes have to be supported. The networked decision-making situation consists of people, goals and requirements of different teams, groups, headquarters, experts and moderators, and obstacles on the way to the fuzzy goals (see Fig. 1). The problem is to find a strategic agreement among all of the networked groups of participants in the shortest amount of time. This problem is ill-defined, incorrect, wherein the emotions, thoughts, feelings and transcendental states of mind of participants advance the decision-making process. The administration and moderators have to control the networked activity so as to ensure the strategic consent of the participants' decision-making. For this aim the moderators have to know the CA at least.

Everybody in a group has to comply with the convergent rules of strategic meeting conduction and structuring the information for ensuring the purposiveness and stability of discussions that can be implemented in the network. The duration of the online networked or apparent strategic discussion (meeting, conversation) should be around 4–8 h. During the discussion each participant has to make a decision in a short time regarding the strategic targets of the group. It may coincide with the global decision of all groups. Sometimes it happens that someone will have to agree with the global decision, but it may coincide with his dissatisfaction. The moderator has to bear in mind that dissatisfaction is the enemy of desire to do anything. The behaviors of various participants are different. The behavior of authority and expert groups may be to obey the strict rules, but the behavior of social networks could bring chaos to mind. These two types of behaviors have to be synchronized.

The information and communication technologies and networked decision support systems help to accelerate the strategic processes; thanks to them the democracy becomes more transparent and direct. It gives people the opportunity to influence policy more directly. However, strategic thinking requires networked group consensus, which differs from votes, when some participants may have their own opinions. Consensus is group agreement when each member of the group accepts the general goals with full responsibility.

Digital democracy activity appears as practices of citizens' control and group decision-making [9]. Nevertheless, in our opinion, these processes have no effective methodology and technology to provide sustained acceleration of citizens' group strategic decision-making. And the CA has to be complemented by the special universal (fractal) constructions that could help to synchronize the processes of strategic planning between various multilevel participants with different types of behavior. There may be at least two fractal constructions: for a multilevel decision-making process and for information representation. The first fractal construction is illustrated in Fig. 2. The idea consists of the recommendation to crowd groups to use Agile technology [14] for organizing strategic processes. As can be seen, in this case the steps of strategic planning on the different levels of control are very similar.

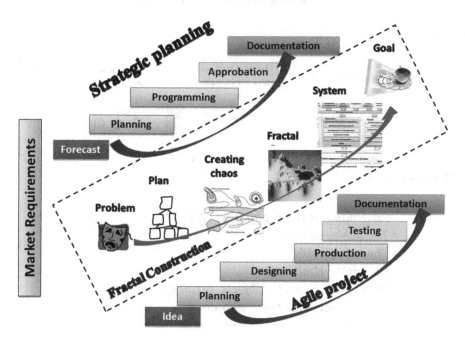

Fig. 2. Fractal construction for strategic planning multilevel decision-making processes.

The fractal construction, represented in Fig. 2, comprises five main elements. The first one is the "Problem" that appears when there is a need to satisfy the market or other external environment requirements. The second is the creation of a draft plan. Thirdly there comes a time of chaotic search that looks like search in a Klondike space [13]. Then, fourthly, there come the ordering spaces in the forms of elements of strategic planning or claims of advances. The result of the fifth point is the system, which may be in the form of production, a prototype of a plan or program. Then come the moments of approbation (testing) and achieving the goal. The goals of strategic planning and creating a product with Agile technology are the same – documentation to advance the results into real practice.

The second fractal construction is illustrated in Fig. 3. It is manual of recommendations for the participants of strategic decision-making, including citizens' groups, the scientific and technical council and board of directors, to put forward their claim in the universal template. It includes the list of information that has to be created by every group during strategic conversation. When groups or individual participants present the results of strategic discussions (the goals, external and internal factors, etc.) in this special fractal construction it ensures the synching and speeding up of SWOT analyses so that the results of all participants have a similar structure.

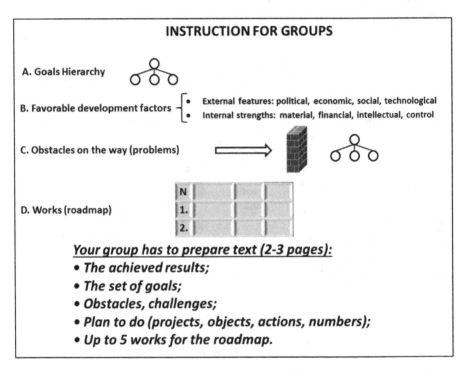

Fig. 3. Universal template for structuring information during group strategic conversation.

4   Networked Marketing Analysis

The Science City strategy must consider not only the global science and technology market. It is more important that the development of science and technology requires a creative atmosphere in the SC. In this way, the connected segments of the market could be very different and may go far beyond merely scientific and technical products. For more general coverage consider one nontraditional and very difficult subject for the SC – cultural heritage reuses. This issue improves the creative atmosphere and SC attraction for the scientific and technological global society.

The processes of improving cultural heritage require networked expert assessments [8] of cultural heritage objects and the events related to these objects. Cultural heritage objects include: churches, industrial buildings, cultural landscapes, archeological sites (not specified yet), cultural heritage monuments, etc. Cultural heritage is not only a link to the past. It is the catalyst of current activity and supports movement into the future. The destiny of every such object is connected with a lot of events. The costs for the adaptive reuse of these assets have to be supported by the public sector, traditional private sector models and special networked expert groups.

The process of cultural heritage reuses demands special marketing analysis and every market segment can have many consumer characteristics. This "gap" could be estimated by different networked experts or groups of experts by using the well-known Quality Function Deployment method, which has to be adapted for the issue (Fig. 4). The numbers in the blocks indicate the order of the implementation process. The detailed descriptions of the scheme are given in [8].

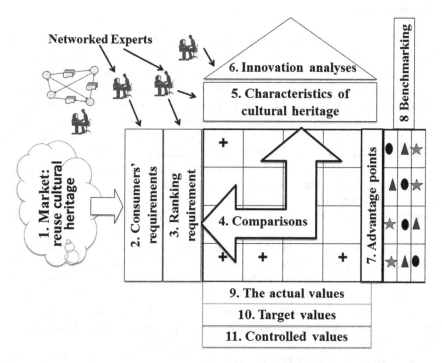

Fig. 4. Decomposition of the cultural heritage reuses estimation process.

The cultural heritage assessments can comprise a desk-based study, interviews of the expert groups from different countries, a wide-area survey, etc. It is very important to choose the right method and create an adequate list of questions. Furthermore, the list has to comprise three groups of questions: holistic, performance-based and sustainability-based [15]. This decomposition helps to obtain the convergence of the decision-making process and implement the CA.

A cultural heritage object can be characterized by different quantitative, geometrical, qualitative and phenomenological parameters. Some of the parameters could be latent or hidden. For example, historical or archaeological places could be of cultural importance to a group of people who are neither historians nor archaeologists, but they may potentially be interesting for them for religious reasons. Moreover, if archaeological research takes place on a site of cultural heritage, the decision-making process regarding reusing the object can be delayed to enable evaluation of the site. This implies the participation of networked experts from different countries and various activities.

Given the multidisciplinary nature of the issue, and the large amount of information that has to be assessed and networked through the distribution of experts, the process of marketing analysis can only be realized with the support of the networked artificial intelligence mechanisms of e-Expertise and Situational Center [8].

5   Conclusions

The aim of this paper is to synchronize and accelerate the processes of SC strategic socioeconomic planning taking into consideration the scientific-industrial complex and cultural marketing analysis and involving networked groups of citizens in the process (civil participants). It provides that in these conditions the CA makes the strategic processes faster, more sustainable and purposeful. This is achieved by structuring information and processes in a special convergent way. The CA is based on some fundamental consistent patterns and artificial intelligence technologies, including cognitive modeling and genetic algorithm for solving inverse problems.

The multi-group self-developing and self-organizing digital democracy processes have been supported by introducing two special fractal templates. They integrate the processes and information structures on the different levels of strategic processes – from administration of the SC to the groups of people, including those who work in a social network.

The main parts of the suggested CA were verified in many cases, for example: the development of the Russian information technology market. It was applied for strategic planning in the fields of: regional higher and professional education, the public health service, social security, housing and communal services, property management, a youth policy and television viewer rating calculations. The results were successfully implemented to develop several governmental situation centers in the Russian Federation and to create business strategies for some commercial companies.

A socioeconomic development strategy for two Russian SCs – the cities of Fryazino [16] and Korolev, Moscow Region – was developed. The strategy describes different aspects of SC life, including issues of complex reconstruction and development territories, high and professional education, the public health service, a social security program, housing and communal services, a youth policy, changing the segments of the market, creating a smart city, etc. Every SC strategy was presented in the form of 50 pages of main document and about 50 optimized points of the road map (action plan). It has been shown that the development of strategies through discussion in different groups of participants can take 2–3 months.

The proposed convergent approach in the condition of self-developing and self-organizing digital democracy processes could be used for strategic planning on government, municipal and corporate levels, mainly by those who have to support high-level group decision-making processes.

Acknowledgments. This work is partly funded by: the Russian Science Foundation, grant 17-18-01326, "Development of socio-humanitarian technologies for a distributed situational center system in Russia based on self-developing polysubject environment methodology"; Russian Foundation for Basic Research, grant 13-07-13165, "Information-analytical system for decision-making support based on the analysis of Big Data in a network of distributed situational centers and cloud computing environments with heterogeneous computing resources."

References

1. Bisello, A., Vettorato, D., Stephen, R., Elisei, P.: Smart and Sustainable Planning for Cities and Regions: Results of SSPCR. Springer International Publishing, Cham (2017). doi:10.1007/978-3-319-44899-2
2. Resin, V.I., Popkov, Y.S.: Urban Development in Transitional Economy. URSS, Moscow (2001)
3. Krogerus, M., Tschappäler, R.: The Decision Book. Fifty Models for Strategic Thinking. Profile Book Ltd, London (2008)
4. Mintzberg, H., Ahlstrand, B., Lampel, J.: Strategy Safari: A Guided Tour Through the Wilds of Strategic Management. Financial Times Prentice Hall, London (2009)
5. Ohmae, K.: The Mind of the Strategist. The Art of the Japanese Business. Tata McGraw-Hill Publishing Company Limited, New Delhi (2004)
6. Larichev, O., Moshkovich, H.: Verbal Decision Analysis for Unstructured Problems. Kluwer Academic Publishers, Boston (1997)
7. Saaty, T.: The analytic hierarchy process: planning, priority setting, resource allocation. University of Pittsburg, Mervis Hall (1988)
8. Gubanov, D., Korgin, N., Novikov, D., Raikov, A.: E-expertise: Modern Collective Intelligence. SCI, vol. 558. Springer, Cham (2014). doi:10.1007/978-3-319-06770-4
9. Simon, J., Bass, T., Boelman, V., Mulgan, G.: Digital democracy: the tools transforming political engagement. NESTA, UK, England and Wales 1144091 and Scotland SC042833 (2017)
10. Raikov, A.N., Panfilov, S.A.: Convergent decision support system with genetic algorithms and cognitive simulation. In: Proceedings of the IFAC Conference on Manufacturing Modelling, Management and Control, MIM 2013, Saint Petersburg, Russia, 19–21 June, pp. 1142–1147 (2013). doi:10.3182/20130619-3-RU-3018.00404
11. Ivanov, V.K.: Incorrect problems in topological spaces. Siberian Math. J. **10**(5), 785–791 (1969)
12. Raikov, A.N., Avdeeva, Z., Ermakov, A.: A big data refining on the base of cognitive modeling. In: 1st IFAC Conference on Cyber-Physical & Human-Systems, Florianopolis, Brazil. 7–9 December, pp. 147–152 (2016). doi:10.1016/j.ifacol.2016.12.205
13. Perkins, D.: The Eureka Effect. The Art and Logic of Breakthrough Thinking. W.W. Norton & Company, London (2000)

14. Sutherland, J.: Scrum: The Art of Doing Twice the Work in Half the Time. Crown Business, NY (2014)
15. Raikov, A.N.: Organizational structure optimization with the questions–criteria hierarchy. In: IFAC Conference on Manufacturing Modelling, Management and Control, MIM 2016, 28–30 June 2016, Troyes, France, pp. 1590–1595, (2016). doi:10.1016/j.ifacol.2016.07.797
16. The socio-economic development strategy of the Science City Fryazino (in Russian). http://www.naukograd-fryazino.ru/assets/files/Strategy/Strategiya_30_05.docx

A Value-Oriented Approach in Smart City Projects Selection and Ranking

Sergey A. Mityagin$^{(\boxtimes)}$, Sergey I. Drojjin, and Olga B. Tikhonova

ITMO University, Saint Petersburg, Russia
mityagin.spb@gmail.com, sergey.drojjin@gmail.com,
tikhonova.ob@gmail.com

Abstract. The article suggests considering a Smart city as a complex of innovative projects implemented in various sectors of an urban economy. The expediency of implementation of the projects is determined, on the one hand, by the requirements of national and international standards and regulatory documents on urban development, and, on the other hand, by the current needs of city residents. The article presents a formalized set of criteria, which can be used to rank innovative projects in accordance to their importance for implementation within Smart cities. Final part of the article includes results of application of the proposed approach to projects ranking in the process of development of a Smart city in St. Petersburg.

Keywords: Smart city · Innovation · Value-based approach · Regional management

1 Introduction

Currently there is no common view on requirements to a Smart city as a system or set of technologies. Implementation of the Smart city concept under the project-based approach may be considered as a complex of innovative projects, which can provide «smart» sustainable development of urban spaces and improvement of the quality of people's life. Under this approach, the most important task is the selection and ranking of projects to be included in the program of a Smart city development.

Obviously, the project should be included only under condition of its compliance with the objectives of a Smart city. In general, the hierarchy of objectives is formed in accordance with the state policy of regional development, determined by regulatory documents, international and national standards. Along with that, the values and needs of citizens are not considered while building the hierarchy of objectives and this may lead to potentially crisis situations in the society and reduction in effectiveness of implementation of Smart city technologies.

It should be noted that present-day indicators and methods, which characterize the sustainability of cities, on the contrary, take the values and needs of citizens into consideration. Among these indicators it is important to mention a City Development Index (CDI) [1], developed by the United Nations Organization, a Better Life Index [2], developed by the Organization for Economic Cooperation and Development, and an Urban Performance Index, developed by McKinsey Global Institute [3]. The

© Springer International Publishing AG 2017
D.A. Alexandrov et al. (Eds.): DTGS 2017, CCIS 745, pp. 307–318, 2017.
https://doi.org/10.1007/978-3-319-69784-0_26

following methods and ratings, developed by analytical departments of major international journals, can be used as additional examples: Mercer («Quality of living survey») [4], The Economist («World's Most Liveable Cities») [5], Monocl («New Quality of Life Top 25 Cities Survey») [6]. At the United Nations level, on the 16th of March 2016 the heads of delegations of the countries of the Eurasian Economic Commission introduced the Prague Declaration during the «European habitat» conference. The declaration included the objectives of improving an environmental performance of cities and quality of living environment by means of introduction of innovative technologies [7].

The necessity of taking into consideration not only objective criteria of quality of life, but also the needs of an urban population, which should be satisfied to form a base for the life quality, is emphasized in the publication [8].

Thus, it can be stated that the significance of a project for inclusion in the Smart city should be defined by two components: the project's compliance with the objective requirements of regulatory documents and its compliance with subjective needs of the population, formed on the basis of the structure of their values and needs.

2 Approach to Selection and Ranking of Smart City Components

2.1 Objective Requirements to a Smart City

At the international level there are a number of guidelines and programs of implementation of the Smart city concept. Rapid urbanization in all countries leads to the fact that the socio-economic development of cities is one of the priorities of the state. Thus, the objectives, urban development strategies, and objectives of national programs, development strategies largely congruent.

This article suggests allocating the following groups of documents related to the creation of Smart sustainable cities:

- international and national standards;
- roadmaps, guidelines, concepts, proposals, reports;
- global benchmarks and indicators.
- International and national standards are presented by the following documents:

(1) ISO/TR 37150:2014 Smart community infrastructures - Review of existing activities relevant to metrics. This paper considers the current activities related to the metrics of «smart» public infrastructure and provides direction for future standardization.
(2) ISO 37120:2014 Sustainable development of communities - Indicators for city services and quality of life. This standard specifies methods for the application of a set of indicators to measure the effectiveness of management and urban services and quality of life.

(3) PD 8100:2015 Smart cities overview – Guide. The document was developed by the British Standards Institution for specialists involved in «smart design» of cities.

(4) PAS 181:2014 Smart city framework – Guide to establishing strategies for smart cities and communities. The document provides basic practical solutions for city leaders, who aim to transform their cities in order to meet future tasks and challenges successfully.

(5) PAS 182:2014 Smart city concept model – Guide to establishing a model for data interoperability. The document provides recommendations for normalization and classification of information from many sources to identify data sets to obtain an understanding of the city's needs and behaviors of the citizens and the business community.

Roadmaps, guidelines, concepts, proposals, reports:

(1) Mapping Smart Cities in the EU - the document produced by the structural subdivisions of the European Parliament with the participation of experts from leading research organizations. The document provides background information and recommendations for establishing Smart Cities in the cities of the European Union (EU).

(2) Green City Index. The document provides measurements and rates of environmental performance of 30 leading European cities from 30 European countries.

(3) Fujitsu's Approach to Smart Cities – the document describes an approach of the Japanese corporation Fujitsu to Smart cities in different industrial fields and reflects the experience of the application of the described approach.

(4) ITU - FG-SSC - Standardization roadmap for smart sustainable cities. The document is a technical report on standardization activities, gap analysis, roadmap and suggestions to International Telecommunication Union study groups for Smart sustainable cities.

Global benchmarks and indicators

(1) European 2020 targets - the limited set of agreed EU-level targets translated into national targets for each EU country.

(2) UN Sustainable Development Goals. This document is a document indicating the priorities for sustainable development. He received the support of civil society, the business community, parliamentarians and other stakeholders around the world.

Russian regulatory documents do not specifically address the concept of a Smart city. However, there are a number of strategic documents covering the implementation of information technology in the priority areas of the urban economy.

Decrees of the President of the Russian Federation from May 7, 2012 № 596-606 emphasize the following priority directions of regional development: economic, social, healthcare, education and science, housing and housing services, demographic.

The Strategy of information society development until 2020 (decree of the Russian Federation Government from October 20, 2010 №1815-r) and the Strategy of development of the information technology industry in the Russian Federation until 2020 and until 2025 in perspective (decree of the Russian Federation Government from

November 1, 2013 №2036-r) cover the implementation of information technology in the following areas of the urban economy: urban environment, transportation, housing and housing services, education, culture and tourism, healthcare, security, government and municipal services, city property management, social support and protection of the population, labor and employment.

The regional strategy of economic and social development of St. Petersburg until 2030 [9] considers improving the quality of the residential environment, enhancing global competitiveness, sustainable economic growth and use of the results of innovation and technological activities as the main goal.

Another regional document, which may be regarded as a good example, is the development strategy of Moscow until 2025 [10]. The strategy covers the following target directions of regional development: the level and quality of life (population incomes, social security and social development, demography and healthcare, education, culture, physical culture and sport, mass media, housing and housing services, housing policy, ecology, security); development of economic potential of the city (gross regional product, industry and science, small business, transportation and communication, development of wholesale and retail trade, financial institutions, tourism); capacity-building for socioeconomic development (human resources, engineering infrastructure, development of the budget system, international and foreign economic activity).

As a result of the initial analysis of these documents, the following directions of development of the Smart city were formed: information and communication technology, energy and natural resources, education and science, structure of the population, transport, economy and finance, quality of life, health, energy, climate and environment, urban development and urban infrastructure, security, technology and innovation, open government and management, safety, culture and tourism. These directions were distributed for 6 structural sections of the model proposed by the Vienna University of Technology[1]:

1. Smart economy:

- Economy and finance
- Technology and innovation
- Smart governance:
- Open government and management
- Smart mobility:
- Transport
- Information and communication technology
- Smart people:
- Education and science
- Smart living:
- Quality of life, health
- Urban development and urban infrastructure

---

[1] European Smart Cities, http://www.smart-cities.eu/.

- Structure of the population
- Safety
- Culture and tourism
- Smart environment:
- Energy and natural resources.

2.2   Subjective Requirements to a Smart City

An urban environment is evaluated by the population primarily on the basis of the objective characteristics, although this evaluation may be influenced by subjective factors of the people's expectations and needs [11]. Interaction between people and the environment they live in is the classic question of environmental psychology [12]. Collision between objective reality and its subjective perception leads to such psychological phenomena as residential satisfaction [13], place attachment [14], sense of place [15], place identity [16] and quality of urban life [17], which are of interest to many contemporary researchers of the system «individual-environment» [18]. A study of values and needs of St. Petersburg citizens was held as a part of the preparation of this article. The study of needs was conducted by means of analysis of urban internet-communities and topics discussed there. The studies [19, 20] resulted in the identification of 10 most important problems of St. Petersburg citizens:

(1)   the problem of provision of urban amenities;
(2)   the problem of garbage and waste disposal;
(3)   the problem of insufficient public participation in planning of the city budget;
(4)   unauthorized parking and dog walking on the lawn;
(5)   the problem of provision of green area amenities;
(6)   the problem of security of adjoining areas;
(7)   the problem of provision of yards amenities;
(8)   protection of children, improvement of kindergartens and playgrounds;
(9)   the problem of excessive number of cars in the residential area;
(10)   lack of public transportation.

The study of values was based on data of a regular sociological survey conducted by St. Petersburg state unitary enterprise «St. Petersburg Information and Analytical Centre» [21]. The results of the study are presented in Fig. 1 in the form of a hierarchy of values.

After analyzing the structure of values of St. Petersburg citizens, it can be noted that almost 50% of values in the 2012 structure falls on such values as «family», «material welfare» and «health». It is also notable that the most specific values have the most considerable weight, while the abstract values («mutual understanding», «happiness», «kindness») have low weight.

In summary, from the perspective of St. Petersburg citizens' needs the most important category is the improvement of the quality of the urban environment, and from the perspective of values it is the development of infrastructure elements of the city, which ensure material well-being of residents and healthcare.

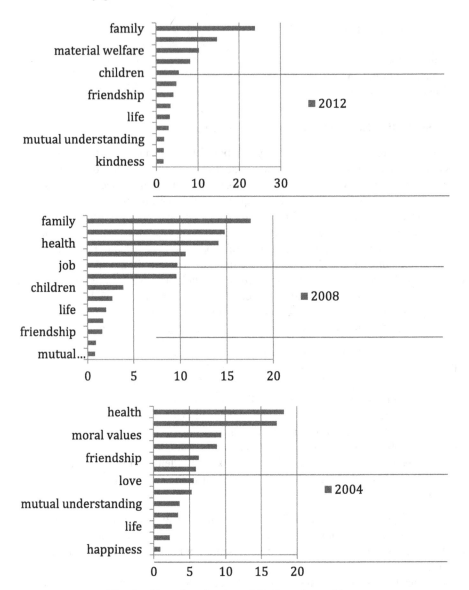

Fig. 1. Hierarchy of values of St. Petersburg citizens

From generalization of approaches to building Smart cities, described in Russian and international documents, and the results of study of the needs and values of the population, the following structure of requirements was developed.

Objectives of a Smart city implementation:

(1) for citizens: gradual ongoing increase in the quality of life;
(2) for a region: ongoing development of the city economic potential and spread of technologies in adjacent areas.

In the context of these objectives three groups of requirements to Smart cities may be considered.

1. Requirements to ensure a high quality of life.

   A pair of interacting components in this case can determine the quality of citizens' life: the living standards of the citizens and the needs of the citizens.

   1.1. The living standards of the citizens are characterized by the citizens' ability to access such components of urban infrastructure as the quality of the urban environment; economic, social and transport components; education and science; healthcare; security; housing and quality of living environment.

   1.2. The needs of the citizens, in turn, may be divided into needs related to the citizens' values, and needs caused by low levels of access to the components of urban infrastructure.

2. Requirements to process management of city development and performance.

   This group includes requirements to management of city development and urban planning, innovation management, waste management and culture development management.

3. Requirements to emergency management.

   This group includes requirements to prediction of emergency situations in the long and short term and to ensuring safety in case of emergencies.

3 Evaluation and Ranking Criteria of a Smart City Components

As mentioned above, under the project-based approach it is considered that the infrastructure of a Smart city is realized by means of introduction of innovative projects, which together can provide achievement of its goals, in various sectors of the economy. For an effective selection of innovative projects for implementation, it's necessary to have a tool for their evaluation and ranking in order of importance, as well as a tool to determine the compliance of the project's results to the requirements of a Smart city.

In this article, the following groups of criteria of compliance of the project's results to the requirements of a Smart city are suggested:

1. target
2. innovative
3. infrastructure
4. image.

Target criteria allow assessing the compliance of an innovative project to the goal of ensuring a high quality of citizens' life by means of developing one or several components of urban infrastructure with consideration of the citizens' values and needs (the first objective of a Smart city implementation).

The structure of target criteria, which was obtained from the studies described in this paper, is given in the Table 1.

Table 1. Target criteria of compliance to the requirements of a Smart city

№	Name of the criterion	Significance coefficient
1	Improvement of the quality of urban environment	0.166
2	Improvement of healthcare	0.166
3	Improvement of economic resilience	0.166
4	Improvement of social services	0.133
5	Improvement of security	0.116
6	Improvement of transportation	0.100
7	Improvement of education and science	0.083
8	Improvement of housing and living environment	0.066

The significance coefficients were established on the basis of the identified citizens' needs and values by means of the method of pair-wise comparison within a group. The first three criteria have the highest weight as they have equal significance from the perspective of the citizens' needs and values.

Innovation criteria allow assessing the compliance of an innovative project to the goal of ongoing development of the city economic potential and spread of technologies in adjacent areas (the second objective of a Smart city implementation).

The structure of innovation criteria, which was obtained from the methodological recommendations [22], is given in the Table 2.

Table 2. Innovative criteria of compliance to the requirements of a Smart city

№	Name of the criterion	Significance coefficient
1	Perspectivity of the applied scientific and technical solutions	0.250
2	Patent clearance of the products and patentability of the applied technical solutions	0.150
3	Perspectivity of application of the obtained results in future projects	0.250
4	Positive impact on other projects	0.150
5	Perspectivity of development	0.200

Infrastructure criteria allow assessing an innovative project from the perspective of its integration into the processes of city life (the second group of requirements to a Smart city). The structure of infrastructure criteria, which was obtained from the studies described in this paper, is given in the Table 3.

Criteria of integration of the project into the Smart city structure and improvement of the quality of management of city development and urban planning have the highest significance coefficients due to the importance of ensuring the integrity of the city's infrastructure.

Image criteria involve an increase in recognizability of the city and are connected to the fact that an important factor for a Smart city is the existence of an idea, which can arrange the objectives and tasks of its development [22].

Table 3. Infrastructure criteria of compliance to the requirements of a Smart city

№	Name of the criterion	Significance coefficient
1	Improvement of the quality of management of city development and urban planning	0.250
2	Improvement of the quality of innovation management	0.100
3	Improvement of the quality of waste management	0.150
4	Improvement of the quality of culture development management	0.100
5	Integration of the project into the Smart city structure	0.200
6	Integration of the information resources	0.200

The structure of image criteria, which was obtained from the methodological recommendations [22], is given in the Table 4.

Table 4. Image criteria of compliance to the requirements of a Smart city

№	Name of the criterion	Significance coefficient
1	Possible positive reaction of public on the project	0.300
2	Recognizability	0.250
3	Improvement of business reputation of the city	0.450

The given set of criteria was used for evaluation and ranking of the projects proposed for implementation as a part of a Smart city in St. Petersburg.

4 Evaluation and Ranking of a Smart City Components in St. Petersburg

For the purposes of preparation of this article, a group of projects was evaluated basing on the given criteria of compliance to the requirements of a Smart city. The projects were proposed by the executive public authorities of St. Petersburg. The proposals were collected by the Interdepartmental Commission for the development and implementation of the project «Smart city of Saint Petersburg» under the Government of St. Petersburg.

49 projects, related to the IT infrastructure of the city, were evaluated in total. The results of the evaluation, summarized by responsible public authorities of St. Petersburg, are given in the Table 5.

The following projects, e.g., were approved for implementation within a Smart city:

- the information system for registering parameters of apartment buildings;
- the decision support system for urban planning;
- the project for processes automation in the field of maintenance of public roads of regional significance;

Table 5. Summary table with the results of evaluation of the projects, proposed as components of a Smart city in St. Petersburg.

Field public authority	Total number of proposed projects	Number of approved projects	Number of rejected projects
Committee for Housing Maintenance	2	2	0
Committee for Civil Engineering, City Planning and Architecture	12	3	9
Committee for City Improvement and Roads	9	7	2
Committee for Tariffs	2	2	0
Committee for Industrial Policy and Innovation	3	1	2
Committee for Tourism and Resort Development	6	1	5
Committee for Transport	3	2	1
Committee for Nature Use, Environmental Protection and Ecological Safety	2	2	0
Committee for Finances	1	1	0
Committee for Labour and Social Protection	1	0	0
Committee for Education	2	0	2
Committee for State Service and Personnel Policy	6	0	6
Total:	49	21	27

- the project for processes automation in the field of planning and control of cleaning and maintenance of territories, as well as immediate informing of the population about the activities conducted;
- the project for improvement of registration of information about sources of negative impact on the environment;
- creation of an integrated center for transport and transport infrastructure management;
- state ecological monitoring for environment in St. Petersburg;
- the project to involve citizens in the budgetary process of St. Petersburg.

The given list of projects is interesting because, in general, it covers the identified problems of St. Petersburg citizens. Besides, it can be noted that the majority of rejected projects was related to autonomous internal functions of the public authorities, which should be automated within the current responsibilities of these authorities.

5 Conclusion

The article presents the results of the study of objective and subjective requirements to a Smart city and the criteria of compliance of innovative project's results to these requirements. It is suggested to differentiate the target, innovative, infrastructure and image criteria.

The developed system of criteria was applied for evaluation and ranking of innovative projects related to the IT infrastructure, proposed by the executive public authorities of St. Petersburg for consideration by the Interdepartmental Commission for the development and implementation of the project «Smart city of Saint Petersburg».

As a result of the application of the criteria system, a part of the projects was rejected as inconsistent with the objectives of a Smart city and the corresponding requirements. The approved projects, mentioned in this article, can be considered as corresponding not only to the objective requirements of regulatory documents, but also to the subjective needs and values of the citizens.

References

1. The City Development Index (CDI). http://www.un.org/ga/Istanbul+5/116.pdf
2. Better Life Index. http://www.oecdbetterlifeindex.org/ru/
3. Cadena, A., Remes, J., Manyika, J., Dobbs, R., Roxburgh, C., Elstrodt, H.-P., Chaia, A., Restrepo, A.: Building globally competitive cities: the key to Latin American growth. McKinsey Global Inst. (2011) http://www.mckinsey.com/global-themes/urbanization/building-competitive-cities-key-to-latin-american-growth
4. Mercer's Quality of Living Reports. https://www.imercer.com/products/quality-of-living.aspx
5. The Economist's Global Liveability Ranking 2016. http://www.eiu.com/public/topical_report.aspx?campaignid=liveability2016
6. Monocle's Quality of Life Survey Is an Alternative Top Destinations for 2015. https://skift.com/2015/06/12/monocles-quality-of-life-survey-is-an-alternative-places-to-go-for-2015/
7. Prague Declaration: Project of the first version from the 7th of December. https://www.unece.org/fileadmin/DAM/hlm/sessions/docs2015/informal_notes/4B_Prague_Declarationdraft.ru.pdf
8. Shen, L., Kyllo, J.M., Guo, X.: An integrated model based on a hierarchical indices system for monitoring and evaluating urban sustainability. Sustainability 5, 524–559 (2013)
9. The decree of the Government of St. Petersburg from the 13th of May 2014 № 355 «On the regional strategy of economic and social development of St. Petersburg until 2030»
10. The decree of the Government of Moscow from the 26th of June 2007 № 513-PP «On the development strategy of Moscow until 2025»
11. Dębek, M.: Towards people's experiences and behaviours within their worlds: the integrative-transactional framework for studying complex people-environment interactions. Soc. Space 8(2), 1–55 (2014)
12. Lawrence, R.J.: Healthy residential environments. In: Bechtel, R., Churchman, A. (eds.) Handbook of Environmental Psychology, pp. 394–412. Wiley, New York (2002)
13. Ramkissoon, H., Smith, L.D.G., Weiler, B.: Testing the dimensionality of place attachment and its relationships with place satisfaction and pro-environmental behaviours: a structural equation modelling approach. Tour. Manag. 36, 552–566 (2013)
14. Lewicka, M.: Place attachment, place identity, and place memory: restoring the forgotten city past. J. Environ. Psychol. 28(3), 209–231 (2008)
15. Campelo, A., Aitken, R., Thyne, M., Gnoth, J.: Sense of place: the importance for destination branding. J. Travel Res. 53(2), 154–166 (2014)
16. Kalandides, A.: The problem with spatial identity: revisiting the «sense of place». J. Place Manag. Dev. 4(1), 28–39 (2011)

17. Marans, R.W., Stimson, R.J. (eds.): Investigating Quality of Urban Life: Theory, Methods and Empirical Research. Springer, Dordrecht (2011). doi:10.1007/978-94-007-1742-8

18. Gifford, R.: Environmental Psychology: Principles and Practice, 4th edn. Optimal Books, Colville (2007)

19. Petrova, M., Nenko, A., Sukharev, K.: Urban acupuncture 2.0: urban management tool inspired by social media. In: EGOSE 2016 Proceedings of the 2016 3nd International Conference on Electronic Governance and Open Society, pp. 248–258 (2016)

20. Gutev, A., Nenko, A.: Better cycling - better life: social media based parametric modeling advancing governance of public transportation system in St. Petersburg. In: EGOSE 2016 Proceedings of the 2016 3nd International Conference on Electronic Governance and Open Society, pp. 242–248 (2016)

21. Amérigo, M., Aragones, J.I.: A theoretical and methodological approach to the study of residential satisfaction. J. Environ. Psychol. **17**, 47–57 (1997)

22. Methodical recommendations on estimation of effectiveness of investment projects and their selection for financing. Official publication. Moscow: The Gosstroy of Russia, Ministry of Economy of the Russian Federation, Ministry of Finance of the Russian Federation, Goskomprom of Russia, 31th of March 1994 № 7-12/47 (1994)

23. Smart Cities – the cities of future. http://greencapacity.ru/ru/information/smart-cities

Data-Based Energy Provision for Smart Cities

Ralf-Martin Soe[(⊠)]

Tallinn University of Technology, Tallinn, Estonia
Ralf-Martin.Soe@ttu.ee

Abstract. This project will demonstrate how ICT-based solutions can contribute to saving energy by motivating behavioural change of energy end-users. The project will demonstrate how energy service providers can be more open (involvement of end-users and other energy market participants) and innovative (open living lab concept for co-creation and co-design practices) in the development of smart energy solutions. This project will develop an effective intervention to change the behaviour of above-average energy users via training them to use smart tools and coaching them throughout the process. The aim is to increase knowledge of the energy market, change thinking patterns, initiate smarter decisions and through this create actual change in consumers' behaviour – in pilot test group energy consumption is expected to decrease by 5–10%. This project will integrate at least seven third party digital energy tools with the Estfeed platform that connects over 600 000 energy users in Estonia. Therefore, we expect to deliver and popularise smart tools for minimum of 100 000 of energy-users, with slightly stronger focus on the large-scale users (both individuals and corporate/public).

Keywords: Smart energy platform · Smart applications · DSO · Digital tools for energy users · Aggregator · Living labs · Open innovation · Social sciences · ICT · Randomised trials

1 Introduction

The project aims to demonstrate how ICT-based solutions can contribute to saving energy by motivating and supporting behavioural change of energy end-users (mainly electricity but also gas and heating) in the case on Estonia as a Large Pilot, Slovenia and Denmark as mini-pilots and Germany as a close follower.

Estonia is chosen as the main pilot country for the following reasons:

1. All electricity meters are being replaced with smart meters (during 2012–2016, 630 000 m were replaced, the total investment was 100 mln Euros).
2. A consortium of companies are developing an open data exchange platform and app store called Estfeed, operated by the main Estonian Government-owned electricity and gas Transmission System Operator (TSO). This platform links data sources and application, and through this makes smart meters' data from the TSO's owned data hubs (electricity and gas at the moment) available over the Internet for end-users but also app developers, close-to-real-time (one hour delay). The platform also provides an app-store where equal visibility for all energy efficiency applications integrated with the platform are presented to customers on equal basis.

© Springer International Publishing AG 2017
D.A. Alexandrov et al. (Eds.): DTGS 2017, CCIS 745, pp. 319–328, 2017.
https://doi.org/10.1007/978-3-319-69784-0_27

3 The Estfeed plafrom runs on the open X-road[1] data exchange layer, which connects all public sector databases in Estonia over the Internet. The X-road is the corner-stone of the Estonian e-government, which is evaluated as the best in Europe according to the EC Digital Economy and Society Index (DESI). In essence, it is a platform that can link whatever data sources with the main ICT infrastructure of Estfeed and through the authentication, authorization and mandates functions, it provides a legal basis for third parties to use this data for processing, testing and developing applications for energy efficiency.

4 Estonia's CO_2 emissions per population are one of the highest in the EU: there is a need for real change.

2 Concept

"A Smart City is a city seeking to address public issues via ICT-based solutions on the basis of a multi-stakeholder, municipally based partnership."

The above definition is part of a 2014 study published by the European Parliament [8]. Although the authors claim it to be a working definition, it is based on the meta-analysis how Smart City has been conceptualised previously. The key point in the continuous and successful development of a Smart City is to understand, that it is not a one-city game. It is a combination of not only multiple stakeholders from municipalities, research, businesses and citizens, but also partner cities, regions and nations. In this paper, the Energy is part of the Environment domain and classified in the following way:

- "Smart energy including renewables, ICT-enabled energy grids, metering",
- Pollution control and monitoring,
- Renovation of buildings and amenities, green buildings,
- Green urban planning,
- Principals: "resource use efficiency, re-use and resource substitution of buildings and amenities",
- Examples: "street lighting, waste management, drainage and water resource" systems "that are monitored to evaluate the system, reduce pollution and improve quality".

Smart Energy is considered an integral part of the main smart city frameworks [1, 3, 7, 9, 11]. There is also discussions regarding the connection between sensing, cloud computing and energy provision [5, 12] and connecting energy to Smart City IoT platforms and testbeds [6, 10].

Dirks and Keeling [4] view Smart City as an important component to integrate city's various systems (transportation, energy, education, health care, buildings, physical infrastructure, food, water and public safety). Balakrishna [2] argues that the prerequisite for Smart City is intelligent infrastructure and a set of cross-sectoral services (energy,

---

[1] https://www.ria.ee/x-road/.

sanitation, health care, transport, farming, governance, automation, and manufacturing). There are as many 'Smart City' definitions as there are 'Smart City' projects.

From the methodological perspective, this project will demonstrate how energy providers can be more innovative and open by using the open living lab concept to implement co-creation and co-design practices of the development of smart energy solutions. The open lab will help to better design smart solutions by both providing competences and access to real user co-design contexts, as well as providing the enabling smart energy environment (including the smart data exchange platform, the energy infrastructure, open APIs and IoT platforms) which serves as a starting point for future innovations. Next generation open living laboratories are also tools for speeding up the take-up of new innovations in an iterative and user-centric, yet managed manner. One of these tools is conducting co-creation workshops with a purpose to involve end-users into the development process, which will also be leveraged on.

In this project, co-creation workshops will be experimental, based on the randomized trials method. That is, we will run two types or workshops:

(1) In the first case (intervention group), we will explain the benefits of energy savings and coach participants throughout the process how to use smart consumption tools offered by the consortium, in addition to co-creating the solutions with end-users;
(2) We will invite the control group only for co-creation purpose, with no guidance on how to save on energy consumption.

This Open Living Lab method (see Fig. 1, developed by Forum Virium) aims to involve end-users of energy services in the development process via the living lab

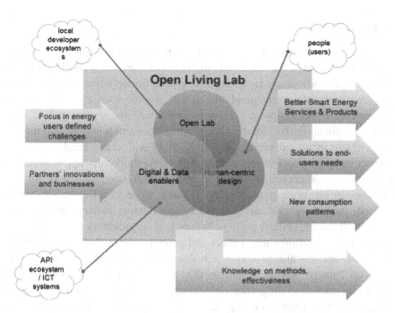

Fig. 1. The Open-Living Lab co-creation model (developed by Forum Virium, https://forumvirium.fi/en/)

model. The aim of the Open Living model is to facilitate the co-creation between the local developers, people (end-users) and ICT systems with specific challenges defined by the public authorities.

2.1 Co-creation Workshops

The co-creation workshops would provide two outcomes:

(1) We will fully involve at least 60 selected end-users (e.g. people with above average energy consumption: house-owners with electrical heating and industrial users) to the smart solutions development process.
(2) We will develop an effective intervention to change the behaviour of above-average energy users via training them to use smart tools and couching them throughout the process. Later on, we will compare the results of the intervention group with their previous energy consumption and the control group. As the outcome, we will measure the two group's energy savings during the time of workshop and also 6 months later. If there are statistically relevant differences between the two groups, we can conclude our intervention to be successful. This could mean that it really makes sense to replicate this intervention (smart solutions and training) for the larger population, both in partner countries but also in Europe generally.

In addition to energy savings, the impact of indoor climatic conditions on personal health, productivity and comfort will be also researched.

3 Project Objectives

The project has three objectives:

(1) Cost-effectiveness: we aim to prove that smart connected meters do provide at least 10% of savings for large-scale energy users: homes with electricity heating and industrial customers. In terms of cost-effectiveness, the idea is also to link customers with data exchange platforms that provide a variety of different energy efficiency ICT tools (app stores) were customers are encouraged to try many different applications for different home appliances and functions and through this also generate increased savings and stronger fit with client needs;
(2) Connect installed smart meters with end-users via third party applications in order to improve interoperability. We will award innovation vouchers for the best solutions. In our main pilot country, Estonia, close to all electricity meters are replaced, partially also smart gas meters and heating meters are installed. This project will integrate third party solutions (e.g. aggregator) and other smart IoT devices to this platform that collect and process data and communicate directly with end-users, this also promotes new data- and platform based business models.
(3) Focus on "smart" saving potential: this project aims to smoothen the energy demand by providing suggestions for energy consumption based on analysed data and energy market behavioural patterns: e.g. suggestions for kindergartens/public offices to switch off their water heaters and refrigerators during the evening peak hours when nobody is in the building anyways.

This project will make this platform available for all third party developers with efficient business plans, independent of their size.

This project consortium has strong capabilities in technology (ICT and Energy) and is coordinated by the eGovernment unit within the Tallinn University of Technology (TUT). The role of TUT is to provide latest insights from social and behaviour sciences in order to understand factors influencing consumer choices and impact on consumer behaviour within such an energy system. In addition to TUT, the consortium involves two EU technology-research centers of excellence (Fraunhofer and Danish Technology Institute), Estonia's government-owned TSO Elering, a Nordic software company with proven Energy record Tieto and an SME for the app-centred pilot in Slovenia (Internet Institute). We have also involved University of Leipzig for Energy expertise. In total, there are 7 partners from 4 countries. The developed solutions will be deployed in a variety of building types (private and public) and the value of the energy services exposed to the end users.

3.1 Estonian Pilot

The Estonian Pilot is targeted at the large-scale electricity users, both private and corporate. In the case of the private customers, only those with electricity heating will be selected. With cold winters reaching as low as minus 25, electricity bills can be remarkable – up to 15%–30% of the average wage, thus the savings potential is the greatest and there is a real need for smart advice. In addition, a selection of corporate buildings will be selected in collaboration with the State Real Estate Ltd. The State Real Estate Ltd is the biggest government-owned real-estate owner with over 1 000 public buildings in the portfolio (e.g. schools, ministries, hospitals etc.). There is potentially larger impact on the smart solutions targeted for large-scale users.

The aim of the Estonian pilot is to develop, test and gather customer feedback to the Estfeed data exchange platform and its energy efficiency applications. Until the beginning of 2017 the main focus has been on developing and building the unique platform that is able to link all different kinds of data sources and applications. Under this pilot the focus is to increase the content quality and user experience of this platform, develop content, services and applications for the client portal, which serves as the user interface of Estfeed. To have a variety of applications and data sources available, this project aims to link the Elering platform with hundreds of thousands of connected smart meters/devices through the Estonian public data transport layer X-road with third party applications like:

(1) Right Amphere ("With the help of this application you can find out how large the main fuse needs to be where you use energy").

(2) Aggregator (the "aggregator helps you to decide how many consumers should band together so as to buy electricity at lower prices").

(3) Virtual Power Plant ("A virtual power plant helps you decide which renewable energy sources would make most sense where you use energy").

(4) Head Monitor ("The heat monitor is able to track energy losses related to your consumption").

Two different kinds of test groups will be formed: the pilot group who receives information, gets access and is educated how to use the platform and its applications and is involved in the development of the platform; and the reference group who will not get any information, training nor access to platform and apps. In addition, pilot data can be compared with their last year's consumption data. Groups of at least 30 + 30 members can prove statistically if our intervention (change in behaviour) has an effect or not.

The outcome of the Estonian Pilot is a Smart Energy platform with at least seven third party smart solutions co-designed and fully integrated to this platform. The integrated solutions will run for at least one year, will be clearly selected, defined and monitored. This platform will utilise the knowledge already gathered on the data exchange layer of the X-Road, an open-source and free-to-use software system, which is successfully used by the governments of Estonia and Finland. The critical requirement for the European Digital Single Market (DSM) is open and secure energy data exchange for the EU-wide consumption. According to the Digital Economy and Society Index 2016, Estonia is ranked as number one in digital government services[2], the cornerstone of this is a successful implementation of the X-road (Fig. 2).

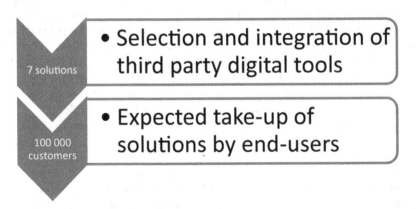

Fig. 2. Design of the Estonian pilot

For this purpose, we will target developer communities but also start-ups, universities and SMES in order to co-develop digital solutions. The selection criteria for these solutions is the maximum reach of customers and savings potential. When complemented with awareness-raising activities, we assume to target 100 000 end-users in Estonia with these new solutions. The technical work (integration with Elering and X-road) will be done by Tieto.

---

[2] https://ec.europa.eu/digital-single-market/en/digital-public-services-desi-dimension-5.

3.1.1   Data Exchange Layer Estfeed

The activities are focused on the development and integration of state-of-the art digital tools and applications and their connection with close-to-real-time-data from smart meters and potentially also from other smart devices. The solutions will empower end-users (building owners, residents, housing associations, public actors etc.) "to engage and collaborate in achieving energy savings and allowing them to explore different means and measures to manage their energy needs over the longer term" (Fig. 3).

Fig. 3. Snapshots from "MyEnergy" application (www.energia.ee/en/tark-tarbimine/mobiiliapp)

One example is "MyEnergy" application in Estonia, offered by state-owned Energy company Eesti Energia. This application connects smart meter data with end-users by offering (1) consumption data, (2) electricity price predictions, and (3) demand-based suggestions for smart energy consumption. See the snapshots from the application below. The application can be downloaded here.[3]

The Estfeed energy data exchange platform[4] is developed by the main TSO Elering, partner this project and uses X-road for data communication. This platform links data sources and applications and provides a user interface for customers to see and manage their energy consumption data and rights. In other words, the platform supports services such as authentication, authorization and mandates that enable to give rights to

---

[3] www.energia.ee/en/tark-tarbimine/mobiiliapp.

[4] http://estfeed.ee/en/.

process and manage the data of customers by third parties, e.g. energy efficiency applications but also tenants who would otherwise have no access to consumption data and therefore also less incentives for smarter consumption management.

The Estfeed is a platform that connects different energy-related data sources and applications that mainly cover electricity, gas and district heating smart metering data but could be also extended to weather forecast and electricity market price data. Data sources can also be machine readable documents (e.g. digital receipts and invoices). Technologically, the Estfeed uses the Estonian government-developed X-road as an data exchange layer that follows highest security standards and is broadly used within the Estonian public sector. This R&D project is the first one of its kind in Europe were a public stock company uses a government developed ICT platform and develops it further in line with the needs of a specific sector, the energy industry and consumers.

3.2   Minipilots in Denmark and Slovenia

Complementing the large pilot in Estonia, a mini pilot will be implemented in Slovenia and Denmark, the aim of which is to test and validate consumer applications from an end-user perspective, hence providing insights about the design of tools and services exposed by smart energy environments towards consumers.

More specifically, the mini pilot focuses on the investigation and validation of mobile apps for energy monitoring and efficiency from various perspectives, including quality of experience, efficiency of use of the available services, transparency of energy-related data and the created incentives for a more energy-conscious user behaviour. Validation workshops will be organised to engage end-users in testing of selected smart energy apps and quantitative and qualitative feedback will be collected to gather and analyse end-users' design insights.

The mini pilot will target involvement of small groups of invited end-users to facilitate a dynamic co-creation and co-design exercise. A validation methodology and key observed metrics will be prepared in alignment with the methodology implemented in the large pilot in Estonia. During the piloting phase, only simulated data will be used.

4   Excepted Results

The aim is to increase knowledge of the energy market, change thinking patterns, initiate smarter decisions and through this create actual change in consumers' behaviour – in pilot test group energy consumption is expected to decrease by 5–10% in the intervention group.

This behavioural change will be initiated through:

1. providing information and training about available smart meters and other measuring devices and sensors, energy efficiency solutions/application and energy data exchange platforms;
2. providing access to ICT solutions and platforms and involving end-users, consumers, clients and their feedback into the continuous development cycle of the

platform and its applications, and through this involvement increasing the usability of the devices, applications and platforms;

3. training consumers and clients how to use the energy data exchange platform and its applications.

This project will integrate at least seven third party energy digital tools with the Estfeed platform that connects over 600 000 energy users in Estonia. Therefore, we expect to deliver and popularise smart tools for minimum of 100 000 of energy-users, with slightly stronger focus on the large-scale users (both individuals and corporate/public).

In more detail, proposed actions of the project will demonstrate the impacts listed below:

- Final energy consumption will decrease by 5–10% in the pilot group prompted by the use of innovative energy efficiency and platform applications introduced and developed throughout the project, e.g. increase of knowledge about changes in energy prices during the day and suggestions how to use energy in a more sustainable way through the platform and apps.
- Novel adoption and deployment of smart energy ICT solution based on user experience (method: open living lab trials).
- Real experimental approach to smart energy applications via randomized trial in order to validate the research approach.

References

1. Batty, M., Axhausen, K.W., Giannotti, F., Pozdnoukhov, A., Bazzani, A., Wachowicz, M., Portugali, Y.: Smart cities of the future. Eur. Phys. J.: Spec. Topics **214**(1), 481–518 (2012). http://doi.org/10.1140/epjst/e2012-01703-3
2. Balakrishna, C.: Enabling technologies for smart city services and applications. In: 6th International Conference on Next Generation Mobile Applications, Services, and Technologies (NGMAST), pp. 223–227. IEEE Press (2012). http://doi.org/10.1109/NGMAST.2012.51
3. Giffinger, R., Haindlmaier, G.: Smart cities ranking: an effective instrument for the positioning of the cities? ACE: Archit. City. Environ. 4(12), 7–26 (2010). http://upcommons.upc.edu/revistes/handle/2099/8550
4. Dirks, S., Keeling, M.: A vision of smarter cities: how cities can lead the way into a prosperous and sustainable future. IBM Inst. Bus. Value 1–6 (2009). http://www-935.ibm.com/services/us/gbs/bus/pdf/ibm_podcast_smarter_cities.pdf
5. Hancke, G.P., Silva, B.C., Hancke Jr., G.P.: The role of advanced sensing in smart cities. Sensors **13**, 393–425 (2013)
6. Jin, J., Gubbi, J., Luo, T., Palaniswami M.: Network architecture and QoS issues in the internet of things for a smart city. In: International Symposium on Communications and Information Technologies, ISCIT (2012)
7. Lugaric, L., Krajcar, S., Simic, Z.: Smart city—platform for emergent phenomena power system testbed simulator. In: PES Innovative Smart Grid Technologies Conference Europe (ISGT Europe), pp. 1–7. IEEE Press (2010). doi:10.1109/ISGTEUROPE.2010.5638890

8. Manville, C., Cochrane, G., Cave, J., Millard, J., Pederson, J.K., Thaarup, R.K., Kotterink, B.: Mapping Smart Cities in the EU. European Parliament (2014). http://www.europarl. europa.eu/RegData/etudes/etudes/join/2014/507480/IPOL-ITRE_ET(2014)507480_EN.pdf
9. Neirotti, P., De Marco, A., Cagliano, A.C., Mangano, G., Scorrano, F.: Current trends in smart city initiatives: Some stylised facts. Cities. **38** (2014). http://doi.org/10.1016/j.cities. 2013.12.010
10. Sanchez, L., Muñoz, L., Galache, J., Sotres, P., Santana, J., Gutierrez, V., Ramdhany, R., Gluhak, A., Krco, S., Theodoridis, E., Pfisterer, D.: SmartSantander: IoT experimentation over a smart city testbed. Comput. Netw. **61**, 217–238 (2014)
11. Soe, R., Mikheeva, O.: Combined model of smart cities and electronic payments. In: International Conference for E-Democracy and Open Government (CEDEM 2017), pp. 141– 148. IEEE Computer Society, Washington (2017)
12. Yamamoto, S., Nakamura, M., Matsumoto, S.: Using cloud technologies for large-scale house data in smart city. In: 4th International Conference on Cloud Computing Technology and Science (CloudCom), pp 141–148. IEEE Computer Society, Washington (2012). doi: http://dx.doi.org/10.1109/CloudCom.2012.6427546

Method GAND: Multi-criteria Analysis for Choice the Most Preferable Geodata-Based Transport Network

Danila Parygin, Alexey Golubev[✉],
Natalia Sadovnikova, and Maxim Shcherbakov

Volgograd State Technical University, Volgograd, Russia
dparygin@gmail.com, ax.golubev@gmail.com, npsn1@ya.ru,
maxim.shcherbakov@gmail.com

Abstract. The paper has deal with the problem of public transport network design. Collected data about people's travelling in urban area opens up new opportunities related to the design of novel solutions for analysing real needs of people. The issue is how to make a rational choice of preferable PTN according to: (i) a set of selected quality criteria; (ii) decision makers preferences. In the paper we propose a multi-criteria decision analysis (MCDA) method adopted for choice of PTN obtained automatically based on geospatial data analysis. The evaluation criteria of the PTN were developed for the particular task: (i) degree of transport demand satisfaction, (ii) coefficient of non-straightness, and (iii) transport network density. This technique was tested on the routes constructed by the expert, as well as on the automatically generated route. The results suggested by the expert and design in automation mode is close to each other in terms of efficiency. It lead to conclusion that data-driven approaches migh be used for urban planning and monitoring with minimal human intervention.

Keywords: eCity · Multicriteria decision making · PTN · MCDA methods · Geospatial data · PTN design · Route planning

1 Introduction

The development of the public transport network (PTN) is an important part of the strategy of urban development for every city. Usually, strategic plan of city development containing actions regarding PTN development as the latter has the significant impact on quality of residential life [14]. PTN development problem should take into consideration many different factors, such as real estate and housing development in the city, trends of residents mobility in the urban environment, evaluation of the optimal ways and routes of residents, and estimation of the fleet properties and its timetable.

© Springer International Publishing AG 2017
D.A. Alexandrov et al. (Eds.): DTGS 2017, CCIS 745, pp. 329–340, 2017.
https://doi.org/10.1007/978-3-319-69784-0_28

The public transport network should provide:

- satisfaction of the needs of residents mobility in the urban environment;
- the equation of demand and supply of transportation system;
- optimal transport fee regarding the points of view of city management and residents;
- Profit making by transportation utilities or companies.

Hence, the general aim of almost all projects of modernization of PTN is in the efficiency improvement of PTN operation. One of the directions related to such kind of projects is the development of solutions based on actual data about residents mobility in the urban environment. These data can be obtained in various ways, but the crucial point is anonymity of data for analysis. Basically, collected data opens up new opportunities related to the design of novel solutions for analysing real needs of people. On the other hand, new geospatial data processing approaches are required, e.g. data-driven techniques for geospatial data analysis [6, 7].

If we apply data-driven approaches for PTN design, usually the several alternatives of PTN are obtained. The issue is how to make a rational choice of preferable PTN according to: (i) a set of selected quality criteria; (ii) decision makers preferences. In this case, a problem of assessing the PTN effectiveness is considered. Specifics of the problem are the evaluation of effectiveness in accordance (i) with performance criteria and (ii) with interest of stakeholders groups. Note, the performance evaluation problem is considered in various methodologies and approaches [4, 7]. Well-known criteria in literature are used for heuristic approaches and decision support procedures based on experts experience and marks. In a case of application in data-driven solutions, these criteria must carefully evaluate in terms of applicability. The data-driven approach provides a set of PTN due to different options (e.g. an arbitrary choice of a number of routes in PTN). Finally, the only one PTN must be selected for implementation. As multiple criteria might be defined, the MCDA need to be applied. It means that existed approaches need to be analysed and adopted for pipelines in automation data-driven approaches for PTN design and evaluation.

The main contribution of the paper is a multi-criteria decision analysis (MCDA) method adopted for choice of PTN obtained automatically based on geospatial data analysis. The MCDA is used the specific set of performance evaluation criteria configured according the task statement. The paper present description of criteria, MCDA method and use cases. Efficiency of proposed method is proven with comparison with human-based approach where the final solution was chosen by an expert.

2   Background

The application of multicriteria analysis for solving the problems of managing the transport system of the city has been widely developed in different countries. The analysis was applied at various stages of management and covers planning, design, maintenance and rehabilitation of transport infrastructure [9]. MCDA methods such as MAVT [5], MCA and GIS combination, DEX [9], AHP, SAW, TOPSIS use for evaluation of a comprehensive project and urban public transportation services [11]. They allow to take wider range of long-term and short-term factors, which are classified into benefits, opportunities, costs, and risks into account [16].

The use of spatial data is one of the directions for improving the methods of multicriteria analysis. The generation of PTN is related to the evaluation of a set of criteria. The objective of these criteria is to reflect the demand for transport services, the vision of development policies and the needs of stakeholders into account. Accordingly, the modern MCDA method should allow to calculate the efficiency of the transport network taking all the factors directly related to the geographical space into account [10,13].

Literature review show existence of different methodologies for PTN design. Basically, every methodology contains the performance evaluation operation based on the set of criteria.

The quality factor K_k was used for evaluation of PTN efficiency most often until recently. The criterion is calculated using formula

$$K_k = \frac{t_p^*}{t_p^f} \qquad (1)$$

where t_p^* – travel time spent on a trip for the theoretically defined comfortable travel conditions; t_p^f – the actual travel time in real conditions.

Norms for travel time for one passenger calculated for bus trip is not taking into consideration during the urban planning [8]. The total travel time includes time for moving to a stop and destination; travel time in transport; time of change or transfer to another route; time of waiting for transport due to denied boarding caused to vehicle overload.

The index of quality of transport services was proposed by [3] is calculated according to the formula:

$$K_k = \frac{t_n}{t_f} - \frac{y_n}{y_f} - R \qquad (2)$$

where t_n – specification of time spent by a passenger on a trip; t_f – time actually spent by a passenger on a trip, min; y_n – standard transport load factor that recommended for urban transport, average no more than 0.3, and in peak hours 0.8; y_f – actual value of the load factor; R – movement regularity index [3].

In [19] the concept of a complex, integrated quality indicator including various factors of passenger service was proposed.

The passenger service level index S presented in [15], is determined as:

$$S = \sum_{i=1}^{6} S_i^{K_i} \qquad (3)$$

where S_1 – reliability of moving right on schedule (travel time); S_2 – availability (frequency of public transport); S_3 – safety (probability of failure-free operation of public transport); S_4 – comfortability (trip quality); S_5 – cost index (transport tariff/fee); S_6 – information service index (level of information support); $K_1 \ldots K_6$ – weights of the corresponding service level indicators.

In [19], a set of criteria that allow to determine the quality and efficiency of the municipal PTN was considered. Those criteria might be divided into two groups: (i) socio-economic indicators of passenger service; (ii) performance indicators of transport utilities.

A municipal PTN might be represents by the following tuple

$$S = \langle P_1, \ldots, P_i, E_1, \ldots, E_j \rangle \tag{4}$$

where P – parameters of the system, which characterize its state; E – demand for transport services. Level of service is a complex indicator including [19]: reliability of vehicles; comfortability of transportation; informing passengers; safety; cost; environmental friendliness.

Summarise, the quality of PTN passengers service might be represented by the indicators [20]:

- availability;
- comfort;
- time spent to movement around the city (minimal is the best);
- high reliability of rolling stock operation;
- traffic regularity with unconditional safety of transport.

In [18] the following system of indicators for value a quality of passenger transportation is given: availability (density of route network, information service, reasonable tariff); performance (travel time, level of transport fatigue); reliability (regularity coefficient, level of denied boarding, traffic safety indicator); use comfortable (coefficient of capacity utilization, compliance with the standards of comfort). Also, the evaluation criteria of the PTN were identified based on (i) degree of transport demand satisfaction; (ii) coefficient of non-straightness; (iii) transport network density.

The system of criteria does not include economic and environmental criteria in this paper.

3   A GAND Method

3.1   General Overview

Based on review we can declare the following task statement. Given a set of PTN with information about all necessary attributes, a set of quality criteria $\{c\}$ and a set of decision makers preferences $\{p\}$ for given criteria.

Need to make a choice of the most preferable PTN using MCDA and decision makers preferences according the criteria.

The following conditions exist for this task. Data representing passenger demand for movement defined as a directed weighted graph $G(K, S)$, where K – set of vertices (formed clusters of destinations); S – weights (passenger traffic). Consider the cluster $k = \{r, c\}$, with r – radius in decimal degrees; c – coordinates of a cluster center in decimal degrees.

Passenger traffic is represented as $s = \{k_i, k_j, n\}$, where $k_i \in K$ – a cluster that has the needs for movement outside (out of cluster), $k_j \in K$ – a cluster that has the needs for movement inside (into the cluster), n – number of people with needs of traveling from k_i to k_j. Route can be defined as $w = \{P\}$, where P – a set of points with coordinates, which are described in decimal degrees.

So, the task can be described by the following tuple:

$$\{G(K, S), R \mid I, O\} \tag{5}$$

where G – directed weighted graph; K – set of vertices; S – set of graph weights; R – set of routes; I – values of criteria; O – results of PTN evaluation.

In order to evaluate the designed transportation network according to the previously presented criteria, we need to know: (i) city area; (ii) the number of transfers between all available points; (iii) the total number of people for transportation. City area can be calculated from the available data or take an already known value for a specific city.

The proposed method GAND to evaluate the efficiency of PTN is based on the SMART method [2]. Figure 1 represent the evaluation algorithm.

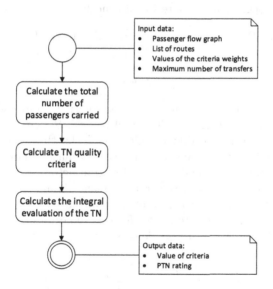

Fig. 1. General algorithm of the method for estimating the effectiveness of PTN in UML 2.0 notation

3.2 Proposed Performance Evaluation Criteria

The following criteria were chosen for the automatic calculation of the efficiency of the PTN:

– degree of transport demand satisfaction;
– coefficient of non-straightness

Degree of transport demand satisfaction is calculated:

$$U = \frac{\sum\limits_{i=0}^{N} u_i}{x} \tag{6}$$

where U – degree of transport demand satisfaction – real dimensionless number $[0, 1]$; N – maximum number of changes; u_i – number of passengers transported with i changes; x – total number of passengers in need of changes.

Coefficient of Non-straightness is defined as:

$$P = \frac{\sum\limits_{i=1}^{M} d_i}{\sum\limits_{i=1}^{M} l_i} \tag{7}$$

where P – coefficient of transport network non-straightness – real dimensionless number $[0, 1]$; M – number of routes in PTN; l_i – length of i-th route ; d_i - distance from the beginning of route i to its end by air.

Transport Network Density is calculated according to the formula:

$$L = \frac{1}{S} \sum\limits_{i=1}^{M} l_i \tag{8}$$

where L – transport network density – real nonnegative number with dimension; M – number of routes in PTN; l_i – length of route i; S – city area.

The first two criteria are dimensionless, and the third one has a unit of measurement. The density of the transport network must be normalized in order to use all these criteria for calculating the integral factor.

The maximum distance from the transport line should be 0.5 km according to experts. Then the maximum length of the transport network per one square kilometer will be 4 km, i.e. is a perimeter for this square. In this connection, the formula for calculating the transport density:

$$L = \frac{1}{4S} \sum\limits_{i=1}^{M} l_i \tag{9}$$

where L – transport network density – real dimensionless number $[0, 1]$; M – number of routes in PTN; l_i length of i-th route; S – city area.

Since, the transport network is better, when the transport network density is less, so the formula 9 takes the form:

$$L = 1 - \frac{1}{4S} \sum\limits_{i=1}^{M} l_i \tag{10}$$

3.3   Integral Criterion

Integral formula for assessing the efficiency of the PTN:

$$O(I,W) = \frac{\sum\limits_{i=1}^{n} I_i W_i}{\sum\limits_{i=1}^{n} I_i} \tag{11}$$

where O – integral assessment of the transport system; I – values of criteria; W – weights for the criteria that determine their importance; n – number of criteria. The decision maker's preferences are defined as weights W.

3.4   Calculation of the Number of Changes

To find all the changes, we need to build a network graph using information about a number of the changes between the routes. As the input of the method, we might have a disjoint set of routes, which is specified by a list of clusters. The task is to build a transport network graph, where the routes will be interconnected by edges (changes between routes) with the lowest value on foot travel between them.

Let us describe the problem in several steps:

1. Initializing the adjacency matrix of data of available routes.
2. Finding edges between pairs of routes with a minimum length.
3. Finding the shortest paths between all clusters in a graph using the Floyd-Warshall algorithm.
4. Counting the number of changes between each pair of clusters.

Consider in details every stage from the list presented above.

Initializing the Adjacency Matrix. The problem is reduced to the initializing the adjacency matrix using about information of connected pairs of clusters. Pseudocode is presented in Algorithm 1.

Note, the *ROUTE* – the route identifier (number). As a result, we get the initial adjacency matrix, where the neighboring clusters in the routes are connected.

Finding Edges with a Minimum Length. The task is reduced to finding the distances between each pair of clusters. Pseudocode is presented in scheme of Algorithm 2.

The `combinations` – function that returns all combinations from the input list as a tuple of two elements, `WALK` – identifier indicating that a change between the routes can be made here (number).

Finding the Shortest Path. The task is to find the shortest paths between all the clusters in the network. In this work, the Floyd-Warshall [1] algorithm is used with the ability to restore paths.

Algorithm 1. Initialize adjacency matrix

Data: R – list of routes, C – number of routes

Result: M – adjacency matrix

1 initialize M matrix;
2 **for** $i = 1 \ldots C$ **do**
3 | Find the length of $R[i]$ and put in N;
4 | **for** $j = 1 \ldots N - 1$ **do**
5 | | $node_1 = $ R[i][j] ;
6 | | $node_2 = $ R[i][j+1] ;
   | | // clusters are connected
7 | | M[$node_1$][$node_2$] = ROUTE // to both sides
8 | | M[$node_2$][$node_2$] = ROUTE;
9 | **end**
10 **end**

Algorithm 2. Search for edges with minimal length and adding them to the adjacency matrix

---

Data: R – list of routes, M – adjacency matrix

Result: M – modified adjacency matrix

1 **for** $(route_1, route_2)$ in $combinations(R)$ **do**
2 | Find the length of $route_1$ and put in len_1;
3 | Find the length of $route_2$ and put in len_2;
4 | Initialize D as empty list;
5 | **for** $i = 1 \ldots len_1$ **do**
6 | | **for** $j = 1 \ldots len_2$ **do**
7 | | | $id_1 = route_1[i]$;
8 | | | $id_2 = route_2[j]$;
9 | | | **if** $id_1 \neq id_2$ **then**
10 | | | | Find distance between id_1 and id_2;
11 | | | | Add founded distance to list D;
12 | | | **end**
13 | | **end**
14 | **end**
15 | Find id_1, id_2 that the distance between them is minimal in D;
16 | M[id_1][id_2] = WALK ;
17 | M[id_2][id_1] = WALK ;
18 **end**

Calculation of the Number of Changes. The calculation of the number of changes is made by a complete search of all possible points of departure and destination. Pseudocode present by Algorithm 3.

Algorithm 3. Counting the number of changes

Data: N – Total number of clusters, M – adjacency matrix, C – correspondence matrix

Result: T – list of transfers

```
 1  Initialize T list;
 2  for i = 1 ... N do
 3      for j = i + 1 ... N do
 4          walk_count = 0 ;
 5          corr_count = 0 ;
 6          Restore path between i and j nodes and put result to route;
 7          Find the length of route and put in L ;
 8          for k = 1 ... L − 1 do
 9              node₁ = route[k] ;
10              node₂ = route[k+1] ;
11              if M[node₁][node₂] = WALK then
12                  walk_count += 1 ;
13              end
                // Number of people moving between node₁ and node₂
14              corr_count = C[node₁][node₂] ;
15              T[walk_count] += corr_count ;
16          end
17      end
18  end
```

---

4   Use Cases and Performance Evaluation

To assess the developed method, we asked the expert to design three routes for the given clusters. For example, the small city was selected with 8 clusters. Figures 2a–c represent the three PTN configurations chosen by a decision maker (a domain expert) marked as Expert-1, Expert-2 and Expert-3 consequently.

This chose has been made among the others based on the analysis of city development from expert point of view and existed documents. It is worth noting that the expert chose only the points entering the routes, and the routes along the roads were built using the OSRM [12] service.

The main drawback is the time that need to design the route by an expert. The proposed in [17] algorithm was used for design the initial PTN.

Figure 2d shows the results of initial PTN design obtain automatically (marked as Zero-Network). Visually, the result in the Fig. 2d is close to the results in Fig. 2c.

Table 1 contains the results of PTN evaluation for four cases according to calculation (11).

Note, that Expert-3, proposed by the expert, is the most effective. Results for Expert-2 is equal to Zero-Network. It mean the automated build PTN is good enough as well. It means, the factor of the choice of initial and final clusters for the construction of a network of routes plays a significant role.

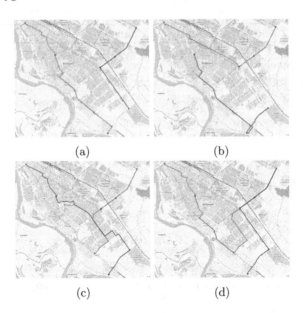

(a)   (b)

(c)   (d)

Fig. 2. PTN configurations

Table 1. Results of PTN evaluation according to the criterion $O(I, W)$ (the higher value is better)

Route network	Evaluation by $O(I, W)$
Expert-1	0.347
Expert-2	0.351
Expert-3	0.366
Zero-Network	0.351

5   Conclusion

Public transportation system is one of the key elements in life quality development of a modern city. Current solutions available on the market do not allow to fully account for population preferences and introduce the necessary changes to the structure of transportation networks, due to the lack of feedback between the population and public transportation planning authorities. Analysis of population preferences and building an optimal and balanced route network based on movement data can provide impetus to the sustainable development of a city as a whole.

The article presents GAND: a multi-criteria method for automated evaluating of public transportation network designed by geospatial data analysis. The main idea of the work is evaluation of the transport network by the efficiency criteria.

There are three quality criteria for PTN estimation proposed: the degree of satisfaction of transport demand, the non-rectilinearity of the transport network, the density of the transport network, and the way to calculate them based on the available PTN data.

These method and criteria are adopted for algorithms of automatic PTN design [6]. It allows to reduce the intervention of expert in PTN design procedure. This method, together with previously proposed algorithms, can be used to modify existing PTN. The disadvantages of these methods can be attributed only to the fact that they were tested on the generated data set.

The development of the project implies functionality and expansion of technological capabilities. In particular, it is intended to be used to collect data collected through sensors, recorders, mobile devices. This requires close cooperation with the city administration, representation of organizations, mobile operators, etc. It is also necessary to intensify actions to attract city residents to participate in the discussion and resolution of infrastructure problems. Carrying out a competent information policy, creating conditions conducive to participation in changes, allows not only to increase the circle of participants in the decision-making process, but also to increase the level of confidence in the authorities. For this, it is necessary to create modern services based on information and communication technologies, which will allow analyzing the preferences of residents and getting them to obtain agreed solutions.

Acknowledgments. The reported study was partially supported by RFBR, research project Nos. 16-37-60066, 16-07-00388_a and research project MD-6964.2016.9. Authors would like to thank anonymous reviewers for fruitful remarks.

References

1. Floydwarshall algorithm. https://en.wikipedia.org/wiki/FloydWarshall_algorithm
2. Smart criteria. https://en.wikipedia.org/wiki/SMART_criteria
3. Bolshakov, A.: Increase in the level of passenger service by buses on the basis of an integrated quality management system. Transport **1**, 74 (1981)
4. Ceder, A.: Designing public transport networks and routes. In: Advanced Modeling for Transit Operations and Service Planning, pp. 59–91. Emerald Group Publishing Limited (2002)
5. Delle Site, P., Filippi, F.: Weighting methods in multi-attribute assessment of transport projects. Eur. Transp. Res. Rev. **1**(4), 199–206 (2009)
6. Golubev, A., Chechetkin, I., Parygin, D., Sokolov, A., Shcherbakov, M.: Geospatial data generation and preprocessing tools for urban computing system development. Procedia Comput. Sci. **101**, 217–226 (2016)
7. Golubev, A., Chechetkin, I., Solnushkin, K.S., Sadovnikova, N., Parygin, D., Shcherbakov, M.: Strategway: web solutions for building public transportation routes using big geodata analysis. In: Proceedings of 17th International Conference on Information Integration and Web-based Applications and Services, p. 91. ACM (2015)
8. Gudkov, V., Mirotin, L., Velmojin, A., Shiriaev, S.: Passenger transportation by motor vehicles: textbook for universities. Hot Line-Telekom, p. 448 (1986)

9. Karleuša, B., Dragičević, N., Deluka-Tibljaš, A.: Review of multicriteria-analysis methods application in decision making about transport infrastructure. GRAEV-INAR **65**(7), 619–631 (2013). http://www.casopis-gradjevinar.hr/assets/Uploads/JCE65201372850EN.pdf

10. Keshkamat, S.S., Looijen, J.M., Zuidgeest, M.: The formulation and evaluation of transport route planning alternatives: a spatial decision support system for the via baltica project, poland. J. Transp. Geogr. **17**(1), 54–64 (2009)

11. Keyvan Ekbatani, M., Cats, O.: Multi-criteria appraisal of multi-modal urban public transport systems. In: Transportation Research Procedia, 10, 2015; 18th Euro Working Group on Transportation, EWGT 2015, 14–16 July 2015, Delft, The Netherlands (2015)

12. Luxen, D., Vetter, C.: Real-time routing with OpenStreetMap data. In: Proceedings of 19th ACM SIGSPATIAL International Conference on Advances in Geographic Information Systems, GIS 2011, NY, USA, pp. 513–516 (2011). http://doi.acm.org/10.1145/2093973.2094062

13. Rybarczyk, G., Wu, C.: Bicycle facility planning using GIS and multi-criteria decision analysis. Appl. Geogr. **30**(2), 282–293 (2010)

14. Sadovnikova, N., Parygin, D., Kalinkina, M., Sanzhapov, B., Ni, T.N.: Models and methods for the urban transit system research. In: Kravets, A., Shcherbakov, M., Kultsova, M., Shabalina, O. (eds.) CIT&DS 2015. CCIS, vol. 535, pp. 488–499. Springer, Cham (2015). doi:10.1007/978-3-319-23766-4_39

15. Shabanov, A.: Regional logistic systems of public transport: methodology of formation and the control mechanism, p. 206 (2001)

16. Shang, J.S., Tjader, Y., Ding, Y.: A unified framework for multicriteria evaluation of transportation projects. IEEE Trans. Eng. Manag. **51**(3), 300–313 (2004)

17. Shcherbakov, M., Golubev, A.: An algorithm for initial public transport network design over geospatial data. In: 2016 IEEE International, Smart Cities Conference (ISC2), pp. 1–7. IEEE (2016)

18. Spirin, I.V.: Organization and management of passenger motor transport: a textbook for students. Academy, p. 400 (2010)

19. Turpischeva, M.S., Nurgaliyev, E.R.: Methodology for assessing the quality of the passenger transportation system. Bull. Astrakhan State Tech. Univ. **1**(57), 42–46 (2014)

20. Varelopulo, G.: Organization of traffic and traffic on urban passenger transport. Transport **207**, 208 (1990)

Hotel Value Dimensions and Tourists' Perception of the City. The Case of St. Petersburg

Nikita Kaspruk, Olga Silyutina, and Viktor Karepin[✉]

National Research University Higher School of Economics,
Soyuza Pechatnikov 16, Saint Petersburg, Russia
kaspruk.nikita@yandex.ru, oyasilyutina@gmail.com, karepin13@gmail.com

Abstract. In this work in progress, we analyze how perceived hotel value dimensions and the perception of city sights are connected with categories of hotels. Applying a topic modelling algorithm to 21,165 reviews from 201 hotels located in Saint Petersburg, we show that clients of hotels of different categories pay attention to different value dimensions. Analyzing local aspect of value perception, we show how existing differences in perceiving the city by guests of the hotels can be explained in terms of the diversity of the socioeconomic status of clients.

Keywords: Value dimensions · Topic modelling · Stratification · Hotels · Reviews · St. Petersburg

1 Introduction

User-generated content (UGC), including on-line reviews, proved to be an important source of information about consumer preferences and experiences as a result of social media diffusion. In this regard, on-line travel reviews have also become an important indicator for different sides of touristic industry [9]. Websites such as TripAdvisor provide customer reviews that reflect significant characteristics of popular tourist attractions and nearby places [1]. To analyse these text data at scale, Natural Language Processing tools can be applied [8], satisfying the need to understand the holistic picture of experiences and opinions with algorithms such as Latent Dirichlet Allocation [2].

In the domain of analyzing tourist customer experiences, the prominent work of Guo et al. [5] applied Latent Dirichlet Allocation to TripAdvisor review data from 25 thousand hotels in 16 countries to understand the dimensions of guests' satisfaction and analyze their relative importance for different demographic characteristics, such as gender and age, alongside hotel classification.

However, looking at tourist value dimensions from glocalization perspective [3], we assume that the local dimensions of experience play at least as important of a role as global ones, being deeply rooted in the specifics of the particular tourist destination [1]. Moreover, leisure tourists choose their destination first,

© Springer International Publishing AG 2017
D.A. Alexandrov et al. (Eds.): DTGS 2017, CCIS 745, pp. 341–346, 2017.
https://doi.org/10.1007/978-3-319-69784-0_29

and the particular hotel second, paying attention to the attractiveness of the city. People form their expectations of potential tourist experience which can then lead to particular practices of hotel consumption. At the same time, sociocultural expectations of tourists define specific destinations that they might visit [6].

Here, we explore how the analysis of hotel value dimensions could be extended to include glocalization of the tourist business: treating the process of the hotel choice as a secondary to destination choice, we look how the hotel customers' preferences and dimensions of value are connected to surrounding context of the city and how this connection is shaped by socio-economic differences of customers proxied by the hotel categories.

2   Data and Methodology

In our study, we concentrate on the case of hotels located in Saint Petersburg. Saint Petersburg is the second-largest city in Russia, known as a cultural center of the country and a very popular destination for different categories of travelers [4] with the well-developed hospitality industry.

Data was gathered from TripAdvisor.ru and consists of 21,165 reviews about 201 hotels in Saint Petersburg, Russia. The hotels were divided into two groups: 2–3 star and 4–5 star hotels. There are no 1-star hotels in the standard TripAdvisor classification. Moreover, we do not consider hotels without a category.

Before conducting analysis, basic text processing steps were performed, including tokenization, removing stop words and stemming [7]. Pre-processed data was used as input to 30-topic LDA model [2].

To come up with the relevant descriptions for obtained topics, three raters examined reviews with the highest probability for each of the topics and extracted 100 of the most relevant words. Only Russian language reviews were included for further analysis.

To analyse associations between topics' saliency and reviews about 2–3 stars hotels and 4–5 stars hotels, we used G^2 log-likelihood ratio for two sub-corpora.

In order to check our hypotheses about the perception of the city by tourists, the list of the city sights was generated from the most frequently-used words in the topics connected with geographical position. Distances from each hotel to each sight were calculated in terms of time and length. After that the G^2 log-likelihood ratios of appearance frequency of the particular sight in the reviews on 2–3 and 4–5 stars hotels were computed.

3   Results

3.1   Extraction of the Dimensions

Table 1 provides information about the topics obtained as a result of LDA analysis based on reviews' text from TripAdvisor. All topics are analytically divided into more general groups describing particular characteristics of the hotel.

Table 1. Topic modeling results

Dimensions	Topics	Example
Patterns of using transport, description of transport facilities	Parking Transport	"The hotel is conveniently located. You can reach the airport by bus. Travel time just as a taxi, but many times cheaper" "There is a private parking, coupons for free parking can be obtained at the reception desk"
Hotel location in terms of the city surroundings	Attractions Closeness to the attractions Location View from the window	"It is located next to Isakievsky Cathedral. The hotel has many rooms with a view of the cathedral" "The main advantage of this hotel is location. It is just 10 min from the Kazan Cathedral"
Purposes of staying at the hotel which require particular facilities	Celebrations Events management Family trip Resort facilities Sleepover	"I could not start the event at the time, because the hall was unprepared" "I was in this hotel in the summer with my father, we came to see St. Petersburg"
Description of living conditions provided by the hotel	Apartment Bathroom Guest facilities Homeliness Location in building Room experience Style and decoration	"There was no cold water at all. Water in the tap and in the shower was literally boiling" "The interior is quite modern, with a focus on the attractions of St. Petersburg. Also I was pleasantly surprised by the old photos of St. Petersburg, hung on the walls"
Assessment of staff performance	Cleaning Checking in and out Politeness of the staff Thanks to staff	"I am especially grateful to Galina (staff) for her caring and responsiveness" "Staff at the reception desk ultimately stated that I would not be checked in. Their behavior was very boorish"
Description of food services provided by the hotel and their availability nearby	Breakfast Dining	"Downstairs is very nice pab- restaurant with good, simple food." "At breakfast there are dishes for every taste..."
Overall evaluation of the hotel based on personal experience	Advice Experience Price and value for money Satisficing	"If you want to spend the night, then it is good, but if you want to stay for a long time, I would recommend you to consider other options" "I will recommend that hotel to all my friends and acquaintances"

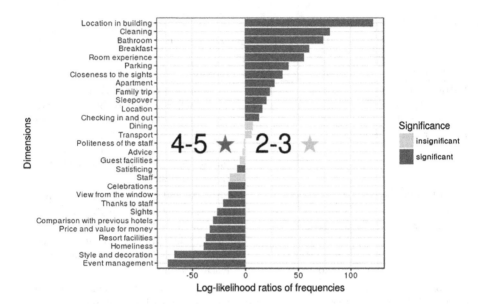

Fig. 1. Prevailing topics in the reviews of 2–3 and 4–5 hotels

Figure 1 presents the 29 most important topics extracted from reviews. To analyse the question about the perception of the city, it is important to examine more closely those dimensions that are somehow connected to the geography of the city. Among them are "Closeness to the sights", "Location", "Transport", "View from the window".

The analysis showed that two of the mentioned topics ("Closeness to the sights" and "Location") are significantly more frequent in reviews dedicated to 2–3 star hotels, while the topic called "View from the window" occurs significantly more often in reviews for 4–5 star hotels. At the same time topic about "Transport" is equally distributed among 2–3 and 4–5 star hotels. The messages with topics "Closeness to the sights" and "View from the window" both often includes names of well-known city sights, such as Aurora and Kazan Cathedral, but carry different contexts. Guests of 4–5 star hotels are writing more about a view from the window, which might include some of those sights, while people who stayed in 2–3 star hotels write more about how close the sights are or how to get there.

Described patterns were taken into further consideration by performing basic spatial analysis. We computed time and distances both by foot and by public transport to get from each of the hotels to the sights, which were frequently mentioned in the reviews. There is no statistical difference between the distances from 2–3 star and 4–5 star hotels to the each of the attractions. Taking into account that finding, we can assume that differences in mentioning the city sights in the reviews are not the consequence of the differences of distances.

Equal distribution of "Transport" topic means that guests from the hotels of both classes write about surrounding transport infrastructure in the same quantity.

To find out more evident distinction in perception of the city by hotel guests, it is useful to look at the likelihood of the appearance of a particular sight in the reviews on the different hotels.

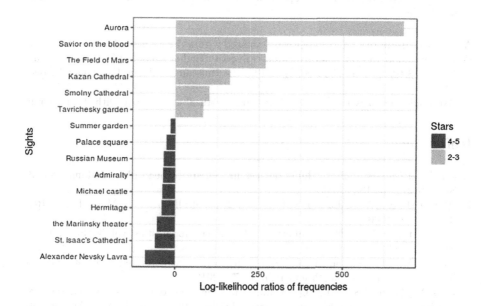

Fig. 2. Log-likelihood ratios of frequencies for sights by stars

Figure 2 represents the probability of mentioning of a particular sight in the review on the 2–3 or 4–5 star hotels. Most frequently mentioned city sights in both classes of the hotels are quite different. These sights can be classified into two groups, those which every tourist can attend for free and those which require some fee to enter. According to this classification, it is noticeable that the major part of sights that are fee-paying, for example, Russian Museum, Michael Castle, Hermitage, the Mariinsky Theatre, are prevalent in the reviews on the 4–5 star hotels, whereas e.g. Kazan Cathedral, the Field of Mars, Tavrichesky Garden are mentioned more frequently in the reviews from the guests of 2–3 star hotels.

4   Conclusion

Practices and patterns highlighted in this paper shed some light on one of the important aspects of "place-making" [1] via UGC-based valuation devices informing tourist experiences.

Using Saint Petersburg, one of the most popular tourist destinations in Russia, we show a connection between perceived hotel value dimensions and the perception of city sights within the different categories of hotels.

Future steps of this ongoing research will take two directions. First, the connection with socioeconomical characteristics of consumers and other determinants of choice will be analysed in more detail. Second, we will focus on studying the role of UGC, ranking and reputation systems as valuation devices informing these choices.

Acknowledgements. The paper was prepared within the framework of the Academic Fund Program at the National Research University Higher School of Economics (HSE) in 2017 2018 (grant No. 17-05-0024) and by the Russian Academic Excellence Project "5–100".

We would like to express our gratitude to Ilya Musabirov for help with this research.

References

1. Baka, V.: Understanding valuing devices in tourism through place-making. Valuat. Stud. **3**(2), 149–180 (2015)
2. Blei, D.M., Ng, A.Y., Jordan, M.I.: Latent dirichlet allocation. J. Mach. Learn. Res. **3**, 993–1022 (2003)
3. Featherstone, M., Lash, S., Robertson, R.: Global Modernities, vol. 36. Sage, Thousand Oaks (1995)
4. Gordin, V., Matetskaya, M.: Creative tourism in saint petersburg: the state of the art. J. Tourism Consum. Pract. **4**(2), 55–77 (2012)
5. Guo, Y., Barnes, S.J., Jia, Q.: Mining meaning from online ratings and reviews: tourist satisfaction analysis using latent dirichlet allocation. Tourism Manag. **59**, 467–483 (2017)
6. Kaya, B.: Transiting with the environment: an exploration of tourist re-orientations as collaborative practice. J. Consum. Cult. **16**(2), 374–392 (2016)
7. Li, G., Law, R., Vu, H.Q., Rong, J., Zhao, X.R.: Identifying emerging hotel preferences using emerging pattern mining technique. Tourism Manag. **46**, 311–321 (2015)
8. Pang, B., Lee, L., et al.: Opinion mining and sentiment analysis. Found. Trends® Inf. Retrieval **2**(1–2), 1–135 (2008)
9. Sung-Byung, Y., Seung-Hun, S., Youhee, J., Chulmo, K.: Exploring the comparative importance of online hotel reviews heuristic attributes in review helpfulness: a conjoint analysis approach. J. Travel Tourism Mark. **34**(7), 963–985 (2016)

NBIC Convergence as a Stage of Transition of Saint-Petersburg's E-Government Information Space to the Sixth Techno-Economic Paradigm

Sergey A. Dyatlov and Oleg S. Lobanov[✉]

Saint Petersburg State Economic University,
21, Sadovaya Street, 191023 St. Petersburg, Russian Federation
thelobanoff@gmail.com

Abstract. Within the framework of this study, the problem of insufficient effectiveness of interaction between information spaces of various departments was discussed, in particular, duplication of hardware, software, data and methods of their processing, which is especially important in the conditions of instability of the economic situation in the country and in a world, and excludes extensive approaches to the region's information infrastructure development by increasing budgetary funding only. In order to deal with this problem, the notion of NBIC (nano, bio, info, cogni) information space was introduced, the content of NBIC clusters was disclosed. Periodization of the evolution of the regional informatization management system had been carried out, key factors of transition to NBIC convergence were shown. The concept of convergence of information spaces was introduced and its role in the characterized process of NBIC convergence was shown. The synergetic effect of the information space transformation to the NBIC information space has been determined. The necessity of transformation of development vector of the information space for the transition to NBIC information space was shown. The economic efficiency of the transition to NBIC information space has been determined. Methods and models for assessing the social effect from the transition to NBIC information space were characterized. Rationale for improving the management of the information space through the transition to NBIC information space was justified. It was proved that the transition to NBIC information space will allow to ensure the convergence of clusters of information spaces. Finally, conclusions are made about the applicability of developed methods and models in the process of managing the informatization of the region and also further prospects for research are shown.

Keywords: Informatization · NBIC · Information space · Convergence · Information systems

The study has been developed under the grant of the russian foundation for basic research № 16–02–00531a.

© Springer International Publishing AG 2017
D.A. Alexandrov et al. (Eds.): DTGS 2017, CCIS 745, pp. 347–361, 2017.
https://doi.org/10.1007/978-3-319-69784-0_30

1 Introduction

A characteristic feature of modern development of the world and Russian economy is the process of radical structural socio-economic transformation, which is caused by the transformation of the industrial-market economy model into a new information-network (digital) economy. Modern emerging digital economy has a complex structural and functional organization and includes a large number of diverse elements and institutions interconnected and integrated through global information networks and cloud technologies. On December 5, 2016, was published a list of instructions on the implementation of creating a digital economy in the country. According to paragraph 9 of this document, a number of ministries must develop and approve the program "Digital Economy", which includes a set of measures to create legal, technical, organizational and financial conditions for the digital economy development in the Russian Federation and its integration into the space of digital economy of the members of the Eurasian Economic Union [1]. The federal program "Digital Economy" should be developed by June 1, 2017.

The new state program "Digital Economy" should be coordinated with the current federal program "Information Society" and with the program on formation of the Eurasian Economic Union digital space. It is planned to create a single information system of control activities based on cloud technologies and Big data. At the same time, great importance should be paid to overcoming the digital difference between the regions of Russia, as well as between the countries of the Eurasian economic space [2].

In this context, it should be noted that the process of managing the information space of state authorities in the region can not occur in isolation from the environment that affects both information space and its components [3]. When considering this management structure in the scale of the region, one should note the existence of information spaces and information systems outside the limits of public authorities, which are subjects of influence on information systems of public authorities that form this information space. This is a necessary and sufficient condition for developing methods for managing effective interaction based on synergy effects from the use of information systems across the region. At the same time, in the process of interpenetration, the existing features of business entities, within which appropriate information spaces are formed, should be taken into account when constructing an effective management system for them.

In addition, in the process of interpenetration, it is required to consider the issues of the synthesis of information technologies that are convergent with cognitive processes, as the basis for making informed decisions, with modern products of high-tech industries, in particular nanotechnology, as well as biological aspects of human activities. These factors in their interrelation provide the possibility of information spaces convergence of the relevant industries and information spaces of the region, which increase the rationality of management decisions in this area and resolves the problems of interdepartmental interaction between these industry sectors.

2 Purpose and Objectives of the Study

2.1 Purpose of the Study

In connection with the presence of these features of managing the informatization processes, the problem of an economic nature is to be solved, which means insufficient effectiveness of interaction between information spaces of various departments, in particular, duplication of hardware, software, data and methods of their processing, which is especially important in the conditions of instability of the economic situation in the country and in a world, and excludes extensive approaches to the region's information infrastructure development by increasing budgetary funding only. From this problem of this subject area follows the problem of a scientific area, consisting of the absence of a unified approach to management of interpenetration and convergence on a semantic and cognitive levels.

2.2 Object and Subject of Research

In order to obtain a clear and objective research, it is advisable to select as an **object** a set of information spaces for economic entities using information spaces on the territory of the region, insofar as they belong to public authorities, municipalities and other organizations with a share of state participation in their authorized capital, whose activities are aimed to the implementation of state programs or the providing of government or other public services. Thus, the **subject** of this study are the processes associated with the interpenetration of information spaces of various sectors and subjects of economic activity.

3 Materials and Methods

3.1 Convergence of Information Spaces

In view of the above features, the construction of a management system for information spaces in the region must begin with the definition of properties and features that allow us to characterize the generality of elements and their properties in independent information spaces. The process describing the identification of the totality of such features in the process of the information spaces interpenetration in various industries and business entities can be characterized as the **convergence of information spaces**.

This term allows us to describe the processes of identifying similar patterns in the information spaces of various industries and business entities, which is a key factor for the integration of these information spaces and the emergence of a synergistic effect of their interaction.

It should also noted that one of the distinguishing features of the information space is generation of knowledge through the processing of data within information systems [4]. With such knowledge, it is possible to build a knowledge-sharing system to exclude the need for their re-generation in other information spaces.

Thus, the process of knowledge sharing between different departments is the integration of knowledge flows generated within the information spaces of these industries and departments, based on the generality of the content of knowledge processed in information systems within each information space, as well as their objects and purposes. In other words, the methodology for exploring the convergence of information spaces should allow us to characterize the methods, techniques and processes of knowledge exchange between information systems that are part of the information space.

A promising method of organizing and structuring the information space is the clustering of regional information systems that involves the transition to the use of universal, multifunctional cloud services, which is a necessary condition for the integration of regions into the information and innovation structure of the national and global information space [5].

3.2 The Concept of NBIC Convergence of Information Spaces

It should be noted that at present humanity is on the threshold of the sixth techno-economic paradigm, where the first one was the beginning of the First Industrial Revolution, the second one was the epoch of steam, the third one was the epoch of steel (Second Industrial Revolution), the fourth one was the oil age, the fifth one was the age of computers and telecommunications (Scientific and Technical Revolution), and, finally, within the sixth one it seems possible to converge technologies that characterize the processes of the emergence of self-organizing structures, emergent, nonlinear and dynamic systems, etc. The information space (IS) of the region, being such a structure containing clusters of information systems, is an element of convergence with other branches of technological development that underlie the sixth techno-economic paradigm, the core of which is NBIC convergence, as shown in Fig. 1. Consequently, the result of the transfer of St. Petersburg IS to the sixth techno-economic paradigm will be the NBIC information space (IS_{NBIC}).

Thus, the process of transition from IS to IS_{NBIC} will be understood as the process of integration of IS in nano- (IS_N), IS bio- (IS_B), IS info- (IS_I) and IS cogni- (IS_C) areas, characterized by synergistic interpenetration of these IS with each other.

This fact of interpenetration will be a cardinal difference from the standard integration of information spaces between themselves, shown in Fig. 2.

The effect of such integration will be: $IS_N + IS = E_{IS\ N}$, $IS_B + IS = E_{IS\ B}$, $IS_I + IS = E_{IS\ I}$, $IS_C + IS = E_{IS\ C}$, where $E_{IS\ N}$ is the effect of integration of IS_N with IS, $E_{IS\ B}$ is the effect of integration of IS_B with IS, $E_{IS\ I}$ is the effect of integration of IS_I with IS, $E_{IS\ C}$ is the effect of integration of IS_C with IS.

In the process of convergence, IS_N, IS_B, IS_I and IS_C information spaces will be integrated not only with the information space of St. Petersburg, but also with each other. In Fig. 3 such integration is shown by a solid line.

Additional connections that arise during the integration process are taken into account in calculating the effect in such a way that the $E_{IS\ N} + E_{IS\ B} + E_{IS\ I} + E_{IS\ C} < E_{IS\ NBIC}$, which can be characterized as the **synergy of NBIC information spaces convergence**. A more detailed calculation of the synergistic effect is presented in Sect. 4.1.

Considering the NBIC convergence of information spaces, it should be noted that, since it was previously proven that the information space consists of clusters of

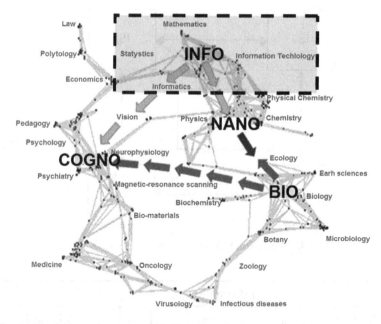

Fig. 1. The information space of St. Petersburg in NBIC technology convergence model

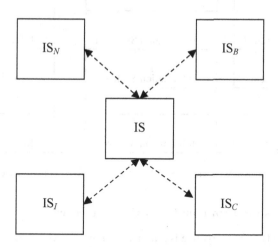

Fig. 2. Integration of NBIC information spaces

information systems [5], within the framework of this study, it is advisable to consider the structure of the information space presented in Fig. 4.

An important consequence of this approach will be the fact that the IS will be considered as IS_{NBIC} if and only if each cluster included in this information space will have signs of NBIC convergence.

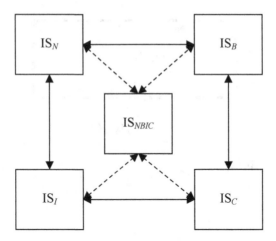

Fig. 3. Convergence of NBIC information spaces

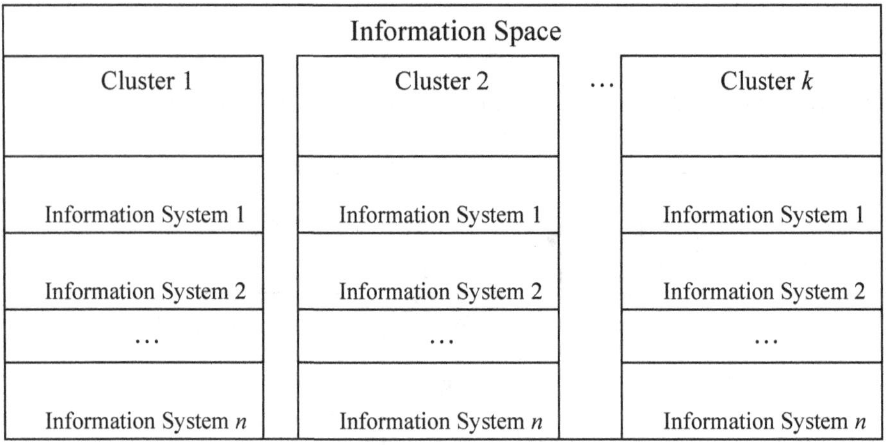

Information Space				
Cluster 1		Cluster 2	...	Cluster k
Information System 1		Information System 1		Information System 1
Information System 2		Information System 2		Information System 2
...		...		...
Information System n		Information System n		Information System n

Fig. 4. The structure of the information space in NBIC convergence process

3.3   Prerequisites for Transition to NBIC Convergence

The transition to NBIC convergence is a logical step in the evolution of the information management system in St. Petersburg. Thus, according to the Gartner study, in the process of periodization of the government information spaces evolution by 2015, the following stages can be identified in accordance with Table 1.

Table 1 shows that at each stage the focus of the use of information technology in the public sector has changed, with each new stage being based on the results of previous ones. At the first stage it was automation of key administrative processes, creation of basic information and accounting systems, and filling them by data. At the next stage, these were state services and inter-agency information exchange in the process of their provision.

Table 1. Periodization and evolution of the management system of the information sector

No.	Year	Name of the stage	A brief description
1	2000	E-government	Operational activities and public services, data was processed in disparate information systems based on various technologies
2	2005	Integrated government	Integrated services and interagency electronic interaction, the emergence of data exchange between disparate information systems
3	2010	Open government	Emergence of open data and involvement of citizens in the processes of data exchange between information systems, the beginning of data transformation into knowledge
4	2015	Digital government	Analysis of information and forecasting, transition to the use of cloud technologies in government structures
5	2017	Convergent government	Synthesis of data and knowledge in the process of interaction of sectoral information spaces, interpenetration of modern technologies and economic sectors in the activities of government agencies

Today, most countries in the world entered the fourth phase of the use of information technology in the work of public authorities, which was named by market analysts, such as Gartner Group, as the "digital government". The digital government is still based on the principles of citizenship/business orientation, a unified view of them, integrated services and application systems. The fundamental difference is in the focus on information and on data transformed into knowledge, rather than on processes and services, as it was at the beginning of e-government, and in the focus on more direct and effective involvement of all parties involved in the provision and consumption of public services [6].

The focus on data and knowledge is the key difference between the concept of digital government and e-government. In the context of cities and regions, analysts today speak of "smart cities" and "smart regions". When we talk about "smart cities" as a trend within the digital government, it is believed that the data, in particular, large data sets ("Big data") generated by the "Internet of things" and operating devices – is what makes cities to be smart cities. Given the beginning of data transformation into knowledge, this stage can be considered as the beginning of public sector transition to the knowledge economy.

At the same time, in the implementation of the digital government, according to IDC, the information and communications technology industry is experiencing a new wave of change and growth that is associated with technologies such as mobile computing, social communications and networks, cloud computing and big data technologies, and these changes will only accelerate. These technological platforms, supplemented (where it makes sense) by active use of the "Internet of things", are key factors to the current phase of information technology usage in the government, which is defined as "Digital Government" [7]. In the context of the transformation of relevant data into knowledge, a transition to new technologies is needed, which ensures the synthesis of these technologies with the sectors of the economy that generate them.

Thus, the process of interpenetration of industries is a regular stage in the evolution of the information management system in the region, while preserving the advantages of the previous stages in the development of information spaces at the same time it is ensuring their convergence at the next stage of this transition, the need for which is determined by the above factors and is an urgent task at the current stage of information-telecommunication infrastructure development.

4   Evaluation and Discussion

4.1   Synergetic Effect

Figure 5 is represents schematically the process of IS convergence into IS_{NBIC}, characterized by interpenetration of information spaces of the four specified spheres.

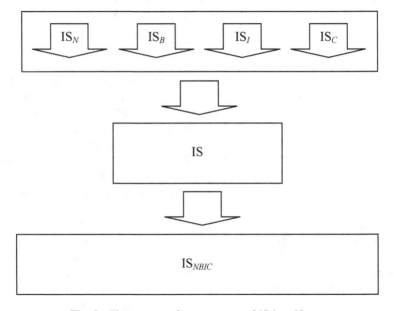

Fig. 5. The process of convergence of IS into IS_{NBIC}

At the same time, in the process of interpenetration of each IS, an effect appears, which is schematically shown in Fig. 6.

In view of the fact that this interpenetration possesses the property of synergy, the effect of this transition will be estimated as $E_{IS\ NBIC} = E_{IS\ N} + E_{IS\ B} + E_{IS\ I} + E_{IS\ C} + \Delta S$, where ΔS is the synergistic effect from the transition to IS_{NBIC}. For the number of clusters n, this effect will be $\Delta S = nk^4$, where k is the number of information systems in the cluster.

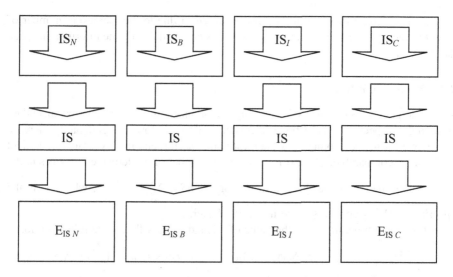

Fig. 6. The effect of IS convergence for each of the four spheres

Thus, the transition to IS_{NBIC} will allow the convergence of IS clusters. In other words, the transition to IS_{NBIC} entails the emergence of **synergistic services**, the essence of which will be disclosed below.

In Fig. 7 is presented a diagram that illustrates the synergetic effect that occurs during the transition to IS_{NBIC}.

As it can be seen on Fig. 7, an increase in the number of information systems in the cluster, as well as an increase in the number of clusters participating in the convergence

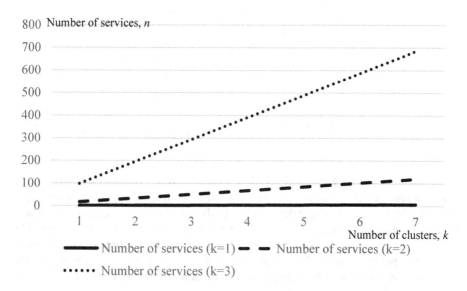

Fig. 7. The synergetic effect that occurs during the transition to IS_{NBIC}

process, leads to an increase in the synergistic effect due to the increasing number of links between the corresponding information systems both inside the information space and beyond it.

4.2 Economic Effect

This synergetic effect is also of economic importance, since in the context of budget financing, the peculiarities of budget legislation do not allow to significantly increase the budget for the development of the information sector, and from year to year budget financing is comparable. Thus, if $P \approx const$ the number of implemented services in the information space will be the following for IS: $nS = \sum_{i=1}^{k} Serv_i \times x_i$, where x_i is the specific weight of current service in the IS cluster.

At the same time, in IS_{NBIC} the value of this indicator will take the following form:

$$nS = (\sum_{i=1}^{k} Serv_i \times x_i)_{IS_N} + (\sum_{i=1}^{k} Serv_i \times x_i)_{IS_B} + (\sum_{i=1}^{k} Serv_i \times x_i)_{IS_I} + (\sum_{i=1}^{k} Serv_i \times x_i)_{IS_C},$$

as it shown in Table 2 for the number of clusters $k = 3$.

Table 2. Calculation of services number by the example of three clusters in IS and IS_{NBIC}

No.	IS	IS_{NBIC}
1	$x_1 Serv_1 = k_1$	$x_1 Serv_1 = k_{1IS_N}$
2	$x_2 Serv_2 = k_2$	$x_2 Serv_2 = k_{2IS_N}$
3	$x_3 Serv_3 = k_3$	$x_3 Serv_3 = k_{3IS_N}$
4	–	$x_1 Serv_1 = k_{1IS_B}$
5	–	$x_2 Serv_2 = k_{2IS_B}$
6	–	$x_3 Serv_3 = k_{3IS_B}$
7	–	$x_1 Serv_1 = k_{1IS_I}$
8	–	$x_2 Serv_2 = k_{2IS_I}$
9	–	$x_3 Serv_3 = k_{3IS_I}$
10	–	$x_1 Serv_1 = k_{1IS_C}$
11	–	$x_2 Serv_2 = k_{2IS_C}$
12	–	$x_3 Serv_3 = k_{3IS_C}$
Resulting number of services	$nS = \sum_{i=1}^{k} k_i = 3$	$nS = \sum_{i=1}^{k} k_i \times x_i = 12$

Figure 8 shows the diagram of the dependence of synergistic services number on clusters number in IS compared to data for a similar number of clusters in the IS_{NBIC}.

Using the example of this calculation, it is shown that the convergence of IS and IS_{NBIC} will enable the deployment of a larger number of services under comparable financing, which, on the one hand, ensures more rational use of limited budget funds, and on the other hand, more effective implementation of state programs which tasks are determined by the current legislation, so it will show the effectiveness of the management system.

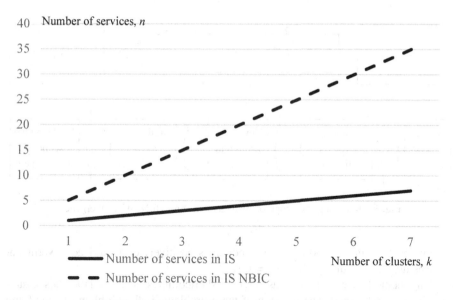

Fig. 8. Number of services in IS and IS$_{NBIC}$

4.3 Effect of Management Scale

Considering the issue of improving the effectiveness of the management system, it should also be noted that in accordance with the principles of budget financing, defined, in particular, by the Law of St. Petersburg of October 10, 2005 No. 531-74 "On the wage systems of employees of state institutions of St. Petersburg", the maintenance of management personnel is calculated by introducing a management scale factor to the base salary in proportion to the number of subordinate employees.

As it was shown earlier, the process of information space convergence will allow, in the course of integration of heterogeneous information systems and their subsequent convergence, to obtain a synergy of services, due to which it will be possible to obtain a synergistic effect from IS$_{NBIC}$ as a whole. These new properties make it possible to reduce the number of personnel by increasing the automation of personnel activities and, thus, to reduce the scale of management, as shown in Fig. 9.

Thus, the use of synergy effects in the management process and the attendant synergy of services will increase the effectiveness of the IS$_{NBIC}$ and thus reduce the scale of human resources management and the related budgetary costs.

4.4 Social Effect

In terms of assessing the social impact of the processes under consideration, it should also be noted that the indicator that characterizes the positive level of perception of public services in electronic form, which in this study is characterized as **public services conversion**, is currently calculated through social surveys using the formula $Ko = K_{survey}$, where K_{survey} is the value obtained by expert way in course of population

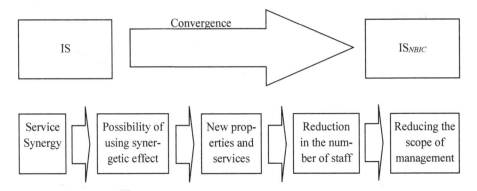

Fig. 9. Reducing the scope of management through NBIC convergence

surveys. For example, if 60% of the respondents positively characterized government services during the survey, then $Ko = 60\%$.

This method of calculation has obvious shortcomings, such as labor costs, subjectivity, low relevance. The solution of these problems is the problem of modifying this index and giving it an integral form. In order to solve this problem, we introduce 4 indicators characterizing each of the IS_{NBIC} spheres, and we characterize them in Table 3.

Table 3. Integral scale of indicators of public services conversion

No.	Indicator	Calculation of the indicator
1	K_N	Data obtained through wearable high-tech devices that use the collection of information necessary to obtain public services
2	K_B	Data of biometric indicators and behavioral aspects of the population in the process of receiving government services
3	K_I	Data obtained through surveys using information technology, for example, an online survey on the government services website
4	K_C	Assessment of knowledge about the use of public services accumulated in knowledge bases for a certain period

Thus, after the transition to IS_{NBIC}, the value of this indicator will be calculated as $Ko = x_1 K_N + x_2 K_B + x_3 K_I + x_4 K_C$, where K_N, K_B, K_I, K_C are values of the indicators for corresponding convergence spheres, x_i is the weight value of this indicator in total set of indicators, where $\sum x_i = 1$.

The values of x_i are calculated on the basis of expert judgment and in approximate form have the values presented in Table 4.

Given the role of the transition to knowledge sharing [8] the most expedient is the maximum value of the indicator x_4, thus giving preference to the largest weight of the K_C indicator in the general model for calculating the public services conversion, which together with other indicators will allow increasing the objectivity and consistency of

Table 4. Values of the coefficients of the public service conversion model

№	Indicator	Coefficient	Value of the coefficient
1	K_N	x_1	0.2
2	K_B	x_2	0.1
3	K_I	x_3	0.3
4	K_C	x_4	0.4

the conducted studies and also will allow fully evaluating the social effect of the conducted events in the field of informatization, allowing, in turn, to increase the relevance of management decisions in this area and to create a favorable impression about the actions of public authorities among the population of St. Petersburg.

4.5   The Effect of Interpenetration of Industries

This transition to IS_{NBIC} will provide both an increase in the effectiveness of regional management [9] and the development of new, high-tech industries at a strategic level. An example of similar structural changes at the level of managing the economy of the region is shown in Fig. 10.

Figure 10 shows that the convergence in the IS_N part will allow the production of nanotechnology elements on the territory of St. Petersburg that besides the development of the relevant industry and the development of information system modules of

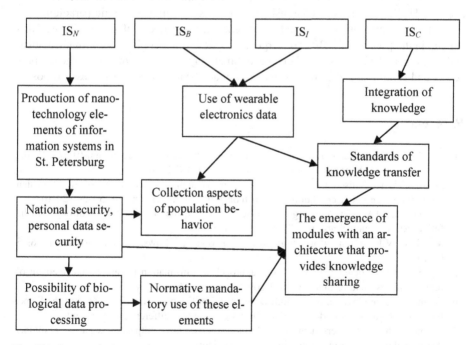

Fig. 10. Structural changes in economic sectors within framework of NBIC convergence of IS

IS_I will provide national security tasks in the face of negative global trends, ensure the safety of personal data, realize the possibilities of processing biological data of the IS_B, and with the mandatory use of the relevant modules at the legislative level [10] – the creation of systems with an architecture that provides knowledge sharing through the implemented standards of knowledge sharing with the IS_C [11], providing an exchange of knowledge about biological indicators, analysis of behavioral factors of the population and increasing innovative hypercompetition of Russian companies [12].

5 Conclusion

In the framework of this study, the concept of IS_{NBIC}, characterizing the transition of the St. Petersburg IS to the sixth techno-economic paradigm, is introduced, and the need for transformation of the development vector of the IS and its clusters for the transition to IS_{NBIC} is substantiated, and the synergistic effect of the IS transformation into IS_{NBIC} is determined. The signs of information spaces convergence in the process of NBIC convergence are determined and the model of information space convergence is developed. The economic feasibility of the transition to IS_{NBIC} is estimated, methods and models for assessing the social effect of this transition have been defined, and the efficiency of IS management has been justified through the transition to IS_{NBIC}.

The proposed features are crucial for the construction of relevant models and allow to effectively manage the convergence processes of information spaces [13] in terms of the possibility of their formalization and description of the corresponding knowledge flows for building an effective system of regional and national informatization management [14] in the process of transition to the sixth techno-economic paradigm.

A further direction of this study is to consider the model of public-private partnership in the process of NBIC convergence, as well as the application of mathematical and instrumental methods for choosing optimal ways of managing convergence processes and minimizing the costs of material and human resources for these purposes.

References

1. ComNews: Digital Economy Takes Shape. http://www.comnews.ru/content/105258/2016-12-22/cifrovaya-ekonomika-obretaet-ochertaniya#ixzz4TY0z709q
2. Dyatlov, S.A., Selischeva, T.A.: Information inequality of countries of the Eurasian economic space under conditions of hypercompetition. Innovations **10**, 50–56 (2016)
3. Kovalchuk, M.V.: The convergence of science and technology is a breakthrough in the future. Russ. Nanotechnol. **6**(1–2), 13–23 (2011)
4. Minakov, V.F.: From information flows to knowledge flows. Nauka-Rastudent.ru **8**, 8 (2016)
5. Dyatlov, S.A., Lobanov, O.S.: Cluster approach to information resources management of regional infrastructure. Innovations **3**(209), 11–15 (2016)
6. Gartner: Digital Government is Both Different From E-Government and More of the Same. https://www.gartner.com/doc/2498215/digital-government-different-egovernment-
7. Gartner: Digital Government Key Initiative Overview. https://www.gartner.com/doc/2715718/digital-government-key-initiative-overview

8. Minakov, V.F., Lobanov, O.S., Artemyev, A.V.: Clusters of consumers of telecommunication services. Res. J. Int. Stud. **6–1**(25), 60–61 (2014)
9. Mussatayeva, A.A.: The Effectiveness of state administration: problems and solution approaches. Middle-East J. Sci. Res. **14**(10), 1331–1336 (2013)
10. Obeidat, M.A.Q., Aldulaimi, S.H.: The role of project management information systems towards the project performance the case of construction projects in United Arab Emirates. Int. Rev. Manag. Mark. **6**(3), 559–568 (2016)
11. Lobanov, O.S.: Construction of the unified information space management system in St. Petersburg, its principles, characteristics and results of the application. Mod. Probl. Sci.Edu. **5**, 444 (2013). doi:10.17513/spno.10611
12. Vasiltsova, V.M., Dyatlov, S.A., Vasiltsov, V.S., Bezrukova, T.L., Bezrukov, B.A.: Methodology of management innovation hypercompetition. Asian Soc. Sci. **11**(20), 165–169 (2015). doi:10.5539/ass.v11n20p165
13. Zwattendorfer, B., Stranacher, K., Tauber, A., Reichstädter, P.: Cloud computing in E-Government across Europe. In: Kő, A., Leitner, C., Leitold, H., Prosser, A. (eds.) EGOVIS/EDEM 2013. LNCS, vol. 8061, pp. 181–195. Springer, Heidelberg (2013). doi:10.1007/978-3-642-40160-2_15
14. Minakov, V.F., Ilyina, O.P., Lobanov, O.S.: Concept of the cloud information space of regional government. Middle-East J. Sci. Res. **21**(1), 190–196 (2014). doi:10.5829/idosi.mejsr.2014.21.01.21138

eHealth: ICTs in Public Health Management

An Ontology Based System for Storing the Research Results on Medical Diagnostics

Aleksandra Vatian[1(✉)], Galina Artemova[1], Natalia Dobrenko[1],
Anton Filatov[2], and Natalia Gusarova[1]

[1] ITMO University, Saint Petersburg 197101, Russian Federation
alexvatyan@gmail.com, g.o.artemova@gmail.com,
graziokisa@ya.ru, natfed@list.ru
[2] Saint-Petersburg Mining University,
Saint Petersburg 199106, Russian Federation
sacateca@yandex.ru

Abstract. This paper proposes an ontology based system for storing information on medical diagnostics. The proposed system is focused on a specific way of storing the medical content – it allows the user not only to store standard information in a medical domain, but gives an opportunity to store the ongoing research. The main contribution of this system is its extensibility to contain all types of medical information and its capability to provide the needed research material at hand, including the quickly way of finding and evaluating the controversial current results. This makes it possible for researchers to work together in team and remotely. The system has been tested on real experimental data we obtained in the diagnosis of lung cancer based on gene expression. The experiments have shown that the proposed system tends to cover the needs of users.

Keywords: Ontology · Medical diagnostics · Medical content · Decision making · Gene expression

1 Introduction

During the last years the ontologies have become the subject of close study in the field of artificial intelligence as a method of presenting information. They are used in the development of various information systems and are represented as a result of the researchers' activity. Ontologies are able to provide the reusability of information and clarify the specification of terms, which help to transmit different information. Knowledge bases can be formed for various intellectual systems on the basis of ontologies [1].

Medicine is nowadays one of the most extensive applications of ontology. There is a large number of projects in the field of medicine that use the ontologies in their applications, mainly accenting in presentation of medical terminology [2]. Physicians have based their research on the use of hierarchy of concepts for various domains, hence extraction technologies, multilingual terms and relationships among them. Such ontologies can help doctors to search documents in various languages in the medical

© Springer International Publishing AG 2017
D.A. Alexandrov et al. (Eds.): DTGS 2017, CCIS 745, pp. 365–373, 2017.
https://doi.org/10.1007/978-3-319-69784-0_31

domian. On the one hand, such representation of medical knowledge provides a great amount of data that can be accessed fluently. On the other hand, medical information systems must be uniquely able to handle complex and contradictory data obtained by physicians and researchers as a result of medical practice. Obviously, this is a complicated task, but it can be solved by constructing ontologies of the medical domain to represent not only standard medical concepts, but also the structured storage of ongoing medical research. Also, they can provide criteria based on semantics to support different statistical sets for different purposes. Therefore maybe the principal goal of medical ontology systems is their ability to transmit the required data among the researchers, physicians and patients [3].

In this work we experimentally explore the possibility of storing general medical data as well as the data that contains the ongoing research. It is important that in the process of doing the research the physicians can obtain data that can represent contradictory results, or even the ones that contain mistakes or controversial data. That is why it is necessary to have the ability to store such results and allocate the features to clarify and simplify the process of further decision making. We use the research about lung cancer based on gene expression levels for the experiment.

Moreover, this paper concentrates on interaction between the researchers during the experiment and remotely. In social communities it is believed that it is important to exchange the research results, but as a rule these results are the completed papers and ready-made results. We offer a system that allows us to support joint work with current results, including conflicting ones. The problem in this case for physicians is the management of a huge number of results and data. System for supporting the distributed work of a group of researchers in the field of medicine.

The paper is organized as follows: Sect. 2 describes the ontology and the proposed system, Sect. 3 contains the information about practical experiment and finally Sect. 4 contains the conclusions and future work.

2 Proposed Solution

In this section the architecture of the proposed system is explained and its components are introduced.

2.1 General Information About the Problem

Basically, medical ontologies are constructed and used as systems containing structured data on diseases and terms that describe them [4]. But in addition, it is important to store numerous data that are not related to standard terminology, and include the knowledge gained empirically from various medical studies. The repeated use of such data for the purposes of secondary research, as well as for the formalization of knowledge about current problems, has recently become important. We present an ontology-supported approach to overcome this problem using the current content storage technique: in addition to defining the basic medical entities at the knowledge base level, we use ontologies to store, organize and describe controversial results. This demonstrates how knowledge representation system are able not only to facilitate the interpretation of clinical data, but also to contribute to decision-making if there are contradictions in similar studies.

To implement this task, we have chosen to create an ontology of lung cancer, but we need to notice that one of the main benefits of the system is its ability to use ready-made ontologies as a basis. The ontology contains the concepts of a lung cancer as well as various medical cases and medical practice. Besides, we store the information about cancer that we receive by practical consideration and our guesses about it. Moreover, the proposed ontology contains the knowledge, received by different methods and algorithms applied to various datasets. The following explanation of ontology structure contains the concepts of our experimental research about the lung cancer, based on gene levels.

2.2 Data Structure

This research offers an ontological model for structuring medical data. The general scheme of the developed ontology is designed as a metaontology and is presented in Fig. 1. The developed ontology describes the structure of medical materials, consisting of three main parts: (1) Part of the ontology of lung cancer (2) Part, containing a classification of methods and algorithms for data analysis (3) Part, containing information about ongoing research.

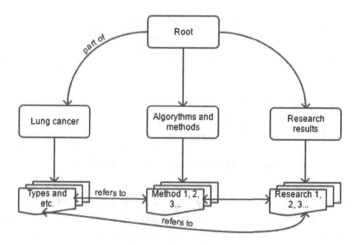

Fig. 1. The proposed metaontology

The open part of the left lung cancer branch is shown in Fig. 2. It stores the data of the standard ontology of lung cancer, which allows us to classify and correlate the obtained data with different types of lung cancer and its characteristics with the help of special bonds. The researcher can create his own ontology, or use the existing ones as a basis.

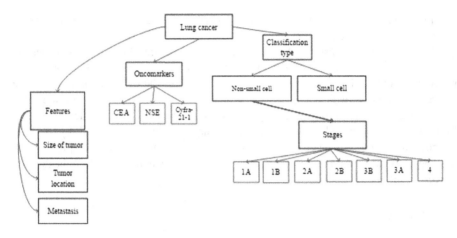

Fig. 2. Lung cancer branch

Figure 3 shows the disclosed part of the middle branch of metaontology - algorithms and methods. It allows the user to store and add data on standard and new methods of lung cancer research, including algorithms for gene expression analysis.

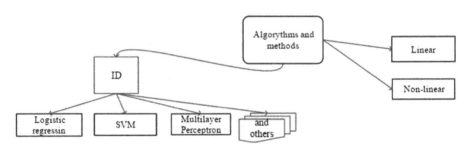

Fig. 3. Algorithms and methods branch

In Fig. 4, we see the entities that store the results of the research. Each entity in our case contains information about itself, and then links to other entities that store data on the investigated data sets and algorithms that are applied to them. Due to the use of special metadata, the researcher can obtain information about the similarity and differences in the presentation of data in different data sets, as well as about the results of applying various algorithms to them. This approach of presenting information allows the user to allocate the necessary signs when working with the ongoing research in order to make the right decision quickly and with less effort.

2.3   The Implemented System

To implement and test the usability of the proposed approach we have decided to deploy the ontology on the base of a wiki-engine, as many authors used this in their

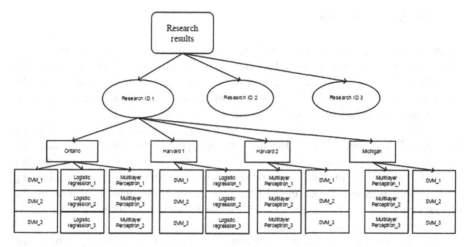

Fig. 4. The results branch

works [5–7]. There are many wiki-engines at the moment [8] and for our project we have chosen MediaWiki – an open-source platform.

The constructed system allows to quickly and effectively deploy the ontology by using the SemanticMediaWiki add-on. Each of the ontology concepts is a web template, which is connected with each other with the various types of relations.

The web template represents a set of medical materials containing general information about the content and special metadata to it. Each template includes the basic structured information about the entity it displays, and its components, for example, the type of cancer, the proposed methods of its diagnostics, etc. Metadata used in templates contain information about types of cancer, its features and are connected with the templates, containing the information about different algorithms, such as the logistic regression, SVM, multilayer perceptron etc.

Moreover, each of these templates is related to those that contain the data obtained in the process of the ongoing research. The metadata used in this templates allows to mark and then quickly and effectively find the necessary information, such as: attributes, overall evaluation, metrics, comments, etc. This allows detecting and sharing common and contradictory signs, obtained during medical work. By using these specified templates, the users will maintain the knowledge base.

When the user adds new documents or even changes some structure of the ontology, all he needs is to simply change the desired information in the metadata and associate a new template with all others which are connected with it. This semantic web structure allows the user to make complex queries and to find necessary information not only on the coincidence of text request, but on the whole structure of the system. The researcher can search for not only child members of a certain object, but also return its parents and search for the related documents such as links, metadata, forms and information about the attached files.

3 Practical Example

In this section, we describe the use of the constructed ontology in the lung cancer diagnostics domain, as it is nowadays one of the most marked problems [10]. The example is based on the real experimental data we gained in the research on the diagnosis of lung cancer based on gene expression. The gene expression is one of the most important methods of cancer diagnostics today [11].

For the study, we have chosen different datasets from open sources – Ontario, Michigan, Dana-Farber Cancer Institute and etc. [9]. Then, different classification algorithms were applied to each data set. The main feature of the comparison was the division of algorithms into linear and nonlinear ones. For the evaluation, the following metrics were selected: F-measure, AUC, ROC area, MCC, which are usually the standard ones in many researches [12, 13]. Weka 3 data mining software was used for feature selection, classifier training and evaluation.

After the research, the following results were obtained: the same algorithms with different combinations of feature selection attributes showed inconsistent results. As you can see in Fig. 5, the ROC curve of the same classifiers applied on the same Ontario dataset, but with various settings is different. The classifier was SVM, the number of selected attributes in the first experiment was 21 and it showed its performance higher that with the selection of all attributes in the second experiment. Therefore, we received the following results as shown in Table 1: the F-measure was 0.792 in the first experiment and 0.671 in the second. For instance, the other interesting result we obtained in the Michigan dataset - the metrics changed inconsiderably even when we used two different classifiers (SVM and Multilayer Perceptron), as shown in Fig. 6.

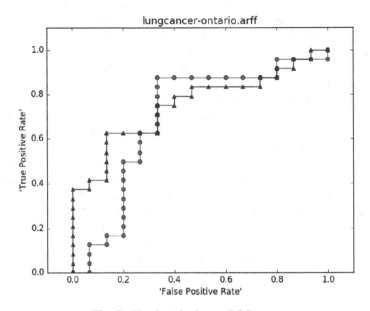

Fig. 5. The Ontario dataset ROC curve

Table 1. Characteristics of the studied algorithms

Classifier	Precision	Recall	F-measure	MCC	ROC area	PRC area
SVM 1	0.683	0.667	0.978	0.687	0.753	0.767
SVM 2	0.793	0.795	1.000	0.664	0.771	0.729

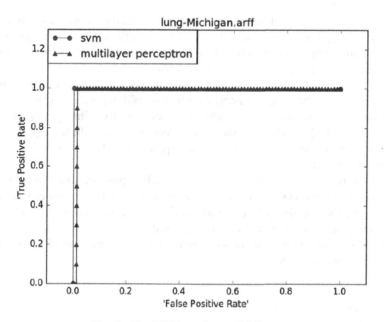

Fig. 6. The Michigan dataset ROC curve

We have imported the results of the experiment into the system, tagging them with the special metadata: the dataset type, the number of attributes, the metrics, overall evaluation, special comments and etc.

Thus, the real storage system that is applicable for further use, has been created - we could label the initial conditions by adding them to the metadata, breaking the attributes into clear and fuzzy ones, and also highlighting stable and unstable features. For instance, the user can make a special query to obtain the results applied to a concrete dataset. In order to find the controversial results, the user can enter [[Ontario :: results :: SVM :: F-measure]], and the system will return all pages with the SVM classifier applied to Ontario dataset, marking the F-measure in different experiments.

In case the user wants to find which datasets showed bad results (based on his research) when non-linear algorithms have been applied, he can enter [[Dataset? :: results :: non-linear :: overallevaluation = 0]], and the system will return all pages, that were marked by "evaluation 0" metadata.

Moreover, Mediawiki has a built-in control version system. This system allows monitoring the changes made and also provides the information about the users that have made changes, and exact time of change of documents and templates. This also helps the user to see the contradictory results while processing a specific query: for example, he can search all the parameters that were considered to Ontario dataset and the results of using them that were different through the last year.

4 Results and Discussion

This paper proposes an ontology-based system for storing information on medical diagnostics. The proposed system is focused on a specific way of storing the medical content – it allows the user not only to store standard information in a medical domain, but proposes a solution to store the ongoing research.

In the process of filling the system will save up enough data on research process, and will be able to be used for improving and simplifying the working process of physicians and researchers in the preparation of medical data. The system search will allow the user to look for the necessary results about applying different algorithms and methods to various datasets, considering the requirements of the specific features that were chosen for them.

Thus, the remote teamwork on medical research is possible with the help of this system. The main advantage of the system is its expandability in terms of information storage, as well as the ability to use ready-made ontologies to fill it. The system also has no limitations in the way the data is processed.

Future works are oriented towards improving the system and extending its database for further implementation.

References

1. Gene Ontology Consortium. The gene ontology (GO) project in 2006. Nucleic Acids Res. **34** (2006)
2. Wu, C.Y., Trappey, A.J.C., Trappey, C.V.: Using patent ontology engineering for intellectual property defense support system. In: Stjepandić, J., Rock, G., Bil, C. (eds.) Concurrent Engineering Approaches for Sustainable Product Development in a Multi-Disciplinary Environment, pp. 207–217. Springer, London (2013). doi:10.1007/978-1-4471-4426-7_18
3. El-Sappagh, S., Elmogy, M.: An encoding methodology for medical knowledge using SNOMED CT ontology. J. King Saud Univ. – Comput. Inf. Sci. **28**(3), 311–329 (2016)
4. Ivanović, M., Budimac, Z.: An overview of ontologies and data resources in medical domains. Expert Syst. Appl. **41**(11), 5158–5166 (2014)
5. Zeshan, F., Mohamad, R.: Medical ontology in the dynamic healthcare environment. Procedia Comput. Sci. **10**, 340–348 (2012)
6. Vitian, A., Gusarova, N., Artemova, G., Dobrenko, N.: An ontology approach to storing educational information. In: Proceedings of the International FRUCT Conference on Intelligence, Social Media and Web, ISMW FRUCT 2016, p. 7584772 (2016)
7. Jung, J.: Computational reputation model based on selecting consensus choices: an empirical study on semantic wiki platform. Expert Syst. Appl. **39**, 9002–9007 (2012)
8. Jung, J., Kim, K., Shin, D., Park, J.: FlowWiki: a wiki based platform for ad hoc collaborative workflows. Knowl.-Based Syst. **24**, 154–165 (2011)

9. Cramerottia, S., Ianes, D.: An ontology-based system for building individualized education plans for students with special educational needs. Procedia – Soc. Behav. Sci. **217**, 192–200 (2016)
10. Podolsky, M.D., Barchuk, A.A., Kuznetcov, V.I., Gusarova, N.F., Gaidukov, V.S., Tarakanov, S.A.: Evaluation of machine learning algorithm utilization for lung cancer classification based on gene expression levels. Asian Pac. J. Cancer Prev. **17**, 835–838 (2016)
11. Artemova, G., Gusarova, N.F., Dobrenko, N.V., Trofimov, V., Vatian, A.: Analysis of the classification methods of cancer types by computer tomography images. In: Chugunov, A. V., Bolgov, R., Kabanov, Y., Kampis, G., Wimmer, M. (eds.) DTGS 2016. CCIS, vol. 674, pp. 526–531. Springer, Cham (2016). doi:10.1007/978-3-319-49700-6_52
12. Paul, A., Sil, J., Mukhopadhyay, C.D.: Gene selection for designing optimal fuzzy rule base classifier by estimating missing value. Appl. Soft Comput. **55**, 276–288 (2017)
13. Deimling, M., Häsler, R., Steinbach, V., Holterhus, P., Spiczak, S., Stephani, U., Helbig, I., Muhle, H.: Gene expression analysis in untreated absence epilepsy demonstrates an inconsistent pattern. Epilepsy Res. **132**, 84–90 (2017)

Boosting Performance of Influenza Outbreak Prediction Framework

Nikita E. Seleznev and Vasiliy N. Leonenko[✉]

ITMO University, 49 Kronverksky Pr., 197101 St. Petersburg, Russia
ne.seleznev@gmail.com, vnleonenko@yandex.ru

Abstract. The work is dedicated to enhancing the performance of the model calibration framework used for influenza prediction in Russian cities. To increase the speed of calculations and to avoid the decreased fitting accuracy due to local minima problem, the parallelized version of the algorithm is introduced and the comparison of the available optimization methods is performed. The numerical experiments were performed on the data of influenza outbreak incidence in Moscow and Saint Petersburg. The obtained speedup of the calibration algorithm allows to work with bigger incidence datasets and obtain influenza dynamics prediction in more reasonable time compared to the initial serial algorithm. The work results can be applied to enhance performance of different healthcare decision support systems, as well as for increasing the effectiveness of decision making in adjacent areas.

Keywords: Mathematical epidemiology · Influenza · Model calibration · Parallel computing · Python

1 Introduction

The increasing popularity of informational technologies in healthcare has brought to life a new term "eHealth". This term, although widely used by scientists and healthcare officials, still does not have one officially recognized definition. Whereas some of the persons refer to eHealth when they speak solely about the local informational systems deployed in clinics and hospitals, the broader definition, for instance, that of WHO [16], also covers the application of IT for the sake of improving public health in general. Hence, the software implementation of decision support systems in the area of public health, aimed at combating diseases and reducing their negative effect, also can be considered a part of eHealth.

It is hard to overestimate the role of information and communication systems in predicting the epidemics of different infectious illnesses and, subsequently, providing data for decision making process. Particularly, the decision makers need to know what funding is required to treat the prospected number of patients, is the number of beds in hospitals enough for all the sick people, what drugs should be prepared in advance in hospitals and pharmacies, and so on. One of

© Springer International Publishing AG 2017
D.A. Alexandrov et al. (Eds.): DTGS 2017, CCIS 745, pp. 374–384, 2017.
https://doi.org/10.1007/978-3-319-69784-0_32

the infections that causes attention of the researchers is influenza that result in 3 to 5 million cases of severe illness and from 250 to 500 thousand deaths annually worldwide [17].

The infection spread in the population is a complex process at times influenced by many external and internal factors [9,14]. Thus the modeling frameworks require a lot of data for the calibration, and the calibration process itself poses big demands on the hardware performance. Due to this reason, the task of foremost importance is to find means of boosting the performance of the epidemic modeling frameworks [2,4].

In the works dedicated to modeling of influenza spread [6] and predicting the epidemic peaks [7] the authors have faced problems with calculation speed. The main reason was low performance of the optimization procedure that finds the best fit for the model curve varying the input model parameters. The optimization function, which is basically the square distance between the model points and the corresponding data points, forms a non-convex surface with various local minima, making it difficult for the optimization algorithm employed to reach global optimum. In this paper we discuss the issues connected with that problem and the ways of overcoming it with influenza prediction in Russia as a case study. The presented solutions can be used as a jumping–off point for optimizing the decision support systems which include model calibration, both in eHealth and the adjacent areas of research.

2 Problem Statement

2.1 The Model and the Fitting Algorithm

The epidemic model employed [1,3,13] was represented by the system of difference equations, with the time step equal to one day. Let x_t be the fraction of susceptibles in the population, y_t be the number of newly infected individuals at the moment t and $\overline{y_t}$ – the cumulative number of *infectious* persons (i.e. those who can transmit flu) by the time t. Then, the equation system may be written in the following manner:

$$\overline{y_t} = \sum_{\tau=0}^{T} y_{t-\tau} g_\tau, \tag{1}$$

$$y_{t+1} = \frac{\beta}{\rho} x_t \overline{y_t},$$

$$x_{t+1} = x_t - y_{t+1},$$

$$x_0 = \alpha\rho. \tag{2}$$

Here α is the initial ratio of susceptible individuals in the population, β is the intensity of infection, I_0 is initial ratio of infected in the population, T is duration of infection, ρ is the population size. The piecewise constant function g_τ gives a fraction of infectious individuals in the group of individuals infected τ days before the current moment t. The function reflects the change of individual infectiousness over time from the moment of acquiring influenza. It is assumed that there exists some moment $\bar{t}$: $\forall t \geq \bar{t}$ $g_\tau = 0$, which reflects the moment of recovery.

The original dataset for model calibration provided by the Research Institute of Influenza [12] contains weekly cumulative incidence for all the acute respiratory infections types (including flu) in three Russian cities from 1986 to 2014. Before the model fitting, we refined the incidence data by restoring the missed values and fixing the under-reporting. We also extracted flu incidence from the cumulative acute respiratory infections incidence data. Corresponding algorithms are described in detail in [5].

Let $Z^{(dat)}$ be the set of incidence data points loaded from the input file and corresponding to one particular outbreak. Assume that the number of points is t_1, which equals the observed duration of the outbreak. The basic idea of the model fitting procedure is the same for the both models. The algorithms vary the values of model parameters to achieve the model output, which minimizes the distance between the modeled and real incidence points:

$$F(Z^{(mod)}, Z^{(dat)}) = \sum_{i=0}^{t_1} (z_i^{(mod)} - z_i^{(dat)})^2, \tag{3}$$

Here $z_i^{(dat)}$ and $z_i^{(mod)}$ are the absolute incidence numbers for the i-th day taken from the input dataset and derived from the model correspondingly. By default the limited-memory BFGS optimization method was chosen to find the best fit [8]. The model parameters that are to be found by the optimization method are $k = \alpha \cdot \beta$ and I_0. Yet another model calibration parameter to be found is Δ_p, the absolute horizontal bias of the modeled incidence curve peak position compared to the data [7], but since it is discrete, and the optimization algorithm works only for continuous variables, we have to find separately the optimal values of k and I_0 for every fixed Δ_p.

Due to the aforementioned existence of several local minima, the algorithm has to be launched several times with different initial values of k, I_0. The best fit is taken as a minimum among the distances achieved from all the algorithm runs. To characterize the goodness of fit we utilize the coefficient of determination $R^2 \in (0, 1]$. This coefficient shows the fraction of the response variable variation that is explained by a model [15]. By definition of R^2 the global minimum of distance function $F(Z^{(mod)}, Z^{(dat)})$ will correspond to the global maximum of the coefficient R^2, so further on we consider our optimization problem a problem of finding the maximum of R^2.

The number of algorithm runs necessary to find the global maximum of the coefficient R^2 depends on the form of the epidemic curve given as an input. In the case if the incidence data dynamics over time has complicated form and is influenced by reporting errors or external factors, the local *maxima* problem is becoming a big issue. In Fig. 1 there is an example of non-trivial form of the epidemic curve which increases the possibility of the algorithm to miss the global maximum and fall into local maximum instead (further on we call this situation "a miss").

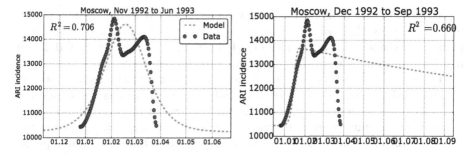

Fig. 1. Examples of the epidemic curves corresponding to the cases of satisfactory fit and a "miss" of a fitting algorithm correspondingly. Blue dots correspond to the incidence data, green dashed line represents the model curve for the continuous SEIR model [6]. (Color figure online)

To minimize the chance of finding the local minimum instead of the global one we increase the number of algorithm runs even more in the case when the value of R^2 is low. But that brought us to issues with program performance. To increase the speed of calibration procedures and hence to boost both the performance and the accuracy of the influenza forecasting framework we have regarded two approaches, which is the employment of parallel computing and the search for the optimization algorithm which can be possibly more efficient than BFGS.

3 Performance Optimization

3.1 Parallel Computing

The model calibration procedure had a definite parallel potential, because it includes several nested cycles with the iterations totally independent from one another. Particularly the model calibration includes the iteration over these parameters:

- City number
- Epidemic season number
- Number j of the algorithm run with distinct initial values for k, I_0; $j \in \overline{1,m}$
- Number i of the incidence dataset (prediction only), $i \in \overline{1,l}$.

The last cycle, unlike the first three, can be employed only for prediction [7], so it is not a very good choice for parallelization. The parallelization of the third cycle seems very perspective. However, since the number of iterations m can be chosen dynamically depending on the value of R^2 obtained on the current algorithm launch, it requires additional efforts for the workload distribution over threads. So we have decided to begin with the first two first cycles. We have defined the smallest independent task as a model calibration to the epidemic curve for the fixed city and the fixed epidemic season (for instance, Moscow,

1993–1994). In case of model calibration on retrospective data (Fig. 1) this task includes m algorithm launches with different initial values for k, I_0. In case of performing the forecast it includes $m \cdot l$ launches, i.e. m launches with different initial parameter values for i-th set of initial incidence points.

The parallel algorithm was implemented using `multiprocessing` built-in Python module. First of all, pool of threads `multiprocessing.Pool` object is instantiated with parameter `processes=multiprocessing.cpu_count()`, which means that amount of tasks executed simultaneously depends on number of available cores for computing. Then `pool.map` function takes the desired procedure reference `func` (which is one independent task) and the list of parameters `iterable`. As a result, it applies `func` to every bunch of given parameter values.

Provided that we have the sufficient number of independent tasks to be distributed, the linear speedup can be observed due to parallelism. This fact is supported by the simulation results performed on all the epidemic seasons available for Moscow – see Table 1 and Fig. 2. All computations were performed using Python 3.5.1 on a laptop with 1.80 GHz Intel CoreTM i5-3337U CPU and 12.0 GB RAM. The CPU had two physical cores with hyperthreading support.

Table 1. Computational time for different number of processes

Number of tasks	1 process, seconds	2 processes, seconds	4 processes, seconds
1	82	82	82
2	160	88	88
3	304	227	186
4	515	308	281
5	609	503	282
6	784	598	417
7	914	605	432
8	1121	660	516
9	1327	764	631
10	1477	1036	706
11	1658	1065	808
12	1713	1085	853
13	1867	1079	906
14	1920	1201	878

3.2   Comparing the Fitting Algorithms: Round 1

The speedup obtained via parallelization of the calibration algorithm facilitated the calculations a bit. Particularly, it allowed to use bigger values of m (number of algorithm launches with different initial values of k, I_0 for the particular epidemic curve), thus reducing the chance to get wrong model parameters due

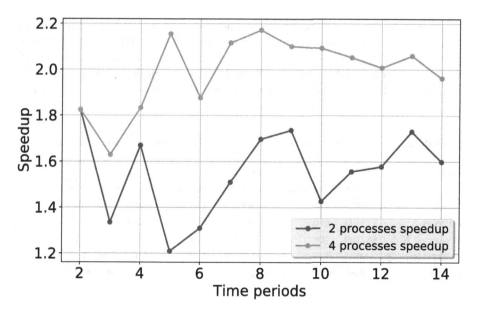

Fig. 2. Speedup curves for different processes number

to local maxima problem. However, the question still remained, whether the local maxima problem could be resolved in a more elegant way than simply increasing the number of simulation runs. We have decided to compare the efficiency of previously employed BFGS algorithm with another algorithms available "from the box" via `scipy.optimize.minimize` routine [10]. Also we have added to the list the genetic optimization algorithm, since this optimization approach is getting popular during the last years [11].

The resulting list of methods included the following ones:

- SLSQP
- L-BFGS-B
- Truncated Newton algorithm (TNC)
- Nelder-Mead
- Genetic algorithm

Let the incidence parameter I_0 be equal 10000 for every algorithm launch. To enhance the accuracy of the comparison, the initial seeds of pseudo-random number generator were chosen equal for each method compared – thus providing the same starting value of k for fixed j-th launch of every optimization method, $j \in \overline{1, m}$. Set the iteration number $m = 25$. The genetic algorithm has a different inner structure than the methods from `scipy.optimize.minimize`, so that it has not got the parameter m. Its parameters are population size and number of generations, which were set to 500 and 50 respectively.

Due to big amount of calculations we have chosen the limited dataset for the experiment. We employed the epidemic curves from Moscow in 1986–1989

(4 epidemic seasons in total). The experiment showed that the speed of convergence of the methods strongly depends on input data. Particularly, for 1986's epidemic curve all considered methods had shown almost similar value of R^2 (with the difference not more than ± 0.001). The calculation time (in seconds) and resulting R^2 estimations for the remained three epidemic curves are given in Table 2.

Table 2. Methods efficiency comparison on Moscow epidemic data, 1987–1989

Method	1987		1988		1989	
	R^2 value	Time elapsed	R^2 value	Time elapsed	R^2 value	Time elapsed
SLSQP	0.832389	225	0.809949	145	0.906502	155
L-BFGS-B	0.829263	650	0.880573	865	0.908231	3493
Truncated NC	0.832390	708	0.905172	993	0.908231	3474
Nelder-Mead	0.909165	2426	0.905333	4176	0.908246	5028
Genetic	0.832380	8027	0.902974	8051	0.908184	8039

Based on the demonstrated results, we can conclude:

1. The genetic algorithm was outperformed by all the others, because to obtain comparatively high value of R^2 it required a big increase in computation time. As a result, this algorithm was excluded from the further comparison.
2. The Nelder-Mead method is slightly more efficient in terms of seeking the best R^2, but it spends about twice much time on calculations. It is decided not to use in calculations.
3. The SLSQP method is much faster than the others, but also it is less accurate. As it can give a good compromise between the accuracy and speed, we decide to leave it for the next stage.

3.3 Comparing the Fitting Algorithms: Round 2

Based on the results of the previous section, the following methods were chosen as the main candidates for the model fitting:

- SLSQP
- L-BFGS-B
- Truncated NC

Analyzing 3D Surfaces. As an input epidemic curve for the current experiment we use the epidemic season of 2000–2001 in Saint Petersburg. Let initial fraction of the infected I_0 be 1.0 for all the simulations performed, $\Delta_p \in [-7, -6, \ldots, 6]$, $k \in [1.02; 1.4]$ [7]. The R^2 values depending from k and Δ_p are shown as 3D surfaces in Fig. 3. Here for the sake of illustration k is taken from the interval $[1.02; 1.4]$ with a fixed step. Three surfaces from left to right in every row demonstrate the ability of the fixed method to increase the found maximum with the increased number of algorithm launches ($n \in \{3, 9, 15\}$). First, n initial parameters sets (K, I_0), uniformly distributed in $[K_{min}, I_{0_{min}}]x[K_{max}, I_{0_{max}}]$ generated. Next, for each particular set, chosen method is optimizing R^2 values within the confines of given range. For instance, for three methods SLSQP, L-BFGS-B, and TNC with $n = 3$, $K \in [1.02; 1.4]$, $I_0 = 1.0$ and RNG seeds equal somewhat arbitrarily chosen as 42, initial parameters sets are the same and equal to $[(1.16233, 1.0), (1.29816, 1.0), (1.38127, 1.0)]$.

Comparison of optimization methods in this experiment is performed in order to understand which of them is less prone to the problem of local *minima*. Having the cases described in Fig. 3 considered, the following observations can be made:

(a) $n = 3$: The greatest R^2 value is shown by L-BFGS-B method, TNC is a little worse.
(b) $n = 9$: SLSQP R^2 value become closer to leaders.
(c) $n = 15$: SLSQP R^2 value is very close to others' values.

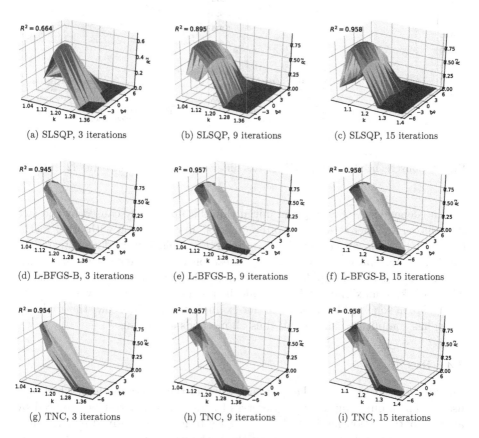

(a) SLSQP, 3 iterations   (b) SLSQP, 9 iterations   (c) SLSQP, 15 iterations

(d) L-BFGS-B, 3 iterations   (e) L-BFGS-B, 9 iterations   (f) L-BFGS-B, 15 iterations

(g) TNC, 3 iterations   (h) TNC, 9 iterations   (i) TNC, 15 iterations

Fig. 3. R^2 surfaces

382   N.E. Seleznev and V.N. Leonenko

Convergence to Global Maximum and the Influence of RNG Initial Seeds. In this experiment we show the gradual convergence of the methods towards the optimal R^2 with $m \in \overline{1, 50}$. The value of the parameter I_0 is set to 1.0 for all measurements. The epidemic curve under study corresponds to Moscow epidemic outbreak in 2000–2001. Since the initial value of the pseudo-random number generator (or, shortly, RNG initial seeds) and, consequently, the initial values of k may influence on the method convergence to global maximum of R^2, we have considered two different values of RNG initial seeds (chosen somewhat arbitrarily as 42 and 420). The results are given in Fig. 4. The difference between Fig. 4a and b shows that SLSQP method depends on the initial seed and, consequently, on the good guess of initial values for k, in order to achieve better convergence, while the two remaining methods are less vulnerable to wrong choice of the initial values. This result was also reproduced on several other input epidemic curves.

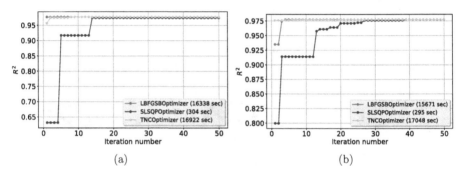

Fig. 4. Convergence to optimal R^2 for two different initial RNG seeds (a) 42, (b) 420

The dependence of SLSQP on initial values is apparently caused by the fact that due to its inner structure it often "misses" in comparison with other methods, and thus slowly converges to optimal R^2. This fact is demonstrated in Fig. 5a, which represents the values of R^2 established by the algorithms on each algorithm launch (2011 epidemic outbreak in Moscow serving as a case study), without taking maximum of R^2 from all the previous launches. However, as seen in Fig. 5b, in some epidemic seasons (for example, 1987 in Moscow) the epidemic curve has complicated shape and thus all methods often "miss".

3.4   Results

Finally, we need to answer the question, whether the BFGS method, which was used so far in our computations, deserves to stay, or it is better be replaced by another optimization method. As we can see from the performed experiments, in most cases the TNC method gives the best result, but at a cost of reduced performance compared to L-BFGS-B. The advantage of the SLSQP method that cannot be disputed is that for the same input it is 20–80 times faster than the

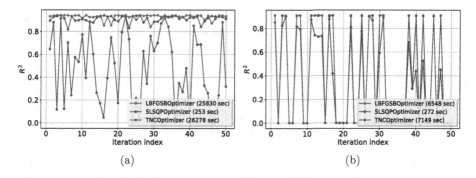

Fig. 5. R^2 values for different iteration numbers of initial k, I_0 in the Moscow city

others methods. We have decided that using SLSQP method with an increased number m of algorithm launches can give us the quality of fitting compared to BFGS and at the same time help us gain a significant speedup.

4   Discussion and Future Works

In this work we have found out that SLSQP method employed along with the parallelized version of the initial serial calibration algorithm demonstrates faster performance and facilitates greatly the model calibration and influenza peak prediction using the modeling framework. The obtained result will help us handle the data of influenza prevalence among different age groups and calibrate the corresponding influenza model to this data.

We need to admit that this conclusion has limited generalization on the calibration models for other input and other differential model types, as probably the efficiency of the different methods is strongly dependent on the shape of the optimization function and the number of local minima it has. The more general conclusion we made is that the methods convergence can strongly depends on the initial parameter values, and the force of this effect is correlated to the complexity of the optimization function shape, particularly – its number of local minima in the selected argument interval.

The future work to be done on the matter described in this paper is to try the alternative parallel version of the program that includes parallelization by the number of simulation run $j \in \overline{1, m}$ with dynamic task distribution over threads. Also it is worth investigating whether we can enhance the SLSQP method productivity by changing its parameters. Current experiments on varying the method maximum precision (`ftol`) and the maximum number of iterations (`maxiter`) did not demonstrated any fruitful results, so our next step is to try the third parameter, the step size for numerical approximation of the Jacobi matrix determinant (`eps`), which apparently has a more complex nature.

Acknowledgements. The authors are thankful to the two anonymous referees who helped to improve significantly the quality of the paper. This paper is financially supported by The Russian Scientific Foundation, Agreement #14-21-00137.

References

1. Baroyan, O.V., Genchikov, L.A., Rvachev, L.A., Shashkov, V.A.: An attempt at large-scale influenza epidemic modelling by means of a computer. Bull. Int. Epidemiol. Assoc. **18**, 22–31 (1969)
2. Emrich, S., Breitenecker, F., Zauner, G., Popper, N.: Simulation of influenza epidemics with a hybrid model-combining cellular automata and agent based features. 30th International Conference on Information Technology Interfaces, ITI 2008. IEEE (2008). doi:10.1109/ITI.2008.4588498
3. Ivannikov, Y.G, Ismagulov, A.T.: Epidemiologiya grippa (The epidemiology of influenza). Almaty, Kazakhstan (1983). (in Russian)
4. Leonenko, V.N., Pertsev, N.V., Artzrouni, M.: Using high performance algorithms for the hybrid simulation of disease dynamics on CPU and GPU. Procedia Comput. Sci. **51**, 150–159 (2015)
5. Leonenko, V.N., Ivanov, S.V., Novoselova, Y.K.: A computational approach to investigate patterns of acute respiratory illness dynamics in the regions with distinct seasonal climate transitions. Procedia Comput. Sci. **80**, 2402–2412 (2016)
6. Leonenko, V.N., Ivanov, S.V.: Fitting the SEIR model of seasonal influenza outbreak to the incidence data for Russian cities. Russ. J. Numer. Anal. Math. Model. **31**(5), 267–279 (2016)
7. Leonenko, V.N., Ivanov, S.V.: Influenza peaks prediction in Russian cities: comparing the accuracy of two SEIR models. Math. Biosci. Eng. **15**(1) (2018). doi:10.3934/mbe.2018009
8. Liu, D., Nocedal, J.: On the limited memory BFGS method for large-scale optimization. Math. Program. **45**, 503–528 (1989)
9. Manfredi, P., D'Onofrio, A.: Modeling the Interplay Between Human Behavior and the Spread of Infectious Diseases. Springer Science and Business Media, Berlin (2013)
10. Optimization and root finding (scipy.optimize). https://docs.scipy.org/doc/scipy-0.18.1/reference/optimize.html
11. Presbitero, A., Krzhizhanovskaya, V., Mancini, E., Brands, R., Sloot, P.: Immune system model calibration by genetic algorithm. Procedia. Comput. Sci. **101**, 161–171 (2016)
12. Research Institute of Influenza website. http://influenza.spb.ru/en/
13. Rvachev, L.A., Longini, I.M.: A mathematical model for the global spread of influenza. Math. Biosci. **75**(1), 3–22 (1985)
14. Tamerius, J., Nelson, M.I., Zhou, S.Z., Viboud, C., Miller, M.A., Alonso, W.J.: Global influenza seasonality: reconciling patterns across temperate and tropical regions. Environ. Health Perspect. **119**(4), 439 (2011)
15. Van Noort, S.P., Aguas, R., Ballesteros, S., Gomes, M.G.M.: The role of weather on the relation between influenza and influenza-like illness. J. Theor. Biol. **298**, 131–137 (2012)
16. WHO: eHealth at WHO. http://www.who.int/ehealth/about/en/
17. WHO: Influenza (seasonal). Fact sheet No. 211, March 2014. http://www.who.int/mediacentre/factsheets/fs211/en/

Dynamically Integrating Electronic - With Personal Health Records for Ad-hoc Healthcare Quality Improvements

Aleksandr Kormiltsyn[✉] and Alex Norta

Department of Software Science, Tallinn University of Technology,
Akadeemia tee 15A, 12816 Tallinn, Estonia
alexandrkormiltsyn@gmail.com, alex.norta.phd@ieee.org

Abstract. Despite the great potential for healthcare professionals, individuals and researchers, the integration of healthcare information from Electronic Health Records (EHR) and Personal Health Records (PHR) systems is complicated because of structural and semantic heterogeneity. Existing ways of PHR- and EHR-collection include harvesting medical and individual data from different data sources that store different medical, not standardized data. Such a heterogeneity increases the complexity of merging PHR and EHR. We focus on the integration process as a main aspect for solving the heterogeneity issue. Thereby, we aim at reducing the merging complexity by defining the requirements for PHR data collection and creating an ontology for a semantically sound dataset merger for personal-centric healthcare systems and we evaluate the results with formal means.

Keywords: Personal health records · Health information exchange · Health information systems · Ontology

1 Introduction

In recent years, Personal Health Records (PHR) have emerged as a patient-centric model of health information exchange [12]. The main principle of PHR is that a person is the author and owner of his/her medical data that can be shared with other individuals including healthcare professionals, or automated clinical decision-support services, e.g., Evidence-Based Medicine electronic Decision Support (EBMeDS)[1]. The growing amount of personal data available increases the role of personal-centric systems in healthcare. The classic explanation of Electronic Health Records (EHR) assumes that EHRs are created and maintained by medical professionals.

The complex analysis and processing of an integrated PHR with EHR improves the quality of healthcare by helping to mitigate diagnosis errors involving patients in healthcare decisions [15]. As EHR contains data mostly of patient

---

[1] http://www.ebmeds.org/.

© Springer International Publishing AG 2017
D.A. Alexandrov et al. (Eds.): DTGS 2017, CCIS 745, pp. 385–399, 2017.
https://doi.org/10.1007/978-3-319-69784-0_33

diseases, PHR contains information about a patient's lifestyle, activity and regular health-state measurements, e.g., blood pressure and blood glucose taken at home. Integrated EHR and PHR cover the whole lifetime period of individuals and thus, enables the understanding of the context for an individual's health state.

Literature review [4,6,24] shows that most researchers provide solutions for integration challenges based on data-heterogeneity reduction in a static way by developing a new ontology, or merging existing ones. This approach is efficient for decreasing the heterogeneity of different EHR standards and a limited number of processes. However, the amount of PHR data is rapidly growing with the development of new applications and devices. The number of processes using PHR is not limited, as PHR data is also used by shared workflows. Therefore, an efficient integration of PHR and EHR requires a dynamic approach that concentrates on the process as a basis for the efficient dynamic integration of EHR and PHR, rather than focusing on data standardization. Paying attention to data-flow processes is an important part of EHR and PHR data integration as health data flows along processes in the distributed system.

This paper fills the gap by researching the integration process of PHR and EHR in the context of dynamic decentralized person-centric systems. The main research question is how to collect and process PHR data in the context of integrated healthcare to improve the quality of diagnostics and cures. The data collection process takes place before the integration and its proper definition helps to integrate only needed data by filtering out noise for a specific healthcare-process goal. We deduce the following sub-questions from the main research question. What are the requirements for the PHR data collection? The answer to this question aims at filtering noise in preparation for EHR mergers. What is the ontology for the integration process? The ontology decreases the integration complexity while data is merged in the contexts of different processes. What is the integration process for merging dynamically EHR and PHR in a targeted way? The definition of an integration process is based on the ontology and results in a better understanding of the context where the collected data is used.

The remainder of the paper is structured as follows. Section 2 presents related work and Sect. 3 discusses requirements for PHR data collection. Next, Sect. 4 gives an ontology for the integration of processes and Sect. 5 address the integration process of PHR and EHR. Section 6 compares the results of this paper to other research work and finally, Sect. 7 concludes the paper together with providing directions for future research.

2   Related Work

We present important background literature that is the foundation for the sequel of this paper. Traditional solutions for solving interoperability issues in the healthcare domain include using a common data standard. Research [21] proves that Fast Healthcare Interoperability Resources (FHIR) [3] support PHR data and can be used for EHR-sharing. Research [23] presents the development of a Systematized Nomenclature of Medicine Clinical Terms (SNOMED CT) [25] query module that can convert a patient problem description, or clinical measurements into SNOMED CT codes. The Health Level 7 (HL7 CDA) [7] may store personal health information in a standardized way in these resulting documents. Logical Observation Identifiers Names and Codes (LOINC) [14] are used for identifying medical laboratory observations and exchanging laboratory-test information between healthcare and laboratory providers.

On the other hand, the use of an ontology can overcome issues of semantic and syntactic heterogeneity of health data to facilitate record linkage [8]. Research [10] proposes an ontology of a context information model as a basis for building u-healthcare services. Ubiquitous Healthcare means a system monitors bio-information in real-time using certain devices such as mobile equipment in a home network and provides medical examination with treatment whenever and wherever needed. Another approach for reducing the heterogeneity of health data is to provide a Wearable KaaS platform [10] to smartly manage heterogeneous data coming from wearable devices in order to assist the physicians in supervising the patient health evolution and keep the patient up-to-date about his/her status. The latter approach describes a wearable healthcare ontology.

Other researchers state that an ontology decreases the complexity of sharing medical data between different healthcare information systems and different databases when being used together with Internet-of-Things (IoT) platforms [11]. In research [16], ontologies are used for giving meaning to the silos of heterogeneous wearable data in healthcare. Furthermore, the ontology focuses on the integration process and does not describe the process of data collection that is performed before the integration takes place.

According to [26], the Agent Oriented Modelling (AOM) approach is geared towards designing socio-technical systems consisting of humans and software that are respectively termed as human agents and man-made agents. Research [13] provides the solution for heterogeneity as development of software agents and systems that attempt to reconcile ontological differences without explicit formal ontologies.

We build non-human agents to support common international healthcare data standards to reduce the complexity of data extraction. We create an ontology to define the integration process supporting agents. The AOM approach is projected to the healthcare domain to reduce heterogeneity problems.

3   Requirements for PHR Data Collection

Processing individual data from different data-sources improves the quality of healthcare processes while it simultaneously creates new challenges. According to research [28], there exists no clear definition of PHR and the PHR data is not on a sufficient level of quality to be useful for medical decision making. Also a graphical user interface for PHR systems should be familiar to the user to reduce possible errors during data input. In contrast to PHR challenges, EHR systems exist on a national level[2] and have common data standards with international classifiers as HL7, SNOMED CT and LOINC. The decentralization of PHR results in a complex merging of PHR with EHR for further processing. To reach our goal, we must explore the requirements for PHR data.

In Sect. 3.1, we analyze the stakeholders for the integration process to place the scope for the domain being analyzed. Stakeholders are then used as human agents in the goal model that guides requirement elaboration. The goal model consists of functional and quality goals, their sub-goals and actors. In Sect. 3.2, we define primary goals for the stakeholders and sub goals. The list of goals and sub goals is used for requirements generation.

3.1   Stakeholders of Integration Process

Before defining system- and software-requirements, the stakeholders are defined [29]. In the scope of integrated healthcare, there are different main stakeholders: individuals, researchers, healthcare professionals, state organizational units as statistics- and social departments, and insurance companies. Individuals are users of PHR systems who receive personalized medical services and use personal information to improve their health state. The improvement is achieved by receiving recommendations and reminders from Clinical Decision Support System (CDSS) processing personal data. Researchers improve the healthcare analysis results by combining both PHR and EHR. Healthcare professionals improve the quality of decision making processes that use both data from healthy and sickly periods of an individual's life. The integration of EHR and PHR improves the healthcare processes of the state by improving preventive healthcare. Insurance companies provide personalized services to individuals and businesses for encouraging a healthier way of life.

3.2   Domain Analysis and Design

Figure 1 presents a goal model, comprising functional- and quality goals with each goal decomposed into sub-goals hierarchically from top to bottom. In the person-centric system, there are both human- and non-human agents. According to [20], analyzing the problem of this socio-technical domain can be performed by using a goal model. The objective of goal models is to serve as communication media between technical- and non-technical stakeholders for generating understandable domain knowledge. We use goal models in the context of requirements-engineering processes.

The main goal is *Prevent disease* that has quality goals. The system offers some advantages to the individual to prevent diseases in the future. Quality goals: scalable, modifiable, integrable, interoperable and secure are the main quality requirements for the cross-ogranizational systems [19]. The main goal splits into two sub-goals: *Provide home care* in a regular manner and *Provide ambulatory care* assuming that it is available. The first comprises two goals: *Monitor health*

---

[2] www.etervis.ee.

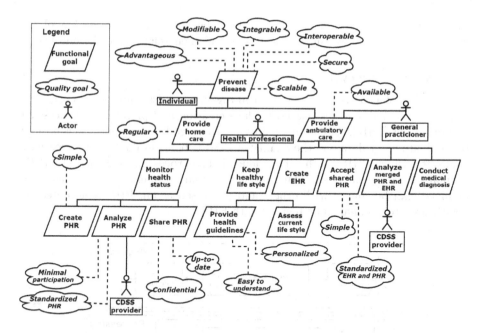

Fig. 1. The goal model for the personal-centric healthcare system.

status and *Keep healthy lifestyle* that involves the role of health professional and includes two goals *Provide health guidelines* and *Assess current life style*. Guidelines should be easy to understand for the individual and personalized to his specific needs. *Monitor health status* goal includes three sub-goals: *Create PHR* in a simple way, *Analyse PHR* performed by the role of CDSS provider with a minimal participation of an individual using standardized PHR, *Share PHR* including quality requirements that correspond to the security and relevance.

The goal *Provide ambulatory care* has four sub-goals. Two of them are related to the processing of shared PHR: *Accept shared PHR* and *Analyze merged PHR and EHR* performed by a CDSS provider. Accepting shared PHR needs to be simple enough for general practitioners in order to improve the results of ambulatory care. PHR and EHR should be standardized in order to prevent semantic heterogeneity. Other sub-goals correspond to the standard ambulatory care process are *Create EHR* and *Conduct medical diagnosis*.

4   An Ontology for the Integration Process

The processing of integrating EHR and PHR requires an ontology definition to reduce semantic- and syntactic heterogeneity. Health and medical knowledge existing in both EHR and PHR is presented as an artifact in an artifact-centric business process model (ABPM) and being processed by different organizations. To build an ontology, we define the lifecycles for EHR, PHR and the merged artifact in Sect. 4.1. In Sect. 4.2, we present a meta-data model for the ontology that covers the surrounding system for the integrated data. Section 4.3 explains in more details the most important classes and their relations in the ontology.

4.1   Artifact Lifecycle

The lifecycle of a common data artifact in Fig. 2, comprises three stages [22]. The acquisition includes states related to data creation and preliminary processing before storing. PHR is entered manually, or generated by smart devices, is filtered to eliminate noisy data and the quality of PHR is being evaluated to increase its value after which PHR can then be amended. The processing stage includes PHR normalization and analysis. During the preservation stage, PHR is classified, archived, can be shared with others and processed again. PHR is accepted by healthcare professional to be merged with EHR.

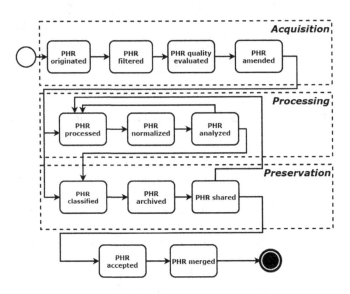

Fig. 2. PHR lifecycle

After an EHR is created in Fig. 3, it is verified and amended. Processing includes three states, i.e., processed, de-identified and analyzed. Depending on the agent type being either human or non human, EHR needs to be de-identified first. Preservation consists of classification, archiving and exporting. After the EHR is available for export, it can be used in other legal organizations and merged with shared PHR.

The merged artifact in Fig. 4, is originated after PHR and EHR are merged, verified and described before processing or preservation. The processing includes states processed, de-identified and analyzed. If an individual restricts access to personal data, a merged artifact is not preserved but can be processed. In the preservation stage, the merged artifact is classified, archived and exported to external systems.

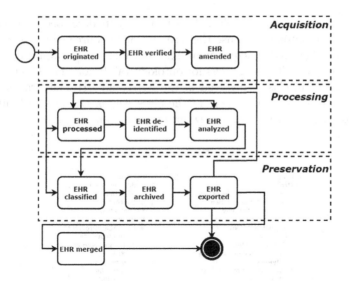

Fig. 3. EHR life cycle

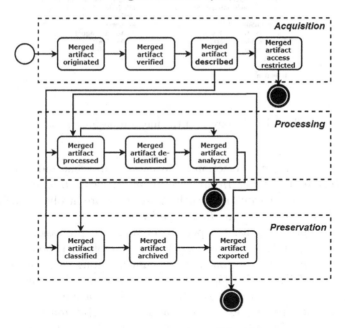

Fig. 4. Merged artifact lifecycle

4.2 A Meta-data Model for the Integration Process

We consider the merged artifact in the context of a decentralized and distributed person-centric system. The meta-data model covers main classes involved in the integration process. We use an ontology engineering approach described in [9] and combine this approach with assistant agents described in research [13]. For building an ontology, we use the free and open source editor, Protégé [18], for systematic knowledge acquisition. The tool includes a graphical user interface, plugins and built-in reasoners for ontology validation. The OWL-ontology[3] describes the main classes involved in the EHR and PHR integration process. In OWL, every class is derived from the class *Thing*. Due to the limitation of space we divided class hierarchy view into two columns and give an explanation below (Fig. 5).

Fig. 5. The class hierarchy of the integration-process ontology

An *Activity* represents the action performed by an agent and can be specific to the healthcare provider as *HealthCareProviderActivity*. *Interaction* describes an action where both person and health professional are involved. Each activity has *ActivityResult* that contains *Reccomendation*.

An *Agent* represents either a person, or a health professional as *Person*, or non-human agent (*NonHumanAgent*). An example of a non-human agent is CDSS, that supports a person with recommendations. We consider believe-desire-intention (BDI) agents [5] as non-human agents. This concept provides a separation of the activity of selecting a plan from a library, or an external planner application from the execution of active plans. *AnthropomorphicProperty* represents features of non-human agents that resemble human behaviour.

HealthKnowledge contains useful information for changing the health status of a person. In our case, it can be either *DiagnosisProbability* or *Risk* specific to a person. The *Information* contains classes responsible for information about a person's health such as *HealthRecord*, or *Guideline*. Health information is needed when a clinical decision happens based on the health knowledge.

---

[3] https://goo.gl/v5ybCY.

Classes *LifeStyle* and *Behavior* are equal from the point of view that a person's lifestyle is the behavior of an agent. A *Resource* is used in the context of activities and represents the resources needed to collect and process PHR and EHR. An *Active* resource is an agent that collects and processes data. *Passive* resource is usually a device, generating the information.

4.3   Ontology Graphs

The following graphs present the most important classes of the ontology from the meta-model. Important related classes and relations between them we described below.

4.3.1   Class Person

The ontology of Fig. 6 focuses on the *Person* class that has *Motivation* to improve his, or other persons' *Health*. *Awareness* of health status helps *Person* to maintain a healthy *Lifestyle*. A *Person* can be at the same time a *HealthProfessional*, or a *GeneralPractitioner*. A *HealthRecord* includes health related information of a *Person* and can be a *PersonalHealthRecord* that is owned by a *Person*, or an *ElectronicHealthRecord* that is created by a *HealthSpecialst*. The *Interaction* involves an *Agent* that can be a *Person*, *HealthKnowledge* is either derived from *ClinicalDecisionSupportSystem*, or a *HealthSpecialist* and *Information* that can be a *Guideline*. *HealthKnowledge* includes *DiagnosisProbability* and a *Risk* related to health.

4.3.2   Class HealthCareProviderActivity

Class *HealthCareProviderActivity* covers in Fig. 7 different types of activities that can be performed in the healthcare center. Those include *Intervention* that

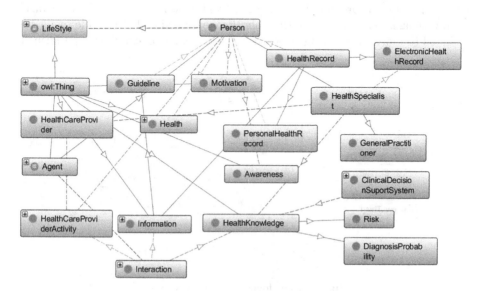

Fig. 6. *Person* focus and neighbouring classes.

attempts to change the status of a persons health, *ClinicalObservation* that generates information about health, *DiagnosticStudy* that describes the actions needed for diagnosis determination. The activity *LogisticsActivity* supports other healthcare-provider processes, such as admission to a ward unit. *HealthCare-ProviderActivity* is an *Activity* that has a transitional relation to *Resource* that can be *Active* or *Passive*. *Interaction* is another type of activity and describes the contact between person and healthcare specialist while class *HealthCare-ProviderActivity* contains only activities specific to *HealthCareProvider*. Each activity has *ActivityResult* that can be a *Reccommendation* to the person.

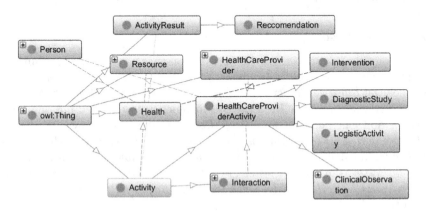

Fig. 7. *HealthCareProviderActivity* focus and related classes.

4.3.3   Class Agent

Class *Agent* that is presented in Fig. 8 has two types: *Person* and *NonHumanAgent*. One agent can have more than one *Role* assigned and also a role might be assigned to more than one agent at the same time. An *Evaluation* is performed

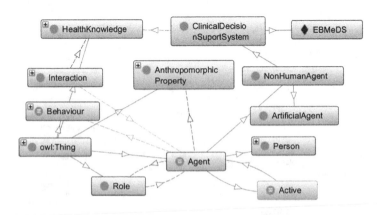

Fig. 8. *Agent* focus and related classes.

by an agent that has a *Behaviour*. The *AntropomorphicProperty* includes features of artificial agents that are made to resemble human characterstics. The sub-classes of *AnthropomorphicProperty* are presented as BDI-agents.

5   Integration Process

We describe the integration process in Fig. 9 with the Business Process Model and Notation (BPMN) [1], a graphical representation for specifying business process model. The integration process is dynamic and involves both human and non-human agents. Non-human agents are software components that communicate with each other and support human agents with appropriate results. To solve heterogeneity issues for the integration process, we use assistant agents as described in research [13]. A human agent initiates the process that has information about data needed to be processed and an agent responsible for processing. After the process starts, the artificial agent defines the required data, that is needed to reach the final goal of the process.

PHR- and EHR data are retrieved in parallel in Fig. 9 by the same, or different agents from a PHR- and EHR-managing system. After the data is retrieved, it is filtered for noise. An agent has information about processing input requirements and if the filtered data cannot be processed as is, it is merged. During the merge task, an error can occur, if it is not possible to merge the data. After the merge, data is validated and then confirmed by a human agent if needed. Different data sources can contain duplicate- or conflicting data. The data collected by each agent is processed and the results are compared. The most appropriate selected data are presented to the human agent.

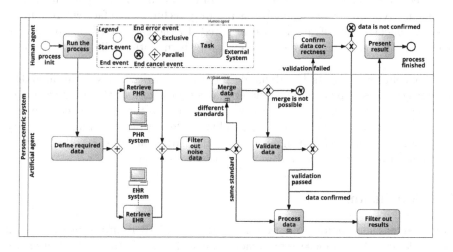

Fig. 9. BPMN diagram for the integration process

6   Discussions

Literature review shows that mostly research focuses on either decreasing the heterogeneity by merging ontologies, or the usage of a common standard. Some research considers the usage of multi-agent systems (MAS) for improving the integration processes in healthcare between EHR systems [2,27]. In our research we use ontology in a different manner to define the integration process itself and not the data processed. Also we extend the usage of MAS to enable integration between EHR and PHR systems.

We define the integration process as a basis for healthcare quality improvement where both individual and healthcare professional are involved. As the number of PHR data sources is not limited, we first define requirements to PHR collection to filter out noise data first. Then we define an ontology for the integration process in order to set up main entities and their relations in the scope of simultaneously processing of PHR and EHR. The ontology includes both the individual's and healthcare specialist's area of responsibility that are in a close relationship. Finally, we define the integration process as an interaction between healthcare professional and assistant agent in MAS that support the human agent with intelligent and dynamic healthcare-data processing.

An evaluation of the ontology we perform with the HermiT reasoner that is based on a novel hypertableau calculus [17] to provide much more efficient reasoning than any previously known algorithm. The integration process we validate with the Signavio[4] tool that checks BPMN diagrams for existing conflicts. We evaluate our solution by analyzing similar research results and using the framework for evaluation in design-science research (FEDS) [30]. We select the evaluation goal as rigor because we want to ensure that our artifact causes an observed outcome. The integration process of EHR and PHR happens in a socio-technical environment and therefore is a purely technical artefact where human risk and effectiveness strategies are required. In the context of this paper, we determine the technical properties to evaluate the maintainability and functionality.

Our solution presents the dynamic integration process. Its maintainability assumes changes implementation via new agent creations, or the modification of existing ones. If we need to add a new data source to the process then we just need to add a new agent. The functionality of design includes interoperability as a main process for collecting and processing data. Data that is collected from different data sources is filtered by its accuracy and context.

7   Conclusion

We consider the dynamic integration of EHR and PHR from the process based point of view. We propose requirements for collecting PHR in the context of healthcare quality improvement. Then we define an ontology for the integration process describing main classes and their relations involved in the integration.

---

[4] https://www.signavio.com/.

Finally, we use an ontology for building the process by using a BPMN notation that includes both human- and non-human agent interactions.

To improve the quality of diagnostics and cures, PHR data needs to be collected continuously by a person. PHR is either entered manually, or imported from external PHR-based system. Processing of PHR requires filtering out noise first and happens in a dynamic way with participation of both human- and non-human agents. Requirements for PHR data collection are aimed to meet the main functional goal of preventing disease. To meet that goal, data is collected by a person in a simple and trustful way and support data sharing options with healthcare professionals. The ontology for the integration process focuses on a person and his activities. The integration process includes BDI agents reducing the problem of data heterogeneity problems by dividing the functionality and responsibility for data collection from different data sources and processing. The integration process starts from a required data definition that limits the scope of valued data. After the required PHR and EHR data is collected, noise data is filtered out first. If collected data is not standardized it is merged and validated. After processing, the results are filtered in order to present only valuable information.

We evaluated the design presented in this paper by comparing the results to other research results in the same area. Literature review shows that other research solves healthcare data heterogeneity problems without considering the merge problem in the context of an integration process. We define a dynamic integration process as a solution for healthcare quality improvement. Still, the design presented in this paper lacks a real use case and social evaluation as it involves individuals and healthcare professionals. Future work comprises conducting a case-study based evaluation of the design and prototyping technical solutions in order to ensure the compatibility with existing processes in healthcare.

References

1. Allweyer, T.: BPMN 2.0: introduction to the standard for business process modeling. BoD-Books on Demand (2016)
2. Bainbridge, D., Brazil, K., Ploeg, J., Krueger, P., Taniguchi, A.: Measuring healthcare integration: operationalization of a framework for a systems evaluation of palliative care structures, processes, and outcomes. Palliat. Med. **30**(6), 567–579 (2016)
3. Bender, D., Sartipi, K.: HL7 FHIR: an agile and restful approach to healthcare information exchange. In: 2013 IEEE 26th International Symposium on Computer-Based Medical Systems (CBMS), pp. 326–331. IEEE (2013)
4. del Carmen Legaz-García, M., Martínez-Costa, C., Menárguez-Tortosa, M., Fernández-Breis, J.T.: A semantic web based framework for the interoperability and exploitation of clinical models and ehr data. Knowl.-Based Syst. **105**, 175–189 (2016)
5. Casali, A., Godo, L., Sierra, C.: A graded BDI agent model to represent and reason about preferences. Artif. Intell. **175**(7–8), 1468–1478 (2011)

6. Dogac, A., Laleci, G.B., Kirbas, S., Kabak, Y., Sinir, S.S., Yildiz, A., Gurcan, Y.: Artemis: deploying semantically enriched web services in the healthcare domain. Inf. Syst. **31**(4), 321–339 (2006)

7. Dolin, R.H., Alschuler, L., Boyer, S., Beebe, C., Behlen, F.M., Biron, P.V., Shabo, A.: HL7 clinical document architecture, release 2. J. Am. Med. Inform. Assoc. **13**(1), 30–39 (2006)

8. Duncan, J., Eilbeck, K., Narus, S.P., Clyde, S., Thornton, S., Staes, C.: Building an ontology for identity resolution in healthcare and public health. Online J. Publ. Health Inform. **7**(2) (2015)

9. Fernández-López, M., Gómez-Pérez, A., Juristo, N.: Methontology: from ontological art towards ontological engineering (1997)

10. Kim, J., Chung, K.Y.: Ontology-based healthcare context information model to implement ubiquitous environment. Multimedia Tools Appl. **71**(2), 873–888 (2014)

11. Kumar, V.: Ontology based public healthcare system in internet of things (IOT). Procedia Comput. Sci. **50**, 99–102 (2015)

12. Li, M., Yu, S., Zheng, Y., Ren, K., Lou, W.: Scalable and secure sharing of personal health records in cloud computing using attribute-based encryption. IEEE Trans. Parallel Distrib. Syst. **24**(1), 131–143 (2013)

13. Lister, K., Sterling, L., Taveter, K.: Reconciling ontological differences by assistant agents. In: Proceedings of 5th International Joint Conference on Autonomous Agents and Multiagent Systems, pp. 943–945. ACM (2006)

14. McDonald, C.J., Huff, S.M., Suico, J.G., Hill, G., Leavelle, D., Aller, R., Forrey, A., Mercer, K., DeMoor, G., Hook, J., et al.: LOINC, a universal standard for identifying laboratory observations: a 5-year update. Clin. Chem. **49**(4), 624–633 (2003)

15. McDonald, K.M., Bryce, C.L., Graber, M.L.: The patient is in: patient involvement strategies for diagnostic error mitigation. BMJ Qual. Saf. (BMJQS-2012) (2013)

16. Mezghani, E., Exposito, E., Drira, K., Da Silveira, M., Pruski, C.: A semantic big data platform for integrating heterogeneous wearable data in healthcare. J. Med. Syst. **39**(12), 1–8 (2015)

17. Motik, B., Shearer, R., Horrocks, I.: Hypertableau reasoning for description logics. J. Artif. Intell. Res. **36**, 165–228 (2009)

18. Musen, M.A.: The protégé project: a look back and a look forward. AI matters **1**(4), 4–12 (2015)

19. Norta, A., Grefen, P., Narendra, N.C.: A reference architecture for managing dynamic inter-organizational business processes. Data Knowl. Eng. **91**, 52–89 (2014)

20. Norta, A., Mahunnah, M., Tenso, T., Taveter, K., Narendra, N.C.: An agent-oriented method for designing large socio-technical service-ecosystems. In: 2014 IEEE World Congress on Services, pp. 242–249. IEEE (2014)

21. Pais, S., Parry, D., Huang, Y.: Suitability of fast healthcare interoperability resources (FHIR) for wellness data. In: Proceedings of 50th Hawaii International Conference on System Sciences (2017)

22. Sinaeepourfard, A., Garcia, J., Masip, X., et al.: A comprehensive scenario agnostic data lifecycle model for an efficient data complexity management. In: IEEE 12th International Conference on E-Science (e-Science), Baltimore, USA (2016)

23. Song, Y.T., Qiu, T.: Standard based personal mobile health record system. In: Proceedings of 10th International Conference on Ubiquitous Information Management and Communication, p. 12. ACM (2016)

24. Sonsilphong, S., Arch-int, N., Arch-int, S., Pattarapongsin, C.: A semantic interoperability approach to health-care data: resolving data-level conflicts. Expert Syst. **33**(6), 531–547 (2016)

25. Stearns, M.Q., Price, C., Spackman, K.A., Wang, A.Y.: SNOMED clinical terms: overview of the development process and project status. In: Proceedings of AMIA Symposium, p. 662. American Medical Informatics Association (2001)

26. Sterling, L., Taveter, K.: The Art of Agent-Oriented Modeling. MIT Press, Cambridge (2009)

27. Tello-Leal, E., Villarreal, P.D., Chiotti, O., Rios-Alvarado, A.B., Lopez-Arevalo, I.: A technological solution to provide integrated and process-oriented care services in healthcare organizations. IEEE Trans. Ind. Inf. **12**(4), 1508–1518 (2016)

28. Urbauer, P., Sauermann, S., Frohner, M., Forjan, M., Pohn, B., Mense, A.: Applicability of IHE/Continua components for PHR systems: learning from experiences. Comput. Biol. Med. **59**, 186–193 (2015)

29. Van Lamsweerde, A.: Requirements Engineering: From System Goals to UML Models to Software Specifications. Wiley, Hoboken (2009)

30. Venable, J., Pries-Heje, J., Baskerville, R.: FEDS: a framework for evaluation in design science research. Eur. J. Inf. Syst. **25**(1), 77–89 (2016)

Survey of Electronic Workflow for Russian Healthcare Services

Irina Sergeeva[✉], Ariadna Aleksandrova, Yulia Ryabukhina,
and Ekaterina Ostapovets

ITMO University, St. Petersburg, Russia
igsergeeva@gmail.com, aariadna@mail.ru,
yvryabukhina@corp.ifmo.ru, kateostapovets@gmail.com

Abstract. The article discusses the issues of using e-health technologies and analyses the quality of Internet access for health care services in Russia and the CIS. The paper presents a critical research of financing the introduction of information technologies in health care services in various regions of Russia and proves the necessity of developing and implementing regional standards, the system of certifying both IT services and new types of health care activities. In order to create a single healthcare space, the authors suggest the principle of systematic approach to introducing information technologies in Russian healthcare services.

To evaluate the economic efficiency of medical information technologies the authors present various methods based on the specific features of Russian healthcare service. The paper suggests using the Total Cost of Ownership method to assess the efficiency of IT systems as it is this method that can provide a comparative analysis of costs incurred in implementation and maintenance of information technologies. The paper provides a detailed analysis of the benefits of implementing electronic health records for outpatient and hospital healthcare services. The assessment of cost and outcome results in the evaluation of the economic efficiency of implementing IT in medicine.

Keywords: E-health · Informatization of healthcare · Experience in the implementation of information systems in medicine · Electronic document management · The effectiveness of information technology in medicine

1 Introduction: IT for E-Healthcare

The progress of modern medicine and healthcare is largely dependent on information technologies (IT). Modern computer science offers the following common, largely non-specific tools:

- global and local networks;
- personal computers with multimedia tools;
- databases, graphic systems and other means of developing automated medical jobs;
- computerized equipment for diagnosis and treatment;
- microprocessor modules for medical equipment.

© Springer International Publishing AG 2017
D.A. Alexandrov et al. (Eds.): DTGS 2017, CCIS 745, pp. 400–414, 2017.
https://doi.org/10.1007/978-3-319-69784-0_34

The entire IT development process is aimed at creating a single medical information space that allows physicians communicate, access archives and libraries of medical knowledge and technologies, and interact with functioning equipment directly from the workplace and in real time.

In modern economic environment, modernization of the healthcare system can be based on the rational use of existing tools and modern IT.

Healthcare models in most countries are based on the market principle of the reproduction of the demand for medical services: demand $\rightarrow$ meeting the demand $\rightarrow$ profit $\rightarrow$ stimulation of the demand $\rightarrow$ new demand.

In fact, modern medical, pharmaceutic and other associated industries as economic entities are directly interested in increasing the demand for medical services. This, as well as demographic reasons, create distortions and elements of crisis in the field of health care.

The main element in the restructuring of clinical processes is the transition to the electronic management of the medical history of a patient, which allows completely abandon the traditional data media in the diagnostic process, i.e. creation and protection of medical information [1].

Information barriers between health facilities will be eliminated, the possibility of continuity of medical observations of patients will help to assist patients throughout their life. A common environment of personal medical data forms the basis of integration for the requests of doctors from any health facility following the functional principle. At the current stage of health care management in the Russian Federation, data will be pooled within the framework of departmental health care. The tasks will be performed at the regional and federal levels [2].

The most important tasks, which include the creation of the State information system for personnel accounting for the provision of medical care to citizens of the Russian Federation are already being met. The project implementation suggests providing the minimum necessary level of informatization for health facilities: creation of a standard software and hardware complex for personalized recording medical care (first stage of PTC), equipping health facilities with computing hardware, software, network and engineering infrastructure for the work of the PTC, connection of medical institutions to the industry-protected Intranet network, ensuring access of medical workers to the information and educational portal, creation of the protected e-mail for interaction between health facilities and with public authorities, ensuring the transition to electronic document management, training medical staff how to work with the system, creation of the means of integration with other types of specialized information systems (for example, ERP, accounting, financial and economic planning systems).

Today, the legal norms for the use of software are almost completely defined. The software already legally becomes not a free application to computing hardware but completely independent component even being an integral part of it. For example, such a notion as a "software and hardware complex" is already receiving its full, originally implied in it meaning.

2   The Current State and Issues of Public Health Services Informatization in Russia

Health care in the Russian Federation still remains an area where information technology (IT) is poorly applied. Improving public health and improving the quality of health services are today the milestone of social policy. And information technology can make a significant contribution to this matter. As of 2011, among the 704 medical institutions only 53 could show a relatively high level of informatization. However, even among this small number of technologically advanced metropolitan institutions, the old methodology of work hampered progress: predominance of manual information input, lack of full automation of the work cycle and integrated information consolidation [3]. There are several reasons why informatization of health care is at a low level.

The following factors can be attributed to the main problems of the slow development of informatization in the healthcare sphere in Russia.

- Insufficient funding of medicine. In 2011, public health expenditures in Russia amounted to 3.9% of GDP (in comparison: the United States will spend 17% of GDP on these purposes, European countries - 8% of GDP, that is, Russia's rates are lower than the European average more than twice). Therefore, spending on medicine among the country's citizens is steadily growing.
- Insufficient number of employees. There is a sorely small amount of nurses and doctors of many specialties. According to the Ministry of Health and Social Development for 2010, in Russia the primary segment of medical care is lacking 80,000 nurses and 49,000 doctors. With the growing demand for health services, this problem will only worsen. And the increase in demand is expected in the near future - as a consequence of the general trend of population aging. The need for medical care for people with diabetes, heart failure, cancer and other diseases inherent in the elderly will grow steadily. The society will have to look for additional resources necessary for the decent functioning of the healthcare system.
- The absence of a legislative base for digital healthcare and electronic document management in Russia.
- The majority of medical workers in the country do not want to switch to new technologies, and the reason for this is the fact that doctors do not see the serious advantages of IT implementation for themselves, since most of the information systems created on the initiative of the «authorities» are oriented toward solving the problems of these «authorities».
- The doctors lack the information on the possibilities of information technologies and the advantages of their use. To solve this problem, medical workers should have much more information about the domestic medical information systems, successes and problems of healthcare informatization abroad.
- Population's mistrust to electronic medical records (EMR). And this makes sense: considering the current prevalence of digital devices, patients have a fair question whether the information system will ensure the confidentiality and safety of personal medical data. It is no accident that the level of EMR systems distribution in the world is rather modest so far. For example, according to Frost & Sullivan, in the United States only about 7% of the population have EMR.

Many issues of the introduction of information and communication technologies (ICT) are associated with the lack of a regulatory framework for the transition to an electronic form of workflow in the field of health and telemedicine services, as well as the lack of industry standards, the certification of ICT and the licensing of new types of activities in medicine.

The level of access to the Internet by medical organizations, states in the CIS countries for 2015 and the availability of system of measures for ensuring the integration of ICT in health care in the CIS countries' strategies and programs are presented in Figs. 1 and 2.

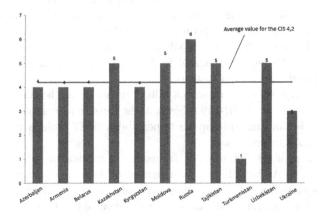

Fig. 1. The level of access to the internet by medical organizations in CIS countries for 2015 (according to the calculations of the National Information and Communication Holding Zerde)

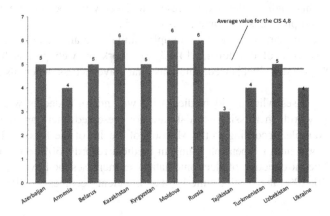

Fig. 2. Availability of a system of measures to ensure the integration of ICT in health care in the strategies and programs of the CIS countries (according to the calculations of the National Information and Communication Holding Zerde)

Informatization of medical institutions is currently taking place both in large cities of the Russian Federation and in remote regions, but more slowly [4]. According to the

Vademecum survey, which involved 100 representatives of public health authorities, the largest players in this market, and according to the analysis of information posted on the public procurement portal, in 2014, the volume of financing of IT projects in this area exceeded 6.5 billion rub. IT-expenses of the federal level are estimated by Vademecum magazine at 745 million rubles, 315 of which went to the Rostech corporation, equal amounts of 200 million rubles each went to the research institute "Voskhod" and "Rostelecom". Rostekh is responsible for the development of an integrated electronic medical record (IEMR) and a federal electronic registry (FER). Research Institute "Voskhod" and "Rostelecom" provide the work of the main and backup data centers. According to the head of the department of IT and communication of the Ministry of Health, there are already 21.6 million electronic medical records in the integrated electronic medical records (IEMR) system. Their number will increase to 38 million by the end of 2015. The IEMR itself occupies 20% of the capacity of the data center, and 80% will be allocated to other federal components of the USHIS (unified state health information system).

The Russian regions spent about 5.8 billion rubles on the health care informatization. At the same time, in 2014 19 subjects of the Russian federation did not spend a penny on IT in health care, shifting the responsibility of IT projects financing to the medical institutions themselves.

Today there are about 290 firms on the market of medical information systems in Russia according to ARMIT. Eighty three percent of them are commercial structures, 14% - state organizations and 3% - non-profit structures (for example, funds). The largest share of information systems developers (about 68%) is in Moscow and the Moscow region, 11% in St. Petersburg and 21% in other regions of the Russian Federation. In the data published in 2008 by CNews Analytics 125 firms across the country were mentioned. Nineteen percent - state organizations, and 81% - commercial organizations. This confirms the ARMIT research. Twenty-two percent are working on highly specialized programs for some areas of work.

Systems used in narrow areas, for example, ambulance and catastrophe medicine are provided by 16% of developers. 14.4% can work on web portals for medical institutions, 8.8% have specialized solutions that have access when using mobile devices [5].

Statistics of cases when rapid medical care was not provided is widely known throughout the world. In Russia such data are not presented, there are only separate studies. For example, according to the Ministry of Health of the Russian Federation, 39% of a doctor's time is spent on filling in medical records, 50% on searching for information. The introduction of electronic databases increases the flow of patients to a doctor up to 10–20%, the waiting time for a sick patient becomes smaller.

3   Experience of Introducing Electronic Technologies in Russia

Unified information space will give new opportunities to doctors in cases of emergency. It is reasonable to create a unified information space for blood services, transplant problems for remote regions such as the Urals, Siberia, etc., as well as to create a unified bases between the states of the world. Processing of the request for problems of providing blood or transplants will be available from any computer.

In order to provide an information medical space, it is possible to introduce the "Electronic Health Passport" system for a Russian citizen. In Europe, such systems were called public health registries [6].

Introduction of information and computer technology will provide:

- monitoring of citizens' health and a clear and rapid assistance system;
- improvement of the medical care to different groups of citizens in general medical examination and in specialized researches;
- expansion of the continuity of information about the patient diseases in different medical spheres, including ambulance;
- effective disease definition while reducing the cost of unnecessary additional examinations of patients;
- strengthening the doctor's decision in diagnosis and treatment, reducing the levels of disability and mortality;
- evaluation of objective territorial health indicators in dynamics;
- improvement of analysis and accounting in clinical medicine, enhancing the effectiveness of medical services in Russia;
- taking responsible decisions by the health authorities in relation to the statistical data of new information systems [7];

With the assistance of medical information systems (MIS), you can create a holistic picture of the patient's health condition and conduct diagnostic and treatment activities in a single cycle: detection - emergency care - hospital treatment - supervision by the attending physician - analysis of trends based on modeling - forecast of the state of health, including the risks of diseases and complications in chronic pathology cases [8].

At present, the principle of a systematic approach is poorly used in large MIS, therefore, many isolated small systems live in them. Because of this, in the terminology of corporate information systems, the state of the existing systems of informatization of Russian health care can be called a "patchwork quilt" [9].

One can quote the ranking of the largest suppliers of MIS for 2014. (Table 1) [10]. According to the table it can be seen that the number of implementations and realized workplaces as a whole increased in 2014 and the growth is projected in 2015 (Tables 2 and 3).

As of April 10, 2014, the total number of entries for a doctor's appointment in Moscow had reached 51 953 253 transactions. Most often, patients use information terminals (20 752 862 records), and the second most popular way is still the registry desks (13 396 874 calls). More than two million records were made by telephone through the appointment service to doctors in Moscow and another 185,000 residents contacted a doctor using the EMIAS mobile application.

To date, all regions of the country are connected to a unified system of reception, although, not all medical institutions have joined it yet. The main place of location for USHIS is the federal data processing center. Regardless of whether you are using your own computing power or leased infrastructure, it should be located on three remote sites - the main data center, the hot standby data center (without stopping the system) and the cold storage reserve center (with the possibility of stopping the system).

Table 1. Major suppliers of MIS: implementation projects for 2012

№	Company	City	Number of implementations per period				Number of implemented jobs per period			
			2012	2011	2013	2013, %	2012	2011	2013	2013, %
1	BARS group	Kazan	1461	348	1833	48	107818	28455	137831	19,2
2	Svan	Perm	450	65	820	80	10081	149	35008	30
3	SofTrust	Belgorod	260	700	N/A	N/A	8000	1500	13000	N/A
4	KORUS consulting	St. Petersburg	166	113	335	20	7305	3012	11100	−50
5	PostModernTechnology	Moscow	290	115	710	-10	4820	4200	19020	−10
6	Smart delta systems	Moscow	338	178	1672	50	4706	2044	29300	40
7	Volga med	Ulyanovsk	12		>100	20	3300		4500	20
8	K-MIS	Petrozavodsk	66	29	204	10	2710	1740	12050	10
9	Samson	St. Petersburg	53	43	364	30-40	1757	1720	14609	
10	Medotrade	Moscow	90	55	480	20	1397	604	10570	25
11	ComTec	Nizhnevartovsk	76	33	130	10	1227	697	2330	10
12	Aksimed	Moscow	102	79	244	18	630	624	4439	10
13	MedInTeh	Novosibirsk	20	8	112	30	618	304	3039	30
14	Softbalance	St. Petersburg	4	3	7	0,5	150	150	300	0,5
15	FORS	Moscow	3	5	8	150	101	100	201	200
16	Medsoft	Moscow	5	6	41		28	34	437	75

Table 2. Top 10 regions for IT healthcare expenditure, 2014. Source: Vademecum 2015

Region	Expenses of IT in healthcare, million rubles
Moscow	3 500
Moscow region	272
Novosibirsk region	200
Bryansk region	180
St. Petersburg	113
Krasnoyarsk region	107
Chelyabinsk region	90
Belgorod region	81
Kamchatka region	75
Sakhalin region	64

Table 3. Top-5 regions by the volume of data transferred to the IEMR, 2015. Source: Ministry of Health, 2015

Region	Share of data transferred from total, %
Altai republic	26
Kaliningrad region	24
Tambov region	17
Republic of Adygea	9
Ulyanovsk region	5

In addition to designing a data center, an urgent task for the ministry is to implement a storage system for archiving images and video of a medical nature. In the US, the annual volume of digital diagnostic images is about 15 petabytes, which should be preserved for 5–10 years. To store such a data set, special systems are needed for archiving, processing and transferring medical diagnostic images. They are called Picture Archiving and Communication Systems (PACS). PACS have become widespread in Finland, the UK and especially Sweden, where almost all medical institutions work with them. In Russia, these technologies are still poorly developed, but there are already first successes. For example, in Chuvashia 12 medical treatment facilities are connected to the Centralized Archive of Medical Imagery. By the end of 2013 more than 34 thousand pictures were transferred to the system [3].

One can also note the "Electronic Medicine" company, which is a web portals developer for public health services in the Rostov region, the Stavropol region and the Republic of Kalmykia.

The company's portal integrates all the sites of medical and pharmacy institutions and contains information about institutions, their structure, services provided, doctors, time of reception and contact information. Currently, more than 60 treatment-and-prophylactic and pharmacy institutions are connected. Also, with the help of portal one can:

- a record for a doctor's appointment via the Internet, preliminary reservation of time and a specialist in health care facilities registered on the portal
- a person who has a federal, regional or municipal benefit can obtain information about the availability of medicinal products in pharmacies that are issuing preferential medicines and book the necessary drug
- it is possible to search for a medicinal product in the city and regional pharmacies registered on the resource; a user can view the on-line stocks of the goods in pharmacies, reserve the necessary medication or order it at the lowest price in case of his absence; connecting pharmacies to the drug search system is free of charge
- there is a possibility of searching health facilities and pharmacies on the dynamic map presented on the portal [11].

The "LPU-EM" MIS scales from a private practice room to a large medical and diagnostic center with a developed regional-level branch structure. "LPU-EM" MIS adapts taking into account the specifics of the regional regulatory framework, medical specialization, the needs of administration and users of the MO. "LPU-EM" MIS provides solutions to urgent problems such as:

- appointment to a doctor in the registry, through the self-recording terminal and the Internet, with the physician's AWP;
- conducting a structured medical record of the patient in electronic form;
- personalized accounting of the use of medicines;
- automatization of accounting for the prophylaxis and vaccination of the population;
- data exchange with laboratory and diagnostic departments of medical organizations and external laboratory systems;
- conducting internal expertise of the quality of medical care;
- the formation of economic and statistical reporting in MHI and VHI systems, internal reporting of a medical institution.

In the catalog of the Association for the Development of Medical Information Technologies (ADMIT) there are more than 50 complex MISs (CMIS) of multidisciplinary medical organizations (polyclinics, diagnostic centers, hospitals, clinics, etc.), 11 information systems of dental medical organizations (DenIS), 12 MIS of specialized medical organizations and units (Special MIS), 11 laboratory information systems (LIS), 7 radiological information systems (RIS).

Despite the seeming variety of solutions, the circle of companies working in the healthcare market, according to CNews, [10] is gradually narrowing. Thus, more than 30 integrators took part in the rating of projects implemented in 2010–2011. In 2012, their number fell to 21, in 2013 - to 13, and in 2014 there were 12, among which there were both those focused mainly on the health IT market companies like «PostModern Technology», «SP.Arm», «K-MIS», «Smart Delta Systems», «Svan», «SofTrust», «ComTec», and integrators of a wide profile, actively developing the direction of automation of medicine within themselves – «FORS», «BARS Group», etc. (Figs. 3 and 4).

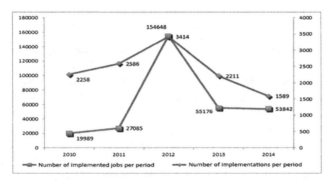

Fig. 3. Number of all types' information systems implementations in the health sector. Source: CNews Analytics 2015

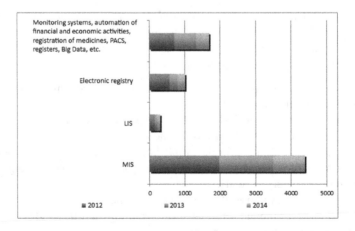

Fig. 4. Number of implementations by a type of system. Source: CNews Analytics 2015

The peak of implementation of projects in the field of health informatization took place in 2012. Then, according to CNews, the rating participants introduced about 3.5 thousand solutions, covering about 150 thousand jobs. Since 2012, CNews has asked the rating participants to specify which type of systems they introduced. According to the data received, the largest number of complex MISs (1969) was introduced in 2012. At the same time, one implementation on average covered 26 jobs. By 2014, the number of implementations of complex MISs has decreased more than twofold to 905, but they have become more large (up to 33 workplaces).

2012 also became the year of mass introduction of the system of remote recording for admission to the doctor (Electronic Registry). Participants of the CNews rating implemented 567 solutions and automated more than 6200 workplaces. In the following years, the number of such implementations dropped sharply, and in 2014, a little over 1,200 users were connected to the "Electronic Registry".

4 Evaluation of Economic Efficiency of Using Information Technologies in Medicine

Evaluation of the economic effectiveness of medical information technology involves a quantitative comparison of costs and results. Estimation of efficiency can be carried out by means of methods of an estimation of economic efficiency of investment projects. The main obstacle to using these methods for assessing the economic efficiency of information technology in medicine is the lack of a clear picture of the results achieved in each year of the billing period.

One of the methods is the Strassmann approach [12]. Since it is often impossible to quantify the economic effect of information technology, the effectiveness of implementing information systems can be viewed from the point of view of their impact on such key financial components as sales volume, working capital, product cost, market share.

Since the subject of our study is the research of methods of assessing the effectiveness of information systems, perhaps only the TCO model (Total Cost of Ownership) might be considered as a general method in this specific field. This model is designed to assess the comparative effectiveness, because it is based on the following premise: two information systems are characterized by the same result, so to choose the more efficient one it is enough to compare the costs associated with their implementation and maintenance. Thus, there is no need to solve the most difficult task - determination of the benefits derived from information systems. However, the field of practical use of the method is substantially narrowed due to the assumption about the identity of the output parameters of the compared projects.

Total cost of ownership is understood as the "fully accounted annual costs of the enterprise (and not just its IT department) associated with the acquisition and, most importantly, the use of information technology in business" [13]. It is intended to take into account not only direct, but also hidden, indirect costs, for example, losses from user downtime.

In the absence of a single, widely recognized and universal methodology, the process of assessing the economic effectiveness of IP is significantly transformed into research work with the need to bind project to a specific facility. In our case, such facilities are medical institutions.

There is an opinion that the introduction of medical information technology, as well as any information technology, is extremely expensive, and their impact is not expressed by cost indicators, but only by qualitative ones: improving the quality of medical services, simplifying the work of medical personnel, improving the health of patients, etc. Essentially, this opinion arose not because of the lack of real economic benefits provided by information technology, but because of the lack of developed methods for measuring the economic effect.

To determine the economic effectiveness of medical information systems, foreign assessments can be used, since there is a long-term experience of computerization in the health care of developed countries. The most significant and revealing among the currently introduced medical information technologies are the systems of electronic medical records (EMR). In European countries, electronic medical records replaced conventional paper cards by 50–90%, in the US - by 70%.

Since the output from the implementation of medical information technologies as a whole consists of resources savings in certain areas of their expenditure, estimates of the achieved economic effect can be obtained by identifying the fullest possible range of benefits provided by information systems.

The most tangible benefits of implementing medical information technologies are:

– Reducing the number of actions with medical cards, the ability to copy records;
– cost savings on drugs;
– saving costs for laboratory and radiological research;
– shortening the hospitalization period;
– benefits of administration when working with payment documents.

It should be noted that the economic benefits of other factors, for example, the exchange of clinical information about patients between medical institutions, are necessarily added to the listed benefits obtained through the introduction of the system of electronic medical cards, provided they are widely disseminated.

A survey [14] gives a more detailed classification of benefits from the use of medical information technologies - in the ambulatory and inpatient sectors:

Ambulatory sector:

– benefits from electronic medical records;
– savings of expenses for extracts from cards;
– savings on laboratory research;
– cost savings on drugs;
– saving on radiological studies;

Inpatient sector:

– benefits from improving the nurses work with documents;
– benefits from electronic medical records;
– savings on laboratory research;
– cost savings on drugs;
– benefits from shortening the hospitalization period.

The quantification of the savings for each of these types of benefits was carried out by timing the work time of medical personnel, interviewing experts, comparing costs before and after implementation of IP, direct costing of medicines etc.

Further consideration should be given to assessment of financial results obtained for each of the advantages of medical information technology.

EMR reduces the need to conduct paper patient outpatient cards. Savings are achieved due to the fact that there is no need for personnel involved in the search and issue of paper cards; Once the patient data is recorded, the doctor can quickly find them and get acquainted with all the resources of the card; Data does not occupy a physical space that can be used more productively. Savings in the cost of record keeping by medical personnel are estimated at 63.4%.

For example, the paper [14] provides the following calculation: an acceptable estimate of the time spent on each statement from the paper card is approximately four minutes. The number of card extracts per doctor per day is more than the number of visits 1.6 times (for example, because some statements are made by telephone contacts between the doctor and patients, between doctors). With an average load of 15 patients per day 5 days a week for 48 weeks, there are 5,760 statements per doctor per year, which occupies 384 h of work, or $ 5,530 annually.

In addition, the use of EMR makes it easier for nurses to access patients' treatment records, save money by reducing processing time and excessive data collection; By reducing the costs associated with paper forms, preventing many accidentally missed procedures.

It was determined that EMR allows to reduce the number of operations with medical cards by 60–70% and to reduce the number of employees engaged in working with medical records by 50%. Saving the time spent working with documentation can be used in at least three ways: (1) to reduce the number of nurses employed; (2) improve care for the same number of patients; (3) accept additional patients for treatment without reducing the quality of the services.

Saving costs for medicines. The cost of medicines is reduced through the introduction of computerized input modules for medical appointments and support for clinical decisions. The electronic system of alternative medicines offers a 15% reduction in drug costs.

Savings on laboratory and radiological research. Savings on laboratory tests are achieved in medical institutions equipped with EMSM with a module for prescribing procedures and tests, as well as supporting clinical decisions, by reducing the number of unnecessary, often duplicate tests. Estimates of savings in these costs account for 22.4% of the total cost of laboratory tests in the outpatient sector and 11.8% in the inpatient.

The benefits of reducing hospitalization. The stay of patients in hospitals is accompanied by a lot of different time losses - delays in the designation of studies and treatment, in the search for documents, in coordinating the appointments of various specialists, etc. According to various estimates obtained through selective control, this reduction is from 10 to 30% of the actual length of stay in the hospital.

Benefits of administration when working with payment documents. A more complete fixation of all performed medical procedures and procedures with the use of EMSM makes it possible to identify errors allowed in billing, which increases the amount of bills by 2% and reduces the quality of errors by 78% [15].

The cost of the EMSM consists of two parts: the capital expenditures of the implementation and the annual, current maintenance cost. At the same time, the cost of maintenance is estimated as a percentage of capital expenditure.

It is assumed that in most cases the capital expenditures for EMSM will be designed for a period of three to five years, including the cost of the EMR software, the cost of local infrastructure (such as network devices and computers), as well as the labor costs of hospital staff involved in installation and modernization of work based on information technology.

In addition to EMR, other information systems are being developed and implemented, in particular, computerizing the work of administrative services. Thus, the introduction of information technology in the administrative services of medical institutions provides savings in the costs of document registration at a rate of 63% of average costs.

Comparison of costs and results of introduction of medical information technologies. In general, financial benefits are calculated for the entire US health care system, which can be obtained through the introduction of medical information technologies (Table 4).

Table 4. Total benefits from the introduction of information technology in medical institutions in the USA. Source: [14].

Type of benefits	The potential savings per year in $ billion	Average annual savings in $ billion	Share in total saving, %
Ambulatory sector			
Benefits of electronic medical records	1,9	0,9	8,4
Cost savings on card statements	1,7	0,8	7,5
Savings on laboratory research	2,2	1,1	10,3
Cost savings for medicines	12,9	6,2	57,9
Saving on radiological research	3,6	1,7	15,9
Total	22,3	10,7	100
Stationary sector			
Benefits of improving the work of nurses with documents	12,7	7,1	22,7
Benefits from electronic medical records	2,5	1,3	4,1
Savings on laboratory research	3	1,6	5,1
Cost savings for medicines	3,7	2	6,4
Benefits of shortening hospitalization	36,7	19,3	61,7
Total	58,6	31,3	100
Total for ambulatory and stationary sectors	80,9	42	

Using the foreign experience of estimating the obtained effect, it is possible to calculate the benefits from the introduction of the EMSM. To do this, you need information about all the articles reviewed by the medical institution: the wages of nurses in the departments per year; Cost of consumed medicines for the year; Total annual costs of laboratories; Total annual costs of the departments that conduct radiological studies; The cost of one bed-day, the number of bed-days in the amount for all patients for the year; On administrative expenses. For the subsequent comparison of costs and results with the purpose of assessing the economic efficiency of investment projects for the creation of medical information systems, data on the costs of implementing and operating the medical information systems themselves are also needed.

5   Conclusion

Thus, based on the study, the following conclusions can be drawn. In Russia and CIS countries, informatization of medical institutions is currently taking place, but slower than in other countries. Among the main reasons of the slow development of informatization in the health sector in Russia, there are such factors as insufficient funding of medicine, lack of staff, lack of a legislative base for digital healthcare and electronic document circulation, reluctance of medical workers to switch to new technologies, lack of information about the possibilities of information technologies and the advantages of their use, as well as mistrust of the population to electronic medical records. In addition, currently in most CIS countries the level of access to the Internet for medical organizations is below the average level. The exceptions are Russia, Moldova, Kazakhstan, Uzbekistan and Tajikistan.

Currently, Russia is gradually developing IT programs for medical organizations. In addition, IT-costs of the federal level are estimated at 745 million rubles. According to ARMIT, about 290 companies work in this sphere. A large share of developers of information systems (about 68%) is in Moscow and the Moscow region, 11% in St. Petersburg and 21% in other regions of the Russian Federation. Among the largest suppliers of MIS are: BARS Group, Svan, SofTrust, KORUS Consulting, Electronic Medicine, MIS LPU-EM and others.

To date, all regions of Russia are connected to a unified system of reception, although, not all medical institutions have joined it yet. The main place of location for USHIS is the federal data processing center.

An important issue is the assessment of the economic effectiveness of medical information technology. The main obstacle to using these methods for assessing the economic efficiency of information technology in medicine is the lack of a clear picture of the results achieved in each year of the billing period.

Using the foreign experience of estimating the obtained effect, it is possible to calculate the benefits from the introduction of the EMSM. The most tangible benefits of implementing medical information technologies are: reduction in the number of actions with medical cards, the ability to copy records; cost savings on drugs; saving costs for laboratory and radiological research; shortening the hospitalization period; benefits of administration when working with payment documents. Thus, the implementation of information technology in the administrative services of medical institutions provides savings in the costs of document registration at a rate of 63% of average costs.

References

1. Electronic scientific journal "Software products, systems and algorithms". http://swsys-web.ru
2. Swan, software and services: The principles of building an unified information space. http://swan.perm.ru
3. The NAAR Journal. Electronic medicine – a healthy life technology. http://naar.ru
4. Kurakova, N.A.: Informatization of health care as a tool for creating a "self-regulated system for the organization of medical care". In: A Doctor and Information Technologies, vol. 2, pp. 9–27 (2009)
5. The Ministry of health of the Russian Federation: The concept of e-health. https://www.rosminzdrav.ru
6. Vyalkov, A.I.: Management and Economics of Health Care. GEOTAR-Media, Moscow (2009)
7. The Pandia: Approaches and first e-health experience. http://pandia.ru
8. Belovodsky, A.A.: Public health in Russia. In: Modern Science-Intensive Technologies, vol. 11 (annex), pp. 21–27 (2009)
9. The Medbe: Classification of medical information systems. http://medbe.ru
10. CNEWS: IT Health Review. http://www.cnews.ru
11. The Electronic Medicine. http://www.elmed-rostov.ru
12. Strassmann, P.A.: http://www.strassmann.com
13. Skripkin, K.G.: Economic Efficiency of Information Systems. DMK Press, Moscow (2002)
14. Girosi, F., Meili, R., Scoville, R.: Extrapolating Evidence of Health Information Technology Savings and Costs. RAND Corporation, Santa Monica (2005)
15. Wang, S., Middleton, B., Prosser, L.A., et al.: A cost-benefit analysis of electronic medical records in primary care. Am. J. Med. **114**, 397–403 (2003)

eEconomy and eFinance: Finance and Knowledge Management

Financial Markets Data Collection Using the Information Model of Interagency Cooperation and the International System of Codification of Financial Instruments

Yuri P. Lipuntsov[1]([✉]), Richard Beatch[2], and Inessa Collier[3]

[1] Department of Economics, Lomonosov Moscow State University,
Moscow, Russia
lipuntsov@econ.msu.ru
[2] Bloomberg LP, New York, USA
rbeatch@bloomberg.net
[3] Bloomberg LP, London, UK
icollierl@bloomberg.net

Abstract. One of the main problems in the organization of inter-system data exchange and the comparison of data coming from different sources is the identification of similar objects. To solve this problem, it is necessary that the users of information services agree on the rules for naming objects and their identification. In global communities, such as the community of stock market participants, the consistency problem requires the creation of a permanently functioning structure that tracks all changes in the sources of data providers, and updates the codification system data in accordance with these changes. The codification system allows comparison of data coming from different sources and provides quality data to end users. The global stock market is one of the most information rich sectors; performing analysis of stock market data assumes the availability of information from various sources: the various tax authorities, statistical bodies, the national settlement depository, stock exchanges and other sources. In order to collect data from different sources, a methodology is needed to transform the data and bring it to a comparable level.

The article describes the experience of applying the information model of inter-agency interaction based on the distributed data core using the codification system. The model presents the organization of a data exchange, which is based on a three-layer core. The article describes the experience of using this model to collect and analyze stock market information. Finally, an example of the model is presented using international identification systems, in particular, a global identification system is considered for the identification of legal entities, and the financial instrument identifier FIGI is considered for the stock market instruments.

Keywords: Codification system · Information exchange · Distributed environment · Domain model · Information modeling

© Springer International Publishing AG 2017
D.A. Alexandrov et al. (Eds.): DTGS 2017, CCIS 745, pp. 417–430, 2017.
https://doi.org/10.1007/978-3-319-69784-0_35

1 Introduction

The availability of relevant and reliable stock market information offers a significant potential for executing business activities of many organizations: market regulators, commercial companies, data vendors, and rating agencies. Making informed managerial decisions requires data from different sources, depositories, registers, trading platforms, securities issue registrars, etc. Despite the fact that the financial sector is the most developed in the field of information technology, most of the systems used (which store huge amounts of data) are focused on solving local problems that do not involve integration with other systems [1]. The problem of data sharing becomes more complex with the proliferation of mobile devices, new types of data, and the constant data accumulation and updating.

Most data vendors provide information related to the stock market either use their own identifiers for stock market objects or simply a set of attributes for identifying objects and for describing them. In addition to the initial data, analytical agencies provide ready-made coefficients and multipliers, while the methodology for calculating them remains behind the scenes. In order to implement a methodology for calculating analytical indicators, many market participants elect to maintain their own databases, solving at the local level the problem of incompatibility of data coming from different sources. Creating a solution for the problem of converting data to a common type will help provide high-quality stock market data in the format "data as a service". Based on this service, it is possible to create components that will allow the end user to develop and implement their own data analysis models. A working prototype of such a solution has been created, which allows creation of company ratings and formation of portfolios using exchange data supplemented by the data from the financial statements, and comparison with analogue data from foreign markets. Working with real data and analyzing representative information on issuers and market participants, the user is provided the opportunity to implement their own analytical models.

The basis for the provision of such a service is an information model that defines the basic principles of the organization of data exchange between systems. The information model should ensure comparability of data related to different objects of the stock market with the necessary sets of attributes whose composition is predetermined by the analysis methods. The informational model of interagency interaction is used as the basis of the information model of the prototype, and the international system of coding is used as the object identification tool.

2 The Information Model of Interagency Communication

The article [12] presents a data exchange model that describes the approaches and principles of maintaining an extensible core of general information and state data. Data providers for information exchange are government agencies and other organizations that are producers of primary data. The model contains several sections that are differentiated based on the subject domain to which they belong. The data core is a three-layer structure: the **universal core**, the **domain core** and the **domain-specific core**. Interaction between layers is carried out using the model of inter-layer relationships. The information model is based on the information modeling principles for a data vault [8].

The information interaction is reduced to the exchange of data related to the state of basic information objects. The data core acts in this case as a data block aggregating a set of information necessary for organizing the exchange. The model allows comparison of information about similar objects coming from different systems, and to monitor the state of the data across change. The informational model of the data core is provided with a description of the semantic links between the objects, which will allow the implementation of semantics using the context. A data mart is formed on the basis of the data core.

The model of each layer includes three categories of elements:

- Basic entities - informational objects of the subject domain, and connections between them.
- Graphical representation of the codification system - a hierarchical representation of objects, which captures the interrelation of objects in the form of a real-world model.
- Additional information resources: Classifiers, Directories, as well as a cross-domain list of codes.

The universal core includes a universal part of the data that are utilized in many subject domains and understood by all of them in the same way. The universal data core includes metadata about individuals, legal entities, location descriptions, and real estate objects. The model helps organize the exchange of data stored in different systems and obtain a sample of data for different sections: the region of registration, the scope of activities, the size of the company, etc.

The universal core is the basis for the domain information exchange. Data is processed, resulting in the basic entities being coded according to the domain ontology. The codification is performed in such a way that all identical objects from different sources receive identical codes. Such a coding system will allow users to find a specific object from across different systems. The data core contains metadata in regards to the data source, the time of the first detection of the object in the local system, the date of its last review, and the time of the data validity end.

Figure 1 shows an example of data representation in the universal core, which includes four basic objects: natural persons, legal entities, location, and real estate objects.

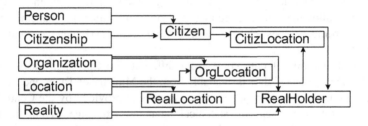

Fig. 1. Example of the universal core codification composition

An extension of the universal core is presented in a **domain core**. It focuses on describing the principles of organization of the activities in this sector of the economy. The stock market describes the principles of regulation, in particular licensing procedures, the process of monitoring activities, the implementation of regulations and other elements that describe the sector activities at the management level.

The **domain-specific core** calls for a detailed description. The data that describes the stock market domain are issuer profile, list of its financial instruments, the venues on which financial instruments are traded, financial reporting data, instrument trading data, various issuer events, such as dividend payments, and other data important for analysis.

The data structure model of the domain-specific core, the stock market sector, includes a graphical representation of the domain and a data integration model. The conceptual representation is reflected in the form of a description of the domain through concepts, their definitions and the relationships between them. The list of concepts of the domain-specific core includes such terms as Company, Financial Instrument, Stock Exchange, Financial Report, and Trading.

Based on the conceptual representation, we can build a graphical representation of the domain-specific part, which will serve as the basis for compiling a data warehouse data model (Fig. 2).

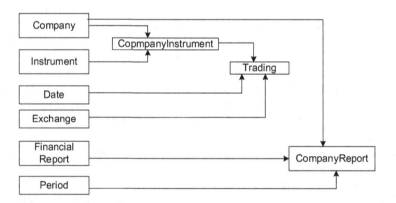

Fig. 2. Graphical representation of the stock market domain

Based on the graphical representation, a conceptual model and a logical model of the stock market data are constructed. The data model of the domain-specific core includes the following objects: company profile (Company), financial reporting (Report), instrument types (Instrument), trading venues (Exchange) and owners (Holder).

Different categories of data come from different participants in the information exchange. The companies' data is available from the Ministry of Taxes and Levies, the data regarding the registration of securities issuance is provided by the Central Bank, financial statements are sent by statistical agencies, exchange trading results are reported by stock exchanges, and data regarding the ownership of the company is supplied by the national depository. A more detailed description of the stock market information exchange model is presented in the previous article of the author [13].

An important element in the organization of data procurement from sources located at different levels of the core is the coordination between individual models, both at the vertical and horizontal levels. Establishing links between them requires creating **a model of inter-level interactions,** which ensures coordination of the way objects are represented in different models. Possible modes of reconciliation can be based on the creation of a mechanism for using a single object codifier, or the establishment of mapping between object representations in different models. Figure 3 shows the version of the agreement between the universal core, the domain core, and the domain-specific core.

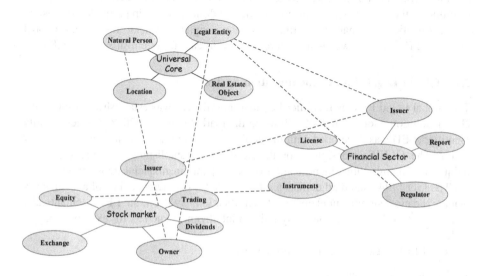

Fig. 3. Representation of inter-layer interactions in the data core

Using the presented model, it becomes possible to create infrastructural elements of data processing operations. In particular, to obtain stock market data, financial reporting data is required, which is reflected at the second level of the model. When analyzing the stock market, financial indicators are important, such as the number of telecommunication companies' subscribers, the volume of cars produced by automotive companies, and the results of an audit of oil reserves for oil companies. Such data can be obtained from domain-specific cores of other domains.

This model of interagency communication is developed based on international experience and reflected in other e-Government's models. The Data Core of NIEM [15] in US and ADMS [10] in EU includes two layers and IMI [9] in Japan has the three layers. These models are utilized to solve the inter-level interaction problem, the solution of which tends to use the codification system.

3   The Codification System

The description of the three layers of the data core makes it clear that the codification system is an essential element in the organization of the data exchange. It is, therefore, necessary to develop a codification system that will be equally perceived by all participants in the information space. Codification is an essential element of many existing information exchange systems. Codification systems are widely used in medical applications [5, 7]. In international practice, coding systems are known that have found application in many countries, including Russia. The Global Legal Entity Identifier Foundation (GLEIF) is the global system for identification of legal entities (it oversees assignment of Legal Entity Identifier - LEI) and can serve as an example of encoding an object from the universal data core. In addition to universal objects such as financial institutions, the prototype uses the codification of domain areas, in particular the system of identification of financial instruments that assigns Financial Instrument Global Identifier FIGI. Below we shall explore each codification system in some detail.

3.1   Global Legal Entities Identification System

The Global Legal Entities Identifier Foundation (GLEIF) was established based on the G-20 resolution adopted in 2009 following the market events of 2008. The legal entity identifier (LEI) was developed with the goal of increasing transparency in the financial sector. The GLEIF is designed for the purpose of establishing a global system of unique and unambiguous identification of participants in financial transactions.

The ISO 17442 standard defines a set of attributes or reference data of a legal entity that are the most significant elements of identification. By itself, the LEI is semantically meaningless, it does not contain any built-in intelligence, such as for example country codes.

The LEI is based on four key principles:

- This is a global standard.
- Each legal entity is assigned one unique identifier.
- It is supported by high quality data.
- This is a public good, provided free of charge to all users.

Once a legal entity receives an LEI, the identifier is published together with the relevant LEI reference data by the local operating unit that issued the LEI. This means that all data from the LEI database is publicly available for unimpeded use by any interested party at any time.

The ISO 17442 standard specifies the minimum list of reference data that must be provided for all LEI codes:

- The official name of the legal entity, which is recorded in the official registers.
- Registration address of a legal entity.
- Country of domicile.
- Codes that represent countries and their regions.
- The date of the initial assignment of the LEI code, the date of the last LEI data update, and the expiration date, if any.

The Global LEI System is coordinated by the Regulatory Oversight Committee (ROC) which is a group of over 70 public authorities from more than 40 countries [11]. In Russia, assignment and verification of LEI Codes is handled by the nongovernmental commercial organization National Settlement Depository JSC, [14]. Currently, 867 RF companies received an LEI code.

One of the aggregators of information about LEI codes is a resource OpenCorporates [17].

While the LEI code was created in order to increase the transparency in the volume of financial transactions, i.e. for the purposes of regulatory organizations, the financial instruments identifier FIGI is focused on the optimization of data management within the organization and serves the needs of both the corporate sector and regulatory organizations.

3.2 The FIGI Financial Instruments Identification System

With the growth of information exchange in the financial industry, industrialization of production, and consumption of data, there is a need for precise data tracking both at the level of elementary and aggregated data objects. An example of the standardization of aggregated data objects can be seen in the FIGI - a codification system designed for the identification of financial instruments across multiple levels of specificity.

The financial instrument identifier FIGI was initially developed by Bloomberg LP in 2010, and in 2014 it became an official standard of the Object Management Group [16]. This identifier system is currently in the review process to become an ISO standard.

The business case for the FIGI is found in the fact that many financial institutions face difficulties in interpreting received financial data because there are different systems for identifying financial instruments. This makes it difficult to compile financial statements, such as balance sheets, and other reports reflecting portfolio management. The presence of multiple identification systems forces companies to maintain cross-system synchronization, which increases costs and increases operational risks. To solve these problems, the system of FIGI identifiers was developed.

FIGIs have a number of unique characteristics that help to serve the broad business needs. First, codes do not change when there is a change in the descriptive components due to corporate actions, such as name change, mergers and acquisitions, etc. The codes are stable, which is important for maintaining the integrity of databases and automated processes. Once the code is assigned, it is never reused - i.e. the FIGI code can be used as the primary identifier. Second, FIGI codes for equities have a 3-tier structure - one identifier attributed at the share-class level, one or more - at the country/regional level, and finally, one or more identifiers at the level of the trading venue. Such a sequence of identification facilitates obtaining and comparing pricing data, execution of commercial transactions and the provision of custody services.

The use of such a code will help avoid mistakes in the preparation of internal reports, and will facilitate an effective exchange of information with external partners, including the regulatory authorities that may require reporting at levels of granularity that are not supported by other identification schemes.

In addition to providing the necessary granularity to differentiate financial instruments, there are over 320 million FIGI codes assigned to various asset types, including stocks, bonds, derivatives, and so on as of this writing. Finally, unlike other identifiers, the assignment, distribution, use and re-distribution of FIGIs is free of charge. These services are provided through the website www.openFIGI.com [3], which offers mapping to the existing codes and ability to request a new code.

Beyond merely providing for identification and an access point for the data, this identifier's methodology is focused on its application in information systems: databases and automated processes required for effective management of financial assets with the active use of metadata. To enable the effective use of the FIGI, the FIGI standard provides a robust semantic model so as to enable effective implementation of the FIGI. The model specifies how each type of identifier functions and how the three levels of identification interact with each other through constraints specified in the Web Ontology Language (OWL). This enables organizations to quickly integrate the FIGI model into their information systems. FIGI can serve as an effective tool for managing databases, compiling operational reports, and can also be linked to other identifiers, such as ISIN, which are required in some legal documents.

FIGI is based on the "meaningless" code approach, which is based on the latest developments in the theory and practice of data management, such as "meaningless" code structure, metadata, permanence and uniqueness. Its main purpose is to provide a single, streamlined methodology that ensures the highest quality of financial data. The FIGI code itself is a twelve character NMTOKEN consisting of two upper case consonants (with some minor restrictions), followed by the upper-case letter "G", then followed by eight characters consisting of uppercase consonants or the numbers 0–9, finally, the last character is a number which is calculated as a check digit to provide for computational validation of the string. For example, the FIGI for Apple common stock at the global level is BBG001S5N8V8.

Because FIGIs do not change, they can be used as the primary key for communication with other market participants. The FIGI also incorporates an inherent understanding of the relationships between instruments and other objects through the provision of descriptive metadata as well as through the relationships specified in the semantic model. Better tracking and analysis of financial instruments requires not only the issuance code but other characteristics as well, such as the trading venue and others, which are taken into account when generating FIGI codes. FIGI explains how things are identified, as opposed to just being an identifier. The purpose of the FIGI code is to create a clear picture that helps us understand how various codes are interrelated. Further, because of the granularity of the identifier, the FIGI code is deeper, compared with the ISIN identifier, because it is assigned not only at the global level, but also at the level of the trading venue. ISIN is assigned to identify the whole security issue and is the same for all trading venues. The FIGI code generation procedure differs from a simple combination of the instrument code and a trading platform accepted for ISIN + MIC (sometimes ISIN + MIC + CUR), as constituent elements of the aggregated code may vary, and the FIGI code provides stability. But from a data management point of view, better data quality and reduced errors are achieve when using a single reference instead of trying to keep two or three pieces of data together through different databases and messaging systems. It could be possible to use a ticker, used on a given trading venue, but then it would be necessary to maintain that cross-reference, which becomes a problem when tickers change. Instead, the ticker, ISIN, MIC, and CFI become metadata associated with FIGIs, thereby providing the structured relationships across these concepts.

FIGI codes are already being used by various financial institutions globally, including the stock exchanges, banks, software vendors, etc. Within Russia, these identifiers are used in the internal systems of a number of large stock market participants.

3.3   Identifier Structure, Properties and Metadata

As noted above, both the LEI (Legal Entity Identifier) and the FIGI (Financial Instrument Global Identifier) are meaningless strings that incorporate check digits and are provided along with metadata. As mentioned before, the 'meaningless' code approach is based on the latest thinking in the theory and practice of data management [6]. This is important in that it has long been recognized that unique identifiers are essential for the management of information in any digital environment. Identifiers represent real world objects or concepts in the data model. The representation of an object or concept should not necessarily have the form of a term from a (natural) language. It can be represented in a computer memory by a memory position, which is the starting position of a 'bit string'. Such a bit string should be an encoding of and should be interpretable as a meaningless but unique identifier (UID) [22]. Information technology recognizes it as an instance of an entity without 'attributes'. Such a unique identifier can represent the object or concept without the use of natural language: there is no term related to the concept yet, and the UID is language independent. The unique identifier should be unique within the context of a managed 'world' of people, organizations and systems that share the UIDs as identifiers of concepts and objects [22].

"Identifiers assigned in one context may be encountered and re-used in another place without consulting the assigner, who cannot guarantee that his assumptions will be known to someone else". Therefore, interoperability between systems requires the "design of identifiers to enable their use in services outside the direct control of the issuing assigner" [18]. The need for systems interoperability dictates that an identifier demonstrates the following characteristics:

- Persistence: the identifier has to be immutable and permanent and not subject to change in any circumstances. It should be globally unique and persist for all time. The objective is to have identifiers that can last longer than any software system that exists today.
- Extensibility: identifiers "users will need to discover and cite identifiers issued by different bodies, supported by different metadata declarations, combine these on the basis of a consistent data model" [18].

Along with language independent unique, persistent and extendable identifiers we need data that can be used to point to the concept and to provide information about the concept, i.e. 'data about data' – metadata - in order to become human interpretable and to become of practical use. A unique and persistent identifier should be able to reference any resource and act as a Unique Resource Name (URN) or an Internationalized

Resource Identifier (IRI). An identifier points to the metadata, and the metadata provides structured information about a resource, so that computer systems can interpret and process the data automatically. "Metadata enables a resource to be found by indicating what the resource is about and how it can be accessed with a series of structured descriptions" [21].

Codification schemes such as the LEI and the FIGI are not unique in the finance sector. Indeed, the finance sector already has a history of using codification systems. One example is the SWIFT code as a standard format of Bank Identifier Code (BIC). SWIFT code represents a unique identification code for a bank or financial institution. Banks rely on these codes for the transfer of funds from one bank to another. SWIFT usage dates back to 1977, and in 2014 BIC was established as the international ISO standard - ISO 9362:2014 [20]. The analysis of the SWIFT code adoption shows [19] that using SWIFT network and a set of standards has significant positive effects on profitability of financial institutions in the long-term; notably, these profitability effects are greater for small banks than for large ones. Further, the usage of SWIFT has proven to provide significant network performance improvements as well as to have a positive impact on the security of financial transactions [4].

3.4   Using the System of Identifiers in the Model of Interagency Communication

Consider the role and place of the codification system in the information model of inter-agency interaction, which involves the organization of inter-agency cooperation through the data core. The information infrastructure of e-government involves integration systems that represent such elements as data structure and technologies for their analysis. Integration of public data is a necessary solution to meet the needs of inter-agency operations for data from different agency and enterprise systems. The structure of the basic elements of the integration platform for e-government infrastructure is shown in Fig. 4.

The diagram shows the delivery of data from the government agencies' and commercial enterprise IT systems. Entities that assign codes for various information objects represent one of the data provider types. Legal entities and financial instruments are examples of such objects in the presented application prototype. The supplied information forms the bases of the up-to-date data of the universal core and the domain s. These two core layers serve as the foundation for generating domain-specific core, which is tasked with providing information to operational processes.

The second but no less important task of the integration platform is to supply data for management purposes. In this case data marts and the results of in-depth analysis act as data providers, while the data is sourced from all three layers of the core. The platform that solves the problem of data exchange and analytical processing simplifies the analysis and publication of results, provides new analytical capabilities, and simplifies the data exchange.

The monitoring function performed by the Central Bank can be considered as an example of such activities. This responsibility involves the assessment of the financial assets under control of market participants, including an assessment of their quality and liquidity, and calculation of financial performance indicators. The data supplied from

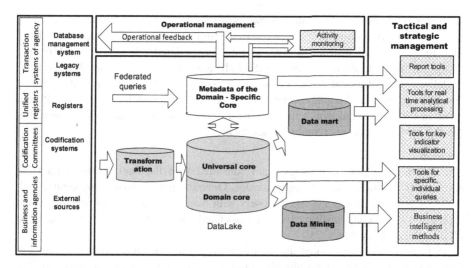

Fig. 4. Framework model of information structure and data flows of public data integration platform

different sources feed into the IT systems of the Central Bank of Russia which enable data analysis. Regional organizations that belong to the Central Bank perform the work of monitoring local enterprises. Geographically-distributed structure of the CB data sources requires use of coordinated data formats which enable carrying out various types of analysis with sufficient granulation.

The problem of transforming data into a common, comparable form is found not only in the public sector; it is typical for large commercial structures as well. The following example of a large commercial bank shows its challenges and the experience of applying a system of standard codes.

3.5   The Role of an Identification System in Global Investment Bank

To keep up with the ever-growing volume of instruments in the market today and to reduce the operational risks of corporate action handling, this Canadian bank urgently needed to upgrade its market data infrastructure to accurately maintain data lineage.

The bank had implemented the Financial Instrument Global Identifier (FIGI) around 2011 to keep market data consistent across the firm, create efficiency and reduce costs.

Problem. The bank, one of the largest and longest-lived financial institutions in the world (it has been operational for more than a century), employs thousands of people in dozens of offices worldwide; it found that its database for maintaining instruments and the associated metadata had grown significantly. One of the bank's challenges was keeping data in sync once a company went through a corporate action.

The bank's processes, previously linked to ISIN as a main identifier globally in multiple countries, had grown inadequate and were now seen to be failing. The bank was unable to store pricing at an exchange level using ISIN—critical to best execution, multicurrency pricing and valuation across positions maintained in different currencies. Additionally, any time an ISIN changed as a result of a corporate action, the linkage back to the original instrument was severed. For example, if company LMN Inc. changed its name to XYZ Inc., and its ISIN changed, the bank was completely unable to deliver the instrument to its clients as a continuous security. This also caused disruption to trade and position management because of rebooking, which resulted in errors in P&L. The bank was struggling with rising costs associated with these errors and the manual processes required to fix them.

Decision

The Bloomberg Open Symbology team consulted with the bank to understand the problems it was facing and its top priorities. Once the bank's goals were established, the Open Symbology team worked closely with bank professionals to develop a new approach to managing instruments and associated metadata using the non-changing FIGI as the primary key.

A joint decision was made: the bank would acquire the FIGI through Bloomberg Enterprise back office products already in place. These products incorporate the FIGI at no additional cost to users. Although the bank had to completely rewrite some of its processes, the mapping of FIGI to replace ISIN in its database was very straightforward. The bank also found that prioritizing the work by asset class and implementing the new processes for the products that caused the most pain first – equities being one – made the solution easier to carry out. The bank moved forward to include other asset classes, such as equity options and corporate bonds.

Results

With the FIGI fully integrated as the backbone to the bank's security master, the bank began to realize benefits immediately. The decision to build its infrastructure around a primary key that never changes, that is more granular and that offers broader coverage than other commercially available identifiers and standards allowed the bank to maintain data lineage. The importance of understanding where the source of the data is coming from, where the data flows to and what has changed over time cannot be overstated and is critical for an investment bank. Additionally, using the hierarchy approach of FIGI assignment for equities, the bank is now able to store information at an exchange level, roll that information up to the appropriate country-level composite FIGI and, ultimately, tie all multiple listings of a stock to its share-class-level FIGI. The bank also no longer needs to worry about cases where ISIN assignment was lacking since FIGI offers comprehensive coverage across all asset classes [2].

4   Conclusion

The information model used for data exchanges plays is very important for ensuring high-quality information support. The information model is designed to solve two global objectives: to determine the composition and names of data objects used in the model, and to determine the procedure for identification of objects. A system based on common codification of objects used by all data providers becomes especially important when organizing data exchange in a distributed environment with many data providers. This solution makes the links between similar objects transparent and helps achieve economic benefits from the use of information technology.

The data model for an information exchange in the framework of electronic government assumes the capture of a sufficiently broad domains of government activity. A data core, as a basis for interagency interaction, consists of a multilayered structure. The use of the codification system is advantageous both at the level of the universal core, as its objects are used in many domains, and at the level of domain-specific models, in particular for the identification of financial instruments. The data flows in the e-government information infrastructure are based on availability of the codification systems for the objects described in the article, as well as for all other objects which are important for ensuring data quality.

This is a major task, and its solution is important for the creation of the e-government IT infrastructure. Creating codification systems for key positions will help provide quality data to the end user: civil servant, citizen or an employee of a commercial company.

References

1. Arms, W.: Digital Libraries. MIT Press, Boston (2000)
2. Bloomberg LP Global Investment Bank FIGI Case Study. https://www.openfigi.com/about/news/2017/2/17/global-investment-bank-figi-case-study
3. Bloomberg LP Open Symbology 2016. https://www.openfigi.com/
4. SWIFT strengthens security after further raids on banks. Comput. Fraud Secur. **2016**(6), 1, 3 (2016). doi:10.1016/S1361-3723(15)30041-5
5. Fenna, D., Wartak, J.: A comprehensive codification for the medical hospital information system. Med. Inform. **10**, 35–42 (1985)
6. Harrington, J.: Relational Database Design and Implementation. Morgan Kaufmann, Cambridge (2016)
7. HL7 Code Systems. Fast Healthcare Interoperability Resources. http://www.hl7.org/Special/committees/vocab/table_0396/index.cfm
8. Inmon, W.H., Linstedt, D.: Data Architecture: A Primer for the Data Scientist. Morgan Kaufmann, Waltham (2014)
9. IPA Infrastructure for Multilayer Interoperability INFORMATION-TECHNOLOGY PROMOTION AGENCY. (IPA). http://imi.ipa.go.jp/IMIOverview-En.html
10. ISA2 ADMS Interoperability solutions for public administrations, businesses and citizens. https://joinup.ec.europa.eu/asset/adms/home
11. LEIROC The Legal Entity Identifier Regulatory Oversight Committee. https://www.leiroc.org/
12. Lipuntsov, Y.: An information model of interagency communication based on distributed data storage. In: International Conference on Electronic Governance and Open Society: Challenges in Eurasia (EGOSE 2016), p. 3. ACM, New York (2016). doi: 10.1145/3014087.3014097
13. Lipuntsov, Y.: Application of information model of interagency data-exchange for the aggregation and analysis of stock market data. In: Selected Papers of the XI International Scientific-Practical Conference Modern Information Technologies and IT-Education (SITITO 2016), pp. 455–460. CEUR, Moscow (2016)
14. NSD National Settlement Depository. http://www.lei-code.ru/ru/

15. OJP National Information Exchange Model. https://www.niem.gov/
16. OMG Financial Instrument Global Identifier, The Object Management Group. http://www.omg.org/spec/FIGI/
17. OpenCorporates LEI The Global Legal Entity Identifier System. openleis.com
18. Paskin, N.: Naming and meaning of digital objects. In: Proceedings of the 2nd International Conference on Automated Production of Cross Media. Firenze Univercity Press, Leeds (2006). http://www.doi.org/topics/060927AXMEDIS2006DOI.pdf
19. Scott, S.V., Van, R.J., Zachariadis, M.: The long-term effect of digital innovation on bank performance: an empirical study of SWIFT adoption in financial services. Res. Policy **46**, 984–1004 (2017)
20. SWIFT Standard Release. Society for Worldwide Interbank Financial Telecommunication. https://www.swift.com/standards/data-standards/bic
21. UK Cabinet Office e-Government Metadata Standard. www.nationalarchives.gov.uk/documents/information-management/egms-metadata-standard.pdf
22. Van Renssen, A.: Formalized natural languages. Definition and Application of a Universal Information Modeling Language. Eindhoven (2013). Gellish.net

Is Russia Ready for Digital Transformation?

Elena Dobrolyubova[1](✉), Oleg Alexandrov[2], and Alexey Yefremov[1]

[1] Russian Academy of National Economy and Public Administration,
Moscow, Russia
dobrolyubova@inbox.ru, efremov-a@ranepa.ru
[2] CEFC Group, Moscow, Russia
aleksandrov@cefc.ru

Abstract. Digital transformation is becoming a mainstream of world economic development providing benefits both to consumers and to businesses adapting to the technological change. Russia, among many other countries, is currently developing a digital economy strategy aimed at supporting sustainable economic growth and increasing productivity. This paper aims to add to the current debate on the priorities of digital economy in Russia by benchmarking Russian ICT development with that in the EU countries and identifying some important preconditions for the digital transformation.

The analysis demonstrates that while the use for Internet and demand for web-based content in Russia is high even by European standards, in Russia, digital technologies in Russia are still seen more as a means of communication rather than a channel for transactions and a source for enhancing business productivity. The lag in terms of connectivity, digital skills, and business adoption of digital technology is significant and is likely to further increase. The economic incentives driving digital economy in the EU countries (such as high labor costs and competition) are insufficient in the Russian context.

Based on the analysis, the new digital economy strategy should be oriented at supporting three main priorities: reducing administrative barriers and creating economic incentives for business digitalization; developing ICT infrastructure with special attention to speed and quality of connection services; and investing in digital skills. These efforts should be complemented by a monitoring and evaluation framework including both core dimensions measured in the EU and sector-specific metrics of digital transformation.

Keywords: Digital economy · Digital transformation · Indicators · Information and communication technology · Factors · Russia · Strategy

1 Introduction

In broad terms, digital transformation denotes a change associated with the application of digital technology in all aspects of human society [32]; it is seen as a key trend that penetrates many industrial and societal domains [17]. Digital transformation strategies often focus on the transformation of products, processes, and organizational aspects due to the innovative technologies [23]; they create new opportunities for customer engagement and meeting consumer needs [8].

© Springer International Publishing AG 2017
D.A. Alexandrov et al. (Eds.): DTGS 2017, CCIS 745, pp. 431–444, 2017.
https://doi.org/10.1007/978-3-319-69784-0_36

The high potential of digital transformation in terms of adding to economic growth and social prosperity makes digital economy a key developmental priority both in developed and developing countries; promoted both by the international community. Developing digital economy is also a priority for Russia, though so far, the research of this subject has been limited. Therefore, in this article, we will focus mostly on economic aspects of digital transformation, while acknowledging the importance of other societal changes that digitalization creates.

International organizations consider digitalization as a key source of economic growth and social development. The World Bank claims that digital dividends to the society (such as growth, new jobs, and services) are largely unrealized, while better use of the technologies available are likely to yield high gains to people, businesses, and governments [37]. In 2016, OECD Ministers and representatives of some of non-OECD countries adopted a Cancún Declaration recognizing that 'the digital economy is a powerful catalyst for innovation, growth and social prosperity' [28]. In 2017, digital transformation was put forward as one of the core subjects for the German Presidency in G20 with significant productivity gains expected [26]. The estimates of the World Economic Forum also suggest that the approaching digital transformation is likely to have a positive impact both on businesses and on the society benefiting from more cost-effective and tailored services, higher security, time and cost savings, reduction in negative environmental effects [36].

Digital economy has become an important part of the current socio-economic agenda both at the international level (i.e., Digital Single Market in the EU [11]; Declaration on Forming Digital Space in the Eurasian Economic Union [16]) and at the national level (i.e. in Australia [1], Canada [14], etc.). Even preliminary review of these strategic documents suggests the change of emphasis from developing e-government [27] (which was a major task for public administrations around the globe in the 2000s and early 2010s) to promoting digital transformation both in the public and, especially, in the private sector. Given the rapid development of digital technologies, more and more attention is being paid to potential risks related to the digital revolution – ranging from the technical issues of cybersecurity and personal data protection to more global impacts of digital technologies on income inequality and labor market.

2 Paper Objective, Literature and Scope

Russia is following the global trend on supporting the digital transformation of economy. The work on a new strategy for digital economy is underway and the strategy is likely to be endorsed before the end of 2017. Given the high competition for the digital leadership with other countries, it seems timely to evaluate the existing pre-conditions for rapid development of the digital economy and assess the gap in adoption of digital technologies in Russia and other countries. This analysis could then be used to tailoring the prospective digital economy strategy to the countries needs and focusing on the key constraints to digital transformation in the Russian context.

While there is vast literature on developing information society in Russia, the research so far has favoured the issues of e-government [10, 18] and the cross-country comparisons have often been limited to the indices produced by the international organizations (see [10, 30]) or to the research aimed at measuring the digital divide among the Russian regions and their readiness to information society. Given the high dynamics of digital development, both the measures used for such comparisons and the aspects of analysis need to be broadened.

So far, the analysis on the prospects of the digital transformation in Russia has either focused on selected sectoral issues, such as digital health [7] or broadband development [29] and policy decisions, such as data localization requirements [24]. Recently some studies on impact of digitalization on business process management [3], internal and external business environment [21], and transformation of design and production [22]. However, most of these publications are devoted to individual aspects of digitalization, without reference to the overall assessment of Russia's readiness for digital transformation.

This paper aims at complementing these attempts and comparing the digital economy in Russia with that in the EU. For this comparison, the components of Digital Economy and Society Index (DESI) used in the EU for measuring the progress towards digital market [13] are applied. The paper then briefly reviews the preconditions for digital transformation and identifies the factors which promote digital economy. In the last part of the paper we focus on developing recommendations on a range of measures supporting digital transformation of economy in Russia.

3 Benchmarking Russia's Digital Readiness

3.1 The Basis for Benchmarking

High pace of digital transformation results in a variety of approaches to measuring and assessing the development of digital economy making cross-country and cross-regional comparisons challenging. Performance measures which were relevant a few years ago, are no longer applicable or adequate for the digital era. The technologies which were considered advanced 5 years ago (such as 3G mobile connections or fixed telephone lines – both indicators used in international ratings of information society), are likely to become obsolete in a few years to come. That is why relatively high positions Russia has achieved in international ICT ratings (i.e., 0,71 points (out of 1) for digital adoption index; 43rd position on the ITU ICT Development Index in 2016 [20], 42nd position in IMD digital competitiveness ranking in 2017 [19] 41st position in Network Readiness Index [36], 32nd position on E-participation index and 35th position on E-government development index in the recent UN E-government survey [35] may be somewhat misleading in terms of assessing the prospects of developing digital economy in Russia.

The use of global composite indices, especially for a large variety of countries, is appealing but it is also often insufficient for policy development purposes. Firstly, the global nature of such indices limits the surveys to the statistics available in most participating states. Such lack of data leads to exclusion of some promising technologies which are not yet widespread. Supporting year-to-year comparability also calls for limiting methodological changes in international rankings.

Secondly, the composite indices use weights and may therefore be biased to highlight some aspects at the expense of others [25]. For instance, in ICT Development

Index only 20% of the total result are related to ICT skills and this assessment is based on overall enrollment data rather than ICT-specific skills. The UN uses similar metrics for its Human Development Index (part of E-government index), but the weight of human capital is higher (1/3 of the total result). The World Bank does not use any indicators related to ICT skills in digital adoption index, while the World Economic Forum uses skills as one of the pillars for constructing Network Readiness Index. In the latter case, the assessment of skills includes an indicator on quality of science and maths education, however, the total weight of skills component is low given that there are 9 other pillars which are calculated [36].

Given the ambition of Russia to gain a visible market share in the evolving global digital economy, benchmarking of the country's readiness for this task should be made based on cross-country comparisons with developed countries. To this end, DESI which has been recently adopted and is used by the EU to track the progress in achieving the Digital Single Market objectives [11] is of special interest. This index includes 5 dimensions which are estimated based on 31 indicators.

Given the lack of comparable statistics in Russia on each of these indicators, we cannot estimate DESI for Russia. However, even benchmarking the data available allows for identifying the gaps and possible points of focus for the future digital economy strategy in Russia. The available comparative data is summarized in Table 1[1] and described in subsections below.

3.2   Connectivity

Measuring connectivity under DESI includes 4 sub-dimensions: fixed and mobile broadband, speed, and affordability. Based on the most recent DESI report [13], fixed broadband is available to 98% of Europeans, and 73.8% of EU households subscribe to fixed broadband. Notably, while availability of fixed broadband connection does not vary significantly by country (the range is from 86.2% to 100% of households), the fixed broadband take-up variation is higher – from 55.2% to 95.7%.

In Russia, there is no official data on the broadband availability. However, given that urban population accounts for about 79%, while the target for 2016 was to ensure availability of modern communication services in 95% of settlements with population of 10–50 thousand, broadband availability in Russia is likely to lag the EU levels. The proportion of households with broadband connection in Russia in 2016 accounted for some 70.7%, which is lower than in most EU countries.

Russia is lagging the EU in terms of mobile broadband take-up: while the EU average is 83.9 subscriptions per 100 of population, in Russia the subscription rate is 68.1[2] (still higher than the EU minimal score of 42.7). There is a gap in terms of 4G mobile networks coverage (84% of populated areas in the EU and about 60% in Russia); some 85.9% of the EU households are covered by 4G/LTE.

Higher coverage levels have impact on the speed of connection. Some 76% of European homes can access high-speed broadband (at least 30 Mbps); 82.2% of

---

[1] Only the data on indicators available both for the EU and Russia is presented in the table.

[2] Hereinafter the data for Russia is for 2015, if not specified otherwise.

Table 1. Benchmarking Russia and the EU on DESI components

DESI dimension	Indicator	EU average	Russia	Comment
1. Connectivity	% of households covered by broadband	98.0	79.0	Estimate
	% of households subscribing to broadband	73.8	70.7	Data for Russia is for 2016
	Number of mobile subscriptions per 100 people	83.9	68.1	
	% of populated areas covered by 4G	84.0	60.0	Estimate for Russia
	% of households which have broadband connection with speed > 10 Mbps	Over 50% in 16 EU countries	48	Data from Akamai 4Q 2016 report both for EU and Russia
2. Digital skills	% of people aged 16–74 who use Internet at least once a week	79.2	71.5	In Russia people aged 15–72 are surveyed
	% of people with at least basic digital skills	77.0	38.8	
	% of ICT specialists in total employment	3.5	1.5	Estimate for Russia for 2009
	% of STEM graduates of all people aged 20–29	18.7	6.4	Estimate for Russia based on 2014 data
3. Use of Internet	% of people who used Internet to read news	57.6	21.1	The EU data is for 2016, the data on Russia is for 2015
	% of people who used Internet to play/download games, images, films, music	78.1	49.6	
	% of people who used Internet to make calls	39.3	41.3	
	% of people who used Internet to participate in social networks	63.1	74.6	
	% of people who used Internet for online banking	59.2	16.9	
	% of people who used Internet for shopping	66.0	26.7	
4. Integration of digital technology	% of businesses using ERP	35.6	9.3	Data is for 2015
	% of businesses using cloud services	20.9	43	Market estimate for Russia
	% of businesses selling online	17.0	18.2	For EU the data is for SMEs
5. Digital public services	% of people sending filled forms to public authorities over Internet	33.6	3.0	Estimate based on service delivery surveys in Russia

Sources: DESI [13], Rosstat, market data

households have connection speed exceeding 10 Mbps. Some 36.9% of the fixed broadband subscriptions are high-speed (ranging from 81.1% in Belgium to 4.2% in Cyprus).

There is no official data on connection speed in Russia. However, based on Akamai Connectivity Report data, the share of households which have high speed broadband IPv4 connection with the speed exceeding 10 Mbps, reaches 71% in Netherlands and is over 50% in 16 other EU countries, while in Russia, only some 48% of households have such connection speed. Notably, the growth of households with at least 10 Mbps broadband connection in Russia in 2016 was the lowest among the 30 countries surveyed. The average mobile connection speed in Russia is 9.5 Mbps which is among the lowest levels in the region [2]. Notably, the share of high-speed mobile connections in the EU went up by 74% in two years [13].

Noteworthy, Russia is among the countries with the most affordable ICT, holding the 2nd place in the world in terms of mobile tariffs and the 10th place in terms of fixed broadband tariffs [36]. However, in terms of the competition in Internet and telephony markets, Russia holds only the 101th position in the same ranking. This factor may be one of the reasons for low growth rates in connection speed which is crucial for adopting digital technologies.

3.3 Digital Skills

This dimension includes indicators measuring Internet usage, digital skills, availability of ICT specialists, and STEM graduates.

On average, 79.2% of all people aged 16–74 in the EU use Internet at least once a week (the indicator ranges from 56.3% in Romania to 96.6% in Luxembourg). In Russia, similar indicator[3] is lower and accounts for 71.5%. Some 77% of Europeans have at least basic digital skills (i.e. use mailbox, editing tools, can install new devices). The evaluation of computer skills in Russia demonstrates lower results: only some 38.8% of adult population used office applications, 8.4% installed a new device or program. The share of ICT specialists in the EU accounts for some 3.5% of total employment. While there is no official comparable data for Russia; the research conducted by IT association in 2009 showed that ICT specialists accounted for some 1.47% of the total employment [4].

An important indicator measuring the prospects of further digitalization is the ratio of STEM graduates (i.e. people with a degree in science, technology, engineering, or mathematics) per 1000 of population aged 20–29. The EU average for STEM graduates accounts for 18.7 per 1000 people. In Russia, the estimate for this indicator made by the authors accounts for 6.44 graduates per 1000 of population aged 20–29 (both for the EU and Russia the latest available data is for 2014). This gap is quite significant and presents an important challenge for the future of digital economy in Russia. The situation is especially worrying as, according to Rosstat, the ratio of graduates with a

---

[3] In Russia, individuals aged 15 to 72 are surveyed which is likely to lead to higher proportion due to more intensive use of Internet in younger age groups. The data on Russia is for 2016.

degree in Computing and IT (per 10,000 of population) has dropped more than twice from 2010 (6.6 graduates) to 2015 (2.8 graduates per 10,000 of population).

3.4 Use of Internet

This dimension includes indicators on the content used by the Internet users, the use of Internet for communication purposes, and for transactions. As demonstrated in Fig. 1, while the use of Internet as a source of communication in Russia exceeds the EU averages (i.e., in 2015, 41.3% of Internet users made Internet telephone and video calls (36.7% in the EU); 74.6% of Russian Internet users participated in social networks (the EU average was 62.9). This prevalence might be partially attributed to the slight difference in age groups used for collecting data in the EU (16–74) and in Russia (15–72), but, nevertheless, the penetration of Internet as a means of social communication in Russia is very high.

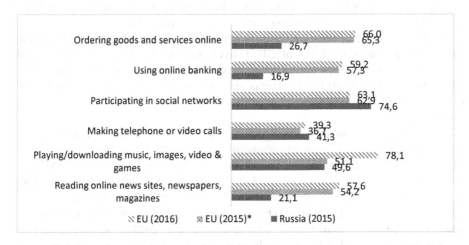

*the EU data on playing/downloading music, images, video and games is for 2014.
The EU data covers individuals aged 16-74; the data for Russia is for individuals aged 15-72.*

Fig. 1. Use of Internet in Russia and the EU, % of individuals who used Internet in the last 3 months (Sources: DESI, Rosstat)

Active use of Internet as a communication tool also promotes using this source for downloading various media content (such as games, video, etc.) – more than 49.6% of Russian Internet users are also users of such type of content. However, the use of Internet as a source of news is far less prevalent: in 2015, only about one fifth of Russian Internet users read online newspapers, magazines, or other news sites while in the EU over a half of Internet users read news on the web.

Russians are much more conservative than Europeans in terms of using Internet for transactions, such as ordering goods and services or online banking. While, on average, 57.3% of the EU Internet users were involved in online banking in 2015 (59.2% in

2016), only 16.9% of Russian Internet users made financial transactions on the web. Similarly, while 65.3% of Europeans ordered goods or services online, only 26.7% of Russians used the web for this purpose. Noteworthy, the variation among the EU member states in using Internet for transaction purposes is very high: the proportion of individuals using online banking in 2016 ranged from 7.41 to 92.0%, ordering goods and services online – from 18.0 to 86.5%.

3.5 Integration of Digital Economy

This dimension includes indicators characterizing business digitalization and e-commerce. The latest data published by the EU demonstrates that European businesses are increasingly adopting digital technologies, such as the use of a business software for electronic information sharing (from 26% in 2013 to 35.6% of enterprises in 2015), sending electronic invoices (from 11% in 2014 to 17.7% of enterprises in 2016) or using social media to engage with customers and partners (from 14% in 2013 to 20% of enterprises in 2016). Cloud technologies are used by some 20.9% of businesses, radio frequency identification – by 10% of EU enterprises.

In Russia, statistical data for business digitalization is quite limited. While most businesses use Internet (88.1% in 2015), have broadband connection (79.5%) and 42.6% of enterprises have websites, only some 9.3% of Russian businesses use ERPs (in the EU - 35.6% in 2015). The market assessments demonstrate that over a half of large businesses and about 43% of small businesses in Russia use two or more cloud services [33].

Some 18.2% of enterprises in Russia engage in online selling. In the EU, the statistics is collected for small and medium enterprises (SMEs). Based on this data, e-commerce by SMEs has grown slightly (from 15% in 2014 to 17% of SMEs in 2016), e-commerce turnover accounted for 7.5% of the total SMEs turnover in 2016. Nevertheless, less than half of these companies sell to other EU countries. In Russia, e-commerce accounted for about 800 billion RUR or 3.5% of retail market in 2016 [12] which represents significant growth (24% as compared to 2015 in nominal terms).

Noteworthy, the existing set of indicators used for DESI does not include many aspects of business digitalization. For instance, there are no metrics used to estimate the value added from using a broad range of new technologies in industrial production, construction, and transport (i.e. smart sensors, robotics, autonomous operations including transport, 3D printing, and the like) which are likely to transform various sectors in the nearest decades [34]. These transformations are likely to bring about significant economic and societal effects, which are still to be measured.

3.6 E-Government

E-government dimension includes the indicators on e-services uptake, online services, as well as open data (including both for the presence and usefulness of open data). The quality of European online public services slightly improved with an increase in the number of public services available online (online service completion score increased from 75 in 2014 to 81 in 2016). At the same time, the score measuring the reuse of user data already known to the public administration as a way of facilitating the delivery of online services remained stable. As for the demand side, 33.6% of Internet users returned filled forms online to the public administration (i.e. have used online public services for more than just obtaining information), up from 27% three years ago.

In Russia, some 39.6% of citizen applying for public services used Internet. However, as the previous surveys revealed, only about 3% of public services were provided fully electronically while in most cases people used Internet for getting information on service delivery procedures [15]. While significant attention has been paid to promoting open data in Russia, both in terms of setting legal basis and introducing monitoring procedures, the use of open data is still low. For instance, the number of requests for open data from the portal per month accounted for less than 300, while the total number of data sets exceeds 12.8 thousand.

4   Preconditions for Digital Economy

The World Bank research demonstrates that digital adoption index is highly correlated with GDP per capita; however, the level of economic development is not the only enabler of digitalization. There is a strong correlation between digital adoption and complements which technology provides such as cutting the red tape, improving institutional quality, and improving skills [37].

High variation of the EU country data on DESI suggests that there are other factors which might influence the extent of digitalization. As it is the business sector which is driving digital transformation, we will focus on two aspects which stimulate businesses to innovate and adopt digital technologies: labor costs and competition.

Labor costs represent an important share of total production costs of businesses; therefore, increasing labor productivity is always on the agenda. Labor productivity varies greatly by sector. In the EU, ICT sector demonstrates the second highest level of productivity (the highest productivity is in finance and insurance – sectors which also use digital instruments intensively). What is also important, it is the ICT sector which demonstrates the highest growth rate in terms of labor productivity as compared to any other sector.

The calculations made based on the EU data demonstrate that there is significant correlation between the hourly labor costs incurred by businesses and the extent of digital integration into business processes (correlation coefficient equals 0,678). Higher labor costs stimulate technical innovation in businesses and motivate entrepreneurs to cut costs using technology advances (Fig. 2).

In the Russian context, with low labor costs, this incentive for business digitalization (and business innovation at large) is limited. It is therefore not surprising that the proportion of innovative businesses (businesses investing in technological innovation) has been declining from 9.1% in 2012 to 8.2% in 2015, while the investment in technological innovation has been stagnating in 2014–2015. However, in the medium to long term with decrease in total labor force, the business motivation to digitalize business operations is likely to increase.

Another factor which is worth considering is competition. There is medium correlation between the independence of telecoms and business digitalization (correlation

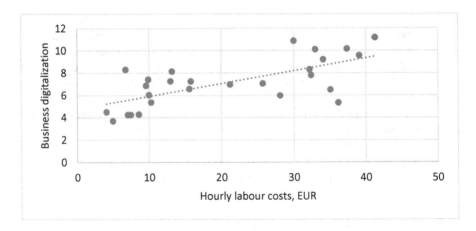

Sources: DESI, Eurostat

Fig. 2. Correlation of hourly labor costs and business digitalization (integration of digital economy) in the EU countries (Sources: DESI, Eurostat)

coefficient is 0,530) demonstrating that the higher is the extent of telecoms independence, the higher is integration of digital technologies into business processes (Fig. 3).

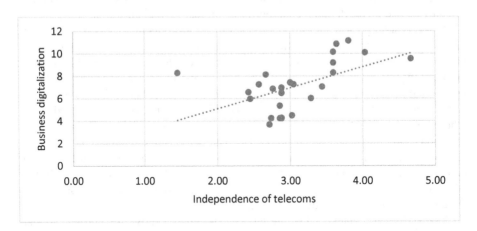

Fig. 3. Correlation of independence of telecoms and business digitalization (integration of digital economy) in the EU countries (Sources: DESI, OECD data [6])

This correlation suggests that the quality of government regulation is an important factor for developing digital economy. This is especially relevant for Russia, as the restrictiveness of public regulation in computer services in Russia is higher than in the EU states [26].

The above example highlights the importance of reducing excessive legal barriers and developing legal framework promoting digital economy. As noted by the Central Bank of Russia, the current legislation regulating the submission and proving value of e-documents, as well as related liability issues, is insufficient [9]. Digitalization and introduction of new products, for instance, software as a service, create challenges for copyright legislation [31]. Another problem is related to regulation of some specific technologies, such as big data [5]. To address these issues systemically, it is important to integrate the assessment of possible barriers to digitalization into the processes of both ex ante and ex post regulatory impact analysis. This measure would help eliminate the existing barriers and prevent the new restrictions for digital economy development.

5 Conclusions

The analysis demonstrates that despite the high levels of Internet use among the population and high demand for digital content and extensive engagement in social media, Russia is still lagging behind the EU average levels in terms of connectivity, digital skills, business digitalization, and digital government. Given the current pace of development in most of these dimensions in the EU and other OECD states, this gap is likely to increase. Economic indicators, such as lower per capita incomes and low labor costs, do not create adequate stimulation for business innovation. In this context, the future digital economy strategy should focus on creating favorable conditions for digital transformation and overcoming the gaps identified.

Firstly, there is a need to reduce administrative and legal barriers for developing digital economy and create incentives to business digitalization. This is especially important given that Russia lacks some of the market incentives driving digital economy in OECD countries (i.e., high labor costs and competition). The possible measures discussed in the context of developing digital economy program include: (i) liberalizing labor market and reducing barriers for using distant labor; (ii) simplifying certification requirements and introduction of declarations of conformity in ICT sectors, including self-certification of systems (i.e. smart homes) rather than individual products; (iii) introducing the notion of 'digital registration address' for businesses which would reduce registration costs; (iv) integrating business accounting systems with tax reporting and statistical reporting on M2M basis, improving the access to public databases and others. Integating identification of digital barriers into the process of regulatory impact assessment could be a useful tool for developing the legal framework supportive to the digital transformation of economy.

Secondly, there is a need for adequate communication infrastructure, which involves improving the efficiency of spectrum use, and ensuring access to high speed broadband for all. To this end, there is a need to pay special attention both to coverage and speed. The latter is traditionally omitted in the Russian strategic documents on ICT development but may become an important bottleneck for using digital technologies in transport, agriculture, forestry, utility sector, and other industries.

Thirdly, the new strategy should focus on developing human capital for digital economy. The analysis in this article shows that while Russia still has high positions in terms of tertiary education, the current trend of decline of graduates with ICT degrees and relatively small number of graduates with STEM degree is worrisome. In the digital economy, there is a need for promoting ICT at all levels of education (primary, secondary, and tertiary), and enable acquiring digital skills as a part of lifelong learning strategies.

Finally, the new digital economy strategy would require monitoring and evaluation arrangements. To this end, adopting DESI indicators used in the EU and complementing them by sector-specific metrics reflecting the progress of digitalization in selected sectors of Russia economy (oil and gas, mining, manufacture, agriculture, transport, and others) is recommended.

References

1. Advancing Australia as a digital economy: an update to the national digital economy strategy. http://apo.org.au/node/34523
2. Akamai. Q4 2016 State of the Internet Connectivity Report. https://www.akamai.com/us/en/multimedia/documents/state-of-the-internet/q4-2016-state-of-the-internet-connectivity-report.pdf
3. Aleksandrova, L., Polushina, I.: Impact of transformation of digital communication technologies and systems on business process management. Humanitarian Inf. **11**, 25–33 (2016). (in Russian)
4. Apkit (2009). (in Russian). http://www.apkit.ru/files/personal2009_final.pdf
5. Arkhipov, V., Naumov, V.: The legal definition of personal data in the regulatory environment of the Russian Federation: between formal certainty and technological development. Comput. Law Secur. Rev. **32**(6), 868–887 (2016)
6. Beiter, P., Koske, I., Naru, F., Wanner, I.: Regulatory management practices in OECD countries. OECD Economics Department Working Papers, no. 1296 (2016)
7. Bereznoy, A., Saygitov, R.: Digital revolution and innovative business models in healthcare: global trends and Russian realities. Vestnik Rossiiskoi Akademii Meditsinskikh Nauk **71**(3), 200–213 (2016). (in Russian)
8. Berman, S.J.: Digital transformation: opportunities to create new business models. Strategy Leadersh. **40**(2), 16–24 (2012)
9. Central Bank of Russia: Barjery na puti razvitija elektronnogo vzaimodejstvija na finansovom rynke [Barriers to the development of electronic interaction in the financial market] (2014). (in Russian). https://www.cbr.ru/finmarkets/files/interaction/1a.pdf
10. Chugunov, A.V.: Russia's concept of "electronic state": the formation of public policy, organizational and legal problems. Vestnik Moscow University. Ser. 12: Polit. Sci. **3**, 78–89 (2010). (in Russian)
11. Communication from the Commission to the European Parliament, the Council, the European Economic and Social Committee and the Committee of the Regions. A Digital Single Market Strategy for Europe – COM (2015). 192 final. https://ec.europa.eu/digital-single-market/en/news/digital-single-market-strategy-europe-com2015-192-final
12. Data Insight (2016). https://www.slideshare.net/Data_Insight/ecommerce-2016-69990938
13. DESI. http://digital-agenda-data.eu
14. Digital Canada 150. http://www.ic.gc.ca/eic/site/028.nsf/eng/home
15. Dobrolyubova, E., Alexandrov, O.: E-government in Russia: meeting growing demand in the era of budget constraints. In: Chugunov, A.V., Bolgov, R., Kabanov, Y., Kampis, G., Wimmer, M. (eds.) DTGS 2016. CCIS, vol. 674, pp. 247–257. Springer, Cham (2016). doi:10.1007/978-3-319-49700-6_23

16. Eurasian Economic Commission. Declaration on Forming Digital Space in the Eurasian Economic Union. https://docs.eaeunion.org/docs/ru-ru/01412001/clco_22112016_186
17. Gray, J., Rumpe, B.: Models for the digital transformation. Softw. Syst. Model. **16**(2), 307–308 (2017). doi:10.1007/s10270-017-0596-7
18. Hohlov, Y., Styrin, E.: E-government in Russia: strategies of formation and development. In: Global Strategy and Practice of E-Governance: Examples from Around the World, pp. 286–303. IDI Publishing, Hershey (2011)
19. IMD Digital Competitiveness Ranking (2017). https://www.imd.org/uupload/IMD.Wcc/PDFSource/RU_digital.pdf
20. ITU Measuring the Information Society Report (2016). http://www.itu.int/en/ITU-D/Statistics/Pages/publications/mis2016.aspx
21. Kuntsman, A.: Transformation of internal and external business environment in digital economy. Manag. Econ. Syst.: sci. Electron. J. **11**, 1 (2016). (in Russian)
22. Kupriyanovsky, V., Sinyagov, S., Namiot, D., Utkin, N., Nikolaev, D., Dobrynin, A.: Idustries transformation in the digital economy – the design and production. Int. J. Open Inf. Technol. **5**(1), 50–70 (2017). (in Russian)
23. Matt, C., Hess, T., Benlian, A.: Digital transformation strategies. Bus. Inf. Syst. Eng. **57**(5), 339–343 (2015)
24. Mikhailova, I.: Could the recently enacted data localization requirements in Russia backfire? J. World Trade **50**(2), 313–333 (2016)
25. OECD: Measuring the Internet Economy: A Contribution to the Research Agenda. OECD Digital Economy Papers, No. 226. OECD Publishing, Paris (2013). http://dx.doi.org/10.1787/5k43gjg6r8jf-en
26. OECD Key Issues for Digital Transformation in the G20 (2017). https://www.oecd.org/g20/key-issues-for-digital-transformation-in-the-g20.pdf
27. OECD C(2014)88 Recommendation of the Council on Digital Government Strategies (2014). http://www.oecd.org/gov/digital-government/Recommendation-digital-government-strategies.pdf
28. OECD C(2016)116 - Declaration on the Digital Economy: Innovation, Growth and Social Prosperity (Cancún Declaration) (2016). http://www.oecd.org/internet/oecd-digital-economy-ministerial-declaration.htm
29. Rossotto, C.M., Gelvanovska, N., Hohlov,Yu., Mačiulė, V., Shapohnik, S.: A Sector Assessment: Broadband in Russia. World Bank Group, Washington (2015)
30. Sadovnikova, N.A., Klochkova, E.N., Dobrolyubova, E.I., Alexandrov, O.V.: Basic trends of information society development in Russia compared to world's leading countries. Int. Rev. Manag. Mark. **5**, 18–29 (2015)
31. Savelyev, A.: Software-as-a-service - legal nature: shifting the existing paradigm of copyright law. Comput. Law Secur. Rev. **30**(5), 560–568 (2014)
32. Stolterman, E., Croon Fors, A.: Information technology and the good life. In: Kaplan, B., Truex, D., Wastell, D., Wood-Harperand, A.T., DeGross, J. (eds.) Information Systems Research: Relevant Theory and Informed Practice, pp. 687–692. Kluwer Academic Publishers, Boston (2004)
33. Tadviser (2017). (in Russian). http://www.tadviser.ru/index.php/%D0%A1%D1%82%D0%B0%D1%82%D1%8C%D1%8F:%D0%9E%D0%B1%D0%BB%D0%B0%D1%87%D0%BD%D1%8B%D0%B5_%D1%81%D0%B5%D1%80%D0%B2%D0%B8%D1%81%D1%8B_(%D1%80%D1%8B%D0%BD%D0%BE%D0%BA_%D0%A0%D0%BE%D1%81%D1%81%D0%B8%D0%B8
34. The Digital Transformation Initiative. World Economic Forum White Paper (2017). https://www.weforum.org/whitepapers/digital-transformation-initiative

35. UN E-Government Survey (2016). https://publicadministration.un.org/egovkb/en-us/Global-Survey
36. WEF Global Information Technology Report (2016). http://reports.weforum.org/global-information-technology-report-2016/economies/#economy=RUS
37. World Bank: Digital Dividends. World Development Report (2016). http://documents.worldbank.org/curated/en/896971468194972881/pdf/102725-PUB-Replacement-PUBLIC.pdf

Digital Economy and Knowledge Barriers: Their Origin and Dealing with Them

Evgeny Zinder[1(✉)] and Irina Yunatova[2]

[1] FOSTAS Foundation, Moscow, Russian Federation
ezinder@fostas.ru
[2] FOSTAS Foundation, St. Petersburg, Russian Federation
iyunatova@fostas.ru

Abstract. This paper presents analysis of problems and applicability of Knowledge Management (KM) methods in enterprise engineering focusing on KM areas for supporting multiprofessional and multiorganizational teams, organizational structures and business processes created and changed dynamically, including engagement of collective and individual agents from the enterprise ecosystem. Knowledge barriers in the way of adequate agents' participation in the dynamic environment of dynamic network business process (DNBP) and knowledge-intensive business process (KiBP) requiring better developed knowledge acquisition methods and information support are examined. As a result of the research, the fundamental reason for the knowledge barriers existence is given, and the organizational and dynamic factors which increase damage caused by barriers are provided. The paper describes the priority set of knowledge elicitation, structurization, and representation methods oriented towards knowledge workers, domain experts, or other human agents for organizing agents' cooperation. The paper suggests the framework of methods aimed at requirements of DNBP and KiBP.

Keywords: Digital economy · Knowledge management · Knowledge barriers · Multiprofessional team · Knowledge worker · Enterprise ecosystem · Knowledge merging · Dynamic business process formation

1 Introduction

ICT development is leading to the capability of the broad enterprise digital transformation (DT) [1, 2] basing on the information connectivity and dramatically diminishing response time, which in turn causes the growth of enterprises dynamics. Under such conditions, dynamic network business process (DNBP which is treated similarly to Dynamic Business Networking described in [3]) formation is accompanied with the engagement of various types of enterprise ecosystem agents, multiprofessional teams formation, and requires support of knowledge-intensive business process (KiBP similarly to [4]). The pivotal role of knowledge demands agents' knowledge integration and sharing which is confirmed by the conception of knowledge enterprises used in [5]. In this paper we will use the term knowledge-driven enterprise (KDE) which is close to the term knowledge-driven organization in [5], but emphasizes the "enterprise" concept.

At the same time, essential problems and knowledge barriers have been revealed in the way of KDE development. Knowledge barriers are here understood as obstacles in

© Springer International Publishing AG 2017
D.A. Alexandrov et al. (Eds.): DTGS 2017, CCIS 745, pp. 445–463, 2017.
https://doi.org/10.1007/978-3-319-69784-0_37

the way of common understanding in multiprofessional and multiorganizational groups, and knowledge management (KM) does not cope with this problem fully enough. While achievements in formal KM methods are quite noticeable, for example, in Artificial Intelligence (AI), this does not rectify the situation in KM on the whole. For instance, Guerino in [6] critically analyzed and evaluated the situation with KM as fairly negative, and this evaluation is largely applicable to practical employment of formal KM methods in dynamic KDE. Academic research into semantic interoperability and knowledge integration is conducted for various industries. However, achievements on this way are still limited, and one of the reasons is limitations of formalized knowledge representation and processing. Ensuring accurate information and adequate knowledge by means of formalized ontology matching is especially poorly applicable in DNBP & KiBP sphere "*due to the difficulties resulting from dynamism in networked businesses*" [3, p. 215]. In particular, short term partnering of parties, various contexts of the parties, and lack of centralized control are listed among difficulty sources generating knowledge barriers.

Besides, overestimated expectations for formal methods applicability have led to insufficient attention to person's roles as knowledge worker (KW) and domain expert (DE) in KM. While KW's and DE's direct performing of the professional knowledge acquisition and integration is needed, such an activity requires mastering special methods for knowledge elicitation and processing.

This paper presents analysis of problems and limitations of KM methods applicability in KDE engineering, especially for supporting multiprofessional and multiorganizational teams assembled on demand for dynamically created and changed business processes, in particular, engaging other agents from the enterprise ecosystem. Formerly it was demonstrated in [7] that it is necessary to ensure appropriate conditions for people involvement in new spheres of activity. In this paper we defined areas where DE and KW are involved in a new kind of activity to undertake certain actions for achieving shared understanding in DNBP & KiBP environment. Our paper proposes the set of KM methods relevant for their exploitation by KW & DE on their own and for these methods application in the highly dynamic environment.

The rest of the paper is structured as follows. In Sect. 2, the used approach and methodology of this research are presented, as well as some concept explanations. Section 3 describes capabilities and fundamental limitations of knowledge merging. Hypotheses defining the areas of our proposals are formulated. Section 4 describes the recommended knowledge elicitation and processing methods oriented toward KW & DE or other human agents in condition of enterprise dynamics. Section 5 suggests the framework "Dynamic KM methods" aimed at meeting requirements of DNBP and KiBP. Section 6 presents the summary of obtained results, direction of further research and the final conclusion.

2 Research Methodology

Our work is based on the search kind of the historical approach which is applied to analyze KDE and KM within the next particular historical period with certain characteristics of the enterprise environment. For our analysis, we are selecting the time horizon from today up to 2030; this horizon corresponds to widely known plans for sustainable economy development [8].

The methodological basis of the research includes two basic components, namely:

- a comprehensive approach to a KDE analysis, including consideration of a human factor, technology, and economy aspects;
- basic provisions of the non-classical and post-non-classical epistemology [9].

The principles of non-classical and post-non-classical epistemology provide background for the expansion of knowledge categories selection for knowledge acquisition and merging.

We use the working scheme of the KM process [10, p. 7, Fig. 2] and the blocks "Acquisition", "Creation" and "Refinement" as the baseline of the main sets of KM tasks in our analysis. Meanwhile, we are treating "enterprise knowledge" as a kind of "knowledge" and define it as part of our proposals. The limitations of enterprise knowledge merging are analyzed using publications about classic and modern endeavors in KM.

We engaged a group of highly qualified experts for evaluating some of our propositions concerning knowledge acquisition methods applicability in conditions of dynamic enterprises. Besides, we also rely upon our own experience gained while performing specific activities in knowledge acquisition and refinement in large and small projects of enterprise analysis in various industries, namely, in aviation, railway transportation, architecture and construction, healthcare, governmental agencies, educational organizations accumulated over 30 years. In addition, we rely upon our background in integrated information systems and databases design and audit, as well as on the experience obtained while running educational projects transferring professional knowledge to students and specialists in enterprise reengineering sphere.

Some key concepts used in this article are widely spread but unfortunately lack generally accepted definitions. For this reason, constructive versions of their interpretation used in this study are provided below.

Knowledge worker (KW) was described by Peter Drucker more than 20 years ago, but there is no generally accepted definition yet. We treat KW, similarly to [11], as a worker whose main contribution to the enterprise results consists of employing his/her knowledge from the specific enterprise subject domain while producing an output product and of creating new knowledge in this domain. Conventionally, domain expert (DE) is a person with deep knowledge in a concrete subject domain sufficient for solving complicated problems specific for this domain. In this study we differentiate roles of KW and DE presuming that KW is a direct performer of the enterprise working processes while DE might not participate in the working processes.

Digital economy is interpreted as a practical economic activity of enterprises and individuals in all economy sectors which is transformed for dramatic performance growth by using ICT ensuring significantly higher levels of connectivity and automation.

The following definitions of enterprise information and enterprise knowledge are an adaptation of some existing ones (subsequent to [12]) by eliminating some redundancy and by specialization for an enterprise.

Enterprise information is the data that have been pre-processed by an enterprise recipient and stored with the resolution that the set of characters and/or signals has or may have definite meaning about something for somebody and sometime in the enterprise. Consequently, respective information has a definite meaning but can provide or not provide some value to any recipient of the enterprise.

Enterprise knowledge is the enterprise information which has been processed to convey understanding, accumulated learning results, and/or expertise as it is applicable to Enterprise problems or tasks and provide some value to a recipient of the enterprise.

3   Capabilities of Professional Knowledge Integration for Dynamic KDE

Capabilities of knowledge dynamic matching/integration are explored by analyzing:

1. an ontology approach with formalized ontologies design and usage as a popular approach in the informatics community;
2. a process-oriented approach for dynamic forming of business process knowledge as a popular approach in the enterprise engineering community.

3.1   Ontology Approach

Initial evaluation of problems and task assignments of an ontological approach for enterprises. The report [13, p. 2] determined that considerable difficulties in the sphere of knowledge integration at enterprises exist due to a fundamental factor – *"due to different needs and background contexts, there can be widely varying viewpoints and assumptions regarding what is essentially the same subject matter"*. We name this factor "a fundamental problem of ontologies" (underlined by the authors of this paper) and consider this problem as a deeper cause for knowledge barriers existence. As this problem leads to negative consequences, the report [13] sets the task of forming and using ontologies as knowledge representations that will explicitly express shared understanding of a certain subject domain (SD), and in such a way that this will help eliminate or diminish abovementioned negative corollaries.

The publications [13–16] introduced meaningful conceptions for knowledge and ontologies at enterprises: types and kinds of ontologies, areas of common ontology application, design criteria and principles for development of ontologies including "modularity", and pointed to significant difficulties in common ontologies development. The report [13] used four ontology formalizing levels: highly informal, semi-informal, semi-formal, and rigorously formal. At the same time, approach limitations were stated in the report claiming that *"... when there are obviously similar concepts defined in existing ontologies, it is rarely clear how and whether such concepts can be adapted and reused"* [13, p. 16]. The paper [15] demonstrated, by the example of four well known and potentially common Upper Ontologies (CYC, Wordnet, GUM, Sowa's), that they are already losing their compatibility on the second level of the semantic graph. Such incompatibility is in fact one of manifestations of knowledge barriers. At the same time, this paper remarked that *"Presumably, the kinds of things that actually exist do not depend on our goals"* [15, p. 23]. However, the latter assumption will be refuted with the careful contemplation of the fundamental problem of ontologies in Sect. 3.3.

Many of abovementioned statements have still been in use, though the most significant ones are often ignored. For example, for different areas and tasks, ontologies of different formalization levels, including highly informal, are most suitable. However, an ontology approach developed in informatics does not take this into account fully enough.

"Ontology matching" direction. In the recent years, matching and harmonizing knowledge from different SD have become the sphere of formalized ontologies application and differentiated themselves forming the "ontology matching" direction where "matching" generalizes such notions as "mapping", "harmonizing", or "alignment". This direction is connected with searching for the best algorithms for alignment of different formal ontologies and developing appropriate program tools.

The report [17] points that *"achieving automatic interoperability among systems"* due to automatic matching of formalized ontologies is *"a goal that has been difficult to accomplish"*. Because of such a difficulty, an open architecture tool with flexible control in different subject areas was proposed in [17]. Our opinion is that such architecture allows using various semi-automated models of ontology matching and solves problems of ontologies matching by means of including a human being as an expert for resolving semantic collisions in the matching process.

The widely cited project [18] indicates that in ontology mapping there are both "reliable mapping" and not reliable mapping requiring the user's direct participation. Hence, a semi-automated matching mode is required as well as a person's participation as an expert for solving arising problems. Later projects like [19, 20] also consider a semi-automated matching mode, though their authors claim an intention to achieve completely automated mapping mode.

Noticeably, the majority of publications indicate the dramatic increase in the problems number during attempts to implement heterogeneous ontologies matching. At the same time, exactly such scenarios correspond to reality which is stated in [21] while describing the search for an ontological tool for dealing with the Internet-of-Things environment.

For these and other tools, evaluations provided in the project [22] on methods validation and ontology matching systems are useful, and the report informs that *"Despite the advances in automated techniques, user validation remains critical in achieving higher quality alignments"*.

Under such conditions, resulting communiqué of Ontology Summit 2016 [23] is meaningful and describes significant problems in the area of semantic interoperability and formalized ontologies application. This communiqué demonstrates a critical glance at the results achieved. In particular, it is suggested to develop bridge ontologies and brokers to mediate different ontologies for solving problems of ontologies incompatibility, as direct integration is often admitted to be impossible. It is stated that new methods and tools for modular ontology design are needed. The conclusion of the communiqué is that *"Even with metalanguages and techniques for expressing ontology mappings, the automatic generation of ontology mappings remains a substantial challenge, particularly for the more expressive ontology representation languages"*. In Sect. 3.3 we provide our recommendation for new initiatives in developing common ontologies considering the reasons mentioned above.

To sum up, knowledge integration or alignment based on formalized ontologies matching is essentially limited. Only semi-automated modes are workable in many significant cases. Because change dynamics of agents participating in a process like DNBP or KiBP is high, heterogeneity of input ontologies is unavoidably growing, and knowledge barriers to establishing sharing understanding are also growing. So, common knowledge and sharing understanding are not supported automatically, but it is clear that partly automated knowledge matching can serve as valuable KW information support in multiprofessional and multiorganizational collaborations.

3.2   Process-Oriented Approach

Main requirements for information and knowledge integration quality in DNBP & KiBP. This subsection concentrates on projects for practical organization of common knowledge for KDE.

In [24] the process of developing The Product Ontology System for the complex of Public Procurement Services of South Korea well-known in e-Government development sphere is analyzed. In comparison to other systems, the one described in [24] might seem simple due to the relative simplicity of the data structure. However, even in such a situation, data semantics analysis forced developers to admit limitations of formal ontological methods. OWL was rejected because of the combination of excessively universal capabilities (named as overkill), and on the other hand, because the users had to work on their own with links of specific types including links defined by the users themselves. The paper also highlights that *"The ontological information model is not a concept easily understood by non-computer/ontology experts... Easy-to-use tools are also essential"*.

The paper [25] presents the knowledge integration approach that is ontology-based, intends to be able to handle heterogeneity and variation of knowledge, to cope with dynamics of distributed knowledge sources, and so to support distributed product knowledge service. The authors note that a small number of works in this area is caused by its high complexity because of heterogeneity of business knowledge with semantic variations. The authors suggest the general model of knowledge collecting channels from product creating participants and suppliers. According to [25], ontologies contain "non-formalized" knowledge of "know-how," "know-why" and "know-with", and this content can be presented in the form of graphics, text, audio and video representations. Knowledge acquisition and storage include permanent elicitation and storage of "practical knowledge", produced by KW in real work (including strategies, effective empirical practices, and tacit knowledge about why and how the product is developed).

In the same period, the paper [26] examines conceptions of DNBP and complex "instant virtual enterprises" created and disassembled on demand. The architectural decision includes several knowledge bases containing not only knowledge of a product, market, and DNBP, but also knowledge of enterprises as potential members of a new virtual enterprise and of teams that should constitute an integrated team. A hope for creating a DNBP Management System as a fully automated system is expressed. Along with that, the authors take into account the complexity of DNBP management which prohibits reaching this goal in a short period of time. The conclusion is that DNBP management *"can use knowledge supported by human users and knowledge stored in knowledge bases, such that a gradual transition from a mainly interactive to a fully automated system is possible ..."*. This reflects objective knowledge barriers on the way of applying common knowledge.

The following publications refer to the period when the Industry 4.0 program had existed for over two years, and this required enterprises to transfer to a higher level of all the works automation.

The paper [27] addresses requirements for knowledge support in the heterogeneous environment of suppliers and designers of automobile electronic equipment. The paper indicates crucial areas of agents' relationships, "product requirements" as these main relationships object, and explicit and implicit usage of agents' experience. The needs are defined for a common ontology, ontological models of engineering artifacts, semi-automated artifacts development, and for ensuring knowledge alignment at different stages of this lifecycle.

The paper [4] analyzes support of KiBP whose requirements add to requirements to KM for DNBP because the process is characterized as *"non-predictable, emergent, goal-oriented, and knowledge-creating"* [4, p. 116]. The most important additions include the aspect of KW participation in KiBP, requirements for the explicit orientation of the basic ontology towards the KW problems and requirements, as well as for changing the basic ontology by the KW themselves.

Additional requirements for Enterprise KM. Valuable additional requirements for Enterprise KM for supporting DNBP & KiBP are stated in other publications, but according to our research goal, only most essential additions are provided below.

In the project [3], requirements for knowledge integration are expressed as the necessity of high quality information on the basis of data coming from different DNBP participants. The project indicates the original existence of information semantic inconsistency and incompleteness, which is also a manifestation of knowledge barriers. The work [12] presents the elaborated approach aimed at the provision of KW and decision makers with needed information when performing KiBP. Suggested means should enable the process-oriented, context-aware, i.e., personalized delivery of process information to process participants. The approach is based on a specially constructed "semantic information network" (SIN) integrating information objects of different types, for instance, instructions and letters, project events and tasks. SIN represents domain-specific knowledge in a structured and machine-interpretable form, not named ontology because it is only one kind of semantic networks. Ontology-based models are also employed as well as models in other forms (e.g., in graphic form) for different project components.

Finally, the approach not only to matching but also to practical using matched and/or merged common knowledge (ontologies) is very important. For this reason, the publication [28] is worth paying attention where Café following other authors suggests ontology integration methods recognized in the area of heterogeneous data bases integration, namely, Global As View (scheme GAV), Local As View (scheme LAV) and hybrid ones. This idea seems perspective, yet it requires further research.

To sum up, the process-oriented approach to Enterprise KM justifies knowledge barriers existence, demonstrates practical solutions for the barriers overcoming, and in the first place, it consists of solving business-process information and knowledge quality management problems. This approach takes into account the necessity not only of using, but also of forming and constant changing knowledge (ontologies) by enterprise KW and DE on their own. Reliance on semi-automated procedures for working with ontologies and employment of ontologies of all formalization levels is anticipated.

3.3   Fundamental KM Limitations and Hypotheses Defining Areas of Proposals

Capabilities and fundamental limitations of knowledge merging. Selecting and organizing efficient KM methods for highly dynamic and knowledge-intensive business-processes is an urgent need. However, to come closer to this goal, it is necessary to get free from excessive optimism towards KM discussed in [6, 21] and develop a pragmatic scheme of dynamic KM.

One of the main KM tasks is development and permanent support of common enterprise knowledge representation relevant for high dynamics. Such common knowledge should express and support shared understanding of several SD referring to a cooperatively manufactured product, business-process, and different parties' (primarily enterprises-partners and KW) participation in this process. To cope with this task, many projects develop automated methods of matching formalized ontologies; however, such an approach in general is unfit as the main one for the following reasons.

Mizoguchi in [14, p. 48] concluded that many ontologies are not portable because "... *ontology always requires HUMAN INTRPRETATION of its meaning*" (capitalization by Mizoguchi), but he considered it possible to elicit at least parts of ontologies not connected with the context. However, later practice demonstrated that even such partial success is not achieved in the necessary degree even at the level of Upper (Top) ontologies forming [15]. Frank [29] analyzes this problem by the example of banking SD and various interpretations of customer, issuer, and other concepts and shows how the subjectively selected interpretation of the task determines the choice of database schema and ontology representation.[1] This subjectivity of understanding is reflected in an old description of the problem in [13] as well as in a recent Sowa's statement [30] about the obligation of stating in ontology its context and the purpose of its development: "*Every ontology should have a formal statement of purpose or intention. Without a purpose, it's just a collection of random sentences*".

---

[1] One of the authors noted similar problems of inconsistent interpretations of the same concept by specialists from different professions in architecture and construction 30 years ago and rectified these discrepancies in collaboration of leading enterprises of the mentioned industry. Checking one of the concepts usage 30 years later showed that mentioned discrepancy not only remained, but also spread wider affecting other professions in that SD.

So, it is important to admit that such situations are generated not by efforts insufficiency, but by existence of the fundamental problem of ontologies (see Sect. 3.1). For enterprise knowledge, the problem reveals itself so that each introduced ontology is the result of agents' subjective choice of their vision of the enterprise task, the way of executing the task, and the choice of the world segment connected with this way. Moreover, agents' subjective vision of this world segment is added which reflects specificities of various collaborating parties' professional cultures. A good example of recognizing and dealing with professional culture and professional barriers can be found in medicine and adjacent spheres [31], but in engineering sphere, observed publications only explore knowledge management aspects outside the wider professional culture context [32].

Thus, ontologies integration problems are primarily defined by the variety of the world cognitive pictures chosen by different people or by the same person but at different moments. That is the reason why the hope of creating stable standard ontologies proves to be unjustified, as it can be realized only basing on refusal of such a variety of own cognitive pictures of the world. Our recommendation for implementing new initiatives to develop common ontologies for enterprises from different industries, like, for example, [33], is the need to take into account the above limitations and their underlying causes.

Nevertheless, in such a situation, it is essential to differentiate various reasons of ontologies mismatching. In some cases, correct ontologies matching is possible, but mostly due to direct DE and KW participation in semantic collisions controlling and resolving. However, such an approach is only feasible when contradictory interpretations of outwardly the same concepts and links are not used in two combined ontologies. Otherwise, using data records or facts collections from databases of one enterprise in information systems of another one can lead to failure in production.

However, it is necessary for cooperative work to form common and combined knowledge from different SD and different situations. Rational decisions are sought for through developing ontology-bridges and intelligent brokers as supplements to original ontologies set, through explicit specifications of the context as a situation where a particular ontology is adequate, and through hybrid systems of knowledge storage and application development. Such hybrid systems combine use of formal and informal ontologies by merging logically stringent concept models and various informal knowledge representations. Upon that, projects oriented towards enterprise goals follow the way of delegating KM functions performing to agents from SD categorized as Knowledge Workers and SD Experts.

Hypotheses. Different variants of harmonious combinations of various knowledge representation forms and methods of working with them are actively developed in many projects and research. At the same time, the authors believe that insufficient attention is given to supporting direct KW and DE participation in dynamic creation of enterprise knowledge. For this reason, the authors set forth their proposals in two areas: (a) enhancing agents-individuals' capabilities to apply some KM methods in DNBP & KiBP conditions, (b) the schema of dynamic KM for DNBP & KiBP conditions with the leading role of KW and DE.

We believe that convenient services for knowledge analysis, refinement, and merging should be provided to DE and KW not as formal ontology matching tools but as intelligent assistants in work with both formal and informal ontologies. In this case, DE and KW could really take leading roles not only in acquisition, but also in merging enterprise knowledge. Accordingly, we are formulating two hypotheses for realization of which proposals are outlined in Sects. 4 and 5:

(1) The hypothesis "Dynamic KW methods" is that the prioritized set of dynamic KM methods exists and that it has a certain value for KW and DE in described conditions and is suitable for practical mastering. Among a big number of traditional Enterprise KM tools there is a compact subset of knowledge acquisition and storage methods, which is useful for overcoming the above mentioned fundamental problem of ontology, and executing the task of knowledge application in DNBP & KiBP dynamics. This subset can be adapted for mastering by KW and DE. Each method can be utilized both in "manual regime" supported by local program services and in the regime of using the method as a part of KM system and even wider − as a part of system for integrated business process implementation.

(2) The hypothesis "Dynamic KM Framework" consists in defining an open KM methods architecture valuable for dynamic KDE and other dynamic enterprises of digital economy. This general Framework incorporates dynamic KM methods for KW and DE, services of information support for these methods utilizing, methods of KDE knowledge consolidating and sharing, methods of solving specific industrial tasks basing on ontologies/knowledge bases, and rules of training KW and DE for utilizing KM methods, taking into account DNBP dynamics and using knowledge in KiBP. This Framework also gives an opportunity to use a business-model "Knowledge as a Business Platform" (KaaBP) for enterprise innovation capabilities development in the digital transformation.

4 Dynamic KW Methods

A compact subset of methods suitable for knowledge elicitation, structurization, and accumulation in DNBP & KiBP dynamics, were selected, analyzed, and tested against their relevance for the situation explored in this paper. The selected methods and techniques were adapted for mastering by KW and DE. This was accomplished basing on literature analysis, especially [34–37], and preliminary talks with acting professionals in relevant areas. After that the modified Delphi method was utilized for refining the list of methods and techniques most relevant to the situation and finding out the popularity of the methods in real practice. This task was completed through the survey of the highly qualified experts carefully selected from business analysis, enterprise engineering, banking, bioinformatics, and education areas. The experts estimated the selected KM methods applicability for enterprises at different stages of an end-to-end "research-production-delivery to client-client feedback" business-process.

As a result, the following list of methods and techniques evaluated by the experts as relevant was produced together with a brief outline of developed working materials.

1. Documents (and/or other information sources) analysis. The secondary highly compressed texts are obtained using summarizing technique for further processing, e.g., creating ordered lists of objects, main ideas, their attributes, relationships, etc. In the case of changes, this facilitates making adjustments. Such kind of summarizing differs from traditional summarizing in that retaining the lexis of the summarized texts is absolutely essential, in particular, for further usage in developing concise multiprofessional glossaries.

2. Expert observation enables acquiring preliminary knowledge for the initial immersion in SD of a new partner and facilitates consequent interviews preparation. This activity often precedes and prepares background knowledge for the subsequent interviews.

3. Unstructured interview facilitates establishing mutual understanding and transition to more formal KM methods, produces initial sets of main valuable ideas, events, conditions, concepts, and procedures employed in the SD of a new partner.

4. Structured interview, for instance, Repertory grid technique, enables grouping concepts according to their attributes, initial analysis of existing links, and preparing checking questions for further rectifications. Such techniques are especially valuable in changing conditions, as there are well-developed procedures producing probable relationships between analyzed items.

5. Semi-structured interview, completed for instance, by Laddering technique, uses the preplanned sequence of questions, mainly, "Why?", to elicit more detailed concepts and hierarchical and other links between concepts, including possible "lateral branches". After initial training, this is an invaluable tool to rapidly acquire knowledge when a new partner appears.

6. Semi-structured interview, applying Socratic questions technique, uses specially designed questions for eliciting, clarifying, and checking knowledge, and helps prioritizing. This widely used and well explored technique provides results that help develop common knowledge in changing conditions.

7. Lateral thinking develops skills for finding unorthodox solutions and dealing with nonstandard situations, and thus it helps resolve semantic collisions, interpret incomprehensible partner's assertions, and find the way out of cul-de-sac situations that can emerge at a dynamic KDE. This technique employing predesigned puzzles and other tasks easily adapted to the specific situation can be used at any stage, in particular, to avoid monotony of training and improving trainees' motivation and creativity.

8. Developing and harmonizing local and integrated glossaries (including bi-directional and later muptiprofessional ones) is absolutely essential, as without them mutual understanding and knowledge sharing between partners from different SD becomes questionable. In dynamic enterprises this is vitally important to develop such glossaries to accumulate validated and easily edited knowledge for sharing and for artifacts translation from one SD to another.

9. Mind mapping is invaluable for fast eliciting, clarifying, establishing hierarchies of concepts, clear and understandable visual representation, and for recording brainstorm results; it creates easy to change maps and is suitable for rapid knowledge acquisition, adjusting, and its further utilization.

10. Concept mapping is relevant for elaborating complex structures representing relationships between concepts and conceptions in a convenient visual form, and it allows adding newly acquired knowledge to the existing. Moreover, developed concept maps are easy to edit which is essential in dynamic conditions.

Note. Mind and concept mapping are considered as techniques that can be used for structuring, visualization, and representation of any interview, documents analysis, and knowledge acquired in any other way results.

KW and DE can use various dynamic KM methods while preparing one stage of an end-to-end business process, and at the same time, one method can be used while preparing different stages of the business-process. Cooperative methods utilizing is anticipated when the result of one method application can be used in planning and implementing another method. This facilitates the adequacy growth, quality, and rate of obtaining working materials presenting knowledge of partners. Utilizing the cooperative methods brings the working materials closer to knowledge merging and formalizing.

5   Dynamic KM Framework

5.1   Framework of Dynamic KM Context, Purpose, and Main Statements

Because of terminology inconsistency in various KM areas and communities, "ontology" and "knowledge base" terms are applied on equal grounds and in the most common meaning, but a combined/merged knowledge of an enterprise is called "Enterprise Knowledge Warehouse", EKWH. It is supposed to be computer-stored in most cases, but this is not obligatory for all application contexts. For brevity, Framework of dynamic KM is called "Framework". Below, each statement or principle is presented as a separate paragraph.

The main conception of the dynamic KM framework. Foundation of the Framework of dynamic knowledge forming and application comprises short-term goals and tasks as well as long-term values, but not short-run methodological rules or technical goals like, for instance, rules of data integration, formalized knowledge representation, or goals of interoperability applications.

Dynamic (highly dynamic) enterprise. An enterprise capable of taking successful instant business decisions correspondingly to the rate of business requirements or opportunities emergence is regarded as [highly] dynamic. This means impossibility of accumulating knowledge necessary for such an enterprise in advance.

Dynamic KM and its purpose. It is regarded as a special KM methods subset and its arrangement intended for supporting dynamic Knowledge-driven enterprise and for other digital economy enterprise activities in conditions of their high changeability. Changeability is regarded as changes in production, business-processes, and structure of the parties engaged in enterprise business-processes from its ecosystem.

Dynamic KM context. Dynamic KM is examined at the chosen planning horizon (Sect. 2). Knowledge is understood as dynamic enterprise knowledge (see below). Wide ontologies interpretation including informal ontologies is used. Fundamental problem of ontologies (Sects 3.1 and 3.3) and limitations of formal knowledge integration are recognized.

"Knowledge as a Business Platform" conception. Dynamic KM principles suggested below comprise the foundation for the business-model "Knowledge as a Business Platform"(KaaBP) which can be regarded as one of perspective platforms for the "EE innovation model" and "EE integration model" in the five-model framework for digital transformation of enterprise [2, Fig. 1].

Enterprise information and knowledge. These conceptions are the part of the framework proposed in this section but were defined in Sect. 2.

Main Dynamic KM statements. They are presented as two groups of principles which are governing rules of Dynamic KM utilizing while organizing KM works in knowledge acquisition, storage, and utilizing, as well as in Framework expanding and its adaptation to specific conditions. The principles are regarded as part of high level enterprise knowledge referring to conceptual and metacognitive knowledge [38]. They are regarded as secondary towards the Framework main conception and Dynamic KM purpose and context. A top level scheme of one possible variant of *Dynamic KM process* based on the principles of this Framework is shown in Fig. 1. This scheme

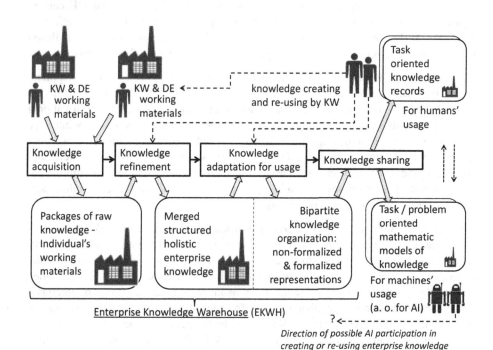

Fig. 1. The scheme of sample KM process basing on dynamic KM framework

points to but does not reflect to the full extent a hypothetical possibility of AI participation in creating or re-using enterprise knowledge.

5.2 Principles of Dynamic KM Implementing

The principle "Dynamism of business-process forming support". Support of rapid achievement of shared understanding of DNBP formation participants' requirements and tasks as well as support of this shared understanding and utilizing constitute the primary task of Dynamic KM. For executing this task, Dynamic KM ensures acquisition of "knowledge about parties' interfaces", the knowledge about mandatory parties interactions, which dynamically forms the common network business-process where parties are connected with "customer – provider" relationships. Knowledge about parties' interface primarily includes knowledge about requirements of the customer to the performer's/provider's result, knowledge about the result transferred by the performer/provider to the customer, knowledge about the result testing method and acceptance procedure, and knowledge about deadlines, etc. Meanwhile, obtaining results by the parties is regarded as a black box.

The principle "Intensive knowledge usage support". All knowledge about the product and its components and about working processes needed for its creation in addition to knowledge about interfaces can be acquired and supported for KiBP organizing and executing. The parties' activity for achieving the result is regarded as a white box in the processes of product creation, and the parties represented by KW and DE can be regarded as co-creators in the creative knowledge-intensive process. For effective executing KiBP, the enterprise can also acquire knowledge for Knowledge Based Problem Solving (KBPS) and knowledge about required workers' competencies.

The principle "KW role in knowledge acquisition and its support". KW are suppliers of practical knowledge, and they are leading or responsible persons in the works on enterprise knowledge acquisition, storage, and actualization. KW can get informational and analytical support of KM information system (KM IS) services. Friendly interface of these services should facilitate easy storing and processing individual working materials with acquired knowledge and organize packages of such materials, preferably supporting the analysis of concept-candidates, their attributes and relationships, organizing working terminology glossaries for various SD and two-sided (multi-sided) working glossaries and thesauri for various SD.

The principle "Support of KW in merging knowledge". Packages of working materials about parties' knowledge at different segments of the end-to-end business-process, other knowledge fragments (for example, reference ontologies, detailed product descriptions) are merged in the enterprise knowledge warehouse (EKWH). It is often reasonable to carry out merging sequentially as knowledge about phases of enterprise value chain is acquired. Organizing and performing merging are regarded as work of KW from the customer party or KW from both parties in the interface of new knowledge fragments and elements inclusion in EKWH (for instance, in the style similar to [39] but with extended functionality and maximum usability of KM IS services).

5.3   The Principles of Knowledge Organizing and Utilizing

The principle "The client as the central object of knowledge". The multi aspect enterprise knowledge about the client is regarded as the central enterprise knowledge about the client's current and perspective values, about his/her demands for production, and about his/her quality criteria. This knowledge is maintained during a relevant part in the enterprise life history including perspective planning horizons.

The principle "KM Framework openness". To retain the dynamism through the enterprise life history, KM Framework is the system of imperative and declarative knowledge, methods, and KM services, having the abovementioned purpose, and open for extension. Dynamic KM is open for utilizing all capabilities developed in other projects of supporting KDE with highly dynamic DNBP & KiBP.

The principle "Controlled modularity". The Dynamic KM openness is based on loosely connected architecture of its components. This architecture is organized in general as a set of relatively independent principles, requirements, knowledge fragments, and loosely connected modules of other types. Individual techniques utilized in KM, procedures for their application (beginning with education), and supporting services also belong to such modules. Modularity principle is extended in particular to include non-formalized and formalized ontologies of various SD, types, kinds, and purposes.

The principle "Various knowledge forms and types support". Dynamic KM supports all types of knowledge in line with their formalization degree and representation form according to the needs and tools for their application. None of the knowledge type or representation form is considered to be preferable in acquisition and storage comparing to others. It is suggested to use the bipartite knowledge organization in EKWH as the primary mode. In this case completely non-formalized and formalized representations of common ontologies are organized as kind of EKWH modules but with establishing and supporting bilateral semantic links between them.

The principle "Knowledge usage for production tasks executing". Common enterprise knowledge is utilized for executing the widest possible set of production tasks. For this purpose, the bipartite knowledge organization might be used as a single storage consolidated by semantic links, bridge ontologies, and intelligent brokers for bilateral connecting the informal and formalized parts of EKWH. Due to such connecting, the enterprise gets an opportunity to use the merged knowledge for executing of end-to-end and local production tasks. Translation of product technical support rules into the user instruction in the end user language can serve as an example of a local problem. End-to-end quality assurance at various stages of design, component production, assembling, and testing the production is an example of an end-to-end task.

6   Conclusion

The large gap between the results in KM sphere and the real needs in the creation, formation, and usage of knowledge at enterprises is the driving force of this study. In connection with this, in this paper we examined KM for practical employment at enterprises in the context of their needs and goals. Relying on our experience and following other authors, we determined the main KM task as provision of shared understanding for cooperative work in conditions of highly dynamic forming of business-process, teams participating in this process, and requirements for the product. At the same time, the analysis confirmed existence of essential knowledge barriers on the way of forming such shared understanding. We analyzed the main ways of forming common knowledge and shared understanding, drew certain conclusions, and made proposals. Summing up, our proposals state that in Enterprise KM it is necessary to:

- take into account the fundamental problem of agents' vision of their world segment leading, in particular, to fundamental reasons for limitations of formalized ontologies automated integration,
- admit that formalized ontologies are inadequate for their wide application by KW and DE categories of the enterprise staff,
- equitably support fully informal and formal ontologies at the enterprise for their direct use in production tasks,
- ensure specific KW and DE professional development for performing leading roles in enterprise knowledge acquisition, structuring, storing, and updating,
- carry out projects for searching and developing methods of semantic matching of ontologies for different levels of formalization and different SD as well as for further developing functionality and interfaces of KM information systems up to the level suitable for their employment in KW and DE work.

Basing on the abovementioned, we determined the set of high-priority dynamic KM methods for knowledge acquisition and structuring by KW and DE and introduced KM Framework for highly dynamic enterprises. Dynamic KM methods were used for professional development of specialists in IT and enterprise architecture areas, and currently the set of methods included in the courses for such education is constantly expanding. Dynamic KM framework is delivered to the project RFBR 16-07-01062: "Development of methods and resources of enterprise engineering based on the smart technologies".

One possible direction of the research might be detailed elaboration of data, information, and knowledge representation layers, for example, employing the semiotic scheme in [40] and other possible stratifications. Another direction might focus on main methods of forming and matching ontologies of different representation forms and formalization levels.

The authors notice that the explored area is vigorously developing, producing at the same time both remarkable results and overestimated expectations. For this reason, the search of most rational endeavors and determination of risk areas should be continued and discussed.

Acknowledgements. This research has been supported Russian Foundation for Basic Research – RFBR under project № 16-07-01062 "Development of methods and resources of enterprise engineering based on the smart technologies".

References

1. Digital Dividends: World development report. International Bank for Reconstruction and Development, Washington, 330 p. (2016)
2. Zinder, E.Z.: Expanding enterprise engineering paradigm. Bus. Inf. **4**(38), 7–18 (2016). doi:10.17323/1998-0663.2016.4.7.18
3. Rasouli, M.R., et al.: Information quality in dynamic networked business process management. In: Debruyne, C., et al. (eds.) OTM 2015. LNCS, vol. 9415, pp. 202–218. Springer, Cham (2015). doi:10.1007/978-3-319-26148-5_12
4. Mundbrod, N., Reichert, M.: Process-aware task management support for knowledge-intensive business processes: findings, challenges, requirements. In: 2014 IEEE 18th International Enterprise Distributed Object Computing Conference Workshops and Demonstrations, 1–2 September 2014, pp. 116–125 (2014). http://dbis.eprints.uni-ulm.de/1069/
5. The KNOW Network. The MAKE research program. http://www.knowledgebusiness.com/knowledgebusiness/templates/home.aspx?siteId=1&menuItemId=25
6. Guerino, F.: Knowledge Management - An Industry Without Focus and Direction (2017). https://www.if4it.com/knowledge-management-an-industry-without-focus-and-direction/
7. Zinder, E.Z., Yunatova, I.G.: Synergy for digital transformation: person's multiple roles and subject domains integration. In: Chugunov, A.V., Bolgov, R., Kabanov, Y., Kampis, G., Wimmer, M. (eds.) DTGS 2016. CCIS, vol. 674, pp. 155–168. Springer, Cham (2016). doi:10.1007/978-3-319-49700-6_16
8. UN Sustainable Development. Transforming our world: the 2030 Agenda for sustainable development (2015). https://sustainabledevelopment.un.org/post2015/transformingourworld
9. Chernikova, I.V., Chernikova, D.V.: Evolutional epistemology and evolutional constructivism as cognitive practices of the modern science. In: SHS Web of Conferences, vol. 28 (2016)/International Conference on Research Paradigms Transformation in Social Sciences 2015, RPTSS 2015 (2016)
10. King, W.R.: Knowledge management and organizational learning. In: King, W.R. (ed.) Knowledge management and organizational learning. AIS, vol. 4, pp. 3–13. Springer, Boston (2009). doi:10.1007/978-1-4419-0011-1_1
11. Tilly, M., Ruiz, C., Dengler F.: ACTIVE D3.2.2. Context-aware Knowledge Processes Fully functional prototype. Institut AIFB (2008). http://www.aifb.kit.edu/web/Deliverable3013/en
12. Michelberger, B.: Process-Oriented Information Logistics: Aligning Process Information with Business Processes. Dissertation zur Erlangung des Doktorgrades, Ulm (2015)
13. Uschold, M., Gruninger, M.: Ontologies: principles, methods and applications. Technical report AIAI-TR-191, University of Edinburgh. http://www.aiai.ed.ac.uk/publications/documents/1996/96-ker-intro-ontologies.pdf
14. Mizoguchi, R., Valwelkenhuysen, J., Ikeda M.: Task ontology for reuse of problem solving knowledge. In: Mars, N.J.I. (ed.) Towards Very Large Knowledge Bases, pp. 46–59. IOS Press (1995)
15. Chandrasekaran, B., Josephson, J.R., Benjamins, V.R.: What are ontologies, and why do we need them? IEEE Intell. Syst. Appl. **14**(1), 20–26 (1999)
16. Perez, A.G., Benjamins, V.R.: Overview of knowledge sharing and reuse components: ontologies and problem-solving methods. In: Proceedings of the IJCAI 1999 Workshop on Ontologies and Problem-Solving Methods (KRR5), Stockholm, Sweden (1999)
17. Giunchiglia, F., Autayeu, A., Pane, J.: S-match: an open source framework for matching lightweight ontologies. Technical report # DISI-10-043, 19 p. (2010). http://disi.unitn.it/~p2p/RelatedWork/Matching/smatch_043.pdf

18. Jimenez-Ruiz, E., Grau, B.C., Zhou, Y., Horrocks, I.: Large-scale interactive ontology matching: algorithms and implementation. In: Frontiers in Artificial Intelligence and Applications, ECAI, vol. 242, pp. 444–449 (2012). doi:10.3233/978-1-61499-098-7-444

19. Mukkala, L., Arvo, J., Lehtonen, T., Knuutila, T.: Current state of ontology matching. A Survey of Ontology and Schema Matching. University of Turku Technical reports, no. 4 (2015)

20. Fellah, A., Malki, M., Elci, A.: Web services matchmaking based on a partial ontology alignment. J. Inf. Technol. Comput. Sci. **2016**(6), 9–20 (2016). MECS. http://www.mecs-press.org/, doi:10.5815/ijitcs.2016.06.02

21. Ganzha, M., Paprzycki, M., Pawłowski, W., Szmeja, P., Wasielewska, K., Fortino, G.: Tools for ontology matching—practical considerations from INTER-IoT perspective. In: Li, W., et al. (eds.) IDCS 2016. LNCS, vol. 9864, pp. 296–307. Springer, Cham (2016). doi:10.1007/978-3-319-45940-0_27

22. Dragisic, Z., Ivanova, V., Lambrix, P., Faria, D., Jiménez-Ruiz, E., Pesquita, C.: User validation in ontology alignment. In: Groth, P., Simperl, E., Gray, A., Sabou, M., Krötzsch, M., Lecue, F., Flöck, F., Gil, Y. (eds.) ISWC 2016. LNCS, vol. 9981, pp. 200–217. Springer, Cham (2016). doi:10.1007/978-3-319-46523-4_13

23. Fritzsche, D., Gruninger, M. (eds.): Ontology Summit 2016 Communique. Ontologies within Semantic Interoperability Ecosystems (2016). https://s3.amazonaws.com/ontologforum/OntologySummit2016/2016-06-02_Communique/OntologySummit2016Communique_v1.2Jun7.docx

24. Kim, D., Lee, S.-g., Shim, J., Chun, J., Lee, Z., Park, H.: Practical ontology systems for enterprise application. In: Grumbach, S., Sui, L., Vianu, V. (eds.) ASIAN 2005. LNCS, vol. 3818, pp. 79–89. Springer, Heidelberg (2005). doi:10.1007/11596370_8

25. Chen, Y.-M., et al.: Ontology-based knowledge integration for distributed product knowledge service. In: Proceedings of the World Congress on Engineering and Computer Science 2009, WCECS 2009, San Francisco, USA, vol. II, pp. 1197–1202 (2009)

26. Green, P., Mehandjiev, N., Kouvas, G., Weichart, G., Eshuis, R.: Dynamic business process formation for instant virtual enterprises. The CrossWork project, supported by the EC, IST 6th Framework. Contract No. 507590 (2009). http://is.tm.tue.nl/staff/heshuis/BETA%20WP198.pdf

27. Tiedeken, J., Herbst, J., Reichert, M.: Managing complex data for electrical/electronic components: challenges and requirements. In: Proceedings of BTW 2013 Workshops, 15th Conference on Database Systems, Technology, and Web (BTW 2013), Magdeburg (2013). http://dbis.eprints.uni-ulm.de/896/1/THR13_BTW_WS.pdf

28. Cafe, A.: Ontology Integration - Heterogeneity, Techniques and More (2014). https://www.slideshare.net/adrielcafe/ontology-integration

29. Frank, W.: Ontological Casting Mistakes in Information Models. Ontology Forum, February 22, the attachment <Casting Mistakes in Informaton Models V3r1p01.docx>, 9 p. (2017). https://groups.google.com/forum/#!topic/ontolog-forum/_WTj3gbcQcQ

30. Sowa J.: Ontology Forum, 23 February 2017. https://groups.google.com/forum/#!topic/ontolog-forum/_WTj3gbcQcQ

31. Hall, P.: Interprofessional teamwork: professional cultures as barriers. J. Interprof. Care. (May), Suppl. 1, pp. 188–196 (2005)

32. Brewer, E.C., Holmes, T.L.: Better communication = better teams: a communication exercise to improve team performance. IEEE Trans. Prof. Commun. **59**(3), 288–298 (2016). doi:10.1109/TPC.2016.2590018

33. Smith, B.: The Industry Ontology Foundry. Ontology Summit, NIST (2017). http://ncor.buffalo.edu/IOF/Ontolog.pptx

34. Burge, J.E.: Knowledge elicitation tool classification. In: Artificial Intelligence Research Group, Worcester Polytechnic Institute, Worcester (2001). https://web.cs.wpi.edu/~jburge/thesis/kematrix.html

35. Turban, E., et al.: Decision Support Systems and Business Intelligence Systems, 8th edn. Pearson, Prentice Hall, Upper Saddle River (2007)

36. Yunatova, I.G.: Analysis and development of professional texts summarizing methods for forming a basic cognitive component of professional competences system in IT sphere (in Russian). In: Proceedings of the XVII Conference "Enterprise Engineering and Knowledge Management", Moscow, MESI, pp. 322–327 (2014)

37. Payne, P., Mendonça, E., Johnson, S., Starren, J.: Conceptual knowledge acquisition in biomedicine: a methodological review. J. Biomed. Inf. **40**(5), 582–602 (2007). doi:10.1016/j.jbi.2007.03.005

38. Krathwohl, D.R.: A revision of bloom's taxonomy: an overview. Theory Pract. **41**(4), 212–218 (2002)

39. Lahoud, I., Monticolo, D., Hilaire, V.: A MAS to assist mechanical engineers in the product's design process. In: IDEAS Workshop, International Conference on AAMAS 2015, At Istanbul, Turkey (2015). https://www.researchgate.net/publication/274019544_A_MAS_to_Assist_mechanical_engineers_in_the_product%27s_design_process

40. Stamper, R.: Information in Business and Administrative Systems. Wiley, London and New York (1973)

Knowledge Management Trends in the Digital Economy Age

Tatiana Gavrilova, Artem Alsufyev$^{(\boxtimes)}$, and Liudmila Kokoulina

Graduate School of Management, Saint-Petersburg University,
St. Petersburg, Russia
{gavrilova, alsufyev, l.kokoulina}@gsom.pu.ru

Abstract. The main objective of this paper is to understand and describe how knowledge management practices are organized in Russian firms of different industries and the extent to which these practices have been adopted to support the business strategy in the digital economy age. Based on hierarchical cluster analysis of 104 Russian companies, this study highlights the specific combinations of KM practices and accents made by Russian managers in this area.

Keywords: Knowledge management · Knowledge management cycle · Russian context · Knowledge management practices · Cluster analysis

1 Introduction

The Age of Digital Economy can be described as « encompassing and revolutionizing phenomenon [fueled] by the convergence of advancements in human communication, computing (computers, software, services) and content (publishing, entertainment and information providers), to create the interactive multimedia and the information highway. This new age is gradually forcing us to rethink the way we perceive the traditional definitions of economy, wealth creation, business organizations and other institutional structures» [24].

The paper focuses on the main areas of knowledge management under the new economy conditions. The empirical study of several Russian companies shows the need for strong progressive leadership who is responsible for the transformation in the company.

The paper studies the communication and networking of employees and managers to combine their knowledge and creativity in the KM framework.

2 Theoretical Background

2.1 Knowledge Management: Brief Overview

For the purpose of this study we define knowledge as a set of information valuable for the organization that is embedded in its employees or any of the production processes, systems and organizational culture [3]. This definition includes the knowledge and

© Springer International Publishing AG 2017
D.A. Alexandrov et al. (Eds.): DTGS 2017, CCIS 745, pp. 464–473, 2017.
https://doi.org/10.1007/978-3-319-69784-0_38

individual skills, norms and value systems, databases, methodologies, software and production experience.

In the literature, there are several knowledge classifications:

- Classification of knowledge based on the content ("knowledge why", "knowledge what", "knowledge how", "knowledge where" [15]),
- Classification based on belonging (to the person or the team [17]), and other criteria.

These classifications could be supplemented by a taxonomy made by [8].

Many authors consider knowledge management as a system determined by organizational, human and technological components (e.g. [15]).

- Organizational knowledge includes principles, skills, routines that provide business activities.
- The human component includes "social capital" of employees, an atmosphere of trust and cooperation that promotes knowledge exchange.
- The technological component that complements KM with IT tools is quite often the most obvious area of investment in KM [2].

However, the focus on investments in technological components may have detrimental impact on the successful solution of more difficult organizational problems [14]. Many authors (e.g. [6]) consider KM in the context of the enterprise management system. KM serves as a "bridge" between the external information management processes (from customers, suppliers, competitors) and internal information management processes (e.g., R&D, marketing, management, and finance).

2.2 Knowledge Management Processes and Functions

In the field of KM there was developed a line of models related to corresponding organizational processes. The authors identify key knowledge management processes. Comparative analysis of these models uncovers the variety of knowledge management processes combinations. For example, the inventor of the term "knowledge management" Wiig classifies these processes into 4 types: building knowledge, holding knowledge, pooling knowledge, using knowledge [28].

As part of knowledge building, knowledge in the organization is acquired, analyzed, renewed, structured and codified. The process of knowledge holding includes keeping knowledge in the archives and embedding it in the existing processes and procedures. Knowledge pooling includes search of new knowledge, coordination and combination with existing knowledge. Knowledge using relates to the analysis of the problem or situation, identification of knowledge useful in this situation, and choosing among the alternative solutions to the problem.

Other authors propose similar classifications. For example, [27] distinguish 4 processes:

1. New knowledge is developed.
2. Knowledge is distributed to those who need it.
3. Knowledge is made accessible both for future use and for use by the whole organisation.
4. Knowledge areas are combined.

Davenport and Prusak describe processes of knowledge generation, codification, distribution and saving [5].

At large extent existing descriptions repeat, detalize or complement each other. For instance, knowledge building [28] includes knowledge generation and codification [5]; knowledge distribution [27] includes knowledge pooling [28], and transfer [5]; while four phases of knowledge spiral represent more abstract description of knowledge sharing, integration and creation.

However, the main assumptions lying in the foundation of the majority of the models have limitations [2, 20]. A number of knowledge process models focuses on knowledge codification, storing and reuse [14, 27, 28]. Particularly, identification of these components (codification, archiving, storing and reuse) is caused by the perception of knowledge management as a function of systematization of already existing knowledge.

Currently companies get competitive advantage not due to existing knowledge systematization and reuse, but due to higher level of absorptive capacity, learning capability and new knowledge creation [10, 25, 29]. In this context, codification and storing of knowledge represent basic supportive functions of KM, but they should not be regarded as key KM functions [1, 20].

Partly solving above-mentioned concerns is knowledge creation model by Nonaka [16]. This model highlights the dynamic aspect of knowledge creation as an ultimate goal of the company. According to Nonaka, knowledge creation is not a separate phase, function or process, but sophisticated concept describing the company's activities in general, targeted at innovation building. The key prerequisite of new knowledge creation are knowledge sharing processes between individuals (socialization) and knowledge transfer in the organization (externalization and internalization).

One of the ways to implement systemic thinking principles in order to build a holistic picture of organization. In the context of KM, systemic thinking means that all elements of the system as well as the system in general are considered: people, valuable knowledge, knowledge sharing culture (or its absence), organizational strategy, technological infrastructure.

2.3 Knowledge Life Cycle Working Model

Cyclical models of KM systems functioning have an iterative character as well as the actual process of KM system creation. Besides, lifecycle models embed the systemic thinking principles reflecting the variety of internal processes of the organization. This is especially important for KM system. That is why it is important to look at the knowledge life cycle as a whole.

On the other hand, lifecycle models have some disadvantages. Firstly, these models usually have prescriptive nature as they prescribe what kind of KM system should be but do not mention the details. Secondly, lifecycle models do not consider the degree of correspondence of KM system to the organizational strategy or cultural context [18].

Lifecycle model developed by Bukowitz and Williams [3] represents the detailed model of working with intellectual and knowledge assets in the organization.

The model consists of 7 stages:

1 Get: Access and filter information to identify relevant and valuable content
2 Use: Combine information in unique ways to enhance and support innovation
3 Learn: Discovery of information in order to apply content based on experience and organizational memory
4 Contribute: Participants share their knowledge and offer their comments into a shared space or 'repository' to assist and develop the overall community or organization
5 Assess: Evaluation of knowledge acquisition and use of the organization in the form of intellectual capital
6 Build/Sustain: Plan and allocate resources to support the attainment of future knowledge for the organization
7 Divest Evaluate: "assets" which do not create value for the organization and allocate the associated resources elsewhere.

The authors highlight that the first four model stages (Get, Use, Learn, Contribute) focus on tactical issues, while the last three (Assess, Build/Sustain, Divest) have more strategic nature.

Overall, organizational knowledge management has been characterized as consisting of three overlapping processes: knowledge creation, knowledge codification, and knowledge. Knowledge is said to be one of the key assets of an organization. Knowledge is not evenly distributed in organizations, and therefore efficient information systems (ISs) are needed to enable timely and effective knowledge flows.

3 Research Methodology

3.1 Knowledge Maturity Measurement

Measuring KM effectiveness is a difficult task because of intangible nature of knowledge assets. There are several approaches towards corporate KM maturity estimation. For example, Balanced Scorecard methodology of Kaplan and Norton (The Balance Scorecard, 1996), is adapted for KM. Other inductive and deductive methods are proposed in [19, 22, 23]. Another example is [11] where authors propose mechanism for KM evaluation including estimation of mental, cognitive, process, technology and institutional levels. One of the limitations of this methodology implementation is difficulty of the measurement process and evaluation criteria choice.

The survey was developed on the base of the PricewaterhouseCoopers [3] survey. Our express-survey estimates effectiveness of the KM system of the company through additive maturity scale.

In order to estimate KM maturity of the company we adapted the survey proposed by Bukowitz and Williams consisting of 140 questions (20 questions for each life cycle stage). We analyzed the questions of five stages included in the theoretical model. In reliance on the results of in-depth interviews and after careful analysis of the survey questions (the questions were translated from English, particularized and simplified) we selected 18 questions measured by 3-point Likert scale: 2 points – Strongly agree, 1– Neither, 0 – Strongly disagree.

Hence the maximum score was 36 points. Based on the results, the average score was 17 points.

3.2   Internal and External Factors Influencing KM System

Apart from the questions related to KM, other questions on respondents' internal factors were added:

- Company size;
- Company age;
- Geographical location.

The size of the organization is the factor that can influence the intensity of knowledge sharing, and in the majority of empirical studies this factor is included as a control variable. In most cases it is assumed that the lesser the size of the firm, the more intensive is knowledge sharing as the employees could communicate more frequently. However the results of empirical studies are controversial: some authors found negative effects [13], positive effects [12], and non-significant effects [26].

The company's age is one of the KM determinants: the more senior the organization or the division, the higher its "organizational inertia" and the less its abilities to learn and to adapt for changing environment [4]. A number of academic papers demonstrated that the more immature firms have various advantages related to knowledge sharing and other knowledge management processes [7].

Geographical location is another factor affecting knowledge management, as proximity to the major cities correlates to intellectual capital level of the region. Of course, the socio-economic context could play a large role in intellectual capital formation of the organizations [21].

3.3   Research Questions

Knowledge management (KM) is the process of capturing the value from the knowledge assets and intellectual capital of the organization. Knowledge and effective knowledge management could be a source of competitive advantage. However, due to intangible nature of knowledge resources managers and academics struggle to evaluate and finally manage these resources of the company.

The main objective of this paper is to understand and describe how knowledge management practices are organized in Russian firms of different industries and the extent to which these practices have been adopted to support the business strategy. Based on a qualitative study of 100 Russian managers from different firms, this study highlights the specific combinations of KM practices and accents made by Russian managers in this area.

This paper investigates the extent to which KM practices have been adopted by Russian firms to gain competitive advantage. Specifically, we address the following research questions:

1. Are firms using KM initiatives strategically to support the business strategy? If so, what are the major KM initiatives these companies adopt?
2. What may be the major problems and areas for improvement if KM practices are to play a more significant role in supporting the business strategy for firms to gain competitive advantage?

3.4   Sample and Data Collection Method

The survey was conducted on a sample of EMBA (Executive Master of Business Administration) program students and alumni at Graduate School of Management in St. Petersburg during 2010–2015. One of the program enrollment conditions is having at least 5 years of managerial experience. Based on the results of the survey, the majority of the respondents represent large companies that are based in St. Petersburg and Moscow.

We conducted the cluster analysis to identify similar groups of companies from the point of KM practices used. These practices are measured by three-point scale presenting the degree of active usage.

Because this study is of an exploratory nature, however, we feel that the number and spread of the cases we obtained are sufficient to provide information needed for this paper's discussion.

4   Discussion of the Results

4.1   Descriptive Statistics

In order to identify the differences between high and low performing in KM organizations we divided the sample in three groups based on their total survey score: top quarter, low quarter, and the remaining companies.

The average score is 17 points. The top quarter of total score distribution has 22–36 points, the bottom quarter of total score distribution comprised the group companies with 0–10 points. The remaining companies were grouped under "middle half" label. The groups' descriptive statistics is described in Table 1.

Table 1. Score distribution within the groups

	Number of respondents	Min. score, points	Max. score	Average score
Top quarter	26	23	35	26.46
Middle half	55	11	22	16.67
Low quarter	23	4	10	8.30
Total	104			

Therefore among the "top quarter" group members there is a noticeable prevalence of large companies. For "middle half" group, large and medium size companies are prevailing. "Low quarter" group is comprised mostly by small enterprises.

The majority of respondents indicated that their organizations were founded during last 15 years. The "top quarter" group was comprised mostly from equal number of the organizations from various ages. In the "middle half" group young companies are prevailing. In the "low quarter" group there is only one company founded before 1990.

Besides, we determined the average estimations for KM characteristics in Russian companies of different size, age, and geographic location (Table 2).

Table 2. KM practices in Russian companies of different size, age, and geographic location

No.	Factor	Index	Characteristics of corresponding criteria			Kruskal-Wallis criteria*
1	Size of organization	*Groups*	*Less than 50 empl.*	*50–150 empl.*	*More than 150 empl.*	0.58
		Average value	16.53	14.40	17.63	
		Number of observations	19	5	64	
2	Age of organization	*Groups*	*1–9 years*	*10–17 years*	*18–24 years*	0.94
		Average value	18.06	17.43	17.71	
		Number of observations	18	21	16	
3	Geographical location	*Groups*	*Moscow and St. Petersburg*		*Regions*	0.58
		Average value	17.89		19.21	
		Number of observations	45		14	

*Kruskal-Wallis criteria showed no statistical differences among the groups based on size (p = 0.58), age (p = 0.94), and geographical location (p = 0.58).

4.2   Cluster Analysis

Based on the KM practices used we were able to get 6 different groups (clusters) of companies with measures of the maturity of KM system within these companies.

Overall, all groups of companies have very low indicators of KM system ranging from 11 to 25 points (out of 54 or 18 questions by 3 points each). But even within this low total score we are able to explore the combinations of practices used so as to show what are the real problems and biases Russian firms have.

The first group represents the majority of Russian companies (n = 38) and scored very low on KM initiatives used (KM = 11 out of 54). This is the lowest result within the largest group with major emphasis on creating necessary KM infrastructure. Investing heavily in databases and ignoring other aspects of KM is by far the most widespread bias in KM initiatives implementation.

The second cluster has a substantial share of companies (n = 29) and has the highest score among other companies (KM = 25), although the score itself is just half of the maximum level of 54 points. These companies pay attention to all aspects of KM in some way, but overlook the "learning perspective", with no particular attention to benchmarking, learning by reflexion and implementing redundancy in job design.

The third cluster of companies (n = 19) is in the middle between the first and the second clusters with the score of 19 points. It is characterized by some developments in KM infrastructure, knowledge sharing, learning and alliances. However, these companies do not have job positions in charge of KM processes, and KM initiatives do not involve all employees. This is the typical situation when KM initiatives are launched by top-managers without support by middle-line managers and specialists.

The next three clusters are outliers from the point of their quantity. They are characterized by above average KM performance.

The fourth cluster (n = 7) has the moderate score of 21 points and is characterized by good developments in KM infrastructure, knowledge sharing and learning (learning organization creation). Main areas for improvement are related to positions responsible for KM, alliances and involving all employees in KM initiatives. The situation repeats the third cluster when top-management in actively involved in KM development overlooking the need to cover employees of all levels.

The fifth cluster (n = 5) with lower score (19 points) focuses on creating job positions in charge of KM processes but does not have well-developed infrastructure, learning orientation. The knowledge sharing system is developing to some extent. Organizational culture supports employees' initiatives but, again, does not involve all employees in the process of KM. From this point of view this cluster is similar to the fourth one.

The sixth cluster (n = 1) with the second highest score of 23 has employees responsible for KM and relevant organizational culture. However, it lacks the appropriate infrastructure, The systems of knowledge sharing, alliances and learning have controversial results.

5 Conclusions

The present research is aimed at identifying the specific characteristics of knowledge management system in Russian companies. The results demonstrated that size, age, and geographic location do not influence the maturity of KM systems in Russian companies.

Descriptive analysis demonstrated that many respondents note high level of top-management support as well as high level of IT as KM tools. This result could be explained by the fact that the majority of respondents consider top-management as an important issue of KM dissemination and development.

Cluster analysis demonstrated that the majority of respondents understood the importance of IT support for all the KM processes. However, this bias could lead to the overall low level of KM maturity.

Second large cluster of companies already has good KM base, but is lacking the strategic goals for KM development. Another problematic point is engagement of all employees in the process of knowledge sharing. Overall, cluster structure of KM practices in Russian companies reflects the internal logic of knowledge management trends with too much emphasis to IT infrastructure at the lower levels of KM maturity.

Acknowledgement. This research was partially conducted with financial support from Russian Science Foundation grant (project No. 15-18-30048) to Tatiana Gavrilova in the part of problem definition and experiments planning.

References

1. Andreeva, T.E., Sergeeva, A.V.: The more the better … or is it? The contradictory effects of HR practices on knowledge-sharing motivation and behavior. Hum. Resour. Manag. J. **26** (2), 151–171 (2016). doi:10.1111/1748-8583.12100
2. Andreeva, T.E., Garanina, T.A., Ryzhko, A.N.: Knowledge management and intellectual capital in Russian organizations – research report. Graduate School of Management SPbGU (2015)
3. Bukowitz, W.R., Williams, R.L.: The Knowledge Management Fieldbook. Financial Times Prentice Hall, Great Britain (1999)
4. Cyert, R.M., March, J.G.: A Behavioral Theory of the Firm. NJ, Englewood Cliffs (1963)
5. Davenport, T.H., Prusak, L.: Working Knowledge: How Organisations Manage What They Know. Harvard Business School Press, Cambridge (2000)
6. Fairchild, A.M.: Knowledge management metrics via a balanced scorecard methodology. In: Proceedings of the 35th Annual Hawaii International Conference, pp. 3173–3180. System Sciences HICSS (2002). doi:10.1109/HICSS.2002.994356
7. Frost, T., Birkinshaw, J.M., Ensign, S.: Centres of excellence in multinational corporations. Strateg. Manag. J. **23**(11), 997–1015 (2002). doi:10.1002/smj.273
8. Gavrilova, T.A., Gulyakina, N.A.: Visual knowledge processing techniques: a brief review. Sci. Tech. Inf. Process. **38**(6), 403–408 (2011)
9. Gavrilova, T.A., Lescheva, I.A., Kudryavtsev, D.V.: Knowledge engineering models implementation for information technologies specialists education. Sist. Program. **7**(1), 90–105 (2012). in Russian
10. Jansen, J.P., Van Den Bosch, F.A.J., Volberda, H.W.: Exploratory Innovation, Exploitative Innovation, and Performance: Effects of Organizational Antecedents and Environmental Moderators. ERIM Report Series Reference No. ERS-2006-038-STR, Rotterdam (2006)
11. Kuriakose, K.K., Raj, B., Satya Murty, S.A.V., Swaminathan, P.: Knowledge management maturity model: an engineering approach. J. Knowl. Manag. Pract. **12**(2), 1–17 (2011)
12. Laursen, K., Salter, A.: Open for innovation: the role of openness in explaining innovative performance among UK manufacturing firms. Strateg. Manag. J. **27**(2), 131–150 (2006). doi:10.1002/smj.507
13. Makino, S., Delios, A.: Local knowledge transfer and performance: implications for alliance formation in Asia. J. Int. Bus. Stud. **27**(5), 905–927 (1996)
14. Milner, B.Z.: The knowledge management concept for contemporary organizations. Russ. Manag. J. **1**, 57–76 (2003)
15. Milner, B.Z.: Knowledge management in modern economics. Tekhnopark **2**, 6–15 (2008). in Russian
16. Nonaka, I.: A dynamic theory of organizational knowledge creation. Organ. Sci. **5**(1), 14–37 (1994). doi:10.1287/orsc.5.1.14
17. Polanyi, M.: Personal Knowledge: Towards a Post-critical Philosophy. Routledge & Kegan Paul Ltd., London (1962)
18. Rubenstein-Montano, B., Liebowitz, J., Buchwalter, J., McCaw, D., Newman, B., Rebeck, K.: A systems thinking framework for knowledge management. Decis. Support Syst. **31**, 5–16 (2001). doi:10.1016/S0167-9236(00)00116-0

19. Skyrme, D.J., Amidon, D.M.: New measures of success. J. Bus. Strategy. **40**, 20–24 (1998). doi:10.1108/eb039905
20. Sergeeva, A.V.: Influence of organizational and managerial factors on knowledge sharing processes in organization (at the example of public schools), Ph.D. Dissertation, SPb (2014). in Russian
21. Stanishevskaya, S.P., Imaykin, E.A.: Intellectual capital management in region based on interrelations between regional educational system and labour market. Her. Perm Univ. Econ. **2**(5), 6–14 (2010). in Russian
22. Stewart, T., Ruckdeschel, C.: Intellectual Capital: The New Wealth of Organizations. Doubleday, New York (1998)
23. Sveiby, K.E.: Disabling the context for knowledge work: the role of managers' behaviours. Manag. Decis. **45**(10), 1636–1655 (2007). doi:10.1108/00251740710838004
24. Tapscott, D.: The Digital Economy: Promise and Peril in the Age of Networked Intelligence. McGraw-Hill, New York (1996)
25. Teece, D.J.: Explicating dynamic capabilities: the nature and microfoundations of (sustainable) enterprise performance. Strateg. Manag. J. **28**(13), 1319–1350 (2007). doi:10.1002/smj.640
26. Tsang, E.W.K.: Acquiring knowledge by foreign partners from international joint ventures in a transition economy: learning-by-doing and learning myopia. Strateg. Manag. J. **23**(9), 835–854 (2002). doi:10.1002/smj.251
27. Van der Spek, R., Spijkervet, A.: Knowledge management dealing intelligently with knowledge. In: Liebowitz, J., Wilcox, L. (eds.) Knowledge Management and Its Integrative Elements. CRC Press, Boca Raton (1997)
28. Wiig, K.M.: Knowledge Management Foundations: Thinking About Thinking: How People and Organizations Create, Represent, and use Knowledge. Schema Press, Arlington (1993)
29. Zahra, S.A., George, G.: Absorptive capacity: a review, reconceptualization, and extension. Acad. Manag. Rev. **27**(2), 185–203 (2002). doi:10.5465/AMR.2002.6587995

Erratum to: Estimation of Relationship Between Domains of ICT Semantic Network

Ravil I. Mukhamediev, Ramiz M. Aliguliyev,
and Jelena Muhamedijeva

Erratum to:
Chapter "Estimation of Relationship Between Domains
of ICT Semantic Network" in: D.A. Alexandrov et al. (Eds.):
Digital Transformation and Global Society, CCIS 745,
https://doi.org/10.1007/978-3-319-69784-0_11

The book was inadvertently published with incorrect chapter author's family name. This information has been updated from "Aligulyev" to "Aliguliyev" to the initially published version of chapter 11.

The updated online version of this chapter can be found at
https://doi.org/10.1007/978-3-319-69784-0_11

© Springer International Publishing AG 2018
D.A. Alexandrov et al. (Eds.): DTGS 2017, CCIS 745, p. E1, 2017.
https://doi.org/10.1007/978-3-319-69784-0_39

Author Index

Printed in the United States
By Bookmasters